D1739128

The Société des Concerts du Conservatoire, 1828–1967

The publisher gratefully acknowledges the generous contribution to this book provided by the Ahmanson Foundation Humanities Fund of the University of California Press Associates.

The Société des Concerts du Conservatoire, 1828–1967

D. Kern Holoman

University of California Press

BERKELEY   LOS ANGELES   LONDON

University of California Press
Berkeley and Los Angeles, California

University of California Press, Ltd.
London, England

Library of Congress Cataloging-in-Publication Data

Holoman, D. Kern, 1947–.
  The Société des concerts du conservatoire, 1828–1967 / D. Kern
Holoman.
    p.   cm.
  Includes bibliographical references (p.   ) and index.
  ISBN 0-520-23664-5 (alk. paper).
  1. Société des concerts du Conservatoire.   I. Title.
ML28.P2S64   2004
784.2'06'044361—dc21   2002032797

Manufactured in the United States of America

13   12   11   10   09   08   07   06   05   04
10   9   8   7   6   5   4   3   2   1

The paper used in this publication meets the minimum requirements of
ANSI/NISO Z39.48-1992 (R 1997) (*Permanence of Paper*). ♾

Contents

Illustrations

Following page 378

Henri Grévedon (1776–1860): Portrait of Beethoven, after
    Ferdinand Schimon, *"propriété de la Société des Concerts du
    Conservatoire,"* 1841
Eugène Guillaume (1822–1905): Bust of Beethoven, 1888
Site plan, the old Menus-Plaisirs and the Conservatoire, 1836
Audience seating plan, Salle des Concerts
A concert at the Conservatoire, 1843
Entry to the Concerts du Conservatoire, 1848
A concert of the Société des Concerts du Conservatoire, 1861
Gaubert and the orchestra, Salle des Concerts, 1937
Program for all-Beethoven concert, 23 March 1828
Handbill for concert of 5 March 1848, following the revolution
    in February
Program for concert of 29 November 1918, El Paso
Marcel Landowski, André Malraux, Charles Münch, Orchestre
    de Paris, 14 November 1967
Lucien Thévet, *horn;* Robert Casier, *oboe:* Salle Pleyel,
    22 March 2002
Robert Doisneau (1912–94): place du Marché St-Honoré, 1948

Acknowledgments

I learned about the Société des Concerts and its archive during my very first research trip as a practicing musicologist, in 1972–73. In 2002, on the day this manuscript went into production, I was still accruing material—in this case during a casual conversation with Robert Silvers of the *New York Review of Books,* where he recalled, with crystal clarity and a few good details, the orchestra's concert of 24 February 1952. So for three decades the Société des Concerts and its successor, the Orchestre de Paris, have been such a central part of my life and work that acknowledging every contributor to what follows, other than with a general but heartfelt salute, became impossible long ago. But the gratitude is very deep.

For virtually all that period my principal mentor in matters Parisian was the eminent French musicologist François Lesure (1923–2001). Lesure helped arrange my first visit to the offices of the Orchestre de Paris, then located in the Théâtre des Champs-Élysées, and did much to smooth over the intrusion of a callow but persistent American into the affairs of a busy orchestra at a critical point in its history. Lesure often looked over my shoulder at the documents treated in this book and was quick to clarify or expand on the issue of the moment—from the TSF (*télégraphe sans fil,* i.e., early radio) to the Vilmorin flower stall blocking access to the Conservatoire. In recent years he would simply growl, *"et la Société?"* when he saw me doing anything else, and, a few weeks before he died, he was the first in with corrections to my manuscript (which he called "your little pamphlet"). I dedicate this book, but more especially the spirit behind it, to his memory.

At the Orchestre de Paris I have to thank Georges-François Hirsch, Nicole Salinger, Geneviève Thomas, Jean-Marie Amartin, Annick Boccon-Gibod, and Didier Allard. The musicians past and present have provided documents and details and countless hours of listening pleasure; chief of these were Lucien Thévet, Robert Casier, Joseph Ponticelli, and the late Fernand Lelong (1939–2002). At the Bibliothèque Nationale Catherine Massip and of course the entire staff have played a central role in bringing this material to light; in the early years, Jean-Michel Nectoux was the library's principal liaison with the orchestra and its archives.

I thank, in Paris and elsewhere in France, Geneviève Ramos Acker, Philippe Brugière at the Musée de la Musique, Anik Devriès-Lesure, Yves Gérard, Pierre Ickowicz at the Musée de Dieppe, Henry-Louis de La Grange, Jean Mongrédien, Cécile Reynaud, Gérard Streletski, and many others. Elsewhere in Europe, Paul Banks, David Cairns, David Charlton, Hugues Cuénod, Suzanne Danco. In the United States, Donna M. Di Grazia, Carol Tomlinson-Keasey, Susan Nelson, Jann Pasler, William Weber—and most especially the trio of Francophiles on whom I rely routinely to read, comment on, and correct my drafts: Peter Bloom, Ralph P. Locke, and Hugh Macdonald.

It has been a particular dividend of strategies adopted in the mid-1990s that I have profited from the vast spectrum of knowledge expressed by visitors to the Internet site. Among cyber-colleagues whom I have never met are Pierre-Paul Corsetti, the flutist Michel Debost, the discographers Eric Derom and Michael H. Gray, Jean-Michel Molkhou, the Cluytens enthusiast Yukihiro Okitsu, and the Raoul Dufy scholar Asuka Wada. Among the many descendants of *sociétaires* who have exchanged genealogical information with me are Hourri Poussard (descendant of the timpanist Poussard) and André Leplus-Habeneck. Marie Anne Corre de Valmalète offered similar information on the concert-managing dynasty of which she was long the queen and is now, there with her web browser, the queen mother.

Two graduate seminars at the University of California, Davis, produced results that have been incorporated here. In 1990 the students and their areas of research were Matthew Daines (Messager—later an M.A. thesis and published article); Carol Hancock (the Haydn *symphonie inédite*); Gregory McCall (Koussevitzky in Paris); Cynthia Meidinger (Fauré); Donald Meyer (the NBC Symphony—later a Ph.D. dissertation); and Michael Shahani (Gaubert). In 2000 the students were Naumy Akhavan (Saint-Saëns); Rebecca Brover (record labeling); Nathaniel Johnson (Ravel); Gavin Kone (Carl Schuricht); John Lutterman (philosophy of performance practice); Angela Mann (Spanish repertoire); and Drew Wheeler (the French school after Ravel). Jonathan Elkus was a constant source of intellectual stimulation. Anthony Lien proofread and mounted the programs on the Internet; Alison Vinande did the same for a portion of the discography; David R. Simpson managed the production of the manuscript editions and refinement of the website. My scholarly work at the University of California, Davis, has been supported by grants from the Academic Senate Committee on Research and the generous sabbatical leave provisions of the University of California. The endowment of my chair at the university by my good friend Barbara K. Jackson reduced the financial worry attending the last stages of work on this kind of project to none at all.

Ralph Locke and my former student Mark E. Brill provided the most detailed readings and corrections of one of the manuscript editions. Gérard Streletski worked carefully through the manuscript to assure accuracy and consistency of French-language material, even if the final result here represents something of a conflation of European and American styles. Additionally I am grateful to the two anonymous reviewers for corrections and suggestions that considerably refined the narrative, and to the anonymous sponsor on the Editorial Committee of the University of California Press (several of whose observations I have drawn whole into this text). The book was acquired for the Press and shepherded through its early stages by Doris Kretschmer, and the Internet strategy was first concluded with Jane-Ellen Long. Lynne Withey, Mary Francis, Rose Vekony, and Mary Anne Stewart subsequently saw the project through publication.

To all of these, and of course above all to my family—our children were born and grew to adulthood surrounded by artifacts of the Société des Concerts; my father, it turned out, was at one of the Liberation concerts, and still had the program—go my thanks, my affection, and my profound admiration.

DKH
Davis / Méricourt

On Documentation

The bulk of the documentation for this project, approximately 3,000 screens, is found in appendices published on the Internet at <www.ucpress.edu/holoman>. To be consulted there are the following:

1. PROGRAMS
   All known programs of the Société des Concerts, arranged by year

2. PERSONNEL
   Alphabetical listing of *sociétaires* with biographical notes
   Chronological listing of *sociétaires* by date of election
   Successions (presidents, conductors, principals, etc.)
   Sociétaires solo and *honoraires*
   Staff personnel
   Rosters by year

3. CHRONOLOGY
   For each year:
   Season (number of concerts, dates of assemblies)
   Personnel (appointments, separations, deaths)
   Links to other information as appropriate (election results, financial summaries)
   Sources

4. SUPPORTING DOCUMENTS AND TABLES
   Statutes
   Decrees

A Note on Currency

The unit of currency at issue throughout this study is the French franc, which replaced the pound as the nation's fundamental monetary unit on 15 August 1795 and was in turn replaced by the euro on 1 January 2002. For the entire period from the foundation of the Société des Concerts until World War I the value of the franc was, except during periods of political calamity, remarkably stable. Rampant inflation between the end of World War I and 1926 is reckoned in terms of an overall increase in cost of living of about 400 percent. Between the end of World War II and the mid-1950s a similar climate obtained, leading to the Gaullist currency reform of 1958–59 and the adoption of the new franc (= 100 old francs) on 1 January 1960. Spoken parlance from then through the dissolution of the Société des Concerts often continued to allude to old francs, emphasizing prices in the millions.

To give some idea of the meaning of these values: the American dollar was worth about 5 francs in 1914, 35 francs in 1938, and 490 francs in 1959. A kilogram of bread fetched about 40 centimes until 1914, 3 francs in 1938, and 60 francs in 1959; cigarettes cost about 60 centimes, 3 francs, and 115 francs in those same years. A schoolteacher made approximately 2,200 francs annually until World War I, 24,000 francs in 1938, and 1 million francs in 1959.

PART ONE

Structure of the Société des Concerts

CHAPTER I

Beginnings

(March 1828)

At promptly 2:00 on Sunday afternoon, 9 March 1828, the violinist-conductor François-Antoine Habeneck, just entering his forty-eighth year, took the crowded stage of the Salle des Concerts at the Paris Conservatoire and gave the summary *premier coup d'archet* for Beethoven's "Eroica" Symphony, never before heard—or so it was believed—in France. Subsequently two students at the Conservatoire, the sisters Nélia and Caroline Maillard, sang excerpts from operas by Rossini; Joseph Meifred, in a work of his own composition, introduced the public to the piston-valved horn he had helped design—and for which he and his colleague (and former teacher) Louis Dauprat were both writing method books; Eugène Sauzay, the incumbent *1er prix* in violin from Pierre Baillot's class at the Conservatoire, played a concerto by Pierre Rode. The concert concluded with three works composed by the director of the Conservatoire, Luigi Cherubini: a chorus from *Blanche de Provence,* the overture to *Les Abencérages,* and the Kyrie and Gloria from the mass Cherubini had composed for the coronation in 1824 of Charles X, the reigning king. The concert lasted some three hours.

Among the listeners were those few of the Conservatoire's faculty and students not already to be found onstage: delegates from the royal government led by Viscount Sosthène de La Rochefoucauld, swashbuckling director of fine arts and promulgator of the decree instituting the concerts; and the artists, journalists, and ordinary music lovers who one way or another had learned of an event not to be missed. A principal eyewitness to that momentous afternoon was the Franco-Belgian savant François-Joseph Fétis, whose successful journal *La Revue musicale* was in its third year of publication. Fétis rightly saw the concert as a turning point in the fortunes of the Conservatoire, closed in the wake of Waterloo and since the reopening still uncertain of its mission and of how to go about claiming its proper measure of international prestige. Fétis called his essay "Rebirth of the Royal School of Music: Société des Concerts" and opened with a tribute to the artists who out of devotion to their art sacrificed self-interest to achieve collective glory—a transaction cited one way or another whenever writers tried to assess the institutional mystique.

> Honor to the [musicians of the old] Conservatoire who, remembering its former glory, have come at the first call to associate themselves with the new school, lend their support, and mold its noble career! Honor to the head of that school, who, motivated only by his zeal for the prosperity of an art he himself has sensibly enriched, gave his council, wrote the proposal, and designed the strategy to return the first musical establishment in France to its brilliant former renown! Honor to the young students who, understanding what was expected of them, showed themselves worthy of their forerunners —like the young draftees of the Empire, proud to fight beneath the gaze of the old veterans of the Revolution, and rivaling them in audacity and valor. They were fired by an ardor hitherto untasted, and they became, in one stroke, distinguished artists.
>
> The concert of 9 March 1828 will be remembered as a great day for the splendor of French music, the moment of its rebirth. The performance was stamped with superiority. The vain attacks on the Conservatoire by the newspapers will stop; the teachers and their students countered them with strength and dignity, and their immense success justifies the government's support of the institution.
>
> What verve, what energy, what ensemble, what perfection of nuance they brought to the Beethoven symphony! They made it seem easy, with fine brush strokes, majestic *pianos* from a huge orchestra, thunderous *fortes*. It was all perfect, admirable, worthy at last of the best artists in the capital of France.

Fétis admonished the young people never to forget their signal victory, striving always to match the level they had achieved at the outset.

He praised Habeneck in general and in particular, noting the salutary improvements that resulted from his conducting with the violin and bow instead of the percussive strokes from the *bâton de mesure* Parisians were accustomed to hear resonating from the pit at the Opéra: "With his violin he gets heated up and joins in the collective atmosphere; with his baton he is glacial and seems bored. Besides, in a concert he can see the orchestra, whereas the stupid arrangement at the Opéra puts the players at his back."

Fétis was pleased and intrigued by the modernity of the repertoire, and thought that what he understood as a decision to focus on new music promised great things for the future of the fledgling association. "Who can believe," he asks of the "Eroica," "that this magnificent composition has never been heard in Paris? But how could it have been, without an entirely new organization?" The old *concerts spirituels* had been done on a single rehearsal, generally dominated by the singers. The symphonies had to have been works already known to the players, and even then the performances were generally mediocre.

Of Nélia and Caroline Maillard, in excerpts from *Sémiramide* and *Bianca et Falliero,* Fétis observed that their student voices, though not without talent, failed to achieve the still-remembered effect of the original stage productions; he found the Rode concerto as offered by Sauzay —a last-minute substitute for Baillot—somewhat cold. (He thus identifies, at the very first concert, what appear from the accumulated press notices to have been the two weakest links of the early years: the limitations of youthful voices and the occasional *froideur* of approach.) Everything else he found "delicious," and he noted that for the first time a chorus from the Conservatoire sang with perfection, an advance he attributed to the new class in ensemble singing:

> The enthusiasm of the listeners equaled their astonishment, and became manifest in noisy and prolonged applause. One seldom leaves a concert satisfied, but here the feeling was better than satisfaction; it was mingled with national pride. Everybody was saying you couldn't find a better performance anywhere in Europe. People who knew the old Conservatoire concerts congratulated themselves for having found the new ones; the rest asked each other in astonishment where this sudden surge of virtuosity had come from.

Fétis's own explanation was persuasively simple: "No undertaking is so difficult that it can't be achieved with enough strong will and enlightened zeal." Superb performances of such a brilliant new repertoire, offered and received with what amounted to patriotic fervor, augured well, he predicted, for the future.[1]

It would be difficult to overstate the degree to which this concert, and the five that followed before the first "session" of "exercises" reached their end, altered the course of music in France and eventually throughout Europe. The critic Joseph d'Ortigue thought the result "a revolution in the world of music; it was, for that art and for art in general, a time of awakening."[2] The young Berlioz, just then succumbing to the throes of nascent Romanticism, found both the direction of his career and the scope of his imagination radically changed by what he heard in the first seasons; Ferdinand Hérold, we are told, studied the work of the Société des Concerts as he composed *Zampa,* and only a few years later Bellini did the same to discover paths toward *I Puritani,* his swan song.[3] Liszt almost certainly conceived his ideals for orchestral sonority and deployment with the Société des Concerts in mind. Wagner says he first understood Beethoven's Ninth in Paris—and Beethoven's secretary Anton Schindler was but one of hundreds of Beethovenians who made the pilgrimage to hear and pay homage to the Paris orchestra. Every French composer from Berlioz through Messiaen and Boulez was formed, at least in part, by what he or she saw and heard in the Salle des Concerts.

The prestige of the Conservatoire was indeed restored as though overnight. In a few short weeks concertgoing had become a welcome alternative to late nights at the theater. Soon it was a habitual Sunday afternoon activity of the nation's leaders in the arts, politics, and business, as well as a growing tourist attraction. Demand for new music sharply increased. Careers and career paths were born. In the medium and long term—and as a direct result—a French school of symphonic music emerged to rival that of Austro-Hungary at its height.

The Société des Concerts lasted 140 seasons, dissolving on 21 June 1967 to make way for the present Orchestre de Paris (still, officially, the Orchestre de Paris / Société des Concerts du Conservatoire). Altogether it presented something on the order of 3,000 concerts—many hundreds more, if engagements beyond the Sunday concerts are counted—before perhaps 2.5 million Paris listeners. The names of some 860 *sociétaires* appear in the registers; perhaps twice that number played or sang as apprentice members of the Société des Concerts before securing employment elsewhere. In sum very nearly all the major French instrumentalists after the Revolution had at least something to do with the organization. Yet there were only twelve first conductors, and no guest conductors at all until after World War I.

Much of the orchestral and orchestra-choral repertoire after Haydn —and until the 1870s, virtually all of it—was first heard in Paris at the Conservatoire concerts. Gainsayers notwithstanding, the Société des Concerts was seldom less than avid in its pursuit of new works to expand the repertoire. If the number of authentic world premieres seems relatively small (perhaps the most significant was that of Franck's D-Minor Symphony in February 1889), the explanation lies in how the musicians conceived of their mission, preferring the widely acknowledged formulation that the very arrival of a work in the hall of the Conservatoire was tantamount to its canonization. This was certainly the case, in France, for works as diverse as *Israel in Egypt,* the B-Minor Mass and St. John Passion, the entire Beethoven corpus, Berlioz's *Roméo et Juliette,* and most of the French masters from Saint-Saëns through Dukas, Ravel, Honegger, and Florent Schmitt. With regard to its almost ritual attention to the post-Romantic "Paris" repertoire, the record of the Société des Concerts is unparalleled.

Beginning in 1918 the Société des Concerts recorded more than two hundred works, including nearly all the French repertoire, many first recordings, and a few unique ones. The records sold well and earned their fair share of awards and grand prizes; most of the better recordings have since appeared in compact-disc format. Additionally the orchestra was engaged under its own name for dozens of film scores, and the management, seeking full employment for its musicians as the twentieth century advanced, brokered many outside jobs where the personnel would be identified as "members of the Société des Concerts" or, just as often, not named at all. The orchestra broadcast concerts from the early days of radio, though it was soon eclipsed in that capacity by the government-funded Radio Orchestra (Orchestre National de la Radiodiffusion Française); a few off-the-air recordings have begun to circulate on compact disc, notably a January 1966 concert under Boulez. Very little film or video footage of the orchestra in concert is readily accessible, though a 1999 documentary on NHK Television included a short clip from *Daphnis et Chloé,* suite 2, recorded during the 1964 tour of Japan, and a DVD of Henryk Szeryng in the Brahms Violin Concerto, probably filmed in December 1962 and broadcast in 1964, is scheduled for release in late 2003 by EMI. Living members recall film cameras being present only in conjunction with the child conductor Roberto Benzi.[4]

With annual concerts in Belgium and Lyon from 1907, then successful tours of Switzerland in 1917 and the United States and Canada in 1918–19, the Société des Concerts began to establish its living presence beyond Paris. Eventually it appeared in much of western Europe and became familiar to audiences in Belgium, the Netherlands, and the United Kingdom—but never, though there were multiple projects to that end, in either Berlin or Vienna. In 1964, essaying air travel for the first time, Cluytens and the orchestra concluded a triumphant journey to Japan. From 1947 the Société des Concerts was in residence for the summer music festivals in both Aix-en-Provence and Besançon.

Directly linked to the national government through its sponsoring academy and its venue, the Société des Concerts ultimately became more or less the official orchestra of France—a role it very much coveted. Summons to provide music for state funerals, visitors of state, and galas or jubilees were received from the outset and became common with the dissolution of the imperial chapel in 1870. Reticent to appear under other conductors or in vast performance spaces, the musicians took relatively minor roles in the exhibitions and world's fairs meant to show off, among many other things, the nation's artistic prestige. But the cultural and political significance of the Société des Concerts was widely understood, and was put to pragmatic use from the very beginning of the concept of propaganda, roughly coincident with World War I. In the 1940s, for instance, the orchestra figured in the public relations strategies of the German occupiers, the Vichy government, and the Allied liberation force.

As a purveyor of fine music in sophisticated surroundings the Société des Concerts ranked for most of its history second in France only to the Opéra. (There may indeed be a connection between the dawn of a new concert life in 1828 and the twilight of French grand opera, clearly in course by 1840.) In fostering serious thought about the central issues of French orchestral music, the society in turn begot imitators and alternative approaches that grew to become worthy rivals. If some of the descendents came periodically to equal the prestige of the Société des Concerts, none ever clearly or for long surpassed it. When, in the 1960s, it seemed that the association might be lost altogether to make room for a new Paris orchestra organized along contemporary norms and practices, the musicians successfully maneuvered to have their old identity commingled with the new enterprise and for many of their colleagues to be absorbed seamlessly into it.

Together with its offspring and imitators, the Société des Concerts created in Paris a large public and an insatiable demand—what the French like to call the *goût de la musique*—that continues strong. Few are left who remember the concerts in the rue Bergère, but their effect on living French music can still be felt all over town.

By the end of the 1828 season the critics were already beginning to run out of superlatives and had begun to take the flair—and the seeming flawlessness—of the concerts for granted. ("I've just about given up heaping praise on the Conservatoire orchestra," wrote Joseph d'Ortigue. "That's to risk endless repetition that doesn't teach the reader much. But every time its performance is so surprising, so prodigious.")[5] Not much changed in the atmosphere from week to week, or for that matter from season to season, and over the years few journalists paused to analyze the Société des Concerts as an institution. When they did, it was often in an attempt to explain how the organization came to be, as one wrote in 1924, the world's "closest to perfect" orchestra, the pride of Paris and glory of France.[6] This superiority was variously attributed to the acoustic quality of its hall; to its rehearsal pattern; or (more correctly) to its organizational stability, with decade-long tenures of virtuosi working in common, subordinating their individual ambition to their collective reputation.

A number of useful assessments came from journalists outside Paris —and thus relatively immune to allegations of chauvinism—hearing the orchestra for the first time and comparing it with others. The *Tribune de Lausanne* of 3 April 1917, writing of a tour appearance there, suggested that

> in Germany you can easily enough find conductors who surpass in genius and personal magnetism the best French *chefs,* but nowhere else will you find an orchestra that even distantly approaches the orchestra of the Conservatoire of Paris. It has a unique gift, the result of the individual merit and artistry of its members. Everybody knows that what they do and possess to do it with far surpasses what even the better orchestras beyond the Rhine can offer. It gives the performances of this unique company a final polish, of an order and perfection that no other conductor will ever obtain—not a Nikisch, not a Richard Strauss, not a Weingartner.[7]

Musicians and critics alike recognized how the collective mission took precedence over any one member's essentially transitory membership. As the violinist Eugène Gautier suggested in 1866, it was by absorbing the confraternal traditions that the Société des Concerts would carry on in perpetuity. "When the hour of repose strikes for us, we will pass on to our successors, intact and strong, this great artwork, which was confided to us and whose mission is ever more necessary, blessed in the present of Art, and safe from the invasion of *faux goût.*" The next year Gautier returned to that sentiment, predicting a happy future for the society, "still young, still strong, destined to last for eternity, it seems, for it is based on mutual esteem, *travail,* and *talent.*"[8]

Fétis was right that the "sudden surge of virtuosity" he sensed in 1828 had, in one sense, simply evolved from the "old" Conservatoire concerts—"the egg," remarked a later observer, "from which our beloved society was hatched."[9] In overall concept, programming, and even initial personnel, the Société des Concerts was descended directly, and strikingly, from the *exercices publics des élèves* of the music school everybody called the Conservatoire, which today reckons its founding from the 1795–96 academic year. A provision of the establishing decree, 3 July 1796 (15 Messidor, an IV), called for six concerts annually, on the twentieth day of the months Brumaire, Nivôse, Ventôse, Floréal, Fructidor, and Messidor—by the evocative Republican calendar—in the academic year. These did not at first materialize, except for the participation of a student orchestra and chorus at the annual prize distribution. At length, in 1800–01, a series of three concerts (6 November 1800, 13 January 1801, and 13 April 1801) was finally presented, but the financial loss incurred threatened the tight budget of the Conservatoire and hence no provision was made for the following year.

The young people, emboldened by the experience, thus organized themselves to undertake a new season in the Salle Olympique at their own risk and peril, adopting the appellation Concerts Français and inaugurating the series on 21 November 1801 in the presence of Mme Bonaparte, the future Empress Joséphine. The season beginning in November 1802 saw the concerts moved to the largest room—about three hundred seats—so far constructed on the grounds of the Conservatoire, the venue that came to be known as the *petite salle,* used by the school for large-ensemble rehearsals and assemblies like the annual prize-giving and the notorious public juries. (It would later be used by the Société des Concerts as a chorus room.) The "Conservatoire concerts," as they soon came to be known, were sporadic—between five and a dozen concerts a year—but ongoing, developing in due course a faithful public and regular notice in the press. Some 140 events were announced over the fifteen years from 1800, of which about 100 appear actually to have taken place. The last was on 11 June 1815, the week before Waterloo.[10]

Nearly every detail of the *exercices publics* set a precedent for the later Société des Concerts. The concerts were Sunday afternoons on the grounds of the Conservatoire, in the rue Bergère, where an impressive new hall was inaugurated in 1811. The low cost of admission, about half the going rate for fully professional concerts (the Concerts de la rue de Cléry, notably), and the inviting combination of youth and exceptional talent attracted overflow houses of sympathetic listeners. The orchestra consisted of nearly eighty players, with tripled or quadrupled winds. Vocal soloists and a chorus were on hand for every performance. If the operatic airs, ensembles, and finales continued to be a significant and popular component of the programming, the focus was nevertheless squarely on the orchestra: symphonies, overtures, and solo concertos played and often composed by the young virtuosi. Haydn was to be heard on every concert, and Mozart nearly as often, with the "Military" Symphony of the former and the G-Minor of the latter favorites of the era. The four symphonies of Méhul were given good performances, and perhaps three symphonies of the intriguing "Betowen" (the First Symphony in February 1807, the Fifth in April 1808, the Third in May 1811). Early suggestions that the repertoire would consist primarily of works by the Old Masters exhumed from a dusty library proved misleading but for a few favorites from the Italian school (Durante, Jommelli, Pergolesi). The pre-revolutionary era was soon forgotten in the clamor for modernity.[11]

Among the personnel were many who in 1828 would bring their experience to bear in organizing the new Société des Concerts: the violinists Rode, Kreutzer, Baillot, and the Habeneck brothers; the violist Urhan; the flutist Tulou, oboist Vogt, clarinetist Dacosta, hornist Dauprat, and timpanist Schneitzhoeffer. The student concerts of 1800–15 established, moreover, a worthy claim to French membership in the august circle of cultures able to sustain a vibrant presence for symphonic music. Prestige in this domain was felt essential to complement the nation's undeniable distinction in science, letters, and painting. And there seems every indication that the performances indeed were, in large measure, distinguished. The press talked of "fire," "youthful ardor" *(vigueur juvénile),* and an "overall superiority" of result; the winds were praised for precision, tone quality, and justness of intonation. The discovery of Beethoven exhilarated everybody; the *Allgemeine musikalische Zeitung* in 1811 noted how the Beethoven symphonies "incited unbelievable passion in the young performers," while supposedly seasoned travelers proclaimed that the students were better than the Viennese musicians who had offered the premieres. One went on to suggest, however, that there were "too many virtuosi" for good Beethoven. Too much detail was lost in the habitually brisk tempos; the musicians of Mannheim and Munich, though less capable than their Parisian counterparts, came closer to the "true German spirit."[12] Given the chronological and geographic distance that separated Paris from Vienna, sharp divergences in performing practice are hardly surprising. That the issue was engaged at all, however, proves the emergence of a major new sphere of influence.

With the second Bourbon Restoration, the Conservatoire, associated as it was with revolution and empire, fell upon hard times. It was closed altogether between 1815 and 1816, and public concerts did not resume until 1823. The irascible but crafty Cherubini, emerging as uncontested head of the Conservatoire in the spring of 1822, led the institution in an imaginative program of reconstruction: righting the budget, dismissing underachievers, developing a curriculum that sought to balance the vocal and instrumental programs, and attending to the library and collection of musical instruments. With the appointments in 1824 of the Viscount de La Rochefoucauld as director of fine arts and of Habeneck, lured from the podium of the Opéra to assume the additional function of "honorary director" of the Conservatoire, a formidable triumvirate of accomplished administrators came to power—all three of them growingly inclined to the notion that assuring serious concert music in Paris had become their most pressing concern.

Which of the three actually turned the corner in resurrecting the moribund concert series is uncertain, and in most respects irrelevant. Six concerts in the spring of 1823 and three in 1824 had failed to achieve either financial or artistic success, and in their wake Cherubini first proposed supplementing the student force with "veterans of the Conservatoire." Fétis thought the plan a shrewd venture in public relations on Cherubini's part, designed to counteract the strident voices arguing that the extravagant use of public monies at the Conservatoire was nevertheless failing to meet the institution's only mandate: "to populate the ranks of the royal enterprises in music and declamation: the royal chapel, the Opéra (the Académie Royale de Musique), the Théâtre-Français, the Odéon, and the Opéra-Comique." Serious negotiations toward organizing a new concert society were well under way during the winter of 1826–27, but by then Cherubini could be found complaining that the public concerts were "a lot of trouble, and disruptive to the curriculum," while Habeneck (according to Guizot's later recollection) continued to maintain their pedagogical utility, an argument he had first advanced three years before. La Rochefoucauld, for his part, took ownership of the project when he wrote his minister, in December 1827: "I have thought it necessary to re-establish the *exercices publics,* at least provisionally, in 1828," proposing six concerts and a government guarantee to cover any deficit. And it was La Rochefoucauld who signed the decree of 15 February 1828 that formally instituted the Société des Concerts.[13]

It was clearly Habeneck, however, who supplied the artistic vision and personal intervention that took the project beyond a mere reiteration of the student concerts toward a lasting association of the most accomplished artists in the land. As first conductor of the Opéra (1821–24), Habeneck had re-introduced the famous Lenten *concerts spirituels,* popularizing among other things the Andante from Beethoven's Seventh

Symphony. Related by his second marriage to the Sieber-Leduc dynasty of music publishers, Habeneck had direct access to the best performance material available for the Viennese repertoire. His father may have played in the Mannheim orchestra. He himself had been a partisan of Beethoven for two decades and in the months just passed had gradually convinced his followers to share his dream of performing the Beethoven symphonies with a fine orchestra, well rehearsed and capably conducted, before an enlightened, faithful public.

Received tradition (as with all legends, the details vary in the retelling) has it that in November 1826, Habeneck summoned an orchestra's worth of his favorite musicians—Opéra players, professors from the Conservatoire, recent prizewinners—to his apartments, purportedly for a *dîner prolongé* on the feast day of St. Cecilia, patron saint of musicians. They were told to bring their instruments, and they arrived to find music stands in the salon holding parts to sight-read (or, as the French language so accurately has it, "to decipher"). They worked on the difficult but unidentified symphony until dark, when the door of the dining room was thrown open and Mme Habeneck proclaimed, "In the name of a grateful Beethoven, *à table!*" During a champagne toast they were told that they had just tried the "Eroica."[14]

There were any number of such occasions, as Habeneck systematically laid the groundwork that would result in the willingness of the finest players and singers to affiliate in a venture that promised only a few hundred francs of new income, a great deal of work, and the vaguest possibility of a lasting place in history. Cherubini and La Rochefoucauld doubtless arranged the other critical pieces of the plan: free access to the better student musicians, use of the hall, and the implied commitment of the government—declining a fund the musicians had collected among themselves—to cover any deficit. The condition that every member of the new society must be, or at some time have been, affiliated with the Conservatoire proved another significant guarantor of solidarity and artistic merit.

Once established, the Société des Concerts charted its own course, more or less independently of the school. Yet one could hardly overlook the rich connections that bound the orchestra to the academy that had given it birth; virtually every member had graduated from the Conservatoire, most of the instrumentalists had garnered a 1er *prix* there, and they assembled three times a week in a hall on its premises. A half-dozen or more times each season the most privileged citizens—politically, economically, intellectually—of France flocked beneath the famous portal, with its boldly chiseled legend CONSERVATOIRE, on their way in to take their seats. Thinking people were quick to celebrate the obviously strong and quite possibly lasting marriage of high art and public education.

This, then, is the story of one of the world's great philharmonic societies. The potent forces of democracy, exclusivity, and revolutionary fever that collided in and around the Conservatoire during the 1820s and 1830s forged and then tempered an organization as flexible as it was strong. The Société des Concerts serves as an important barometer of the culture as it adapts to changing circumstances and perceptions. The repertoire mutates; prevailing practices are altered in response to external events. Cycles of growth, complacency, and crisis develop. Some of the story is particular to its place and time—how the orchestra survived, for instance, the turbulent years of 1830, 1848, and 1870, then 1914–18 and 1937–44, sometimes by subterfuge, sometimes by overt collaboration. Some of it is peculiar to the traditional ways government and art interact in France, and to the unique brand of national pride cultivated by its citizens.

And some threads of the story are common to orchestras of any time or place. Effective governance of an orchestra requires scrupulous nourishment of three constituencies: the musicians, composers living and dead, and the public. A library and equipment must be acquired and safeguarded. Relations with civil authorities and colleagues and rivals must be kept cordial, but competitive position not compromised by careless partnerships. The finances must be in some semblance of order.

Portions of this story have been told before.[15] Antoine Elwart's *Histoire de la Société des Concerts du Conservatoire Impérial de Musique* (Paris, 1860) chronicles the first period of the orchestra's history, to June 1860—just over a month after the musicians had elected their third conductor, Théophile Tilmant *aîné*. (A reprinting of 1864 carries the documentation to the end of Tilmant's tenure, in 1863.) Elwart had personally attended all the concerts except those of the 1835 and 1836 seasons, the two years he was abroad as a Prix de Rome laureate; for a time he led the summer *concerts d'émulation* of the Conservatoire student orchestra. His attachment to the Société, as we will note in due course, bordered on the parasitic, but it resulted in his apparently having been the first non-member to gain access to the archives and registers. Hence, in addition to annotated transcriptions of all the programs from 1828 to 1863, his work offers texts of the major decrees, the bylaws, and an important sampling of the rosters and financial accounts. Elwart provides the starting point for all subsequent studies, including this one.

The prolific music historian Arthur Pougin (1834–1921) embarked on a similar project to assemble and annotate all the concert programs but does not appear to have completed his work or published the results.[16]

Elwart's approach was imitated in the next epoch by E.-M.-E. Deldevez, the fifth conductor of the association and author of *La Société des Concerts, 1860–1885* (Paris, 1887). Deldevez, conductor at the time of the fiftieth anniversary of the society, was a capable writer who had already published a conducting treatise (1878) and who had the advantage of being able to consult the documentary sources anytime he liked. In 1890 he published *Mes Mémoires,* with a sequel in 1892, completing a formidable written legacy—the only one left by any of the conductors.

Sequels to Elwart and Deldevez were offered by Arthur Dandelot, sire of the dynasty of concert promoters with whom the Société des Concerts came to work closely in the 1940s and 1950s. First published in 1898, Dandelot's work was later (1923) substantially revised, bringing the published history well into the twentieth century: *La Société des Concerts du Conservatoire (1828–1923) avec une étude historique sur les grands concerts symphoniques avant et depuis 1828.* But Dandelot does not attempt to present more than an abstract of each season, and by comparison with Elwart and Deldevez his assessments seem summary and on the whole disappointing. A twenty-four-page illustrated *Notice historique* by Jean Cordey, published in July 1941, adds documentation through the tenure of Philippe Gaubert (1919–38) and the accession of Charles Münch in 1938; its first iteration, in fact, had been as a public address welcoming Münch to the podium.[17] A much later period, that of the transition from the Société des Concerts to the Orchestre de Paris, is elegantly treated in Nicole Salinger's *Orchestre de Paris* (Paris, 1987), published in connection with the new orchestra's twentieth anniversary and presenting a definitive chronology and discography for the period 1967–87. The 150th anniversary of the Société des Concerts, in 1978, was recognized in a major exhibition and a published brochure that included a number of previously unfamiliar images and source citations.[18]

Every *sociétaire* was conversant, by virtue of the rituals of appointment, with the outlines of the institution's history, and there were always several members who took a particular interest in safeguarding the tale and its sources. Each year the secretary would offer a retrospective of the season; some of these reports became major orations backed by real historical competence, as was the case with Théodore Heymann's address at the end of the eighty-second season, 1908–09.[19] Every couple of decades someone would assemble "notes on the origins of our society" or set down its major turning points. Albert Vernaelde, a bass singer and a four-term secretary of the Société des Concerts, wrote the extended article on the Paris symphonic associations that appears in Albert Lavignac's great *Encyclopédie de la musique,* the first to analyze the difficult decades since the turn of the century and among the most coherent accounts of the interlocking fortunes of the several orchestras that had sprung up in town. (His contribution was written ca. 1920, then updated after his death in 1928 and just before publication by the *sociétaires* Tracol and Bleuzet, the conductor Straram, and the impresario Kiesgen.) Vernaelde was well qualified for the task, having steered the Société successfully through a period of crisis in 1909–11 caused at least in part by increased competition from its own descendents. The conductor André Messager praised Vernaelde for the "truly remarkable fashion in which he fulfilled his functions."[20]

Supplementing these assessments from within are the late- and post-career reminiscences of the participants, from the manuscript memoirs of the violinist and founding member Eugène Sauzay, through Eugène Gautier's charming *Un Musicien en vacances* (1873) and Charles Dancla's *Notes et souvenirs* (1893), and on to the autobiography of Charles Münch, *Je suis chef d'orchestre / I Am a Conductor* (1954–55).[21] From just outside the membership are the memoirs of Piero Coppola, who produced and recorded the extraordinary electric-microphone recordings of the early 1930s (*Dix-sept Ans de musique à Paris, 1922–1939* [1944]), and those of Marcel Landowski, the composer-administrator—and arch-rival of Pierre Boulez—who engineered the transformation of the Société des Concerts into the Orchestre de Paris (*Batailles pour la musique* [1979]; *La Musique n'adoucit pas les mœurs*—i.e., "Music does *not* soothe the savage breast" [1990]).

Finally, any study that touches on the Paris Conservatoire must begin with a salute to the two original documentary histories of that institution, Théodore Lassabathie's *Histoire du Conservatoire* . . . (Paris, 1860) and Constant Pierre's monumental *Le Conservatoire National de Musique et de Déclamation: Documents historiques et administratifs* (Paris, 1900).

The present book is based primarily on the administrative archive of the Société des Concerts, which began to be available for scholarly research in 1975 at the Music Division of the Bibliothèque Nationale in Paris. Berlioz scholars, led by the young British musicologist Hugh Macdonald, had been drawn to the library of the Société in the mid-1960s during the course of assembling the sources for the New Berlioz Edition; a century earlier, in 1863, Berlioz had given all his performance materials to the Société des Concerts, thinking it "the sole musical institution in France whose future [promise] inspires confidence in a composer."[22] The Berliozians arrived, as it happened, just as the Société des Concerts was being dissolved and the Orchestre de Paris created, in the summer of 1967. The collections were in disarray and were dispersing. One portion was apparently still at the Salle des Concerts on the site of the "old" Conservatoire in the rue Bergère. Another was to be found at the "new" Conservatoire in the rue de Madrid. Scores and parts of potential value to the Orchestre de Paris as well as the administrative records necessary for the transition were relocated to offices on an upper floor of the Théâtre des Champs-Élysées, the historic venue that had served as the orchestra's primary hall since the end of World War II. Three reputable historians active at the time concur in their accounts of at least one incident where primary Berlioz sources were found in trash bins in the rue de Madrid.

As the Orchestre de Paris prepared, beginning in about 1972, to move its administrative offices to the new Palais des Congrès at the Porte Maillot (the unpopular "hall in the mall," as it came to be known), and to relieve the growing anxiety of the Berlioz scholars, arrangements were completed to bring the most historic items in the collection, and especially the Berlioz sources, to the Bibliothèque Nationale. There the long task of organizing and cataloguing the materials in a more formal fashion was begun. Letters from Jean-Michel Nectoux at the Bibliothèque Nationale to the Orchestre de Paris—dated January 1975, July 1976, and May 1977—document the progress of the transfer.

In May 1973 I prepared a list of the Berlioz parts already at the Bibliothèque Nationale by verifying the library's master registers against the collection itself and against Hugh Macdonald's original notes; this list enabled us to identify items seen by Macdonald in the late 1960s but not included in the original delivery from the Orchestre de Paris. In March and May of 1978, Nectoux and I returned to the library of the Orchestre de Paris, then in the third sub-basement of the Palais des Congrès, to verify what remained there, and a third handlist was prepared by the two of us. (It was there that I found and identified the two fine pages of sketches for the *Marche pour la présentation des drapeaux* in Berlioz's Te Deum. I presented my first assessment of the collection and its meaning in a public paper delivered in July 1980.) On 18 September 1981, the library of the Orchestre de Paris moved once again, this time to the Salle Pleyel at 252, rue du Faubourg-St-Honoré—a hall that had been inaugurated by the Société des Concerts in 1927 with a gala concert conducted by Gaubert, Stravinsky, and Ravel. To simplify that move, the orchestra deposited yet another portion of its heritage at the Bibliothèque Nationale; the cataloguing was completed and verified by the summer of 1982. I located the missing last volume of personnel registers, with the kind assistance of Nicole Salinger and Geneviève Thomas, at the Orchestre de Paris in the summer of 1998.

At first, scholarly attention centered on the Berlioz materials, and these were soon incorporated into the relevant volumes of the New Berlioz Edition and my *Catalogue of the Works of Hector Berlioz* (1987). Other exciting materials came to light as well. David Charlton, for instance, identified orchestral parts to the otherwise lost third and fourth symphonies of Méhul and readied the edition (1982) that served for the first complete recording.[23] Annie Mary evaluated documents from the Gaubert years in a six-volume typescript *mémoire* in musicology for the Conservatoire, *La Société des Concerts du Conservatoire: Étude historique, 1919–39* (1977).[24] What follows in these pages is the result of my ongoing effort, begun seriously in 1990, to read every file in the archive.

The archive of the Société des Concerts as presently preserved, not counting its library of scores and parts, consists of several dozen bound registers and perhaps a hundred boxes and envelopes of loose paper.[25] Of these thousands of pages the most comprehensive and least interrupted are minutes of the weekly meetings held by the administrative committee and minutes of the annual general assemblies. Since these minutes served as the source of formal, legally binding transcripts and held answers to the often contentious issue of the order in which members were appointed, they were scrupulously assembled to begin with and rigorously conserved later on. Anything that might be needed later for reference or adjudication is set down, often verbatim, and in the case of the committee meetings the record of each *séance* is signed by every member in attendance. Yet by the same token authors go out of their way to protect their colleagues' reputations, to the extent that some of the most delicate incidents in the history of the society are masked or all but hidden completely by the elegant prose. Generally the minutes are recorded in the third person and with detachment, though from time to time a secretary will slip into the first person or, during journeys away from Paris, use the register as a diary. A single volume of the minutes, covering 1931–34, has been lost.

Documents associated with the general assemblies include, in addition to the minutes, the supporting materials collected for presentation to the membership: the secretaries' orations, for instance, and the petitions that first moved amendments to the bylaws. Transcriptions of historic ministerial decrees and excerpts from the statutes were kept nearby for consultation during debates. Where these materials can be reconnected with the meetings for which they were prepared, significant evidentiary threads begin to emerge.

The personnel registers, essentially complete from March 1828 to April 1967, record the names of the members, their instrument or voice part, and date of appointment. For most periods the entries also include the date and place of birth, offices held and appointments received, and occasionally the death date. The few discrepancies generally descend from copying errors incurred in preparing duplicates, though for several blocks of time an attempt to reconstruct the past from flawed sources is clear. More regrettable still are the sharply abbreviated entries, not even including first names, for the hundred or so founding members. Supplementing the personnel registers, with regard to end-of-career matters, is the information to be found in the extensive records of the retirement fund and, later, the social security service. This group of sources suggests any number of corrections to commonly accepted data concerning the more celebrated members, and for the others establishes the very foundation of their biography.

The run of programs is reasonably well intact; the lacunae, mostly from the twentieth century, can usually be filled by consulting concert listings in the press. Last-minute changes to the announced programming, however, can be only haphazardly traced.

Preservation of the correspondence, both incoming and outbound, is sporadic at best and is complicated by a decision at the Bibliothèque Nationale to take letters by and to noteworthy figures away from the archive in order to append them to the existing collection of *lettres autographes.* Much of the outbound correspondence, kept in the form of handwritten drafts—and, after the conspicuously late acquisition of a typewriter, carbon copies—is formulaic: annual announcements to the press, notifications of appointment, letters of thanks for services rendered. Most correspondence received at the Conservatoire is either from candidates desiring appointment—a statutory condition of employment was the submission of a letter of application—or from those desiring engagement as soloist; in addition, there are, of course, hundreds of notes from members begging to be excused from engagements.

We are left a useful overview of the day-to-day business of the early years, and of the language in which it was carried out, in a register of all outgoing correspondence from January 1833 to December 1835, and for brief periods in 1836 and 1846, apparently kept by Joseph Meifred during his tenure as secretary and brought back to the Conservatoire by his heirs.[26] Exceptional correspondence is almost always mentioned in the registers of the committee meetings—though too frequently, as in the case of the condolences addressed by the society to the Mendelssohn family in 1847, the resulting letter itself can no longer be traced.

Naturally, the archive includes a great deal of material related to accounting functions, from daily attendance records to start-of-season lists of subscribers and end-of-year summary reports. The contracts for outside engagements, including recording sessions, are quite carefully kept—again, out of the need for documentary evidence in the case of potential disputes—and are comprehensive for much of the twentieth century.

There were, inevitably, minor errors in the classification scheme and more substantive lapses in the process of carrying it out. The particulars, for instance, of the violent rupture between Charles Münch and his general manager, Jean Savoye, that led to the dismissal of both have crept into a dossier marked "Taffanel's succession" (of 1901), which also contains materials on the election of George-Hainl in 1863.[27] Some of the most precious documents—texts of governing legislation, for example—are buried in piles of loose, unsorted paper, and so far as I can tell there are no remaining copies at all of the frequently updated member handbooks that contained the full text of the bylaws after 1865. Conscientious archivists were forever imploring former officers to deposit their paperwork but were not often successful. As late as 1902 a committee member was complaining that "to have an archivist there must be archives."[28]

The souvenirs and memorabilia include the *livre d'or* of the Société des Concerts, inaugurated by Saint-Saëns in November 1908 as a guestbook to be signed by celebrated visitors. It was soon used to mount significant memorabilia discovered elsewhere in the files, ordinary requests—to appear as soloist, to be appointed to a vacant post, to be sent a complimentary ticket—from extraordinary correspondents: Cherubini and Berlioz, then Lamoureux, Garcin, Sarasate, Thomas, Franck, and Gounod, on through Milhaud, Karajan, Stravinsky, and Hindemith.[29] The *livre d'or* was acquired concurrently with Messager's accession to the podium and kept assiduously until the beginning of World War I, then again from 1947, when the star system had gained irreversible hold.

Of the artifacts elsewhere one might note especially the bronze bust of Beethoven by the sculptor Guillaume (1887) in the administrative office of the modern Orchestre de Paris. Several dozen instruments in the Musée de la Musique (formerly the Musée du Conservatoire) were owned by members and played in the concerts; in the same museum are Romagnesi's plaster medallions and the younger Dantan's justly celebrated *portraits-charges* of the great founders—Habeneck, Vogt, Tulou, Dauprat, Duvernoy, Plantade.[30] A few of the commemorative medals in bronze or silver presented by the society to each new member and every guest soloist are preserved in the Musée de la Musique; the six given to Saint-Saëns are at the Château-Musée de Dieppe. And it is worth repeating that the most precious of all the artifacts left by the Société des Concerts are the sound recordings—the audible and greatly revealing archive of the music that both occasioned and resulted from all the paper.

No single volume, even so long a one as this, can take into account every known source. For every letter preserved in the society's own archive there is commonly, after all, its mate somewhere else. Significant caches are also to be found at the Archives Nationales of France: *fonds* AJ[37] (Conservatoire), F[21] (Beaux-Arts), O (royal and imperial household), and the Minutier Central des Notaires de Paris—though my research suggests that these materials either duplicate or confirm the findings presented here.[31] Nor is there the opportunity to go as richly as I would like into the results of the thriving research on related matters of culture, institutions, and politics of nineteenth- and twentieth-century musical life in France. Representative of the several recent works that have affected my thinking or approach in these areas are *La Vie musicale sous Vichy* (2001), the work of a research group led by Myriam Chimènes; and *Les Affaires Culturelles aux temps d'André Malraux* (1996), the proceedings of a two-day colloquium in 1989 that brought most of the surviving characters back together. The European Science Foundation's ongoing project on Musical Life in Europe 1600–1900 embraces a work group on "The Concert and Its Public in Europe" that devoted a session of its 1999 colloquium to "Les Sociétés de concert au XIXe siècle." In Paris the 1995–96 celebration of the bicentenary of the Conservatoire, coincident with the inauguration of its new campus—the "Cité de la Musique" at La Villette—resulted in major new research and two published volumes that have much to say about the Société des Concerts and its personnel.[32]

   Such essays complement and extend the work of established leaders in the field, notably Jeffrey Cooper, Katharine Ellis, Jane Fulcher, Jann

Pasler, and William Weber.[33] I salute them all and acknowledge their precedence and preeminence, especially in matters of novel methodology. My principal concern here, however, is get the facts of the Société des Concerts du Conservatoire set out—unlike the archive itself—in some trackable order. It is for that reason that I have preferred the chronicle approach, starting in chapter 5, to an organization by themed critiques—for example, repertoire and canon, economics, reception, interaction with other conductors and orchestras.

Nevertheless there *is* a theme, which is that the story of the Société des Concerts is to some degree a microcosm of French history, where a corporate, guild-like body with roots to the *ancien régime* responded both positively and negatively to the larger forces that buffeted French culture and society as a whole, safeguarding with remarkable success its identity and original principles.[34] Embedded in the narrative, then, are the implicit sub-themes: how urbanization, for instance, changed the habits of the ticket-buying public; how the orchestra responded to war; how broadcasting and recording and the star system redefined everything; the prices of state subvention; the meaning of Malraux. The three overviews—1828–72, 1872–1919, 1919–67—attempt to clarify that strategy.

The story of a great musical institution differs from the biography of a great musician not only in lifespan but in the number of voices that recount it. It seems essential to let the characters themselves tell as much of their story as possible, for their insights are keen and their manners of expression memorable. They themselves, for instance, recognized that "we instinctively divide our history into reigns stamped with the character of the conductor—'under Habeneck,' 'under Girard'—to designate an era dominated by thus-and-such a current of artistic and administrative concepts." [35] This book proceeds accordingly, after four chapters that establish the society's overall structure, in chronological order separated into conductors' tenures. In fact the most illuminating vignettes from the archive are often about, and nearly always written by, others: the hitherto unknown deliberations on how to ease the ailing Habeneck into retirement; Rossini's re-emergence in 1861; the poignant communications to Paris from members displaced all over France in 1870; the thick dossiers on the French *manière de voir* and its American counterpart that formed the aftermath of the disputatious 1918 tour of the United States and Canada; the tender farewell in 1964 of the venerable secretary-general André Huot. From these episodes of everyday life and hundreds like them coalesces a greatly more meaningful history than could have been written before.

It is a story of unusually strong beginnings and consistent adaptability later on, characterized by a tactical imagination that led the Société des Concerts to prosper early and to weather the storms of its epoch, emerging each time proud and—the members would have always publicly argued—strong. It is about ancestors and descendents; about competition bred from admiration; about the astonishing ability of Paris, for all its idiosyncrasies, to maintain its position as arbiter of European taste. The archive of the Société des Concerts opens a window over one of the *grands boulevards* of French musical practice to 1967—a broad and blossomed avenue of which we have known too little.

CHAPTER 2

The Musicians

To be elected by one's peers a *sociétaire* of the Société des Concerts du Conservatoire was a signal recognition of expertise, sought by nearly all self-respecting graduates of the institution. The typical field of candidates for a vacant post consisted of the *aspirants*—apprentice members already appearing with the group—as well as the most recent prize-winners from the Conservatoire. All had certified in a letter of candidacy that they had met the conditions of French nationality and ongoing or past affiliation with the academy. Appointment was by decision of the executive committee, most often by unanimous vote endorsing the senior apprentice. The practice of auditioning for vacant positions seemed unnecessary for many decades, since the nominators were already familiar with the results of the juried examinations at the Conservatoire. Auditions began in the late nineteenth century when filling the highly coveted first *(solo)* chairs; competitive auditions for every vacancy were uncommon until well into the twentieth century, as was auditioning to reseat entire sections.

The musicians were expected to appear, when convoked, at rehearsals and Sunday concerts (some sixty services per year during most of the society's first century); to excuse themselves for any absence; to attend the annual general assembly, where officers were elected and the season's proceeds divided among the members; and, when called upon, to take administrative office. They were not to lend their services to any other concert-presenting organization during the season. Tenure was assumed to last until end of career; the modest remuneration was considered, at least publicly, coincidental to the artistic satisfactions of membership.

Virtually all the instrumentalists had a simultaneous appointment with one of the theater orchestras, for which they played something on the order of two hundred services per year (for about 1,200 francs altogether, in the early decades). Wind players often belonged to the military bands, singers to the local theater companies and churches. A few earned the bulk of their livelihood in other enterprises; in 1848, for instance, the violinist Joseph Lecointe explained abandoning a daytime rehearsal owing to the sudden illness of an employee covering for him at the office where he was postmaster. The tenor Arthur Jacquin had sung with the chorus for fifteen years when he was appointed, at age forty-three, head of the insurance company that employed him by day; he wrote the society's first fire insurance policy and went on to provide valuable financial expertise when the retirement fund was in danger of failure in the 1880s.[1]

Most of the principal players were professors at the Conservatoire, where they wrote the treatises and tutorials that changed the face of music making (Hyacinthe Klosé's *Grande Méthode* for clarinet, for instance, still in use today) and trained their own successors. Indeed the clearest indication of a musician's unrivaled seniority in Paris would be concurrent appointments as principal with the Société des Concerts, soloist in the Opéra orchestra, and professor at the Conservatoire. Some pursued an interest in chamber music—for instance, the hornist Dauprat, who popularized the wind quintets of Anton Reicha; Berlioz describes a breathtaking early performance of the Beethoven Piano Quartet with the pianist Hélène Mazel and four *sociétaires:* Veny, Klosé, Kocken, and Dauprat.[2] Many of the most prominent French string quartets were organized from within the membership (including that of Baillot, with Vidal, Urhan, and Norblin). Nearly everyone had composed etudes and exercises, and a surprising number of the members had successful ballets and light operas to their credit. Some of the serious composers had major works performed at concerts of their own society, as was the case with excerpts from the Fifth Mass by V.-F. Verrimst, a doublebassist, played at the *concerts spirituels* of April 1873. Any number of the players earned their principal livelihood as conductors elsewhere.

By and large the musicians sat by order of seniority within their sections, with the senior member acting as *chef d'attaque* in the strings and *solo* in the winds. One member who believed strongly in the principle of seniority (and its corollary, that every member was as capable as all the rest) was the violinist Henri Berthelier, who served some ten seasons in the late nineteenth century as the designated *1er violon solo,* but preferred to render the solo work from the middle of the first violin section, where he sat according to his years of membership.

Occasionally, a player sensing diminished capacity would retreat to the back of the section, relinquishing his seat to a younger player favored by his colleagues; perhaps he would change sections entirely, moving to the viola section, the chorus, or to cover bass drum and cymbals. By contrast, Émile Schvartz served briefly as a viola player, then became chorusmaster, a role he filled with notable success. But when the violist Henri Aumont (who had garnered a *2ᵉ prix* in violin) asked in 1851 to move to the violin section, he was refused, the committee wishing to save those vacancies for the apprentices already in the section and not wishing to open any floodgates.

In one unusual case, the violinist Jean-Jacques Masset transferred in 1839 to the tenors—not an unprecedented shift, but one usually associated with instrumentalists suffering some form of digital incapacity. Masset, a student of Habeneck who had won a *2ᵉ prix* in 1828, played violin in the orchestras of the Théâtre des Variétés and Théâtre-Italien and viola at the Opéra before being named conductor at the Variétés in 1835. His flute concerto was performed by Dorus at concerts in 1835 and 1836, and excerpts of a violin concerto offered by Charles Dancla in 1837 and 1839. Accepting the challenge to join the Opéra-Comique, Masset made his debut in late September 1839 in Adolphe Adam's *La Reine d'un jour* and consequently applied to fill a vacant spot in the tenor section of the society's chorus. He went on to a colorful career in Italy and Spain and the Paris Opéra (1848–49), returning to the Société des Concerts in January 1850 as tenor soloist in a romance of Martini. After his retirement from the stage he worked more than three decades as professor of voice at the Conservatoire.[3]

A defining feature of the Société des Concerts, and a major shaper of its repertoire, was the chorus. Some forty or so of the original members were singers; the rest of the chorus had been assembled from the *classe d'ensemble vocal* at the Conservatoire and from the considerable ranks of graduated aspiring opera singers. Those elected to full membership as *sociétaires* included, in addition to the star soloists treated below, principals at the Opéra (the tenor Wartel in the 1830s; the brilliant bass Florentin Auguez in the 1870s) and those whose main contribution was in the oratorio repertoire offered by the society itself (J.-U. Boussagol, with a forty-year career; A.-É. Narçon, soloist from 1890 to 1914). In the case of women singers, the situation was considerably more ambiguous, with a few being named as *sociétaires solo* but most holding apprentice or, at best, adjunct membership. The result, combined with the inevitable disappearance of women to marry and become *mères de famille,* was a rapid turnover each season in the sopranos alongside great stability in the tenors and basses.

By the end of the century, maintaining a full-time, full-sized chorus was no longer viable. The last chorus members, Thomas Bonnefoy and Jean Saraillé, were elected in June 1914; beginning with Gaubert's tenure in 1919, there was no effort to schedule choral works at every concert. The affected members were allowed to serve in other capacities as attrition took its course (twelve members were left in 1926–27, eight in 1928–29); the tenor Marius Mille, appointed in 1904, went on after the war to participate as percussionist and keyboard player, while Saraillé was *inspecteur de la salle* for two decades (1920–41) at full compensation.[4]

One was expected to resign when the obligations of membership could not routinely be met. After ten years of service, departing members were usually granted the title *membre honoraire,* which gave them access to their retirement accounts and to vacant seats for the concerts. Honorary members were welcome at the general assemblies, where they frequently appeared to "protect the traditions" of their society. Obituaries would note that a long-retired member had been sitting among them when last they had met—Charles Dancla, for example, "an octogenarian, full of youthful ardor."[5]

In the early 1840s the mandatory retirement age was set at sixty, also the age a member gained access to the pension offered by the Association des Artistes-Musiciens, forerunner of the musicians' union. Those having reached the *limite d'âge* without significant impairment might be granted two or three extensions, or *sursis,* but seldom more. The doublebassist Eugène Tubeuf was denied his *sursis* in 1889 because it was discovered that he had altered his birthdate while serving as personnel manager in order to extend his years of possible service. By contrast, the violist Julien Gaillard was granted seven *sursis* (1920–26) so that he might continue his capable and popular work as *archiviste-caissier.* When Jean Bouvenne, a bass in the chorus and a founding member, was retired at the *limite d'âge,* Mme Bouvenne, a soprano, resigned simultaneously—though whether in pique or to join him in the rustic pleasures of retirement is not recorded. An effort to establish mandatory retirement for singers at age fifty or fifty-five was never successful.

Except during periods of general upheaval, surprisingly few musicians resigned their posts early. Something on the order of half the *sociétaires,* perhaps three-quarters of the instrumentalists, served from the beginning to the end of their active careers. Those who went away left to seek more glamorous work abroad, generally as recitalists, or to accept attractive offers from the provincial conservatories. The doublebassist Mathieu, a founding member, resigned in 1851 to become a farmer, but his contribution had by then been long and distinguished. Singers sometimes left owing to irreconcilable conflicts between their jobs as church choirmasters and their mandatory presence on the bleachers at 2:00 each Sunday. Members failing to resign before accepting other engagements were dismissed by the committee—in their elegant usage, "considered as having resigned" *("considéré comme démissionnaire")*—as habitual absentees.

Otherwise, the decision to quit the society usually had to do with ill health, declining faculties, or simply *fatigue,* the culture's universally accepted reason for abandoning one's *métier.* Resignation was not always taken seriously. When Tulou, nearing his sixtieth birthday just as mandatory retirement went into effect, offered to vacate his seat, the committee rejected his proposal as "without the slightest value" and sent his letter back "so that it doesn't clutter our archive."[6]

Almost without exception, members announced their intention to depart, or their acceptance of the suggestion to depart, in grateful, graceful terms. In the late 1860s the violinist Rignault expressed his thanks for the granting of a *sursis,* which allowed him to "stay in the bosom of this great and beautiful society where every artist would be happy and proud to find himself," noting that he was certain the recognition was "more for my zeal than for my talent."[7]

More than one, in departing, reflected that his reason for staying in Paris at all had been membership in the Société des Concerts. In May 1885, after two *sursis* and nearly twenty years of service, the tenor Paul Juette wrote:

> I was still fully occupied by a career as a leading tenor in the provinces when, in 1868, I went to the auditions for the Société des Concerts. I did not think I would stay long, preferring new theatrical engagements. But the moment I participated in such perfect performances, I became a fanatic. It seemed to me that I was hearing true music for the first time. After that, I lacked the courage to leave a place where they did such beautiful things. Thus I attached myself to the chorus so that every Sunday my ears could revel in the lyric temple, "the Louvre of Music," as M. [Narcisse] Girard once said to the Empress Eugénie. I can never forget the delicious sensations I felt at the concerts of the Société.[8]

On her husband's death in 1929, the widow of Julien Gaillard, violist and longtime officer of the society, remarked simply that "the Société des Concerts was the great artistic love of his life."[9]

Active musicians were expected to attend the funerals of their colleagues, and in the early decades such attendance was mandated by statute. This noble provision became burdensome once there was a large cohort of the retired; those who lasted into their eighties and nineties after retiring to the provinces would have been forgotten by the active membership, and families routinely neglected to notify the society of their loss. At mid-century, the full membership was convoked to funerals of active members who had died during the season. By the death of the noted cellist L.-J. Jacquard in 1886, however, the official response was limited to a floral offering at the society's expense, duly noted in the minutes as though setting a precedent.[10]

Most of the *sociétaires* had first become affiliated with the Société des Concerts as *aspirants,* on the whole a normal career step for prizewinners from the Conservatoire. (The routine use of enrolled students had come to an end after the first seasons, as the ranks filled with graduates.) Qualified players would first be placed on the list of apprentice *aspirants en cas,* to be called as substitutes and in emergencies. On assuming duties for a full season, a young player took the title *aspirant actif,* awaiting a vacancy by retirement or resignation. Eventual election as *sociétaire,* by order one was first invited to serve as an *aspirant,* was virtually assured.

Sometimes the whole process took only a year or two for the strings, somewhat longer for the winds since there were many fewer positions. But when the complement of *sociétaires* was filled with young and middle-aged musicians, access could be blocked for years. The violist L.-J. Henricet waited eight years as an *aspirant.* Jules Garcin, who became the orchestra's sixth conductor in 1885, had waited three years from his 1er *prix* of 1853 to be named even an *aspirant en cas,* then three seasons before becoming an *aspirant actif,* and another four before his election as a *sociétaire* in 1863 — a decade in all. At one point he wrote to remind the committee that he had petitioned for appointment as *aspirant* every year since 1848. Charles Lamoureux, who won the next 1er *prix,* in 1854, noted sourly in 1859 that his violin teacher, no less a figure than the conductor Girard, had tried to secure his admission for three years without result; Lamoureux, too, was appointed in 1863, two months after Garcin — both profiting from the round of retirements and resignations that tended to accompany a change in conductor.[11] Auguste Tolbecque *fils* became an *aspirant* on winning his 1er *prix* in cello in 1849, at the age of nineteen, but was not elected to full membership until 1873.

Nevertheless, the Société des Concerts was utterly reliant on the *as-*

pirants for filling its ranks and treated them both fairly and, in the long run, generously enough to prevent raiding from rival organizations. For young people it was a useful arrangement, since there was a certain amount of leeway in expectations; unlike the *sociétaires, aspirants* could be excused to accept other engagements, and if serious employment opportunities opened in the provinces or abroad, they could leave for entire seasons without jeopardizing their chances for eventual election. Several musicians, indeed, served as *aspirants,* established good careers elsewhere, then returned as *sociétaires* of relatively advanced age.

What was important, in the case of the long waits for a vacancy to open, was that the written record of a musician's first engagement as *aspirant* be correct in the personnel registers. Election of a new *sociétaire* sometimes took place in a climate of urgency or confusion, and even within so tradition-minded an organization the institutional memory of seniority could be short. In one bitter case the violist Jean Conte, an *aspirant* given to complaining about his situation anyway, challenged the preferential seating (and thus the probable order of subsequent election) of a younger player, Cassaing. This favor Conte attributed to the protection of "an over-zealous friend." Favor had been extended to Cassaing, the committee replied, because he was principally a viola player and not, like Conte, a redirected violinist. Conte angrily set out the true facts: both had begun as violinists (and his rival also as a tenor); Cassaing was still playing violin at the Concerts Pasdeloup; they had begun to substitute for missing violists in the same year, but Conte was violist at the Opéra while Cassaing served at the less prestigious Opéra-Comique. "Thus," Conte summarized, "M. Cassaing is no more a specialist than I: he simply plays viola like any decent violinist does."[12] Moreover, Cassaing had never taken classes at the Conservatoire. The case was won; Conte was elected *sociétaire* in 1876, and Cassaing disappeared.

Following World War I, in an effort driven primarily by competition for the best graduating musicians, a new and perhaps more reassuring title was developed for musicians awaiting permanent vacancies, that of *sociétaire adjoint.* (An older use of that title had disappeared with the chorus; it was also occasionally used as a title for permanent musicians who were either of foreign birth, as was the case with the tenor Marcel Devriès in 1904, or who had been prevented from attending the Conservatoire by external circumstance, as was the case with the violist Emmanuel Elissalde in 1926.) The three categories of membership were, thereafter, *aspirant* (the old *aspirant en cas*), *sociétaire adjoint* (the old *aspirant*), and *sociétaire*. In the 1960s, when apprentice workers throughout France were said to be *en stage*, the usage mutated to *aspirants, stagiaires, sociétaires*. It was not uncommon, in this period, to convoke the best nineteen- and twenty-year-olds from the Conservatoire to serve as substitutes, then see them elected decades later as *sociétaires*. This was the case, for example, with the violinist Fernand Datte and the violist Marcel Laffont, whose names appear in the pay manifests of the late 1920s but who were not elected until the 1950s. Both became founding members of the Orchestre de Paris in 1967.

Some important, essentially permanent players preferred not to be bound by the requirements of full membership but instead to remain *externes*, compensated with a fee for service roughly equivalent to the value of a member's share. The *externes* agreed to give first priority to activities of the Société des Concerts but, unlike the *sociétaires*, were not required to be present when they had nothing to play, thus leaving them available for other work. Long-term engagement of external players tested some of the most delicate house practices. On the one hand, it was the only arrangement to which certain of the most prominent players would agree (the noted timpanist Joseph Baggers, for instance, who played in the orchestra from 1907 to 1918 but was never a *sociétaire*) and the only practical way to deal with intermittent needs for percussion, harps, and keyboard. On the other, since fees paid to ad hoc players reduced the overall income to be distributed among the *sociétaires* at the end of the year, it was often suspected that the *externes* were making away early with more than a fair share—and without the risk borne by all the others. In this regard, however, it is telling that an 1838 proposal to reduce the payment to external members to a rate calculated as one-third less than that of the *sociétaires* failed soundly when brought to a vote.[13]

A closely related problem was the hard feeling that sometimes erupted concerning the practice whereby full shares were paid to, and full attendance expected from, *sociétaires* who often had nothing to play: the third-chair players in the woodwind sections, and of course the low brass and timpani players. In 1845 the matter came to the fore when Leplus (flute III and piccolo), Hugo (clarinet III and bass clarinet), and Dieppo (trombone I)—all of them longtime and respected members of the orchestra—were invited to join the committee in studying the nuances afoot.[14] It was already obvious that the repertoire would continue to demand growth in overall size of the orchestra, and a way of establishing new positions would have to be found. Over the years, successive administrations adjusted the balance of *sociétaires, aspirants,* and *externes* in their attempt to find advantageous conditions for all; in general the trajectory was toward eliminating singers in order to open posts for an extended orchestral complement. Yet not until 1908 was it thought necessary to have a slot for the tuba player.

Until about 1850 there was another category of membership, that of *sociétaire solo.* This title was reserved for the most prestigious, and most highly paid, musicians in Paris, with the mutual understanding that they would appear for a modest honorarium (twice that of the rank and file) when needed but be otherwise exempt from the provision of mandatory attendance. All but two, the violinist Pierre Baillot and the pianist Frédéric Kalkbrenner, were stars at the Opéra: Dérivis, Levasseur, Nourrit, Duprez, and Bataille; Mmes Cinti-Damoreau, Gras-Dorus, and Stolz; both M. and Mme Dabadie; and Mlles Falcon and Nau.[15] Baillot's unusual appointment—he was already in his mid-sixties and had helped establish not only the Société des Concerts but also its predecessors—followed his participation in the concert of 29 March 1835 (the solo from Beethoven's *Missa solemnis,* the Romance in F, and his own Andante *con sordini*). He had later stopped into a committee meeting to offer the members his heartfelt thanks for the title and assurances of his "entire devotion to a society that has rendered, and is certain to continue to render, such great service to art." When he declined payment of any sort, it was decided to offer him the commemorative medal cast in gold.[16]

Mme Viardot and the tenor Gustave Roger were included on various lists of the *sociétaires solo* but never formally entered into the master registers of personnel. This is a curious state of affairs in both cases; Roger had, among his several services to the society, translated the text of their popular rendition of *The Seasons,* and Mme Viardot was beloved of the Société des Concerts—as she was by all who knew her—and fastidious in her service to it. When in 1841 she took care to inform the committee of a forthcoming trip to London, she also offered to participate in any concert before she left. A delegation was sent to call on her forthwith, resulting in her memorable appearance in arias of Handel and Mozart on 7 February 1841.[17] The practice of appointing *sociétaires solo* began to fade as the great stars of the lyric stage increasingly declined to accept long-term affiliations; the last was the soprano Sophie Boulart, elected in 1856.

The title had, in truth, been used simply to retain on the rolls the names of celebrated artists no longer able to lend themselves regularly to the society. Prosper Dérivis politely resigned his post before leaving for Italy in 1841, but his resignation was declined in favor of the largely honorary title *sociétaire solo*. Mlle Lefebvre, an *aspirante,* wrote in 1851 that she could not continue to come to chorus rehearsal owing to the fatigue resulting from her theater career; she asked for, and received, the title of *sociétaire solo,* but disappeared entirely before being entered in the record.[18]

While most of the celebrated French divas of the mid-nineteenth century served at least some time as *sociétaires solos,* and while many dozens more young women sang in the chorus, there was in the history of the Société des Concerts only a single woman instrumentalist—the harpist Alys Lautemann. She seconded, as *aspirante,* the veteran soloist Victor Cœur beginning with the 1926–27 season, then at his retirement in 1942 advanced into his seat. In the spring of 1944 she petitioned for the full appointment as *sociétaire* that many thought her just due, but on 6 June 1944 the minutes say, tersely, that "the committee, following the statutes, declines this request."[19]

For many decades it was customary to recognize the unpaid guest soloists and others who had offered special service to the Société des Concerts with a letter of thanks and the gift of "a small token" (*faible témoignage*) of their gratitude: the commemorative medal bearing the young Habeneck's likeness and the simple legend "*F. Habeneck / fondateur*"—proof positive, incidentally, that Cherubini's role in the foundation was regarded as secondary. The medals—in bronze or, on conspicuous occasion, silver or gold—were cast at the national mint and had some commercial value (unlike the tiny *jetons de présence* on which they were based); each *sociétaire* had been given the opportunity to purchase one as a formality of appointment and perhaps as an investment. In 1836, to choose a representative season, medals were sent to the pianists Thalberg and Billet, the violinist Molique, the flutist Dorus, and the hornist Bernard for their solo appearances. Medals were also sent abroad, with letters in ceremonious prose, to foreign artists whose compositions had been presented and admired in Paris, among them Friedrich Schneider, Schwenke, and Mendelssohn. Over the years Saint-Saëns was given six medals by the Société des Concerts. As fees for concerto appearances became the norm, presentation of the medals declined accordingly.

Particularly affectionate or generous relationships with an outsider were ceremoniously acknowledged with the title of *sociétaire honoraire* (or occasionally *membre honoraire*—but a quite different sort of honorific than the one extended to retiring members). The great Wagnerian soprano Gabrielle Krauss was the first to receive this title, in 1870; similarly honored were the pianists Louis Diémer (in 1899) and E.-M. Delaborde (in 1906). The trumpet player Édouard Lachanaud was so saluted in 1920 for coming out of retirement to cover a defection in the ranks, as was the New York Symphony conductor Walter Damrosch on the occasion of that orchestra's visit in May 1920. Francescatti was recognized in 1935 for donating the fee from his solo appearance (in Lalo's *Symphonie espagnole* and Dohnányi's *Ruralia hungarica* for violin and piano) to the pension fund. A donor, Mme Louise Maillot, was named a *sociétaire honoraire* in 1929.

Compensation of the players was merely honorific at first, and never more than modest. For years the musicians earned 240 or 250 francs per season. At the end of the society's first century, in 1928–29, the tax and compensation records suggest that a conscientious full-time *sociétaire* made 3,770 francs for his year's work; *aspirants* who had played the whole season earned about half that—1,350 to 1,950 francs. The leftover chorus members with nothing to do made 1,551 francs, while Saraillé, as *inspecteur de la salle,* made 3,226 francs. Gaubert's income that year from his orchestral conducting was 18,057 francs, between five and six times the orchestra's compensation. Münch, writing in 1954, suggests that his players made about 500 old francs, or $1.45 per service—or on the order of $6.00 a week for three rehearsals and a Sunday concert. Münch talks of the eighteen-hour day as common, which may not be exaggerating by much; a workday that began with a 10:00 A.M. rehearsal and concluded with an opera would take sixteen hours from the time a musician left the house at 8:00 in the morning until he returned home at midnight. The treasurer André Huot reckoned in 1947 that every *sociétaire* at the Assemblée Générale had earned 1,950 francs per concert, which given the total number of concerts that year would have brought the season income of an ordinary *sociétaire* to something approaching 60,000 francs—just over $200.[20]

What had begun as formal association of some 100 artists and several dozen "supernumeraries" stabilized as an organization of about 160— 80 instrumentalists and 80 singers—of whom between 100 (in 1828) and 120 (in 1843) were full *sociétaires.* Of the founding members, a little over half were orchestra players (including an essentially full brass section—four horns, three trumpets, three trombones, ophicleide—and a timpanist); the rest were chorus members, soloists, and staff (conductor, chorusmaster, accompanist). The increase from 64 to 74 orchestral *sociétaires* in 1857 represents a significant change, both in the practice of securing soloists and in the explicit reservation of two-thirds of the posts for the orchestra.

Notions of ideal orchestral strength and disposition were at the outset based on the composition of the Opéra orchestra, with its 12–12–8–12–8 strings. That 24 violins was somehow the natural size for a splendid orchestra goes back—in concept, if not in the particulars—to the celebrated *violons du roi* of the seventeenth century. Within a decade of the society's founding, living composers and new repertoire put increasing pressure on a structure that at first reckoned for only 60-odd orchestral *sociétaires* altogether. From the beginning, Habeneck preferred to use 60 strings: 15–14–10–12–9. There were about a dozen woodwind *sociétaires* (3–3–2–4) and modest brass: generally 4 horns, 2 trumpets, 2 trombones, and a timpanist. The odd E♭ or bass clarinet part and supplementary brass were played by the *membres externes;* percussion parts were covered by young *aspirants* in the doublebass section or, in the 1890s and early 1900s, by Couppas, the contrabassoonist.[21] But this was a plainly untenable arrangement for long, and ultimately places had to be found for quadrupled winds and 3 percussionists. Among the *externes* there had to be a place for a harpist, then 2, and for an organist as well. Münch's orchestra of the 1940s generally numbered 87: 14–14–10–10–8, triple winds, quadruple brass, a timpanist and 2 percussionists, 2 harps, piano, and organ.

The ideal chorus numbers were generally thought to be 16 each, sopranos I and II; and 10 each, tenors I–II and basses I–II—a total of 72, often rounded up. When the four-part chorus became the norm, it consisted of 20 of each voice part, as listed, for instance, in the rosters for 1904–05.

It is worth noting that in the twentieth century, the full complement of players seems seldom to have been achieved. None of the photographs shows anything like the 56 string players just enumerated, but rather something on the order of 10 violins and 8 of each lower string. Nor, as the decades passed, were all 120 *sociétaires* active in any one season; attendance at the general assemblies averaged between 90 and 105.

Authority to govern and the responsibility for stewardship of the society were vested by the general assembly in its Comité d'Administration, called henceforth simply the committee. Its eight-man membership—president, vice president / conductor, secretary, *commissaire du personnel, commissaire du matériel, agent comptable, archiviste-caissier,* and *membre adjoint*—was stable for many decades. After Habeneck's death it was acknowledged that both the structure of the committee and the habit of populating it with the strongest personalities in the organization had been calculated to check and balance any autocratic leanings that might develop in the conductor, and what we know of Habeneck's temperament suggests that this strategy was not ill advised. The committee was hardworking from the first, and had secured effective control of the organization within a year and for all intents and purposes complete administrative authority by the time the bylaws of 1 January 1834 were drafted.

Though not required by the first statutes, the office of president was filled from 1833, with only one exception, by the director of the Conservatoire. Habeneck, presiding over the early years, had reported to Cherubini as director, who in turn was charged with carrying out the ministerial edict of February 1828. Cherubini took formal office as president in November 1833 in the process of ratifying the bylaws, and after somewhat petulantly noting that he had never been made *sociétaire.* The next directors, Daniel Auber (1842–71) and Ambroise Thomas (1871–96), each served as president of the committee from the time of assuming their post at the Conservatoire until their deaths. After Thomas's death, specific language connecting the two offices was added to the rules. The authority cited was a decree of 13 December 1832: "The Director of the Conservatoire will convene and preside over the committee."

In ordinary times, the presidency was largely ceremonial, limited to routine and often quite brief appearances to open the general assemblies. There was the occasional dispute to mediate, and the intervention of the director of the Conservatoire was essential to securing the attention of "notable personalities" in high authority. Letters to these individuals, though written by the secretary, were always signed by the president. But for a director of the Conservatoire to take particular interest in the daily activities of the Société des Concerts was the exception to the rule. Ambroise Thomas and his wife occasionally gave receptions after concerts to honor distinguished foreign soloists. Fauré's tenure (1905–20) embraced periods of active hostility between the orchestra and the administration of the Conservatoire and was further complicated by his particular interest in the Société Nationale, which some considered a competing organization. It was thus a considerable relief when Fauré was succeeded by Henri Rabaud (1920–41), raised in the shadow of the Société des Concerts; his father, the cellist Hippolyte Rabaud, had been principal cellist and an important officer, and his ancestry extended back to founding members.

After World War II, interaction between the director of the Conservatoire and the orchestra became rather more commonplace, notably in developing responses to the crises that, more and more, came to dominate the affairs of the Société des Concerts. Claude Delvincourt (1946–54) and Raymond Loucheur (1956–62) each presented a warm discourse on assuming office and tried to attend every meeting of the general assembly. Raymond Gallois-Montbrun (1962–67) was a major architect of the plan to absorb the Société des Concerts into an independent Orchestre de Paris and of the ideas for a new Conservatoire that finally resulted in the Cité de la Musique at La Villette.

"The conductor," it says simply in the rules of 1828, "will lead the performance and will be the only one with the right to beat time." "The conductor," Deldevez later remarked, "reigns but does not govern."[22] It was a brilliant political stroke in 1833, especially for an ensemble of theoretical equals, to put the conductor second in the chain of authority, as *vice-président / 1ᵉʳ chef d'orchestre*. In practice the post was nevertheless the most prestigious in the country, all the more so since its incumbent was usually also *1ᵉʳ chef* at the Opéra and, after its establishment, professor of the *classe d'orchestre* at the Conservatoire. Assaults on what amounted to life tenure were repeatedly turned back. In 1890, for instance, reasoning that "even though our society is an exemplary case of the republican system in its most advanced form—in equality of salaries, universal suffrage, and ongoing adjustment of its constitution," the members recognized the necessity for "absolute autocracy" and defeated a measure to renew the conductor's mandate every five years. Further it was acknowledged that non–re-election of a conductor in mid-career would be humiliating.[23]

Remuneration of the conductor was set at twice that of the musicians, increasing to eight times under Philippe Gaubert—a reflection both of new scales throughout the orchestra and of Gaubert's own earning power in the world at large. Habeneck earned about 750 francs annually from the Société des Concerts and carried less than 1,000 francs into his retirement. Gaubert, we noted above, made just over 18,000 francs from the Société des Concerts in 1927–28; a decade later, Münch's annual salary was 140,000 francs, some eight times what Gaubert had made.[24]

On Henri Rabaud's retirement from the Conservatoire in 1941, Charles Münch, who had been conductor for three seasons, engineered his own election as president; Rabaud's successor, Delvincourt, served as "honorary president" until the abrupt departure of Münch in 1946. A similar arrangement was discussed when André Cluytens was conductor (1946–61), but by then the orchestra was effectively being run by a general manager, and most of the conducting was done by guests. Such distinctions held little meaning for Cluytens, and the administrative power of the director of the Conservatoire to secure governmental intervention was more essential to the society's best interests than ever.

In the early years, the principal first violinist—the *chef d'attaque*—had seconded the conductor in emergencies; in 1848, provision for a 2^e *chef*, seated in the first chair of the violin section and a statutory member of the committee, was added to the bylaws. A statute limiting candidacy for the position to existing members of the society was passed in 1860. Until that time, the main attraction of the post was in establishing succession to the podium, since the *chefs* had near-perfect attendance records. With Deldevez, whose health was unpredictable, there were good opportunities to conduct the great orchestra before the public. Lamoureux, Ernest Altès, and Garcin succeeded each other as assistants to Deldevez; Garcin ultimately took his place. Paul Taffanel and Philippe Gaubert were both known to the membership from their tenures as assistant conductor when they were elected 1er *chef*. The bitter departure of the reputable violinist / conductor Désiré Thibault, 2e *chef* from 1892 to 1901, prompted numerous adjustments to the bylaws and a string of unsuitable incumbents, then stabilized with Gaubert's long apprenticeship (1905–18). Issues of how, from what constituencies, and for how long to appoint assistant conductors arose again in the 1920s. Jean Martinon served briefly as assistant conductor and heir apparent to Münch, after which the question of sub-conductors was swept into the overall, rather nuanced, matter of engaging guest conductors.

The secretary, later the secretary-general, was the chief administrator of day-to-day activities, partly because he established the agenda and kept the minutes of the committee meetings, but mostly because it was the secretary who delivered, each year, the *rapport moral* concerning the season's work and who thus in some measure seemed responsible for it. The secretary was also charged with preparing an analysis of each issue brought to the vote of the general assembly. Both types of addresses were usually written out word for word and approved in advance by the rest of the committee.[25] The secretary's term was for two years.

A small notebook is preserved in the archives in which a secretary of the 1850s has listed things to do at the opening and close of each session:

OPENING OF THE SESSION

1. A week before the first concert, go to the offices of the Assistance Publique, avenue Victoria, no. 3, to renew the subscription for the *droit des indigents* and sign it.
2. Write to the emperor and empress (having the letter signed by the president), the minister of the imperial household, the minister of fine arts, and the director of theaters at the imperial household, to announce the opening of the session. For the first concert, write a letter, enclosing tickets and a program, to the directors of the Imperial Opéra and the Opéra-Comique.
3. Write the prefect of police a few days before the first concert, inviting him to send personnel to the concerts, remembering to include dates and times. Recommend that the officers come at noon.
4. Before the first concert, give the *inspecteur de la salle* the list of members of the press to be admitted to the concerts.
5. Taking note of the date of the last general rehearsal for each concert, prepare the large piece of paper that needs to be signed by the students for admission to the rehearsals.

NEW PROCEDURES

1. The secretary will stamp the letters, record the expense, and present the bill at the end of the session to the *agent comptable*.
2. Every Friday before a concert, put a program and two tickets to the ministerial *loge* in an envelope to Count Baiocchi.
3. At the beginning of each committee meeting, read the minutes of the previous meeting, have them adopted, and transcribe them into the register of minutes.

CONCERNING POSTERS

1. First posting of the season: twelve days before the first concert.
2. First posting of program the Thursday preceding the concert.
3. Second, corrected posting Saturdays after the rehearsals.

CLOSE OF SESSION

1. Prepare the report on the work of the session to read to the committee before the Assemblée Générale for the reckoning of accounts. Post the agenda for the assembly before the beginning of the meeting.
2. The day after the last concert, go the office of the high chamberlain (at the Tuileries), between noon and 3:00, to announce the end of the concerts and ask reimbursement for the price of the imperial box.
3. Take the notary a stamped document containing the family names and first names of *sociétaires* admitted during the season.
4. Make sure that the new *sociétaires* have signed the acts of association before the day honoraria are paid.

5. Give the notary, as a stamped document, extracts of the minutes of any Assemblée Générale in which the modifications or additions to the statutes were voted.

6. Send or take medals of the society to guest artists not in the Société des Concerts who lent their participation as soloists, along with letters of thanks.

7. The secretary is responsible for making any public announcements at concerts.

8. At the committee meeting following each performance he annotates the program and copies the annotated program into the archive of programs.[26]

Deldevez suggests that it was the common practice for each committee member to pass such a notebook of duties on to his successor.[27]

The secretary acted as chief correspondent for the Société, and was delegated the power to sign letters on behalf of the organization. Additionally he counted ballots, acted as liaison with the Conservatoire, and collected signatures of each committee member following the adoption of the minutes of the previous meeting.

The more powerful secretaries did as much to shape the success of the Société des Concerts as anyone, devoting essentially all their spare hours to assuring its prosperity. Though limited to two-year terms, they would merely rotate to another office, returning at their next eligibility to be elected again, hence administering the organization for terms that rivaled those of the conductors. Among the most prominent, with dates of their overall administrative tenure, were the ubiquitous Meifred (1828–53); the cellist Charles Lebouc (1856–78), for whom Saint-Saëns wrote "The Swan"; the violist Alfred Viguier (1869–87); Taffanel (1875–91; the following season he was elected first conductor); Vernaelde (1897–1911); the violist Albert Seitz (1904–26); and the violinist André Tracol (1913–30), also concertmaster and assistant conductor. Albert Ferrand and his conductor, George-Hainl, kept the Société des Concerts alive through the troubles of 1870–71—the Franco-Prussian War and its aftermath; Seitz and Tracol steered the organization through World War I and the American tour and its litigious aftermath.

In 1937, during what amounted to a takeover of the Société des Concerts by the dissatisfied younger generation, the violinist Jean Savoye emerged as secretary, a position he retained uninterrupted until his dismissal in 1948, from 1941 styling himself secretary-general. Savoye was succeeded by his companion-at-arms, the violinist André Huot (1948–63), easily the most admired administrator of the twentieth century. The principal second violinist, Georges Tessier, guided the society through its dissolution and re-emergence (1965–67) and served for three seasons as the general manger of the new Orchestre de Paris. In early 1961, after the resignation of André Cluytens as conductor and vice president, the offices of secretary-general and vice president were considered the same. In May 1965 this arrangement was ratified by a change to the statutes, which thereafter called for a "vice president who, in his exterior relations, will carry the title secretary-general." [28]

The personnel manager, or *commissaire du personnel,* convoked the players to rehearsals, concerts, and general assemblies. His most public duty was to call the roll at every gathering of the membership; when the orchestra and chorus rehearsed simultaneously in different rooms, he was allowed to delegate the chorus roll call to the chorusmaster. Following this formality the *feuilles de présence,* large-format lithographed rosters of the year's personnel, would be completed for forwarding to the accounting officers. Since each *présence* amounted to an eventual share of the financial proceeds, with each tardy arrival or early departure incurring a fine, the position was one of considerable authority. Certainly it demanded diplomatic skills, and not infrequently entailed risks to the incumbent's standing among his peers. From time to time it would happen, as a result, that no one would stand for election and a colleague would have to be pled with. The statutes note presence of the *commissaire du personnel* to be indispensable for every function during the season.

The *commissaire du personnel* kept, too, both the annual and the permanent registers of membership. At the beginning of each season a copyist would prepare a clean copy of the previous year's personnel notebook, into which the new year's resignations and retirements, appointments, and adjustments would be entered as the season went by. It was critical that the old and new notebooks be on hand when each incoming committee came to assess, while the players were away on their summer holidays, the present state and future needs of the personnel. In the summer before the 1840 season, apparently owing to illness, the bassist Kilian failed to turn the personnel records over to the incoming commissioner, Gustave Vogt, and chaos ensued; this was especially vexing for Vogt, who had served with distinction in that office on and off since 1832. The accuracy of the personnel records declined noticeably over the next three decades. [29]

In 1876, following the events of 1870–71 and increasing pressure from Deldevez to clean up the books, the *commissaire du personnel* Charles Turban went back through the archive to reconstruct the employment history of each *sociétaire*. His work led to the preparation of the main personnel registers, still being kept as of the dissolution and preserved intact today.

The personnel manager came to exercise still more influence in the twentieth century, since it was he who chose and summoned members to extra work: film and recording sessions and any supplementary engagements where the name of the Société des Concerts was invoked. As contracting musicians for outside work became more frequent, more politically charged, and less possible to achieve effectively, it proved necessary to have two personnel officers, one each for strings and for winds. The 1950s saw the organization of a *conseil de solistes* (first-chair players), whose principal purpose was to act as a liaison between the committee and the personnel.

The *commissaire du matériel*, originally the *bibliothécaire* ("librarian"), was to assure the copying of parts and the acquisition by purchase or loan of "the objects necessary to the Society," both instruments and furnishings. He was to see that all this was in good order and good repair, properly arranged for each rehearsal and concert. Effectively he was both librarian and equipment manager, thus overseeing an ever-increasing inventory—doublebasses, percussion, harps, keyboard instruments—and the roster of functionaries and purveyors *("employés et fournisseurs")*. He, too, was to keep a register to be audited and cleared each year by the accounting officers. Once the Société des Concerts began to venture away from its hall, in the 1880s, then with the routine out-of-town appearances from the first decade of the twentieth century, the commissioner inherited the substantial burden of arranging the drayage.

Even though the famous library of the Conservatoire was adjacent to the Salle des Concerts, it is fair to say that few *sociétaires* ever developed a taste for assembling, maintaining, and ultimately cataloguing the collection of scores and parts that over the decades accumulated into a real treasure. The parts were distributed at rehearsals and performances by a *garçon d'orchestre* working under the commissioner's supervision, then taken back again at the close of each function. This system worked to the disadvantage of the chorus rank and file, who were naturally less gifted at sight-reading than the instrumentalists. In 1837 it was decided that thereafter the chorus parts would be distributed well in advance, with the artists obliged to master them before the rehearsals. Singers responsible for loss or mutilation of these materials would be counted absent and lose their share of the proceeds for that particular concert.[30]

Calls from conductors and *commissaires de matériel* to return the music were, nevertheless, legion—as they are in any orchestra anywhere.

The financial staff consisted of an *agent comptable* and the quaintly but aptly named *archiviste-caissier*, whose duties were thought to check and balance each other. The *agent comptable* was simply to administer the expenditures and receipts, reconciling the books in time for their presentation each year to the general assembly. A statutory two-week delay between the last concert and the annual general assembly gave the *agent comptable* time for this task.

The *archiviste-caissier* held the funds of the Société des Concerts in a cashbox, and thus was responsible for paying the daily expenses, satisfying the tax collectors, and counting out each member's yearly compensation at the close of the general assembly. More significantly, he became the supervisor of the box office when this duty was relinquished by the Conservatoire; he was thus the principal point of contact between the Société des Concerts and the public. This was not always an easy position, given the potential for aggressive demands for admission to a room that generally could not be stretched any further. "One of these days," remarked Meifred, "you may see a charge for armed guards, hired to protect the *archiviste-caissier*'s life."[31] The job became associated with the oldest active member of the organization, in part because the box-office duties often precluded his being on stage for the concert.

Unlike most of the other offices, that of *archiviste-caissier* was renewable, and thus was held for long terms by distinguished incumbents: the violinist Charles Saint-Laurent (1833–49); the violist Auguste Seuriot (1850–55); the great hornist Frédéric Duvernoy (1856–64); the violinist Ernest Altès (1864–70), called Altès *jeune* to distinguish him from his older brother the flutist; the cellist Hippolyte Rabaud (1872–98); the violists Julien Gaillard (1898–1927) and Pierre Chavy (1904–19); the cellist Émile Deblauwe (1927–34); and the trombonist Raphaël Delbos (1934–41). In 1941, when Savoye named himself secretary-general, the offices of *archiviste-caissier* and *agent comptable* were combined into the ordinary post of treasurer, filled from 1942 to 1948 by Savoye's comrade Huot. The violist Lucien Wesmaël, serving as treasurer from 1956 to 1967, was a critical member of the governance in the period of transition.

Money handling was on the whole primitive, with a strong preference for cash transactions. The earning power of the large sum of money held on the premises between the taking of the subscriptions in the fall and distribution of the proceeds in late spring was first explored in the

1840s, as the lessons of the successful retirement fund were learned. Bankers and brokers were eventually invited to assist in managing the financial affairs of the society, albeit with a certain reluctance.

Disagreements between the treasury officers were common. One dispute that took place between two trusted officers—H.-M. Trévaux as *agent comptable* and Saint-Laurent as *archiviste-caissier*—required the intervention of the notary, Mᶜ Bonnaire; he proposed improved checks and balances and weekly in-person meetings, Thursdays at 3:00, until the books were regularized. The cellist Émile Deblauwe was dismissed from both offices, *agent comptable* in 1925 and *archiviste-caissier* in 1934, for financial irregularities. After a potentially scandalous bookkeeping discrepancy in that same period, two independent *contrôleurs aux comptes* were elected to provide an annual outside review. For all that, and despite the enormous fiscal challenges of the period after 1870, the Société des Concerts never incurred any sustained period of rank insolvency.

The *membre adjoint* was elected annually for a one-year term of office to substitute for any member of the committee unable to fulfill the responsibilities of his office. Though the *membre adjoint* was not considered a full-fledged member of the committee unless acting in another office, the post was keenly sought in order to establish credentials for subsequent advancement into the next major vacancy. Hence the most interesting election in a given year was frequently for that otherwise unpromising office. And as often as not the *membre adjoint* had plenty to do, covering for illnesses, unexpected resignations, and a variety of contrary turns of events. In a standoff in the summer and fall of 1836, Habeneck, disinclined to work with the incoming committee, refused to preside over its meetings, thus causing an organizational crisis and the resignation of all concerned; the committee was persuaded to return to office on the condition that a provision would be added to the statutes allowing it to function, in the absence of both the president and vice president, with the *membre adjoint* in the chair. This amendment of 4 December 1836 increased by one the checks on a conductor's authority, and greatly enhanced the importance of the *membre adjoint*.

In the early twentieth century the contrabassoonist Couppas, as *membre adjoint,* came to the rescue during a linotypers' strike, taking the program materials to a one-man printing establishment in the Marais, correcting the proofs there, then taking the materials home to fold with his wife and children. The same Couppas was sometimes to be found playing percussion when not needed in the bassoon section.

A *commissaire de publicité* was attached to the committee in 1922, not long after the orchestra had returned from the United States and Canada full of admiration for what they called *publicité à l'americaine*. By 1946 the bulk of this work was being contracted to an outside agency, with the post converted to a second *membre adjoint* to help keep up with the rapidly escalating general workload.

The two other members of each season's government were the chorusmaster and the *inspecteur de la salle*. The *inspecteur de la salle* was typically an older, semi-retired member. He was expected to review the condition of the hall with regard to the upholstery, lighting, and heat, and to oversee the house staff for the Sunday concerts. In the 1840s, when a black market for places was being run by the ticket-takers and ushers, the *archiviste-caissier* reminded his colleagues that this job was not a modest one, and should go to a member who would fulfill his duties with "zeal and exactitude." (The outgoing *inspecteur* took temporary offense.)[32]

Originally the responsibility for preparing the chorus was assigned to the professor of the *classe d'ensemble* (i.e., the choruses) at the Conservatoire, Kuhn, assisted by the institution's accompanist and *répétiteur*, Adèle Croisilles. When Kuhn resigned in 1837—Habeneck had taken over the chorus practices—it was necessary to find an independent chorusmaster; the statutes were rewritten to provide for a *répétiteur du chant* who would also chair, owing to his presumed ability to read full score at the keyboard, a subcommittee meeting biweekly during the summer hiatus to identify and study works that might be added to the repertoire. The best of these works would be forwarded for the *répétitions d'essai* that took place at the start of each season. But the *répétiteur du chant* was listed, alternatively, as the *accompagnateur*, and this title may be a good indication of what many thought to be his principal task. Eventually the more stylish designation *chef des chœurs* became current.

Of the succession of colorful chorusmasters, Alexis de Garaudé *fils*—natural son of the singing teacher Garaudé and his favorite pupil, Clotilde Colombelle (Mlle Coreldi)—served from 1850 to 1854; known for his gifts in score reading, he was often called to the committee meetings for a little *déchiffrage*. The noted composer Théodore Dubois served briefly in the capacity (1871–72) and later as interim director of the Conservatoire. The popular and famous Alexandre Samuel-Rousseau—father of the composer Marcel Samuel-Rousseau—served from 1892 to 1901 and narrowly lost election as first conductor to Georges Marty.

The committee functioned for over a century more or less as it had originally been conceived. Meifred described it as a sort of tribunal to assure
talent, loyalty, conscientiousness, and exactitude in the ranks—with the
added obligation to re-examine changing times and circumstances in
order to fine-tune every operational practice. Its members were, with
remarkable consistency, the strongest in the society. Some effort was
made to keep the committee balanced, though on one occasion the secretary (Vernaelde, a singer) complained that all the parliamentary wrangling of the era was being caused by "too many violists" on the committee.[33] The officers served with no compensation other than their
complimentary tickets, or *billets de service*. These had some commercial
value; in 1872, for instance, Ferrand was thanked by the committee for
reselling his *billets de service* and donating the income to the Société.[34]
But mostly they went to friends and family, and meanwhile the officers
incurred substantial out-of-pocket expenses for which the tickets were
modest enough tokens of reimbursement.

The committee met weekly, usually on Tuesday or Wednesday morning, reducing to once a month out of session and generally taking the traditional August holiday. A week or so after the spring general assembly,
the outgoing and incoming committee members would meet together
once to review outstanding items on the agenda and the status of the
treasury. In September of each year the season's work would begin in
earnest with the annual housekeeping chores as to the personnel (including the tiresome matter of auditioning for a full chorus), the subscribers, and the authorities and press. There would be pro forma correspondence with royal agencies to secure use of the house, with local
authorities to arrange for the tax rate and police and fire protection, and
with the syndicates for performance rights. The more engaged committees would remember to nominate one or two distinguished colleagues
for recognition in the January honors lists with the appropriate palms
and rosettes, including those of the Légion d'Honneur and, more frequently, of the title Officier de l'Instruction Publique. Final dates for
the concerts might not be set until late autumn.

As the first concert approached, the rhythm sharply increased. In late
October 1871, for example, the committee met nearly every day. On several occasions they assembled on Christmas Day, once grumbling in the
written record over the absence of several members, scornfully assumed
to be still asleep after their services at midnight mass. By spring, always
an inviting time in Paris, there would be little to do but choose the programs, and that could be done out of doors. At one point the minutes

note somewhat disapprovingly that "from the sixteenth of March to the twentieth of April the committee, having nothing to do but attend to the programs for the last concerts, met most infrequently and often *en plein air*." [35] Very occasionally its members would simply chat, the minutes carefully noting that these *causeries* nevertheless concerned business of the society.

Most often these meetings were at the Conservatoire, but it was not uncommon to assemble at the conductor's apartment—and nearly always so when he was ill, since it was impossible to finish a program without his approval. In the twentieth century, as the orchestra took to the rails, the committee enjoyed meeting in a train compartment. The committee meeting of 20 November 1928 was held in a *café* across from the bank in the rue Bergère, to the bemused annoyance of the members. They had arrived at the Conservatoire to find a note posted on the door of their *loge* by a semi-literate employee: "Starting today, these gentlemen are invited to have their committee in their library or in the alumni room." A protest to Rabaud—neither of the proposed venues was heated, *cher maître,* and they could not go to Gaubert's office at the Opéra because they were expecting delivery of proofs for the week's posters, which would need correcting on the spot—suggested that this arrangement was neither practical nor worthy of the Société des Concerts. Rabaud, ever a diplomat, appeared in person the following week to offer his apologies and alternative solutions. They chose the *foyer* outside the organ loft, both heated and proximate to a telephone, and Rabaud made the necessary arrangements for a table and a cabinet for their archives.[36]

Most decisions were reached by show of hands, with the vote recorded in the minutes; on simple matters a unanimous vote was customary. But the privilege of a secret ballot could be invoked at any time, and the most difficult decisions—the retiring of a venerable colleague, for example, or a vote that might run counter to the will of the conductor—were reached by the time-honored system of depositing white *(oui)* and black *(non)* marbles in an urn.

The committee's correspondence was enormous—requests from aspiring musicians, composers hoping for a performance, journalists desiring free entry, subscribers with a complaint—and, owing to the practice of having all the mail read aloud by the secretary, time consuming. Prospective members, soloists, and composers were all expected to present their candidacies in a formal written statement of qualifications. In one im-

pressive session, significant proposals from Stephen Heller, Gustave He-
quet, Alkan, and Berlioz were treated in a single morning.[37] Other deliberations were more mundane, as in the discussion of a 1911 complaint
from a disgruntled patron demanding that ladies remove their hats, as
was the custom at the cinema. The committee declined to intercede in
matters of fashion.

The musicians applied to the committee for leave, or *congé*, for every conceivable reason. In 1886 the concertmaster Édouard Nadaud
asked for extended leave in conjunction with his forthcoming wedding,
granted on the condition that the conductor, Garcin, ascertain in person whether or not this purported *raison de famille* was legitimate.[38]
But excuses that could be attributed to the obligations of family life
were nearly always accepted. One *sociétaire* was excused with the notation "neglected wife"; another, to go to Brussels for a year for "intimate
reasons," having promised to return when things got better at home.

Next the committee would turn to disciplinary measures, mediations,
condolences, and various other housekeeping functions. Chief among
these was to assure punctuality and seemly behavior in the ranks. Habeneck would often complain of a musician that he showed *"peu de zèle"*
in fulfilling his duties; another typical charge was *"inexactitude dans ses
services,"* leveled, for instance, against the violinists Cuvillon and Sauzay
and the tenor Andrade in February 1833.[39] The committee would generally respond with a gentle letter reminding a wayward *sociétaire* of his
responsibilities, expecting a letter of apology in return. Ongoing disruptions would result in a letter of *blâme* and, for cause, the dreaded
amende: usually a half-share of the proceeds for tardiness and a full share
for absence. Three unexcused absences resulted in expulsion.

The soprano Mlle Printemps *jeune* was dismissed in 1851 for all of the
above: *manque de zèle, inexactitude,* and a poor quality of voice. Mlle
Dellanoy met the same fate in 1845, "no longer having a voice." The aspiring cellist Garry wrote that he was stunned not to be called to replace
an absent member; he was told that he had developed a reputation for
inexactitude, then was stricken from the on-call list when he replied in a
letter than contained "offensive language"—the committee always looking with great disfavor on correspondence deemed *peu convenable* or *offi-
cieuse.* Another *aspirant* was dismissed for not being in his place in time
to sing a solo part. Three sopranos were fired for having "troubled the
order" backstage.[40]

Other infractions incurred less severe response. The oboist Triébert,
who had sent another player to cover his absence, was reminded that
only the committee could choose a replacement. While his gesture was

appreciated, it was concluded that "he erred through an excess of zeal." Pierre Chevillard was fined 15 francs for showing up without his cello. So distinguished a colleague as the cellist Franchomme was chastised for playing unauthorized outside engagements and had to write a humble letter of apology.[41] From time to time a letter would be dispatched urging a woodwind player to attend to the repair of his instrument, or to one of the highly visible players on the risers to improve his attire.

There were also discordant events that would lead to an officer's resignation, the *grand geste* of French politics. Typically it would be refused by the rest of the committee, as was the case in 1835 when H.-M. Trévaux's resignation was declined and his motive was "found erroneous" —the "wrongful interpretation of a remark made in the heat of a rather animated discussion."[42] The same Trévaux found himself at the center of another controversy in January 1846 when, acting as a member of the committee during a rehearsal, he accused his colleague Koenig, also a tenor, of never singing, thereby wounding his self-esteem. Koenig had lanced an ill-advised retort, and an altercation ensued in the presence of orchestra and chorus. Summoned to explain himself to the committee (they were meeting at Habeneck's apartment, and Trévaux excused himself to another part of the flat), Koenig attributed his inadequate performance to a cold but refused to apologize for a remark that had "escaped naturally." The committee, exhausting every effort at reconciliation, suspended him from the next concert, Trévaux abstaining from the vote.[43]

The committee was always anxious for proof that its worries were unfounded. The capable violinist (and conductor) François Seghers was dismissed, to his great surprise, for unexcused absences. Upon asking for a formal explanation of this assault on his dignity, he was invited to appear before the committee; on 27 December 1844 he successfully implored his colleagues "to change their opinions relative to his zeal and character" and was restored to his usual place.[44] A few months earlier the violist Henricet had been dismissed for *"grande négligence"* and, after a personal apology to Habeneck and promising to be more "exact," had been restored.[45]

By twentieth-century standards, the deference of the committee toward its correspondents and the courtesy of its prose are striking. The language developed in the 1830s to decline offers from composers and soloists is a model of its kind:

> You must not doubt, sir, the esteem in which your talent is held by the artist-members of the committee, nor the haste with which they would like to grant your desire, but the quantity of proposals already before it, and the de-

cisions already reached with regard to the concerts, do not permit the committee to contract with you in this matter. It directs me to convey its every regret, and to tell you that it has noted your kind offer and very much hopes to profit from it, in the interest of the society, if changes in the program make that possible.[46]

The language of dismissals was equally respectful: "[the committee] sees itself, with regret, in the necessity of replacing you as a *sociétaire*." Or "Know of my regret at having to let you know of this decision."[47] Meifred was a master of this style, writing the senior trombone players, Devise and Bénard:

The mission I must fulfill toward you today, my dear sir, makes my duties as secretary of the society profoundly disagreeable; the committee directs me to convey to you its decision—thoughtful, carefully considered, and without any personal disrespect for an estimable artist—that in the best interests of the performances a change in the trombone section is necessary. Ever mindful of your contributions to the society and desirous that you lose neither the glory it has acquired nor any that might henceforth befall it, the committee proposes to name you *membre honoraire*.[48]

The committee took equal care to express the satisfactions of its duties. To the famous, on delivering their medals, a secretary might write: "I take great joy, on this occasion, to be the one to convey the society's sentiments."[49]

Committee members did most of the work themselves; not until the 1870s was the first salaried office employee engaged. Such functionaries as were required up until then were either reimbursed privately by the committee members themselves or considered production expenses.

The *garçon d'orchestre* would typically inherit his post and its modest stipend from his father. In due course, he would petition the committee for an increase of his *gratification,* noting plaintively the number of years he had served at the same pay accorded his father, and his initiative would be rewarded with a raise of one or two francs per service. His principal task was to set the stage and distribute the parts for rehearsals and performances, but from time to time he would be asked to do other chores, notably copying. Among the duties of M. Renouf, the *garçon d'orchestre* in the 1830s and 1840s and by all indications a highly valued employee, was to hand-deliver calls to the new season and agendas for the general assembly to the domicile of each *sociétaire*. For large events and in emergencies, the *garçon* would be assisted by other employees of the Conservatoire, where he would have had additional weekday employment and in some cases a room to live in. In 1951 the committee recorded a decision whereby the *garçon d'orchestre* was forbidden from living in the *bibliothèque* and was instructed to use a folding bed in another room.[50]

There were house employees for the Sunday concerts—ticket-takers, cloakroom personnel, ushers—and such functionaries as the man who brought the firewood and the woman who filled and lit the oil lamps. The famous luthier C.-F. Gand (and his successors, C.-E. Gand and Gustave Bernadel) supplied the cellos and doublebasses and some bows. One of the firm's employees would be on hand for emergency repairs and, it appears, some tuning.[51] (The luthier's bill for 1846 occasioned alarm owing to the number of instruments and bows broken and lost during the season, which had to be replaced at societal expense.) In 1873 —by then in their forty-fifth year of service—the Gands complained that their duties to the Société des Concerts had doubled since the foundation and successfully petitioned for a *billet de service*.[52] An ongoing relationship with a notary, Mᶜ Florestan Bonnaire, figures in the records from the late 1830s; after Bonnaire's retirement, the reassignment of his complimentary seat to a successor prompted a bitter dispute.

The most colorful of Mᶜ Bonnaire's several successors was Mᶜ Roger Hauert, art collector, noted attorney to celebrity artists and companies, ubiquitous photographer of their public and private moments,[53] and devotee of amorous dalliance and the scandals that resulted. Hauert is remembered in some quarters for his particular focus on stars in distress. Certainly he enjoyed his *coups de théâtre,* as when he saved the eighty-six-year-old Marguerite Long from eviction (for "troublesome usage of the piano") by the landlord of her apartment in the avenue de la Grande-Armée; instead he negotiated a ten-year extension of her lease. "Fine," she replied, "but what happens after that?"[54]

From 1868, on the advice of the admitted hypochondriac Deldevez, the Société des Concerts retained a physician by offering him free entry to the concerts. His service consisted largely of dealing with medical emergencies in the hall and assuring that musicians struck by illness had proper care, but from time to time he would be called upon to verify the medical condition of suspected laggards. In 1873, after two warnings for unexcused absence, the tenor Édouard Ambroselli excused himself from his duties pleading illness and was sent to Dr. Levrat, "physician to the society," who reported that he was unable to find an indisposition that might prevent Ambroselli from working. The excuse was found invalid and, having reached three unexcused absences, Ambroselli was dismissed.[55] Later physicians guided the administration in developing its relatively inflexible policies toward the frequent petitions for excuse based on fatigue. In mid-November 1912, for instance, the violist Louis Bailly, following a death in the family, pled nervous depression and on the advice of his personal doctor begged leave for the remainder of the calendar year—some six weeks. The committee reckoned, on the contrary, that it was "in the best interests of M. Bailly's health" not to ask leave of absence and that "absorbing work would constitute a powerful counterfoil to his grief." [56]

The first true employee, a bookkeeper and box-office assistant, was engaged in 1873. Thereafter the ever-increasing workload was managed by a combination of office staff and such external agents as the publicity bureau, the *agent de change,* and eventually the Paris impresarios. The social security records from the 1940s forward suggest a full-time administrative staff of three, headed by Mlle Yvette Paviot (1943–61) and her successor, Mme Élisabeth Beurdouche (1962–dissolution).

The committee was designated by election from among the membership at large, convened as the Assemblée Générale. The principal purpose of the end-of-year annual meeting, at it was put in 1868, was to come together after the concerts "to hear the reports from your stewards, acknowledge the importance of your work, and receive the new members that come to fill the vacancies retirement or death have left in our ranks." [57] The meeting was set to take place fifteen days after the closing concert—in practice, the Saturday morning two weeks after the last Sunday concert—generally at 7:00 A.M, in order to have the musicians free for their next appointments. The assembly would last for two or three hours, after which the *sociétaires* could present themselves to the *archiviste-caissier* to collect the modest monetary reward for their labors.

A typical Assemblée Générale began with a roll call (matched against a closing *contre-appel,* to assure that the members sat through the whole session) and welcoming remarks by the presiding officer, usually—and certainly when controversy was expected—the director of the Conservatoire. ("I am not embarrassed," said Raymond Loucheur at the start of a difficult session in 1961, "by the issues we are about to face, since we are all among friends.") [58] The secretary would then be recognized for the delivery of his solemn oration, the *compte-rendu* or *rapport moral* on the work of the previous session, its text having already been studied and approved by the entire committee.

The *rapport moral* was the centerpiece of the meeting, and several of the secretaries developed it into high theater. Whereas the reports of the 1860s and 1870s are but a few paragraphs long, others—for instance, those of Albert Seitz (1905–07)—are over two dozen manuscript pages, elegantly copied and bound with red ribbon. For a time in the 1880s the *rapport moral* was even printed. The oration began with a review of the season's particular successes, first performances and new additions to the repertoire, and distinguished visiting artists; the work of the conductor and chorusmaster would be complimented briefly and sometimes almost parenthetically. The secretary then addressed changes in the membership, welcoming the young, saluting the newly retired, and eulogizing those who had died during the season. There would be a hortatory injunction or two—to "be on guard," for example, "against indifferent performance, against spontaneous naysaying, and other systematic assaults that tend to sap a beautiful and great institution"—and an eloquent close: "an invitation to redouble our zeal and energy to be able to preserve the reputation we have acquired with such labor." Or, more colorfully: "Let us seek to enrich our already rich repertoire; let us endeavor to perfect our already perfect performances. . . . There can be no victory without struggle."[59]

The secretary's remarks were followed by the drier, and sometimes even longer, reports from the financial officers and directors of the retirement fund. Someone always rose to contest the magnitude of the expenses, which after all amounted to deductions from their salaries. The elder Dancla complained of bills for works copied but not performed; Tulou, of the charge for the *fumiste,* or heating technician—to which the testy response was that the civil authorities required it and that in any event the same expense had appeared in the treasurer's report for fourteen years.[60] Once the floor was so opened, squabbles and petty concerns were apt to erupt and the meeting to veer off course, brought back to order by the intervention of the president. Since the general assembly was the last resort for resolving differences, members could also bring their appeals to the floor, as in the case of a member seeking to overturn a fine for having been caught smuggling a fur coat across the Belgian border at the close of an orchestra tour.

An Assemblée Générale *extraordinaire* might be called at any time, either by the committee or by petition of the members. The usual reason was to approve changes in the bylaws, the extraordinary session being necessary to have enough time for adequate deliberation. Election of a new conductor usually required an extraordinary assembly, sometimes two. Now and then a complex grievance would be resolved during an extraordinary session.

As with the committee, decisions of the Assemblée Générale—election of officers, changes of policy, response to member petitions—were reached by vote of the full membership. After World War I, when it became customary to accept outside engagements, the orchestra would be asked to vote decisions during rehearsal breaks to spare the cost of convening a general assembly, for which chorus personnel and retired members would need to be paid. Inviting the visiting New York Symphony to a reception in 1920 required a petition, a committee vote, presentation to the members during a rehearsal, and, when they failed to agree on how to pay for it, an Assemblée Générale *extraordinaire* to reach closure. Votes were sometimes taken on whether to vote, followed by votes on how to vote.

Matters provoking little dissent might be decided by voiced acclamation. A simple majority vote might be taken by show of hands or sitting and standing *(assis et levés)*. Any member could demand a secret vote, where written ballots would be deposited in an urn watched over by attendants. Some ballots would be recorded as *blanc* (no vote, abstaining) or *nul* (supporting none of the proposed options or candidates, protesting), and these would figure in the recorded totals. Members might also suggest the presence of a *cas grave*, which, if approved by a majority show of hands, would require a two-thirds vote for passage. Maneuvers to invoke a *cas grave* are the sure sign of a hard-fought battle in course.

Elections with multiple candidates were managed through a system of *scrutins* (ballots) followed by *ballottage* (runoff). In the early rounds, those with minimal success often withdrew their candidacy in favor of a likely winner. If, after four *scrutins,* an absolute majority (or in some cases a two-thirds majority) had not been reached, the voting would shift to *ballottage,* in which the top two candidates faced each other in a runoff. Ballots *blanc* and *nul* could still prevent a majority for either candidate, sending officials off to study their parliamentary procedure. More than one heated runoff resulted in a tie, broken by the president.

In the ordinary course of affairs, the two-year terms of office were arranged so that only half the major posts needed filling in any one year. Even so, the elections were tedious, and in periods of rapid turnover caused by unexpected deaths or resignations *en masse,* they could last for hours. If time ran out, the assembly would reconvene in a week. Only when the elections were done were the members invited to present themselves at the *caisse,* open from 11:00 A.M. until 4:00 P.M., then for a few days the next week, to settle their accounts for the session and collect their earnings in cash.

The committee prepared carefully for each Assemblée Générale. The secretary read his *rapport moral* to his colleagues a week or two in advance, soliciting their advice as to style and content; the financial reports would be reviewed for accuracy and propriety of expenditure. Issues of substance, notably petitions to change the bylaws, were studied at length, with the committee's recommendation presented in a rigorous and generally lengthy report that would establish the factual history of the matter and treat the advantages and disadvantages of the various proposed solutions. Hardly a word was improvised. The speaker read from his prepared manuscript and would have the supporting documents at hand, each read aloud as well. In 1862 the report to the membership on the case of the hapless Victor Mohr, who had appeared as horn soloist with the Pasdeloup orchestra without prior authorization, took two dozen manuscript pages with eight supporting documents.

The records of the administrative committee and general assembly thus afford keen insight into the working of a French *société:* the dignity of the overall governance, its seriousness of purpose, its commitment to equality of standing, the pleasure it took at a well-reasoned argument. One is impressed particularly by the eloquence of language as an exemplary sort of democracy plays out in a context of studied fraternity and individual responsibility. Even the outbreaks of rowdiness are characterized by their joviality. The boisterous are also witty.

Most members were usually content, however, to leave the business of the Société to the committee. As a result, the rank and file often needed reminding just how powerful they were as a deliberative body. "Your committee, which is charged with administering the Société, does not presume to dictate your decisions," remarked Lebouc. "Its duty is to illuminate the issues, to the best of its ability, when a proposal of great significance is submitted to your judgment. It remains to you to ponder carefully the vote you will sustain, a vote for which the consequences may be decisive for the Société des Concerts du Conservatoire."[61]

What gave the institution its palpable *esprit de corps* was the simple nobility of its commitment to art music. What made it permanent was a strong constitution—the *Statuts règlementaires,* or simply, "the statutes." This *"règlement en 50 articles"*—the best source gives fifty-two—had been read aloud and agreed to at the first Assemblée Génerale on 4 March 1828, the date from which the founding members reckoned their appointments.[62] The change of governments following the revolution of 1830 prompted a new authorizing decree of 13 December 1832 and a general revision of the bylaws during 1833, a project led by the secretary, Charles Plantade. The updated *règlement,* now numbering fifty-four articles, was published in a lithographed broadside given to each member and approved at a general assembly on 1 January 1834 (see website).

The statutes were well reasoned from the first, with safeguards against wanton meddling. After the formative years, passing an amendment required a two-thirds majority. Elwart thought the statutes "broad, liberal, and above all practical" [63]—and, one might add, resilient. By 1828 French legal codes were conceived to survive political upheaval, increasingly regarded as inevitable but not necessarily consequential, at least in terms of concert life; bureaucrats typically honored long-standing governmental commitments when dated documents could be referenced.

Several of the guiding principles of the Société des Concerts—low ticket prices, shared income, free admission for authorities, annual accounting, and above all the Conservatoire pedigree required of all musicians—were present in La Rochefoucauld's founding decree of 15 February 1828. Its nine brief articles began with praise for the old *exercices publics,* which he correctly characterized as a powerful opportunity for students and their professors to work together, and concluded by conveying authority for their implementation to the director of the Conservatoire. What La Rochefoucauld did not attempt to establish was a structure of governance; this was first outlined in the statutes of 4 March 1828, which call for an administrative committee headed by the conductor. The 1834 revision separated the office of president from that of conductor, but neither specified the director of the Conservatoire as president nor the conductor as vice president.

By 1840 the statutes had been tested by more than a decade of experience. The post of chorusmaster had evolved, along with mandatory pre-season rehearsals and a growing insistence that, where public concerts were concerned, *sociétaires* appear exclusively with the Société des Concerts. Moreover, the founding members had encountered, or were at least beginning to think about, the frailties and financial challenges of old age. Concern for the widows and orphans of deceased colleagues seemed to demand the kind of formal pension funds already developed for foreign orchestras and local theater companies. The new capitalism promised interest of 3 percent when an institution invested its reserve, but such a strategy would require considerable refinement in how the Société handled its funds. Mc Bonnaire, the notary consulted on the matter of the pension fund, also recommended formally reconstituting the Société des Concerts with a particular eye toward the kinds of eventualities—catastrophe, dissolution, disposal of the property—that lawyers are more accustomed to considering than musicians. This new *rè-glement* of eighty-four articles, embracing the familiar language of the 1830s and adding a new part II of twenty-two articles establishing the Caisse de Prévoyance, was registered with the government on 30 December 1841—as an association *"double et commune."* Thereafter each new *sociétaire* would visit the notary to sign the articles of association and receive his passbook *(livret)* containing the latest version of printed statutes and a record of his payments into the pension fund.

The three early iterations of the statutes (1828, 1834, 1841) have in common much of the organizational structure and the bulk of the language. Administration by a small but powerful committee of peers held firm, and the size of the society stayed about the same. In 1841 both Cherubini and Habeneck, the two moving forces at the foundation, were still alive, but their days were clearly numbered (Cherubini died in 1842, Habeneck in 1849). Bonnaire's draft quietly set the stage for the succession, leaving options for a president not the director of the Conservatoire, and a vice president not the conductor. Both eventualities came to pass a century later. Bonnaire also included provisions for separation from the Conservatoire and the disposal of assets that in large measure guided the dissolution in 1967.

Subsequent amendments to the statutes recognized the natural evolution of the Société des Concerts, both internally and in its relations with the world at large. Challenges to the orchestra's pre-eminence in Paris were met with ever-tighter language designed to achieve exclusivity in use of the hall and the allegiance of the musicians. As the use of unpaid Conservatoire students waned, attention was paid to assuring the *aspirants* a decent wage and guaranteed elevation to full membership. Attitudes toward the chorus—involving, as they did, the delicate question of the women members—mutated, as did the approach to engaging assistant and guest conductors. Among the amendments that may be seen in retrospect as historic turning points for the Société des Concerts are the following:

- In 1841, a system for judging and adopting music by living composers
- In 1843, the formal interdiction of women *sociétaires* and the institution, for them, of the category *sociétaire adjoint*
- In 1848, the post of second conductor, member of the committee
- In 1857, the abandonment of *sociétaires solo* and increase to seventy-four orchestral *sociétaires*
- In 1858, improved status for *aspirants* and *externes*

- In 1858, the institution of a mandatory retirement age of sixty
- In 1865, improved stipends for *aspirants*
- In 1874, provision for an office employee
- In 1905, agreement that the orchestra could appear without the chorus, thus allowing frequent tours
- In 1926, the establishment of a patron organization, Les Amis de la Société des Concerts

In 1911 a separate legal contract, consisting of the *engagement* and a brief *règlement* of nine articles, began to be used for all new hires, both *aspirants* and *sociétaires*. By the late 1950s the bylaws were divided into *statuts* and a *règlement intérieur;* typed, mimeographed copies of 1962 include twenty-four articles of statute and fifty-seven house rules. Both codes incorporate formulations of the past alongside the radically increased legalisms of the advancing twentieth century. The Caisse de Prévoyance disappeared, having been swept into the modern social security system. For all the changes of format, however, the duties of the musicians remained about the same, and the ring of the language quite familiar.

Copies of the statutes of the Société des Concerts were often solicited by potential imitators, notably including the organizers of the Vienna Philharmonic in 1872.[64] Over the years, transcripts were lent to orchestras in London, Brussels, and the French provinces; in 1928 a philharmonic association in Soviet Moscow, drawn to the egalitarian politics it assumed to be in play, directed inquiries to the committee and received a polite response.

Always it was a benevolent society, and within a few months of realizing their initial artistic success, the members set about assuring their financial welfare in retirement and providing for aid to their colleagues, widows, and orphans in distress. The Caisse de Prévoyance, established in 1838 as the Caisse de Secours (and later called the Caisse d'Allocation de Post-Activité), was consolidated from the proceeds of benefit concerts and member dues—a *droit d'admission* of a few francs followed by an annual contribution in the same amount. Each member's account was recorded in his passbook, its totals updated annually as a function of his share of the overall sum. On retirement a member would generally elect to liquidate his account and collect his principal and interest as a lump sum. In 1841, when the *livrets* were first printed, Habeneck carried 228 francs forward. His input rose each year, from 45 francs in 1842 to 110 in 1848, and at his death his widow and daughters collected 890 francs.[65] By contrast, in 1872 the wildly fluctuating interest rates caused the recently retired George-Hainl to lose 30 percent of the value of his purse; his protest was referred to the notary, who could do little but explain the drawbacks of speculative finance.

Management of the retirement fund was by a committee of three older *sociétaires* with long records of service to the society: a secretary, *agent comptable,* and treasurer. Membership was renewable and often held for many years; each year one of the three members was selected by lot to stand for re-election, which was essentially automatic.

In addition to retirement benefits, the Caisse de Prévoyance provided emergency allocations to widows in need and to *sociétaires* suffering from debilitating illness. In 1845, when the doublebassist Durier broke his arm and applied for emergency relief, he was granted the maximum stipend of 300 francs. Protecting the Caisse de Prévoyance, the trustees noted at the time, was serious business that required careful examination of each claim; but Durier was the head of household of a large family, thus warranting payment of the full benefit for a relatively inconsequential complaint.[66] The violinist Javault, a *1*[er] *prix* and concertmaster at the Opéra-Comique, was felled "in the flower of his youth" by a paralyzing stroke in 1845; he immediately received the customary 300 francs in *secours,* recognizing that his condition deprived him of any possibility of earning his livelihood. These annual stipends were continued until his death, supplemented by payments from Baron Taylor's Association des Artistes-Musiciens. With "almost no hope of continuing his functions," Javault was retired in October 1846 and made a *membre honoraire.*[67]

The violinist Paul Renaux, appointed in 1906, died in 1908 at the age of thirty-three, leaving his widow "in profound distress." She was sent 200 francs in direct aid from the current-year budget and 200 francs from the Caisse de Prévoyance. The same year, Draux, a vocal soloist *externe,* also died prematurely; in his case the Société des Concerts contributed 30 francs to a fund established for his widow by the *Figaro.* In the course of dealing with the matter it was discovered that a number of retired chorus members were living in precarious circumstances, and they were sent an *encouragement* of similar size.[68] In 1928 the eighty-five-year-old cellist Victor Cabassol, who had since his retirement at age sixty-two lived in a single room and been cared for by his landlady for 50 francs a month, needed to enter a nursing home in Neuilly. The committee, few of whom could have known him well, saw to it that the entry fee was paid.[69]

Frivolous or inappropriate requests, on the other hand, were turned down. Désiré Thibault, for instance, lost his job as a theater conductor in 1874 and asked for 300 francs to avoid financial embarrassment. The vote against his request was unanimous.[70] By the same token, the committee generally declined requests for short-term loans.

The nine hundred or so members of the Société des Concerts were certainly the best and arguably among the most interesting graduates of a dozen generations at the Conservatoire. In pursuing their entire careers at and around the Conservatoire they built impressive lineages, both professional and domestic.

The violinists traced their line to Pierre Baillot, who had played a formative role in the foundation and who appeared from time to time as soloist. (When Chrétien Urhan asked to play the Beethoven Violin Concerto in 1836, his proposal was welcomed on the condition that Baillot did not want to play it himself.)[71] Baillot's successor at the Conservatoire, Lambert Massart, did not become a *sociétaire,* but appeared as soloist. Jean-Pierre Maurin played in the society for twenty-five years before becoming professor at the Conservatoire in 1875; his students filled the violin sections well into the twentieth century.

The Cuban violin virtuoso Joseph White (José Silvestre de los Dolores), who took his *Ier prix* in 1856, was welcomed as a *sociétaire* on his naturalization as a French citizen in 1866. He left Paris in 1874 to establish his solo career in the Americas and ended up in the service of the Emperor Pedro of Brazil. Prolonging his official leave from the Société des Concerts by an exceptional three years, despite an ultimatum to return by January 1876, he resigned in 1877 to the considerable regret of his colleagues.[72] White returned to France in 1889, where he died in 1918.

Among the notable later violinists were four concertmasters: Édouard Nadaud (*soc.* 1884–1903, with significant service to the administrative committee and as second conductor); P. Alfred Brun (*soc.* 1887–1924); Henri Merckel (*soc.* 1929–35); and Pierre Nérini (*soc.* 1946–67). All four can be heard in recordings of the Société des Concerts. At least two legendary violists—in addition to Urhan, who premiered the solos in *Harold en Italie* and *Les Huguenots,* but who played violin with the Société —figure on the rolls: Théophile Édouard Laforge (1863–1918), named *sociétaire* in 1887, and who became the first professor of viola when a class was established at the Conservatoire in 1894; and the great Maurice

Vieux (1884–1951), appointed to the Société des Concerts as an *aspirant en cas* at age nineteen and as principal viola solo in 1905 at age twenty-one. In December 1907 he played his first *Harold en Italie* with the orchestra. Louis Bailly (1882–1974) served only briefly as a *sociétaire*, but as professor at the Curtis Institute of Music shaped an American school of viola playing.

The first generation of cellists was particularly fine, including Louis-Pierre Norblin (*soc.* 1828–47), also a member of the Baillot Quartet; Auguste Franchomme (*soc.* 1828–69); Alexandre Chevillard (*soc.* 1830–69); and their successor, Charles Lebouc (*soc.* 1849–84). The equally famous Charles Vaslin (*soc.* 1828–46) resigned when Franchomme was chosen to succeed Norblin in the principal's chair. Similarly, Prosper Seligmann played with the orchestra as an *aspirant* from late 1838, but soon took to the road as a traveling virtuoso recitalist. Though he was elevated to the rank of *sociétaire* in December 1840, the decision was withheld from him until the committee could learn more about his plans and establish his seniority. Seligmann was given his position in November 1842 on the condition that he return to Paris to fill it by February 1843; instead the committee was obliged to dismiss him that April, and later declined his appeal.[73]

Among the eminent later cellists were Hippolyte Rabaud (*soc.* 1868–98), C.-E. Cros-Saint-Ange (*soc.* 1882–1906), and Auguste Cruque (*soc.* 1925–52). Cruque's forced retirement, at age sixty-two and after three *sursis*, was protested in a petition signed by all the musicians in his section, in part because the mandatory retirement age for theater musicians had increased from sixty to sixty-five. The committee agreed, *"par déférence et par amitié,"* to hear his appeal, but maintained their decision after he delivered himself of what was held to be an unseemly outburst. Maurice Maréchal, a celebrated cellist, served a few seasons with the Société des Concerts (1921–24) and is to be heard with the orchestra in a 1947 recording of the Andante from Honegger's Cello Concerto. Though it was a coup to secure Paul Tortelier as an *aspirant*, he served only his apprentice year (1934–35) and, after returning from engagements with the Monte Carlo and Boston Symphony orchestras, one year as *Iᵉʳ violoncelle solo* (1946–47) before more lucrative pursuits lured him away again.

Many of these players had superb instruments at their disposition, including not a few by Stradivari. Some eleven preserved Strads carry names of *sociétaires:* the violins called Habeneck (1734), Alard (1715, later played by Joachim), Dancla (1703), Maurin (1718) and Maurin-Rubinoff

(1731), Garcin (1731), Lamoureux (1735, later played by Efrem Zimbalist), and Nadaud (1734); and the cellos Baudiot (1735, later played by Piatigorsky), Vaslin (1725, bought by Narcisse Girard for Vaslin's use), and King of Portugal–Chevillard (1726). Alard also played—and named— the "Messiah" Strad of 1716, Lamoureux the Rode (1722), and Garcin the Cremonese *ex* Joachim (1715). Joseph White played the "Song of the Swan" instrument thought to be Stradivari's last (1737). Auguste Franchomme played the Duport cello of 1711, later acquired by Rostropovich. The "Thibaud" violin passed from Baillot to Sauzay to Jacques Thibaud before being destroyed in the 1953 plane crash that claimed Thibaud's life. Charles Münch owned the violin now called the King David.[74]

Those hearing the Société des Concerts for the first time often commented on the extraordinary sound of the doublebass section, more accurate and in tune, it was said, than was the case with any other orchestra. A Lyon journalist, for instance, wrote in 1908 of the "unbelievable agility of the doublebasses."[75] The section's high reputation apparently emerged in the 1840s, under the leadership of Victor Gouffé (*soc.* 1842–67).

But none of the successions is as remarkable as that of the principal flute, descending from Jean-Louis Tulou—"incontestably," remarked Fétis, "the most accomplished flute player in France, and apparently all of Europe."[76] Tulou's extraordinarily long career was never matched, but among his successors were not only the avatars of flute technique but at least two superstars (Adolphe Hennebains, Marcel Moyse) and two who became chief conductor of the Société des Concerts (Taffanel, Gaubert; see table 1, "Succession of Principal Flutists"). Tulou and Dorus were seconded by the equally fine Henri Altès (*soc.* 1845–69), who served as principal for a year before ceding his place to Taffanel. The third member of this formidable section, also the piccolo player, was Louis Leplus (*soc.* 1835–66), Habeneck's son-in-law.

"French oboists," remarked Charles Münch, "are as much in demand as the greatest wines of Burgundy and Bordeaux."[77] At the Société des Concerts the lineage began with the legendary and exotic Gustave Vogt, who had been at the battle of Austerlitz and was one of the few *sociétaires,* other than Cherubini, to have made the acquaintance of both Haydn and Beethoven. (Vogt had missed the 1828 season owing to solo concerts in London.) The founding oboist, Henri Brod (*soc.* 1828–39), was equally celebrated. Their successors were Louis Verroust, whose plummet is described below; Charles Triébert (*soc.* 1853–67), of the dis-

TABLE I. Succession of Principal Flutists, 1828–1967

	Lifespan	*Sociétaire*	Principal
Jean-Louis Tulou	1786–1865	1828–56	1828–56
Louis Dorus	1813–96	1839–68	1856–68
Paul Taffanel[a]	1844–1908	1867–1901	1869–92
Adolphe Hennebains	1862–1914	1893–1913	1893–1913
Philippe Gaubert[b]	1879–1941	1901–38	1913–19
Marcel Moyse	1889–1984	1920–38	1919–38
Lucien Lavaillotte	1898–1968	1923–60	1938–58
Henri Lebon	1911–?	1948–64	1958–64
Michel Debost[c]	1934–	1962–67	1964–67

[a]Conductor, 1892.
[b]Conductor, 1919.
[c]Orchestre de Paris, 1967–90.

tinguished family of woodwind builders and uncle of the oboist Raoul Triébert (*soc.* 1882–88); the celebrated Georges Gillet (*soc.* 1877–1900); Louis Bas (*soc.* 1889–1904, recalled 1918), whose English horn playing and Baroque work were much admired; Louis Bleuzet (*soc.* 1901–38); and Robert Casier (*soc.* 1958–67), who contributed his recollections to this study.

The founding clarinetists were I.-F. Dacosta and the multi-talented Claude-François Buteux (*soc.* 1828–55), also a professor of cello at the Lycée Louis-le-Grand. Upon Klosé's appointment for the 1843 season, Buteux moved to second chair, deferring to Klosé's greater virtuosity, though his name was still listed first in the program, according to seniority, as it would be for the rest of his long career. (This may have been at least in part to avoid the hard feeling that had occurred in 1833, when Dacosta had been displaced by the committee to make way for Buteux himself.) The middle period was dominated by Cyrille Rose (*soc.* 1857–87), who popularized the Weber concerti in France; Charles Turban (*soc.* 1872–1902), praised on his death as one of the most gifted soloists of his generation; and Prosper Mimart (*soc.* 1896–1914). Both Turban and Mimart were devoted administrators of the society; Turban, as noted above, revised and re-established the master personnel registers, and his restructuring of the Caisse de Prévoyance was regarded as the key administrative reform of his era.[78] After World War I the section was dominated by three long-term members, Louis Costes (*soc.* 1914–33), François Étienne (*soc.* 1933–56), and André Boutard (*soc.* 1956–67).

The bassoon section was molded largely by J.-F.-B. Kocken (*soc.* 1833–65), whose longtime second and successor at the Conservatoire was Eugène Jancourt (*soc.* 1843–69), pioneer of the French-system bassoon and author of the *Grande Méthode* (1847) still in use — the bassoonist's Klosé. The twentieth century boasted François and Fernand Oubradous, father (*soc.* 1920–36) and son (*soc.* 1928–42), admired for their *charme méridional*. Oubradous *fils*, with his *Enseignement complet du basson* (1938–39), was as important a didact as Jancourt; he was also a major figure in woodwind chamber music, establishing the Société des Instruments à Vent in 1939 along the lines of Taffanel's precedent organization.

The universally admired cadre of horns was assembled and taught by the two colleagues who had essentially founded the school of modern valved-horn playing: Louis Dauprat (*soc.* 1828–39) and Joseph Meifred (*soc.* 1828–53). The orchestra's trademark rendition of the overture to Méhul's *Le Jeune Henri* using twelve horns — later sixteen — was made possible by their students; Berlioz remarked of the work that "this must have been difficult during the composer's time, but for our young artists it seemed nothing but a plaything."[79] In fact there were so many horn players around that when Meifred took a brief leave in 1832, the hornist Duvernoy — another in the distinguished lineage — asked to replace him and was told that five hornists were still in place and would suffice.[80]

Meifred, indeed, with his colorful history as a secretary to the Empress Joséphine, military bandsman, teacher, poet, journalist, memoirist, and twenty-five-year administrator of the Société des Concerts, must be counted the second most influential of the founding *sociétaires* after Habeneck himself. The unhappy fate of their successor, Victor Mohr (*soc.* 1854–62), has already been mentioned; among the other important horn virtuosi were J.-F. Rousselot (*soc.* 1828–67), Louis Vuillermoz (*soc.* 1894–1904 and 1925–35, with hiatus as principal hornist in Monte Carlo), and Lucien Thévet (*soc.* 1939–67).

The founding trumpet player, François Dauverné (*soc.* 1828–ca. 1848) hailed from a dynasty of French brassmen. Perhaps the most important of the trumpeters was Xavier-Napoléon Teste (*soc.* 1875–96), who first mastered the high trumpet playing necessary for the Bach-and-Handel repertoire that came to vogue in the 1880s. The "lightning brilliance, fearless and error-free," of his B-Minor Mass (1891) did much to assure the success of that daring premiere; his eulogy praises Teste as "renowned of the trumpet, and the trumpet's renown."[81]

Various solutions to staffing the low brass were tried over the years, with one full-fledged *sociétaire*, the trombonist Antoine Dieppo (*soc.*

1838–67), supplemented as necessary by *externes;* in the twentieth century the trombonist Raphaël Delbos (*soc.* 1914–41) was admired not only for his musicianship but for his willingness to devote his considerable offstage time to duties with the treasury and box office. Permanent provision for a tuba player was realized in 1908, followed by an impressive succession of incumbents: Joseph Brousse (*soc.* 1909–24), Louis Appaire (*soc.* 1925–35), Arthur Pavoni (*soc.* 1936–42), and Fernand Lelong (*soc.* 1964–67). Lelong retired from the Orchestre de Paris in 1999 and contributed reminiscences and photographs to this project before his untimely death in November 2002.

The founding timpanist, Schneitzhoeffer, a favorite of Berlioz and others, resigned in 1833 to be able to play elsewhere freely and to attend to his other careers as composer and chorusmaster; his most distinguished successors were Joseph Baggers *(externe),* first professor of timpani at the Conservatoire, and the gregarious Félix Passerone (*soc.* 1936–54), one of the most colorful musicians of his generation.

Among the 150 or so active musicians at any given time would be more than a dozen important conductors, *petits chefs,* and chorusmasters. Of the founding members, François J.-B. Seghers became a successful conductor in Paris, then established a highly regarded concert series in Brussels, the Société Ste-Cécile. Pantaléon Battu was second *chef* at the Opéra, in which capacity he conducted the famous Paris *Le Freyschutz* of 1841. Habeneck's successors Girard and Tilmant were also founding members; Deldevez, Garcin, Taffanel, and Gaubert had all served as second conductors before being elected 1er *chef.* The Société des Concerts was also, of course, the proving ground for second conductors who left to take—or build—major positions elsewhere. Charles Lamoureux was a longtime member of the orchestra; Édouard Colonne served briefly as an *aspirant en cas;* Ernest Altès, Désiré Thibault, and Jules Danbé all became major conductors. Among other significant conductors who passed through the orchestra at the beginning of their careers were Robert Siohan (as a violist), Eugène Bigot, Jean Martinon (*aspirant en cas* from 10 May 1939), Serge Baudo (as a percussionist), Jacques Bazire, and the oboist Jean-Claude Malgoire, founder of La Grande Écurie et La Chambre du Roy (1974).

The early decades, as noted above, could boast among the *sociétaires* and *sociétaires solo* the first casts of the Opéra and Opéra-Comique—Duprez, Nourrit, Mme Cinti-Damoreau, Mme Gras-Dorus, and later Mme Viardot. Since for these stars their lucrative stage contracts always came first, their tenures with the Société des Concert were relatively short and prone to disagreement or hard feelings when the time came for separation. The best younger soloists—Mlle Nau, for instance—had sung with the Société des Concerts as students and there found valuable career contacts, but they would resign as soon as their first engagement at a provincial opera house took them away from Paris. Nevertheless, Deldevez saw the relatively inexpensive flow of big-name singers from the national theaters to the Salle des Concerts as the best state subvention one could imagine.[82]

As always, musical aptitude ran in families. The qualifiers *père* and *fils* are common in the records; so, too, are *aîné* and *jeune,* used for pairs of brothers, cousins, or uncles and their nephews. For example the Dancla brothers—Charles (violin, 1817–1907), Arnaud (cello, 1819–62), and Léopold (violin, 1822–95), called, respectively, *aîné, cadet,* and *jeune;* their sister Laure (1824–80) played piano—had each been sent to Paris from distant Bagnères-de-Bigorre, at the foot of the Pyrénées in the Midi, to study at the Conservatoire. In turn each garnered his 1er *prix* and established a major career in Paris. Charles Dancla, a runner-up for the 1838 Prix de Rome, played at the Opéra-Comique, then fled Paris in 1848 to work in a provincial post office until his belated appointment as professor of violin at the Conservatoire; Arnaud became principal cellist at the Opéra-Comique and wrote a successful method book; Léopold, who had first prizes in both horn (as a student of Meifred) and violin (as student of Baillot), alternated playing horn in military bands and violin in theater pits. Charles and Léopold appeared together several times in the 1840s in a Duo Concertant and a popular Symphonie Concertante of the elder's composition. Arnaud, the cellist, died young after a long illness, and it was noted how many of the musicians had known him since his childhood visits to his older brothers in Paris and how kindness, simplicity, and devotion to the cult of art ran in the family.[83]

In the nineteenth century the largest of the string dynasties was the Tolbecques; in the twentieth, it was the Benedettis. Of the four Tolbecque brothers who came to Paris from their home near Namur, just north of the Belgian border, three—the violist Baptiste and the violinists Auguste and Charles—played with the Société des Concerts; Baptiste and Charles were founding members. Auguste Tolbecque *fils* (1830–1919) was born in Paris and as student of Vaslin took his 1er *prix* in cello in 1849. After a successful career in Marseilles, he returned to Paris in 1871 as a member of the Lamoureux and Maurin Quartets and to play with the Société des Concerts, only to resign five seasons later to locate his famous *lutherie* in Niort. There, for more than forty years, he built violins and lovingly restored early stringed instruments.[84] Altogether six Benedettis passed through the Société des Concerts, two brothers and a cousin (the violinists Marcel, Paul, and Robert), all from Toulon, and their sons born in Paris. Charles Benedetti played viola for a time, and the famous violin virtuoso René Benedetti appears to have played in the orchestra at least as a student. The cellist René-Michel Benedetti, elected 1965, was in one of the last classes of *sociétaires*. Three Benedettis (Paul, Marcel, and René-Michel) were on the roles at the dissolution.

This list of relatives goes on and on, from the three Mesdemoiselles Maillard—Nélia, Hortense, and Caroline—who came into the public eye at the first concert, to the three tenors Ponchard (apparently father, son, and grandson), and the brothers Verroust (oboe and bassoon), Pickett (doublebass; Lucien Pickett styled himself Gasparini), Dubois (trumpet), Turban (clarinet, violin), Marx (cello), and Zighéra (cello, violin; a third Zighéra, Bernard, played harp, eventually in the Boston Symphony Orchestra). The trombonist brothers Alloud, calling themselves Allard, came from Puerto Rico to the Conservatoire in the 1870s and were simultaneously elected in December 1886 after their naturalization as French citizens. Auguste served six years before his death, while Louis, who has the longest name in the rosters—Louis-Philippe-César-Auguste-Frédéric-Victor-Oscar—served twenty-six years, retiring at age sixty in 1912. The bassoon section had three father-son pairs—Letellier, Jacot, and Oubradous—and the founding bassoonist, Antoine-Nicolas Henry, was father of the gifted soprano Mlle Laure Henry (and of her sister Clarissa, also a singer). The trumpeter David Buhl, composer of the trumpet calls still used by the French military, was the uncle of the even more famous trumpeter François Dauverné.

Henri Rabaud, director of the Conservatoire and in that capacity president of the Société des Concerts, had perhaps the most august ancestry of all. His father was the noted cellist Hippolyte Rabaud, a senior officer of the society; his maternal grandfather was Louis Dorus, the celebrated flutist, whose sister, in turn, was the great Mme Gras-Dorus, married to the violinist and founding member Victor Gras.

The marriage in 1833 of Gras and Dorus was by no means the only one contracted in and around the Conservatoire, where the young men of the orchestra and chorus and the several dozen unattached women of the chorus came into frequent contact. The famous soprano Mme Dabadie and her husband the bass (who created the role of Guillaume Tell) were already married when they lent their support to the society's foundation. The violists Henricet and Dubreuil and the oboist Bleuzet all married singers. In the chorus were to be found M. and Mme Bouvenne, M. and Mme Jansenne, M. and Mme Sangouard, and M. and Mme Sureau-Bellet, the last a very popular and promising singer who was forced into early retirement by an unspecified traumatic event.[85] Mme Garaudé was a member of the chorus before the appointment of her husband, Alexis Colombelle de Garaudé, as chorusmaster in 1849; later she tried, unsuccessfully, to promote improvements in the status accorded women members.

It was not unknown for spouses of the members to appear as soloists. On 23 March 1828, at the second concert of the society, Mme Brod played a movement of Beethoven's Third Piano Concerto. Mme Willent-Bordogni's husband was the bassoonist Willent, or Villent, professor at the Conservatoire, engaged for solos on 25 February 1838 and 7 March 1841. Mme Viguier was a pianist, appearing in the Beethoven Third Piano Concerto in March 1873. Mme Georges Marty, an alto, appeared as soloist both before and after her husband's untimely death. But the committee went to great lengths to avoid any impression of impropriety in the engagement of family members; in the case of Mme Viguier, for instance, her husband left the room as the committee discussed the possibility, and they took care to note in the record that she had been invited after a formal vote.[86]

On retiring from the Société des Concerts the musicians would ordinarily relocate to their country houses or to an inviting village somewhere in the south of France. With some luck they would enjoy two decades or more of respite from the frenetic pace they had known in Paris during the concert seasons. The noted violinist Cuvillon, for instance, died in 1900 in Fontainebleau after leaving the orchestra at age sixty and a thirty-one-year retirement; he had played in the very first concert. Most kept in at least some touch with Paris for a time and would try to attend the annual Assemblée Générale if they were in town. A few remembered the Société des Concerts in their wills, as did Gustave Vogt in 1870 and the violinist Alcide Poirier in 1956, with a gift of 100,000 francs to what was then called the Caisse de Post-Activité.[87]

Not everyone lived long enough to retire. Two, the tenor Matthieu Tramasset and the oboist Lucien Leclerq, were killed in battle in World War I and listed in the roles as *morts pour la France*. Others died in the epidemics of cholera (four, for instance, in 1850) and influenza that occasionally reached the membership. The committee attributed the death in 1843 of the violinist Demouy to overwork, an *excès de travail* that hastened his end. The violinist Wacquez died at his post, working on the accounts for the Caisse de Prévoyance. Old Triébert, the oboist, died after the particular strains of the Exposition Universelle in 1867. In the most dramatic of the death scenes recorded in the archives, his young successor, Berthélemy, collapsed and died in the arms of his colleagues just after being named *sociétaire*.[88]

The committee tried to exercise great deference to musicians approaching retirement, especially in cases of demotion or failure to grant the customary suspensions *(sursis)* of the mandatory retirement rule. Leaves of absence were given freely as musicians approached the end of their active careers. The violist René Michaux was given "unlimited leave" in 1936 owing to "notorious incapacity," presumably of hearing; the oboist Boudard was similarly edged out in 1939 for deafness.[89] On the other hand a decision to retire the violinist Louis Franquin was reversed to allow him to reach the fifteen years of service necessary to assure his full pension.

Among such an exuberant collection of artists there were inevitably troublesome characters—the timpanist of slovenly dress; the principal oboist Louis Cras, of whom Lamoureux complained in 1874 of habitually late arrival in inappropriate attire and with his instrument in bad repair—and black sheep. In 1874, presumably during the Mendelssohn "Italian" Symphony on 29 March, the basses Lejeune and Jolivet stood just outside the stage entry to quarrel and exchange blows; the *inspecteur de la salle* had to be summoned to quell the disturbance. The guilty parties expressed their regret and begged indulgence for the "scandal" they had caused, but were sent letters of censure nonetheless.[90]

Strong drink was sometimes at issue. In 1838 Habeneck succeeded in having the trombonist Barbier dismissed for arriving at a rehearsal in a condition thought to "compromise the dignity of the Société des Concerts,"[91] but he was apparently reinstated shortly afterward. The oboist Verroust the elder, praised by Fétis for his "exceptional talent, delicacy, and expression, with a good sound and great certainty in the playing of the most difficult passages," nevertheless conceived an "invincible passion for wine." The committee first notes having received "unfavorable reports" on his account in mid-January 1853. Two days later Verroust's brother, the bassoonist, came in tears to an extended urgent committee meeting, asking that his brother's punishment "be the most severe possible" in order to return him to his senses. He was given a blunt letter to remit to his brother, a document meant to serve as "a moral lesson."[92]

Verroust was in decent enough condition by mid-year to have been appointed professor at the Conservatoire and to the new imperial chapel. But by December 1853 his salary had been attached by legal injunction, and the committee insisted that his legal situation be corrected before he could reappear with the Société des Concerts. The *affaire Verroust* continued; another complaint was received in May 1854 and he was dismissed, but in November Girard thought the better of this course of action and returned Verroust to the rolls as *externe* at full wage. Ultimately, according to Fétis, having lost all his positions and ruined his health, Verroust finished his life "in acute catatonia."[93]

Similarly problematic, and often also related to alcohol, were the cases of musicians whose financial affairs had got out of hand, usually signaled by the arrival of an official of the court (a *bâtonnier* or *huissier*) with a stamped document attaching the musician's salary for payment of back debts, as was the case with Verroust. The officers looked particularly askance at such situations, owing to the manner of the finances; one musician's liabilities were, in a way, the liabilities of all his colleagues. The committee would move quickly to distance the society from such proceedings, usually by dismissing the member.

Such was the outcome with the tenor Robert. A *huissier* came twice in early 1844 to claim 225 francs from Robert's future earnings; on these occasions the *archiviste-caissier* responded that his responsibilities concerned the whole of the society, not the complications of individual members, and sent the agent away. When another *huissier* presented himself in the spring of 1847, the *archiviste-caissier* complained to the committee of encountering the same problem "every year," deploring the "sloppiness and disorder" of his colleague. Robert was dismissed on 2 November 1847, with the committee sufficiently concerned about this state of affairs to leave a lengthy extract in the minutes:

> The good reputation of the Société des Concerts is a responsibility left in the care of its administrators, who must watch over it without ceasing. M. RO-BERT, *sociétaire,* one of the singers, having been warned for several years that if the disorder in his finances continued to oblige the committee to respond to claims, stamped documents, and oppositions concerning him, there would be occasion to consider the question of his dismissal, and this artist not having taken, nor taking now, any account of the multiple warnings that have been given him, it is decided that his name will be removed from the registers. This decision, reached unanimously, will be conveyed to M. Robert by the secretary, who will express to him the committee's regret at having to

meet its onerous duty, and at being forced to deprive the Société des Concerts of the participation of an artist whose zeal and talent have always been valued.[94]

On three or four occasions members of the Société des Concerts had more serious encounters with the law. Among these was an *aspirant actif* named Léonard, *alias* Vicini, arrested in July 1874 on a morals charge and dismissed from the society after having been condemned to prison for corruption of the public morals and resisting arrest.[95] There were periodic grumblings afterward about assuring moral probity among the recruits, and the record shows that in the aftermath the committee was known to ask: *"Que savez-vous de la moralité de la susdite?"*[96]

This sampling of the peccadilloes to be traced within the Société des Concerts ought not conclude without reference to the matter of the musicians and their cigarettes, an addiction that was virtually universal by the end of the nineteenth century. The vogue for cigarettes coincided with, and aggravated, the vigorous campaigns for improved theater safety in the 1890s—danger of fire caused by a cigarette butt remains the principal concern of the *sapeurs-pompiers* charged with protecting the opera theater in the palace at Versailles—as the players were begged to extinguish their cigarettes in new receptacles put for that purpose in the *foyer* of the Salle des Concerts. Smoking (and the reading of newspapers) during rehearsals was strictly forbidden, but a photograph of an early recording session shows every player smoking while simultaneously fiddling.

Whatever their individual foibles, the musicians of the Société des Concerts du Conservatoire realized their common dream on a grander scale than any of the founders could have imagined. Each passing decade brought challenges and lessons that reconfirmed the permanence of the principles that associated them. Charles Münch put it simply, and well: "They know that they are completely dependent on one another, and they place all their talent at the service of the musical collective of which each is but a part. They teach us an important lesson in human solidarity."[97]

CHAPTER 3

The Hall

The thousand-seat Salle des Concerts du Conservatoire was by all accounts a venue of acoustic perfection. Elwart called it the Stradivarius of concert halls, a formulation that had been in use among the players for years, and most subsequent observers followed suit. An unforgettably lush presence of sound gathered as orchestra and chorus set the chamber resonating; this was a function of its rectangularity, high ceiling, and modest volume. No one was very far from the performing force, a circumstance that allowed listeners to hear details of the playing they habitually missed in the big theaters. And the unique personality of the Salle des Concerts went beyond how the music sounded to what a concert felt like, for there was also an almost religious mystique surrounding the Sunday concerts. It was something of an accomplishment to be admitted at all, and the room was typically packed beyond its seating capacity with standees in every corridor and nook. Once inside, subscribers would find themselves in the heady company of ministers, senior bureaucrats, barons of trade, and—usually in the cheaper seats—the intellectual aristocracy of the day: composers, writers, a painter or two, and of course the nation's leading journalists, all at close range. Concerts were thus aurally and visually captivating, psychologically fulfilling, rich with social and political subtext.

The *théâtre* consisted of a flat stage extending well forward from the proscenium and thus covering the pit. Its surface was nevertheless crowded, since it held both the choristers and the upper strings. About halfway back there rose a series of sharply raked bleachers that accommodated the low strings, winds, and percussion. The space was closed with a hemicycle of panels—later decorated with representations of the muses—that seemed to surround the timpani player at the center of the top tier. From the audience perspective the stage was thus filled, both horizontally and vertically, with the musicians.[1]

The auditorium, or *salle,* measured 15 meters across and 35 meters from the proscenium to the back wall.[2] Seating at the *parterre* level— the flat floor before the stage—was, during the first decades, on simple benches accommodating 180, with standing room for 150 to the rear. The *parterre* was circled with the 30 boxes of the *rez-de-chaussée,* above which rose the first and second tiers of *loges,* 30 and 35 boxes respectively, and above these at the back, 4 third-tier *loges* and an amphitheater of about 90 seats. From the wall before the first tier there hung an unusual horseshoe balcony accommodating a single row of seats, much sought after by the stylish set.

The original *décor* featured dark green fabrics embroidered in vio- let, with contrasting cream-colored—some say gray—linen wall fabric and painted wood- and plasterwork. (The altogether different neo- Pompeiian *décor* in dark reds and turquoise, still preserved, dates from the remodeling of 1865.) *Appliqués* to the balcony front were of fes- tooned vines articulated with masks of Tragedy and Comedy and im- ages of the musical instruments. Larger *bas-relief* medallions evoking the mythology of music and theater were to be seen in the walls and arch of the imposing vault that defined the proscenium and contained the forwardmost boxes. Compared with the ubiquitous burgundy-and- gold color schemes of the other Paris houses, the overall effect was sur- prisingly ebullient, perhaps somewhat fanciful, a sensation emphasized by the floating balcony.[3]

Daylight—for most concerts were in the afternoon—was diffused though a large rectangular skylight covered in translucent glass. By night, as for the Lenten *concerts spirituels,* the four huge chandeliers glittered with whale-oil flames that played off the green upholstery and ivory walls. Gazing over the hall packed with its audience of the *élite* was, according to Elwart, *"vraiment admirable! Quel silence! Quelle attention!"*[4]

The Salle des Concerts was not, however, a comfortable room. Crowding was endemic, not only in the *parterre* and amphitheater, where that was to be expected, but also in the narrow balcony and even the boxes, where seven and eight people were often wedged into spaces meant for six. Listeners gladly accepted placement in the corridors and blind boxes, called *purgatoire musical* by the regulars; indeed standing in one of the thirty-two spots in the four corridors leading from the room carried the cachet of a listener's seriousness of purpose. The shortage of seats worsened as the years elapsed, since with each theater fire in town new exit passages would be required by the civil authorities, eliminating aisle seats, *strapontins,* and any other temporary seating that had accrued. By 1890 it was observed that while with every passing year the disfavor associated with the places called *de couloir* augmented, the better seats were still routinely sold out and frequently the objects of dispute.[5] Tortoni, whose ice-cream establishment around the corner was always similarly packed, shrugged: "Well, if they were comfortable, they wouldn't come back."[6]

With regard to temperature, the Salle des Concerts was all but life-threatening. The early morning orchestral rehearsals began in the bitter cold, a condition remembered by everyone from Sauzay at the beginning to Charles Münch and his musicians during World War II. The hall was often damp, that part of town having risen over a swamp at the foot of Montmartre, so much so that the singers refused to rehearse in one of the antechambers for fear of contracting pneumonia. As concerts progressed and the offstage furnace and porcelain stoves on each floor belted out their calories uncontrolled by thermostats, the temperature rose to infernal levels. When gas jets at length replaced the oil-burning lamps, the heat intensified. The amphitheater seats were known colloquially as the Turkish bath; among professional journalists the atmospheric conditions of the two press boxes, where more than fifty journals vied for twelve seats, were the stuff of legend—and many a droll essay.[7] At the concert of 11 February 1883, three people seated in the amphitheater fainted from the excessive heat, and the physician to the Société des Concerts had to intercede with the authorities to correct the problem, while the committee was occupied for weeks responding to the many complaints that followed the incident.[8]

Those preoccupied with matters of fashion found fault, too, with the diffuse illumination afforded by the skylight. It was not, primarily, that the orchestra seemed engulfed in shadow, but that the incoming light as swallowed up by the dark fabrics rendered the faces of the listeners "pale and yellowish, which is scarcely flattering to the ladies," who "complain exceedingly of the disadvantage to which their beauty is subjected in the boxes." And a bright day, it was felt, betrayed the mysteries of the *toilette.* The heat was "disagreeable in more than one way," with results that were "little calculated to beautify."[9]

Nevertheless, listeners came back religiously, enduring the discomforts with the same philosophy Parisians adopt in cathedrals during the winter or in the Métro at rush hour. Attending the Sunday afternoon performances of the Société des Concerts in the Conservatoire's famous hall was widely deemed a privilege of the good life.

From the street the main approach to the auditorium—whether one arrived by horse-drawn conveyance or by foot, whether via the portal and passageway from the rue du Faubourg-Poissonnière and into the courtyard of the Conservatoire or through a great gate that led from the rue Bergère into a formal garden—began beneath a colonnade, or peristyle, designed to protect the public from inclement weather (see site plan, following p. 378). The box office, or Bureau de Location, was at one's back, in the building that extended from the far end of the gallery to the rue Bergère. Originally adorned with statues of the muses after antiquities at the Louvre, the colonnade became over the years something of a hall of fame, with memorial busts of Cherubini and Habeneck, a marble plaque listing the conductors of the Société des Concerts, and another honoring the society's victims of war. Some of the pavement, in squares of black and white marble, still exists.

The grand staircase rising from the colonnade to the main *foyer* was dominated on the left and right by Giuseppe Serangeli's wall-sized paintings *The Descent of Orpheus into the Underworld* and *Sophocles Confounding His Sons Before the Areopagus* (by reading *Œdipus*)—thus saluting music and drama, the two arts to which the hall was dedicated.[10] Over the doorway at the landing hung a famous *bas-relief* of Minerva distributing crowns to the laureates of the Conservatoire, in reference to the annual prize-giving ceremony that took place in the hall. The staircase then split into two and reversed, rising to the long room over the colonnade that was intended to be the reading room of the Bibliothèque du Conservatoire, a provision not fully realized until 1860. While the elevation of the various architectural elements is difficult to envisage from prose descriptions, an 1821 cutaway (see website) clarifies the overall layout. Among its details are the statues in the colonnade, one of the large paintings, and the *décor* of the walls and hemicycle.

The door from the main landing gave into the great *foyer,* with corridors to the left and right leading to the first-tier boxes and, just in front, the door to the royal box—the *loge d'honneur.* (Subsidiary stairwells allowed access to the balcony and boxes, as well as the possibility of escape during an emergency. Access to the *parterre* was through corridors to either side of the main stairs.) Each Sunday the *foyer* would be mobbed as the public arrived and negotiated last-minute arrangements for seating, and hardly a season went by without a least one serious altercation there.

The *loge d'honneur* was reserved for the king or his representatives in exchange for an annual remuneration of some 1,500 or 2,000 francs. The royal *gratification* was greatly prized, not so much for its amount —hardly more than the same box might have fetched in conventional subscriptions—as for the way it indicated national recognition on a par with that accorded the Opéra and leading theater companies. In later years the precedent was often cited as evidence that the Société des Concerts had always been the official orchestra of France. While the record does not seem to specify a visit by the king himself, it does often document visits by members of the royal family, and a high-ranking official would nearly always attend the opening concert of a new season. On such occasions the government garnished the royal box with food and drink and appropriate insignia.[11]

Later in the season the box was often unoccupied, though occasionally a diplomat or visiting head of state would be offered its use. So long as the annual compensation arrived in due course, this conspicuous emptiness was regarded philosophically. In years that the money failed to come, the committee would doggedly pursue ministerial officials to secure it: while not a munificent sum, it was nevertheless critical to balancing a budget reckoned to the *centime,* and its loss for a season would be a formidable setback. Occasionally there would be a threat to release the seats to the box office, and it may have been the quiet practice, in the absence of honored guests, to allow members of the general public to occupy seats in the royal box at the last minute.

Disposal of the *loge d'honneur* was of particular concern when the government underwent radical change. In 1851, as Louis-Napoléon edged the nation toward a second empire, it was vacant more often than not. In truth the future Napoléon III was a musical ne'er-do-well, said to be tone deaf, and is remembered in music history primarily for his failures of judgment in patronage. Originally he had been disposed to "accept with pleasure the *loge* that the Société wishes to place at my disposal, and pleased to be able to encourage an institution where art so prospers." [12] In 1852, however, he tersely refused it. In late December of that year Auber, as president of the Société des Concerts, was sent to the office of the prince-president to see whether "changed circumstances" —that is, his forthcoming investiture as emperor—might lead him again to the Salle des Concerts. With the question still unresolved in 1853, during the beginning-of-year housekeeping, Auber left a formal communication with the administrative committee imploring it to take no action on the royal box; he himself would attend to such nuances under the new government.[13] Later national leaders were more enthusiastic in their use of the *loge d'honneur*, notably Maréchal and Mme Mac-Mahon (1873–79). The blind king of Hanover was accorded the box on 3 November 1874; in 1871 the emperor of Brazil was not, and ambassadorial requests for its use were routinely declined.[14]

After a single box was found insufficient, two boxes, some twelve seats in all, were reserved for the press. Shortly before each season began, the secretary would write the leading newspapers, inviting them to announce the new season and to submit the name of a correspondent to receive a single pass to the press box. This would be issued on heavy paper, later a wooden plaque, and verified each Sunday against the master list of complimentary passes. No-shows would be dropped to accommodate new applicants. For the three seasons 1833–35 there were about a dozen papers on a list always led by *Le Moniteur* and the *Journal des Débats*. Altogether some eighteen papers were sent invitations during those years;[15] by mid-century fifty-three papers were credentialed.

Only established journals gained free admission for their critics. In 1833 the satirical paper *Charivari* was made to wait, not because of its approach but on account of its youth; the next year both Maurice Schlesinger's new *Gazette musicale* and the English-language *Galignani's Messenger* failed to get their credentials.[16] Another paper had its privilege withdrawn when a writer informed the committee that his employer would accept his work only if it reflected negatively on the Conservatoire.

Journalists' requests for a second ticket were regularly denied;[17] those suspected of smuggling guests into the press boxes were rebuked. In January 1845, to stem abuses by the press, the *cartes d'entrée* were proclaimed non-transferrable and issued thereafter on wooden plaques, thus provoking a skirmish of several weeks. Hippolyte Prévost, who was in the habit of letting his wife have his pass, complained that the Société des Concerts had no business interfering with house practices at a newspaper; a journalist had the right to use his passes however he liked. The committee, finding this argument risible, returned a blistering response: "The two *loges* sacrificed by the Société in the interest of publicity are assigned to the press, not their wives—nor the friends of their friends."[18]

In 1869 there was renewed concern over the sighting of a woman in the press box. This was almost surely Mme d'Ortigue, widow of the distinguished critic Joseph d'Ortigue, who retained the favor of her *entrée* long after her husband died in 1866 and was finally turned away with great regret in 1872–73.[19]

The rear portion of the *parterre,* behind the benches, was used as standing room for *sociétaires* until they were found to be selling their passes to third parties—including women, who "distracted" the performers. Members of the public willing to spend Saturday night waiting outside the box office—or to send a footman to do it—would often gain access to the standing room the next day. In 1844, to discourage the all-night vigils and the inevitable rowdiness of distributing coupons just before the starting time, it was proposed to keep a waiting list; but on 11 November of that year the *billets de parterre* were instead retired altogether, with the space retained for the *membres honoraires.* This was also the occasion to withdraw the long-standing privilege of the *parterre* from students of the École Polytechnique.[20]

From 1829, students of the Institution Royale des Jeunes Aveugles (Royal School for Blind Youth) were admitted to backstage *loges publiques,* one of several miscellaneous areas used to accommodate non-paying guests of the society. Berlioz, in 1835, describes the arrangement in terms of benches placed on a catwalk meant for the service personnel and goes on to note the students' particular appreciation of the gesture. The annual correspondence with the service organizations for the blind suggests that the Société des Concerts, in turn, considered this custom not only an obligation but a special pleasure. The blind and war-wounded were eventually invited to the Saturday morning rehearsals— to which the Conservatoire students had had passes from the start. When these were opened to the paying public in November 1920, a blind patron complained of the new admission charge; he was told that henceforth the price would be 5 francs for all, but that his guide could enter for free. As late as 5 June 1947 there was a concert, under the direction of Henry Jollas, to benefit blind youth.[21]

Offstage the musicians had their own *foyer,* through which they would pass on their way to work and where announcements of the day were posted and committee members made themselves available for consultation. A *petit foyer* with a fireplace adjoined the larger room. Here the women singers assembled, prepared their *toilette,* and waited to go on-stage. Chaperones of the young ladies of the chorus—preferably their mothers, but if necessary a maid—were allowed to wait for their charges in the *petit foyer;* hence it was made off-limits to the public and the men of the society by an act of the committee in 1837.[22]

Mostly the offstage areas *(dans les coulisses)* were used for milling around. Every couple of weeks a complaint would be received, or a warning issued, about the noise of conversations reaching the hall from offstage. This would frequently be attributed to the chaperones attending the young ladies of the chorus, but in truth most of it came from the musicians themselves. Nearby, too, were the few rooms accorded the Société des Concerts for administrative purposes. Storage of the large instruments and their trunks was beneath the stage.

The faubourg Poissonnière in the eighteenth century was a suburban area north of the boulevards where *petits artisans* skilled in carpentry, cabinetmaking, *décor,* and costume had gathered to live and ply their trades. The Folies Bergère, also one of the enterprises of that neighborhood, was just around the corner. The focal point of the neighborhood was an enclosed block traditionally entered from the rue Bergère, with for a time a makeshift stage in the courtyard that had been rescued from the nearby Foire-St-Laurent (the plot now occupied by the Gare de l'Est). The court was ringed with the workshops and warehouses of the theater industry.[23]

In 1762, representatives of the crown acquired the entire lot to accommodate the Argenterie, Menus, Plaisirs et Affaires de la Chambre [du Roi]—in brief the royal furnishings—and from this period the locale was known colloquially as the Menus-Plaisirs and more formally as the Garde-Meuble de la Couronne. Since the block was both crown property and also traditionally associated with the lyric stage, it was thought the ideal location for a school that began to be envisaged in the 1780s to supply singers for the Opéra. Such a school was formally established in 1784 on roughly the southeast quadrant of the property. The largest existing room, later known as the *petite salle,* was refashioned for rehearsals and occasional public events like the annual awarding of prizes.

During the Revolution, First Republic, and Empire, the area became busier than ever as the *ateliers* produced the big *fêtes nationales* and the storehouses became the Magasins du Matériel des Fêtes. Concurrently the national bandmaster, Bernard Sarrette, was instructed to increase the supply of qualified instrumentalists for the national bands, thought in the 1790s a higher priority than the theaters. So it was that singing school and military band academy coalesced on the premises into the national Conservatoire, which dates its foundation from August 1795. The Paris Conservatoire began to offer formal instruction in October 1796.

On 3 March 1806 a decree was issued to replace the *petite salle* of the

Menus-Plaisirs that had thus far served for the *exercices publics* with a larger, more glamorous hall appropriate to the prestige of the institution. The language was typical of the imperial aspiration: "This monument, unique in Europe and standing in the heart of the new metropolis of the world, should rightly bear the imprint of the grandeur of the Imperial Government . . . and testify to the high patronage that the latter accords the fine arts."[24] The work was confided to François-Jacques Delannoy (1755–1835), architect of the iron-and-glass passage Vivienne and of various *hôtels* in the quarter. It appears that the "miracle of acoustics" achieved by Delannoy was essentially an accident, arrived at by the need to squeeze a fully appointed theater onto a small rectangular footprint—thus, for example, the high ceiling that was thought responsible for the exceptional resonance. The rectangularity of the hall was considered a liability, "the most unfavorable arrangement for a concert hall. From time immemorial, it has been recognized that circular halls succeed far better with regard to acoustics."[25] But that perfection had somehow been achieved with the Salle des Concerts was acknowledged as early as the gala inaugural concert, on 7 July 1811. The student orchestra, joined by Mme Branchu, Dérivis, and the elder Nourrit, offered works of Haydn, Mozart, Piccini, and Gossec. Outside, the sun beat down; inside, the temperature was said to have reached 45°C (100°F).

The campus of the Conservatoire, and indeed the whole of the neighborhood, was a work in progress for much of the nineteenth century. In 1835 there is reference to construction in one of the courtyards, a project that blocked the Sunday carriage traffic that was by then in the habit of entering from the rue Bergère, having passengers alight in the colonnade, and leaving through the passage into the rue du Faubourg-Poissonnière. This was probably the construction of the majestic portal in the rue du Faubourg-Poissonnière seen in an engraving of ca. 1848 and a photograph of ca. 1906 (see website). In 1836, again with the comfort of the public in mind, the benches of the *parterre* level were upholstered; by 1845 there was a first plan to convert the entire *parterre* to conventional seating.[26]

In 1853, during Haussmann's reworking of the IX^c Arrondissement, the enormous lot—bounded by the rue de Trévise, rue Richer, rue du Faubourg-Poissonnière, and rue Bergère—was quartered by the opening of a street running south to north along the west face of the Conservatoire's buildings, the present rue du Conservatoire, and an east-west street, today's rue Ste-Cécile, extending the rue de Montyon to intersect with the rue du Faubourg-Poissonnière. The gate in the rue Bergère and the buildings that had housed the Garde-Meuble de la Couronne (and the lodgings of the director of the Conservatoire) were torn away, and in the narrow strip that was left between the street and the Salle des Concerts were positioned a new carriage entrance and forecourt, as well as modernized spaces to house the academic collections and administration of the Conservatoire (see website). This in effect left the Conservatoire the only inhabitant of its block. For a time, on the occasion of the society's fiftieth anniversary, the widow Habeneck and the musicians of the Société des Concerts hoped to name one of the new streets after the founding conductor, but today only Ambroise Thomas is recognized with a street name in the area.[27]

The wear and tear on the Salle des Concerts from its unrelenting use was substantial. Projects to remodel the hall were proposed from the early 1860s by the Société des Concerts, feeling that the gradual deteriorations had made it "unworthy" of an organization of their prestige.[28] The Bibliothèque du Conservatoire above the colonnade had finally been completed in 1860, and the Musée Instrumental on the ground floor along the new rue du Conservatoire had been opened to the public in 1864. Good economic conditions and an effective working relationship between Auber and the ministers he reported to made it a propitious time to undertake new work on the concert hall.

The renovation begun in 1865 and completed in 1866 was dramatic, since the old interior décor of ivory, deep green, and purple was abandoned in favor of the reds and turquoise of the mosaics at Pompeii. The hemicycle around the orchestra risers, with its flamboyant neoclassical renderings of the muses, is spectacular even today. Additionally, the conversion of the entire *parterre* to fixed seating was completed, and the standing room in the corridors replaced with *strapontins*. Lighting by hydrogen gas was finally introduced, forty-five years after its installation at the Opéra, resulting in a much improved view of the players and singers.

At approximately this same time, Aristide Cavaillé-Coll began to build a pipe organ in the Salle des Concerts, primarily to serve the curriculum of the Conservatoire. Once it was done he exerted his considerable influence on the society to have the instrument heard during the famous Sunday concerts, with the result that César Franck was invited to inaugurate the forty-sixth season (1872–73) with Bach's E-Minor Prelude and Fugue (29 December, 5 January).[29] The organ was a critical factor in allowing the Société des Concerts to take the lead in the Bach-and-Handel revival in France, also to popularize the Third Symphony of Saint-Saëns. Alexandre Guilmant first played a Handel organ concerto on 5 and 12 December 1875 and thereafter was sought out for his recommendations of repertoire. He was appointed organist to the Société des Concerts on 23 April 1878, as an external member at full fee, and listed on every program. Guilmant's successors were Georges Jacob and Maurice Duruflé.

Having an organ and organist meant extra expense and considerable administrative bother. The records show, in addition to the occasional payment of a bellows operator (M. Lescot *fils* in 1873, for instance, was paid 2 francs each time he assured the *soufflage*),[30] ongoing complaints to the Conservatoire about the organ's mechanical condition and frequent requests to have it tuned. The instrument was enlarged in 1881–82 with the addition of a new *buffet*. The following year the committee discussed removing enough of the hemicycle behind the risers to reveal the new structure—and to realize a little more floor space on the top tier for the expanding percussion section.[31] This may have been the standard arrangement for unusually large works and is visible in one of the twentieth-century photographs.

After the watershed political events of the early 1870s, the administration of both the Société des Concerts and the Conservatoire began to be driven by the continuing decline of the overall property: "All the functions of the Conservatoire are overburdened: teaching, library, and museum are insufficient for proper operation. The concert hall is too small; though it has an exceptional acoustic property, we need to build a second, bigger hall, one more like the places the students will find work."[32] The institution had nearly tripled in number of faculty and student body, with new classrooms and studios carved out by dividing exiting space into ever more haphazard arrangements. The large rooms were nearly always overbooked with master classes, juries, and ensemble rehearsals; it was impossible to keep to a schedule.

Projects to rectify this situation came and went. In March 1878 Charles Garnier, architect of the new Opéra (the "Palais Garnier") was asked by the government to study the problem. He returned with two options: either to build a new Conservatoire on another property or to remodel the existing facility completely. A subcommittee of the standing commission on civil buildings and national palaces, examining the proposal on 9 December 1878, elected the second alternative. A budget of 5.6 million francs was proposed in November 1881:

Acquisition of nos. 19, 21, 23, rue du Fbg-Poissonnière	Fr. 1,315,000
Demolition of same; reconstruction	Fr. 4,325,000
Total	Fr. 5,640,000

This budget included rebuilding the amphitheater of the Salle des Concerts as well as improvements to the adjoining library and museum, alongside new classrooms, studios, and lodging for the staff. Projects for any refinement to the hall were soon abandoned, however, and in January 1883 the entire project was withdrawn by the president of the Republic.[33]

Meanwhile the administrative committee of the Société des Concerts continued on its own to address the limitations of the room, especially with regard to seating capacity and ventilation. The first effort was thoroughly unsuccessful. The architects consulted in 1877 about the possibility of adding new seats deferred to Garnier's study. In 1881–82, during the overhaul of the pipe organ, there was another opportunity to increase the seating; instead, in April 1882, the Conservatoire notified the orchestra of radical reductions required by the municipal authorities for improved fire safety. At the very least, the corridor seating would be removed, some fifty seats in all, reckoned to be worth 600 francs in lost revenue per concert. Intense diplomatic efforts reduced the total places lost to only a few, but ticket prices were increased for only the second time to avoid a net season deficit.[34]

The episodes of fainting from the heat in the amphitheater, combined with the fire-safety movement, prompted an interest in electrifying the hall. In February 1884, representatives of the Edison Company proposed to light the Conservatoire with incandescent bulbs, invented in 1878 and just being commercialized in France. They would be less expensive than gas, it was promised, and would emit neither noise nor heat. In the course of the project, buzzers *(sonnettes électriques)* were installed in the lobbies and corridors. These were used successfully during the Prix de Rome competition of winter 1884–85, but the committee thought it best to wait until the beginning of the 1885–86 season to introduce this possibly frightening innovation. Electrification brought with it, however, new expenses for replacement bulbs. In May 1889 the treasury was first charged with 200 francs for the "repair" of the electric lights.[35]

The new electric lighting also brought up the problem of power failure. In April 1907 there was a strike of electrical workers, causing the secretary and *commissaire du matériel* to be found scouring the bazaars and boutiques with other hoarders in search of oil lamps. The *garçons d'orchestre* spent the afternoon arranging the lamps about the house, taking care not to block the new emergency exits or to put a single nail in the wood and plaster. The musicians were able to rehearse by 9:00 at night, bringing *Harold en Italie* to life as their brigandly shadows danced on the walls. The next day the electricity had returned—"but the lamps are ours." Two of them stayed in the committee room as souvenirs.[36]

Already in the early 1860s there had been talk at the Société des Concerts of abandoning the Salle des Concerts altogether. This idea was driven in part by the excitement surrounding the new opera house under construction by Charles Garnier, in part by Pasdeloup's success at drawing audiences of six thousand and more to the Cirque Napoléon. Elwart alludes to the possibility in his volume of 1863, and Deldevez, in the 1880s, takes a strong position against it: "The quite delicate and flowery style of the symphonies that constitute the core of the repertoire make it law at the Société not to abandon [the hall], so perfect is its sonority."[37] But when the project to rebuild the Conservatoire in the faubourg Poissonnière failed in 1883, the academicians began to look toward building a new Conservatoire with a modern hall somewhere near the Gare St-Lazare, while Paris planners started to talk about alternative exploitations of the cité Bergère. In either event the Salle des Concerts was sorely threatened.

In the aftermath of the tragic fire at the Bazar de la Charité in 1896, the Salle des Concerts was closed as unsafe, and a decision to demolish the whole block was announced by the government. The concerts of 1897–98 were given at the new Opéra while a commission of bankers and industrialists considered what to do with the property occupied by the Salle des Concerts. Protests of the music lovers—"you don't demolish cathedrals to widen streets"[38]—prevailed, and the panic over public safety eased somewhat with the passage of time. Within the year it was decided to allow the Société des Concerts to resume concerts in its own hall, though with the loss of another 150 seats:

1828	1,078 seats (including standing room but not press)
1860	956 seats
1897	992 seats (921 paying, 71 service)
1899	845 seats (774 paying, 71 service)
1928	874 seats (817 paying, 57 service)[39]

Meanwhile the Conservatoire concluded its arrangements to occupy the former Collège des Jésuites in the rue de Madrid, but dropped plans for a public concert hall there. The move across town took place in the summer of 1911.

The Société des Concerts was now alone in its hall, with both the Opéra and Conservatoire gone to more modern quarters in Haussmann's new Paris. The plot at the corner of the rue Bergère and rue du Faubourg-Poissonnière —with its historic courtyard—was given over to a large building for the PTT (Administration des Postes, Télégraphes, et Téléphones), soon to house the telephone exchange for that part of town and, interestingly, equipment for early radio broadcasts. The *sociétaires* had become the sole purveyors of fine art in a venerable but outmoded neighborhood.

After World War I, with the room's every appointment considered sacred by some and with no one particularly interested in investing in its restoration, the most trivial repairs and adjustments were resisted. Threadbare *fauteuils* were preferred to the new folding seats, and the lighting was seldom modernized. The overcrowding and lugubrious atmosphere were accepted as part of the mystique. The Société des Concerts continued to appear in the hall from time to time even after transferring the bulk of its enterprise to the Théâtre des Champs-Élysées in 1945. But the photographs of the 1930s and 1940s show the orchestra crammed into a dark, dimly lit, and by that time rather grimy sanctuary.

On the separation in 1946 of the Conservatoire into two separate institutions, the Conservatoire de Musique et de Chant and the Conservatoire National Supérieur d'Art Dramatique, the hall fell under the aegis of the new drama school. Subsequent changes to the envelope have included the creation of a fore-hall and studios (1951), the addition of new floors and a new library (1972), and new stage machinery (1987).[40] The interior, now seating about five hundred, has been enchantingly restored to how it must have looked shortly after the redecoration of 1865–66 and is used for plays and an occasional chamber concert. In 1991 it served for the video recording of Berlioz's *Symphonie fantastique* as conducted by John Eliot Gardiner, from which a good sense of a concert of the era can be gleaned.[41] Otherwise the capacity is far from large enough to sustain orchestra concerts. Yet of all the artifacts left behind by the Société des Concerts—the programs, a few illustrations, recordings made for the most part elsewhere—it is the Salle des Concerts itself that most excites the imagination as to how things must have been in the nineteenth century.

Permission to use the Salle des Concerts was granted not by the administration of the Conservatoire but, since it was associated with the royal household, by a higher authority.[42] Generally this was the director of the Office of Fine Arts, the position occupied in 1828 by La Rochefoucauld.

The director reported upward to a minister of the interior and simultaneously, in some periods, to a minister charged with the oversight of public buildings—in 1830, the Ministry of Commerce and Public Works.[43] Not until the 1960s under André Malraux, long after the Société des Concerts had left its hall, was there a true cabinet associated with a minister of cultural affairs; only then did Marcel Landowski emerged as a strong director of music.

The custom was for the Conservatoire to occupy the hall for the prize distributions in November or early December, then turn it over to the Société des Concerts for the season. Authority for its use would already have been granted in response to a simple letter of application from the committee to whichever bureaucrat was in charge. From time to time the officials would add a new condition, usually the commandeering of more complimentary seats. Whatever the details, the overriding goal of the Société des Concerts was to achieve regular and, for all intents and purposes, exclusive use of the hall during the concert season, at least as far as ticketed concerts of symphonic music were concerned.

This arrangement was workable enough until an outside party presented a legitimate call on the facility, often breaking the established chain of authority. It was a root of ongoing antipathies, for instance, that Cherubini had opposed Berlioz's application to use the hall for the first performance of the *Symphonie fantastique* in 1830 and resented his success at obtaining authorization directly from La Rochefoucauld.[44] The Société des Concerts generally yielded to the ministry when it came to using the Salle des Concerts for events to benefit the infirm or victims of some meteorologic, public health, or political disaster; indeed the society often participated in these events. It tolerated concerts given in conjunction with the teaching program at the Conservatoire. But it looked with great disfavor on "foreign" interlopers and on any exception to ordinary practice that might set a precedent for ongoing shared use of the hall.

As early as 1833, for instance, there was a dispute over conditions of use that led to the formation of a special committee to look into the matter. In 1834, as a result, the hall was granted to the Société des Concerts without conditions, and it is to this decree that the membership always pointed in claiming the "sacred principle" of priority use. By 1837 the hall would be assigned exclusively to the Conservatoire from the *distribution des prix* until the end of the season's concerts.[45]

Berlioz took it as a personal affront when the Conservatoire and Société des Concerts proclaimed on 25 April 1850 that thenceforth from

the end of October until the close of the season, the hall would be reserved exclusively "for the purpose of teaching and the service of the
Société des Concerts."[46] This was, in fact, a great victory for the orchestra, however, and the pages to come recount dozens of skirmishes
designed to protect that right. But misunderstandings intensified as the
interests of the orchestra and the Conservatoire grew ever further apart
and as Parisian concert life broadened to include dozens of concert-
giving societies of every description. After 1870–71 the republican government exercised its authority to grant the hall to others with a certain
amount of relish. But at least for Saturday morning dress rehearsals and
Sunday afternoon concerts, the privilege of the Salle des Concerts was
by then essentially inviolable.

Diplomatically negotiating the several levels of government oversight
while relinquishing very little, however, was one of the committee's
most difficult ongoing assignments. The historic alliance with the Conservatoire had always to be recognized, but in situations where the
society and the Conservatoire were competitors, their joint director /
president would generally side with the interests of the school. The relationship with the Opéra was nuanced by competing designs on singers
and library, to say nothing of the overlap in orchestral personnel; thus
it was a societal policy to oppose recurring initiatives by the Opéra to
present public concerts. At the beginning, too, the Opéra sought to tax
the income of the Société des Concerts, following a provision of the
governmental mandate recognizing the Opéra as the state "academy"
of music. In short, bureaucrats of every description needed keeping at
bay, for any one of them could make trouble if, for one reason or another, they became unhappy with the Société des Concerts.

The best insurance of good will in these circles was purchased with
complimentary admission. Generally six boxes of six seats were reserved
for government officials: one each for the director of the Conservatoire;
the inspector-general of the royal chamber; the architect of the Conservatoire (Henneville in 1833); the conservator of the crown properties in
the area (Conservateur d'Immobilier de la Couronne—Zimmermann
in the early 1830s); the secretary of the Conservatoire (Beauchesne);
and the collector of the *droit des pauvres* (Saint-Julien and his dreaded
successor, Mantou). Individual seats were offered to the directors of the
Opéra and Opéra-Comique and to the members of the Académie des
Beaux-Arts de l'Institut de France; one document that appears to be a
liste d'entrées gives the names of Berlioz, Félicien David, Reber, Thomas,

Gounod, and Saint-Saëns. In 1834, Sarrette, Auber, and Rossini were among those reminded by letter that they were on the *liste d'entrées;* Rossini was reminded again on the occasion of his return to the concert hall in 1861.[47]

These privileges were considered by their recipients valued perquisites of employment, highly enough prized that they sometimes had to be wrenched away from outgoing officials. For instance, in January 1837 Germain Delavigne, in his new capacity as Conservateur d'Immobilier de la Couronne, wrote Cherubini that he had succeeded Zimmermann and invited immediate transfer of the customary privilege.[48] Meanwhile the administration of the Société des Concerts watched closely for any opportunity to recoup a complimentary seat for the generation of income. In 1851, for example, it was noted that the seat reserved for the director of fine arts had remained empty all year, representing a monetary loss that could not be continued.[49]

With the move to concert pairs in 1866–67 there was some relaxing of pressure for seats. As noted in the previous chapter, such providers as the lawyer, physician, and luthier were granted free entry; in 1871 the singer Boussagol asked for and was granted places in return for his distributing and collecting the chorus parts. For some time, perhaps from the beginning, admission to the backstage had been granted to music publishers in exchange for parts and rights to their use—to Aulagnier, for instance, in 1837. In another case, Victor Wilder, translator of Schumann's *Manfred,* was given seats in apology for the program's having listed the wrong collaborator (Benjamin Delaroche)—despite the "hardly acceptable language" of Wilder's complaint letter.[50]

Expenses of occupying the hall—lighting, heating, staff, and security— were paid from the beginning by the Société des Concerts. After World War I, during Henri Rabaud's long tenure as director, it became the working arrangement to pay a set price of 600 francs per concert for the use of the hall, including heat and light; the house staff was paid in a lump sum as well, totaling about 350 francs per concert.[51]

Whatever the acoustic properties of the Salle des Concerts, its audience capacity was never more than barely sufficient, nor, once the size of an orchestra grew past eighty, was its stage area satisfactory for the needs of the repertoire. With the crisis of 1897 and the relocation of the Conservatoire in 1911, the matter of finding a new venue came to the forefront and stayed there. For three decades the problem seemed insurmountable. For one thing, Fauré held, a Société des Concerts housed at neither the old nor the new Conservatoire could no longer rightly claim to be *du Conservatoire*. There was no financial apparatus by which the orchestra might remit weekly rent to a privately run house and still maintain its system of payment by division of the annual proceeds. The promised hall at or near the new Conservatoire in the rue de Madrid failed to materialize, and no one was quite certain which theater in Paris could be adapted to meet the society's requirements and be made available for concerts every Sunday afternoon.

In terms of its ability to attract large paying audiences, the Société des Concerts was probably capable of surviving a move, and even of separating from the Conservatoire altogether, by 1911. But when approached by the impresario Gabriel Astruc to become a principal tenant of his new Théâtre des Champs-Élysées, scheduled to open in 1912 or 1913 with a great hall accommodating 1,900 patrons, the society did little but to embark on its typically methodical and leisurely analysis of the financial ramifications.[52] By the time the committee was on the verge of experimenting with the notion, Astruc and his enterprises had gone bankrupt, and Europe was plunged into world war. The possibility came to the fore again in June 1920 during the course of four triumphant *matinées* at the Théâtre des Champs-Élysées with Isadora Duncan, but a satisfactory contract could not be agreed to. In 1923 the orchestra finally began to appear at the Théâtre des Champs-Élysées in a marginally successful series of Thursday afternoon concerts.[53]

In 1927 the Société des Concerts inaugurated the new Salle Pleyel in the rue du Faubourg-St-Honoré, a short walk down the avenue Wagram from the place de l'Étoile. This would have been an ideal permanent venue for a large orchestra—the Salle Pleyel, seating 2,300, was home to the Orchestre de Paris between 1981 and 2002—but the society could only manage the necessary internal expansion of personnel and budget in stages. And the initial scheme of four Salle Pleyel concerts mingled with the conventional season in what was by then being called the Salle de l'Ancien Conservatoire was a miserable failure at the box office. Fearing for their very existence, the musicians retreated once more into their drab but seemingly safe quarters in the faubourg Poissonnière.

During World War II the society contented itself with concerts in its traditional home and, from 1939, with big populist events in the Palais de Chaillot, opened in 1937 on the site of the former Palais du Trocadéro. Over the years the society experimented with other halls as well, notably the Salle Gaveau. But it was to the Théâtre des Champs-Élysées—all along, the only practical solution to the situation—that the Société des Concerts moved the minute the war was over. Here it found a workable new home and came to adapt itself well to its fundamentally changed circumstance.

The momentousness of this occasion was scarcely remarked, overwhelmed as the organization was in becoming a full-fledged, postwar philharmonic society of the mid-twentieth century. Still less did anyone note, three years later, the last appearance of the Société des Concerts du Conservatoire in its venerable old hall. On this occasion, 20 March 1948, André Cluytens conducted an all-French program: Yves Baudrier's *Le Musicien dans la cité*, Marcel Mule in Tomasi's Ballade for Saxophone, Lucette Descaves in a *Rapsodie concertante* of Thierac, and the *España* Rhapsody of Chabrier.

CHAPTER 4

The Concerts

Public performances of the Société des Concerts were given for more than a century on Sunday afternoons in the Salle des Concerts du Conservatoire—as unbroken a tradition as exists in orchestral music anywhere. Equally certain, for the better part of the first century, was that the house would be filled with its regular subscribers. Tourists who expected to hear the famous orchestra during visits to Paris were usually disappointed. Consulting their Baedeker in 1910 they would have found the following entry:

> *Concerts.* The celebrated concerts of the Conservatoire de Musique, Rue du Conservatoire 2, take place on Sunday at 2:15 P.M. from November to April. Only the highest order of classical music is performed. Conductor: M. André Messager.
>
> As all the seats are taken by subscription, admission for strangers is possible only when tickets are returned by subscribers (apply at the office Rue du Conservatoire 2, on Sat. at 1:30–3 P.M. or on Sun. at 1–2 P.M.). Adm. 4–15 fr.[1]

For the non-subscriber to have any hope of securing a place, it was necessary to be both intrepid and lucky. Such was the case in April 1851 for two *habitués* of the London Philharmonic. Admittedly prone to "John Bull prejudices" and having heard that the Conservatoire "had fallen off much since the revolution" of 1848, they found themselves in Paris on Easter Sunday, 20 April 1851, and took in the *concert spirituel* that evening at 8:30 P.M.: "There is something about a Beethoven Symphony no Philharmonic man can resist—an Alderman would as soon refuse turtle." Their lengthy account is worth citing *in extenso*:

Accordingly we entered one of the indescribable vehicles which, under an immense variety of the prettiest feminine appellations, do the duty of cabs, and proceeded to the Rue Poissonniere in search of tickets. We found immense difficulty in procuring them, but on mentioning the Philharmonic, we were supplied with the only two billets left, with which we proceeded to our hotel, and in due time to the appointed place. We were ushered into a large hall, on each side of which were a range of plain columns; and on exhibiting our numbers were told on which side to enter. Half Paris seemed to be there, and every one seemed full of interest and anxiety. By and bye we were marshalled to our place by an old woman in a spotless white cap, who acted as box-keeper, and we found ourselves in the Salle des Concerts. This in truth is a theatre, and not a concert-room, in our sense of the word. It is of oblong form, but it has its tiers of boxes, balcon, stalls, parterre, couloir, &c., like any other theatre. The place of the stage is occupied by some seats placed on the level, and then side benches, which run rapidly to the back. Its decorations are distemper and seem only temporary. In fact the arched ceiling appears to be covered with nothing but common paper-hanging. The part occupied by the orchestra is painted as if ornamented with hangings, and inscribed with the names of the most celebrated composers, in which we gladly saw those of Handel and Bach. There was an evening dress. The French are always *bien ganté, bien chaussé*—but the ladies wore their bonnets, and white chokers were not visible.

There is a marked difference on the part of the auditory. Alas! that we should have to say it, but the finer part of the Philharmonic members seem as much interested in themselves as in the music—like the Roman ladies in the time of Horace in Juvenal. There is no rustling of silks—no light breathings, that amount almost to a titter, as young ladies enter. The mammas do not faint, nor the *chaperons* turn out a whole row, that their fair charges may take their seats, while the band are playing the "adagios" of the first movement. Nothing of this sort at Paris. No; they come for the music! and every one is seated quietly and silently in their places. In the meantime the band enter and take their seats. The first and second violins are disposed in front, on two sets of benches, facing each other. In the centre between them are benches for the chorus. Behind these, facing the audience and crossing the ends of the violin benches, are the tenors. From these the benches rise rapidly, and are filled on the right side, as you look at them, by the violoncelli, each one attended by his contra basso, and on the other side are the wind instruments. All these benches, except the violins, face the audience. It will be understood that the wind band and the basses each form a mass, while the violins are divided. Here was another marked difference in favour of the French arrangements. There was none of that fearful dissonance at tuning the instruments; no rasping of basses, howling of horns, squeaking of fiddles, and blowing of trombones, that form such an unpleasant overture to the programme, and dull the ear to the first chord of the symphony. Except a few slight touches, almost inaudible, to make sure all was right—not a sound was heard. The band consists of somewhat less than our number, and about our own proportions, except that there are four bassoons instead of two.

In the meantime our neighbour has discovered that we were strangers, and pointed out to us, with the gentlest politeness, all the men of distinction—the principal being Auber, for whom there seems an esteem and respect we scarcely ever saw fall to the lot of any musical man. A short time elapsed and the conductor, Monsr. Girard, took his place and was warmly received; and the band began the famous E-flat of Mozart.

The first chords seemed hardly so full as at the Philharmonic, and the drum began with too much of a bang, as is the general custom in France; but the rich piano echo notes of the wind band compensated for this. The scale passages for the violins seemed much like our own; but those for the *tutti bassi*, both in the forte and piano parts, were much better; they were as clean as a run on a pianoforte. . . . The allegro began deliciously, the horns were so rich and so well in tune. . . . The *crescendo* was fine, taken with great judgment, and the burst into the forte splendid. Again, the excellence of the basses, their extraordinary clearness of execution and ensemble, attracted our notice. The wind instruments played perfectly in tune, and with much judgment. . . .

The *andante* began, the violins playing with marvellous delicacy. The basses gave the *rallentando* ["by the way," the footnote reads, "this is not marked in the Leipsic score of (Breitkopf) and Härtel"], as they descend splendidly. It was like a gleam of sunshine. . . . At last began the *finale*. The violins led off the rapid passages like one single instrument giving as much light and shade in the forte passages, as delicacy in the pianos. Instead of unmeaning divisions, the air in the forte came out with all the energy and beauty of Mozart, but when the second piano part came, with the imitation and answer from instrument to instrument, my friend leaned over to me, and whispered in the interval of the pause—"Ah! Old fellow, we have nothing like this at the Philharmonic; in fact we have not got a piano there." Alas! it is too true. We felt in the presence of superior intelligence; and when the symphony ended, we both sighed—"Well, this is the first time we ever heard the 'Swan' symphony done perfectly."

Then came the chorus in their hallmark polychoral *O filii:*

The chorus entered. It did not appear so numerous as our own. The band struck a single chord; and they began, without accompaniment or forte strains a very original motett of Leisring's—"O Filii." The voices went together as perfectly as the "Dom-Chor" of Berlin, but not so "aigu" in tone. The strains are simple and mournful, and are echoed by the same chorus (always without accompaniment) *pianissimo*. Such an echo we never heard. It was so perfect as if the mocking nymph herself had repeated it from the side of a wooded hill. . . . The composition itself had not much to recommend it except originality; but it was most effective as a *tour de force* for a chorus, and it was most rapturously encored.

Another hallmark rendition followed: excerpts from a string quartet performed by the full string ensemble.

As if to give us the greatest possible contrast, the next piece was the andante in G, and presto movement in D, from Haydn's Quartett, No. 5, performed by the whole string band; and it was executed as we never heard anything done before. The andante was like the performance of two finished players of the deepest feeling. The violoncelli were surpassingly excellent. The presto was given with the most sparking effect—the rapid divisions as clear as a Genevian box [i.e., a Swiss music box]. . . .

As if to carry the system of contrasts to its uttermost, the next piece was the 18th Psalm of Benedetto Marcello—"In cieli immensi narramo." (We called it the 19th.) . . . It begins with a fire and energy unusual to this writer, and reminds one of the some of the spirited movements in Haydn's masses. It is but repetition to say that the chorus was superb. One thing, however, puzzled us both amazingly. There was an accompaniment for full orchestra; written so exactly in the spirit of the time, that we began to doubt whether our recollection of the old Venetian had not failed us, and that, instead of the simple basses, with a figured part for harpsichord, or organ, he might not have scored this composition. On inquiry, however, we found it had been scored in modern times, and certainly most cleverly. Instead of giving the trumpets mere holding notes, they took a prominent part, while the oboes, &c., moved with the voices, as they do in most of Handel's choruses. Better musicians than ourselves might have been mistaken without any great shame.

This simple psalm preceded the mighty Symphony of Beethoven in C minor—certainly the most inspired work of the kind ever produced. There was a pause, during which every person seemed to be concentrating his attention; the same quiet examination of instruments went on—a careful look from the conductor was cast round—and amid breathless silence the great symphony began. . . . The very first four notes were given with a force and precision we never heard before. The fortes and pianos again attracted our admiration at their exquisite light and shade. The little bit of solo for the horn rang out as clear as a bell, and as round as a diapason. The long notes, which alternate as echoes between the stringed and wood band, were perfectly smooth and in tune, a thing we hardly ever hear in England; the basses were as clear as the violins themselves, and altogether the symphony seemed to develop fresh beauties at every bar. The same remarks will apply to the andante, particularly where, for the sixteen bars preceding the fortissimo reprise of the subject, the flute, oboe, and the two clarionets have the field to themselves, and their notes seem to twine round each other in the most graceful melody; their tones were perfectly silvery. The *scherzo*, however, deserves a few words of notice. It was taken much slower than in England, and the *rallentando* more *cantabile*, and very judiciously so; for as the time is accelerated at the *fugato*, it gives the instruments an opportunity to execute their notes accurately. The basses gave the subject as clearly as the notes of an organ, instead of the puff-a-puffs with which we are usually treated. We cannot understand the reason of hurrying over this movement; it is not marked so either in the German or French scores, and its effect is marvelously enhanced by steady treatment. The oboes and horn again excited our admiration, but the treat was to come; the pianissimo was perfect—the orchestra seemed asleep except the dull beat of the drum; the *crescendo* was regular and gradual, not as ours getting into a *fortissimo* long before its time, and trusting to the blare of the trombones for a burst, but increasing only to the forte, and then bursting with *fortissimo* on the first chord of that wondrous triumphal march; and here appeared the vast superiority of the brass band . . . and silver it was, each playing *with* the band and not endeavouring to drown everybody else: blowing, as a facetious friend of ours says, enough to carry off one's "whiskers." We will not attempt to describe that march; let the reader remember what we have said, and then let him fancy what the different points must have been, with such horns, bassoons, and oboes as these. The end was followed by a short pause; every one seemed to draw a long breath, and then followed such a burst of applause as we hardly ever have heard. No soul attempted to move till all was over. There was no fidgetting for hats, turning boas round necks. No: it was clear that the audience were as refined in appreciation as the band in execution. We parted with heartiest shake of hands from our neighbours, who seemed positively charmed to see how we enjoyed the music. "Vive la Société des Concerts," said we, as we resumed our hats, and made our last bows to our polite friends.

The music lovers go on to summarize their comparisons. "Their contrabassi are as superior to ours as a Bottesini is to all other players—they *really* play, and don't make a fuzzy sort of sound." They give the advantage, surprisingly enough, to the London violins. Equally surprising is how they find the solo bassoon in Paris richer in tone ("our bassoons use too weak a reed") but not superior in execution; one would generally put it the other way around with French bassooning—that is, unmatched technical skills but narrower, softer tone quality (presumably the rationale for using four bassoons with pairs of the other winds). The English visitors found the French oboes, horns, and trombones vastly superior, and the flutes and trumpets about the same. "We have nothing like the pure tone of this wood-band, . . . nor have we anything like the rich tones of their brass band: theirs is music, ours is blare. Only the timpanist stands out: no one at the Conservatoire can rival [Thomas] Chipp." They left with an overall sense of "discipline—obedience—no one thinks of himself, nor plays for himself; every one is subservient to the whole."[2]

All this may have been in response to a remark in the same journal a month before to the effect that "English executants are for spirit and energy superior to the French *Conservatoire,* though not equal in the minute refinement of execution." That particular writer regarded performances at the Conservatoire as cold: "The effect produced upon me was that of frigid correctness; there was none of that irresistible *entrain* which is the great characteristic of our own London performers. . . . Mendelssohn and Spohr . . . both preferred the rough energy of the Philharmonic . . . to the cold refinement of the Conservatoire."[3]

The great majority of the short-term visitors, however, shared the same kind of thrill at hearing the "Paris Conservatory Orchestra" that the British *amateurs* recorded at such length. Another sojourner, Wagner, famously remarked that the scales fell from his eyes on hearing Beethoven's Ninth Symphony at the Conservatoire. But the best evidence of the orchestra's allure is the loyalty of the subscribers, who returned season after season, learned and came to love the repertoire of the great classics, and aged along with the orchestra itself.

A grandfather, for instance, who had his seats in the third row, orchestra right, on Sundays enjoyed the company of his impressionable grandson Jean Cocteau, who later wrote:

> There in that painted wood sarcophagus full of venerable mummies, pell-mell I found Beethoven, Liszt, Berlioz, and Wagner. It was a kind of miracle, that room. And if in my childhood the curtain, the scarlet panels, the steep risers, the flaming sword of the archangel at Heaven's gate were wasted on me, I delighted in the bleachers' garish kaleidoscope of chorister beards, binoculars, princess dresses, golden epaulets, and black velvet neck ribbons installing themselves, chattering over a tuning note cruelly prolonged by the conductor until the last cough, until the last poor old myopic lady, overcome with embarrassment, finally found her seat number and sat down.[4]

A subscription to the Société des Concerts was one of civilized life's treasured luxuries. Each autumn, on cue from the *archiviste-caissier*,[5] those so privileged took care to send a footman with written authorization to collect the coupons for their *fauteuils* or *loge;* and upon their worldly demise, with equal certainty, they would pass their subscription on to their senior male heir.

Elwart puts it more poetically:

> More than one head of hair whitened, more than one man, ripe at the foundation, reached old age there. Empty seats would be retaken when good health returned. Then a seat occupied for twenty-five years by the same listener would be taken by an "unknown."
>
> But no, we are mistaken: it's the son or the nephew of the subscriber who took the Great Journey. For one leaves his stall, or a *loge* seat, or an entire *loge,* as one wills a painting, an *objet d'art,* a house—so few are the invitations to the sanctuary where Beethoven is pope.[6]

Those not having places would spend a chilly Saturday night in the late fall hoping to claim subscriptions that would come back on the market the following afternoon. Patrons who lost their subscriptions by negligence or inadvertence—often those who had not returned from their summer holidays in time to answer the call to renew—would be informed, elegantly or tersely according to the terms of their inevitable complaint, of the committee's great regret that nothing further could be done for them.

Later there would be an official waiting list, ordered as scrupulously as the list of *aspirants* awaiting election as *sociétaires*. But the waiting list was many seasons long and subject to disruption with the ongoing loss of seating capacity. So simple a change in habit as Maréchal and Mme Mac-Mahon's intent to occupy the *loge d'honneur*, after its having been abandoned by Napoléon III, resulted in hard feelings as patrons were ejected from what had become their customary places to accommodate the new head of state. The confusion in the years following 1870–71 was widespread, as founding subscribers—Jules Lefort, for instance—lost their privilege during the chaotic struggle to resume normal concert life before the patrons got back to Paris from wherever they had taken refuge. Meanwhile nobles sat on *strapontins*. Well-placed musicians and famous composers waited in the wings and *foyer*.

To these arrangements there were very few exceptions. Occasionally, by committee decision, the rich or powerful might jump the queue. Victor Schoelcher, deprived of his spot in 1848, had it reattributed in 1872 in thanks for the gift of his scholarly edition of Handel's works. The publishers Brandus and Heugel were bumped to the top of the list that year as well, presumably on account of the services they were likely to render in providing music at no charge. But in September 1856 even Cherubini's son was reduced to imploring two places for his family, already knowing how difficult this was; Gounod sought to know if "by happy coincidence," a place might be found to accommodate M. Pouquet.[7]

A black market thrived. To the committee this amounted to piracy, pure and simple, demanding aggressive response. But in fact such commerce was barely controllable, practiced as it was by the public, the press, and even the *sociétaires* and *membres honoraires*. Chorus members regularly slipped guests onto the chorus bleachers or into their *foyer;* boxholders tried to insinuate seven and eight people into their six-seat boxes. (One patron was reluctantly allowed to squeeze an extra child into his box, in thanks for services he had rendered the society.) At the second concert in December 1869 a woman went so far as to enter the box office to resell her tickets on her own; the prefect of police was invited to station a foot patrolman in the area to discourage such practices in the future.[8]

"Even employees charged with preventing the invasion of strangers" were apprehended in the act. In 1833, for instance, the secretary wrote the personnel chief of the crown properties, Lambert, to complain about "the woman Fallague, a worker on the left-hand side of the orchestra level," who had been "persuaded to favor the entry of persons without tickets," asking that she be banished to work the amphitheater on the third floor, with her door assigned to someone more trustworthy. Lambert replied that he could not simply punish an employee on hearsay after the fact; he must be notified immediately of any irregularities, in which case he engaged to counter abuses at once. The complaint was pursued, and eventually "closed in a conversation of Lambert, Habeneck, and Seuriot" (a member of the committee). But two years later Mme Fallague and her colleague Mme Grosset were charged with a similar *abus de confiance* and suspended for two weeks and one week respectively. In another case a patron complained that the usher had introduced *une personne étrangère* into his box.[9]

Brothers and brothers-in-law feuded over the right to take the seats of a deceased parent. Women patrons discovered that the policy of male-only succession was waived only for insiders. Mme Labadens, childless widow of the violist and founding *sociétaire* Isidore Labadens, asked in 1873 to transfer her places to her nieces and their heirs, and in view of her personal connections was granted the favor. The widow Habeneck, with two daughters, left her two prime seats to her lawyer, who was reminded that only direct descendents could inherit; one of the daughters, it was suggested, could take the tickets and give them to the attorney. When this arrangement was found unsatisfactory, and after considerable unpleasant correspondence, Habeneck's tickets were passed to his son-in-law, Louis Leplus, a *sociétaire*. The daughter of Vogt, the oboist, was given priority on the waiting list. Mme Lassabathie, in 1871, complained bitterly but apparently to no avail at losing her seat after the death of her celebrated husband, the founder of the Musée Instrumental; his seats had been complimentary, and the committee saw no reason to continue the privilege.[10]

Glancing through the patron lists, though Rothschilds and other wealthy families are well represented alongside the ministers and bureaucrats, one is struck especially by the number of names of professional musicians. The major composers held subscriptions, and a very large number of the seats appear to have been occupied by relatives of the *so-*

ciétaires themselves. This seems another indication of the society's on-going enthusiasm for its noble mission.[11]

D'Ortigue writes memorably of how the society intoxicated its clientele:

> The concerts of the Conservatoire: today's haven of art. Not *soirées,* but *matinées;* not a place to get together and chat, but a sanctuary where the writer, the painter—all serious artists flock. Listen, when leaving the hall, to the exclamations from every corner of the vestibule. Note the emotion showing on every face. See the blind students who are taken to harmony's temple to forget the loss of their sight and who come back with that mysterious insight of the hearer. Now musical Germany is ours; . . . we young musicians have Vienna and Munich at the Conservatoire.[12]

Both famous nineteenth-century images of the Sunday concerts, one outside the Conservatoire in the rue Bergère, one inside the Salle des Concerts, evoke particulars of the atmosphere (following p. 378). In the exterior view a crowd is arriving before the outer portal of the Conservatoire. A carriage drawn by white horses has paused to deliver an aristocratic *amateur de musique.* It is a bright winter day; of those pressing forward on foot, the women wear fur stoles and muffs, with the men in greatcoats and top hats. A foot-patrolman stands before the carriage, with two mounted officers looking on—members of the staff required by the Préfecture de Police for public spectacles. In the foreground, a couple and their child, perhaps on their Sunday promenade, pause to observe the excitement.[13] A photograph of perhaps 1874 (see website) shows almost exactly the same scene from a different angle.

The excitement continues within. Fashionably dressed women struggle to reach their seats in the narrow balcony; indeed the majority of the recognizable figures are women. We have a good view of the *loges* and the way the best of them give directly onto the performance force. The grand chandeliers invite one's gaze. The room is packed.

The artist gives a decent approximation of the distribution of orchestra and chorus, with the sharply rising bleachers for the winds and a not-quite-accurate row of doublebasses at the top. The hemicycle can be seen encircling the group. The chorus women are seated at the front of the stage; at dead center of the aggregation, a conductor leads with his bow and a violin soloist stands alongside to the left. This engraving comes from 1843, and thus must suggest the concert of 29 January 1843,

the only one that season with a male violin soloist—Sivori. In that case the conductor is not Habeneck but Tilmant, who substituted that day.

The disposition of the orchestra in choirs follows Habeneck's preference and is on the whole not dissimilar from modern configurations with antiphonal violins. The seating plan published by Elwart shows the chorus on the forestage separating violins I and II to the left and right.[14] Violas complete the box. On the tiers are cellos and doublebasses to the right, woodwinds and brasses to the left, with trombone, ophicleide, timpani, and battery at the top, along with a lone stand of contrabasses. Later there were alterations, of course, but the photograph of Gaubert and the Société made in the 1930s (following p. 378) shows essentially the same layout, though with five risers, not four, for the winds and brass, and the cello section now opposite the violins.

One of the intriguing components of Elwart's seating plan is the way the front two stands of low strings each consisted of a cellist and a doublebassist, an arrangement also suggested by Berlioz in his orchestration treatise and, for that matter, by the British tourists. This could only have worked for the early decades, where the prevailing repertoire could be notated on a single cello-and-bass part. (Beethoven and Schubert begin to treat the lines separately. Berlioz continues the "emancipation" of the bass line, ordering separate parts for cellos and doublebasses from the late 1830s, and in some respects it is surprising that he recommends the society's practice.) Having the principal desk of cellos so far from the conductor, and the whole of the cello-and-bass section behind the violas, seems musically problematic, however, and it was the one detail of "historic" practice that Roger Norrington felt compelled to abandon in his "Berlioz experiences" of the 1970s.[15]

The other unusual feature of the disposition of performers was, of course, to have the chorus surrounding the conductor—and with the bass singers separating the opposing violin sections—in front of the orchestra. The singers would wait offstage until their portion of the program, then occupy benches much like those of the *parterre* level, with the strongest voices on the forward bench of each section. Particular attention was paid to the appearance of the women, who being in the direct line of public view, were to expected to wear full-length supple gowns *(robes de Mousseline)* and gloves. In April 1840 there was an incident over two women who ignored (or, they said by way of apology, had not understood) the call for somber dress for the Good Friday concert, appearing instead in long overcoats *(spencers)*.[16] Concern with the deportment of the chorus, not only in matters of dress but also with regard to tasteful taking and leaving of the stage and the seldom-observed rule of silence in the wings, was a frequent feature of committee meetings.

Those who have tried the chorus-in-front arrangement for such works as Beethoven's Ninth and Berlioz's *Roméo et Juliette*—Berlioz specifically advocates it in both the "Observations" that precede the score and the *Grand Traité d'instrumentation*[17]—naturally admire the rich choral presence. But the need for the forwardmost women and tenors to turn away from the audience in order to see the conductor cannot have seemed graceful, and the use of the chorusmaster to mirror the conductor's gestures was positively cumbersome.

It is worth noting again that the chorus, appearing on every program, was an integral part of the Société des Concerts from its inception. One is tempted to argue that the organization could not at first have sustained weekly concerts with the limited repertoire of symphonies and concertos available to it in the 1820s and 1830s. Certainly the chorus made possible the revival of Holy Week *concerts spirituels,* and the research it conducted on its own behalf popularized a sizable *a cappella* repertoire of the sixteenth and seventeenth centuries. At the close of the nineteenth century the big orchestra-and-chorus works were the main drawing card for the Société des Concerts.

In other respects the attempt to maintain a complete, full-time chorus was dubious from the outset. For one thing, the equivalence of stature—artistic, financial, even social—purported to exist between orchestral and choral musicians was a fiction. It was never intended that young women singers would advance naturally to full membership—nor for that matter was the turnover of young men singers especially slow. Meanwhile even modestly compensated opera singers commanded fees manyfold higher than anything the Société des Concerts could ever offer, and the notion that they would long sing in a chorus, whatever its prestige, was folly. The result was a chorus of which half or more were students or semi-professionals. It seems likely, to judge from both the press and accounts of episodes we will have occasion to consider, that the artistic quality of the choral component was often low. Running the chorus was quite costly in administrative time, and the expense of translating the texts—except for Latin sacred music, the works were sung exclusively in French—formidable.

At the foundation there had been little alternative but to rely on the Conservatoire's own investment in choral training—the *classe d'ensemble*—to organize and staff a chorus. Singers and players maintained at least the appearance of solidarity until after the turn of the century, when the orchestra insisted on appearing away from Paris as the "Société des Concerts du Conservatoire de Paris," unencumbered by the chorus. The "extinction" of the chorus through gradual attrition was decided in a formal vote on 30 May 1919. By this time there were any number of superb choral organizations in Paris: descendents of the Orphéon movement, the better church choirs (though some of these still forbade women), professional ensembles organized by graduates of the several fine singing schools, and even a university chorus at the Sorbonne. From the early 1920s the remaining choristers supplemented the Chœur Mixte de Paris for such few chorus works as were programmed. Later collaborators included the choir of St-Eustache and, notably, the Chorale Yvonne Gouverné, with whom, for example, Charles Münch and the orchestra recorded Honegger's *Danse des morts* in 1940.

During the last years the Chœurs Élisabeth Brasseur became the principal chorus of the Société des Concerts. Brasseur (ca. 1900–1972) was the founder of the Schola Féminine of the Church of St. Joan of Arc, Versailles, where she was organist-choirmaster. Her women's ensemble, organized in 1934, was expanded into a mixed chorus in 1943. The Brasseur chorus appeared with the Société des Concerts for the first time in 1948 with Florent Schmitt's Psalm 47, André Cluytens conducting; later in the season came their first joint Ninth Symphony. In 1952 they made their first recording together when the chorale backed Janine Micheau in Debussy's *La Damoiselle élue,* and the Brasseur singers are to be heard on more than a dozen later records, among them Cluytens's great Fauré Requiem with Victoria de Los Angeles and Dietrich Fischer-Dieskau (1962). Their 1958 Ninth Symphony, under Carl Schuricht, won a Prix Charles Cros, and in 1963 they were awarded the *grand prix* of the Académie du Disque for Milhaud's Third.[18]

The matter of a resident chorus came nearly full circle when it became a principal tenet of discussions in the mid-1960s that the new Paris orchestra would emerge with a companion symphonic chorus numbering in the hundreds. This is the present Chœurs de l'Orchestre de Paris, organized and led until 2002 by Arthur Oldham (1926–2003).

The early seasons began in January and continued through Lent, with the original series of six statutory concerts and a closing benefit for indigents quickly extending in both directions with *concerts supplémentaires*—any, that is, past the statutory six, sometimes open to the non-subscribing public. In 1830 there were ten concerts in all: the designated six, three *concerts spirituels,* and a benefit. By the mid-1930s the season had settled into seven or eight ordinary Sunday concerts, a *concert spirituel* on Easter Sunday or Good Friday night (later both), and a closing concert to benefit the new emergency fund. However described, the normal expectation during the first four decades was a season of some ten concerts. In 1866–67 the schedule moved to seven pairs, "odds and evens," with the same program repeated on successive Sundays; in 1873, to nine pairs, running from the beginning of December to the end of April. After World War I there were twenty separate concerts, then twenty-two and twenty-four, extending from October until the Good Friday *concert spirituel* or beyond. While the program was different every Sunday, there remained two subscription series, called Ire and IIe, later pink and blue.

One of the several ways the Société des Concerts steadfastly refused to acknowledge that its imitators—the Pasdeloup, Colonne, and Lamoureux orchestras—were in fact competitors was in its traditional time of opening—not at the *rentrée,* but in December, a full two months after the rivals. The limited number of performances was another factor that kept the house full, and fully subscribed. It was possible to attend every concert as a matter of course, and the session was over before good weather attracted concertgoers to their outdoor pursuits.

During the concert season the committee's main work was to set the programs. Rough ideas were generally set down three or four weeks in advance and the necessary soloists contacted. The program was expected to be definitive and irrevocable no less than two weeks before the concert time, largely to meet the printer's deadline. On 1 February 1848, for example, the committee first recorded its ideas for the concert of the twentieth:

1. Overture by M. Chélard
2. A solo by Alexis Dupont
3. [A concerto with] Verroust, or Dorus, or Arban
4. Scene from *Alceste*
5. "Pastoral" Symphony

The overture by Hippolyte Chélard, chapelmaster to the grand duke of Saxe-Weimar, was to Chélard's opera *Hermann et Varus* (*Die Hermannsschlacht,* 1835). Dupont, when approached by the committee, suggested Cherubini's *Ecce panis angelorum* for tenor and orchestra (1816). Two of the soloists considered for the instrumental solo were leading wind players in the society, Verroust the oboist and Dorus the flutist—neither, incidentally, a principal at the time. Arban, not a member, wanted to demonstrate a new chromatic trumpet, and later in the season did so. In the event it was none of these, but rather the principal clarinetist Klosé, who appeared, playing an unidentified work of his own composition.[19]

The orchestra's own benefit concert, to the profit of its Caisse de Prévoyance, was usually the last of each season, a tradition that extended back virtually to the beginning. In this case and a very few others, the members would receive no compensation and the full ticket income would go to the worthy cause; more frequently a global fee for the orchestra was reckoned as an expense to be deducted before recording a profit. Proceeds of the first concert of 1831 were directed to the wounded of the July 1830 revolution; a similar event followed the revolution of 1848. Additionally there was a benefit for Habeneck in 1835, possibly to assist him during one of his periodic financial shortages, and another in December 1847, almost certainly with his retirement in mind. Later benefit concerts assisted the two widows—Mme Girard in 1860, Mme Marty in 1908—of conductors who had died suddenly and in active service. Otherwise the proposed beneficiaries were victims of natural disaster: floods in 1840, 1846, and 1856; a crop failure in 1863; and a spectacular explosion of a Pas de Calais coal mine in March 1906, which killed 1,200.[20] During three wars and their aftermaths the benefit concerts became almost a *raison d'être* for continuing the apparent luxury of orchestra concerts; they gave everyone involved a sense of purpose in troubled times. After 1870 there were benefits for the war-wounded, the reparations fund, the drive for the return of Alsace and Lorraine. Any profits of the 1918 tour of the United States and Canada were intended —or so it was announced—for the Red Cross. In 1940, there was a concert to support a national day for hot wine for the soldiers; in the years that followed, any number of events where proceeds were destined for the Red Cross or to aid prisoners of war.

Another form of participation in the world outside the faubourg Poissonnière was for the Société des Concerts to lend its support to the erection of statues and monuments honoring its associates. Few seasons passed without an approach from some commission of worthies reminding the society, unnecessarily, of its noble position as custodian of the past and urging its participation in their particular enterprise: the Beethoven monument in Bonn (1837), for instance; monuments to Cherubini in Paris (1841) and Florence (1861); a marble frieze commemorating Habeneck (1849). From time to time a benefit concert would be specifically connected with one of these projects, as was the case with the 22 December 1861 concert for the Cherubini monument in Italy. More frequently, since benefit concerts were not certain of any profit at all, the musicians would tax themselves or draw from the income of one of their own benefits to pay for a subscription; this was the approach taken in 1882 with regard to the Berlioz statue in the Paris square now named for him. In 1870 the Bavarian consulate approached the Société des Concerts, apparently unsuccessfully, to support a Gluck monument; in 1912 the musicians declined to participate in a benefit for a statue of Lalo. That same year they elected to draw from the reserve fund for their contribution to a plaque commemorating Alexandre Guilmant, who had been organist to the society.

The first command performances were on 11 May 1828 and 3 May 1829, both ordered by the Duchesse de Berry, widow of the assassinated heir to the throne of Charles X and mother of Henri de Bourbon, expected at the time to become Henri V. In 1845 there was a concert at the Tuileries, possibly in the presence of the queen; in both 1855 and 1856, concerts at Napoléon III's palace at St-Cloud. These first away-from-home appearances gave the society valuable production experience. A concert at the Hôtel de Ville in the summer of 1851, for instance, posed such unfamiliar tasks as dealing with other employees, rental and transport of equipment, and coaches for the women of the chorus. The most elegant command performance to have taken place in the Salle des Concerts may have been that of 16 May 1857 for the Grand Duke Constantine of Russia, brother of the czar, Alexander II. Ministers of the republican governments called increasingly on the Société des Concerts for state ceremonies, notably funerals. These appearances established an important evidentiary thread in the effort to have the society designated the national orchestra of France.

Rehearsals lasting from three to four hours took place on Friday and Saturday mornings, with chorus rehearsals on Wednesdays. Roll was called by the personnel manager or the chorusmaster at twenty minutes before the appointed hour and, during periods of close attention to policy, again at the end. The results were recorded in the *feuilles de présence* that formed the basis for dividing the receipts among the musicians at the close of the season.

The music would already have been placed on the stands and chorus benches by the *garçon d'orchestre*. Irregularities in the distribution of parts had the potential to disrupt the orderly flow of a rehearsal right from the start, so from time to time a *sociétaire* was delegated to assist the *commissaire du matériel* in inspecting and approving the work of the staff personnel before the musicians began to arrive.[21] Any business items to be brought to the immediate attention of the membership would be announced by the secretary, though on the whole it was preferred to communicate with the membership in writing, either by announcements posted in the *foyer* or through printed materials delivered to each member's residence. The vice president / conductor would then assume complete control of the rehearsal.

For the sixty-fifth season (1891–92), and doubtless for others, a pocket card was printed for the membership listing rehearsals and performances, with the orchestra obligations on one side and those of the chorus on the other. The card called for seven preliminary rehearsals on Fridays and Saturday in November—the season began on 6 December—then weekly Friday and Saturday morning rehearsals for the orchestra, with Wednesdays substituted for Friday conflicts. The chorus had a separate rehearsal on Thursday evenings.

Seemly behavior and dress were expected of all members at rehearsals. So, too, was punctuality, with stiff fines for late arrival and early departure. Marathon rehearsals were out of the question, as the players had early-afternoon teaching duties before needing to return home to dine, dress, and depart on time for their theater obligations. Occasionally one of the opera singers, trying to avoid the rush, would show up in costume or makeup.

Infractions of deportment called to the attention of the committee most often centered on offhand, usually disrespectful, remarks made by musicians to their colleagues or—less frequently, but with inevitably dramatic results—in the earshot of the conductor and soloist. There are incidents of displeasure at trombone players reading newspapers and missing their entry, instruments in bad repair, and late taking of seats before the next work. Concern over noise drifting in from conversations offstage or in the *foyer* peppers every volume of the record; signs were posted, fines levied, stern lectures read aloud. But all these are typical shortcomings of working musicians, and on the whole the corrective measures were to little avail.

With the growth of social and political activism among professional musicians, which may be said to have dawned in the 1870s and flowered after the world wars, came a pronounced increase in rowdiness among the rank and file. This alarming trend, many believed, was accompanied by an overall decline in pride of workmanship and musical result that led to artistic crises in the 1940s, 1950s, and 1960s. But in the nineteenth century, the sobriety—some would have said chill—of working habits seems the distinguishing feature of the rehearsals.

Rehearsals carried on in weeks without a Sunday concert. These might be used to continue to piece together monumental undertakings: Beethoven's Ninth and *Missa solemnis,* the B-Minor Mass, Berlioz's *Roméo et Juliette*—each of them rehearsed for years before being presented complete. Found rehearsal time could also be used for polishing works, usually first performances, planned for a particular season but not so far ready. Programs were very frequently modified between the Wednesday and Saturday rehearsals, most often because of a last-minute changes of soloist. Even when concerts began to be advertised on the Morris columns about Paris, there was a preliminary posting early in the week and a final reposting after the Saturday general rehearsal. If there were any uncertainty about a new work, it would be postponed in favor of something from what was by the mid-1830s already a large standard repertoire. Few objected, at least in the first half-century, to rehearing a Beethoven symphony or scenes from a familiar opera—all the more so as the public seldom knew what might have been.

The final *répétitions générales,* or "dress" rehearsals, were Saturday mornings at 10:00. With the exception of Conservatoire students bearing a valid *carte d'entrée,* these were closed to guests. Organizations that had been granted the privilege of entry at other theaters—for instance, students from elementary school and the physically handicapped— found their requests to attend dress rehearsals of the Société des Concerts routinely denied. So, curiously, did visiting professional musicians. Composers were invited to hear the final rehearsal of their new works and in some periods to preliminary rehearsals as well; they were allowed to offer brief observations and their thanks to the musicians just afterward. From time to time, on the occasion of a much-anticipated premiere, a diligent critic or two would manage to slip into the house to study the new work. Otherwise the doors were blocked.

Admission of a paying public to the Saturday morning general rehearsals followed the overall reorganization of the Société des Concerts after World War I. The possibility began to be broached toward the end of the 1919–20 season and was adopted for 1920–21, beginning with the rehearsal of 7 November 1920.[22] The public rehearsals were hugely successful within two seasons, often attracting a full house with standees, and were a key to the orchestra's financial survival during the economic chaos of the 1920s and 1930s. They brought a new public, too: unescorted women, young people, and music lovers of limited means— enthusiasts who may have acquired their taste for art music from radio broadcasts and from the good-quality phonograph recordings just then becoming universal. The *répétitions générales publiques* were continued even after the orchestra moved to the more spacious quarters of the Théâtre des Champs-Élysées, where the income was in fact critical to making the change of venue possible at all.

Members, critics, and other witnesses agree that the technical perfection of the Société des Concerts as perceived by the public was the result in equal measure of precedent-setting rehearsal schemes and an unwavering determination not to present works until they had been mastered. This feature of Habeneck's legacy may well have been more important in the long run than his having introduced Beethoven to the French. Beethoven would have arrived anyway.

Before the concert season got under way, and from time to time as it progressed, there would be the vitally important *répétitions d'essai,* at dead center of the theory and practice of the Société des Concerts. Here a half dozen or so new works would be read and one or two selected for further work and presentation in the forthcoming season. Two preseason rehearsals were customary at first, and when these were found insufficient to read all the music that had attracted the attention of the conductor and committee, the number was increased to four or more. The *répétitions d'essai* brought the central issue of sustaining a vibrant repertoire before every *sociétaire* every year.

The Société des Concerts took its mission of giving life to the great masterworks seriously indeed. The chief commitment of the early years, incontestably, was to the Beethoven repertoire. To be heard in the first season were the Third and Fifth Symphonies, the Violin Concerto and Third Piano Concerto, the *Egmont* and *Coriolanus* overtures, and excerpts from *Fidelio* and *Christus am Oelberge* (called in French *Le Christ au Mont des Oliviers*). Within five years all nine symphonies were mastered, and during Habeneck's two decades the society acquired, studied, and performed everything of Beethoven that anyone had ever heard of —including not a little chamber music. Second in their allegiance were Mozart and Haydn, with Haydn having the slight edge owing to his especially warm connection with Paris. The late Mozart symphonies were heard from the first, along with some of Haydn's London and Paris symphonies and, frequently, the orchestra's very popular excerpts from *The Seasons (Les Quatre Saisons).* Overtures and excerpts from the operas of Gluck and Weber were staples. Two Parisian composers, Cherubini and Méhul, figured prominently in the early years.

The repertoire broadened naturally toward Mendelssohn, Meyerbeer, and Schumann, with enthusiasm for Mendelssohn reaching by 1850 all but the same level as that accorded Beethoven. Meanwhile the chorus popularized a few Renaissance and Baroque works, including in addition to their famous *O filii* an *Alla beata Trinita* said to be of the fifteenth century. This was a period of rapidly growing music historical awareness, stimulated in part by the vogue for *concerts historiques* established by Fétis.

To say that the Société des Concerts introduced these composers and works to the most cosmopolitan of European publics is greatly to understate the situation. It made them familiar, and current. Some passages the society made as popular as the light-opera tunes played in the salons and hummed on the street. In 1850 Schonenberger, following practices customary with popular stage works, began to publish piano reductions of the signature works—his *Répertoire des morceaux d'ensemble exécutés par la Société des Concerts du Conservatoire,* delivered in nearly two hundred installments and priced from 35 *centimes* for the quartet from *Fidelio* and an excerpt from Rossini's *Moïse* to 3.50 francs for the "Eroica." Among the works chosen for anthology are Beethoven's first three symphonies, the Mozart G-Minor, Haydn's "Surprise" Symphony and C-Minor Symphony, No. 95, the overtures to Weber's *Oberon* and *Euryanthe,* Méhul's *Le Jeune Henri* overture, and the victory chorus from Handel's *Judas Maccabaeus* and Chœur des Sauvages from Rameau's *Les Indes galantes.* In 1851 Aulagnier sought to imitate the series, asking to publish the society's version of choruses from Rameau's *Castor et Pollux,* but was refused. Both the pianist Charles-Valentin Alkan and the violinist Charles Dancla composed and published, in the 1850s, musical *souvenirs* of the Conservatoire concerts.[23]

Habeneck and his musicians were keenly aware that they had inherited little by way of a French symphonic tradition. They imagined themselves to be on the lookout for, even encouraging, worthy French successors to Beethoven, though as self-proclaimed curators of a museum of Old Masters—"the Louvre of music"—their qualifications seem a little suspect. Certainly they did their share of looking, diligently reading the symphonic work of Georges Onslow, Louise Farrenc, Elwart, and Deldevez, on through such forgotten figures as Nicolas Baudiot, Joseph-François Turcas, and Alexandre-Charles Fessy. It is to their credit that little of this music passed through the cumbersome adoption process and into the repertoire. That they were slow to be attracted to Berlioz and, later, to Gounod and Franck shows among other things how particularly they were looking for four-movement orchestra pieces called symphonies. It also suggests how the values of working orchestral musicians tend to lag behind the ideals of forward-looking composers.

Habeneck himself became disillusioned by the quest for a French Beethoven as his tenure approached its end, and his immediate successors seem, despite their protestations to the contrary, mightily disinterested in carrying it on. Not until after the Franco-Prussian War did the French "moderns"—Reyer, Saint-Saëns, d'Indy, Franck—begin to have any measurable share of the repertoire, and the Belle Époque was well under way, as was government insistence on programming French composers as a prerequisite for subventions, before the works of Bizet, Roussel, Dukas, and Ropartz began to tip the balance of the repertoire to the French patrimony. Messager and Gaubert undertook and succeeded in an ambitious program of catching up, helping to canonize Debussy and Ravel, among others. Charles Münch, for his part, was an avid modernist, having arrived at the Société des Concerts with a repertoire that included Honegger, Milhaud, Schmitt, Françaix, and Aubert. By this time it was clear to everyone that the French had made a symphonic tradition to call their own.

From the outset the players were naturally interested in the repertoire for soloist-and-orchestra. The Société des Concerts had a major role in fostering both the concerto in the nineteenth century and the custom of allocating the center slots of the program to one or more soloists. The ordinary Sunday concert of the early decades consisted of two parts: the 1re *partie,* opening with a major work, usually the featured symphony, and the 2^e *partie,* closing with another. Toward the middle, sometimes before a short intermission, would come the soloist, often as not playing a work of his own composition: a full concerto, perhaps, but just as frequently a fantasy or variations on a theme or themes, often operatic, by another composer. The orchestra's own virtuosi established this practice, but by the mid-1830s the focus began to shift to foreign artists, a vogue established by Liszt, Chopin, Thalberg, and Sivori (billed as a student of Paganini, who never appeared with the orchestra). The Société des Concerts also welcomed visiting principal players from foreign orchestras: Belgians, Prussians, Austrians, and Dutch by the dozens. If one would not characterize the repertoire they brought to Paris as lasting, the personal interactions were exactly that. The foreign players would go home with marvelous accounts of what was happening in France, while the Parisians, in turn, would absorb new ideas of tone quality, technique, and instrument building—and sometimes be invited, tit for tat, to appear abroad.

By the 1860s the vogue for real concertos was in full swing. Clara Schumann, who as Clara Wieck had asked to be invited as early as 1839 (listing her credential as "pianist to His Royal Highness the Emperor of Austria"), appeared in 1862 in the "Emperor" Concerto. Among the soloists over the next several seasons were Théodore Ritter, Saint-Saëns, Henri Vieuxtemps, Joseph Joachim (in the Beethoven concerto), Georges Pfeiffer, and Louis Diémer. In 1864, after a season that had included half a dozen major concertos, Lebouc in his *rapport moral* congratulated the *sociétaires* on the critical role the Société des Concerts had played in stimulating the vogue for the solo concerto in France. For years they had recognized how their concerto performances had become audience favorites; whole evenings of concertos were beginning to be organized in Paris, which meant more pickup work for the musicians. And the most popular works were also of the highest quality. "Where it comes to good taste and elevated style, we can only rejoice at this development, [embracing] serious works instead of frivolous stuff." [24] Saint-Saëns and Lalo soon profited from the trend, and their concertos were adopted by the society straightaway.

Meanwhile the committee was deluged with petitions from young keyboard virtuosi, mothers and fathers of prodigious *demoiselles*—and an insistent Monsieur Franck, who wrote repeatedly of the accomplishments of his son, César-Auguste. The A. Duvernoy who played a Mozart piano concerto in March 1867 was a nephew of the *sociétaire* and celebrated hornist Duvernoy, and got the job at least in part owing to his uncle's intervention. By that time, however, the Société des Concerts was only really interested in the world's leading virtuosi. Most of them passed through over the years, and in a few cases—Saint-Saëns playing Mozart, Marguerite Long playing Chopin with Gaubert conducting—the affection exchanged between orchestra and soloist was so substantial as to define the local performance tradition. Both Münch and Cluytens were esteemed for their concerto work, and both left strong concerto discographies.

In sum the contention that the Société des Concerts did little to renew the symphonic repertoire is grossly unfair. It was a delicate matter, however, since many of the players and perhaps most of the subscribers were openly hostile to aggressive modernism. No one wanted an invasion of lesser works, but it was often difficult for the members to articulate the difference between intrinsic lack of quality and their own distrust of the unfamiliar. Nor could they quite get past the notion that their fundamental purpose was to present "Old Masters, particularly Beethoven";

Girard went so far with the museum analogy as to suggest that "nobody complains when they don't change the paintings on the walls." There was a real risk of the orchestra and its repertoire becoming immutable: "Its makeup," Deldevez proclaimed in the 1880s, "can never change."[25]

Nevertheless, nearly everyone was interested in expanding the repertoire, so long as there was at least some promise that the investment of their time and resources would return a sturdy title with a long life. In some periods the repertoire was discussed at nearly every committee meeting, from excited reports of a newly found work by Haydn or Beethoven to the latest accomplishments of a living master and even, from time to time, how to encourage a promising young composer. Every fall the conductor would propose a list of new music to study. Parts would be sent for, and the work would be scheduled for a *répétition d'essai* as soon as they arrived. Some ideas fell by the wayside for want of availability or performance rights; German choral works had first to be sent to a French translator. Difficult music might take several seasons of study and would be introduced, as we have already noted, movement by movement over several seasons. Habeneck first talked of doing entr'actes from *Egmont* as early as 1835, but this staple of the repertoire was not ready to be introduced until 1855, well after his demise. The committee had an animated discussion of Schubert symphonies in 1841, though the orchestra did not end up playing one until the premiere of the "Unfinished" in January 1883—four conductors later.[26]

Then came the question of how to reach a fair decision on the essayed works, backed by enough authority to insulate the administrators from the inducements and sometimes hostile reactions of living composers. Habeneck, who was a co-designer and strong partisan of the *essai* system, proposed in 1838 that uniform questions evaluating each work be put to a commission of committee members and other representatives.[27] Article 33 of the 1841 statutes called for a commission of twelve (customarily eight players, four singers), drawn by lot, to be added to the committee in order to vote answers to four questions in a secret ballot:

1. Shall the work be essayed again?
2. Shall it be programmed in its entirety, as it stands?
3. Shall it be essayed again after revisions?
4. Shall excerpts [only] be played?

The language grants permission to "the composer alone" to hear the audition, and goes on to specify that in the event the work is adopted, the composer must immediately remit the score and parts to the *commissaire du matériel*, not to be returned until after the performance.

This process succeeded admirably in weeding out most of the dross and was particularly useful when the work of a *sociétaire* introduced questions of *amour-propre* and *camaraderie*. It was perhaps less to be admired for the way it encouraged piecemeal renditions. That was the case in 1872 with Franck's *Ruth,* Lenepveu's Requiem, and a Saint-Saëns symphony, all excerpted—though Saint-Saëns was already a favorite of the society. Théodore Dubois, the new and popular chorusmaster, heard only two of his *Sept Paroles du Christ* performed that season.

The system of *essais* and votes did little to stem—in fact it may have aggravated—the avalanche of works submitted by living composers to the attention of the Société des Concerts. Composers of greater or often lesser note—Täglichsbeck, Rousselot—dedicated works to the orchestra in the hope of having them played. Carl Czerny apparently composed and dedicated a symphony for the Société des Concerts and gave the manuscript to Habeneck.[28] Local composers were shameless in promoting their works, and those who had had one successful premiere could be counted on to return annually with new music. Deldevez himself was always ready with a composition. Gounod's habit of dropping into committee meetings unannounced to propose his latest work was tolerated owing to his stature and unfailing good humor; other in-person callers were sent away with the instruction to put their request in writing.

Antoine Elwart became a laughingstock at the committee with his annual late-fall proposals. In 1837 the orchestra had rehearsed the Credo from his mass, presenting it on 25 February 1838. That December Elwart offered an engraved copy of the score, hoping for a full performance. In 1839 the committee agreed to rehearse an aria from *La Reine de Saba,* but only programmed it for the concert of 26 April 1840 after considerable badgering; the next day Elwart thought to propose himself for the title *membre honoraire*.[29] Thereafter he came forward with an *Ave verum* ("in homage to the Société des Concerts") in 1843, his oratorio-symphony *Le Déluge* in 1845, an *Oratorio de Noël* in 1846, a symphony in 1847, an elegy on Mendelssohn's death (within a month of the event) in 1848, symphonies (plural) in 1849, and multiple works in 1850. The most memorable of his tactics, in January 1844, was to send the committee his best wishes for a happy new year, congratulating himself that he had nothing to propose; instead he invited the committee to come hear his new *Ave verum* and *Pie Jesu,* attaching a copy "for the library."

"Thank M. Elwart," the secretary noted in the margin of his letter, "pure and simple."[30]

Persons of note would intercede on behalf of their friends, generally without success. In 1868 Victor Massé wrote to Hainl (as "*mon cher Georges*") to indicate that the ambassador and crown prince of Prussia were interested in the work of Count Waldemar de Pfeil, one of Massé's students at the Conservatoire; he proposed the wedding march from an opera called *Amilla*. It lasted five minutes, noted Massé, calling for two harps but no trumpets, trombones, or timpani. The parts had already been copied.[31]

Then there were the composers' widows. Mme Le Sueur wrote in March 1840 asking for her husband's work to be heard that spring; it was too late for the chorus to begin rehearsing a new piece, but the secretary offered to discuss the possibility with prospective soloists, and in fact Alexis Dupont offered to sing the Offertoire from the third *Messe solennelle;* but when all was said and done he appeared in the trio from Rameau's *Hippolyte et Aricie*. Mme Charlot, widow of the chorusmaster, urged the committee to program her husband's *O Salutaris,* which the chorus had premiered just before his death in 1871, in his memory. Marguerite Holmes pestered the committee yearly to program works of her late husband, Alfred. In 1937 Mme Alfred Bruneau pled with the secretary to resume performances of her deceased husband's work, which, she said with some justification, they had played regularly before his death in 1934. (*"Cela est très remarqué par beaucoup d'amateurs,"* she wrote.) Gaubert returned affectionate wishes and his intention to follow through with her request the next season, but shortly thereafter announced his retirement. In the same year, Nadia Boulanger renewed her efforts of behalf of her late sister, Lili: *"Je vis dans le souvenir de ma petite sœur."*[32]

The system of *répétitions d'essai* and voted adoptions of new repertoire continued more or less uninterrupted into the 1870s. In 1874, however, it was decided to end the practice of reviewing every unsolicited work, choosing instead only to examine compositions recommended by the conductor or one of the more curious members of the committee—a decision that in some ways freed the society to embark on its Bach-and-Handel projects of the next decade. Garcin, as early as 1872, attempted to move all the works by living composers to supplemental concerts; versions of this formula were often tried in the twentieth century. Eventually the government stepped in with a *cahier des charges* that required attention to French composers living and dead and to French soloists. In 1937, the requirement was for three hours of new music.

Enough of the *sociétaires* recognized their responsibilities as player-educators—concepts of the orchestra as agent of public education came to be persuasive arguments for government support—that explaining the repertoire naturally accompanied expanding it. Annotated programs began to appear in the late 1880s, during Garcin's tenure, with notes by Louis Bourgault-Ducoudray, the first professor of music history at the Conservatoire. Both Arthur Pougin and Julien Tiersot annotated programs in the 1890s; later Maurice Emmanuel had a long and impressive tenure in the role. In 1937 an ancillary Programme-Revue with feature stories began to appear, during the same epoch that saw the dawn of young people's concerts with spoken commentary. In the 1950s the illustrated season brochure *(dépliant)* made its appearance, with polemics by Bernard Gavoty that became rallying cries for the reorganization of music in France. The program notes were central to making the case for the B-Minor Mass, offered translations once the chorus began to sing in original languages, introduced the Russian repertoire—and told the story of *L'Apprenti sorcier.*

The conflicts of interest inherent in having important reviewers provide the program notes—Gavoty, for instance, wrote for the *Figaro* (under the name of Clarendon)—was either quietly overlooked or overtly acknowledged as being in the society's best interests. Maurice Emmanuel, a powerful critic, was not above threatening to stop the flow of program notes if the Société des Concerts refused to perform his music.

In 1912–13 the committee engaged in a contract with the publicity agent Lusinski (or Luczinsky), and later with the Strenger agency, whereby program booklets containing advertising were distributed to the public free of charge. The committee assured the *sociétaires* that it would censor material of "doubtful taste," whether in the text or in the illustrations. At first the advertising was unpopular with both the subscribers, who wrote in great number to complain about it, and the players, who objected to the possibility of promoting rival musicians in the pages of their own publication. Emmanuel "deplored" how the ads broke up his narrative and, he believed, contributed to the "arbitrary shortening" of his essays.[33] In a few months, however, the advertisements became accepted as a price of the modern life. As artifacts of the culture the ads have just about as much to say as the program notes, not only in their precious documentation of broadcasts and recordings, but also of the other interests of the leisured set: rail excursions, elegant garments, face creams, and headache remedies.

The library at the foundation consisted only of such parts for the Viennese repertoire as Habeneck and Sieber might have presented to the new society and whatever else might have been inherited from the old *exercices publics*. Parts for the operatic excerpts were lent by the Opéra, with those that went on to gain a foothold eventually copied for permanent addition to the library. Soloists and living composers were expected to lend materials without the society's incurring an expense, and various interpretations of this policy held sway until the dissolution.

The library thus grew slowly. Its most precious property consisted of the material for orchestra-and-chorus works acquired from distant places and refashioned, with new French texts, to their liking: Beethoven's *Les Ruines d'Athènes,* for instance, or Mendelssohn's *La Nuit du Sabbat* and *Ode-Symphonie* (*Die erste Walpurgisnacht* and the *Symphonie-Cantate* in B♭ Major, "Lobegesang," respectively). *La Nuit du Sabbat* was popular enough in France for the material to be in demand by organizers of the summer casino concerts. Otherwise acquisitions were somewhat random, and until the late nineteenth century the committee was routinely loathe to invest its cash in published materials. The need for economy in music copying was noted in the late 1830s—so, too, the unacceptable level of disappearances from the library. The state of the library greatly vexed Deldevez, himself something of a bibliophile, who often complained about it and eventually set a project of modernization in place.[34]

Berlioz presented his priceless gift—scores and parts, manuscript and printed: three trunks weighing hundreds of pounds each—in 1863. It was accepted at a general assembly of the Société with *"marques nombreuses d'approbation."*[35] He himself borrowed items back from time to time, and later Ernest Reyer approached the committee to borrow the bulk of the most important materials for a *grand festival* to be held at the Opéra on the first anniversary of Berlioz's death, 8 March 1870.[36] The same material made possible the great resurgence of interest in Berlioz at the Société des Concerts that took place between then and the centenary of his birth in 1903.

Other treasures and curiosities, though none so rich as the Berlioz material, were to be found in the library. The manuscript symphonies of Étienne Méhul got there by accident, having been lent temporarily by Daussoigne at the Société Libre des Émulations in Liège to Cherubini in Paris and lost, they alleged, on the *diligence;*[37] in fact they were simply misplaced in the archives. Much commotion surrounded the recovery in the mid-1870s of a manuscript C-major symphony attributed to Haydn, performed for several seasons as the "exclusive property of the Société des Concerts." Manuscripts of Carl Schwenke's Mass in E♭ and Friedrich Schneider's Symphony in B Minor had been composed for and presented to the society. Several of the conductors made important gifts to the library; George-Hainl, for example, presented five full scores on his accession to the podium in 1863. When first insured against fire in 1870, the collection was valued at 25,000 francs, incurring a premium of 26 francs.[38]

Deldevez and Ambroise Thomas began to exert pressure on the Société des Concerts to acquire a true library of modern published materials. The Bach repertoire, for instance, was developed from scores and parts bought directly from Breitkopf & Härtel, thus based on the Bach-Gesellschaft edition. Paris publishers, notably Enoch (with Chabrier's *Gwendoline,* for instance) and Durand, presented new scores and sometimes all the materials for works performed, more or less in exchange for the promotional opportunity. In the early twentieth century Mme Costallat donated a full score of Berlioz's *La Damnation de Faust;* Mme Pelletan's executors gave a copy of the latest score in the Gluck edition, *Écho et Narcisse,* even though the Société des Concerts was not among the subscribers to the project. In 1907 it was noted of the collection that "a great proportion of its riches" had been donated by Durand.[39] By the time of the dissolution of the Société des Concerts in 1967 its library, like so many of its other features, was not dissimilar from that of any other major orchestra. The manuscript materials were for the most part remitted to the Bibliothèque Nationale, while much of the published material was retained by the Orchestre de Paris in the working collection. Some of it is still in use.

Otherwise the property of the Conservatoire and the Société des Concerts was essentially interchangeable. The institution owned dozens of string instruments and kept them in good enough shape that it became the custom of many of the players to leave their own instruments at home. In late 1837 it was decided to require violinists and violists to bring their personal instruments to both rehearsals and performances; cellists could use the Conservatoire's instruments for the rehearsals but were required to bring their own to concerts. The *commissaire du matériel* would oversee the particulars.[40] The doublebasses were at first the property of the Conservatoire, gradually transferred—along with the not inconsiderable expense of their maintenance—to the Société des Concerts. In the 1930s and 1940s it was policy for the orchestra to rent the low string instruments, harps, and percussion from the primary resident of any hall it visited and in turn to rent out the instruments backstage at the Salle des Concerts to guests of the Conservatoire. This arrangement was preferred to the costly and dangerous alternative of frequent drayage.

In 1885 François Brémond, principal of the French hornists, arguing that their personal equipment "compromised the performances," convinced the committee to finance the purchase of four matched piston horns. The noted house of F. Besson (i.e., Mme Fontaine-Besson, widow of the founder) provided the instruments, horns of three pistons and their cases, for 1,350 francs, including a discount of 25 percent; the committee, always anxious to save a franc, tried unsuccessfully for 30 percent. The orchestra began to acquire its own percussion in 1894, following an attractive promotional arrangement concluded with Monsieur Tournier, *facteur d'instruments.* In the mid-1920s it began to purchase the instruments necessary for the Impressionist repertoire—celesta, tam-tam, chimes—with surpluses left in the travel fund *(caisse de voyages)*.[41] If these are the percussion instruments heard on the recordings of the 1940s, they were very fine indeed.

The first century of the Société des Concerts took place simultaneously with the revolution in instrument building that permanently changed the sound of the symphony orchestra. This was most audibly the result of the wholesale refashioning of violins for volume, a movement led by the luthiers J.-B. Vuillaume and the firm of Gand and Bernadel. (Since Vuillaume was the father-in-law of Delphin Alard and Gand the official luthier to the society, it is safe to assume a widespread, early adoption of the "modern" violin.) As professors at the Conservatoire, the instrumentalists were naturally interested in the mechanical innovations and adopted the more promising changes in due course. The Triébert family of woodwind builders, for instance, was well represented in the oboe section during the latter half of the nineteenth century. But aside from one or two pioneers—notably Klosé and Meifred—the instrumentalists do not appear to have been consumed by a search for novelty. Tulou refused to adopt a modern key system. The four-string doublebass coexisted with the three-string model favored by Bottesini—Mendelssohn was surprised to find the latter still in use—for many years. Tuning the doublebass in fourths had been decreed after a bitter struggle at the Conservatoire during the 1810s, but more than a century later, in 1920, the doublebass section is to be found objecting to the practice of their young colleague J. Rousseau of tuning his instrument in fifths. Rousseau's name does not appear on subsequent programs.[42]

The instruments left to the Conservatoire by the founders—precisely because, it must be said, they had become historic—seem positively old-fashioned for an orchestra that was cultivating Mendelssohn and Schumann: Vogt's oboe, to which five keys had been added; Jancourt's bassoon, a primitive instrument of 1826 by Savary; Franquin's simple trumpets; and Delisse's tiny tenor trombone.

The many advances—and not a few false paths—promoted at the exhibitions and fairs with which Paris was so taken in the nineteenth century appear to have made few inroads on their daily life. There is no mention, for instance, of Adolphe Sax or his instruments anywhere in the record until the saxophone concertos and *Pictures at an Exhibition* in the twentieth century. The pipe organ, we have noted, was built in the late 1860s and used frequently thereafter; a pianist (Jacques Delécluse) was not appointed until 1960. Concerto pianos were lent, upon promotional consideration, by Érard and Pleyel.

After the declined offer by a harpsichordist to appear in 1837,[43] the next mention of a harpsichord is in conjunction with a performance of Bach's *Phoebus and Pan* cantata in 1912, where the continuo was realized by the young Marcel Dupré; in the 1950s Marguerite Roesgen-Champion was greatly popular with the orchestra for her harpsichord performances and recordings. The *ondes Martenot* was recorded in 1943 and heard occasionally from 1950, owing to compositions for it by Messiaen, Jolivet, and Landowski in their repertoire. Ginette Martenot, sister of the inventor Maurice Martenot, was the usual soloist—and their father had been the harpist of the Société des Concerts from about 1906.

What, then, did the Société des Concerts du Conservatoire sound like? From first to last its primary characteristic was technical perfection on a level few had ever heard—at least until the major orchestras started touring widely in the mid-twentieth century. When asked by the government to describe the orchestra's character, the secretary cited refined good taste, an intimate understanding of the French style, respect for tradition, sensible and sensitive interpretations, flawless technique, and an unrivaled richness of sonority. He proudly closed with a quotation from the foreign press: "One evening spent with the Société des Concerts is worth more to the French cause than many volumes of propaganda."[44]

To draw overall conclusions from the fifty years of recordings left to us by the Société des Concerts has its obvious risks, and it would be better to put off any substantial remarks about them until the proper place in the chronicle. Nevertheless one is tempted to identify an idiomatic Paris Conservatoire sound much in keeping with what the journalists described in prose. To compare Piero Coppola's recordings with the Société des Concerts and those he conducted with his "Orchestre du Gramophone" is to hear an obvious difference in standards. Much the same can be said of the disappointing Schumann Fourth under Bruno Walter, recorded in June 1928 with a "Mozart Festival Orchestra" where the Société des Concerts was joined by lesser players; this should be heard alongside Gaubert's recording of two of the Debussy *Nocturnes,* recorded the previous March. Often the individual technique—if not, always, the ensemble—is indeed dazzling, as in the case of the 1941 *La Mer* conducted by Münch, his first major recording with the orchestra outside the concerto repertoire. The often cited splendor of the cello and doublebass sections can be heard on nearly every recording; take, for example, the opening of the Rachmaninov Second Piano Concerto with Clutyens and Gabriel Tacchino of 1959. With both Gaubert and Münch, the lines and phrases are unusually short, a practice that may have been at the root of the "cold and methodical" criticism that some journalists enjoyed making.

One would not characterize the Conservatoire sound as big, or broadly limned. The tone quality cultivated by the winds is biting and very narrow of envelope, a sound, the oboist Robert Casier told me, that was criticized as "too bright, not round enough."[45] A rapid and very tight vibrato is apt to color solo and section work in all the winds, oboe and clarinet included. Lucien Thévet says that it was he who introduced prominent vibrato in the horn solo of the Ravel Pavane, and indeed horn vibrato begins to be heard in the early 1940s, just after he was appointed. Gaubert's *La Valse* of 1927 embraces pronounced string portamento; this unusually sensuous effect disappears with the Coppola and Münch recordings.

Thévet was animated in his description of guest conductors encountering the Paris sound. They tended to deplore the horn and trombone vibrato and other local practices, but Thévet insisted on their propriety; when one was a guest of the Société des Concerts, one needed to accept its manner of performance. (The bassoonists had already been pressured to abandon the Buffet-Crampon French *basson* for what they called, perhaps with some scorn, the German *Fagott*.) Thévet regretted that by the time of the recordings of the 1960s the taste of conductors, and presumably of the record-buying public, was for the increasingly standard practices of the American orchestras and those of Berlin and Vienna as the Paris idiom began to disappear.

Both Casier and Thévet had much to say of unusually high pitch to which the orchestra tuned in the late 1940s and the 1950s. In principle, and by decree, the orchestra had played at A = 435 / C = 552 (at 15°C, or 59°F) from the adoption in 1859 of a "universal" pitch standard. Now and then they were "re-invited" by craftsmen's guilds to maintain that standard, despite its increasing divergence from international practice, as was the case with an approach in 1924 from the Fédération Nationale du Commerce et de l'Industrie de la Musique.[46] There are one or two other references over the decades to the use or purchase of tuning forks, but in general it does not appear that a standard pitch was a matter of great concern.

Casier attributes the conspicuously high pitch of the post-war recordings to the conditions of World War II. Most rehearsals and many concerts were played in the bitter cold—"we wore sweaters, jackets, and overcoats all at once"—and the woodwinds were often, as a result, much too low to match the piano for concertos. Gradually the woodwind players had their instruments altered to lessen the struggle, to the extent that when the heating came back after the war the pitch went still further up. "Besides," said Thévet, "we always sounded better playing sharp."[47]

The recordings of the Société des Concerts add a new dimension to an archival study otherwise based largely on paper in boxes. There is undeniable excitement to be heard in their recordings of *La Valse* and *Le Tombeau de Couperin* while Ravel was still alive, *élan* and *savoir-faire* in the Gaubert discography, and a certain evangelical touch in the crusades of Coppola and later Cluytens to set down the new French tradition entire. In the solo passages the characters of this written tale—the concertmaster Henri Merckel, Moyse and Lavaillotte, Casier and Thévet, and many others—come to aural life. We sense something of the *exactitude* and *zèle* that were equally the pride of Habeneck and his colleagues in 1828.

At season's end, there remained only the balancing of the books before the closing Assemblée Générale and distribution of the proceeds. The theory was quite simple: each *sociétaire* received a *jeton de présence*— a "share" of the potential income—for every service. Eventually, annual expenses would be subtracted from annual income, and the balance would be available for distribution *(répartition)*. This net balance was

TABLE 2. Hypothetical *Répartition,* 1830

Subscription income per concert	Fr. 5,000
Number of concerts	7
Total income	Fr. 35,000
Expenses	Fr. 5,000
Amount available for *répartition*	Fr. 30,000
Number of services *(jetons)*	50
Number of members	100
Number of *jetons* outstanding	5,000
Value of *jeton*	Fr. 6.00

divided by the total number of *jetons* to produce the value of a single *jeton;* each member would then draw out his payment, reckoned as the number of *jetons* he had accrued times the value of the *jeton.* Table 2 gives an approximate example of the practice of the 1830s, in round numbers; a member who had played fifty services would have received 300 francs. In 1831, the actual income of an ordinary player was 213 francs.[48]

The true reckoning was a good deal more complicated. For the rank and file, concerts and the Assemblées Générales earned 2 *jetons* and the *répétitions d'essai* only ½. Soloists and the conductor earned a good deal more. Table 3 reproduces the scale of remuneration given in article 52 of the 1841 statutes. Attendance varied from player to player, both for personal reasons and owing to uneven requirements of the repertoire; some musicians would incur fines, reckoned as the deduction of full or partial *jetons,* more frequently than others. So the *jeton* system allowed differential honoraria within a context of theoretical equality.

The figures for 1832 and 1833 are shown in table 4.[49] The cash value of the *jeton,* as can be seen, was rounded down to the nearest 5 *centimes,* mostly to simplify the cash transactions but also to leave a few dozen francs in the treasury for carrying forward into the next year: 88.32 francs in 1832, 119.89 francs in 1833. The worth of the *jeton* stabilized around 8 francs for many years; in 1870–71 it had reached 10.25 francs, though it fell abruptly thereafter.

What made the financial system painful was its very success. By 1833 all seats were taken by subscription at an average ticket price of roughly 5 francs (from 2 to 9 francs, in 1830). Barring what was for three decades an unthinkable increase in ticket prices, the income could never rise substantially. Reselling of vacant places might bring in a few dozen francs;

TABLE 3. Remuneration, in *Jetons,* 1841

Function	Assemblée Générale	Répétition d'essai	Répétition générale	Concert
Conductor	2	1	2	4
Soloists	0	0	2	4
Sociétaires	2	1/2	1	2

SOURCE: Statutes of 1841, article 52: D 17338 (8).

TABLE 4. Actual *Répartition,* 1832, 1833

1832	
Income	Fr. 26,630.32
Expenses	Fr. 3,557.72
Amount available for *répartition*	Fr. 23,072.60
Number of *jetons* outstanding	4,213.00
Value of *jeton*	Fr. 5.45
1833	
Income	Fr. 34,526.85
Expenses	Fr. 4,374.28
Amount available for *répartition*	Fr. 30,152.57
Number of *jetons* outstanding	3,787.25
Value of *jeton*	Fr. 7.95

SOURCE: Rapport moral 13 May 1832 and 19 May 1833: D 17341.

the number of concerts could be modestly increased but would also incur substantially increased expenses. Meanwhile, the orchestra was still young, with little by way of property, library, or staff assistance. Every purchase represented a loss of revenue to the players. So modest a change as the 1834 increase from 150 to 200 francs in the poor-tax—a total of 400 francs for that season of eight concerts—was crippling, especially as it came close on the heels of an 1833 decision to pay each student player 35 francs for the season. The committee had promised to be extraordinarily vigilant; perfecting the administration of the new society would certainly involve correcting any abuses that tended to "compromise the amelioration of receipts." Taking an ultra-conservative stance toward incurring new expenses, the society managed to keep a remarkably consistent budget for almost a century.

TABLE 5. Admission Prices, in Francs, Winter 1956

	Série rose (6 concerts)	*Série bleue* (5 concerts)	*Répétitions* (11)
Loge de corbeille	4,200	3,750	5,950
Fauteuil de corbeille			
d'orchestre	4,200	3,750	5,950
Baignoire, Ire loge,			
Ier balcon, Ire série	3,400	3,050	4,750
Ier balcon, 2e série	3,100	2,700	4,200
2e balcon	2,200	2,200	4,100

SOURCE: Winter 1956 brochure (boxed programs).

Subscription prices rose only twice in the nineteenth century, in 1857 and 1881–82. From the mid-nineteenth century the value of the house was reckoned to be 8,000 francs per concert, based on roughly 800 seats at an average ticket price of 10 francs; by World War I this was 12,000 francs, the same 800 seats at an average price of 15 francs—by consequence the orchestra valued its per-concert fee in those years as 12,000 francs. Ticket prices were raised every year during the runaway inflation of the 1920s, and from then on adjusted seasonally according to prevailing national economic conditions. Table 5 shows the prices listed in the winter 1956 brochure (before the conversion to new francs in 1960). Average admission was roughly 585 francs for concerts and 430 francs for the Saturday rehearsals, something on the order of $12 and $9—no longer cheap, but still modest.

The recurring expenses increased along the same gentle trajectory, but usually somewhat faster than the income. The official authorization to hold public spectacles, granted each year by the Prefecture of Police, would begin by recognizing the ministerial decrees of 13 December 1832 and 30 October 1850 and go on to attach conditions: paying the poor-tax, arranging with the society of authors and composers for rights to perform works not in the public domain, submitting each program in advance, and of course enlisting police protection. One typical order for police assistance at Sunday concerts lists:

4 patrolmen *("sergents de ville")* and a brigadier

4 mounted police and a brigadier

4 firemen and a coal-man, with the recommendation to come at noon, when the fire is lit

1 [plainclothes] security agent, at 12:30, to prevent commerce in tickets around the box office

The police and firemen did very little but stand around. From time to time, as for a series of thefts following a concert of 9 March 1834, the police were asked to increase their patrol, though the record fails to note any arrests. There is a single reference to a fire extinguished in the Salle des Concerts—and one complaint from the women of the chorus about a fireman, probably a *fumiste* (and a voyeur), who had not waited to put out the main fire in the foyer until after they had "completed their *toilette*." [50]

Additionally the *entrepreneur d'éclairage* was one of several functionaries who wanted raises of a few francs per concert at the beginning of each season.[51] Later there was the substantial expense of the poster-mounting service *(service affiches)*. Always there were vexing little taxes, as for example the periodic requirement for stamps on printed programs; in 1851 the society was fined 79.50 francs for non-payment of a stamp tax.

The infamous *droit des pauvres,* or poor-tax, sometimes called the provision for *indigents* or *hospices,* was galling both in its amount and for the way it epitomized government meddlesomeness. It vexed and alienated organizations of every ilk—orchestras, opera and theater companies, circuses, cabarets—from its inception in 1830 until its gradual abandonment in the 1960s. In concept the *droit des pauvres* was a luxury tax levied on those who could afford seeking their pleasures in the elegance of the theater on behalf of those who could not. Reckoned as a tax of 12½ percent, or the *huitième,* of the gross receipt, it was levied, quite like the similar tax on gaming, by a semi-private *régisseur* (the notorious Mantou in the 1830s and 1840s) and his employees. On the one hand the *régisseur* could be reasoned with, offered inducements, or instructed by higher authority to adjust the arrangement; on the other, his enterprise derived its authority from the Prefecture of Police, and an aggressive agent could theoretically seize the tax directly from the cash-box or prevent the curtain from going up.

In the economics of serious concert life, where nobody made much money, the *droit des pauvres* felt like an unjust tax on the artists themselves. Too often it was the expense that explained the financial loss of a public concert. To composers or soloists risking substantial personal funds for the generally laudable purpose of making their work known, the tax therefore lacked any redeeming merit at all; Berlioz is the noisiest—and the most bitter, and once again the most powerfully expressed—but by no means the only major artist to have found it crippling. To collectives like the Société des Concerts the tax represented the largest sum to be deducted each year from their subscription income before its *répartition*. It was money directly out of their pockets.

In its earliest years the Société des Concerts had successfully argued its case, in annual political maneuvers with the Conseil des Hospices, for exemption from the percentage tax. Instead it paid a flat rate *(abonnement)* of 100 francs per concert—a very substantial privilege, since even in the first decade 12½ percent of the gross receipt for a season of seven concerts would have been in excess of 4,000 francs. The *sociétaires* naturally cited this precedent whenever they were approached by the dreaded agents of the poor, and were quick to invoke higher authority when it was challenged. They managed to keep the principle of a per-concert honorarium intact, but had to resign themselves to its steady growth:

1828	Fr. 100 / concert
1832	Fr. 150
1834	Fr. 200
1857	Fr. 300
1872–73	Fr. 400
1875–76	5 percent of gross receipt (ca. Fr. 430)

Holding even that line was not easy. Each adjustment began as a skirmish with the authorities and ended in full-fledged battle. They would write to ministers citing their public utility and service to their art, the devotion of 160 artists "who find compensation for their sacrifice in the honor of belonging to the loveliest of associations" despite having their income frozen by a fully subscribed house, and the dignity with which they had always paid their due tribute to the disadvantaged. They would note their lack of an official subvention like the ones enjoyed by the state theaters and major opera houses. On one occasion they even cited the precedent of special courtesies extended to Hiller and Berlioz for their private concerts in the same room.[52]

The ongoing confrontations over the *droit des pauvres* are as much an identifying feature of the history of the Société des Concerts as they are of Berlioz's concert career. Their record fills many hundreds of paragraphs in the documentation, more even than the question of a royal or imperial subvention, where similar effort is expended to secure both the fact and the principle of 1,000 francs or so. There is reference to the *droit des pauvres* as late as the statutes of 1962.

The society was somewhat more supportive of the principle of paying performance rights, the ultimate purpose of which seemed largely justifiable. These demands, first asserted more by librettists and translators than by composers, emerged in the late 1850s and for art music coalesced into the powerful Société des Auteurs, Compositeurs, et Éditeurs de Musique (SACEM, not to be confused with SAMUP, the Syndicat des Artistes-Musiciens de Paris). Like the *droit des pauvres,* the performance rights payment began as a token amount and mounted inexorably:

to 1870	Fr. 25 / concert
1869–70	Fr. 100
188	Fr. 110
1890	Fr. 150
1900	Fr. 200 + two balcony seats
from 1920–21	4 percent of gross receipts + Fr. 25 to emergency fund + Fr. 25 per public dress rehearsal

The customary charge, it was noted during the negotiations in 1890, was 5 percent of the gross receipts of the house. In 1924 SACEM demanded a 10 percent surcharge for their retirement fund, which appears to have become the custom thereafter.[53]

The reluctance of the committee to incur expenses, laudable as it may have been in the overall politic of maximizing individual income, had its amusing moments. So outstanding a servant of the society as Meifred begged permission to buy a new dispatch box, having worn the first one out during his twelve years as secretary; the similarly devoted Saint-Laurent thought it necessary to seek committee approval before buying an almanac of twenty-five thousand addresses. Much later, when the administration of the Conservatoire complained in 1913 of the number of ticket-related phone calls being received across town in the rue de Madrid, the committee agreed to acquire their first telephone in the box office at the Salle des Concerts and to reimburse the Conservatoire for the installation fee of 200 francs. Within the month, discovering that there was a subscription charge for telephone service, they had it removed.[54]

Some indication of the market value of the orchestra can be found in what it charged to appear elsewhere in Paris or on the road. For an early road concert, that of 30 May 1920 at the Théâtre de la Monnaie in Brussels, the proposal was for a public dress rehearsal and a concert on the same day:

Conductor	Fr. 1,300
Solos	Fr. 150
Others	Fr. 130
Per diem per musician (hotel, 3 meals)	Fr. 25
Train fare	at cost

(Here, "solos" refers to the first-chair players, "others" to the rank and file; later the usage is "firsts" and "seconds"). In this case the theater was provided for free; costs of lighting, theater staff, and publicity were deducted from income before turning any net profit over to the Société des Concerts.[55] Instead of adding road profits to the amount to be divided up at the end of the year, and since the musicians had already been paid a fee, the orchestra allowed these small amounts to accrue in a *caisse de voyages*. This was most often used to purchase percussion instruments and equipment.

For the Isadora Duncan *matinées* on 19–20 and 26–27 June 1920 the fee schedule was as follows:

	REHEARSAL	PERFORMANCE
Conductor	Fr. 200	Fr. 600
Solos	Fr. 25	Fr. 80
Others	Fr. 20	Fr. 60 [56]

The following season, for two concerts in Marseille on 16–17 April 1921, the fees were

Conductor	Fr. 3,000
Solos, *externes*	Fr. 350
Others	Fr. 280

Travel was billed at cost; an individual per diem was not quoted, but rather a global figure for collective costs *(frais sociaux)* of 1,000 francs.[57] The Sunday subscription concert income for the same year (1920–21) totaled 183,468.50 francs, of which 5,000 represented a subvention from the government; per-concert income ran from 5,704.50 francs to 9,185.60 francs.[58]

When the government of Spain solicited two concerts of Spanish music for the Exposition Internationale de Paris 1937, the proposal was to provide ninety musicians (table 6). Rehearsals and concerts were not

TABLE 6. Estimated Costs, in Francs, for Concerts
of Spanish Music, 1937 (Orchestra of 90 Musicians)[a]

Rehearsals (2½ hours, with a 15-min. break)	
Firsts: 30 players at Fr. 50	1,500
Seconds: 60 players at Fr. 45	2,700
Total each rehearsal	4,200
TOTAL for two rehearsals	8,400
(+ Fr. 5 per musician per 15-min. unit of overtime)	

Concerts	
Firsts: 30 players at Fr. 100	3,000
Seconds: 60 players at Fr. 90	5,400
Total each concert	8,400
TOTAL for two concerts	16,800
(+ cost of transportation and incidentals)	

Production expenses	
Hall	6,000
Ticket takers	200
Police	300
Stamped posters and posting on Morris columns	5,000
Printing: 8,000 programs, tickets, flyers, reprinting for change of program	2,000
Advertisements: 4 newspapers, 5 lines each	3,000
Postage: flyers sent to homes	3,000
General handling	3,000
TOTAL	22,500
ESTIMATED GRAND TOTAL	47,700

SOURCE: Corresp. September 1937: D 17263 (10).

[a]Proposed orchestration: 60 strings (16–14–12–10–8), 12 wood-winds (3–3–3–3), 11 brass (4–3–3–1), 1 timpanist, 3 percussion, 1 piano, 2 harps.

to extend past midnight; the estimate calls for two of each, to be paid at the union scale *(tarif syndical)*. The final bill for the concerts of 21 and 22 September 1937 came to 63,278 francs, which presumably represented three rehearsals with overtime and two concerts (table 7).[59]

Compensation for an engagement during this period, inclusive of rehearsals, thus averaged 200 to 250 francs per musician. Gaubert's fee was 2,000 or 3,000 francs. Ordinary soloists were commanding 1,500 to 2,000 francs; Jacques Thibaud required 10,000. These figures are to be

TABLE 7. Final Bill, in Francs, for Concerts
of Spanish Music, 1937

Orchestra, *garçon*	52,325
Seven 15-min. units of overtime	7,570
Radio broadcast	2,100
Transportation, notices mailed to musicians	1,283
TOTAL	63,278

SOURCE: Corresp. September 1937: D 17263 (10).

compared with Busoni's "handsome gesture of [monetary] disinterest"
in late 1913, when he declined invitations from both the Colonne and Lamoureux orchestras in order to appear twice with the Société des Concerts (18 and 25 January 1914) for a global fee of 1,500 francs.[60]

The metamorphosis of the Société des Concerts into a full-time symphony orchestra was already, in 1937, well under way. Year-round, fully
booked calendars came in the form of recording sessions, film work,
non-subscription concerts ("organized concerts") backing star soloists, tours ("always at a deficit," it was noted), and summer festivals.
Guest conductors became commonplace as Münch and Cluytens took
long leaves of absence. The one-composer "festival" concert—a genre
Münch detested—drew huge crowds, as did big-name soloists who
would extend their stage time with sonatas and multiple encores. The
impresarios who by then controlled concert life in Paris—the Dandelot, Valmalète, and Kiesgen families—would promote the vogues that
first drew African-American artists to the Société des Concerts (Mattiwilda Dobbs, Dean Dixon), the new generation of foreign virtuosi
(Claudio Arrau, Aldo Ciccolini), and even the occasional child prodigy
(Idil Biret, Roberto Benzi). The annual budgets, owing both to the fees
accorded guest artists and to the post-war value of the franc, were as-
tronomical. The budget of the 1880s had been less than 100,000 francs;
in the 1950s it was reckoned at some 7.5 million.

Governmental subvention of the Société des Concerts had been
established at the foundation with the privilege of the hall and the
1,000 francs of royal *gratification,* and there was at least the informal assurance that early deficits would be covered by the Office of Fine Arts.
In fact the organization stayed generally in balance without substantial government support until the upheaval in global economic circumstances in the twentieth century. The first true subventions came from

the propaganda wing of the government, the Office d'Action Artistique à l'Étranger, in conjunction with the Swiss and American tours of 1917 and 1918. Utter reliance on government support—in the 1950s, between 1 and 2 million francs, their share of the 6 to 8 million francs distributed among the four Paris orchestral associations—followed World War II. Once subvention of that size—some 25 percent of the budget—became the norm, the Société des Concerts had effectively become national-ized, subject to a stern *cahier des charges* that, increasingly, dictated rep-ertoire and artistic policy. That was a far cry from the heroic ideals of the foundation.

The apparent identity of the Société des Concerts had by 1966–67 mutated in many particulars. The concerts now began at 5:45, to allow the patrons their Sunday luncheons and weekends in the country. The Théâtre des Champs-Élysées was an hour's walk, a half hour's ride, from the faubourg Poissonnière. The chorus was long gone. But no one could argue that the twenty Sunday afternoon concerts from October to March that season were not part of a venerable tradition that had grown and amazingly prospered.

The English visitors of 1851 congratulated themselves on hearing Mo-zart's "Haffner" Symphony and Beethoven's Fifth. Subscribers in 1966–67 would have heard both those symphonies, along with more than a dozen other pillars of the Viennese canon, including Beethoven's Third and Seventh. They heard Schubert, Schumann, Chopin, Berlioz (in-cluding an excerpt from *Les Troyens*), and Liszt—but no Mendelssohn; Brahms, Tchaikovsky, and Dvořák; Wagner and Strauss; Franck, Dukas, and Roussel; Debussy and virtually the whole of the Ravel orchestral repertoire; even Bondeville and Loucheur. And not a few of them would have regretted the last *adieu*.

François-Antoine Habeneck
(1781–1849; *soc.* 1828–48)

Narcisse Girard
(1797–1860; *soc.* 1828–32, 1848–60)

François George-Hainl
(1807–73; *soc.* 1863–72)

E.-M.-E. Deldevez
(1817–97; *soc.* 1839–85)

Jules Garcin
(1830–96; *soc.* 1853–92)

Paul Taffanel
(1844–1908; *soc.* 1867–1901)

Georges Marty
(1860–1908; *soc.* 1901–08)

André Messager
(1853–1929; *soc.* 1908–19)

Philippe Gaubert
(1879–1941; *soc.* 1901–38)

Charles Münch
(1891–1968; *soc.* 1938–46)

André Cluytens
(1905–67; *soc.* 1946–60)

Joseph Meifred, *French horn*
(1791–1867; *soc.* 1828–53)

Charles Lebouc, *cello*
(1822–93; *soc.* 1849–84)

Joseph White, *violin*
(1835–1918; *soc.* 1866–77)

Albert Vernaelde, *bass singer*
(1859–1928; *soc.* 1893–1914)

André Boutard, *clarinet;*
Michel Debost, *flute;*
Robert Casier, *oboe:*
1963

PART TWO

1828–1872

However sweeping the success of the Société des Concerts in its first seasons, the period after its inauguration was, perforce, focused most of all on locking into place the measures that would assure the new institution its permanence. Already before the third season, stability was threatened by the gathering clouds of revolution, and for three seasons after July 1830 crisis followed upon crisis as the government of Louis-Philippe sought to preserve the substance of *ancien régime* musical institutions in republican guise. On at least two occasions the dissolution of the society was but narrowly averted. Mendelssohn encountered the contorted world of institutional restructuring when he came to Paris expecting his work to be featured in the 1832 concerts, only to find the entire season in doubt.

Other degrees of permanence came easily enough. The musicians, including many of the founding members, were intrigued by their work and willingly continued their affiliations, thus putting into place the tradition of life tenure. Every indication is that the patrons were equally tenacious. Within a decade of its foundation, much about the society seemed fixed and immutable: budget, repertoire, audience. For a substantial proportion of the constituents, this was a suitable outcome, amounting to a comforting certainty as to what might take place each Sunday afternoon. Intellectuals, soon enough, began to sense more than a hint of stagnation in the aesthetic.

Within two decades the founding generation had obviously begun to recede, engaging for the first time the many issues of succession that came rapidly to the fore—those regarding Cherubini and Habeneck most notably, but also such matters as how to establish priority in orchestral seating and subscription fulfillment. The age at which singers and players should retire was much at issue, as was the financial stand-

ing of *sociétaires* in retirement and of their widows and orphans after
they were gone.

Above all there was Beethoven, mastered systematically by the musicians and their conductors in a disciplined approach for which there was
no precedent in the history of concert music. It took the first few seasons—the militant years, as Sauzay had it—for both the musicians and
the listeners to digest their discoveries, devoured week by week in an atmosphere of excitement for which there is likewise scarce precedent.
Beginning in January 1838 Berlioz, whose chief assignment at the prospering *Revue et gazette musicale* was to cover the Sunday concerts, began to explain Beethoven to its readers. His cycle of articles on Beethoven's symphonic *œuvre* is arguably the first great critical treatment of
that corpus in any language.[1] To read it at a stretch is to be reminded
again how thoroughly Berlioz's conceptual world was shaped by Beethoven; it is often as though each new sentence speaks at once of the
Beethovenian subject matter at hand and its eventual reflection in Berlioz's own music.

Even in the first seasons, with all-Haydn and all-Méhul concerts, there
is evidence of a concern to expand the programming beyond the inherited concert repertoire and Beethoven symphonies. Habeneck, sensing
that the Beethoven fever would run its course, insisted on a variety of
measures meant to refresh the programs and encourage the development
of a national symphonic school. The chief of these was the formal system of *essais;* and if it did not succeed in finding much to program, that
was because there was not much to be found, at least in France. A huge
body of new music, including just-composed works of both Mendelssohn and Wagner, was nonetheless seriously rehearsed. Indeed Mendelssohn soon came to share Beethoven's preeminence in the programming.

Habeneck's successors were by and large content with this body of
staples, happy enough to cultivate—as the exclusive clientele was to accept—the related concepts of the Salle des Concerts as the Louvre
of music and of a work's arrival there as its canonization. This was the
identity of the Société des Concerts when Napoléon III and his empress
came to use it to convey the merits of French culture to the nation's
most distinguished guests. (But I do not concur with the notion that,
before, the concerts had "helped to legitimate the Orleanist monarchy
on an elite level imbuing it with a patina of high culture";[2] in those
years the society's relationship with the government was as often as not
adversarial.)

The 1860s brought many indicators that the inaugural period was reaching its end. Pasdeloup's concerts, begun in 1861, constituted not only the first enterprise to offer the society serious competition but also a fundamental re-thinking of the economic and social principles of the public concert of classical music. The remodeling of the Salle des Concerts erased visual connections with the foundation. A pipe organ acknowledged new compositional directions and the growing interest in performing music of the Baroque era. Preparations for the emperor's Exposition of 1867 reframed the politics of concert music as a tool of national aggrandizement. Meanwhile the statutes of the society, its code of behavior and identity, had essentially frozen the institution in Habeneck's image. The apocalyptic turns of 1870–71 put that status quo to a critical test.

CHAPTER 5

Habeneck

(1828–48)

Whether or not Habeneck indulged his fondness for snuff during the first performance of the Berlioz Requiem is beside the point. François-Antoine Habeneck was by all accounts a distinguished musician, a devoted teacher, and in matters of the orchestral repertoire the great visionary of post-Napoleonic France. He was held in esteem by working musicians of every ilk and spontaneously returned their affection with loyal friendships. "His heart," said Elwart, "was as generous as his character was elevated." To Escudier he was "one of the glories of France."[1] Berlioz gives Habeneck due honor for having "revealed in France the genius of Beethoven" but cannot resist casting him as the personification of an establishment that made younger composers feel unwelcome and in turn stifled the necessary progress of musical art.[2] That was unfair, since it was one of Habeneck's fondest hopes to establish an ongoing program whereby the Société des Concerts would somehow encourage the younger generation of composers in their symphonic pursuits.

The evidence also suggests a psychologically complex artist prone to depression and sometimes haunted by feelings of inferiority as he came into daily contact with the young virtuosi of the Romantic era. Such a diagnosis might account for Habeneck's episodes of churlish behavior and help explain his sad decline. In one of several descriptions of Habeneck's public ridicule of his musicians, Charles de Boigne recalled in 1857 that "at every wrong note he turned around and used his violin bow to point out the culprit to the vindictive public."[3] Saint-Saëns, observing that the disposition of the chorus in the Salle des Concerts often caused it to separate from the orchestra during performances, remembered how

on such occasions Habeneck would turn toward the unfortunate choristers, and thus also to the listeners, and make faces. "Since he was very
ugly, the only result he got was bursts of laughter from the audience."[4]
(Both these accounts, and for that matter Berlioz's *Mémoires,* come
from well after the fact. Saint-Saëns would have been only thirteen when
the old man conducted for the last time.) Habeneck was also sharp of
tongue, often offending those of tender sensibilities with outbursts of
unseemly language.

Habeneck may well have been disappointed by not having achieved
the notoriety as a concert violinist enjoyed by his mentor, Kreutzer, and
his own contemporary Baillot, and it may be telling that he appeared
only twice as soloist with the Société des Concerts—once in the first
season playing a work of his own, and in January 1840 with the slow
movement of a Bach concerto. His intimates knew of his considerable ambition and need for admiration; they grew accustomed to how
he could be good-humored one moment and intolerably arrogant
the next. He had everything, remarked Escudier: honor, triumph, renown—everything but happiness.[5]

But there was no disputing Habeneck's erudition, taste, and wondrous ear. His musicians sensed supernatural powers in how he seemed
to command the secret of his art. Both his admirers and his critics understood that in the concert hall of the Conservatoire, where he was at
his best, he was a worker of miracles.

Like so many of his colleagues and successors, Habeneck came from a
musical family. His father, Adam Abneck, born and possibly trained in
Mannheim, was a musician in the French military service; his younger
brothers, Joseph and Corentin, also became prominent violinists in
Paris. He was born in Mézières, between Limoges and Poitiers, where
his father was stationed. The young Habeneck learned violin from his
father and by the age of ten had established the usual credentials of
prodigy: solo concerts and a portfolio of compositions. He is to be
found in Brest in 1799, at the age of eighteen; shortly afterward, having exhausted the possibilities of distant Brittany, he matriculated at the
Paris Conservatoire as a student of Baillot.

Habeneck quickly became Baillot's star pupil and from 1801 his *répétiteur,* garnering a *1ᵉʳ prix* in 1804. Tradition has it that the empress
Joséphine took an interest in his career and offered him financial encouragement. As incumbent *1ᵉʳ prix* he also led the *exercices publics des
élèves* from the concertmaster's seat, with such success that the rules were
changed to allow him to continue as *chef,* a post he held from 1806 until

the closing of the Conservatoire in 1815. At the orchestra of the Opéra he began as a section violinist in 1804 at the age of twenty-three, soon rising to the position of adjutant to the concertmaster, Rodolphe Kreutzer, then succeeded Kreutzer both as *1ᵉʳ violon solo* and on the podium.

In 1804, too, he married his first wife, Anne-Charlotte Gardel, daughter of Gabriel Gardel, ballet master at the Opéra. She died, childless, in 1817. In 1818 he married Marie-Adèle Sieber, daughter of the music publisher, and they had two children, Antoinette-Marie-Juliette-Caroline and Marie-Mathilde. Caroline later became the second wife of Louis-Gabriel Leplus (usually called Louis but also Gabriel and occasionally Ludovic), the flute-and-piccolo player who seconded Tulou, Dorus, and Altès for three decades.[6] Marie-Mathilde was still living at home as of her father's death in 1849, at the family's apartment in the rue de la Tour d'Auvergne. She eventually became a successful actress, married to Romain Touttain-Bignault and called in the society's records Mme Bignault-Habeneck, Bignaux-Habeneck, and once Mme Touttain-Habeneck. The descendents were formally authorized to add -Habeneck to their names by a decree of 16 June 1883, signed by Jules Grévy, president of the Republic.[7]

Habeneck had achieved genuine, and for all intents and purposes unrivaled, prominence as a conductor long before the foundation of the Société des Concerts. By 1828 he had grown accustomed to playing an important role in the creation of new music enterprises at the national level. He had been a member of Louis XVIII's chapel and led that of Charles X; later he would organize the chapel of Louis-Philippe. He inaugurated the Opéra's new theater in the rue Le Peletier—completing, for that occasion, Nicolas Isouard and Angelo Benincori's *Aladin, ou la Lampe merveilleuse* (with a gas-lit diorama by Louis Daguerre, 1822)—and was its general director from 1821 to 1824. His Légion d'Honneur was conferred there in August 1822.

As first conductor at the Opéra until his retirement in 1846, Habeneck led the premieres of the great majority of the Romantic repertoire, including the major works of Rossini, Auber, and Meyerbeer. He reintroduced the Holy Week *concerts spirituels* and there continued, as in the *exercices publics,* his Beethoven readings. With Rossini's *Le Comte Ory* (1828) he began to conduct with the violin bow, abandoning the infamous audible strokes *("tacks")* that were commonplace. Musicians preferred him to any other conductor of lyric theater.

Habeneck's appointment in 1824 as inspector-general, or honorary director, of the Conservatoire was a political maneuver designed to curb Cherubini's megalomania and of no particular interest to the conductor himself, except insofar as it led to the creation in 1825 of his professorial post in violin. This work he relished, both the nourishing of one young virtuoso after another and the lifelong affections that would blossom as a result. Of his habitually warm heart, the story was told of a former student who died leaving a destitute mother; Habeneck, though never himself long on money, signed over to her the rights to one of his concertos, representing some 1,800 francs in royalties. The first 1er *prix* from his class was won by Cuvillon in 1826; from later classes came Delphin Alard, Masset, Clapisson, and Sauzay—all productive members of the Société des Concerts.

Habeneck was also, like most musicians of his caliber, a sometime composer. His ballet *Le Page inconstant* was produced at the Opéra; his violin method enjoyed some success. Additionally there were two violin concertos, a Grande Polonaise for orchestra, and various string and chamber pieces. Only two of these were played by the Société des Concerts (1828, 1833), neither of them identified. Gradually Habeneck gave up composition, finding it "thankless work."

The draft decree circulating as late as 11 February 1828 foresaw "six concerts annually by the students of the Conservatoire"—little more, that is, than a re-introduction of the *exercices publics*. It seems likely that the decision to constitute the Société des Concerts primarily of alumni and professors was forced by Habeneck on the authorities at the last minute. The letter from La Rochefoucauld to Cherubini transmitting the formal decree of 15 February 1828 mentions "a few changes" that had been made to the text, presumably to that effect, and within the week Cherubini was securing the necessary administrative approvals to release alumni from the exclusivity clauses of their theater contracts in order to play in the Sunday concerts.[8]

Sosthène de La Rochefoucauld's decree of 15 February 1828 begins, as we have seen, with the notion of returning to the Conservatoire "the reputation it had acquired by virtue of the perfection of its public exercises," certain in the view that the giving of concerts was a powerful stimulus for the students "and even the professors." Nine articles follow, outlining what became a familiar landscape:

- Six public concerts separated by no more than two weeks, beginning no later than 1 March
- The use of students, alumni, and—"to give a good impression"—the professors, joining their "disciples"

- Interdiction of any participant "foreign" to the Conservatoire
- Mandatory, uncompensated participation by the designated students
- For the others, indemnity by division of the annual proceeds, with section principals receiving double shares
- Use of the Salle des Concerts and admission by inexpensive tickets, here priced at 2–5 francs
- Free entry for the staff of the Conservatoire, officials of the Office of Fine Arts, and the directors of the national opera companies
- An end-of-year accounting
- Delegation of administrative authority to the director of the Conservatoire

A document probably circulated between 15 and 22 February lists the signatures of fifty-nine *anciens élèves de l'École Royale de Musique* agreeing to participate in first season according to the conditions of La Rochefoucauld's decree.[9]

Meanwhile an ad hoc committee was at work on a draft constitution. Meeting on Tuesday, 4 March 1828 in their first Assemblée Générale, the prospective associates heard their provisional secretary, the flutist Guillou, read the proposed fifty statutes governing their society. Forty-nine musicians, now calling themselves *membres de la Société des Concerts,* ratified a copy with their signatures, and it is from this date that the founding *sociétaires* reckoned their appointment.[10] Some ninety-five came to be counted in the list of founding members, with five others added before the end of the first season to bring the total to the statutory hundred. Almost certainly they rehearsed every morning that week for their inaugural concert on Sunday, 9 March 1828. The last stage of organizing the Société des Concerts, then, had taken just less than a month.

Two days after the inauguration La Rochefoucauld wrote to convey his satisfaction with the "remarkable performance" of the *anciens élèves* and their young comrades, the manner in which Habeneck had "presided," and Cherubini's zeal in having seen the project through. The next day La Rochefoucauld wrote twice, once with his assurance that the hall would be repaired and refurbished before the 1829 concerts and once to waive payment of the tax the Opéra had sought to levy on the proceeds. In June, on reviewing the accounts, he would write again to compliment young and old alike, this time singling out each member of

the new committee—Habeneck, Guillou, Brod, Dauprat, Meifred, Halévy, Kuhn, Amédée-Lanneau and Albert Bonnet—for particular praise.
Not being able to send them all medals, despite the obvious goodwill
and devotion everyone had shown in this "memorable circumstance," he
presented one to Habeneck in salute of a "remarkable zeal and talent." [11]

The 1828 season, lasting through a sixth concert on 11 May, continued
much as it had begun, to the ongoing excitement of the public, press,
and the musicians themselves. The second concert was "dedicated to the
memory of Beethoven," including a second reading of the "Eroica," excerpts from the C-Major Mass and Third Piano Concerto, the quartet
from *Fidelio* and *Le Christ au Mont des Oliviers,* and what for many was
the high point of the first season: Baillot in the first Paris performance
of the Violin Concerto. Beethoven's Fifth Symphony was heard at the
third concert. The fourth, "dedicated to the memory of Mozart," presented the E♭ Symphony (K. 543), the finale of the "Jupiter," an unidentified piano concerto, excerpts from *Idomeneo* and the Requiem,
and the *Magic Flute* overture. Later in the season came the first movement of Mozart's G-Minor Symphony (K. 550), Beethoven's *Coriolanus*
overture, and more movements from the C-Major Mass. The French
repertoire was represented with sacred music and opera excerpts by
Cherubini, Boieldieu, and Auber. Only two works of Haydn, both short
excerpts, were to be heard in 1828. The last concert was billed as "by order of the Duchesse de Berry," with repeats of both Beethoven's Fifth
and the Violin Concerto with Baillot; in 1829 the duchess would "express the desire" to select the program herself.[12]
    To judge from Elwart's listing of the orchestral and choral personnel
in 1828 (constructed in part, he says, from memory),[13] the first concerts
were offered by an orchestra of 86 (15−16−8−12−8 strings, 4−3−4−4
woodwinds, 2−4−3−1 brass, and a timpanist) and a chorus of about 80
(Elwart lists 17−19−22−21); additionally there were perhaps a half-dozen
unnamed Conservatoire students and, among the sopranos, five boys
listed as *pages de la musique du roi.* This is in keeping with the general
performing force on hand for many decades, an orchestra of 80 and a
chorus of 80, but by no means all of the names listed by Elwart show up
in the official registers. Some disappeared after the first concerts, unwilling to commit to the long-term requirements; some doubtless were students who did not make the grade. The opera stars he lists as belonging
to the chorus—the entire casts of *La Muette de Portici* and *Guillaume
Tell,* for instance—would not have showed up with any regularity. But

there was no question that the new concert society had put before the public the best assemblage of musicians the nation could boast, and in the best possible light. In so doing, the political goal of the concerts, to restore the reputation of the Conservatoire, was achieved at the outset.

Eugène Sauzay summarizes the excitement and courage of the first years: "It was not without difficulty that this admirable ensemble of works, in which everything was new in spirit and in form, was put together. We would rehearse three times a week, from nine until noon, sometimes until one o'clock even, without having eaten, without a fire, in that damp and cold room so well heated today. We were, if not martyrs to art, at least valiant and industrious artists." [14]

In October 1828 the prefect of police for the city of Paris, who granted the authority for public gatherings, invited the committee to his office to propose what amounted to another command performance, this one to support his "fund for the extinction of mendacity." La Rochefoucauld heartily endorsed the project and the membership approved it, leading on 21 December 1828—well after the first season, well before the second—to the society's first *concert extraordinaire*. The program was drawn from the existing repertoire (Beethoven's Fifth, an excerpt from the C-Major Mass, and a pairing of the *Coriolanus* overture with the finale of *Le Christ au Mont des Oliviers* that became a regular offering), supplemented with solos by Vogt, the tenor Adolphe Nourrit, and Baillot in the first performance of the Beethoven Romance in F. This established the model for the many benefits and *concerts extraordinaires* to come, and it began the gradual but certain increase in the number of concerts from the prescribed half dozen. But it also had the effect of levying the first *droit des pauvres,* a precedent to which the Société des Concerts appears to have consented all but inadvertently. [15]

The governing committee met for the first time, and began its first register of minutes, on 14 November 1828. Its initial order of business was to dedicate the opening concert of the second season to the memory of "the celebrated Haydn." [16] This was not only to correct an obvious shortcoming of the first season, but to provide the venue for the first (or possibly second) performance of Cherubini's *Chant sur la mort d'Haydn,* for three soloists and orchestra, notoriously composed before Haydn's death. In the fall of 1805 Cherubini had traveled to Vienna, where he conducted a concert for Napoléon at the Schönbrunn palace, attended the first performance of *Fidelio,* and was received by both Haydn and Beethoven—an encounter remembered largely for Cherubini's subsequent characterization of Beethoven as "an unlicked bear."

His return to Paris coincided with the Europe-wide rumor that Haydn had died, prompting Cherubini to organize a memorial concert that was to have included his own cantata and a Kreutzer violin concerto after themes by the late master. The announcement published by the Berlin *Musikalische-Zeitung* reached Haydn, said by C. F. Pohl to have remarked, "The good gentlemen! I am really much indebted to them for this unexpected honor. If I had known of the ceremony I would have gone there myself to conduct the [Requiem] mass in person." [17]

The Haydn concert on 15 February 1829 included both the *Chant sur la mort d'Haydn* and, with Auguste Tolbecque as violin soloist, the Kreutzer concerto; also an unidentified symphony, *La Tempête et le calme (Der Sturm,* for soloists, chorus, and orchestra), "The Heavens are Telling" from *The Creation,* and two excerpts from *The Seasons.* Both of these, the introduction and opening chorus of "Spring" and the fine hunting chorus that concludes "Fall," became audience favorites. Haydn's music went on to regain its customary place in the affection of the Parisian musicians and audience.

The second season also offered the premieres of Beethoven's Sixth and Seventh Symphonies, the "Hallelujah" chorus from Handel's *Messiah,* and—confirming the latest vogue—Weber's overtures to *Oberon* (also called *Le Roi des génies*) and *Der Freischütz (Robin des bois)* and excerpts from *Euryanthe.* For her command performance the Duchesse de Berry chose the Fifth and Seventh Symphonies of Beethoven and a second hearing of a new Septuagesima motet by Cherubini.

In the third season, 1830, the orchestra premiered Beethoven's First, Second, and Fourth Symphonies. They dedicated the concert of 7 March 1830 "to the memory of Méhul," thus putting a French composer in the heady company of Haydn, Mozart, and Beethoven. At least the two overtures, *Stratonice* and *Le Jeune Henri,* would stay in the central repertoire. The rest of the program was selected from Méhul's operas, as though the musicians were still unaware of his symphonies. Two other French composers of the old school, Catel and Gossec, were introduced to the repertoire.

It was the longest season so far, with the six statutory concerts, closing *concert extraordinaire,* and three nighttime *concerts spirituels*—on Holy Wednesday, Good Friday, and Easter Sunday. The predominant composer to be heard at the Holy Week concerts was Cherubini, with excerpts from his masses. It could be that the frequent programming of movements from the *Messe du sacre,* composed for the coronation of Charles X in 1825 at the cathedral in Reims and now numbering a half-dozen performances since 1828—and for that matter, the unusual choice of Le Sueur's *Urbs beata,* also a coronation anthem—had as much to do with currying royal favor as with Cherubini's intrinsic popularity. Beleaguered as it was, the monarchy might have responded tangibly to these evocations of a more comfortable time. Elwart records a disquieting incident at the last concert of the season, on 30 May 1830, where Her Royal Highness, presumably Queen Clotilde, was hissed when she arrived ten minutes late. The orchestra, very exceptionally, had deferred its prompt starting time at Cherubini's request.[18]

The revolution that toppled Charles X took place at the end of July— the *Trois Glorieuses,* 27–29 July 1830—while the Société des Concerts was out of session, and so passes unnoticed in the written record. But in its wake came a governmental reorganization that prompted a succession of short-term crises, fundamental budgetary change, and a revised constitution for the Société des Concerts. The benign patronage of Sosthène de La Rochefoucauld was lost; so, too, were retirement pensions of former employees of the Conservatoire and Opéra. The society's own 2,000-franc subvention failed to arrive in 1831. The minister of commerce and public works, Count d'Agout, had both the Opéra and the Conservatoire in his new portfolio, but delegated most of the day-to-day administration to a Commission of Oversight for the Opéra and Conservatoire (Commission de Surveillance auprès de l'Académie Royale et du Conservatoire de Musique), chaired by La Rochefoucauld's successor, the meddlesome Edmond Cavé. His first priority was the franchising of the Opéra to a semi-independent impresario.

It took some time for the Société des Concerts to understand how radically it was to be affected by these changes. The 1831 season, like that of 1830, seemed little different from years past, as though the institution was following its usual course, insulated well enough from the distractions of politics. Of the seven concerts that year, only the first, with its proceeds dedicated "to the July wounded," took any note whatever of the previous summer—whereas in 1848, when the revolution took place during the concert season, the programs embraced republican allusions nobody could miss. The musicians stayed focused on their mission, completing the cycle of Beethoven symphonies on 27 March 1831 with the much-anticipated Ninth featuring a marvelous quartet of soloists: Mme Dabadie, soprano; Mlle Dorus, alto; Alexis Dupont, tenor; and Dérivis *fils,* bass. Two weeks later the orchestra introduced its first authentically French symphony, by Georges Onslow—probably the First, in A major, op. 41.

In the interval between the fourth and fifth seasons, however, the new government began to clarify its designs. When the Count d'Agout, in late 1831, authorized the 1832 concerts, he attached the condition that the society offer a benefit on behalf of those at the Conservatoire who had suddenly lost their retirement pensions in the wake of the July revolution. Not only did this come as a surprise, but the language in which the count expressed himself did not seem to promise a warm relationship: "I do not doubt that the members of the Société des Concerts, who have always given proof of their true disinterest, will learn with pleasure that I have thought to offer them a way to care for their comrades, and thus have decided that a seventh concert, at least, would be given where the proceeds would be reserved for them." [19] Mendelssohn, newly arrived in Paris, wrote his sister that, as a result, "The concerts in the Conservatoire, which were my great object, probably will not take place at all, because the Commission of the Ministry wished to give a Commission to the Commission of the Society, to deprive a Commission of Professors of their share of the profits; [to] which the Commission of the Conservatoire replied to the Commission of the Ministry that they might go and be hanged [a pun on 'suspended'], and even then they would not agree to it." [20]

Cherubini had the good sense to refer the question to an Assemblée Générale *extraordinaire* on 8 February 1832. A lively discussion ensued, noting that however worthy the cause, a dangerous precedent was being set when the government began to attach conditions to its support—in this case, conditions that adversely affected the season's monetary outcome. At length the assembly agreed, by the narrow vote of 41 to 32, to meet the governmental charge, but they immediately drafted a written summary of their concerns. On 12 February they wrote Cherubini to protest the notion that the new authorities would impose such a condition on "an artistic association that for five years had spared nothing to sustain musical art in France." They consented to offer a *"concert extraordinaire donné au profit des pensionnaires du Conservatoire de Musique,"* but instead of depositing the proceeds into a "momentarily embarrassed" government account, they meant to distribute them directly to their distressed comrades.[21]

A particularly troublesome agent of the new order was Cavé, whose primary allegiance to the Opéra was a given and who almost certainly felt threatened by the fast emergence of a serious competitor. The charge of his commission, moreover, was to establish sound business practices requiring minimal subvention, and using the Conservatoire's only money-making activity to clear away the problem of its pensioners—

much as the Opéra itself meant to do—seemed only sensible. Cavé told his superiors that he was "stunned" at the attitude expressed by the *sociétaires* in their letter of 12 February and overruled their obviously unworkable plan to deal with the income themselves.[22]

The benefit concert was given without further incident on 29 April 1832, consisting of symphonies of Haydn and Beethoven, excerpts from a piano concerto composed and performed by Valentin Alkan, solos by Mlle Dorus and Vogt, and the finale of Cherubini's *Médée*. Box office receipts were 2,858 francs, representing a two-thirds occupancy. After expenses of 1,054.08 francs were deducted, a balance of 1,803.92 francs was deposited in the Caisse des Dépôts et Consignations. The matter of a pension or retirement fund for the *sociétaires* themselves—every one of whom was, after all, a potential pensioner of the Conservatoire—was thus indirectly broached, and it would occupy them for some time to come.[23]

How bitterly the *sociétaires* resented the intrusion of the government and its oversight committee, and how seriously they thought their finances threatened by it, is clear from the tone of the secretary's report to his colleagues at the end of the year: "The Conservatoire may owe its very continued existence to the superiority and reputation of the Société des Concerts, now on the point of being stopped in its course by new rules that the opera commission (which includes not a single musician) thinks it has a right to impose under the ridiculous pretext that the government lends the room, the equipment, etc."[24]

And there was worse to come. The crisis re-erupted in December when the Société des Concerts received two documents from a ministry now achieving its stride: on 1 December a preliminary authorization for the society to present its 1833 season in the Salle des Concerts, and on 13 December 1832 a new decree replacing La Rochefoucauld's of 1828.[25] The first of these began innocently enough, requiring the orchestra to pay the expenses of "employees, box office, ushers, porters, agents of the Garde Municipale, firemen, transportation, heating, and lighting. There must be no postings without advance approval." Then came the astonishing requisition of places: "the *grande loge* for the Intendant General of the Civil List [Montalivet], *loge* no. 14 for the Curator of Crown Furnishings ['Conservateur du Mobilier de la Couronne'], *loge* 17 for M. Cherubini, *loge* 15 for the Architect of the Conservatoire, *loge* 13 for M. Lambert, manager *(chef de bureau)* of the Office of Crown Furnishings, . . . *loge* 2 for M. Bazin, charged with ceremonies and oversight of the house, 2 places in the second *loges* for Zimmermann, the

Building Inspector . . ." and, of course, places for d'Agout, Cavé, and the directors of the opera houses. The total number of places commandeered was about two dozen.

The decree of 13 December 1832 had only five articles:

- Administration by a committee of twelve, presided over by the director of the Conservatoire, with the conductor as vice president
- Seven bi-weekly concerts, to begin in January 1833
- At every concert, a solo appearance by a prizewinner from the Conservatoire; and, likewise at every performance, a composition by a Prix de Rome laureate who had completed his three years abroad (two in Rome, one in Germany)
- An eighth concert to benefit the pension fund at the Conservatoire
- An end-of-year budgetary report to the Commission of Oversight, which was invited to attach its comments

Count d'Agout, as though meaning to force the issues, called for "serious attention" to the concluding three provisions. In sum the conditions for 1833 included insistence on the vexatious matter of the pension fund, a manifestly unworkable charge to offer a new composition by a junior composer at every concert, and the withholding of a number of complimentary seats sufficient to crush the budget. It was clear that an Assemblée Générale *extraordinaire* would be necessary before the committee could proceed to plan the season.

In fairness to the administrators it must be said that the idea of conferring advantage on young laureates of the Conservatoire was almost surely supported by both Cherubini and Habeneck, and that this *cahier des charges* was in general keeping with the kinds of things expected from the theaters. (The twentieth-century *cahiers des charges* insisted on similar privileges for French soloists and composers.) Moreover, in late December 1832, the society was returned its royal compensation. Montalivet wrote that Louis-Philippe would take the royal box and the six places immediately underneath for a sum of 1,500 francs "in encouragement of the arts and principally of a Society composed of the distinguished artists whose reputation has become European"—plus any revenues that might accrue for use of the box when the royal family did not appear. ("Here is written, in the Hand of the King," the letter concludes, "'*approuvé*. L. P.'") This arrangement survived until 1848, and in 1834 the gratuity was increased to the 2,000 francs originally accorded by the Bourbon monarchs.[26]

At the general assembly of 6 January 1833 the secretary, Charles Plantade, began his report by objecting to the clause requiring works by Prix de Rome winners on every concert: "episodes to bore the public" and overburden the library with "extra weight." The matter of the benefit concert was more than anything else an annoyance. "But the condition of gravest consequence," he went on, "is the reserving of places by the household of the king and his ministers." He noted that since the foundation in 1828 it had been the society's own privilege to decide which places to offer, either to promote its own best interests or as simple courtesy. A member of the royal household (the Duchesse de Berry in 1828 and 1829, the queen herself in 1830) had always taken and paid for a box, and the royal subvention of 2,000 francs had been customary until 1831. Plantade valued the seats required by the government as worth 384 francs per concert, a total of 2,688 francs in lost revenue. Even with the 1,500 francs just granted by the king, there would be an annual loss of 1,118 francs. The committee made no particular recommendation: "That is for you to decide."[27]

By a unanimous vote, the membership refused to accept the new charge, threatening to cancel the season if a solution could not be negotiated. They designated Meifred and Kalkbrenner, two of their most persuasive representatives, to join the committee in a delegation to visit the Ministry of Commerce and Public Works. Received in early February 1833 by Montalivet, the delegation managed to secure a "light fix" in the release of four places, two in each of two *loges*. This reduced the value of the complimentary seats, it was now calculated, to 188 francs per concert for seven concerts, a total of 1,316 francs in new season expenses. But one potentially lasting victory was secured: the exclusive use of the hall during the season, as well as the moral satisfaction of "the opportunity to tell [Montalivet] about the origins of the society and the value of its work to the prosperity of musical art in France."[28] The conference was sufficient to allay the most pressing concerns, and the sixth season began on 17 February 1833, about a month later than first envisaged.

The revolutionary stance taken by the membership on 6 January 1833 was not specifically addressed by the government until after the season. On 3 June 1833 a new minister of commerce and the interior, the great Thiers, responded that he would "tolerate the inexecution of all the conditions, but for one: the benefit for the pensioners"—and suggested a certain irritation that he had delivered the same opinion orally to Habeneck during the season without the benefit concert having taken place.[29] In fact the matter was allowed to die. The crown retained the same seats in 1834 as in 1833, when the secretary remarked that, having already consented to the unfortunate precedent, there could be no turning back. The financial loss would simply have to be absorbed.[30]

Little of this upheaval became public knowledge. The patrons of 1832 and 1833 would have perceived business as usual, a generally familiar repertoire, the comforting certainty that—for most of them—their usual seats would be waiting each Sunday. So far the Société des Concerts had little if any competition from other providers of serious symphonic music. By 1835 the Gymnase Musical would be offering a concert series, and as the century progressed any number of promising organizations would be formed to similar effect. But in the early 1830s the only other live concerts, excepting the kind of ad hoc single-composer events pioneered with such tenacity by Berlioz, were those of the pleasure garden and dance hall—the Musard quadrilles.

Mendelssohn had high hopes of his own for the 1832 season, expecting performances of the *Midsummer Night's Dream* overture and his new Symphony in D Minor (No. 5, "Reformation"): "Habeneck talks of seven or eight rehearsals." The overture had been read twice by mid-February, and though it does not appear on the printed program, Mendelssohn writes that it was played at the end of the second concert, 19 February 1832, where "it went admirably, and seemed also to please the audience." The symphony was delayed until further notice, such that Mendelssohn's Paris sojourn concluded with his premiere of Beethoven's Fourth Piano Concerto on 18 March. He was ebullient after the last rehearsal: "If the audience to-morrow are only half as enchanted as the orchestra to-day, we shall do well; for they shouted loudly for the adagio *da capo,* and Habeneck made them a little speech, to point out to them that at the close there was a solo bar, which they must be so good as to wait for. You would be gratified to see all the little kindnesses and courtesies the latter shows me. And the end of each movement of the symphony, he asks me if there is anything I do not approve of, so I have been able for the first time, to introduce, with a French orchestra, some favourite *nuances* of my own." After the concert, he reported, "The French say that it was *un beau succès,* and the audience were pleased. The Queen, too, sent me all sorts of fine compliments on the subject."[31]

Among the important premieres in that era were another Onslow symphony in 1832, probably the Second—that is, the one in D minor—and Berlioz's *Rob-Roy* overture in 1833, clearly an effort to meet the spirit of the governmental charge. The curiosities included in 1832 the hunting chorus from *Der Freischütz* with sixteen horns, and an *a cap-*

pella vocal work of the sixteenth century identified only as *Laudi spiri-tuali*. In 1833 there was a succession of featured virtuosi from the ranks, perhaps also in the spirit of the ministerial decree: the strings in a *symphonie concertante* for four violins by Ludwig Maurer (Tilmant, Urhan, Claudel, and Cherblanc); the woodwinds in a Reicha quintet (Tulou, Vogt, Buteux, Henry, and Dauprat—a stellar ensemble); and the brass in a quintet by Jacques Strunz (Meifred, Jacquemin, Bailly, Dauverné, and Dufresne). Good theater came with the attendance on 18 March 1832 of the new queen, Marie-Amélie, and her retinue of fourteen to sixteen. News of the visit, requiring not only the royal box but the *loges* on either side, reached the committee only two days before. The queen desired to hear, she said, "one of the most beautiful movements of your great symphony." This the committee interpreted as a request for Beethoven, and rearranged the program to open with the "Pastoral" Symphony.[32]

The supremacy of Beethoven was unchallenged. The 1832 season closed on 15 April with a second hearing of the Ninth Symphony. Attendance was, unusually, poor, owing to the cholera epidemic that had reached Paris; receipts suggest that the house was at about 60 percent capacity. Habeneck chose to separate this new performance of the Ninth into two halves, with the first two movements at the start of the program—the second identified as "minuet"—and the last two at the close. The Ninth had been deemed too long to be absorbed continuously, and this solution had the obvious advantage of putting a work that rendered everything else anticlimactic in both places of honor. In 1834, the Ninth was separated into a "first part," consisting of the Allegro, Adagio, and scherzo played in that order at the start of the concert, and the finale as a "second part" at the end. The disadvantages of dividing the Ninth became clear with repeated hearings, and from 1837 it was generally heard intact.

All nine symphonies were now in the repertoire, the Third and Fifth having been introduced in 1828; the Sixth and Seventh in 1829; the First, Second, and Fourth in 1830; the Ninth in 1831; and the Eighth, still unpublished in France and for which it had been difficult to acquire the parts, in 1832. Of the piano concertos only the first movement of the Third and the complete Fourth had so far been heard (Mme Brod, 1828; Mendelssohn, 1832)—again, probably, for lack of the parts; the Fifth Piano Concerto ("Emperor") would be premiered in 1838. Baillot's appearances in the Violin Concerto and Romance in F were remembered fondly from 1828. All the known overtures had been gradually added: *Egmont* and *Coriolanus* in 1828, *Fidelio* in 1829, one of the *Leonore* overtures in 1834, *Prometheus* and *King Stephen* in 1831.

Having begun to exhaust this repertoire, at least for premieres, Habeneck led his players to the chamber music, presenting the Beethoven Septet, one on a part, in 1831, and in 1832 embarking on the quartets op. 18 and 59 as played by the full string orchestra (of 54: 14–14–10–10–6).[33] The Septet, too, would soon have this treatment, with pairs of clarinets, horns, and bassoons added to the strings in a famous and long-lasting rendition. Chopin was among the connoisseurs who knew the Beethoven quartets already and, not surprisingly, disliked the custom: "You think you're hearing four gigantic instruments: the violins like a palace, the viola like a bank, and the cello like the Protestant church."[34] But from Habeneck's point of view it made good sense to keep the voyage of discovery at full sail.

The chorus had learned *Le Christ au Mont des Oliviers* and the Gloria from the Mass in C during the first season. In 1832 they presented *Le Calme de la mer (Meeresstille und glückliche Fahrt)* and what seems to have been an unsatisfactory reading of the Kyrie and Gloria from the *Missa solemnis*. In 1835 the Credo and Benedictus were heard, the latter featuring Baillot as violin soloist. Mlle Falcon premiered *Ah! perfido* the same season. Excerpts from *Fidelio* would be tried and added to the repertoire when they met with success.

From the mid-1830s on, it was a matter of obtaining the music and painstaking mastery of what remained to be learned, notably the rest of the *Missa solemnis*. Habeneck called for acquisition of materials for the *Egmont* entr'actes in 1835, for instance, but the project was waylaid by a dispute over the French translation. He apparently conducted *Wellington's Victory (La Bataille)* at a semi-private reading for guests of the *sociétaires* after the last concert in April 1839; he put one of the *Leonore* overtures—presumably No. 3, since the *Fidelio* overture and another *Leonore,* probably No. 1, had already been done—into first rehearsal the following October, programming it at the opening concert of 1840.[35] Excerpts from *The Ruins of Athens* were first heard in 1844, with the full performance coming in 1847, perhaps Habeneck's last major premiere.

Berlioz did not approve of the society's frequent practice of offering excerpts from the major Beethoven works. Of the performance of the scherzo of the Ninth at Habeneck's benefit on 26 April 1835, he said he would reserve judgment until he heard the whole work: "In general these planks of the great scores lose three quarters of their merit by being offered in isolation and without the preparation that had preceded them."[36] Nor was Habeneck's Beethoven always a model of good sense. Berlioz and others complained of his habit of omitting the doublebasses from the fugal trio of the Fifth Symphony, movement III. Dancla wondered why Habeneck insisted on playing the famously redundant two measures at the return of the scherzo in the same movement—but nevertheless considered his interpretation ideal, better than Beethoven himself could ever have heard.[37]

Behind the scenes, the Société des Concerts went on refining the scope and order of its dreams, working out, as the months passed, business practices meant to assure it a long and productive life. The minutes of the first half decade record delicate, often antagonizing, deliberations on every aspect of administering an orchestra and chorus, from matters of programming and the engagement of soloists and temporary personnel to how retirements might best be handled. The committee took care to claim its authority to name substitutes, replacements, and successors, thereby counteracting early on the common practice of players' sending their students to rehearsals. When Fétis wanted to engage the society for his *concert historique,* it declined to appear, at least under its own name, for an independent sponsor. (The decision to participate was left to the individual players, and Fétis was admonished not to have the posters carry the words "Orchestre du Conservatoire," since that would mislead the public, and since only the Société des Concerts could be said to be "in residence" at the Conservatoire.)[38] During performances, the chorus was sent offstage when it had nothing to sing. As conditions in the press box came to cause the organization more harm than good, it was decided to commit a precious second box, then four more places, to the journalists.

By 1832 it had become necessary to invoke measures to prevent "inexactitude" in the ranks. That season was "long and painful," according to the secretary, owing largely to extra rehearsals of the new repertoire—the *Missa solemnis* and Beethoven quartets.[39] Habeneck insisted on mandatory attendance at rehearsals and performances, invoking article 38 of the statutes ("three unexcused absences constitute a tacit resignation") against two members, and warning four, including Narcisse Girard, for "lack of zeal."

Girard eventually responded that his commitments elsewhere were indeed compromising his work for the Société des Concerts but that he hoped nevertheless to maintain his affiliation. At least in part owing to Girard's high rank in the society, and as a first experiment, he and a few other members of his standing were offered the option of reverting to the status of *aspirant* on an interim basis, with the assurance of eventual reinstatement to the rank of *sociétaire* by order of original seniority. Such reinstatement would occur upon renewed demonstrations of "zeal, talent, and exactitude." The tenor Louis Révial was dismissed a few seasons later for vacating his place without explanation. At first he offered the feeble excuse that he had not received the rehearsal schedules, but the *garçon d'orchestre* testified that he had attempted delivery and been turned away from the door. Révial thereupon sheepishly visited the committee to accept the blame and its consequences, and as he was desirous of continuing his work was also accorded the courtesy of starting over as an *aspirant*.[40]

But the violist Isidore Labadens, who asked for an extended leave, was refused so as not to set a precedent with the rank and file and subsequently resigned. The tenor Doineau was denied a leave and, "persisting in separating himself from the work of the Société," was dismissed. The noted violinist Halma, who had left Paris in 1833 without telling the committee, was refused reinstatement when he returned two years later, having "betrayed" his colleagues.[41]

As the Société des Concerts achieved permanence, however, several of the most influential *sociétaires* began to realize, like Girard, that the ongoing commitment was more than they could manage. Jean-Jacques Vidal, second violinist in Baillot's quartet, had been one of the first to go, resigning in December 1828; another was Fromental Halévy, the founding accompanist, upon his move from keyboard player at the Théâtre-Italien to *chef de chant* at the Opéra. The tenor Alexis Dupont left Paris in 1832, his brusque abandonment of the organization noted with disapproval in the secretary's report that May, regretting the manner in which he had "suddenly, one might say dishonorably, broken his relationship with colleagues highly qualified to appreciate his contribution and thus meriting the courtesy of his confidence when he arrived at his intention to retire."[42] Yet the committee soon enough understood that goings and comings of the star singers were a matter of professional necessity; Dupont was welcomed back late in 1836 and appointed for the 1837 season, by unanimous vote, a *sociétaire solo*. He went on to serve faithfully until his retirement in 1848 as a *membre honoraire,* though his tenure was not without other periods of conflict, notably during Holy Week in 1842.[43]

The two new soprano soloists appointed in 1838, Mlles Hyrne and d'Hennin, both found the conditions of appointment too burdensome. Hyrne left Paris almost immediately after her election, giving notice that she would not be available until mid-December; d'Hennin said she would come to rehearsals only when it was convenient and in fact seldom showed up at all.[44]

The vagaries of maintaining a first-rate chorus—no young singer could be faulted for wanting to accept employment in the provincial theaters, and the young ladies were of marrying age—were an ongoing source of consternation. The autumn chorus auditions each year stretched everyone's patience. Some young singers would register for a hearing before a half dozen of the busiest professional musicians in the nation and then fail to appear. Many were found to be "not yet musicians." The *amour-propre* of some of the more experienced professionals was such that they refused to audition at all, expecting appointment on the basis of their prizes and entitlements elsewhere.

The committee fought every *sou* of new expense. Ticket sales had been handled at first as an uncompensated extra duty by F.-H. Réty (1789–1877), the *contrôleur-caissier* of the Conservatoire. In early 1833 he demanded an honorarium of 25 francs per concert and when offered only 20 asked to be relieved of the responsibility;[45] later in the year he declined a request from the commission revising the statutes to return to duty. (Réty and his son E.-E.-H. Réty, who served as business manager at the Conservatoire from 1867 to the end of the century, remained bulwarks of support in matters of accounting. Two other important functionaries—Alexandre Laty at the Conservatoire and Simon Leborne, librarian at the Opéra—were tenors in the chorus.) Thereafter the tickets were handled by the *archiviste-caisser,* who as a member of the committee received no compensation. But the matter of staff support at the box office would not go away. Albert Bonnet, as *archiviste-caissier,* employed a Conservatoire student to deliver the weekly ticket coupons to subscribers—the practice, he held, of all the theaters and public establishments. It was nevertheless determined that this expense could not be billed to the operating costs but must borne by the *archiviste-caissier* personally. Similarly a superfluous employee who placed the music on the stands was eliminated, with his duties transferred to the official *garçon d'orchestre.*

Campaigns to control the *parterre* were waged without success. In 1832 the committee offered one coupon for the *parterre* to each *sociétaire,* then almost immediately had to rescind the privilege to control the reselling that attracted "mobs" to the courtyard before each concert;[46] later the *sociétaires* had to claim their passes a week in advance, and demand for them diminished accordingly.[47] The violinist Lagarin was found guilty of selling his coupons at elevated prices and resigned, with his victim reimbursed 12 francs and awarded Lagarin's pass for the rest of the season.[48] After discussions in October 1835 and September 1836, women—largely family members of the musicians—were banned from the *parterre*. "During the recent seasons," it was reported to the membership, "we had noted that the presence of ladies on the *parterre* seemed to paralyze the effect that one might have expected the performance to have on that part of the house."[49]

In the ongoing struggle with the agents of the poor-tax there were both victories and disappointments. With the new government the flat rate increased at once from 100 to 150 francs per concert. In 1834 the agency now calling itself Assistance Publique demanded the full *huitième*, or 12½ percent, levied on all theatricals, and it was necessary to agree to a new per-concert fee of 200 francs. Another skirmish was fought again in 1836, this time won by the Société des Concerts. The fee stayed at 200 francs until new subscription prices went into effect in 1857.

The first serious altercation between the musicians and their conductor broke out during the Assemblée Générale preceding the 1832 concerts, when the pianist Frédéric Kalkbrenner demanded that authority for inviting guest soloists be transferred from the conductor to the committee, which would then be free to embark on a program of encouraging the visits of foreign artists. Habeneck contested the idea, wanting to withhold the flood of star virtuosi "until the Beethoven symphonies no longer excite and incite the public."[50] Kalkbrenner was reminded of article 50 of the statutes, which required that new business be presented to the assembly in the form of a petition from ten members. That was enough to table the motion for the time being.

The famous foreigners were not long, however, in coming. Mendelssohn had already visited. He was followed by Liszt and Chopin in 1835 and Thalberg in January 1836. In his review of Thalberg's appearance, Berlioz (considering Liszt and Chopin to be countrymen) congratulates the Société des Concerts for having "bent the rules," at last, for a foreign virtuoso. Traveling virtuosi of every ilk and description rapidly became an important component of the programming in the late 1830s and the 1840s: J. Faubel, first clarinet to the king of Bavaria (15 January 1837); Wolfram, flutist to the duke of Baden (14 March 1839); Grassi, violin *solo* to the czar of Russia (8 March 1840); Ernest Cavallini, first clarinet *solo* of La Scala (28 January 1842); the doublebassist Hindl (6 March 1842); van Gelder, cellist to the king of Belgium (14 January 1843); Belche, first trombone to the king of Prussia (14 January 1844); J. Blaes, first clarinet to the king of Belgium and professor at the Brussels Conservatoire (8 February 1846); and dozens of others. Each received for his services a letter of thanks and the society's commemorative medal.

It is not precisely clear how the statutes grew from the fifty articles that were read to the members in March 1828 to the fifty-two articles of the first preserved constitution and finally into the fifty-four statutes of early 1834. In December 1829 a commission, chosen so as not to include any members of the provisional committee, was appointed to "revise and perfect" the rules of the society. Its members were Tulou, Laty, Alexis Dupont (who left Paris in January 1832), Auguste Seuriot, and its chairman, Dominique Tajan-Rogé (who left Paris in early 1833). The entire membership discussed the process for drafting new statutes at an Assemblée Générale *extraordinaire* in June 1830, and these were adopted without dissent on 1 December 1831, thus taking effect at the start of the fifth season, 1832.[51]

In all probability the Tajan-Rogé text consists of a close editing of the original fifty articles to bring them into conformity with existing practice. The director of the Conservatoire is called to preside at the general assemblies and the conductor to preside over the committee; the concept of a president and vice president / conductor has yet to be formed. The numeration of the articles accords with references in the minutes of the first half decade.

But there must have been a second commission at work almost immediately. By May 1832 it had been agreed to have the general assemblies at the close of each session, so that officers could be elected and begin their work over the summer. Certainly refinements were needed after the ministerial decree of 13 December 1832, calling specifically for the director of the Conservatoire to serve as president of the Société des Concerts. Cherubini had a new draft in hand in 1833, when he testily invited the committee's attention to the fact that he himself was not a *sociétaire*, a situation remedied by unanimous vote at an Assemblée Générale *extraordinaire* on 7 November 1833. More significantly, the members went on to elect Cherubini their president, again unanimously. Notifying him the next day of their actions, the committee remarked that "these artists were, for the most part, formed beneath your gaze and under your care, and they could not but vividly hope you would accept this title, for it will cast new glory on the society where Cherubini's name now heads the list."[52] Even accounting for the flattery, this language suggests that having Cherubini as president may have been their intent all along.

At a general assembly of 5 January 1834 each statute was discussed and adopted, with the new constitution signed by the committee and dated as of that day. A second assembly on 4 April put final touches on the document, which was then lithographed so that a copy could be presented to each *sociétaire*—the first time every member had one—at the regular end-of-year Assemblée Générale of 4 May 1834. Members were invited to sign the original of "the constitution on which we depend" before leaving the room.[53]

The statutes of 5 January 1834 represent a thorough overhaul of the first constitution to bring it into accord with existing practice. Most of the new provisions had already been introduced in 1833:

· A new committee structure, with an elected president, a conductor, and an optional vice president

· Increase in the number of *sociétaires* from 100 to 112

· Delegation of authority for the chorus and its repertoire to the professor of ensemble singing at the Conservatoire

· Remuneration of students and supernumeraries called to participate

· The possibility for exceptional election of foreigners, as *membres honoraires*

· Detailed analysis of expenses

· Detailed instructions for the system of *jetons* and *répartition,* including a system of fines for infractions

Substantial amendments would be voted in 1836 and 1837, and the statutes would be rewritten entirely by a lawyer in 1841. Stable as it was in underlying design, the constitution, like the society itself, was still being shaped.

The *concerts spirituels* as given in Holy Week 1830 had been abandoned, perhaps as a result of the 1830 revolution. In 1834 Habeneck suggested adding to the subscription series a *concert extraordinaire* on Good Friday night, 28 March 1834, when the theaters would be closed by ministerial decree. Kalkbrenner and Mme Gras-Dorus agreed to participate, and the Good Friday concert was successful enough to earn a permanent place in the season. In 1838 it was paired with a regular concert that fell on Easter Sunday, and beginning in 1840 the term *concert spirituel* reappears in the program for both Good Friday and Easter Sunday.

In 1842 the Easter concert was moved from the traditional 2:00 time slot to 8:30 at night, the Sunday luncheon having begun to detract audience.[54] This return of the *concerts spirituels,* which lasted until the calendar was adjusted in 1927 to conclude before Easter, was appreciated far and wide and credited by the members to Habeneck. The extra concert in 1834 devalued the *jeton* slightly, from 7.80 francs to 7.15, owing in large measure to the extra cost of lighting a night concert, but since there were more *jetons,* each member enjoyed a modest increase in compensation.

The original series of six concerts grew quickly. In 1838 it numbered ten concerts that stretched from mid-January to late April, usually the Sunday after Easter.

1834	8 concerts (7 + Good Friday)
1835	9 concerts (7 + Good Friday + benefit for Habeneck)
1836	8 concerts (7 + Good Friday)
1837	9 concerts (8 + Good Friday)
1838	10 concerts (9 + Good Friday, with Good Friday and Easter Sunday pair)

Attendance remained high, and the income showed small but certain growth, the result in part of some newly built seating. The benches at the front of the *parterre* level were converted into fixed seating; addition of a seventh seat to some of the *loges* caused enough discontent among the subscribers that the practice was short-lived. Great care was taken to maximize the resale of unused coupons *(places disponibles),* bringing attractive financial results. With some trepidation the committee placed the fall proceeds in treasury bonds and included the interest in the overall amount to be distributed in the *répartition* of 1834.[55]

Before the opening of the eighth season, 1835, the committee made its first decision to invite the resignation of members in good standing, the trombonists René Bénard (age fifty) and Devise.[56] There was certainly some dissatisfaction with their artistry; additionally, they took up memberships in very short supply for what was, in their cases, part-time work. Probably the committee wanted to assign their spots to Charles-François Poussard, the timpanist appointed two weeks later, and to the Swedish-French trombone virtuoso Antoine Dieppo, who appeared as a soloist that season and went on to have a brilliant career with the Société des Concerts. Meifred, as secretary, proposed to lessen the indignity to his outgoing colleagues by offering them the title *membre honoraire,* so far used only for active appointments of non-French musicians.

Devise accepted the suggestion and gracefully noted his willingness to continue as ophicleide player on a per-service basis. Bénard came to the committee to protest. Habeneck explained "with the grace and dignity due an estimable artist," that the title *membre honoraire* was intended to "indemnify artists whom age and fatigue oblige to retire." Bénard complained of the lost income, countered with the observation that his twenty-two years of service at the Opéra left him a generous pension; he demanded to appeal his case to an Assemblée Générale *extraordinaire.* Vogt, as *commissaire du personnel,* counseled him to "reflect carefully on that possibility," suggesting that "this slight wounding of his *amour-propre*" was best left in the relative privacy of the committee room. Bénard, refusing to resign, was then retired by a unanimous committee vote; a week later, having had time to reflect on his situation, he accepted the title *membre honoraire.* The important new category of retired *membres honoraires* was thus established, and with it Meifred found an elegant way for long-term *sociétaires* to end their careers. Behind closed doors the committee members acknowledged that the exercise had amounted to a "purge." [57] Gradually, led by Habeneck, they were approaching the still more delicate question of mandatory retirement.

The 1835 season introduced, in addition to the Credo and Benedictus of the *Missa solemnis,* an overture by Fesca and works of the *sociétaires* Clapisson and Masset, as well as a concertino for pedal harp composed by Nadermann and played by one of his pupils. Mlle Nau, soon to become a star soprano, was introduced in an Auber aria as a "student of Mme Cinti-Damoreau." The season concluded memorably: for the Good Friday *concert spirituel,* 17 April 1835, Liszt appeared in Weber's E♭ Piano Concerto; then, in a benefit for Habeneck on 26 April, Chopin played his Introduction and Polonaise, op. 22. He had petitioned for an invitation three years before, writing on 13 March 1832 of his fond ambition to be heard at one of the society's "admirable concerts" and reminding the committee that he lived just around the corner, at Cité Bergère, no. 4.[58]

Habeneck's benefit was a resounding success from start to finish. Also on the program were Mlle Falcon in the premiere of Beethoven's *Ah! perfido* and Adolphe Nourrit introducing Parisian audiences to Schubert's *Erlkönig (Le Roi des aulnes).* He had sung *Die Nonne* (D. 208, as *La Religieuse*) earlier in the season, and Mlle Falcon would present *Gretchen am Spinnrade (Marguerite)* the next season. Berlioz records a full house and the turning away of five hundred people, with magnificent musical results despite ensemble problems in the Beethoven symphonic works—the "Pastoral," the finale of the Fifth, the scherzo of the Ninth. Curiously, he does not mention Chopin, and he did not go to the Liszt concert.[59] Nor is there any indication in the press or the minutes as to precisely why Habeneck would have been given a benefit that particular season.

Baillot, as we have noted, declined payment for his three solos on 29 March. By contrast, Brod, who was already a *sociétaire,* insisted on receiving a fee for his two appearances as oboe soloist. Brod was a self-absorbed, rather flamboyant musician, always ready with a new show-piece of his own composition: a waltz and a fantasy on Swiss airs that season, a fantasy *à l'espagnole,* with castanets, in the next. The committee pointedly noted that appearing as a soloist was a privilege, to be accepted as proof of one's "artistic devotion."[60]

High on the agenda for 1836 was to improve the caliber of the chorus. The singers themselves were unhappy, having petitioned formally with their desire "to have the sung portions earn as much success and reputation as the orchestra has long enjoyed." They needed more rehearsal time—this would mean a decided increase in *jetons*—to find and master an expanded repertoire of choice materials. The committee concurred that this could be done without modifying the statutes, deciding instead that "during the year, as often as possible, there will be choral *répétitions d'essai,* which M. Benoist, the society's accompanist, is charged to direct."[61] Compensation would be ½ *jeton* for each rehearsal. The petitioning singers came to the committee meeting of 27 May 1835 for a leisurely discussion of their detailed plans, which included rearranging their benches and maintaining custody of the music at their own risk and peril.[62] Habeneck agreed to attend the rehearsals and help choose the new repertoire; the delegation expressed their confidence in his support and their satisfaction with the new measures. They hoped to put them into practice immediately.

What went unspoken but understood was the general dissatisfaction with the chorusmaster. Since the foundation of the Société des Concerts, the chorus had been the responsibility of the Conservatoire's professor of ensemble singing, Kuhn; it was thought a natural extension of his duties, very much like the equally untenable situation where Réty had been expected to undertake the ticket sales. Kuhn had already been warned for repeated absence in 1835, when he pled over-commitment with his responsibilities for *Robin des bois* at the Théâtre Feydeau.[63] He would have noted both Habeneck's undertaking of the chorus rehearsals and the rapidly advancing career at the society of his talented accompanist, François Benoist, appointed to full membership in late 1834 and conspicuously welcomed—"a choice to be applauded, adding to our reputation, and certain to attract favorable notice of the administration"; Benoist was a Prix de Rome laureate, professor of organ at the Conservatoire, and *chef de chant* at the Opéra. Kuhn took these hints and stepped aside. In his letter of resignation of 3 May 1837 he wrote that he had wanted to help since the foundation; now he had reason to believe his work was no longer so construed. He agreed that the chorus left "something to be desired, if not in quality, at least in the variety of its repertoire."[64]

Within two weeks a new article 17 was drafted, establishing the post of *répétiteur du chant*. Benoist was its first incumbent. The 1837 season saw a satisfactory Ninth Symphony and the first public hearings of an excerpt from Cherubini's new Requiem for men's voices and orchestra, presented complete in 1838. In 1838 there is also reference to moving the tenor Moreau to the post of accompanist and having him lead unreimbursed chorus rehearsals that December from the portable organ.[65] The chorus was on the mend.

The chorus had also been the center of a controversy in the autumn of 1835, when the parish priest at the Church of St-Roch and the archbishop of Paris invited the Société des Concerts to present a mass for St. Cecilia's Day, 22 November, under royal patronage. Tulou pronounced himself strongly against a proposal that would ostracize a portion of the society, since women were forbidden in the chancel; when a counterproposal to use a boys choir passed comfortably, Tulou then proposed taking up a collection after the mass to distribute to the women who had been denied their fees. The archbishop, after meeting with Habeneck, vetoed this plan, and the St. Cecilia mass was abandoned at the last minute. Explanation was sent to the newspapers, and a letter to the king, signed by each committee member, presented abject apologies. The society held its ground in November 1836 when the matter came up again; although the proposal passed a vote of the general assembly, the margin was so narrow that they were unwilling to proceed.[66]

Habeneck, deprived of the presidency of the Société des Concerts since late 1833, grew bored with his administrative responsibilities and increasingly hostile toward his colleagues on the committee. He had come to have little contact with them during the week and almost none at all outside the concert season. In the fall of 1836 he failed to appear for the traditional discussions of the forthcoming season. By late November his absence had become critical, since there was no statutory provision for the committee to meet without a presiding officer. On 29 November the committee wrote Habeneck that with Cherubini's authorization they had met to begin planning for the season, "which has not, as you know, so far taken its ordinary course. And last Thursday, an audition of new student members, which you called, had to take place without you." [67] The committee would meet the following Thursday at 11:00 in Cherubini's office to confront the crisis, and Habeneck was enjoined to attend and present the reasons for his absence.

He replied, bluntly, that he was too busy with legitimate duties elsewhere to bother with administrative chores. Attaching, to everyone's astonishment, his resignation as vice president, he said he meant to retain only his function as conductor, which he promised to fulfill with his customary industry. Since the committee had forced the confrontation to begin with, it had no choice but to continue it. On 2 December all six elected members of the committee—Prosper Dérivis, secretary; Saint-Laurent, *archiviste-caissier;* Kilian, *commissaire du personnel;* Nargeot, *commissaire du matériel;* Seuriot, *agent comptable;* and Trévaux, *membre adjoint*—submitted their resignations to Cherubini *en masse.* Cherubini convoked an emergency Assemblée Générale for 4 December.[68]

This was attended, most unusually, by both Cherubini and Habeneck. Saint-Laurent, as senior member of the committee and almost surely the leading *provocateur,* read their letter of resignation aloud. The question was called as to whether to accept the resignation of the committee as a whole. Of 73 present, the six committee members abstained and all 67 others voted to decline the motion. Habeneck left the meeting. The committee, too, withdrew for a few moments, then returned to accept their mandate, but requiring a new clause in the statutes to allow it to carry on in the absence of its presiding officers: "In the case where both the president and the vice president find themselves unable to fulfill their duties, they will be replaced by the *membre adjoint."* A member rose to suggest that the secretary notify Habeneck of these results by letter, to which would be appended the customary transcript of the minutes. The secretary closed the mandated correspondence with the remark, "I thus acquit myself, sir, of that mission, but must observe that your decision not to participate in the committee's deliberations painfully surprised the society, which was in turn happy to learn that your absence was due only to your occupations elsewhere. Convinced of the merit of having its founding member participate in every detail of the administration, it hopes you will continue to sacrifice yourself, as you have done for nine years, on its behalf, and continue to fulfill your duty toward us."[69]

The committee and conductor somehow reached a wary truce in order to get on with their business. They concurred in insisting that no *sociétaire* participate in other public concerts without the express permission of the committee, posting a warning in the *foyer* that such engagements were "contrary to the best interests of the institution," then drafting an amendment to that effect. This measure, remarked the secretary, was meant to protect the "immense reputation and artistic independence of the Société des Concerts," so that it "might not be confused with enterprises that don't hesitate for a moment to prostitute noble and great music, and who mingle, pell-mell, the quadrilles of Musard with the symphonies of Beethoven."[70] In April 1837 the membership ratified an earlier decision to contribute 500 francs toward the Beethoven monument in Bonn, though whereas Habeneck had proposed a tax of ½ *jeton* on each *sociétaire* to pay for it, the members decided simply to bill it to the modest reserve fund they had accrued.[71] In May the officers brought the final language of their year's work to the floor of the closing Assemblée Générale and had the measures adopted into the statutes:

- Provision for the *répétiteur du chant*, who would be allowed to call the roll at chorus rehearsals (new article 17 and related clauses)
- Provision for mandatory *répétitions d'essai* during the interval between seasons, paid at ½ *jeton* (article 36*bis*)
- Interdiction of musicians from playing outside concerts during the season, except with express permission of the committee or conductor (article 39*bis*)

One of Habeneck's major frustrations was the inability of the Société des Concerts to find its way with regard to the modern French repertoire. Few of the essays of contemporary works—in January 1836 a symphony of Fessy, a year later the symphony Rousselot had written for them—had much promise; Girard's overture to *Antigone* was played only once, in 1836. The most fruitful cultivation in the early years was of George Onslow's symphonies, introduced in 1831 and 1833, with the First Symphony reprised in 1836, but Onslow's work—long-winded, and pale by comparison with that of the Viennese—had very few partisans. On the whole the three symphonies the orchestra premiered by the German composer Thomas Täglichsbeck (1836, 1837, 1840) attracted more interest. ("Good scholastic music," said Berlioz, however: "nothing more.") And there was too much focus on the display pieces for Habeneck's liking. (In an unusual incident surrounding one of these, a Thalberg fantasy on "Là ci darem la mano," the soloist Billet *aîné*, a student of Zimmermann, had to give up within a few bars owing to the tuning of the piano.) The major advances were in other repertoire, especially the excerpts from Gluck's *Iphigénie en Tauride, Armide,* and *Alceste.* Berlioz, naturally, gave the honors of the 1836 season to the "Scène des Scythes" from *Iphigénie.*[72]

It was clear that the trial readings needed to be doubled or tripled if there were to be any hope of finding good contemporary works to add to the repertoire, but equally clear that Habeneck could not himself bear the full brunt of the responsibility to identify them and rule on their merit. He needed insulating from external pressures, as well as broader participation from the musicians in the decision making. And he was in a potentially troublesome bind with regard to a proposed new symphony by J.-F. Turcas, Cherubini's son-in-law. ("It will be terrible," said Cherubini.)[73] Habeneck wanted to promote Turcas, but needed the ratification of his musicians.

Accordingly, Habeneck proposed that a commission of the players, perhaps twelve, be added to the committee with fully delegated authority to decide which new music was to be programmed. He drafted language that foresaw a vote after a single reading, attaching the specific condition that such a reading would not even be scheduled until finished parts had been presented to the committee. The *sociétaires* were in general sympathy with the plan but, finding the provision about the parts unworkable, amended it to the effect that the committee would "remember to discuss this matter" with each composer.

More significantly, many objected to the idea of deciding the fate of a work of art on a single hearing. It was decided to allow for a second hearing if that seemed warranted, the three votes of the commission then being whether to admit, reject, or proceed to a second hearing. So amended, Habeneck's proposal was adopted unanimously on 1 February 1838.[74]

The first experience with the new system came, as expected, with the symphony of Turcas. (Louise Farrenc was also invited to submit a work, but did not respond until two years later.) The reading took place on the morning of 1 April 1838, after which the orchestra retired to the *foyer* to elect its commission of 12. Adding the 6 votes of the committee brought the total to 18: when the results were counted, 8 favored performing Turcas's work, and 10 were opposed.[75]

This was an outcome Habeneck had not expected and would not accept. He felt obliged, he told the electors, to program the work, in appreciation for "the many services Turcas has rendered the art." At this point the jury of 12 withdrew to allow the committee to reach a solution. In a spirit of compromise it was agreed to schedule another reading of the second and third movements, after a rehearsal of the "Eroica" on 19 April; the secretary would explain the change in strategy to the players. The results of the subsequent vote, now cast by only the six elected committee members, were barely more favorable than before:

For programming the Andante only: 1 in favor, 5 opposed

For programming the minuet only: 5 in favor, 1 opposed

For programming both movements: 1 in favor, 5 opposed[76]

The minuet was thus presented on the concert of 22 April 1838, the last in the season. Habeneck tried once more in 1840 to get Turcas programmed, but to no avail.[77]

Habeneck now urged that the article adopted in February be rewritten to allow the possibility of presenting excerpts of works that had been denied programming in full, suggesting the four questions subsequently asked of every essayed work (see chapter 4, page 112). The end-of-year assembly adopted the new wording on 13 May 1838 after recommending that a reduced ensemble be used for certain readings. The final wording appears as article 33, "*Des Jurys pour l'admission des ouvrages nouveaux*," in the statutes of 1841.[78]

The Turcas case, contorted as it was, nevertheless demonstrated precisely why the system was needed and how valuable it could be. Having to play the minuet was a small price to pay for regularizing the approach. The system was followed more or less scrupulously from the moment of its adoption. Table 8 shows the results in the first year. (The tied vote on excerpts from Henri Reber's symphony was broken by the president in favor, and it was then decided to premiere the second and fourth movements. Circumstances to be encountered presently led to a more favorable outcome still.)[79]

It was apparently at Habeneck's own initiative that a reading of Wagner's *Columbus* overture was slipped into a pre-season rehearsal, almost certainly in December 1839. This was also, probably, the occasion Wagner was present for a rehearsal of Beethoven's Ninth—when, he says, the scales fell from his eyes. That would have been concurrent with Ber-

TABLE 8. *Répétitions d'essai*, 1838–39

Composer	Work	Date Essayed	Votes Cast		Date Played
			Oui	*Non*	
Deldevez	Symphony	2 Dec 1838	12	5	10 Mar 1839
Baudiot	Overture	[19 Jan 1839]	—	—	Canceled
Riegel	Chorus	19 Jan 1839	8	10	—
Riegel	Chorus, 2nd audition	19 Jan 1839	1	17	—
Elwart	*La Reine de Saba*	28 Feb 1839	15	2	26 Apr 1839
Baudiot	Overture	16 Mar 1839	4	12	—
Sauzay	Overture	16 Mar 1839	3	13	—
Reber	Symphony	16 Mar 1839	5	11	[23 Feb 1840]
Reber	Symphony, excerpts	16 Mar 1839	8	8	23 Feb 1840

SOURCE: Com. winter 1838–39: D 17345 (2).

lioz's first performances of *Roméo et Juliette* with essentially the same musicians. ("I felt myself a mere schoolboy beside Berlioz," Wagner recalled.)[80] The confluence of stimuli—Habeneck, Berlioz, the Ninth, and most of all the quality and force of the Paris players—represents a turning point in Wagner's conception of what an orchestra could do.

Extending the repertoire backward in chronology was rather easier. The *concert historique* had been around since Fétis, and music-historical inquiry was gaining its stride. The patrons were as curious about Bach and Handel—and Schubert—as they were concerning Egyptian antiquities and the excavations at Pompeii. This interest was not lost on Habeneck, who in late 1838 asked the committee to develop a program of "old" music for chorus and orchestra, perhaps with historical details provided in program notes. The idea of annotated programs was seized immediately, with notes added for the premieres of a Handel *Jubilate* and excerpts from an oratorio by Ferdinand Ries, *Le Triomphe de la foi,* at the first concert of the new season, 13 January 1839. In mid-January, the society agreed to appear, exceptionally, in a *séance de musique ancienne* organized by Joseph Mainzer (founder of the *Chronique musicale*) with the participation of Baillot. Mainzer introduced each work—Janequin's *Bataille de Marignan,* a Clari duo, scenes from *Orlando* and *Acis and Galatea* of Handel, a Palestrina madrigal, and a movement from one of the Bach violin concertos—with an oral *notice historique.*[81] These experiences almost surely shaped the first program of 1840 as well, which included an aria from one of the Bach passions, Habeneck playing the

Andante of a Bach concerto, and works of Marcello and Rameau. The Jannequin, Clari, and Palestrina facilitated the resurgence of the chorus; the parts stayed in the library, and all three works entered into the standard repertoire of the Société des Concerts.

Habeneck's deep involvement in the repertoire of those seasons is one of several strong indications that he had regained his "customary zeal." In December 1838 he summoned the committee to discuss what would become its overriding goal in the decades to come: recognition as the official orchestra of the state. He was optimistic, he said, that the state was on the verge of granting a permanent subvention in exchange for an agreement whereby the society might be called upon by the nation to provide music for *fêtes et cérémonies publiques.* The results of this particular initiative are not clear, though there was talk of an official contract throughout the next year; in effect, the discussions themselves established a firm course.[82]

In the spring of 1838 Meifred and Kilian had written to propose the introduction of an emergency fund, the Caisse de Secours et de Prévoyance. Their draft was enthusiastically received, with its original concept of funding one-time grants to those in distress expanded to include an invested retirement account for each member. The strategy and interim language was developed at a series of meetings in May and June 1838, where the membership agreed to have 20 francs per *sociétaire* deducted from the season's proceeds to establish the fund, and to the deduction thereafter of an annual premium. The first governing committee was elected: Kilian as secretary, Meifred as *agent comptable,* and Alexis Dupont as treasurer.[83]

The new Caisse de Prévoyance was garnished with *jetons* collected in fines, gifts and bequests, and the proceeds from one concert annually designated as a benefit. In 1838 the government subvention was late to arrive, so in order to close the books the committee directed these 2,000 francs to the new account as well. Funds not claimed either by guest soloists—Mme Viardot, for one, never collected her fees—or by heirs of the deceased would revert to the Caisse. The possibility of a windfall to the fund was behind the dubious decision of the 1846 committee to take 500 francs' worth of tickets to a lottery sponsored by the Association des Artistes-Musiciens, the collective devoted principally to assuring working musicians a comfortable retirement; the members of the Société des Concerts overwhelmingly opposed this form of speculation (22 favoring, 44 against), approving instead a simple gift to the benevolent society in the same amount. The fund was placed originally in a low-risk government account; in 1872, after other investment schemes had been put to work, the Caisse de Prévoyance generated some 10,500 francs in interest. Members' shares were recorded in their passbooks *(livrets)*, and their holdings would be paid out at retirement, or to their heirs, in the form of coupons redeemable at the current market value.[84]

The first payment from the new fund was made in April 1839 to the widow Brod in the amount of 300 francs.[85] Brod, the principal oboist, had died suddenly on the morning of 6 April 1839, the first active member to succumb during the session. The committee, meeting urgently, summoned the membership to his *convoi* the following Monday at 8:00 A.M. and assumed responsibility for the music, then sent a commission of the oboists Vogt and Veny and the bassoonist Barizel off to confirm the funeral arrangements with a priest. In May the committee presented a new statute to the Assemblée Générale calling for mandatory attendance of the *sociétaires* at funerals of their colleagues and the provision of appropriate music. Habeneck asked if they seriously meant to offer music at every musician's funeral, and given the melancholy circumstance the unanimous response—for the moment—was in the affirmative.[86]

Brod's sudden death brought several questions to the fore. One was the immediate question of closing the accounts of deceased members; shortly three widows, including Mme Brod, were reimbursed their late husbands' holdings.[87] Another was how to evaluate calls on the emergency fund. The trombonist Jules Barbier—the same Barbier who had been censured for showing up drunk in 1838—begged succor for his wife with the unlikely story that she was about to have the big toe of her right foot amputated. The commissioners agreed to pay her medical debts up to 300 francs directly to a physician; in no case would they be given to her husband. A deputation sent to verify her condition found it *"très déplorable,"* and she did not survive; Barbier was eventually given 100 francs plus what was left of the allocation to his wife.[88] Further, there was general concern for the health of other key wind players, "any one of them as important as an entire section of strings"; Vogt, fifty-eight, and Meifred, forty-eight, were both suffering from prolonged illness.[89]

Finally there was the question of how the retirement fund might treat members who left the society either before accruing the required five years of service or before the first five-year vesting delay was done in the spring of 1843. Kilian, a founding member who retired in 1841, was not reimbursed until 1843, and even then somewhat reluctantly. The tenor Mocker, resigning in 1843, insisted that he had five years' service by counting his first tenure of 1830–32, thus prompting the committee to add the word "consecutive" to the guidelines. The tenor Charpentier was the first *sociétaire* to be retired by committee decision before completing five years of service. In his case, benevolence seemed the correct course of action: "Barring serious infractions of the rules, it was unfair to deprive an artist who had suffered the bad luck of losing his talent or his voice, of the funds that he had legitimately acquired, no matter how long his service." He was returned his full investment and interest.[90]

Probably the most valuable introductions during this era were not of new music but of personalities. In March 1839, the young César Franck appeared as soloist in a Hummel Fantasy in E♭ for piano and orchestra, after his father had approached the committee suggesting a concerto by Moscheles.[91] Henri Vieuxtemps performed one of his own concertos in 1841; later in the season Léopold de Meyer played his piano solo arrangements of "Casta diva" and the *Freischütz* overture. Mme Viardot's first appearance with the Société des Concerts in February 1841 contributed to the growing enthusiasm for Handel—excerpts from *Judas Maccabaeus* were being programmed as fast as they could be learned —with arias from *Rinaldo* and *Scipione* alternating with choruses from *Samson* and *Alexander's Feast;* she concluded her appearance with an aria from *Così fan tutte*. In 1842 she was featured in three concerts, offering her already famous scenes from Gluck's *Orphée,* an aria from *Cenerentola,* the soprano solos in Mozart's cantata *Davidde penitente* and the Pergolesi *Stabat mater,* and arias from Weber's *Oberon* and *Euryanthe*. When the grateful committee asked her to accept the title *sociétaire solo,* she accepted with her customary grace and assurances of her best intentions to reserve herself for the Société des Concerts; she indeed appeared again in March 1843. But through shoddy bookkeeping Mme Viardot was never entered into the registers—nor were Habeneck's nominations of the tenor Gustave Roger and the bass Hermann-Léon in December 1844.[92]

In January 1840 there arrived a letter from the government announcing that the intendant, ceding to orders from a higher authority—the words *"ordre élevé"* are underlined—had granted the Salle des Concerts to the young composer Henri Reber for a Sunday afternoon program of his works on 19 January, just a week after the opening of the season. The committee returned a sharp note of protest to Montalivet, suggesting that the Société des Concerts would cease to function if its hegemony during the season were so threatened. But before the situation could get out of control, Reber wrote in highly conciliatory language offering to change any conflicting rehearsals and asking respectfully if there were any possibility of releasing some of their players for his concerts.

Impressed by the polite terms of his request, they agreed to "suspend their work"—that is, cancel two standing rehearsals—to free the hall during the week in question. "With every possible regret," however, they found it necessary to hew firmly to the rules, and "with the greatest rigor" would refuse to authorize the participation of the *sociétaires*. Reber wisely renounced his plans, and the committee, appreciating the "delicacy" of this gesture and "in recompense for his voluntary sacrifice," agreed to add his symphony to their own program for 23 February. It was an unusually satisfactory ending for this sort of confrontation; the orchestra already had two movements of the work in rehearsal, their association with Reber went on to be warm and mutually profitable, and the precedent could be expected "to paralyze the effect of the hall's concession to others."[93]

Louise Farrenc at last responded to the committee's invitation of 1838, proposing her new overture in a letter received on 10 February 1840. The reading was scheduled for the very next rehearsal, on 13 February, and the work was successfully introduced on 5 April;[94] in 1849 her symphony would be premiered, somewhat reluctantly, by Girard. Farrenc's overture was the last significant work by a younger composer to enter the repertoire for some time. No new work at all was presented in 1841, and the readings were suspended for 1842.

The river Seine flooded in the early autumn of 1840, leaving many hundreds homeless and the threat of a new outbreak of cholera. In November Habeneck invited his forces to offer a benefit for the victims, a proposal that gained unanimous consent from both the committee and the assembly. Admission prices were raised for a non-subscription concert on 20 December 1840: favorites from lyric repertoire sung by the reigning stars, a popular Duo Concertante by Charles Dancla for the composer and his brother Léopold, Méhul's *Jeune Henri* overture with the sixteen horns, and Beethoven's Fourth Symphony. The house was full, generating the not inconsiderable sum of 3,896.50 francs forwarded to a government bank account. The degree of the public and financial success encouraged the society to accept the responsibility for other benefits, where it became the practice to double the ticket prices in order to increase the proceeds paid to the beneficiary.

Three years of experience with the Caisse de Prévoyance convinced the committee to seek professional legal counsel, in part out of simple concern for the security of a growing sum—and for their personal liabilities—and in part because a Société des Artistes-Dramatiques had invested its pension fund with positive result. For so conservative an organization as the Société des Concerts the idea of speculative investment was a significant departure from prevailing financial practice, and it was strongly opposed by two of the three governors of the fund, Kilian and Meifred—both of whom resigned their duties before it was over. Nevertheless the notary who had designed the theater fund, Mc Bonnaire, was consulted. He recommended a considerably more formal version of the standing statutes and an entirely new second part devoted to the Caisse alone.

A commission of four senior members—Cuvillon, Leborne, Plantade, and Seuriot—joined the three governors of the pension fund to confer with the *notaire* and his associates in drafting the new code, suddenly razor-honed in its precision and thick with legalisms. Ten conferences later the authors presented it to an Assemblée Générale *extraordinaire* called to vote the measures. Bonnaire summarized the work of the commission, and the secretary quite probably read all eighty-four articles aloud. Toward the end came the investment plan, envisaging a portfolio of treasury bonds and bonds on the Mont de Piété (the government pawn shop), a commercial bank, and a savings bank. (In 1845, there were 48,000 francs in these accounts: 42,000 francs in 5 percent bonds and 6,000 in the savings bank.)[95] Discussion focused on the known problem of outgoing members with less than five years' service, with an understanding reached where existing members could choose to belong or not according to their own best interest. The new statutes then passed handily, with Meifred vigorously opposed. The members were invited to go to the notary's office at their early convenience to sign the *acte sociale* and pay their first *cotisation* of 20 francs. This task they accomplished between 27 October and 26 December 1841. The new statutes were registered on 31 December 1841.[96]

A new *livret* with the statutes published at the front—the better that "each member can study his rights and duties"—was prepared for every *sociétaire*, a task that took the better part of the following year.[97] We owe the preservation of the hitherto unpublished 1841 statutes to a single *livret*, Habeneck's, now preserved with his personal papers. It is a precious document in its detailed description of how the Société des Concerts functioned for the rest of the nineteenth century, and without it, countless references to article numbers elsewhere in the written record would be impossible to follow.

Like every other structural change, the new statutes brought some members temporary hardship. For one thing, many of the *sociétaires fondateurs* would retire before there was a substantial return on the investment. For quite some time there were *sociétaires* with and without coverage, and for a couple of years every change of employment status seemed to pose a new problem to be resolved. But for most members the new arrangements meant a major step forward in their social welfare—in "the security of their pecuniary interest."[98] And, as a fine by-product of the exercise, the services of Mc Bonnaire were retained, and he was given a medallion engraved *"Mr Bonnaire, notaire de la Société des Concerts."* He steered the society through its legal encounters—and enjoyed his free admission to the concerts—for twenty-five years.

On at least one of his several visits to Paris between 1839 and 1841, Anton Schindler—Beethoven's former secretary—was the society's guest (and was also present at one of the first performances of Berlioz's *Roméo et Juliette* in late 1839). In token of thanks, Schindler offered his hosts the privilege of copying the portrait of Beethoven that hung in his apartment. By 1841 Henri Grévedon had reproduced the work on stone, and the lithographer Lemercier printed copies on fine *papier de chine* for each *sociétaire* as a sort of "certificate of membership," it was said, in the hallowed organization. Copies were sent to each *sociétaire fondateur*, to the artist and lithographer, and, handsomely framed, to Schindler himself. A certain M. Pierret, who engraved the legend, was given for his efforts a complimentary subscription to the 1842 and 1843 concerts. Several dozen copies were kept to offer future *sociétaires* upon their election. The stone itself became the property of the Société des Concerts, so as to prevent circulation of the precious artifacts beyond the immediate membership.[99]

The fifteenth session, 1842, began with Habeneck in a combative frame of mind. He subjected the members to the indignity of a formal reading of article 38, forbidding *sociétaires* from appearing in public concerts during the session without express written consent of the committee; then he fought such senior members as Alard, Chevillard, both Tilmant brothers, Franchomme, Dorus, and Veny when they applied for permission to appear elsewhere, typically as concerto soloists. He insisted the committee follow a strict interpretation of the statute in considering leaves. Members meanwhile contested the definition of a public concert; having to apply for authorization to appear in one's daughter's recital—as two members felt obliged to do—seemed a study in folly. It was in this context that the committee regretfully and quite tactfully refused Berlioz's request of November 1844 for musicians to play in the impressive series of concerts he was planning for the Cirque Olympique on alternate Sundays from the Société des Concerts, but nevertheless during the season. The committee observed that for some years it had bent the rules in order to accommodate Berlioz, but this time was forced to say no. The minutes note that this was a particularly difficult letter to compose.[100]

Habeneck was also vexed by the "useless" National Guard band drills that conflicted with his Friday and Saturday morning rehearsals. The woodwind players were showing up at the end of the rehearsal and claiming their full *jetons;* the brass had begun to skip Saturday mornings altogether. He convened and scolded the band directors who were members of the society, though they eventually reached an agreement whereby the bandsmen were excused from early Saturday morning duty in exchange for Habeneck's promise to begin his rehearsals no later than 9:00 A.M.[101]

Habeneck repeatedly advocated the unpopular concept of a mandatory retirement age of fifty-five for the players and fifty for the singers. He began to levy fines on faithful servants of the society whose transgressions had been traditionally overlooked—notably, in April 1842, Alexandre Laty, who was often retained by duties at the Conservatoire post. The committee was guardedly sympathetic to the argument that Laty could not be two places at once, and refunded the fines for his tardies. But Laty was the next in the long list of overworked artists who could no longer meet the expectations of a *sociétaire;* in December 1843, he resigned in pique, later apologized so as to be named *membre honoraire,* and from time to time thereafter was convoked as an emergency accompanist.[102]

Habeneck's position in the bizarre discussion of the status of women members, which took center stage in 1842–43, seems somewhat equivocal. The confrontation appears to have been engaged by the husband-and-wife pair, M. and Mme de Garaudé: she, a soprano, insisting on election to full membership, and her husband threatening to quit his appointment as accompanist if she was not. (His resignation was eventually accepted, though he returned as a *sociétaire* and chorusmaster briefly in the 1850s.) On the face of it, the excuse offered her—that women would have "difficulty taking part in the debates of the committee and the other duties imposed on each active member of the society"—seems preposterous. The better women recruits, notably Mme Sainte-Foy, were already disinclined to accept appointment as permanent *aspirantes.* The solution to the problems of *femmes sociétaires* was apparently Habeneck's: a new title, *sociétaire adjoint,* at full pay, to which the senior women were now regularly elected (Mme Sainte-Foy, Mlle Laure Henry, Mme Jourdan *née* Mercier, Mme Meyer *née* Picard, and Mme Petit, who retained the name Mlle Grimm). Habeneck wanted ten positions for the women members; the committee approved eight. Yet he seems to have concurred in the strong—to modern eyes blatantly offensive—language of the new statute adopted in May 1843: "Women may not be made active members of the society: they take the title *sociétaires adjoints,* in which capacity they are entitled to the same *jeton* as the active members, though without ever being called to become involved in any manner with the administrative operation of the society; nor can they be vested in the Caisse de Prévoyance. Their number will be eight." [103]

And there was a curious stagnation of the repertoire. In December 1841 and January 1842 Habeneck and the committee discussed his imaginative list: Mendelssohn's *Paulus* for the first concert, an aria from Salieri's *Last Judgment* with Alexis Dupont, and for the fourth concert a full program of excerpts from *The Marriage of Figaro* with a superb cast—Alizard as the Count, Paul Barroilhet as Figaro, Dupont as Basilio; Ferdinand Prévost as Bartolo, Mlle Nau as Susanna, Mme Flamment as the Countess, Mlle Rouvroy as Cherubino, and Mme Widemann as Marcellina. None of these came to pass, though *Fingal's Cave* and an excerpt from *The Magic Flute* were heard. Then it was suddenly ruled, without further explanation, that there would be no "new music" for the season. [104]

Cherubini's death on 15 March 1842 would, as Meifred noted in his *rapport moral* of 1844, have been perilous to an institution less well established than the Société des Concerts. Instead, no administrative or artistic duty went undone as Habeneck moved in with almost unseemly speed to preside. There was no memorial concert, despite the fact that Cherubini's second Requiem was already in the repertoire— and intended by the composer himself to serve that purpose. Instead, two short selections from other works by Cherubini were hastily added to the program already schedule for Sunday, 3 April 1842. Vogt and Mc Bonnaire were assigned to organize a subscription drive for a monument, seeded with 1,000 francs from the current-year budget. [105] Plantade promoted the idea of a second commemorative medal bearing the likeness of their "*grand patron* and illustrious founding executive," but this initiative died for lack of attention. Not until December 1861, at the invitation of the Italians erecting a monumental tomb in Florence, was there a commemorative event.

The uninterrupted routine of the Société des Concerts in 1842 masks a considerable turning point, for the matter of Cherubini's succession as president was by no means predestined. The ministry, and probably the committee, expected the election of Auber, his successor at the Conservatoire. Meanwhile a strong and vocal contingent, the majority as it turned out, favored Habeneck. Five nominees for the post of president reached the Assemblée Générale of 1 May 1842: Habeneck, Auber, Vogt, Zimmermann, and Trévaux. Habeneck, presiding, thanked the membership for this new proof of their affection but discouraged his candidacy and announced that he would not accept the presidency even if elected. It was noted that the election of a president was a *cas grave,* thus requiring a two-thirds majority to elect: some 44 votes. A heart-stopping four ballots ensued:

	1st	2d	3d	4th
Auber	30	37	36	50
Habeneck	39	27	28	13
Vogt	1			

Between the second and third ballots an argument erupted as to the propriety of requiring a two-thirds majority; between the third and fourth, after "forceful" but "most honorable" wrangling during which Habeneck reiterated his intent to decline the presidency, it was agreed to accept a simply majority, with the dissent noted in the record. A week later the outgoing and incoming committees called jointly on Auber to announce, officially, his election as president of the Société des Concerts. The tradition that the society's president and the director of the Conservatoire were one and the same was thus established. And Auber quickly became popular with the *sociétaires,* who were pleased to see on their rostrum "a personality who carries, and has long carried, the flag of the French school." [106]

There were significant mutations elsewhere in the ranks. Antoine Henry, founding principal bassoonist and father of the sopranos Laure and Clarissa Henry, died on 29 March 1842 after a brief illness; the members were called to his *cortège* and funeral at 8:30 A.M. on 31 March. [107]

Dacosta, the founding principal clarinetist, retired and was replaced by Klosé and Buteux. Vogt, too, retired at the end of the season, pleading ill health at the age of sixty-one. He continued to accept administrative assignments until his death nearly three decades later, at the age of eighty-nine.

Habeneck's true feelings at losing the presidency to Auber are a little less easy to deduce. His decline can certainly be traced to the beginning of the next season. On 5 October 1842 the committee received his unexpected letter of resignation, owing, he said, to his poor health and over-extension at the Conservatoire. The secretary, Henry Deshayes, hurried to call on Auber with the news; the committee was assembled at 3:00 the next day, with the venerable Meifred invited to lend counsel; and by 4:00 everyone was in Auber's office, successfully convincing Habeneck to withdraw his resignation.

But on 29 January 1843 the concertmaster, Tilmant, was called to conduct when Habeneck pleaded "indisposition," an exceptional event in the society's history thus far. In December Habeneck told the committee that his state of his health would be "compromised by the fatigue of rehearsing new works during the session," asking that Tilmant be allowed to conduct the *répétitions d'essai* while he listened.[108] He begged them to limit the programs to "composers of the rank of Haydn, Mozart, and Beethoven." In late February 1844 Habeneck sustained an unspecified accident in which he broke both his arms and was in consequence gravely ill—as much psychologically, it was noted, as physically. Tilmant conducted again on 25 February 1844 and for the rest of that season; he began to attend committee meetings from 13 March.

The committee met at Habeneck's bedside through the end of April, attending to his detailed instructions. The secretary later noted that Habeneck "did not cease for a single minute to preside over the committee, enlightening it with the advice of his high reason and long experience."[109] It was agreed that an anecdote would be placed in the minutes, in consideration of the committee's esteem for Tilmant and his work: "Arriving by the sickbed to present his best and most sincere wishes, Tilmant said several words, to which M. Habeneck responded, 'I have two broken arms, but since I still have you, I haven't lost my right arm.'"[110] In his year-end oration on 12 May 1844, the secretary's references to Habeneck's devotion, to the "talent and intelligence" with which M. Tilmant *aîné* had performed his duties, and to Auber's committed support were vigorously applauded.[111]

For Tilmant these emergencies represented something of a *retour à la vie* at the Société des Concerts. He had been dilatory in his attendance owing to his duties as chief conductor at the Théâtre-Italien and his frequent engagements as violin soloist, and he had been elected *commissaire du personnel* but failed to serve. Now he had regained the confidence of the *sociétaires* and not a few cries of *bis!* from the public. And for all intents and purposes the great Habeneck had designated him as his successor.

Habeneck's own circumstance did nothing to lessen his advocacy of a mandatory retirement age for a membership now so obviously aging. The committee discussed two specific options in December 1842. The first — envisaging a commission of nine, none of whom had reached their forty-ninth birthday, to decide whether those over fifty would continue for two more years — had been rejected by a vote of 2 favoring and 5 opposed. The second was proposed to the full membership in May 1843:

> After the distribution of honoraria each year, the singers and wind players who have reached the age of fifty, and the other instrumentalists at fifty-five, will cease to be members of the Société. The secretary will identify these *sociétaires* in his annual report, and a new general assembly, meeting a week later, will decide by ballot, and without discussion (1) which of these artists should be retired, and (2) which of them might continue their service. This decision would apply for a year and could be renewed. This article is not applicable to members of the committee until they have completed their mandate.[112]

The updating of the statutes that spring thus unraveled into a marathon conflict, requiring five assemblies (6, 13, 21, and 27 May; 30 October 1843) to bring under control.[113] The violinist Claudel began the fray by presenting a "long and very tedious" counter-measure urging that retirement decisions be made by an independent commission of the musicians; Meifred, reading from a prepared text, responded at similar length and more convincingly that deciding on retirements was, and always had been, the committee's business. Meifred's position, supported by a resolution Seuriot composed on the spot, began to take sway, and the draft language prepared in committee was defeated by a large majority. The assembly then adjourned for a week to study the Meifred-Seuriot text and because Habeneck, author of the original, had left the meeting. They had failed to elect officers.

On 21 May Habeneck urged his position once again, and a secret ballot was called; again it was rejected, 4 favoring the original proposal and 63 opposed.[114] Habeneck shouted his inalterable opposition to leaving retirement decisions to the committee; Cuvillon tried to read a prepared statement supporting the committee's statutory rights but could not be heard "through the hubbub." In the general disarray the Meifred-Seuriot text was called and defeated with 27 ayes, 41 nays, and 2 disqualifications.

By this time no one was certain where the membership stood on the basic question of mandatory retirement. It was proposed to direct the committee to return a new resolution once the membership had voted a basic stance. The results were dramatic: on the first ballot, 33 voted in favor of mandatory retirement, 21 were opposed, and 12 abstained, leaving no majority. On the second vote was a tie, 33 to 33. Habeneck voted "aye," and the principle of mandatory retirement seemed at last adopted.[115] The officers could finally be elected.

On 27 May 1843 the members returned to lend precision to the votes taken in confusion the week before. Cuvillon was asked to repeat his statement but replied that he lacked "sufficient lung power to overcome the interruptions" and refused to speak. Meifred rose to observe that the brouhaha of the last meeting, while reprehensible, might be excused in view of the fact that the Société as a whole had too little experience in debate; now the members needed to give their full attention to developing their ideas, since everyone had come to understand the gravity of the subject. The issue was ruled *grave* by a vote of 38 favoring, 35 opposed. Now the question of mandatory retirement would be put yet again, this time requiring passage by two-thirds majority, reckoned to be 48 votes. The secretary reported 43 white marbles and 30 black ones deposited in the urn, such that further resolutions were deemed useless. Once again, the specifics of a mandatory retirement plan failed to pass.[116]

The *répétitions d'essai* of January and February 1843—works of Chélard, Deldevez, Elwart, and Farrenc—found nothing for immediate addition to the repertoire.[117] Enthusiasm for Mendelssohn's music, however, began to gather full steam. *Fingal's Cave,* first performed in 1842, came to rival the Weber overtures in frequency of programming. A Mendelssohn symphony led off the next three seasons: the "first" (probably the "Italian," No. 4, but possibly the "Reformation," No. 5) in 1843, a "new symphony" (the Third, "Scottish," in A minor) in 1844, and another in 1845; for the "new" symphony Mendelssohn was sent the society's medal cast in gold.[118] Habeneck and his players were especially pleased to establish relationships with living German composers, counting Mendelssohn alongside Schwenke and Friedrich Schneider, "the dean of German composers," on their list of special friends. Music, they believed, overcame "*malentendus* of nationality," and they were proud "to raise their banner over every great and noble work without regard for its national origin."[119] The affiliations with Schwenke and Schneider went back to 1838, when sacred music of each had been performed. One of Schwenke's symphonies was played in both 1843 and 1844, and in the same period Schneider sent the handsome manuscript of a symphony he had written, headed as follows:

Sinfonie
dédiée à la Société des Concerts du Conservatoire Royal de Musique à Paris
par Frédéric Schneider,
Maître de Chapelle de S.A.R. le Duc régnant d'Anhalt-Dessau[120]

Both composers were sent effusive letters and the society's medal, but there is no evidence the Schneider was ever performed.[121]

Mendelssohn was soon, by a wide margin, the favorite living composer of the Société des Concerts and its public. The musicians were stricken at the news of his death in early November 1847, which reached them late in the month. They stopped to draft a letter of condolence to the widow Mendelssohn and her family, taking such care to perfect its language that it was not ready for signing and dispatch until 28 December. They went on to dedicate the opening concert of the 1848 season to his memory: the "Scottish" symphony, the excerpts from *Paulus* that had long attracted Habeneck, *Fingal's Cave,* and what appears to have been the first Paris performance of the Violin Concerto, played by Delphin Alard. He used a Stradivarius violin inherited from his father-in-law, the celebrated violin maker Vuillaume.

The opening of the 1846 season was marked by a confrontation with César Franck's aggressive father, who had managed to reserve the Salle des Concerts for a concert by his son on 4 January 1846, and by a command on 3 January from the foreign minister Guizot for a concert three days later. Concerning the first problem, the officers argued unsuccessfully to the authorities of their society's sole right to the room, then purposefully scheduled a rehearsal for 4 January, suggesting that Franck take 21 or 28 December. When Franck *père* responded that rescheduling was impossible at that late date, the committee countered by denying Tilmant authorization to conduct and forbidding five musicians (Tilmant *jeune,* Klosé, Michiels, Chevillard, and Maussant) permission to appear.[122] For the concert at the Ministry of Foreign Affairs, a program of their signature pieces was quickly arranged: movements from Beethoven's Seventh and the Septet, the *Oberon* overture, and their standard rousing vocal works: excerpts from *Moïse, Armide, The Creation*, and "Chantons victoire" from *Judas Maccabaeus*. Guizot's honorarium, when finally it arrived, was an insulting pittance, "unworthy" of the Société des Concerts. Unable to decide, however, how much the concert was worth, the committee declined payment altogether, settling the account for true expenses alone.[123]

For the sixth year running, Habeneck took no interest in the *répétitions d'essai* before the 1847 season. The committee went about its work without guidance from him, declining works of Elwart, Mathieu, Sowinski, and Zimmermann on the grounds that "the society cannot come to the aid of works not certain of success."[124] Onslow's newest symphony was scheduled without a preliminary reading.

Habeneck's interest appeared to be limited to introducing Beethoven's *Les Ruines d'Athènes* in the French setting of Maurice Bourges. He had urged appointment of a resident *homme de lettres* since 1839; now Bourges was named the society's *poète-traducteur*, to whom they might regularly turn to "translate into our language works written in foreign tongues" in exchange for admission not only to performances but also, for purposes of study, to any rehearsal where one of his texts was being sung.[125] Meanwhile the committee wanted to return Beethoven's Ninth to the repertoire and publicly billed it for 14 March 1847; but the chorus was not ready, and it was necessary to program the Seventh Symphony and the *Euryanthe* overture intead.[126]

More embarrassing still was the case of Halévy's new *Prométhée enchaîné*, written for the Société and on which the musicians had been working for some time. It had attracted the keen attention of the press. Originally scheduled for 11 April, it was delayed for a week, then postponed with the composer's consent until the next season. A note was left in the minutes: "The committee of the Société des Concerts, not finding that the study of M. Halévy's scene *(Prométhée)* has been completed, and thinking that the full rehearsal which took place that morning [Wednesday, 14 April 1847] was not satisfactory enough to hope for a good performance of this work, felt it necessary to have an emergency meeting. After having conferred with M. Halévy and expressed to him its fears, it was decided, *unanimously*, that in order not to compromise the success of this work and the reputation of the Société des Concerts, there was reason to postpone the performance until the next season."[127] Halévy's scene was eventually premiered by Habeneck's successor, Narcisse Girard, on 18 March 1849.

Violence erupted in the streets of Paris in the week following the fourth Sunday concert (20 February 1848). On the 24 February Louis-Philippe abdicated, and on 26 February the Second Republic was constituted. By the committee meeting of 29 February the theaters had been closed and public gatherings forbidden; the Salle des Concerts had been "sequestered." The society slipped past the interdictions by billing their fifth concert as a *concert extraordinaire* to benefit the wounded. The program was as overtly political as anything the orchestra had ever done: the *Marseillaise* to start; "Affranchissons notre patrie" from *Euryanthe;* and their popular standby, "Chantons victoire"—the march and chorus from *Judas Maccabaeus.* There were dilemmas at every turn: whom to ask to authorize the hall, how to secure leave for the members of the Garde Nationale called to active duty, which officials to invite to the royal box. The profit of 1,840.80 francs was mediocre; by contrast, a benefit for flood victims in November 1846 had brought 8,000 francs. There was nowhere to deposit the money, which was eventually left in the hands of the mayor of the IIᵉ Arrondissement. And in a wonderful reversal of the usual roles, the committee had to remind Mantou, the collector of the *droit des pauvres,* to come do his duty. It was impossible to schedule the *concerts spirituels,* which were abandoned altogether. This lowered the income for the year, but by season's end the secretary was predicting that the worst was over and that the society would easily regain its customary privileges. Congratulations were sent especially to Tilmant, who had conducted at least two and possibly several other concerts in 1848.[128]

Habeneck did not attend the Assemblée Générale closing the session, on 7 May 1848. His formerly robust constitution had declined dramatically since 1842; he had retired from the Opéra in 1846. Probably he was suffering cerebral accidents; eventually he lost the use of his arms and legs, and his reason was affected as well. The political events of February 1848 appear to have confused him and left the orchestra rudderless in a time of crisis, in stark contrast to the way George-Hainl would steer it through the agonies of 1870 and Münch through World War II. Increasingly Habeneck was to be found in his country house at Chatou, near St-Germain-en-Laye. His closest friend among the musicians and a frequent companion in last years was the flutist Tulou, with whom he enjoyed hunting until he was no longer able. He would talk aimlessly about the past, said Tulou, and of a future in which he knew he would have little part; the privation of physical powers caused him "intense anguish."[129] His colleagues at the Société des Concerts had already begun to search for some gentle way of removing him from the podium, to assure the power of the institution over even the most august of its members.

Habeneck reported that he was still *en voyage* in August 1848, when the new committee returned to address the manner in which he would be removed. Charles Saint-Laurent, the old *archiviste-caissier*—as old as Habeneck, and also in declining health—had tried to signal the turning point in May 1845 when he first proposed a statute making it possible to elect a *président d'honneur;* it seems likely that this idea gained a certain momentum when Habeneck was ill in November 1845 and may have been discussed with him at one of the meetings the committee held in his home. The committee for 1848–49, strategically put in place by nominations from the outgoing members, included three of the strongest administrators the Société des Concerts had ever had: Meifred as secretary, Saint-Laurent as *archiviste-caissier,* and Trévaux as *membre adjoint.* Thus constituted, the committee arranged for the necessary twelve *sociétaires* to submit a petition for action, received and approved on 2 September, and called an Assemblée Générale *extraordinaire* for 7 September 1848 to ratify the simple amendment: "The Société, in witness of its great esteem and consideration, may accord the title *président d'honneur à vie* to those of its members who retire after at least twenty years of service." [130]

Auber presided; neither Habeneck nor Saint-Laurent attended. Immediately after the formal reading, a member asked for the meeting to be suspended for fifteen minutes so that the musicians could discuss the situation. They returned understanding that they were about to retire their conductor, and Seuriot proposed to amend the language to that effect: "to a *chef d'orchestre* who retires . . ." Elder members, including Tulou, objected to passing the measure behind Habeneck's back, and others wondered who would take him their decision. On the third reading, "each phrase was considered, each word weighed," and at the end there were no modifications proposed. Adding to the record that "the society appreciates the motives behind the proposition addressed to the committee," the members voted passage, 60 favoring and 3 opposed.[131] On the 10 September a letter accompanying a transcript of the minutes was signed by each member, and the next day, assembled in Auber's office at noon, the committee received Habeneck's written resignation.

One paragraph of Habeneck's angry letter accused members of the previous two administrations of disloyalty and a conspiracy to unseat him. For the moment that was ignored as the committee hurried to compose their first-ever agenda for the election of a new conductor. It was likely to be agonizing, since Tilmant, Habeneck's hand-picked successor, had serious competition from Girard, and there would need to be face-saving strategies for the loser. Nor, in view of experiences just past, did the officers want to go forward without a formally elected second conductor—a provision Tilmant himself had been urging since 1843.[132] They called the assembly for 18 October and published a deceptively simple agenda: "(1) election of a 2e *chef;* (2) nomination of a 1er *chef;* (3) election of a *président d'honneur à vie.*"[133]

But at the committee meeting two days before the general assembly, Meifred returned to Habeneck's "incriminating" language. It seemed to him that for the dignity of the orchestra's governance, and so as not to enfeeble its authority, the members cited by Habeneck—himself, Saint-Laurent, Claudel, and Benoist—should tender their resignations. A new agenda was prepared with that in mind. It was agreed, too, that after the election of an honorary life-president, the *archiviste-caissier* would propose according him a 1re *loge* in perpetuity.[134]

Virtually all the *sociétaires* were present for the Assemblée Générale at 8:00 A.M. on 18 October 1848, chaired by Auber. Habeneck's letter was read aloud, with the observation that it would be placed in the archives as no. 1. Meifred then proceeded to outline the reasoning behind the resignations, beginning with testimony of affection for Habeneck and his family; he swore on his honor that no member of the committee ever acted out of disrespect for their distinguished founder or his reputation. He invited his colleagues to name a new secretary, *archiviste-caissier, agent comptable,* and chorusmaster. But they would not discuss the incident further.

Seuriot, speaking on behalf of the committee members who had left office just before the events, rose to object that Meifred's solution did nothing to correct the dishonor Habeneck had visited on them; the accusation applied to seven *sociétaires,* not three. He then moved a new resolution: "The members of the Société des Concerts, persuaded that the administrative committee for the session 1847–48, far from incurring blame, acted consistently with every courtesy required by the difficult situation in which they found themselves, decide that the resignations of Messrs. Meifred, Saint-Laurent, Claudel, and Benoist are not accepted, and they are kindly engaged to continue their duties as a committee." The motion carried unanimously. Meifred thanked his colleagues of the rank and file: "[We gave] all our zeal, all our devotion, to the best interest of the society; but in the difficult situation we faced, the efforts of your committee would have been in vain if it could not have relied on your energetic support. It is through indifference and lack of commitment *(laisser-aller)* that great institutions are lost, and our great stature must never perish." [135]

The election of a first conductor was thus almost anti-climactic. With 78 members present, the necessary two-thirds majority was 52. On the first ballot Narcisse Girard had 50 votes, Tilmant 23, and Valentino 2, with 2 blank ballots and 1 disqualified. On the second round, Girard was elected with 54 votes, Tilmant 21, and 3 blank. Tilmant was then named second conductor on the first round, with 74 votes (Valentino, 1; Poussard, 1; 2 blank). On the proclamation of Tilmant's sweeping though surely disappointing victory, the room broke out in spontaneous applause, which continued as Auber accepted Habeneck's election as honorary life-president by unanimous acclamation. The members then unanimously voted Habeneck and his family the most precious thing they had to offer: a box, the one over the first violins, assigned to the *maître* and his heirs for the life of the Société des Concerts.

With that the wrenching effort to remove Habeneck was done. Both the committee and then the entire membership had met their responsibilities with the dignity and delicacy they knew from the beginning the circumstance warranted. Each separation with the succeeding great *chefs* of the Société des Concerts—Deldevez, Messager, Gaubert, Münch, and Cluytens—was in its own way equally painful. But for the institution, the turn away from Habeneck was the most dangerous step of them all: a purposeful step into an unknown future, where the first principle of the association—a collective of the nation's best artists, acting as equals—would surely be put to the test.

CHAPTER 6

Girard, Tilmant, and George-Hainl

(1849–72)

Narcisse Girard ought to have seemed a more dubious choice to head a great concert society than in fact he was. After the first round of balloting on 18 October 1848 he held more than twice the votes of his closest rival, Tilmant, the concertmaster.[1] This was largely, it appears, a matter of institutional loyalties, for Girard had succeeded to Habeneck's post at the Opéra in 1846 and before that had been (among his many other appointments) conductor at the Opéra-Comique—the two enterprises that employed most of the electors. Then, too, the undeniable prestige of having the first conductor from the Opéra on the podium of the Société des Concerts, following Habeneck's precedent, doubtless assured the results well in advance of the election.

Although a founding member of the society, Girard had left it in 1832 to pursue his career as conductor and composer for the lyric theater. In both professions he enjoyed some success. He became chief conductor of the Opéra-Comique in 1836; his comic opera *Les Deux Voleurs* (1841) had a good run; he was awarded his Légion d'Honneur in 1843. Berlioz's scarcely flattering assessments of Girard's abilities, however, suggest a pedestrian artist at best; for it was Girard who failed to master the *réunion des thèmes* in the third movement of *Harold en Italie,* thus prompting Berlioz to undertake conducting for himself.[2] Aside from one or two references to Girard's "spirituality," the record offers little hint as to his personality or artistic character; in contrast, a good dozen or so of his players left indelible stamps, some of them as orchestra conductors. His only photograph is not flattering.

Girard's career had been shaped principally by Habeneck, and it followed much the same path. Born 27 January 1797 in Mantes, halfway between Paris and Rouen on the Seine, he took his 1er *prix* in violin in 1820, then began his steady rise through the theater orchestras—section violinist for the *opéra-buffa* at the Théâtre Feydeau, principal violinist and conductor at the Odéon—to the podiums of the Théâtre-Italien, Opéra-Comique, and Opéra. He earned a chair as professor of violin at the Conservatoire in 1847, thus effectively completing his sweep of his mentor's positions. He had just turned fifty-two when he conducted his first Conservatoire concert.

Elwart writes that the musicians, even Girard's competitors, welcomed him warmly back into their midst.[3] His inaugural concerts were promising: on 14 January 1849 the *Zauberflöte* overture, a new arrangement by Adolphe Adam of Martini's popular *Plaisir d'amour,* and a Ninth Symphony that drew cheers of approval; on 28 January, Beethoven's First and Haydn's "Surprise," and an excerpt from Félicien David's *Christophe Colomb*. Within a few weeks Girard, his musicians, and his public had begun to settle into what seemed very much like business as usual. A pair of sudden developments then showed everyone just how much had changed.

Habeneck died of a stroke on 8 February 1849. "Pale, suffering, he went walking like a ghost," wrote the effusive Escudier of his last months, "through this long, living cemetery we call Paris. His friends dared not pause to talk with him, so sad was his expression." He had spent sixty years, Escudier mused in his next column, "in pursuit of the phantom called Glory." The essay went on to lament how quickly Paris had forgotten him, suggesting that abandonment had hastened his end. In fact the Société des Concerts had been anything but remiss in honoring its founder; given the tensions of his last years, their treatment might well be characterized as deferential in the extreme. They immediately canceled their third concert, scheduled for 11 February, to mourn his loss— a gesture that had the effect, one journalist suggested, of putting the "brusque rupture with their venerable chief" into a past best forgotten.[4]

The funeral was at noon on Monday, 12 February 1849. Though the family and colleagues would have preferred the ample Church of St-Roch, the curate of Notre-Dame-de-Lorette insisted on his parish church, then demanded an extra fee to open the main front doors for a crowd estimated at three thousand. Habeneck's surviving brother escorted the widow and her daughters at the head of the procession from the mortuary to the church, followed by Verroust leading the National Guard band. The funeral awning was borne by an imposing quartet: Spontini, Meyerbeer, Auber, and Baron Taylor. Members of the Opéra and Société des Concerts, some two hundred musicians in all, were waiting in the church, where they offered selections from Cherubini's Requiem, a chanted *De profundis,* and—acknowledging an expressed desire of the deceased—the "Eroica" funeral march. Many must have reflected, as did *Le Ménestrel,* on how often the late master had himself conducted this same army of musicians in this same symphony, so deliriously applauded at the Salle des Concerts. *"Quelle page sublime! Quel langage touchant et harmonieux! Ô Beethoven!"*[5]

Orations were delivered by Meifred for the Société des Concerts, Elwart for the Conservatoire, and Baron Taylor for the Association des Artistes-Musiciens; Cuvillon spoke on behalf of Habeneck's many students, and Adolphe Adam improvised, in his halting manner, on behalf of the composers. There were the particular ceremonial gestures accorded members of the Legion of Honor. Burial followed at the Cimetière de Montmartre, toward which the canopy was now carried by Taylor, Adam, Zimmermann, and Tulou. In an ordinary practice of the time, the coffin was placed in a temporary grave to await arrangements for a permanent resting place and a fitting monument.

Mme Habeneck and her daughters liquidated his retirement account by appearing before the notary on 14 July and 8 November 1849. It contained 890 francs—probably enough to last them a year.[6]

The Société des Concerts allocated 1,000 francs from their season earnings toward a monument, as they had done for Cherubini. Meifred returned a written project for an allegorical *bas-relief* in two sections:

> Habeneck arrives in the Elysian fields. Cherubini, the first president [of the society], presents him to Haydn, Mozart, and Beethoven and seems to say to them, "Here is the man who popularized your masterpieces in France." In the second section, we perceive Adolphe Nourrit, our former colleague, the only person who interpreted the scene from *Orphée* with proper dignity. He is talking to Gluck and pointing out their newly elected colleague: "Your works," he says, "were covered in dust and forgotten. There is the man who exhumed them and showed the beauties of *Armide, Orphée* and *Iphigénie* to a new generation, for they had always been in the forefront of his mind."[7]

The society endorsed the widow Habeneck in her long, but eventually unsuccessful, effort to have a street named for him. To this day no celebration of the Société des Concerts or Orchestre de Paris is without its salute to Beethoven and Habeneck in practically the same breath.

As it happened, however, Habeneck never occupied the box reserved for him in perpetuity, and after he was gone Mme *veuve* Habeneck was not much interested.[8]

Saturday, 24 February 1849, less than two weeks after Habeneck's funeral, was the first anniversary of the republic born from the revolution of 1848. With only a few days' notice the new director of fine arts, Charles Blanc, convoked the Société des Concerts and the forces of the Opéra to participate in a patriotic ceremony intended to promote the modern order of things, its elements borrowed from the *fêtes nationales* of the 1790s as well as from church, royalty, and empire—a true *fête religieuse et patriotique*. Blanc wanted music—"so powerful, so well loved," as he put it—to play the principal role.[9] The event would begin with a Requiem and a Te Deum in the Madeleine and military music outdoors near the column in the place Vendôme. Neither the liturgical nor the Napoleonic associations of the locale had much to do with the ideals of 1848, but the result made for a good Parisian spectacle nonetheless. The church was lavishly decorated; the cardinal archbishop of Paris convened the service at 10:00 in the presence of the president and vice president of the Republic, its new Assemblée Nationale, and its military chiefs. The music was recycled from Habeneck's funeral: the Dies irae from Cherubini's Requiem and the Lacrymosa from Mozart's, the *De profundis,* and the Beethoven funeral march; the Te Deum included Le Sueur's *Urbs beata* from the first *Oratorio du sacre* and a Hymn to Ste-Geneviève.[10] The service ended with *Domine salvam fac republicam,* a celebratory motet for chorus and orchestra hastily composed to order by Auber. Lefébure-Wély improvised at the pipe organ Cavaillé-Coll had just completed. Outside, the National Guard band played its fanfares and *chants nationaux* at the column. Drums sounded the retreat from the church, and as the high government officials appeared at the door, the crowds roared, *"Vive la République!"*

One journalist, considering Narcisse Girard in command of the musical force, saw evidence of revolution on that score as well.[11]

Girard had his share of triumphs during his eleven-year tenure but never outdid his first season. The Sunday concerts resumed on 18 February 1849 with a long excerpt from *La Vestale* that built on the scenes Habeneck had introduced in 1845. Spontini was present for the "thundering triumph." Elwart, congratulating him afterward, took the opportunity to lament that his works had not been heard more frequently at the Conservatoire. "That favor," replied Spontini, "is so rarely accorded to contemporary composers that to be played ten times they would have to live at least two centuries." [12]

Fromental Halévy's long-delayed *Prométhée enchaîné,* to a text by his brother Léon after Aeschylus, was ready in March. The stumbling block had been the harmonic challenges of the chorus of Oceanides, which tried to suggest the quarter tones thought at the time to have been a feature of the Greek harmonic system. And eight of the nine Beethoven symphonies were heard in Girard's first season, with the cycle completed at the start of the next.

For a time Girard and his committee went methodically about settling obligations that had for some years gone unattended. Early on they approached Berlioz, who proposed selections from *La Damnation de Faust. Faust* had had an unhappy birth in Paris in 1846, and even if the excerpts selected for 15 April 1849—the sylphs' scene (Dupont as Faust, Depassio as Méphistophélès) and *Marche hongroise*—were relatively short, some twenty minutes in all, the gesture was significant. Berlioz is certain to have been pleased by the framing works, Beethoven's Seventh and a rehearing of the selections from *La Vestale.* A week later, on 22 April 1849, Girard led both the premiere of Mme Farrenc's First Symphony and the symbolic reprise, as though formally accepting Habeneck's mantle by reviving his last great project, of the movements from *Les Ruines d'Athènes.* Louise Farrenc, having now had two first performances, immediately proposed a third. There was no interest: "The society has fulfilled all its obligations toward her, and because of us she has come to be known and appreciated by the public; consequently, the proposal is denied." [13]

The season closed on 29 April 1849 with echoes of Meyerbeer's *Le Prophète,* triumphantly premiered at the Opéra on 16 April with Mme Viardot and Gustave Roger. Both appeared in the Sunday concert, with Mme Viardot singing an aria from Handel's *Rinaldo* orchestrated for her by Meyerbeer himself. More significantly, the Société des Concerts offered the first performance of two movements cut from *Le Prophète,* a "Chœur des mères" and a "Marche des jeunes filles otages."

Just after the season closed, a "plague," probably cholera, swept through the membership and claimed the lives of a valued employee and three *sociétaires:* the *garçon d'orchestre* Renouf (died ca. 5 May 1849), the bassoonist Blaise (d. 15 June), Charles Saint-Laurent (d. 16 June), and the trumpet player Kresser (d. 27 June). Allocations from the Caisse de Prévoyance of 100 francs each were presented to Blaise's three small children, Charlotte, Marie-Antoinette, and Zoé, "struck so young by this terrible disaster." A solicitation of the *sociétaires, aspirants,* soloists, and purveyors to the society yielded 862 francs for the widow Renouf. Mme *veuve* Saint-Laurent collected her husband's retirement benefits and notified the society of the 1,650.49 francs left in the cashbox he kept as *archiviste-caissier.* A memorial service for Saint-Laurent, whose long service to the society was as distinguished as that of Meifred or Vogt, was clearly in order; out of respect for the others, however, this was delayed and broadened into a joint commemorative ceremony on 15 June 1850 at Notre-Dame-de-Lorette.[14]

The new government, ignorant of the society's privileges and traditions, brought with it new crises. It was discovered that an English impresario named Lumley had successfully petitioned the ministry for authorization to give a series of "costume concerts" *(concerts costumés)* in the Salle des Concerts. Meifred, sensing a serious threat, summoned the committee to plot their strategy with Auber. Together they approved a draft letter to the minister of the interior, threatening to abandon the hall if tasteless spectacles were to be permitted there. An Assemblée Générale *extraordinaire* was hurriedly convened to ratify the letter, since the theater commission was to meet on the issue forty-eight hours later. Drastic action was the order of the day, Meifred told his colleagues, who agreed that in the event of any administrative decree that interrupted their scheduled rehearsals or performances, they would simply cease to function, reimbursing the patrons for the value of their seats. A blistering resolution to that end passed unanimously:

> Whereas the exclusive possession of the Salle des Concerts was accorded to us from the start of December through April, inclusively, for the preparation and performance of our *séances;*
>
> Whereas the mission taken on by the society and fulfilled for twenty-two years requires serious and ongoing work;
>
> Whereas the incursion of any kind of speculator meaning to give concerts, spectacles, etc., into the bosom of the Conservatoire during our session would require stage settings that would make it impossible for us to devote ourselves to our work;
>
> Whereas it would be better to leave completely than to fall in the opinion of the public;
>
> And in view of the committee's report on the letter addressed to the Minister of the Interior:
>
> Now, therefore, the Société des Concerts in its general assembly of 2 February [1850], resolves as follows:

"The committee is authorized to take any steps, including the most radical, it judges necessary to safeguard the dignity of the art and of our institution." [15]

Three days later the chastened minister wrote to assure the Société des Concerts that he would do nothing to trouble its rehearsals. Not only did he deny Lumley's proposal, but on 30 October 1850 he issued a vitally important decree conveying "the use of the hall of the national Conservatoire [uniquely] to its teaching needs and to the Société des Concerts." [16] This confirmed two precedents the society typically cited when claiming exclusive use of the hall: Cherubini's stance of 1837 and the 1843 decree of a previous government—the one reckoned by Berlioz to have been aimed directly at him.

Berlioz and the Société des Concerts had in fact formed a certain symbiosis from the beginning. In one of the earliest accounts of Berlioz, the *Revue musicale* describes how at the premiere of the *Fantastique:* "He runs about among the hundred musicians who fill up the stage of the Conservatoire, and although all these regulars in the Société des Concerts make up perhaps the most admirable orchestra ever heard, he begs, he growls, he supplicates, he excites each one of them. This man is Berlioz." [17] The society's first two seasons brought life to scores Berlioz had only imagined and fundamentally changed his perception of his own destiny. No longer a composer of music for the church and theater in the mode of Le Sueur and Cherubini, he promptly cast himself as a disciple of Beethoven.

In 1833, in one of its only attempts to meet the ministerial charge to perform works of Prix de Rome winners, the committee programmed *Rob-Roy,* forerunner of the first movement of *Harold en Italie.* Meifred conveyed this news on 15 March 1833 with obvious warmth: "The committee, my dear Berlioz, has taken note of your letter of the thirteenth of this month in which you indicate the hope that the Société des Concerts would perform your *Rob-Roy* overture. The article of our constitution that forbids *trial readings ("essais")* that we invoked *against you* two years ago no longer being applicable to you today, the committee invites you to have the orchestra parts copied promptly and with *the greatest care.* I am pleased to be charged with conveying this decision in the absence of the secretary [Tajan-Rogé], a decision for which I would have argued with all my eloquence had it been necessary." [18] The performance on 14 April 1833, however, was not a success; Berlioz says he burned *Rob-*

Roy after the performance because it was "long and diffuse." (Another copy of the overture survives.) In its *séance publique annuelle,* the Académie des Beaux-Arts de l'Institut de France noted in passing that "the composer has been judged by the public and it is no longer up to us to comment"—a dismissive formulation if ever there was one.[19]

In 1837 Berlioz appeared in the percussion section during a Sunday concert and was sent a medal in appreciation: "At one of our concerts you offered your services to M. Habeneck by covering a cymbal part that would have gone lacking altogether without your help. The committee, hoping that this will not be the only relationship between you and the Société, has charged me to address its sincere thanks and to beg you to accept the medal of the society as a token of its thanks."[20]

Habeneck conducted four of Berlioz's self-produced concerts in the Salle des Concerts, as well as the Requiem in 1837, the brief run of *Benvenuto Cellini* in 1838–39, and one version of the *Symphonie funèbre et triomphale.* Girard conducted some ten Berlioz concerts and Tilmant two; altogether Berlioz used the Salle des Concerts for his concerts some two dozen times, and even after the 1843 ruling went on to hire the *sociétaires* whenever he could. By the mid-1830s he was easily the most gifted journalist covering the Société des Concerts—and the most diligent, sometimes writing different essays on the same concert for the two papers that employed him. One of the several reasons he stayed in Paris for nearly a decade before leaving in 1842 to take his music east of the Rhine was his dream of succeeding Habeneck at the Opéra and Conservatoire.

Berlioz and Girard had been on good terms for the better part of the 1820s and 1830s. The *Messe solennelle* of November 1827 used Girard's players from the orchestra of the Odéon, and it was probably Girard who gave Berlioz his pass to the Shakespeare performances there. Girard composed his *Antigone* overture for a joint concert they gave in 1835, and Berlioz suggested the title. In one of his columns he also promoted Girard's arrangement for full orchestra of the "Moonlight" Sonata.[21]

Berlioz describes himself in April 1849 as "waiting backstage with the firemen, trembling like a beginner" while Girard conducted the excerpts from *Faust.* Both the movements were greeted with warm applause and calls for more—a good sign from what Berlioz regarded as "a difficult public generally ill disposed to living composers." Girard conducted well, Berlioz was forced to admit, but refused to grant encores, pleading that he could not find his place again in the thick score.[22] This *contretemps* rekindled their old hostilities. Berlioz's description of the concert

in his *Mémoires* is decidedly sour, and Girard programmed no further
Berlioz during his long tenure at the head of the Société des Concerts.

The headline of Jules Janin's review for the *Journal des Débats,* on the
other hand, trumpeted *"Berlioz au Conservatoire, enfin!":* "These compositions that in recent days so delighted the Conservatoire's public
have been long familiar to the *amateurs* of London and St. Petersburg.
Must Berlioz make a circuit of 1200 leagues to arrive at the rue Bergère?
. . . Now that Berlioz doesn't give any more concerts, they play his music everywhere. Tired of moving toward the mountain, he quit; now the
mountain has begun to move toward him." [23] Tilmant programmed Berlioz twice during his tenure as the society's chief conductor; George-
Hainl, an old friend, introduced *La Fuite en Égypte* in his first season.
But the Société des Concerts did not get serious about Berlioz's music
until after his death. In the early 1870s it began to master *Roméo et Juliette,* thought by the mid-1890s to be one of the society's triumphs; the
rest of the Berlioz repertoire followed along. What is interesting about
the Girard era is that after twenty years of militant search for a French
successor to Beethoven, and even after Berlioz's well-publicized triumphs abroad, the society still failed to acknowledge the obviously
Beethovenian elements in his music.

By the time Girard returned to the Société des Concerts, it would seem,
he was no longer especially interested in new music. He disliked the system that left initiative for programming new works with the composers,
and he was not alone in thinking that far too much time was spent trying to decipher mediocre music. Among Girard's first duties had been
to lead readings of an overture by Molet and a symphony by Théodore
Gouvy; in the fall of 1849, the first year he was fully in control, three *répétitions d'essai* were devoted to reading nine works—among them symphonies by J.-B.-M. Chollet and Mme Lavauine, an overture by Alexandre Montfort (Berlioz's Prix de Rome companion), a piano concerto by
Édouard Silas, and Gounod's dramatic scene *Pierre l'hermite*—of which
not one was deemed suitable for adoption. Nor was he fond of the arrangement by which concerto soloists were chosen from a roster of the
self-nominated. In November 1849 applications from pianists were suspended outright, and in December the committee began to draw away
from the "essay" system that seemed to make everyone involved—composers whose works were adopted but waiting in a long queue, those
whose music was heard and declined, and those who were presented and
then expected to be heard every year—unhappy.[24]

The result was an abrupt decline in the programming of new music during the tenures of Girard and Tilmant. Elwart mentions the trend in his notes on the repertoire for 1852 ("the more the concerts advance, the fewer are the new composers to be presented") and again for 1857 ("the further the Société des Concerts distances itself from the foundation, the less varied are its programs"). He goes on to analyze it in his essay "On the Past, Present, and Future of the Société des Concerts," with which his book concludes.[25] Meanwhile the journalists, with nothing much to report, trickled away.

Even the Empress Eugénie, wife of Napoléon III, noticed. Recognizing in 1856 the name of only one living composer—Rossini—on the program, she inquired of Girard, "And do you play only compositions by dead people in your lovely Conservatoire concerts?" "Madame," replied Girard with a bow, "the repertoire of our society is the Louvre of musical art."[26] It says a certain amount about Girard that he is remembered to posterity largely for failing in *Harold en Italie* and for that remark.

By contrast, Girard was tireless in advancing the music of Haydn and Mendelssohn. We know the "Surprise" Symphony to have been a pillar of the programming, with at least its familiar Andante heard nearly every season. Girard brought what seem from the listings to have been a half-dozen more Haydn symphonies into the active repertoire, probably including the "Oxford," "Military," and "Clock" Symphonies (Nos. 92, 93, 101) and Symphony No. 102 in B♭ Major.

In 1851, for instance, he called for pre-season readings of four new ones; he then spent the summer of 1852 researching the Haydn symphonies, which, he reported back to the committee, numbered 120.[27] On this occasion he instructed the librarian to borrow and copy A.-F. Marmontel's collection of twenty-four symphonies in two large volumes. Following Habeneck's treatment of the Beethoven chamber repertoire, he began to program Haydn quartet movements for the full cohort of strings; in 1852 he introduced, as *Hymne d'Haydn,* the theme and variations from the "Emperor" Quartet, one of his signature works. Another popular Haydn excerpt, listed in the programs merely as a Benedictus, was probably the famous movement from the "Lord Nelson" Mass, with its stern trumpets and timpani.

Girard also continued to piece together *The Creation* and *The Seasons,* hoping to have both oratorios fully assembled during his tenure. *The Seasons* was heard in its entirety on 22 March 1857, the first time the society devoted a full concert to a single composition. The translation was by Gustave Roger, who sang the role of Lucas; the role of Jeanne was shared by two sopranos, Mlle Ribault and Mlle Boulart, and the bass Bonnehée was Simon. *The Seasons* was reprised in January 1858 and again from time to time by Girard's successors. Excerpts continued to be heard every year, as they had been since the foundation. *The Creation,* called *La Création du monde,* was first heard on 6 February 1859 and was Girard's last major premiere. Connoisseurs were pleased, but its length made *The Creation* fit less comfortably into the Sunday format than *The Seasons,* and by the same token it was difficult to find adequate rehearsal time. Only "The Heavens Are Telling" and one or two other choruses stayed in the repertoire.

In January 1851 Girard instructed the secretary to contact Härtel in Leipzig for the score and parts to Mendelssohn's incidental music for *A Midsummer Night's Dream,* introduced to the Paris public on 23 March 1851 as *Fragments du Songe d'une nuit d'été*—a "perfect performance," according to Charles Dancla, leaving "a vivid and profound impression."[28] Over the next several seasons there were several experiments with the number of excerpts and the order of the intermezzo, nocturne, and scherzo, resulting (in March 1858) in a six-movement suite with the nocturne and duo in the center:

Ouverture − Allegro appassionato [= Intermezzo] − Andante tranquillo [or Adagio; = Nocturne] − Couplets et chœur [= Lied] − Scherzo − Marche [= Wedding March]

Other organizations clamored for the parts and French translation of what they heard, but the society regarded the *Songe d'une nuit d'été* as its "exclusive property" and refused to release the material.[29]

The January 1852 performance of the "Italian" Symphony, No. 4 in A Major, opening the twenty-fifth season, was probably a premiere; in any event the three main Mendelssohn symphonies ("Reformation," "Italian," and "Scottish") were now in place, with the "Lobgesang" *symphonie-cantate* soon to come.

The society's experience with the *Midsummer Night's Dream* music had been so positive that it was decided to undertake another ambitious Mendelssohn project, *Die erste Walpurgisnacht.* Materials were acquired from Friedrich Kistner in Leipzig, and within a month of receiving them the musicians had given the work a reading; the decision was soon reached to begin the long process of readying it for a French premiere. Goethe's text was given to the translators Leroy for the prose and Bélanger for the poetry, the latter well known for his translations of the Schubert songs as well as Mendelssohn's *Midsummer Night's Dream* and *Saint Paul* and Beethoven's *Egmont.* Bélanger demanded an exaggerated price for his *travail poëtique.* Girard, remonstrating with him, appealed to his higher instincts: "You help us popularize an important work," he said; "some of the glory . . . will fall to you. Join us in the sacrifice we are making to present this work."[30] Bélanger relented, and *Die erste Walpurgnisnacht* appeared on the program of 20 March 1853 as *La Nuit du 1ᵉʳ Mai, ou le Sabbat des sorciers; ballade de Goëthe, trad. de M. Bélanger, musique de Mendelssohn.* The overture and nine episodes were explained, unusually, with twenty-four lines of text in the program. *La Nuit du 1ᵉʳ Mai* was initially a success, though interest in it soon faded. Later on Girard was to introduce the first act of *Die Loreley,* the *Ruy Blas* overture, and one of Mendelssohn's psalms for double chorus.

There was attention, as well, to the other masters of "music's Louvre." Mozart's symphonies, so far represented by the "Jupiter" and G-Minor, were pursued to the extent that the mysteries of their order and publication could be unraveled in Paris; there was a "Fourth" symphony in the repertoire, and Girard called also for a "Second" and "Sixth." The Beethoven repertoire was enhanced with *Der glorreiche Augenblick* (called simply *Grande Cantate*), four excerpts from *The Creatures of Prometheus* (called *Gli uomini di Prometeo:* Ouverture, Tempesta, Adagio, Allegretto), and one of the woodwind trios in a setting for two oboes and English horn. The *Egmont* incidental music, which Habeneck had wanted to undertake, was finally premiered in 1855, with a new French text by Henry Trianon.[31] Of Handel, Girard added choruses from *Alexander's Feast* and *Samson* and a theme and variations with fugue arranged by Adolphe Adam from a harpsichord work. Adam had also prepared, at Louis-Philippe's request, "Dans ces doux asiles," a version of the minuet-chorus from Rameau's *Castor et Pollux* that was introduced to subscribers in January 1851 after a performance at court.[32]

These were significant new forays into territory where the Société des Concerts already had a considerable stake. But in other respects the programming of individual concerts had grown formulaic: a Beethoven symphony, a Haydn quartet, something by Mendelssohn, perhaps a chorus of Handel or overture of Weber—and all, or at least most, of the Beethoven symphonies every season. The effect must have been similar to playing one's favorite recordings again and again. There was no objection from the subscribers, and the musicians much preferred learning new music by composers whose idiom came naturally—and only once or twice a year.

The city of Lille offered its third Festival du Nord in June 1851, where Girard succeeded Habeneck and conducted, among other things, the Lacrymosa from Berlioz's Requiem. He returned a staunch partisan of the movement to establish something similar in Paris. Music festivals, like industrial exhibitions, were much in vogue. Yet when a government commission invited the Société des Concerts to organize a festival concert at the Panthéon, the committee declined, doubting that their eighty-piece ensemble would sound rich enough in the venue and knowing full well that the organizers had little feel for such basic practicalities as moving a symphony orchestra and paying its fees.[33]

Girard took advantage of the invitation to open a discussion of how the society might take the lead in some festival "manifestation of musical art," the sort of thing that might draw sympathetic attention from the national and municipal governments on whose good will they depended. It would, he thought, require a festival venue like the one in Lille. Responding to his initiative, the committee sent Auguste Seuriot to Lille to discover "everything necessary to enlighten the discussion" of a possible new venue. Seuriot met with Lazard, builder of the pavilion in Lille, who would not venture a guess as to the cost of a similar structure in Paris until he came to talk with potential contractors; doubtless the expense would be prohibitive.[34] We hear no more of a festival hall for the Société des Concerts, but the episode is instructive on two counts. First, it might be reasonable to infer from Girard's ardent enthusiasm a character trait he probably brought to his readings of Haydn and Mendelssohn (and, earlier, to Berlioz). Then, too, there is the suggestion that the society had begun to think about other venues. This would become one of the overriding concerns of the 1870s and beyond.

In late November 1851 it was decided to approach the great Dauverné, a founding member, and ask him to relinquish his place as principal trumpet. The *commissaire du personnel* was sent to call on him and explain the need for rejuvenating the section, begging in turn for his indulgence. Dauverné instead took offense and wrote both the *archiviste-caissier* and the *agent comptable* insulting letters to the effect that their colleague had been trying to accept a resignation not yet tendered. The visit had been intended as a *démarche amicale,* the committee replied as they unanimously upheld Dauverné's forced retirement; further, in view of the offensive tone of his retort, they discussed the possibility of withholding the customary distinction *membre honoraire* and even his retirement benefits. But Meifred in his wisdom—and, like Dauverné, a founding member—argued successfully that passing indiscretions of language could not really be made grounds for such penalties; Dauverné was due this "mark of esteem and consideration as recompense for his long and honorable service, in both the orchestra and its administration." He was then named *membre honoraire* by unanimous vote, with full rights to the Caisse de Prévoyance and, with an unusual flourish, "entitled to all the prerogatives attached to this title."[35]

The agitated state of the capital caused the committee to adjourn its meeting of 2 December 1851 early, as they learned of the dissolution of the National Assembly and the possibility Paris would fall under martial law. Serious work was impossible, and several of the members were "preoccupied" with their desire to take to the streets.[36] But the immediate danger passed as quickly as it had come, with the Second Empire proclaimed the next day, 10 December 1851.

Adapting to an imperial government taxed everyone's patience, and to some extent offended the natural republican sentiments of the institution. To become an appendage of the imperial household, subject again to the whims of personal decree, was all too reminiscent of the months following July 1830. Soon enough, in fact, the society was denied access even to its furniture when the routine annual request for the Salle des Concerts was answered with a finding that loans of imperial property were denied until further notice.[37] In a return to the patronage arrangement for the royal box, a system that had never functioned especially well, a cash "gratification" was promised but seldom delivered. To secure the money one or another of the officers had to trek from the accountants in the Office of the Lord Chamberlain to the accountants in the Ministry of the Imperial Household, to the secretary of the Imperial Cabinet, and so on. There was friction with Auber, who did not want the society dealing with the government except through his offices, so great was the danger of a *malentendu*.[38] The bright side, that Her Imperial Highness would become more interested in the work of the Société des Concerts than any of her recent royal predecessors, was so far not to be seen.

From the minutes of 13 January 1852:

INCIDENT

The session was interrupted by the unexpected return of the *commissaire du matériel*, thought to have gone to the library. He appeared to be in the grip of substantial agitation.

"*Messieurs*," said he. "Guess what's happening to the Société?"

"What, then?"

"They've come for the kitchen sink."

"The kitchen sink?"

"A black man is downstairs, *chez le concierge,* armed . . . I'm still over-whelmed . . . he's armed with a stamped document that demands, in the name of a Russian prince, considerable damages and interest."

"And? . . . "

"The prince contends that he had everything in order and on time for the occupancy of his box and when he sent someone to collect the tickets, it had been let to another person, said to have been its proprietor for fifteen or six-teen years! The factotum, armed and dangerous, is pestering, threatening, and swearing by St. Nicholas that even if it costs the Russian prince 100,000 francs, he intends to pursue it to the end."

The committee finds in the excessively unpleasant humor of the noble subscriber the manifest proof of the society's musical excellence, and relies on the zeal and intelligence of the *archiviste-caissier* to resolve this business.[39]

It was a testy season all around, beginning with complaints from the au-dience about the noise offstage and a terse warning posted in the *foyer.* In February 1852 a scheduled Beethoven's Ninth had to be abandoned and the work postponed for a year when Girard demanded four extra rehearsals the committee was unwilling to budget. He, meanwhile, was complaining bitterly of the "impatience" the musicians showed with his style. He thought a certain remark lanced in his direction highly offen-sive and became furious when its source, remaining "incognito," as he put it, refused to come forward; the next rehearsal began with a long re-monstrance to the musicians at large. Two weeks later there was an un-pleasant episode when the violist Nargeot asked Girard for permission to leave a rehearsal early, was refused, and left anyway. The committee found this behavior *très blâmable* and a bad example to set so early in the season. Nargeot was rebuked "with all the forms and courtesies owed to an excellent *sociétaire* who has rendered great service to the so-ciety and who is held in esteem by everyone," to which he replied with an improper letter displaying a "scarcely motivated ill will" that only made his situation worse.[40]

Evidence of an uneasy relationship between the conductor and his musicians crops up periodically from that point on, but there seems little explanation for Girard's sudden resignation in the spring of 1854. There had been a significant turnover in management. Meifred, long the so-ciety's peacemaker, had retired at the end of 1853–54; the chorusmas-ter, Garaudé, died suddenly at the age of thirty-three; Seuriot resigned briefly as *archiviste-caissier* (and, altogether, from the Opéra orchestra), possibly for reasons of health. Girard may have had a dispute with one of the new officers, though for the most part they were familiar and trusted servants. The case of the drunken Verroust was at its height; there may have been trouble surrounding the complete performance of Rossini's *Stabat mater* at the Good Friday *concert spirituel* of 14 April 1854.

Whatever the case, Girard convoked an Assemblée Générale *extraordinaire* for Wednesday, 19 April 1854, three days after the closing Easter Sunday concert, without specifying a reason. The members arrived to find his chair vacant; in his absence the secretary proceeded to read the letter of resignation, which began with an apology for the mysterious call and went on to conclude that conductors who no longer have the support of their musicians have no choice but to step down. The secretary explained, but did not record, the "allegations" made by Girard, then recommended declining his resignation. The assembly so voted, 88 out of 93 present. The burst of applause that greeted the announcement of the results was recorded as the "true expression of their sentiments toward M. Girard and of their gratitude for his immense service to the Société des Concerts."[41]

The committee then proceeded to Auber's office to announce the outcome, and Auber joined them in a delegation to present the news to Girard personally. Girard received his colleagues warmly, assured them of his intention to devote his every energy to the society, and suggested that it was as good a time as any to get on with urgent business—that is, to have a committee meeting. Later it was decided to offer him one of the society's commemorative medals, this one cast in gold and engraved *"La Société des Concerts à son Chef, M. Girard."*[42] Six *sociétaires*— Bussine, Deldevez, Mercadier, Gaillod, Rivals, and Montsimon—joined the committee in a delegation to present the medal. Meeting at 8:30 on Saturday morning, 5 May 1854, by the clock outside the Opéra, they walked again to Girard's apartment, where he welcomed them again, and the misunderstanding—whatever it was—was over.

The new chorusmaster, Eugène-François Vauthrot, had first appeared with the Société des Concerts in 1839 as a boy soprano *(le jeune Vauthrot)* in Cherubini's motet *Inclina, Domine.*[43] He was the accompanist at the Opéra-Comique, thus familiar to Girard; in 1856 he became chorusmaster at the Opéra. He was an able arranger of piano-vocal scores, a skill put to good use at the society. In his first season he helped prepare the *Egmont* music, then worked closely with Girard on the Haydn oratorios; additionally he introduced the chorus to the motets of Bach. Vauthrot served for twelve years, an unusually long tenure in that office.

Just after the 1855 season concluded, the society was forced to take a position on the difficult question of what engagements the musicians should be allowed to accept during the summer interval. Paris was awash that summer in ceremonies and evening spectacles surrounding Napoléon III's Industrial Exposition, meant to rival the English Crystal Palace Exhibition of 1853. Pasdeloup and his young musicians had been engaged to offer a series of Saturday evening concerts at the Hôtel de Ville, and the one on the evening of Saturday, 7 July, was to be especially festive, followed by a grand ball and reception for the visiting Lord Mayor of London. Pasdeloup invited many of the *sociétaires,* both singers and players, to complement his ensemble. The committee was sufficiently alarmed by the thought that the public would perceive a "foreign" conductor at the head of the Société des Concerts to rewrite the sensitive article 38 specifically to thwart Pasdeloup. Previously it had read:

> For the duration of each concert season, no *sociétaire* will participate in other public concerts without the assent of the committee.
>
> In the absence of the committee, the president or vice president will grant, if there is reason, provisional authorization.

Now it was to say:

> No *sociétaire* may participate in orchestra concerts given by formally constituted societies, nor play or sing in public concerts and official ceremonies led by a conductor of one of these societies.[44]

The provision had never been popular with the musicians, and the proposed text seemed on first reading to threaten their freedom to take the summer casino and spa work with which many supplemented their season income. Discussion at the assembly of 6 June 1855 began with an observation from the floor that the Société des Concerts was strong enough not to be concerned with rivalry, and that it was counterproductive to deny the musicians their right to earn a little extra money. The leadership argued that there was in fact cause for grave concern over this particular situation. Pasdeloup was an interloper, presenting seasons in the Salle des Concerts with an organization he called the Société des Concerts des Jeunes Artistes du Conservatoire. His orchestra had the same president, Auber, and the same *garçon d'orchestre.* Alard and Desmarets asserted that the two groups were increasingly confused in the public mind. And the new wording was carefully contrived, actually allowing musicians to take other work year round, so long as it was not a question of "formally constituted societies" or ad hoc assaults by their conductors. (Pasdeloup was not the only one to fall into that category;

Berlioz, for instance, was at the time conductor of a rival but short-lived Société Philharmonique. And there were others, though none but Pasdeloup who could so far be considered a threat.)

So argued, the new text impressed the musicians, who adopted it overwhelmingly, 64 in favor out of 79 voting. Then, since the question of a *sociétaire*'s right to appear as concerto soloist with other orchestras had come up before and was certain to come up again, they proceeded to improvise an amended second clause: "Authority to play or sing solos can always be granted by the committee. In the absence of the committee, the *chef d'orchestre* will accord, if there is reason, authorization." The approach from Pasdeloup was thus temporarily staved off, and the hastily written article ended up as something of a turning point, allowing—even encouraging—new career patterns, especially for the leading instrumentalists.[45]

The Société des Concerts had its own occasion to be part of the summer festivities when the minister of state for foreign affairs commanded a performance for Prince Albert of England on 26 August 1855 at the emperor's palace in St-Cloud. This time the committee took care to require a reasonable fee, 6,000 francs. To the objection that no room in the palace would accommodate all the players, the producers responded with their plan to transform the *orangerie* into an elegant concert venue. The musicians proceeded to St-Cloud and back in a convoy of carriages that must have impressed both them and the bystanders with its novelty. The incident of the evening was caused by the *aspirant* trombonist Cerclier, who, not having anything to play, occupied himself by making a bouquet from the cut flowers decorating the room. Reprimanded by the *commissaire du personnel,* he compounded the offense by not finding it significant, and was issued a "most formal" reprimand for unbecoming conduct.[46]

This first imperial command performance, and first out-of-town appearance, was well enough appreciated that another came from the palace at St-Cloud in May 1856—the occasion for the empress's inquiry about dead composers and Girard's arch response—and a third, in May 1857, for a concert to honor His Imperial Highness, the Grand Duke Constantine of Russia, in a gesture of reconciliation between France and Russia after the Crimean War. The program was typical of Girard's last years: Beethoven's Seventh, parts III and IV of *The Seasons,* and Weber's *Oberon* overture. The grand duke was "enchanted," reports Elwart, and applauded vigorously.[47] Additionally, a concert to benefit the victims of the Loire floods of 1856 produced excellent financial results, as had the grand duke's concert. Such supplementary events would sell out in any case, because they were the only ones not filled in advance by the subscribers.

In early 1856 an aristocratic subscriber, Mme d'Haussonville, wrote that the society's patrons were anxious to hear Mme Viardot again. She observed in patrician terms that this might add a new "ornament" to their concerts, where "the singing corresponds so little to the incomparable perfection of the instrumental music."

"*Madame,*" Lebouc responded:

> M. Girard has forwarded to the committee of the Société des Concerts the letter you did the honor of addressing him, wherein you express on behalf of a great number of subscribers the desire to hear Mme Viardot again at the concerts of our society. The committee recognizes as you do the eminent talent of Mme Viardot and likes to recall the great success she has had with the Société des Concerts. But it regrets that in support of your request, you offered an opinion on the vocal component of our concerts that we are far from sharing.
>
> I am charged as secretary to answer you that the committee has received on precious few occasions requests like yours from subscribers concerning artists, and that it has always thought it necessary to reject anything that seems to be pressure from a fraction of the public. In consequence I regret, *madame,* not to be able to act on the request you have represented to us.[48]

This blunt rebuff suggests that the society's heightened profile among aristocrats, and perhaps its quickness to respond to imperial command, were now recognized as having certain disadvantages. The language is dangerously cold, very different than anything Meifred might have written. And to some degree it is dishonest, since the committee members knew better than anyone how often the quality of the singing was a source of alarm.

Fundamental changes in the membership structure resulted from the decision in November 1857 to abandon the category of *sociétaire solo* and raise the number of orchestral *sociétaires* from 64 to 74. This made room for full appointments of a third oboe / English horn player, a third clarinet / bass clarinetist, a third bassoon / contrabassoonist, a third trumpet, and a timpanist. Twenty-two new *sociétaires* were named—10 orchestra, 12 chorus—to fill the ranks that November and December, the largest incoming class since the foundation. The total number of *sociétaires* now stood at 118 (table 9).[49] The intention was to recognize pre-

TABLE 9. Number of *Sociétaires*, 1857

	1841	1843	1857
Orchestra	64	64	74
Chorus	36	—	—
Men	—	36	36
Women (adjunct)	—	8	8
Solos	12	12	0
TOTAL	112	120	118

SOURCE: AG 21 November 1857: D 17345 (6).

vailing practice, since increasingly it had been necessary to offer prominent soloists at least a modest fee.

But for a time the change of policy caused as many problems as it
solved. For one thing, it made no provision for the incumbent soloists,
and the classification of the women *sociétaires adjoints,* established in
1843, was still misunderstood. For another, the increase in ticket prices
that would be necessary to sustain a new system of fee payments had
been discussed and defeated the previous season. And there was the substantial new cost in time of recruiting soloists case by case, since a resident cohort would quickly disappear. The best singers were notoriously
prone to last-minute cancellations. Regarding a particularly difficult
season, ca. 1910, Vernaelde writes: "There were too often modifications
to the program owing to the solo singers. Oh! the singers! They are the
terror of the committees, the fear of the conductors. What tribulations
they cause! They are indispensable for rehearsals at the theaters to which
they are bound. They earn high fees everywhere, whereas the Société des
Concerts, by statute, only pays 100 francs. For the secretary, this means
darting about through Paris and the suburbs—since many artists, seeking tranquility after the hour of battle, live *extra muros.* Often he only
finds a savior at the last minute."[50] Deldevez held that the hiring of outside soloists had been the "germ of a complete revolution" of which he
did not approve, though he also sensed that neither the chorus nor the
resident soloists had developed as well as the orchestra. Scudo thought
that the society purposefully engaged mediocre singers in order to put
the instrumentalists in a better light.[51]

The debates of late 1857 and spring 1858 concerning personnel led
inexorably back to the question of mandatory retirement. On 26 December 1858, more than two decades after it was first discussed, a new

article 7bis adopted a retirement age of sixty with the possibility of exceptions, or *sursis,* to be granted by the committee: "Except for the president and first and second conductors, every *sociétaire* reaching the age
of sixty ceases to be an active member of the society. Those reaching
that age during the session, that is, between 1 January and the general
assembly for the division of accounts, continue their functions as active
members until the end of the session. The committee, in emergency situations only, can delay the retirement of an outgoing member; this delay will not exceed one year, but may be renewed." [52] The vote was 71 favoring, 30 opposed, 2 blank, 1 disqualified. The measure was exercised
for the first time in the fall of 1859 for the orchestra of 1860. Three members having reached the *limite d'âge*—Leborne, Nargeot, and Baptiste
Tolbecque (the violist)—were given a first *sursis;* Maussant was retired.[53]

Both the empress and Rossini attended the concert of 17 April 1859,
which featured the finale of act III of *Moïse.* The audience rose to applaud both *grandes entrées,* hers to the imperial box and his to Auber's.
The commotion after *Moïse* was prolonged, and finally Rossini was "led
away in triumph by a crowd of avid admirers wanting to express their
admiration one last time." [54] As Girard turned to begin the closing se-
lection, Weber's *Oberon* overture, he had the first of what appears to have
been a series of heart attacks. (Other accounts suggest that he "almost
died twice" on the podium of the Société des Concerts, though he conducted four more concerts in 1859 and the opening concert in 1860.)

Girard died early in the morning of 17 January 1860 after collapsing
at the Opéra the night before during a performance of *Les Huguenots.* He was sixty-three, and had led 112 Conservatoire concerts. The
committee discovered the news as they gathered that day for their
weekly meeting at the Conservatoire. They paused in silence to honor
his memory, then chose the Mozart Requiem and funeral march from
the "Eroica" for the funeral and convoked the musicians to a rehearsal
the next morning. An allocation of 300 francs was approved for the
priest and expenses of St-Roch, Girard's parish church of St-André having been thought too small to accommodate the expected guests; Lebouc, as secretary, was designated to speak on behalf of the society. The
faire-part invited guests to the procession, service, and burial beginning
Thursday, 19 January 1860 at 9:00 A.M.[55] The concert scheduled for
22 January was postponed for a week in Girard's memory.

Since the conducting duties would naturally devolve to Tilmant, and
since his abilities were well known to them, it was also agreed to post-

pone formal election of a new conductor until the end of the season already under way. Tilmant's first concert, like Girard's, featured the Ninth Symphony; sustained applause greeted his approach to the podium, tending to affirm a succession never much in doubt. With two notable exceptions—Félicien David's Symphony in E♭ on 19 February, and Spohr's Eighth Violin Concerto on 1 April, played by his student Kœmpel—the season's repertoire was inherited from years past. The Easter Sunday *concert spirituel* was offered as a benefit for Mme *veuve* Girard, concluding with the scene from Rossini's *Moïse* her husband conducted the night of his first heart attack. She responded with fulsome thanks for their kind gesture of "profound homage" to the memory of her dear husband.[56]

On 5 May 1860, less than a week after the last concert of the season, the *sociétaires* assembled to choose their first and second conductors. Tilmant, to no one's surprise, was elected *vice-président/ 1ᵉʳ chef* on the first round of balloting: 98 favoring out of 104 voting. The musicians had been uncertain whether he wished to continue, but that being the case it was only fitting that the man who had served eleven years as second conductor and as heir apparent long before that—indeed the only conductor to have substituted on the podium of the Société des Concerts—should have his chance. His tenure could not last long: he was already nearly sixty-two, well past the retirement age they had just adopted for the rank and file.

In consequence the election of a *2ᵉ chef* on this occasion amounted in turn, or so it seemed, to choosing Tilmant's heir. The successful candidate would also become concertmaster, as specified by the statute adopted in 1848 ("the second conductor is the principal of the first violins"). Three candidates—the principal second violinist Delphin Alard, Philémon de Cuvillon, and E.-M.-E. Deldevez—came forward in advance; Charles Dancla and Édouard Millault nominated themselves from the floor. (Dancla had quit his job at the post office on his appointment to a chair in violin at the Conservatoire, where he served for more than thirty years, until 1892.) All the senior violinists, in short, ran for election. The committee announced its recommendation of Alard, causing Cuvillon, chronologically the eldest, to withdraw in his favor.

Dancla maintained his candidacy, pledging to uncouple the two positions. Deldevez agreed that the functions of a second conductor and a concertmaster were fundamentally different, and, following Dancla, engaged to modify the statute if elected. That was probably a turning point for them both, since Deldevez was already known to be a capable conductor and Alard, Baillot's successor at the Conservatoire, was by some distance the more eminent violinist. After the first round of balloting, Deldevez led comfortably, with 49 votes to 39 for Alard, 3 for Dancla, and 2 for Millault. On the third ballot Deldevez accrued the necessary two-thirds of the votes, 81 out of 104, and was proclaimed second conductor.[57] Delphin Alard became *1ᵉʳ chef d'attaque* by acclamation. Following up on the commitment to legitimize this arrangement, the assembly proceeded to modify the statute concerning second conductors, dropping the linkage with violin players: "The second conductor must be chosen from among the active members of the society."[58] Most of the subsequent second conductors were indeed violinist / concertmasters, but among the others were the flutists Taffanel and Gaubert, both of whom acceded to the podium.

Antoine Elwart, who had just published his book on the Société des Concerts, was among those who expected Tilmant to retire instead of standing for election. He drafted a nine-paragraph letter applying for the post of first conductor and summarizing his platform—as outside candidates, not having the opportunity to address the general assembly, were encouraged to do. He asked that the committee consider his candidacy "only in the event M. Tilmant might decide to avail himself of a glorious rest." Learning from Tilmant that that was unlikely, he withheld the letter until after the election, then submitted it for the ideas it contained, and went on to give the text in full in the second edition of his book. His suggestions were three:

- That the society not look to the outside for vocal soloists, whose reputations were too often merely local and whose abilities did not always rise to the level of even the most modest *sociétaire*

- To pursue Habeneck's dream of a state subvention, which would permit summer study of works of the Old Masters and contemporary composers, forming a reserve of programming that need not diminish their "Beethovenian prestige"

- Again following Habeneck's model, to return to the practice of using the orchestra's own virtuosi—"now relegated to a kind of silence that paralyzes even the liveliest talent"—as concerto soloists

Elwart assured the committee that while his activities as a composer gave him "special familiarities" that might be of use to the society, he would never program one of his own works.[59]

Elwart had thought as much about the Société des Concerts as anybody, certainly more than any non-member except perhaps for Berlioz. The ideas expressed in his letter of candidacy and the essay that concludes his book provide a useful counterpoint to the society's own, increasingly rigid attitudes. He was among the constituents for whom the Société des Concerts of the present paled in comparison to the happy memory of how it was in the early days of trial and discovery. Elwart's second edition of 1863 carries his chronology to the end of the Tilmant years, just before his unsuccessful run for first conductor. As he fades from the scene we lose his eccentric but precious week-by-week commentary. No later chronicler—not even Deldevez, who did not join the orchestra until 1831—could say he had been present at the foundation.

Théophile Tilmant, called *aîné* to distinguish him from his brother the cellist, was a thirty-two-year veteran of the Société des Concerts when he took over as chief conductor. Beginning with his emergency appearance on 29 January 1843, he had already led more than a dozen concerts as de facto, and later official, second conductor, and by 1860 had acquired his legendary distinction as Habeneck's "right arm." He was well liked by the musicians in a way Girard was not, and apparently lacked enemies or even detractors. "His modesty," it was said at his death, "equaled his talent." [60]

A student of Kreutzer, Tilmant had won the 1er *prix* in violin in 1819 and by the time the Société des Concerts was founded had established a good professional reputation, notably in string chamber music. He had been Habeneck's choice as concertmaster for the nascent society, occupying that seat from its inaugural concert. The great success of the Gymnase Musical concerts of 1834 and 1835 was in large measure owing to his organizational and artistic leadership. He left the orchestra of the Opéra to become first conductor at the Théâtre-Italien in 1838, then succeeded Girard in 1849 as first conductor of the Opéra-Comique; he shared with Auber the musical direction of the imperial chapel from its organization in 1852. The committee immediately set about securing his appointment to the Légion d'Honneur; Lebouc, noting that Tilmant was too modest to seek the distinction himself, cited his record of service to the theaters of Paris, his long tenure as second conductor of the Société des Concerts, and his essentially unanimous elevation following the death of Girard. The ribbon arrived in 1861. [61]

There was little incentive for Tilmant to do anything more than continue with the now canonic repertoire and the financially successful policies of the 1850s. His three major contributions all came in 1861:

Mendelssohn's *Symphonie-cantate* (the *"Lobgesang"* Symphony No. 2 in B♭ Major, op. 52), Hérold's *Zampa* overture, and Weber's *Jubel* overture. (The Mendelssohn, though seemingly a perfect choice for the society because of the way it combines a long instrumental introduction with eight vocal movements, was not a great success. Elwart complains that the text was not understood, and there was no explanatory note in the program.)[62] Tilmant also reprised excerpts from *La Damnation de Faust* in 1861, adding the finale of soldiers and students from part II; and in 1863, shortly after the premiere of Berlioz's *Béatrice et Bénédict* in Baden-Baden, he programmed the lovely *duo-nocturne*.

By contrast there was significant advance over the Girard years in the quality of the guest soloists. The debuts of Sarasate and the great pianist Francis Planté came at the very start of Tilmant's tenure, in January and February 1861, with Planté returning the "Emperor" Concerto (last heard in 1838) to the repertoire. The young Théodore Ritter, a *protégé* of Berlioz, played the Beethoven Fourth Piano Concerto in February 1862, followed in April by Clara Schumann in the "Emperor" again— her reception polite, but not more; the Parisians knew little, so far, of her husband's music. In April 1862 the young Saint-Saëns appeared in the Beethoven Choral Fantasy, thus beginning an illustrious half-century of association with the society and with that work in particular. Mme Viardot appeared in all three of Tilmant's seasons, with particular interest surrounding her selections from Gluck's *Alceste* in both its French and Italian versions, presented just prior to the production built for her at the Théâtre-Lyrique. In 1863 she was splendidly paired with Mme Vandenheuvel-Duprez, daughter of the celebrated tenor Gilbert Duprez, in Beethoven's Ninth and the Berlioz *duo-nocturne*.

It took two stimuli from beyond the Salle des Concerts, both during the 1861–62 season, to rouse the society from its contented routine. One of them, the dawn of real competition from a new "pops" orchestra led by Pasdeloup, shook the institution at its very foundations.

The other was the announcement in September that a monument to Cherubini was to be constructed in Florence, his native city. A subscription was opened by King Victor-Emmanuel, and assorted nobles and city fathers had already accrued 5,000 *louis d'or*. The Société des Concerts pledged its moral support and was considering the particulars of its financial gesture when none other than the great Rossini stepped forward to suggest that this would be a fine occasion for him to premiere his aptly titled *Chant des Titans,* seventy-nine bars of music for four unison bass-baritones (*basses de haute-taille*) and an accompaniment he promised to orchestrate for the society. Rossini's offer was accepted straightaway and the Italian text, by Giuseppe Torre, sent to Émilien Pacini for its French translation.[63] The performance was arranged for 22 December 1861 and billed as a *concert extraordinaire, donné au profit de la souscription pour élever un monument À LA MÉMOIRE DE CHERUBINI.*[64]

Rossini approached what became overnight the talk of the town with his customary good humor. He told the committee that while he had not orchestrated anything in three decades, it would be good to put all the horns and the tam-tam player—someone to cover "the Titans' piccolo"—on notice. Applying to Royer, director of the Opéra, for the loan of the four singers (Belval, Cazaux, Faure, and Obin), he promised that

> . . . there isn't even the slightest *roulade,* nor chromatic run, nor trill, nor arpeggio: it's a simple song, of titanic rhythm and a bit enraged. One short rehearsal with me, and all will be done.
>
> If my health permitted I would willingly come myself, as would be my duty to your valiant artists, to secure the favor that I make bold to ask. Alas, my friend, my legs collapse with every heartbeat, but that heart comes in advance to plead its true thanks: it guides my hand to reiterate the feelings of highest esteem and true friendship of
>
> Your affectionate
> GR
> Fourth-rate pianist.[65]

He sent the widow Cherubini his portrait of her husband as a young man with the *envoi: "Voici, chère madame Cherubini, le portrait de ce grand homme, resté aussi jeune dans votre cœur que dans mon esprit."*[66]

Rossini's little piece amounted to a parenthesis in a concert where the atmosphere was all but religious, the hall redolent with memories and with Mme Cherubini in the *loge d'honneur.* The audience exchanged Cherubini anecdotes, then listened with rapt attention to the overture from *Anacréon* and selections from *Blanche de Provence.* The unfamiliar excerpt from *Elisa, ou Le Mont Bernard* apparently succumbed to struggling soloists (Cazaux and Grignon) and the orchestra's swamping the chorus. The same was said of the Rossini: "All the basses from the Opéra would have been needed to overcome the orchestral assault on Jupiter." ("An irreparable problem," remarked the reviewer. "The orchestra of the Société des Concerts, owing to its natural sonority, its brilliance, and the way it dominates the little stage of the Conservatoire, literally swamps the voices.") Beethoven's Fifth closed the concert with "incredible perfection," and the applause came in an avalanche.[67]

Elsewhere in town Jules Pasdeloup had unveiled his Concerts Populaires de Musique Classique at the Cirque Napoléon. His partner was
François Bazin, partisan of the Orphéon movement and experienced organizer of the concerts at the Hôtel de Ville. While the Société des Concerts was giving its Cherubini benefit, Pasdeloup was conducting Beethoven's Ninth.

The Pasdeloup concerts took the familiar Sunday afternoon time
slot, during the window between the opening of the Paris season and
the start of the Conservatoire concerts in January. The orchestra of
110 players was a third larger than that of the Société des Concerts, the
repertoire essentially the same: Haydn, Mozart, Beethoven, Weber, and
Mendelssohn. The first program was all but indistinguishable from offerings at the Conservatoire: the *Oberon* overture, "Pastoral" Symphony,
Mendelssohn Violin Concerto with Delphin Alard (concertmaster of the
Société des Concerts), theme and variations from Haydn's "Emperor"
Quartet, and overture to Méhul's *Le Jeune Henri.* Berlioz's orchestration of Weber's *L'Invitation à la valse* took the honors at the second concert. What was radically different was the price and availability of tickets.
The best seats were 2.50 francs, with intermediate places at 1.25 francs
and, revolutionarily, third-class seating at 75 *centimes.* Even so, the public response surpassed every projection: six thousand came to the first
concert, and the venue, which theoretically held only five thousand, was
sold out from there on—a "vast enclosure, . . . packed to the rafters." [68]

The Concerts Populaires, soon called by everyone the Concerts Pasdeloup, offered the great masterworks to a huge public for loose change.
In a stroke the French had their festival, monetarily viable from the first
and destined for a measure of greatness, to compete with England and
the Rhineland. A reviewer summed it up as "decidedly one of the hap-
piest ventures we've seen over the last while." Comparisons with the Société des Concerts were abundant, one for instance urging Pasdeloup's
public to observe the tradition at the Conservatoire and restrain its
"tempestuous cries for encores, which interrupted the train of the discourse." [69] As something altogether new, the Pasdeloup concerts were
thrilling and, for the Société des Concerts, immensely troubling.

So it was considered a major affront when Victor Mohr, the principal hornist of the Conservatoire concerts, cut rehearsals for the Cherubini benefit in order to be the featured soloist in Pasdeloup's concert of
17 November 1861. As much to serve as a warning to others as for any
other reason, the committee of the Société des Concerts summarily dismissed him and withdrew his pension. "Human societies, *messieurs,*" re-

ported the secretary at the end of the year, "exist only by strict observation of their laws—pacts contracted by all to be respected by each. No one has the right to put them into question."[70]

But the *affaire Mohr* caused serious upheaval in the ranks. There was a hostile correspondence, then a petition from thirty-one players demanding review of the meted punishment. The membership assembled twice more after the season to confront the problem, on 31 May and 28 June 1862, concluding with an overwhelming vote (72 favoring, 23 opposed) to maintain the interior rule of order and, thus, Mohr's dismissal. The ousting was noted in the press and discussed by the public; Elwart refers to it as regrettable in one of the last notes in his book.[71]

Pasdeloup had launched the first arrow of a campaign that would become fierce and begin to affect every decision at the Conservatoire. In proving the capacity of Parisians to absorb more classical music, he broke the hegemony of the Société des Concerts in a way that Berlioz, Seghers, Henri Herz, and others like them had failed to do. Charles Dancla, noting that "from the first day victory for Pasdeloup's enterprise was assured," praises in particular a repertoire that the Société des Concerts "kept in oblivion": the music of Bizet, Reyer, Massenet, Lalo, and Wagner, among others.[72] If the orchestra of the Conservatoire was never seriously challenged in quality—and that assertion is a stretch—it was nevertheless forced to rethink its mission, and more importantly its self-perception, in every particular.

On the occasion of Deldevez's election as second conductor, an anonymous subscriber began to submit, in the form of jottings on his printed program, his *conseils d'un amateur au 2ᵉ chef d'orchestre de la Société des Concerts*. Deldevez was amused enough to include them in his book (which begins where Elwart's first edition leaves off). The anonymous correspondent has much to say, commenting on the performers—of Battaille, for instance: "He will never understand Mozart: he's too concerned with himself"—and the performances, often assessing the choice and arrangement of the repertoire. He liked the *Zampa* overture ("I see you've hesitated to play *Zampa*, but it's much better than a lot of weightier things") and enthuses over the great works of Handel, Weber, and Beethoven (*"toujours, toujours"*). Like Berlioz he is enamored of Gluck—indeed one would suspect Berlioz of being the anonymous author were it not for the remark *"Je ne sais pas un mot de contrepoint."* Toward Mendelssohn his opinion is mixed, sorry that the *Midsummer Night's Dream* music was put aside in favor of the symphony-cantata and *Saint Paul* ("not very imaginative, and quite labored"); the Violin Concerto he found "too long." He thought Haydn's "Military" Symphony passable but inferior to a dozen others. He suggests adding a Boccherini quintet to the repertoire and for the first time anywhere in the annals brings up Wagner: "If the Société des Concerts had an impartial spirit and a charitable heart it would, in reparation due the unhappy Wagner, play the Pilgrims' March [from *Tannhäuser*] or one of the other orchestral works obviously a thousand times better than the symphony of Félicien David you played last year." The mysterious patron carried on for the whole season, concluding his missives with a touching *envoi*—"God bless you for the noble impressions that emanate from your house! In the world of the dead, I see nothing more truly alive than the Société des Concerts"—before they stopped altogether.[73]

A general assembly of 15 November 1863, called to approve two preseason concerts to benefit the retirement fund, found itself diverted by the case of the tenor Charles Marin, dismissed earlier in the fall for having lost his voice. Koenig, his compatriot in the tenor section, was charged by the singers to represent the case. "M. Marin's voice is not as feeble as the committee says," he argued, and urged the assembly to overrule the committee. But the *sociétaires* refused to take a stand until hearing the voice in question, so Marin was called to audition before all his colleagues after the rehearsal on 21 November. Faced with this daunting prospect, he retired his appeal at the last minute and accepted a *congé*.[74]

Not notified of this development, the members assembled on 21 November 1863, expecting to hear Marin of the feeble voice. Instead they found themselves being read Tilmant's letter of resignation. He had become disheartened by editorials favoring the Lyon conductor George-Hainl for the vacancy created at the Opéra by the dismissal of Pierre Dietsch. (Dietsch's ineptitude had been legendary since the *Tannhäuser* debacle in 1861. As he struggled toward the final curtain of his last *Les Vêpres siciliennes,* the chorusmaster Vauthrot was heard to remark, "There's a fellow who hasn't got more than twenty minutes left.")[75] A delegation called on Tilmant in the hope of dissuading him—a goal not especially advanced when Mme Tilmant caught one of her corset stays on her husband's violin, left on the bed, and sent it crashing against the wall. ("They fixed it," Deldevez noted, "and it sounded better than before.")[76]

But Tilmant wisely realized his career was over and held firm. His retirement was accepted with unanimous acclamation of the title *président d'honneur,* recognizing his thirty-six years of uninterrupted service. He would be accorded lifetime entry to the committee's box.[77]

The benefit concerts of December 1863 were thus confided to Deldevez, who conducted well despite "the saddest of circumstances": the death of his father. Financially they were a triumph, adding 107.30 francs to the book value of each member's account. For the first time, a consecutive pair of concerts was open to non-subscribers, and they had flocked to the box office. It is as though the society were attempting with the extra concerts to meet Pasdeloup's challenge. Very possibly the idea of pairs represents the dawn of an understanding that the short, fully subscribed seasons in a small room had no choice but, one way or another, to grow. The de facto season inched back into December; in 1863–64 it numbered a record twelve concerts: eight subscription program, two *concerts spirituels,* and the two *concerts extraordinaires* for the pension fund.

For Deldevez the concerts amounted to the most important audition of his career. By every traditional measure, he was the obvious candidate to succeed Tilmant—an incumbent second conductor and capable violinist who was already well respected by the electors. But in 1863, with Habeneck's lineage manifestly approaching its end and decided ferment in Parisian fine-music circles, there was no counting on tradition. Already in early November the field of announced candidates was strong. From within the orchestra there were the same nominees as in 1860: Alard, Cuvillon, Dancla, Deldevez, and Millault. From the outside there were the aging but now venerable Berlioz;[78] L.-M.-A Deloffre, first conductor of the Opéra-Comique; the irrepressible Elwart; and François George-Hainl, just appointed first conductor at the Opéra.

It was a perplexing circumstance, and the assembly called for 21 November 1863 to elect Tilmant's successor suspended deliberations almost immediately in order to allow the musicians to assimilate the situation and caucus among themselves.[79] Dancla, who had disliked the electoral process three years before, urged that the field of candidates be limited to the existing membership; if the members were unaware of each other's talents, that was the fault of a system that failed to encourage the several fine conductors in their midst. He hoped they would take the time to audition the unfamiliar candidates, and that in the future they might from time to time confide rehearsals to colleagues who aspired to the podium. Both suggestions were ruled out of order for the time being, though they returned soon enough to the fore. Time ran

out before the assembly was ready to make its decision, and it was agreed
to suspend the question for another month—until after the benefits.
When the members regathered, there were two more candidates, Auguste Placet and Prosper Sain d'Arod, and Deloffre had withdrawn.

On Monday morning 21 December 1863, the day after the second of
the supplementary concerts, the Assemblée Générale gathered again at
8:00 A.M. to elect the new conductor. The secretary read the letters
of candidacy from the external candidates, an admonishment from old
Meifred to proceed with dignity and care, and a discourse emanating
from the committee in favor of George-Hainl. Someone suggested appointing two conductors—thereby assuring at least one from within
the society—and two assistants; another, in view of the various uncer-
tainties they faced, proposed electing a conductor for only three years.
Auber, presiding, tabled both proposals until the committee could study
them, then called the question. The number of eligible constituents
was reckoned to be 102, requiring a two-thirds majority of 68 to elect.
George-Hainl emerged from the first ballot in the lead, with 49 votes;
Deldevez had 32, Berlioz 10, Alard 7, Dancla 2, and Millaut 1. Alard and
Dancla then withdrew in favor of their colleague Deldevez.

The second ballot gave Hainl 53 votes, Deldevez 46, and Berlioz 4.
As of the third, Hainl began to lose ground and Berlioz was effectively
eliminated: Hainl, 52; Deldevez, 49; Berlioz 1. The fourth and last preliminary ballot had breathtaking results: Hainl 51, Deldevez 50, and
1 blank ballot—with 52 needed to elect. What the minutes characterize
as a *vive agitation* took hold. Auber, challenged as to how he would rule
in the event of a tie, refused to commit himself. In the runoff George-
Hainl was elected by a vote of 53 to 49 for Deldevez.[80]

Deldevez took the turn of events philosophically, reasoning in his
memoirs that at least the situation was settled for a while.[81] His tenure,
when at length it came, would be longer and a good deal more memorable. The membership, meanwhile, congratulated itself on having ral-
lied around the will of the majority. Hainl accepted his marginal victory
with aplomb, presenting the library five published scores from his collection in token of his gratitude and humility.

So began inauspiciously the nine-year tenure, at age fifty-six, of the viva-
cious, hirsute François-Georges Hainl, known to his friends as George,
to his musicians as Monsieur George, and formally as George-Hainl.
He had won his *1er prix* in cello in 1830 and worked as a chamber musician and traveling virtuoso until his engagement as music director of the

Théâtre Municipal in Lyon, probably the most prestigious theater position in France outside Paris. He may have played for a time as *aspirant*
with the Société des Concerts, and in January 1838 appeared on a Sunday concert in an otherwise unidentified *solo de violoncelle*. Berlioz, who
was in Lyon in 1845, describes a gregarious, good-hearted host, determined to see that every detail of his concert, from the quality of the
personnel to the attitude of the press, was made right well in advance;
Hainl even learned enough harp to get through *Harold en Italie*.[82] He
continued to compose orchestral works, and in 1853 published a history
of music in Lyon. At the Opéra he had gained control within a few weeks,
righting *Les Vêpres siciliennes* and later leading the world premieres of
L'Africaine, Don Carlos, and *Hamlet*. His wife, the pianist Marie Poite-
vin, was also popular with the *sociétaires;* much later, in April 1891,
she appeared with Clotilde Kleeberg in the Mozart Concerto for Two
Pianos.

Inevitably at this clear break with the past, nearly four decades from the
foundation, there was a substantial turnover in personnel. Nine members separated during 1863–64, including Charles Dancla (having failed
to be elected second conductor in 1860 and first conductor in 1863) and
the founding members Battu, Gras, and Tolbecque *aîné*. The retirement
a year later of Simon Leborne, noted scholar and professor of composition, deprived them of a workhorse who never missed a season despite the obligations of a distinguished academic career. Delphin Alard,
their concertmaster, professor of violin, and pioneer in France of the
Mendelssohn Violin Concerto, decided to retire before the 1866 season,
though promising to return whenever his services were needed.[83]

A few weeks later the chorusmaster Vauthrot chose the same course.
His resignation had already been accepted and an assembly called to replace him when Hainl and Auber, acting on their own initiative, found
him at the Opéra and persuaded him to withdraw it, "pure and simple."[84]
Vauthrot saw the 1865–66 season out, then resigned definitively on 9 October 1866. At this point the membership declined to ratify the committee's nomination of Vandenheuvel, husband of Mme Vandenheuvel-
Duprez, to succeed him; Vandenheuvel was not a French citizen, had
not attended the Conservatoire, and was not a member of the society.
Auguste Charlot, winner of the 1850 Prix de Rome, was elected to the
post, narrowly ahead of Bizet on the first ballot and comfortably on the
second.[85] Charlot served from 1866 until his death from epidemic disease in 1871.

To replace the outgoing cohort came a brilliant new generation:

the violinists Jules Garcin, Charles Lamoureux, and Albert Ferrand; the violist Alfred Viguier; new trumpet and horn players. Lamoureux and Garcin were soon to be concertmaster and principal second violinist, respectively; each became second conductor, and eventually they were both to occupy positions of great influence in France. Ferrand was an important quartet player and a sometime conductor, at length advancing to second chair in the violins; Viguier was principal violist for more than a decade until his eyesight failed. All five became devoted administrators of the Société des Concerts, with Viguier and Ferrand soon emerging as the most capable officers of their era.

Hainl conducted the Société des Concerts for the first time on 10 January 1864. Until that Sunday he had been primarily an opera conductor, and he must have spent his first three or four Paris seasons mastering the society's repertoire week by week. The programming on his first concert of the "Chœur des nymphes" from Ambroise Thomas's *Psyché* may hint at his personal taste, which tended toward opera overtures and big choral excerpts. An *Ave verum* of Gounod was heard in March, and in April Berlioz's *La Fuite en Égypte* (part II of *L'Enfance du Christ*), reprised in 1866 and 1872 and thereafter carrying sturdily into the twentieth century. One of Hainl's first errands in Paris had been to inquire of Berlioz which of his works should be programmed for 1864— "not long," he had specified, thinking perhaps of the four symphonic movements from *Roméo et Juliette*. Berlioz would have preferred to hear Mme Charton-Demeur in excerpts from *Les Troyens,* since *Les Troyens à Carthage* had played the previous winter at the Théâtre-Lyrique and was still the talk of intellectual circles. But Mme Charton declined to sing unless they included the love duet, and when the committee decided to program only the septet Berlioz withdrew the project altogether.[86] On the whole, Hainl's commitment to Berlioz was surprisingly modest, limited to the *Hymne à la France* for the Universal Exposition in 1867—an event Berlioz had been scheduled to conduct—and after Berlioz's death the *Faust* excerpts.

In any case it is difficult to know just how much the leadership in programming came from Hainl himself and how much rested with the committee at large. Collectively the committee was well disposed toward rejuvenations of any kind. None of the three ex officio members— Hainl as conductor, Deldevez as assistant conductor, and Vauthrot as chorusmaster—was as ardently conservative as Girard had been, nor was the secretary, Lebouc. Lamoureux and Ferrand were staunch progressives. At least they defined the problem, describing, in response to some public grumbling about the modernisms of 1863–64 (minimal though they were), a weekly juggling act between the old and the new. It was the familiar problem of revitalizing a repertoire intellectuals knew to have grown stale, while watching the subscribers "revolt at seeing the name of a living composer on the program, arguing noisily that the Société des Concerts should limit its attention to dead people."[87]

The front-page composer of 1863 and 1864 was Giacomo Meyerbeer. *L'Africaine* was finished (though it would not open at the Opéra until April 1865), its triumph already assured by the decade of anticipation that had preceded it and one of the most memorable effects—the wrecking of a ship—ever seen onstage. The Société des Concerts began its program of 24 January 1864 with the overture to *Struensee,* just a few weeks, as it turned out, before Meyerbeer's death and elaborately staged funeral in May. They dedicated the opening concert of the thirty-eighth season, 1864–65, *à la mémoire de G. Meyerbeer,* with a chorus from *Marguerite d'Anjou,* the overture to *Le Pardon de Ploërmel,* and the always popular "blessing of the daggers" scene from act IV of *Les Huguenots.* The overture entered the standard repertoire, and the following season a double chorus, *Adieu aux jeunes mariés,* began to overtake Leisring's *O filii* in frequency of programming on the *partie vocale.* Deldevez later made a four-movement suite from *Struensee,* to which Garcin added an entr'acte in 1885:

> Ouverture − La Révolte − Le Bal (Polonaise) − L'Auberge du village (Entr'acte) − Le Rêve − La Bénédiction − Marche funèbre − Dernier moment

The overture and polonaise remained in the repertoire well into the twentieth century.

Hainl's first seasons were quite successful at the box office, with improved global income generated through rigorous economies and the selling of makeshift attic seating to *amateurs* who clamored for it; the December concerts dramatically garnished the pension fund. At the end of 1863–64 some 102,673 francs were distributed to the *sociétaires,* each taking away 537 francs in cash and 376 francs in their retirement accounts; the next year's income was still better, at 103,574 francs. The *jeton* held firm at about 10 francs for each of some fifty-four services (roughly eighteen public events and thirty-six rehearsals)—a total of something over 500 francs per *sociétaire* per annum. That the income was essentially fixed and costs were rising was nothing new; at the time the burning question was how to answer the public demand for entry.

The season grew to thirteen concerts in 1865 with a May gala at the Opéra for a charity called the Amis de l'Enfance; in 1866 there were fourteen: six subscription concerts, five non-subscription *concerts extraordinaires,* two *concerts spirituels,* and a command performance for the Grand Duchess Marie of Russia. (The command arrived on 1 June for a concert four days later.) That unusual number of supplementary concerts was a preliminary response to a petition signed by twenty-three suggesting conversion to two series of seven concerts each—an idea that had been in the air for some years.

A second petition concerned the necessary remodeling of the Salle des Concerts, thought to have become *"insuffisante et peu digne de notre publique."*[88] Remodeling began in the summer of 1865, forced the pre-season concerts into 1866, and was "just finished" by the Assemblée Générale of 13 May 1866.

The new *décor* was brilliant, and the gas lighting at last lifted the orchestra from its "Stygian obscurity." For the musicians who had made their debuts amidst the "good old decoration" it was an occasion for nostalgia and some melancholy. The loss of seating left some subscribers "troubled and inconvenienced," but the *archiviste-caissier* and his assistants worked overtime to satisfy each patron, and in the end the committee maintained that relationships with the public had never been better. The secretary likened the change to a refurbished vessel once again flying its proud standard: *"le Drapeau de l'art respecté et de la noble et grande Musique."*[89]

The fortieth season of the Société des Concerts, 1866–67, thus consisted of twelve subscription concerts in six pairs, each program repeated the next Sunday except when problems with the soloists forced a last-minute change. At the beginning the *concerts spirituels* were considered non-subscription events, though eventually the first series would include Good Friday and the second, Easter Sunday. Patrons cultivated in 1866 became the new subscribers to the second series.[90] The reduction by half of titles performed was inconsequential, at least at the outset, since there was little novelty in any event.

With these fundamental changes in practice successfully negotiated, the society could turn its attention to the Exposition Universelle of 1867. The minister invited them to give "several concerts" in their capacity as an artistic monument, a pride of the nation worthy to be offered before the thousands of citizens of the world who would come to visit France.[91] The two evening concerts they provided in response, 2 and 14 June 1867, were relatively short: a Beethoven symphony, choral selections, excerpts from the *Midsummer Night's Dream* on one and the Beethoven Septet on the other, and a Weber overture. On Thursday 11 July 1867 (postponed from 8 July),[92] George-Hainl led the huge festival concert in the Palais de l'Industrie, with 500 orchestral musicians, 500 singers, and a military band of 200. This event was very long, with a dozen works separated by two intervals. Rossini's *Hymne à Napoléon III et à son vaillant peuple* and Berlioz's *Hymne à la France* were featured— neither was a first performance—alongside such crowd-pleasers as the Soldiers Chorus from Gounod's *Faust,* the Coronation March from *Le Prophète,* and Méhul's overture to *Le Jeune Henri,* all with a 60-piece drum-and-bugle corps for the fanfares. Berlioz, who probably suggested most of the program, had meant to conduct, but was in mourning for his son, Louis, dead of yellow fever in Havana.

Wagner's music arrived at the Salle des Concerts in March 1866 with the Pilgrims' Chorus from *Tannhäuser.* That turning point became the more memorable when Liszt was recognized to be occupying Auber's box. The public, delighted to catch a glimpse of the legendary pianist now dressed in a cleric's black, grew restless; the agitation reached fever pitch when Liszt, who thought the Wagner should get more applause, stood and demanded a *bis.* The musicians responded accordingly, but the audience, oblivious by now to *Tannhäuser,* cried *"Vive Liszt!"* until the concert was over. Auber regarded the incident as unknown in the annals of concertgoing.[93] The excerpt from *Tannhäuser* was joined in 1869 by the wedding march with chorus from *Lohengrin;* both were popular, but soon to be dropped in the wake of the Franco-Prussian War.

By the decade's end the Société des Concerts was well embarked on a program of thoughtful enhancements to the repertoire. Gounod's *Près du fleuve étranger* ("By the Waters of Babylon"), a motet for unaccompanied chorus, took its place alongside the Meyerbeer *Adieu aux jeunes mariés* in frequency of programming. Schumann's "Spring" Symphony (No. 1, in B♭ major) opened the 1867–68 season; Mendelssohn's Psalm 42 came a few weeks later. Jules Garcin and Anton Rubinstein played concertos of their own composition, and at the concert of 10 April 1868 a new pedal piano by Érard was demonstrated, with the young E.-M. Delaborde playing a chorale and Toccata in F by J. S. Bach. Saint-Saëns appeared in his Third Piano Concerto in December 1869. Meanwhile the committee set in motion a scheme to divide the works of Beethoven and Mendelssohn into roughly equal parts, rotating through the repertoire of both composers every two years.[94] The primary goal was to restore works that had inadvertently fallen by the wayside—chief among them the Ninth.

For some of the musicians, the new order had its tribulations: "The committee thinks it its duty to tell you, *messieurs,* how often it is discouraged in its search [for new work] by the marks of impatience and disregard that a good number of the members think it necessary to offer during the sight-reading sessions—judging without favor works signed by composers of merit, sometimes even the great masters. First readings nearly always leave something to be desired, and we think it imprudent to manifest any opinion whatever of the value of a work before its performance is satisfying."[95]

Just before electing George-Hainl, uncertain of his promise and knowing that all three previous conductors had declined in capability while serving them, the *sociétaires* had passed a short but significant modification to the statutes: "A conductor who reaches the age of sixty shall be re-elected every two years."[96] Hainl turned sixty in November 1867 and thus needed to stand for re-election at the general assembly of May 1868; he did not attend, pleading indisposition.

There was consternation over what was actually happening, Lamoureux favoring a yes-or-no plebescite and other officers maintaining that it was an open election, requiring a two-thirds vote. After long, "agitated" debate, ratification by a two-thirds majority was called for. The first ballot showed Hainl well short of a two-thirds majority, with 56 votes to 30 for Deldevez, 5 for Lamoureux, 4 for the retired Charles Dancla (nominated at the last minute by his brother, Léopold), and 1 each for several others. In succeeding rounds Hainl never reached the two-thirds vote, and it was only when the slate was reduced to two candidates in the runoff that he secured a decent margin, 80 to 35 for Deldevez. His mandate was thus extended for two years, 1868–69 and 1869–70. Somewhat later an anonymous *sociétaire* placed a sharply negative assessment of George-Hainl's first half-decade in one of the major papers, to the committee's obvious consternation.[97]

The onstage collapse and death of the young oboist Berthélemy, and a generally hard winter, brought the appointment of a physician to the Société des Concerts who was to occupy the committee's box and stand "ready to bring the aid of his science not merely to the members of the Society, but also to our public."[98] This distinction went to Dr. Laroche, *amateur de musique,* who died—leaving them his pharmacy—during the next season, then to Dr. Levrat, physician of the IXe Arrondissement; from 1877–78 the assignment was taken by Dr. Firmin, personal physician to Deldevez and later dedicatee of his 1887 volume on the Société des Concerts. Tilmant, incidentally, was discovered to be in poor health and financial need, and the society went to his aid.[99]

Another sort of leadership crisis began during the usual pre-season review of personnel in the autumn of 1868, when the committee retired one older singer, Lebourlier, outright and summoned others to audition. One of these, Lebaron, was found to lack vocal means and also retired involuntarily. The general assembly called to hear his appeal heard instead the secretary's account of the "poor state of his voice" and a letter received the night before in which Lebaron excused himself from the meeting owing to a case of the flu, appending a certificate from his physician. Hearing, however, that he was actually on the grounds of the Conservatoire, the presiding officer summoned the hapless Lebaron, who apologized for the gross inconvenience and promised to sing for them after the rehearsal on 14 December, subsequently delayed until the eighteenth.[100] There, with 103 colleagues again present, Lebaron asked for yet another delay of two weeks.

With nothing else to do, the members launched into a debate on the premises of forced retirement.[101] The violinist-composer Millault presented the artistically suspect but doubtless widely supported view that every *sociétaire* had the right to remain until age sixty, "whatever the impairment of his means." Lamoureux argued to the contrary that not only had the committee properly exercised its mandate in the case of Lebaron, but that the unjust element in the equation was that it did not require the same verification of the orchestral personnel. Sauzay, himself on the verge of sixty, leapt to his feet in protest, as the meeting adjourned to await the promised audition. Lebaron's audition was finally heard by 106 colleagues on 9 January 1869. The first-round vote, dramatically, was tied: 52 favoring dismissal, 52 favoring a reversal of the committee decision, and 2 blank ballots. Auber refused to break the tie, calling instead for a second ballot. The members now narrowly voted to retain their colleague: 54 favoring reversal, 29 approving the committee decision to dismiss, 1 blank, and some two dozen abstaining.

With Lebaron thus maintained as a *sociétaire* and the committee's decision overridden, its members began to tender their resignations, provoking pandemonium. "In view of the agitation and fatigue of the assembly," the president summarily closed the meeting to allow the situation to clarify. The members assembled once more on 19 January 1869—for the fifth time in a month—to end the debate. The singers, assuring their continued confidence in the government, asked the committee members to withdraw their resignations. Viguier was inclined to resume his post, though not likely to change his *manière de voir;* Altès said his action was irreversible, and was replaced.[102]

The rejuvenation in programming continued to gain momentum. The 1868–69 season had opened with Gouvy's Symphony in F, and in 1869–70 there was not only a new violin concerto by Victorin de Joncières but also Schumann's *Manfred* overture, two movements of a new Requiem by Gounod, and an ambitious cantata by Auguste Vaucorbeil, *La Mort de Diane,* with the reigning diva Gabrielle Krauss in the title role. (Later in the year Krauss joined J.-B. Faure and Mlle Nilsson in a light concert sponsored by the Ministry of Naval and Colonial Affairs: duos from *Don Pasquale, Così fan tutte,* and *The Barber of Seville;* arias from *Figaro* and *La Traviata;* the Schubert *Ave Maria;* and a concluding trio from Cimarosa's *Il matrimonio segreto.* By the end of the season Krauss was as popular with the patrons as Mme Viardot had been.) Friedrich Gernsheim, professor at the Cologne Conservatory, visited with a piano concerto of his composition, and an *O salutaris* by the chorusmaster, Charlot, had one performance before being abandoned because of a soloist's indisposition. Viguier's *rapport moral* on 15 May 1870 briefly noted his satisfaction with that kind of season, then turned to consider the great *solennité musicale* being planned for the centenary of Beethoven's birth in December.

There would be no Beethoven centenary concert in 1870. During the summer France was invaded by the Prussians, who laid siege to Paris and ultimately occupied it, effectively severing the capital from the rest of the nation. The situation became menacing in August; on 18 September, after the German victory at Sedan, the last remaining communications with the outside world were cut. December 1870 and January 1871, during the siege, saw bombardment, famine, and bureaucratic collapse. Historians reckon the winter of the siege as the most devastating chapter of modern Parisian history, as the citizens were forced to eat domestic animals, then the elephants—Castor and Pollux—in the zoo, then common rats. The horror began to subside with the armistice of 28 January and the punishing capitulation signed at Versailles.

Many of the musicians fled France altogether, finding work in London, Brussels, and Geneva. Others remained or established themselves in country houses as far away as they could get from what at first they called the *tristes événements,* then the *terrible catastrophe* and *désastre* that had befallen Paris. Normandy and Brittany were popular for refuge, as they offered the possibility of eventual escape by sea to England; one member waited out the crisis on the Isle of Jersey. Some bragged of dodging the draft and general mobilization (whereas the young Vincent d'Indy served faithfully and even wrote a history of his battalion). In Paris, the Conservatoire was used as a hospital.[103]

The Société des Concerts managed to assemble remnants of its membership and enough young people to present two concerts during the period before the siege: a benefit for the Ambulances de la Presse — the historic drive to establish field hospitals to treat the war wounded — on 31 October 1870,[104] and a solemn performance of the Cherubini Requiem in the Madeleine on 23 December. The day-to-day concerns of the society were capably administered by George-Hainl and the *archiviste-caissier*, Albert Ferrand. When the siege lifted, the musicians were immediately summoned to rehearsals in the hope of salvaging a season of five concerts from Sunday, 5 March 1871, with a benefit for the wounded on Monday, 6 March.

But this was impossible. The telegraph lines were still down, and the mail was delayed for days when it was not lost altogether; the *convocations* posted on 28 February were still being received in mid-March. Those in Brussels could not return through the militarized zone; the Trouville contingent had to await the repair of the rail line to Paris, while colleagues in Switzerland discovered that the Geneva–Lyon service was still out. An accounting of the absent that February lists 30 members: 8 violins, 4 violas, 4 cellists, a contrabass, a clarinet, and 12 singers including the chorusmaster Charlot. Among the *aspirants actifs*, 3 violinists, a cellist, and 14 singers were out of town, for a total of 48 absent—more than a third of the typical force.[105] Adolphe Blanc, the *agent comptable,* would not return to Paris for fear of contracting disease, but neither would he reveal the location of the account books in a letter he would have to confide to the post. Ferrand at length prevailed on him to come home to do the banking, appealing to his colleague's sense of duty and noting that he himself had not missed a single one of the twenty-three committee meetings that took place during the fall and winter.[106]

Many were indeed ill with life-threatening gastroenteritis. Diarrhea made travel unthinkable. Charlot and his wife were stricken in one part of France, along with three generations of his in-laws elsewhere. There is more reference to sick wives and children in the minutes of 1871 than in all the rest put together: the dossier is plaintive, bitter, appallingly poignant.[107]

Life in Paris was again thoroughly disrupted by the Commune, 18 March to 27 May 1871, with street fighting at its peak in late May. The musicians who had returned to town dispersed again—for example, Boulard, who in late March concluded that his wife and daughter were too impressionable to be living in Montmartre. Ferrand and Hainl spirited the institution's funds out of Paris for deposit in Le Havre. The octogenarian Auber died in mid-May, his remains stored in a vault at the Church of the Trinité to await a more appropriate occasion for farewell; Charlot died in July. And for the first time in its history, a season of the Société des Concerts was lost.

By mid-summer a semblance of normalcy was settling in. Auber's funeral took place on 15 July with the society at sufficient strength to offer the Cherubini Requiem again and the "Eroica" funeral march. In September it was decided to schedule ten concerts, five pairs, from 29 October to 31 December 1871, thus maintaining the illusion of a forty-fourth season (which would ordinarily have run from Christmas 1870 to Easter 1871); the forty-fifth season, of fourteen concerts in seven pairs, would begin in January 1872. Rehearsals were announced, and the subscription process went into operation as usual.

In truth, the situation was anything but normal. The musicians had lived in severe distress for ten months. At least one had lost most of his personal belongings when his house was destroyed in the bombardment. The committee was overwhelmed with requests for leave and exceptions to the rules, as the instrumentalists begged to play in the casino orchestras and Jules Danbé's concerts at the Grand Hôtel: "Given the unhappy events that have taken place, we have to be heard, to make some money." More often than not the committee had to yield priority, and so there were still not enough musicians to go around. The *aspirants,* meanwhile, jockeyed hungrily for the forthcoming round of vacancies and wrote the committee to make sure their places on the seniority list were secure—the violist Jean Conte, for instance, who protested that his colleague Trombetta was wrongly ahead of him in the queue, a situation that "wounded his *amour-propre* and deprived him of an artistic satisfaction he highly valued."[108]

There was comparable confusion in patron seating, as places were reassigned when old subscribers failed to renew, only to return to Paris expecting their customary seats. The direct impact of the war continued for a couple of years more, indirect results—for there was a new republic—for much longer still.

On 4 October 1871 the membership reassembled for the first time since May 1870 to hear a report on where things stood, be introduced to the plan for two seasons in one, and start to fill the many vacancies in their ranks. They began by electing as their president Ambroise Thomas, Auber's successor as director of the Conservatoire, in an essentially unanimous ballot. (One *sociétaire* cast his vote for Gounod, who had declined the Conservatoire post—a "senseless pleasantry," Hainl grumbled.)[109] To succeed the deceased chorusmaster Charlot the committee recommended two candidates, Théodore Dubois and Ernest Guiraud; Dubois won on the second ballot by a vote of 54 to 44. Three days later Thomas signed the *livre d'or*, noting his humility at the thought of taking up the offices of Cherubini and Auber.[110]

The forty-fourth season was inaugurated on 29 October and 5 November 1871 with, symbolically, the "Eroica" Symphony and Gounod's lamentation on the fall of Paris, *Gallia*, a motet for soprano, chorus, organ, and orchestra. Gounod had composed the work for the opening of the London International Exhibition that summer; his mistress, Mrs. (Georgina) Weldon, came from England to sing the solo. The publisher Choudens nearly prevented the performance by suggesting 300 francs rental for the materials. When that was declined he asked for four seats to the concerts, also refused, this time with the observation that something had to be done to stop pretentious demands from music publishers.[111]

In a turn of immense significance, the Société des Concerts resumed aggressive *répétitions d'essai*, some five between the end of November 1871 and the end of February 1872. Proposed works now had a preliminary reading at the piano before the committee alone, with the full jury convened only for those that passed to the orchestra reading. As before, most of the work essayed failed by a wide margin: overtures by Matthias and Taudou and Pfeiffer; excerpts of a symphony by Dancla; a piano concerto by Castillon; an Andante by the violinist Michiels (0 favoring, 20 opposed; when told of the decision, Michiels swore at Hainl and incurred a brief suspension); and a *Stabat mater* of Mme de Grandval.[112]

What was surprising was the number of new works programmed— the effect, it may be surmised, of Deldevez and Dubois joining forces on behalf of new music: the Andante and scherzo of a "new" symphony by Saint-Saëns (quite probably drafts of the "Organ" symphony), excerpts from Franck's *Ruth,* the Introit and Dies irae of a Requiem by Charles Lenepveu, and two of *The Seven Last Words of Christ,* by Dubois. By all appearances Dubois had emerged as a pivotal figure before the end of his first season, both for his organizational skills and for his musical tastes. He set the chorus to work on Vittoria's *O vos omnes,* two new Bach motets, Mendelssohn's *Paulus,* and Schumann's *Paradise and the Peri* (not performed until February 1888, in a French translation by Victor Wilder).

The third concert of 1872 was to have fallen on 28 January, the first anniversary of the shameful "armistice"—the fall of Paris—that had lifted the siege but cost France its army, an indemnity of 200 million francs, and Alsace and Lorraine. On Friday, 26 January, Hainl asked his committee if they wished to cancel their Sunday concert, given the lugubrious associations of the date, but they preferred to continue on the course already charted. At the dress rehearsal the next morning, however, a letter from the prefect of Paris decreed closure of all the theaters and "invited" the orchestra not to play. Committee members rushed to arrange postings and notices in the Sunday papers; subscribers were, for the first time, sent telegrams notifying them of the change.[113]

There was also the need to arrange a benefit of some kind for the victims of 1870–71, the society's standard gesture of citizenship in the world beyond the Salle des Concerts; since November they had been discussing the possibility of a *Missa solemnis*. The concert took shape instead as a benefit on 3 March 1872 for the benevolent organization calling itself L'Œuvre de la Délivrance, dedicated to raising charitable donations for the war reparations and "the patriotic work of liberating the captive territory"—that is, Alsace and Lorraine. Ticket prices were increased by 50 percent, and both the committee's *billets de service* and press boxes were sold to the public; women volunteers would collect an offering. The government authorized them to note the patronage of the president of the Republic and volunteered 1,000 francs for the *loge d'honneur*. Mme Viardot agreed to sing her celebrated arias from *Alceste* and *Orphée*.[114]

At the last moment there were political misunderstandings, and the government withdrew its sponsorship and permission to collect donations. The box-office proceeds, on the other hand, were quite substantial. This left the Société des Concerts with the curious problem of what to do with the money. It was suggested that it go to a women's club, the Société des Femmes de France, which was supporting the occupied departments through an arrangement with the Bank of France. At length the national treasury agreed to take the money, earmarked "payment in support of delivering the territory." It would be conveyed to the proper authorities when Alsace and Lorraine were free of German occupation. The society remitted a remarkable total of 17,267.30 francs, its contribution to restoring the national honor—reckoned by Germany to be worth 3 billion.[115]

The long march of concerts, some two dozen without a Sunday's break from the end of October 1871 until mid-May 1872, showed the players all they could do and whetted their appetite for more. They were, in their non-demonstrative fashion, stimulated by the new music. There was surprisingly little concern in the ranks occasioned by the new Société Nationale organized at and around the Conservatoire with arguably as strong a backing as the Société des Concerts had ever had. (It was rather quickly observed, however, that both George-Hainl and Dubois were on the organizing committee of what might well be thought a rival philharmonic society, a situation long forbidden by the rules. Hainl agreed to sever his connection with the Société Nationale; Dubois's conflict of interest was resolved with his resignation from the Société des Concerts in October.) [116] The new government had taken the *loge d'honneur* for every concert, and by April there was serious progress toward an ongoing subvention.

The Good Friday *concert spirtuel* of 31 March 1872 was conducted by E.-M.-E. Deldevez, owing to Hainl's sudden indisposition. Mme George-Hainl quietly let Deldevez know that her husband had suffered a heart attack two nights before. George-Hainl had not missed a concert since his election; Deldevez had last conducted the orchestra for a benefit in March 1867, and in the interim had seen a number of upheavals in his own artistic life. Hainl was back on the podium for the Easter Sunday concert and led the rest of the season, but at the last rehearsal, presumably on Saturday, 11 May 1872, he shocked his colleagues by announcing his resignation. His co-director at the Opéra, F.-A. Gevaert, had returned to Belgium to succeed Fétis as director of the Brussels Conservatoire, leaving Hainl alone during a period of rebuilding and stress; he had become the "artistic conscience" of the house, he said, and was needed there full time. He did not mention his health.

Turning to Deldevez, he indicated a "loyal friend" worthy of taking the role. *"Vous avez à vos côtés,"* he said, *"un successeur tout indiqué."*[117] At the Assemblée Générale of 25 May 1872, accordingly, Deldevez was elected to succeed him, with 94 votes out of 104.

Hainl's name appears in the minutes a few more times, mostly regarding a disagreement over the rate at which his shares in the Caisse de Prévoyance were liquidated. Otherwise he simply disappears, and does not seem to have been especially regretted. He died just over a year later; after that the next time he is mentioned is in 1877, when his daughter, Mme *veuve* Le Corbellier *née* George-Hainl, following the wishes of her late husband, established a prize of 1,000 francs for the 1er *prix* in cello at the Conservatoire.

PART THREE

1872–1919

If today E.-M.-E. Deldevez has lost stature by comparison with the attention naturally focused on the founding conductor Habeneck and on the stardom of the twentieth-century *chefs*, then it is all the more important to emphasize his centrality in his own era. Deldevez, a consummate performer and a composer of not inconsiderable merit, was also a good philosopher. His assessment of the repertoire dilemma was sensitive to the many nuances afoot, and his strategy in response—to keep to the middle of the road—was, though not especially daring, workable. On the face of it his approach to programming seemed most often to cater to the patrons. Yet gradually doors were opened, first with Bach and Handel, then Berlioz, later with the Prix Rossini for young composers. Deldevez would leave the stage in readiness for the four defining productions of his immediate successors: the *Missa solemnis,* Franck's D-Minor Symphony, the B-Minor Mass, and Berlioz's *Roméo et Juliette.*

Dramatic change in the economic and social condition of musical institutions was accommodated by the Société des Concerts with comparative ease. Taxation rose hugely in the Third Republic, in part to pay for the war reparations. The musicians' union (SAMUP) and the performance rights organization (SACEM) began to dictate major shifts in internal policy. The political health of the nation, in its new democracy, was fragile at best and soon deteriorated with the multiple crises surrounding the Dreyfus Affair. A strongly competitive, capitalist environment for concert music became a way of life, not only for the "four associations"—the Colonne, Lamoureux, Pasdeloup, and Conservatoire concerts—but also for the several institutions established, in an atmosphere of sharply aggressive nationalism, to promote new French music.[1]

The era of Garcin, Taffanel, and Marty, 1885–1908, was the last period of sustained political and economic tranquility the Société des Concerts was to know. Not since the 1830s had music and the other arts so flourished in Paris. The popularity of concertgoing coincided with stasis at the Opéra, yielding a more balanced and thus more wholesome environment for art music in all its manifestations. *Fin-de-siècle* intellectual ferment and the decorative exuberance of the Belle Époque afforded an uncommon level of stimulus even for so tradition-minded an association as the Société des Concerts. To the orchestra prosperity meant, above all, freedom from crisis and the concomitant luxury to enjoy their *métier* as guarantors of the great classics in long-perfected interpretations. But it also encouraged them to invest in progress, to risk the unfamiliar more routinely than before.

And there was fine progressive music to be had for the looking. Gradually at first, then with gathering momentum, the Société des Concerts saw its mission transformed—and, one might well argue, its overall outlook improved. It became in effect a beacon of the French national school and, as politics deteriorated in western Europe, a significant organ in the formal propaganda effort to promote the superiorities of the French culture. Though Garcin's tenure began without special excitement, in the ordinary exercise of an established pattern of succession, he left indelible marks of an exciting new orientation, with the old "Louvre of music" sentiment a thing of the distant past. He found a commercially viable niche, promoting works of size and substance that only the Société des Concerts was capable of delivering.

With Messager's strong commitment to new music, notably that of Debussy, the Société des Concerts found too a workable balance between veneration of the past and full membership in the present of art music, no longer to be dismissed as either retrograde or dabbling in modernism. As a business, thanks largely to Taffanel's stewardship, the society was in excellent shape. Impresarios emerged, capable of negotiating —better than the musicians themselves—the complex agreements necessary to secure new venues and the best concerto soloists. In the single most important step taken by the Société des Concerts in the twentieth century, it undertook what would rapidly become a flourishing program of touring, thus reaching a large new populace. Though achieved at the formidable price of dismissing its chorus, the orchestra's experience on the road proved the key to its triumphal emergence from World War I.

CHAPTER 7

Deldevez

(1872–85)

Aftershocks from 1870–71 continued for many months. The *sociétaires* and their dependents struggled to overcome the grave assaults on their health and financial security. The stress that always accompanied a change of conductors was compounded at this juncture by the general atmosphere of uncertainty, as well as the melancholy realization in hindsight that Hainl had been lost to the society just as he was reaching his stride. The institution, likewise, had been on the verge of finding its place in a post-Romantic world, welcoming new musicians, new patrons, and even a few new works. Suddenly the very foundation of its success, the certainty of the Sunday concerts played to a faithful clientele, had been swept away in direct consequence of war. Thoughtful artists pondering the loss within a few months of both Berlioz and Auber could not help concluding that their aesthetic had passed with them, for that was the case. It did not take much further thought to recognize the number of fine French composers—two generations: Gounod, Franck, Lalo; Saint-Saëns, Bizet, Massenet—with whom the Société des Concerts had so far had little, or nothing at all, to do.

Given all these things, the vigor and vibrancy of the post-war Société des Concerts are remarkable indeed. The orchestra and its new 1er *chef* embarked on their forty-sixth season, 1872–73, with assurance; they were well organized, intellectually engaged, artistically excited. It is as though the *tristes événements* cleared the way for what needed doing. By the end of 1873–74 the *rapport moral* could boast of maximum receipts, a house in perfect order—of a Société des Concerts "never greater, never more admired, never more respected."[1]

That Edme-Marie-Ernest Deldevez, born 1817, would sooner or later become first conductor of the Société des Concerts was, by the time it occurred, universally understood. He had been a member of the orchestra for nearly four decades, having served as an *aspirant* from 1833 and a full *sociétaire* from 1839. Habeneck, his principal mentor, had groomed him for conducting; he had been *2ᵉ chef* since Tilmant's elevation to the podium in 1860. Nearly half the members supported Deldevez on the occasion of George-Hainl's election in 1863, and Hainl had seen fit to designate him in the course of his own resignation speech. The musicians were excited to have one of their own at the helm again.

For Deldevez himself, elevation to the post he had long expected was a genuine professional comeback and something of a personal triumph. He was given to both rheumatism and depression, a *maladie morale* that had troubled him since childhood. His duties as *2ᵉ chef* at the Opéra, where he was called at the last minute to conduct difficult works on no rehearsals, were agonizing on psychological grounds as well as artistic ones. Eventually he was unhappy enough with his lot that in June 1870, after years of threatening, he held firm in his decision to give up the post. He immediately fell ill with rheumatism and was still convalescing when he returned to Paris just before the siege, there to pass his days alone at his desk, hungry and cold, composing religious music and exchanging a few words with a faithful domestic servant named Henriette. By night he would go the Opéra to observe what he called the *tristes soirées du siège,* the room hazy with smoke from the whale-oil lamps that had been substituted for the useless gas jets. He waited out the Commune in the village of Dinan in Brittany, homesick for orchestral hurly-burly, for the *mélange* of instruments—in short, for sonority itself—that would come with better times.[2] He could not know that they were at hand, and so consumed himself in misery.

And his frame of mind did not at first improve with the dramatic change in his station. Between his election in May 1872 and the first rehearsal for the new season that October, his psyche spun out of control, swinging "between terror and hope, desire and despair, success and failure." He concluded he was losing his faculties and once again penned a letter of resignation, intended to take effect even before he began his new duties. Friends talked him into destroying the foolish letter and led him to conclude that the act of resignation was merely a "charlatan's cure for bad luck."[3]

His career as *1ᵉʳ chef* of the Société des Concerts, though not without its stressful periods, was distinguished both in length and in artistic result. Honors commensurate with his achievement were not long in coming, notably election in June 1873 as *1ᵉʳ chef* at the Opéra and appointment to a professorship in conducting at the Conservatoire a few months later (October 1873). These were followed by the Légion d'Honneur (1874), a knighthood from the *mélomane* King of Hanover (1875), and the coveted title Officier de l'Instruction Publique (1878).

Deldevez was the most academically inclined of all the conductors of the Société des Concerts. His inclination to solitude made him most comfortable at his desk, where he was a natural composer, researcher, writer, philosopher, organizer. It is fair to say that he was the first really good composer in the lineage of the society's conductors, with three symphonies published by Richault to his credit, a successful Requiem, and a number of smaller works. His four major books—*Curiosités musicales* (1873), *L'Art du chef d'orchestre* (1878), *La Société des Concerts du Conservatoire* (1887), and *Mes Mémoires* (1890)—are solid and engaging, and important sources for this particular volume.[4] If his autobiography focuses on a conductor's "misfortunes and griefs" with positively Berliozian melancholy, there is nevertheless an underlying current of amusement at how his many tribulations worked themselves out for the best. He takes a certain pleasure, for instance, in reprinting his 1833 reprimand from the committee for having missed three services; once threatened with dismissal, he was now in charge. He was historically curious and widely read, and by the standards of his generation unusually well informed on the arcana of the Haydn corpus, the music of Schumann, and the lost works of Schubert.

In extension of these interests, he was actively involved with the society's library. At one of his first committee meetings he complained of the *mauvais état de la bibliothèque,* and in the weeks following issued calls for rebinding abused and aging scores, the copying of a Gluck *De profundis* for the *concerts spirituels,* retranslating and recopying the chorus parts for Beethoven's Ninth (and insisting that the translator be a member of the writers union; the faithful Bélanger was chosen), and a proper inventory of the collection. This last task was undertaken, at the suggestion of Deldevez, by the bassoonist Jancourt, a *membre honoraire* recalled to service. During his year's work on the project, the usual courtesy loans to other organizations were suspended.[5]

Deldevez was delighted when Fanny Pelletan and Berthold Damcke

presented a copy of their lavish new edition of Gluck's *Iphigénie en Au-*
lide and again when Victor Schoelcher offered the Bibliothèque du Conservatoire a copy of his Handel edition—one of the main stimuli of the
French Bach-and-Handel revival. Deldevez led the effort to purchase
new printed parts for the standard repertoire, and when Ambroise Thomas complained of an "embarrassment of riches" in their availability,
knew to select Breitkopf & Härtel publications. Alone of the *sociétaires*
he had direct access to the libraries of the Opéra and imperial chapel;
this later caused problems when he was ill and could not fetch the music himself.[6]

In his contemplative mode Deldevez theorized orchestral practice
with an eye toward identifying the ways of greatness and a philosophy
of governance that would assure and maintain it. From the outset he
took an aggressive role in determining the society's repertoire, properties, and business practices. He became an outstanding leader, easily the
best since Habeneck and probably to be numbered with the greats—
Habeneck, Gaubert, and Münch. The musicians proved their loyalty as
they stood unwaveringly with him through his several crises of health,
always disinclined to look for anyone else. Another measure of his success lies in how the Société des Concerts was perceived, during his
tenure, from the outside. The conservatives continued to see the bas-
tion of tradition they so desperately needed, while outsiders abandoned
their idea that the gates were barred and instead began to think of the
arrival of their works in the Salle des Concerts as the ultimate stamp of
success.

Deldevez enjoyed the collaboration of an unusually strong inner circle:
Charles Lamoureux as second conductor and *1er violon solo*, Jules Garcin
as principal second violinist and secretary, the distinguished cellist Hippolyte Rabaud as *archiviste-caissier*, and for a short time Théodore
Dubois as chorusmaster. Every member of his first committee was or
became an outstanding servant of the Société des Concerts.[7]

With Dubois the association was short lived. The popular chorusmaster resigned in September 1872, "profoundly pained" but overworked as *maître de chapelle* at the Madeleine; perhaps he also sensed
the onset of what proved to be divisive changes in attitude toward the
chorus. There was scurrying to prevent the election of the unpopular
Adolphe Fétis as his successor: "*Effectivement il est d'origine belge,*" it
was complained, and could not be appointed without a change in the
statutes. The only other candidate was another outsider, Alexandre La-

fitte, choirmaster at St-Nicolas-des-Champs. The singer Koenig testified in his behalf, assuring Lafitte's promise and availability, and he was
elected with the strangely non-committal vote of 59 favoring, 49 blank.[8]
Dubois would return to the Société des Concerts in 1896 as its president, when he served briefly as interim director of the Conservatoire.

The strongest voice on the committee—certainly the loudest—was
that of Charles Lamoureux, Alard's successor as concertmaster. Articulate and vociferous, sometimes belligerent, he seethed with new ideas:
assigning numbers to each chorus member and every manuscript or
printed part, calling for new committees to balance the books and organize the subscribers.[9] He took the lead in promoting the Baroque
repertoire that was soon to preoccupy everybody, but became so hot-
headed about it as to provoke a crisis. Meanwhile he served a vital role
as substitute conductor during the long illnesses of Deldevez, establishing during his apprenticeship the credentials for a major career.
He would almost certainly have risen to the podium of the Société
des Concerts had he not abandoned it in 1877 on his engagement as conductor at the Opéra and, more significantly still, to cultivate his own
chorus-and-orchestra society—what became the celebrated Concerts
Lamoureux.

Jules Garcin was, after his long wait in the ranks of the *aspirants,* in
his tenth year as a *sociétaire* and second year as secretary; he had some
assignment on nearly every committee until his election to succeed Deldevez in 1885. He appeared as soloist on several occasions, including in
a violin concerto of his own composition, and in 1874–75 returned
Beethoven's Romance in F to the repertoire. Before anyone else in the
inner circle, he promoted the music of Bizet and Massenet. But his first
recorded proposal, though offered for all the right reasons, was fundamentally misguided: to extend the season with supplementary end-of-
year concerts reserved for music of living composers—by extension limiting the main season to established repertoire.[10] This very scheme, as it
came to be practiced in the 1940s and 1950s, marginalized the contemporary repertoire and divided the public, and was on the whole bad for
everyone concerned.

Their first season together was the forty-sixth (1872–73), opening in
December with Beethoven's Seventh, excerpts from *La Damnation de
Faust,* and familiar works of Gluck, Mendelssohn, and Weber. Cavaillé-
Coll had asked that the new organ in the Salle des Concerts be heard
during the Sunday concerts, to which end César Franck appeared in

the second pair to play the Bach Prelude and Fugue in E Minor (BWV 548). This was the first general audition of an instrument soon to be used, with Alexandre Guilmant at the console, for continuo in the Bach-and-Handel vocal repertoire and, later, for the Handel organ concertos.[11]

Schumann's *Manfred* was on the same program; at the next, the First Cello Concerto of Saint-Saëns was played by Auguste Tolbecque *fils*, fifty-two, recently returned to Paris after an absence of more than two decades in Marseille. Beethoven's Ninth, purposefully scheduled for mid-season, was the centerpiece, given a third performance for non-subscribers (9, 16 February, 16 March 1873).[12] Two movements of a new Symphony in F by Charles-Marie Widor were introduced in early March. Adolphe Thiers, first president of the new republic, announced a few days before the event that he would be in attendance on 23 March and would like to hear Beethoven's Seventh, so that program was rearranged accordingly.[13] The season drew to a close with the Kyrie and Gloria of a fifth Mass by Victor-Frédéric Verrimst, a doublebassist in the orchestra, and, after a year of rehearsals, the first half of Mendelssohn's *Saint Paul*, "The Martyrdom of Saint Stephen." Altogether there were a record nineteen concerts: seven subscription pairs, three *concerts supplémentaires*, and two benefits.

The Widor and Saint-Saëns had been approved during the fall readings, where the musicians continued working through the long list Hainl had just begun. Three works failed the piano auditions: an *O Salutaris* of Adrien Boieldieu, an overture of Godard, and excerpts from Lalo's *Fiesque*. A symphony by Joncières went on to the orchestra reading and failed there. Still in the queue were another work of Lalo, Franck's *Rédemption*, a work of Alfred Holmes, and yet again a composition by Elwart. Optimists all, the committee had agreed to listen to every new work submitted.[14]

The two benefit concerts of 1873 were the next in the myriad of events for which the charitable participation of the Société des Concerts was by now regularly solicited. Days after the benefit of 3 March 1872, "for the deliverance of the territory," a number of musicians were excused to play in support of the Œuvre des Saints Anges, then forbidden to appear on behalf of the Œuvre de la Miséricorde and again the Œuvre des Orphelins de Guerre; in December 1872 representatives of a Société de Protection des Alsaciens-Lorrains Demeurés Français (Comité de Secours aux Colons Algériens) asked for a benefit, to which the committee responded was that it had already done its part in March; neverthe-less a concert toward the same end was given in April 1873.[15]

In early February 1873 Mme Jules Simon, wife of the minister of pub-lic instruction, approached the committee with a proposal that, given status of the sponsoring personalities, could not be refused: a concert under the patronage of Mme Thiers and featuring the baritone J.-B. Faure, to benefit the amputees of war. The committee attached the con-dition that a fee of 9,000 francs be counted an expense of the concert, thus guaranteeing the musicians their ordinary *jetons*. Viguier called on the sponsors to explain that this would result in only a modest profit to their cause, then scheduled the concert for 23 February. But sales were poor, just approaching 10,000 francs gross, and after the dress rehearsal on Saturday, 22 February, it was decided to give away the 450 remain-ing seats—more than half the house—to the personnel of the society; the *archiviste-caissier* stayed in the office until midnight distributing the coupons. The final reckoning showed a mere 1,544 francs to be passed on to the good work: 10,544 francs in receipts minus 9,000-franc fee. For the concert of 27 April 1873, billed as a benefit in favor of the Œu-vre des Alsaciens-Lorrains, the net financial result was a considerably im-proved 6,612 francs.[16]

The following season Mme la Maréchale Mac-Mahon—Thiers and his government having fallen and been succeeded by Marshal Mac-Mahon—endeavored to sponsor a benefit for the "orphans of the two sieges of Paris," but without success.[17] The society had learned its les-son, and thereafter declined outside benefits except when they were po-litically unavoidable. In July 1875 they declined a benefit for victims of the floods in the Midi on the grounds that the public was on summer holiday; the alternative idea of a *messe en musique* was compromised by the archbishop's remaining "firmly and formally against" the presence of women singers in the choirloft. So "in order that it could not be said that the Société des Concerts did nothing under this circumstance," they withdrew 1,500 francs from the Caisse de Prévoyance to send to the afflicted.[18]

On the whole, the experience of 1872–73, close on the heels of the back-to-back seasons of 1871 and 1872, suggested that the Société des Con-certs was prepared to move successfully to a formal season of nine pairs: the seven pairs in place since 1868–69 (and de facto since 1866–67) plus the *concerts spirituels* and *extraordinaires*. The musicians had not in fact succumbed to the fatigue they so feared, and on the contrary there had been a measure of exhilaration at both a victorious comeback and their clearly enhanced posture with the national government. Their purses had fattened as well. An extended schedule would permit abandoning the non-subscription supplementary and benefit concerts, for which demand was beginning to recede as the second series became fully subscribed. And it afforded what was by this time seen as the opportunity to present a wider variety of compositions. Lamoureux even led a petition submitted in May 1873 to proceed to not nine but ten pairs.

The calendar would need to run from the week before Christmas until mid-April, with the last two Sundays in April reserved for extenuating circumstances—and they wanted exclusive rights to the hall for the entire period. Ambroise Thomas, as director of the Conservatoire, objected that this was a thinly veiled effort to control the Salle des Concerts for the entire Paris season; in any event, the Conservatoire required one Sunday a month for its own purposes, and failing that he would not recommend the proposal to the ministry. The necessary Sundays were found by moving the inaugural concert to the beginning of December, and the plan was approved by the minister in August 1873. The formal adoption of an eighteen-concert season in nine pairs was reckoned from that date.[19]

Just how significant a step this was is suggested by the length of the secretary's oration on the subject in his *rapport moral* of 26 May 1874, as he reported the new policy and explained the impossibility of the proposed ten pairs. He traced the history of their sessions—the original six statutory concerts, the growth to nine and then ten (seven ordinary concerts, two *concerts spirituels*, and a benefit for the Caisse de Prévoyance), the move in 1866 to seven pairs—and observed that in those years the idea of fourteen concerts had risked "troubling the personal affairs" of the membership. "But since that time," he went on, "the taste for music has grown and grown,"[20] a taste they themselves had largely created. Other organizations—the Concerts Pasdeloup, and that season Édouard Colonne's Concert National—had come along to play every Sunday from the beginning of October without interruption. As the "driving force" in French musical life for forty years, the Société des Concerts had little alternative but to meet its competition head on.

One of the oldest and most sacred privileges of the Société des Concerts, its exemption from the full *droit des pauvres*, began to be challenged by the new civic administration of Paris that coalesced in 1871 and 1872. The confrontation escalated into a major crisis in a matter of months, as the reorganized Assistance Publique undertook a relentless assault on the society, called by the *sociétaires* on more than one occasion a *guerre sans trêve* ("a truceless war"). It dominated the work of the committee for over five years until a more or less definitive settlement was reached in 1875.[21]

For the twenty-seven years from 1830 until 1857, when the price of seats was increased by a third, the poor tax had been 200 francs per concert in lieu of 12½ percent of the gross receipt; thereafter it was 300 francs per concert on receipts of approximately 8,000 francs. In administrative parlance of the era, the arrangement had been for a "subscription" payment of a flat fee instead of a "proportional tax." During the 1871 season, representatives of the Assistance Publique notified the society of their intent to collect 4½ percent on the gross receipts of the October concerts, rising to 9 percent within the year.

A tax collector came to the performance of 29 October 1871 expecting to leave with a cash payment; the *archiviste-caissier* refused to release the money, and the following Tuesday the committee pled its case in a call on the prefect of police. Failing to get a satisfactory response, they threatened, at the end of the week, to cancel the rest of the season. On 14 November they noted with satisfaction that the Assistance Publique had abandoned its "pretentions" and that the *droit fixe* would hold through the end of spring 1872. In his *rapport moral* on the 1871 concerts, however, the secretary concluded that the days of this preferential arrangement were numbered, and that members should expect a markedly lower net income when the time came, since the potential liability was 1,760 francs per concert.[22] Put another way, they were threatened with a 600 percent increase in taxes.

The scenario was repeated at the start of the 1872–73 season. On the Saturday afternoon before the second concert, and despite assurances to the *archiviste-caissier* that the arrangement would hold firm for the year,[23] the Assistance Publique notified the box office of its intent to levy the 9 percent announced the year before. The secretary sent directly to the prefect of police for clarification, without result. The collector showed up on the next day to count the house and tax the gross receipt, this time refusing to leave without his cash. At the end of the concert he was still there, provoking an altercation when the *archiviste-caissier* refused to comply. Again, a delegation (Deldevez, Garcin, Viguier) had to visit the prefecture the next Tuesday. They returned to report that the prefect had received them gracefully and promised a favorable resolution, but that they would need to do their part by accepting a 100-franc augmentation, to 400 francs per concert. After extended debate, the committee agreed by a vote of 5 favoring, 4 opposed, to accept the new rate, remarking that this was the most they could possibly afford. Under no circumstance could they manage 9 percent.

But the authorities clearly regarded this outcome as a one-time exception to policy, and for another two years the absurd drama of a tax collector appearing in the fall and provoking an urgent visit to the prefecture repeated itself. In 1873–74 under a new prefect of the Seine, Ferdinand Duval, the situation deteriorated. In October he told the society of his firm intent to levy an 8 percent rate. Lamoureux complicated matters by taking it upon himself to lobby an acquaintance in the prefecture, and somehow an inflammatory account of where things stood appeared in the *Paris-Journal* under the headline "Les Concerts du Conservatoire and M. Ferdinand Duval." Apologies were penned, the infuriated Duval relented so far as to re-authorize the 400-franc rate, and the senior members of the committee went off once more to the prefecture to express their thanks in person. The situation, they were assured, would soon be regularized; the minister of fine arts and the minister of finance were working out a solution.[24]

But in the fall of 1874, the full 12½ percent was levied again pending a direct instruction to the contrary from Duval.[25] Still smarting from the events of the previous year, he let it be known that he was disinclined this time to intervene. In November the collector showed up to claim 1,073.77 francs for the concert of 22 November and 1,075.87 for that of 29 November; the *archiviste-caissier* gave him 400 francs for the first concert and sent him away from the second. On Tuesday 24 November the committee received a final offer from the authorities of a proportional tax of one-eleventh of the gross, or 9 percent: 744.64 francs for the first concert and 782.85 for the second. They unanimously refused the augmentation and summoned an Assemblée Générale *extraordinaire* for 25 November.

The membership at large was inclined to force the issue by abandoning the season in the face of these "vexatious measures." One *sociétaire* argued that the cure—effectively a strike, with loss of income—was worse than the disease, but another replied that "when the dignity of the Société is attacked, everybody has to make sacrifices."[26] The strike vote carried unanimously, though Ambroise Thomas urged the musicians not to carry out their threat, whatever transpired. On Christmas Eve the director of the Assistance Publique replied to their ultimatum that he maintained his levy, but would out of courtesy collect only the first 400 francs until the dispute was resolved at a higher level. The matter was still on hold in the spring, with neither party having yielded any ground at all. Higher authority had not ruled. "It is impossible," Viguier optimistically told his colleagues, "that a society which has rendered such unanimously appreciated services to music will not at some point be recognized as in the public utility and absolved from any tax at all." [27]

Resolution came with a law passed on 3 August 1875 by the National Assembly: "The tax to be levied on the gross receipt of non-daily concerts given by artists or associations of artists will not exceed 5 percent." [28] This was bad news to the contingent who imagined returning to the 300-franc rate, but effectively pre-empted any work action. It was good news for the budget, since on an average gross of 8,600 francs the society now paid 430 francs, whereas since 1872 they had paid 400. Yielding to the proportional tax was clearly an "aggravation," but the necessary consequence of a privilege that had reached its end.[29]

The poor tax was but one of many new obligations incurred as both the national and city governments struggled with the war reparations and an uncertain financial picture. For the society, each new expense was a further burden on a budget that could barely stretch as it was. A stamp tax on tickets was passed on to the subscribers. Postage was rising. A tax on personal income included in the tax code of 1872 was a serious new threat. While the society managed to secure exemption for its members during the 1870s and 1880s—one of the tax collectors, the Directeur du Timbre, was an avid patron who tried to protect their interests—the *sociétaires* were regularly warned to expect an income tax at any moment. It was becoming more urgent than ever to secure permanent exemption from all taxes, for the Société des Concerts to be proclaimed *"d'utilité publique."*

The new era also brought increasing pressure from the Société des Auteurs, Compositeurs, Éditeurs de Musique (SACEM), a powerful rights organization that traced its foundation to 1851 in the flurry of syndication that had also seen the establishment of Baron Taylor's benevolent Association des Artistes-Musiciens (1843; in his autobiography, W. C. Handy notes with envy the French leadership in this realm).[30] Like the *droit des pauvres,* the royalty had long been fixed as a token payment. In the 1869–70 season it quadrupled from 25 francs to 100 francs per concert, with the expectation that a new agreement would be negotiated every season. Though the personal connections with the authorities at SACEM were much closer than was the case with the poor-tax collectors, the fall ritual was similar, with the added twist that no works controlled by the organization—nearly all new music, certain published editions of old music, and French translations of texted music—could be programmed until the annual agreement was signed. Impasses often compromised the fall planning, and on more than one occasion an important premiere was delayed. The society was less supportive of SACEM than it might have been, holding that for a living composer to be played in the Salle des Concerts at all, and moreover in the hallowed company of Mozart and Beethoven, was sufficient compensation.

The personnel had to be replenished as well, especially in the lower strings—one of the reasons Tolbecque was induced to return to Paris. Thirty new *sociétaires* were appointed between 1871 and the end of 1874; two of these, the trumpet player Teste and the doublebassist de Bailly, had not been to the Conservatoire and were admitted under the emergency provision of the statutes. Changed circumstances had also to be accommodated; for instance, members of the National Guard, since there was no longer a standing army, found their obligations greatly increased and were sometimes called for guard duty on the ramparts of Paris when they should have been at rehearsal.[31] The Caisse de Prévoyance had been converted from securities to cash in May 1871, when the funds were taken to Le Havre for safekeeping, and needed reinvesting.

It took time, finally, to straighten out the patron seating in the Salle des Concerts. Thiers and the Mac-Mahons were inveterate concertgoers, pre-empting the *loge d'honneur*. The Mac-Mahons went on to requisition the box for both series, thus displacing six permanent subscribers to the second. George-Hainl and his wife needed to be accommodated with adjoining seats, and Mme George-Hainl continued to exercise her privilege after her husband's death. Ambroise Thomas reorganized and expanded the administration of the Conservatoire, requiring new seats for his staff. And the minister of the interior and fine arts assured them, in calling for a box, that he would be "among their most faithful listeners and admirers."[32]

Mme Mac-Mahon was a problematic patroness, settled in her tastes and not afraid to state them—meddlesome, in a word. In February 1874, communicating through her secretary, Count Walsh, she let it be known that she intended to hear Beethoven's Ninth and the *Midsummer Night's Dream* music during the season already well under way. On this occasion, since the Ninth had been scheduled, luck was with the orchestra and her requirements could be met in the ordinary course of business. But in mid-March she directed the committee to prepare a benefit concert for her charity of the moment, the Œuvre des Sourdes-Muettes (deaf-mute girls). Suspecting that Madame did not comprehend how the Société des Concerts operated, a delegation called on Count Walsh to explain the impossibility of scheduling extra concerts without an Assemblée Générale *extraordinaire;* they would, however, be prepared to dedicate an ordinary concert to her purposes, where an offering could be collected. Or she could pay a set fee for a supplementary concert and take any proceeds past that expense. To this latter option she agreed, though now thought the proper beneficiary should be the orphans of "the two sieges of Paris." She assured the committee of her ability to place all the tickets, and the committee reluctantly billed her benefit— essentially a repeat of the 17–18 April concert pair, with Beethoven's Ninth—for 26 April 1876. They made quiet arrangements to distribute leftover tickets in the event of a disastrous pre-sale, another lesson of the failed benefit for the amputees.

On Friday before the concert on Sunday, Mme Mac-Mahon sent notice that she was canceling her concert, leaving them to tally the expenses already incurred—and the delicate task of collecting reimbursement.[33] She was back in January 1875, again after the season was fully under way, inviting the engagement of the Russian cellist Karl Davidov (1838–89, Rubinstein's successor as director of the St. Petersburg Conservatory). On this occasion the committee concurred as to the merits of a "remarkable artist" and rearranged its programs—going so far as to delay a performance of the Ninth—to allow a pair of appearances in February before Davidov left to return to Russia. It appears that the concerto of his own composition, played at the first of the concerts, was a failure, since it was replaced on the second with a short excerpt from one of the Bach cello suites.[34]

In 1872 Lamoureux formally proposed that each year, for "artistic and patriotic reasons," the Société present an oratorio of Bach or Handel in supplementary concerts. Interest in Bach had been building since the 1850s: Mendelssohn's championing had not gone unnoticed, and the Bach Gesellschaft edition had made quality scores and parts available. For some time the critic Scudo had been calling for the Société des Concerts to popularize Bach, *"qui sort des catacombes."* Handel enthusiasm had followed close behind and was somewhat more directly associated with Paris, where Victor Schoelcher lived and worked. Both composers had admirers on the faculty at the Conservatoire, and one of Deldevez's favorite works was "the magnificent [victory] chorus from *Judas Maccabaeus* of Handel."[35]

Lamoureux already had a good reputation for his chamber performances of Bach. He vigorously renewed his proposal in the late spring of 1873, as planning for the forty-seventh season began and the idea of festival concerts at the end of each year was gathering support anyway. Now he suggested that the St. Matthew Passion be performed on Holy Saturday in an external venue that could accommodate an expanded chorus of about 100 and an orchestra of 74. The committee was intrigued by the proposal, suggesting as it did a mission along the lines of the Beethoven crusade of the early years.

It nevertheless foresaw numerous and probably insurmountable difficulties. Most notably there was the matter of the woodwind and brass players, who would need to be excused without pay, and the soloists, who would require substantial fees. Increasing the size of the chorus could be accomplished by inviting students from the Conservatoire and the theater choristers, but finding the rehearsal time was a major obstacle. There was the onerous cost of the material, including a new translation, for a work of such substance. Rehearsals for a Holy Saturday concert would doubtless cause the personnel "excessive fatigue" that might compromise the traditional Good Friday and Easter Sunday *concerts spirituels.* Then there was the matter of venue; for the orchestra to leave the hallowed halls of the Conservatoire, where it was "sovereign," was a step it seemed not yet prepared to take. The Salle des Concerts boasted new decoration and its new organ, but could only accommodate the force Lamoureux envisaged with the greatest difficulty. Finally, conservatives argued that in the mission of the Société des Concerts the "symphonic element reigns," and that it would be "disadvantageous to pursue a route entirely opposed to the goal for which it was founded." [36]

Lamoureux held his position vigorously. The Bach passions were done annually by sister institutions in Germany and England, he said, with great success. The student singers could do their rehearsing in ensemble class; the society's own chorus could manage its time better, anyway, and they were always complaining about being too little used. As for their mission, he rightly held, the Société had been devoted from the start to big works for chorus and orchestra—notably the Ninth Symphony.

But the committee voted Lamoureux down, 2 favoring and 6 opposed to the St. Matthew Passion. Lamoureux insisted that the incident be fully recorded in the minutes, where it is far the longest debate recorded so far; Deldevez quotes it copiously in his book.[37] Thus defeated, Lamoureux, who had married well and controlled a large fortune, simply organized the performance anyway. His Société Française de l'Harmonie Sacrée emerged forthwith, presenting three performances of *Messiah* in December 1873 and three performances of the St. Matthew Passion the following March and April; in subsequent seasons he offered *Judas Maccabaeus* and *Alexander's Feast,* along with oratorios of Gounod and Massenet. The committee excused Lamoureux himself for these concerts, though it declined his request to waive article 38 for the *sociétaires* he wished to engage. It was later agreed that Lamoureux's advocacy of the St. Matthew Passion had been honorable and that "thanks to his initiative our country can now know this immortal masterpiece." [38]

For its own part the Société des Concerts was enthusiastic enough about the general concept of programming Baroque oratorios. They agreed in principle to a *Messiah* in 1874, then a full *Israel in Egypt,* and went so far as to consult the famous Charles Garnier, architect of the Conservatoire, about re-designing the stage platforms. But so far the chorus was not up to the task of learning big works in one season, and instead the singers fell back on their traditional formula of building up from excerpts. From *Saul* the chorus "Envie, fille d'enfer" ("Envy! Eldestborn of Hell!"—the opening chorus of part II) was popularized; from *Israel in Egypt,* two, then three choruses: "La grêle tombe à flots," "Ténèbres funèbres," and "Tout peuple entendra" ("He gave them hailstones for rain," "He sent a thick darkness over the land," and "The people shall hear and be afraid"). Not until January 1911, under Messager, did *Israel in Egypt* reach a full performance.

George-Hainl's death on 2 June 1873 was as unexpected as his resignation. Deldevez, badly shaken by the news, rushed from his dinner table to comfort Mme George-Hainl and spend a few last moments at Hainl's side. The funeral was at the Church of the Trinité on the morning of 5 June. The committee assembled at the mortuary to take its place in the procession. Deldevez gave the main eulogy, praising Hainl for having made of the Société des Concerts a venerated cult. He described Hainl as a good man, affable, and fair. He and Mme George-Hainl led the procession to the cemetery for the final *adieux.* There is no mention of music at the funeral, nor evidence of a memorial concert.

Deldevez opened the 1873–74 season with the love scene from Berlioz's *Roméo et Juliette,* the first step in a five-year project to learn the entire work, and Haydn's Symphony No. 97 in C Major (Deldevez No. 44). Sarasate appeared in the second concert pair with Bruch's Violin Concerto; the committee would have preferred the Beethoven Concerto but yielded to Sarasate because they had earlier declined his offer of a Spohr concerto.[39]

In the bitter cold of late December, Deldevez suffered a severe attack of his rheumatism, with Lamoureux called to conduct the reading sessions and the seven concerts through 22 February 1874. It was a tempestuous few weeks, as Lamoureux, who rehearsed slowly and with minute attention to detail, behaved imperially and filed multiple complaints about the musicians. He was particularly cross with the unpredictable principal oboist, Louis Cras, and annoyed more generally with how the musicians had "let their impatience be known in an inappropriate way." A warning was posted in the *foyer*.[40]

Lamoureux nevertheless had a brilliant debut, introducing in succession a Handel concerto grosso, the first half of Bach's Suite No. 2 in B Minor (the second half, with the Badinerie played by Paul Taffanel, came in April under Deldevez), and Schumann's Fourth Symphony in D Minor, op. 120. On his return Deldevez premiered two works that had survived the *répétitions d'essai:* the overture *Marie Stuart* by the baron Zuylen de Nyevelt and excerpts from Weckerlin's oratorio *Le Jugement dernier*. These were cited, in the *rapport moral,* with the curious construction: "For the [very] last time this year, you were asked to devote two *séances* to contemporary music." In the last pair, the bass Jacques Bouhy (Bizet's first Escamillo) sang a recitative and aria from Mendelssohn's *Elijah,* apparently and quite surprisingly the first time anything from that great work was presented at the Conservatoire.[41]

In the fall of 1874 Alexandre Lafitte, Dubois's successor as chorusmaster, was stricken with illness and had to relinquish a post he had held only two years; he died in 1877. Joseph Heyberger, chorusmaster from Mulhouse, was elected to the post over Jules Cohen, the accompanist at the Opéra. It was an unusual choice, owing much to a recommendation delivered from the rostrum by Ambroise Thomas—an uncommonly partisan gesture from the society's president. Later he apologized for any misunderstanding; his interjection had been intended to be purely informational, and was offered in good faith.[42] Heyberger went on to enjoy a brilliant career of nearly two decades with the Société des Concerts.

The 1874–75 season opened with the premiere of the "remarkable" Schumann Piano Concerto, played by Alfred Jaëll in December; the Schumann repertoire, already including the First and Fourth Symphonies and *Manfred* music, was beginning to be quite respectable. Along the same lines, two new works of Berlioz were added, the *Francs-Juges* overture and, for the chorus, *La Mort d'Ophélie*. In January the first excerpt of the B-Minor Mass was presented to the public: the portions of the Credo through the Crucifixus. Deldevez missed six performances, two in December and four in the spring, giving Lamoureux the opportunity to conduct Beethoven's Ninth Symphony for the first time.

For living composers it was a banner year. From Gounod there was a new *Salutation angélique;* from Vaucorbeil a second performance of *La Mort de Diane,* premiered in 1870; and a second performance of the G-Minor Piano Concerto by Saint-Saëns. Saint-Saëns had hoped to premiere *Le Rouet d'Omphale,* but this was delayed for a year in deference to Mme Montigny-Remaury, the concerto soloist. Massenet made his debut with a four-movement suite of scenes after Shakespeare *(The Tempest, Othello, Romeo and Juliet,* and *Macbeth).* Bizet at last crossed the threshold of the Salle des Concerts with the *L'Arlésienne* Suite No. 1 in February; he died in June.[43]

It was, the secretary remarked with pride, the kind of superb season that could be achieved when—unlike the previous year of confrontation with Lamoureux—everyone worked together in harmony.[44] There had been considerable success in establishing an equilibrium of old and new. But at the same time, the members found their attention focused again on the costs of the system of *répétitions d'essai,* to which they had recommitted themselves with such vigor not so long before.[45] The administrative burden was substantial, requiring a considerable exchange of correspondence with composers, significant rehearsal time, and an unwieldy apparatus for making the decisions. The musicians, and both conductors, really wanted to devote their time to Bach and Handel, to Schumann and Berlioz. Composers like Bizet and Saint-Saëns would, they reasoned, gain access to the programs without the *essais.* Like his predecessors, Deldevez grew weary of the chore of winnowing out.

The society remained committed to providing, "with prudent reserve, access to modern works both French and foreign," though always keeping in mind about the patrons that "enthusiasm for new works, we say under our breath, is not their predominant quality."[46] Yet it was critically important to gain some freedom from the demands of *compositeurs vivants.* Beginning in September 1874, new proposals were declined with the terse response: "The committee no longer accepts requests to try out compositions." Or "By virtue of a recent decision, the committee is unable to admit any requests from a composer for readings."[47] In 1875, a more delicate response to composers and potential soloists was framed:

> Sir:
> I am honored to acknowledge receipt of the letter you have addressed to the committee of the Société des Concerts. In view of the large number of requests the committee receives annually, to which it is practically impossible

to do justice, henceforth it reserves to itself the entire responsibility for finding new works and choosing soloists.[48]

Concerto proposals from both Rubinstein (probably Nikolai, who was
coming to Paris to conduct concerts of Russian music at the 1878 Exposition) and Eduard Reményi were declined.

All the next year the leadership discussed options for dealing with
compositeurs vivants and the possibility of modifying the jury system
described in article 33 of the statutes. Finally, at an Assemblée Générale in October 1877 the members adopted a much simplified wording:
"When the committee judges it opportune to submit the work of a
living composer to the vote of the society, it will have it tried at a rehearsal, following which the admission to the repertoire of that work will
be judged at a secret ballot of all the *sociétaires* who took part in the
trial."[49]

In truth, the task of organizing eighteen concerts annually had begun to surpass the capabilities of an all-volunteer executive. It was not
the musicians but the committee members who found themselves suffering from an "excess of fatigue scarcely in keeping with the material
benefits to be found" in administration.[50] Of these it was the *archiviste-
caissier* who was most over-burdened, having to wrestle daily with the
ticketing and overall financial management. When his private assistant,
M. Jullien, disappeared, Rabaud proposed that the Société des Concerts
take the unprecedented step of hiring a salaried employee. The employee would come every day to the Conservatoire to help members of
the committee, and in any unused time he could copy music. Leudet,
the *membre adjoint,* counter-proposed that each member of the committee have an assistant, elected from among the *sociétaires,* who would
automatically succeed to the position, but this was too radical a shift
from established practice to gain any support. A revised article 20 of the
statutes, allowing this one employee but continuing to specify that any
other assistance would be at the personal expense of the member requiring it, was thus proposed and adopted by the members at their assembly on 26 May 1874. The position was filled by M. Frémaux, former
equipment manager for the Opéra-Comique and retired horn professor
of the Marseille Conservatory (and father of the cellist Paul Frémaux,
soon to join the society). Frémaux agreed to a salary of 1,200 francs a
year, payable in monthly installments, but reserved the right to ask for
more at the end of the first year if this modest remuneration proved in-
commensurate with the duties required. He was to report each day for
four hours of box-office work and copying, with a holiday on Mondays

after the concerts.[51] Frémaux was succeeded by MM. Housset *père* and *fils* in 1878 and M. Bergin in 1880.

The suddenly unquenchable public thirst for art music exacerbated the two weakest points in the structure of the society: its inability to control the Salle des Concerts, and compensation so low that the members were tempted to play for rivals. An 1873 project of Louis Bourgault-Ducoudray, professor of music history at the Conservatoire, to present oratorios of Bach and Handel in the Salle des Concerts brought both problems to the fore. Jules Danbé, one of the society's leading violinists, conducted the first of these with his orchestra of the Grand Hôtel concerts—mostly *sociétaires* who had been authorized in 1871 to appear in the hotel concerts largely to help them restore their income. The committee protested to Ambroise Thomas of the "fateful consequences" of establishing such a precedent. Previous authorizations of the hall had been for living composers to present their works or for non-traditional repertoire; in this case an organization of long standing was involving itself in repertoire the Société des Concerts had presented since 1840. Thomas sighed and intervened with a letter to the authorities, and a compromise was reached allowing the *sociétaires* to appear under the billing "with the participation of the Société des Concerts." Neither Danbé's name nor words "Grand Hôtel" were to appear on the poster.[52]

Yet the minister of fine arts went on granting the hall to others: a few weeks later, for instance, to Heugel, impresario for a program of piano concertos with Francis Planté. The minister would listen politely as the delegations routinely protested, but not commit to cease and desist; Ambroise Thomas grew reluctant to endorse the society's stand.[53] The committee's patience reached the breaking point in February 1875, when Thomas brought the unwelcome news that the minister had lent the hall for an orchestra-with-chorus concert by a Society of St. Vincent de Paul—unlike Bourgault-Ducoudray or even Heugel and Planté, without a remote connection to the Conservatoire. Thomas was as surprised as anyone else, thinking that the minister had expressed his good intentions toward the society after their recent visits. Sharing the view that this was an issue of consequence, and alarmed to see a posting in the courtyard of his own institution that suggested the unauthorized participation of artists from the Société des Concerts, he took the minister aside at the concert of 7 February 1875 in an unsuccessful effort to persuade him to withdraw his accord. The minister agreed, however, to allow the society's representatives to visit the following Tuesday and—again—state their case.

On 9 February the minister, "typically benevolent and welcoming," received the official delegation—Thomas, Deldevez, Lamoureux, and Viguier. Thomas presented the usual arguments supporting their claim to the "rigorous privilege" of the Salle des Concerts, doubtless citing the decree of 30 October 1850 that committed "the use of the hall of the national Conservatoire to its teaching needs and to the Société des Concerts." The minister responded with his disinclination to alter a commitment already made—a privilege granted, he explained, on the spur of the moment, but that he now saw the merit of their position and would not repeat his error. He offered, moreover, to frame those sentiments in a letter for their archive, "engaging, in some respects, ministers to come." The letter, couched in heartfelt praise for the Société des Concerts and its work, arrived within the week. Discretion prevented the society from releasing it to the press.[54]

Neither Lumley and his costume concerts of 1850 nor the Society of St. Vincent de Paul, nor even the likeable Bourgault-Ducoudray and his students, could have caused the Société des Concerts any real harm. Their own progeny, on the other hand, raised that decided threat. The Concerts Pasdeloup remained greatly successful. Édouard Colonne's orchestra now took its place as the second direct descendent of the Société des Concerts; the conductor and much of the personnel had passed through as *aspirants,* and the governing statutes were altogether similar. Colonne (1838–1910) had studied violin at the Conservatoire with Sauzay and had had courses with both Elwart and Thomas; he played briefly with the society before moving to the Opéra as principal violinist. He had also played in Pasdeloup's Concerts Populaires, Danbé's Grand Hôtel concerts, and Lamoureux's oratorio society, so was as experienced as anybody in how concerts ought to be produced. His Concert National series began at the Odéon in 1873, soon becoming the Concerts Colonne at the Châtelet. Colonne's appointment as administrative director and first conductor of the music for the Exposition Universelle in 1878, and again for the Centennial Exhibition of 1889, constitute one of many indications that the hegemony of the Société des Concerts was approaching its end.

Charles Lamoureux's defection in 1877, meanwhile, freed him to create another *association symphonique,* with his Société des Nouveaux Concerts—the Concerts Lamoureux—formally constituted in 1881. This brought to four the number of philharmonic societies offering Sunday afternoon concerts, and the multiplicity of *concerts dominicaux* was soon recognized as a particular attraction of the French capital. As early as 1875 the October start of the Pasdeloup and Colonne concerts had begun to exert pressure on the Société des Concerts to announce subscriptions and concert dates weeks before it was customary; by 1878 competition from the other orchestras was being cited in calls for renewed vigilance in recruitment and "confection," as they put it, "of the programs."[55] The newer associations, being hungrier, were more progressive on several fronts. For one thing, they found programming niches the Conservatoire concerts seemed to overlook: Colonne, for example, with Berlioz's *La Damnation de Faust;* Lamoureux with Wagner. Later they would take the lead in out-of-town appearances, recordings, and broadcasts. The Société des Concerts went on assuming its place to be a rung above the offspring—artistically, historically, even spiritually—and thus without peer, but rivalries both conscious and unconscious now became a way of life for all.

Lamoureux's autocratic manner as *2ᵉ chef* was not popular with the musicians, and he too had his share of competitors. Chief among these was Désiré Thibault, violinist in the society and conductor at the Théâtre-Lyrique. In autumn 1875 Thibault collected eighteen signatures on a proposal to set the term of office of the first conductor to five years and limit the second conductor's term to three. His initiative provoked a lively debate in an assembly that November. Taffanel, as secretary, presented the committee's strong objection to a proposal in which it saw "extreme danger": a lessening of the authority of both conductors, too-frequent elections, and the development of rivalries "prejudicial to the unity of the society." Thibault, craving Lamoureux's job, led the arguments in favor. Standing for periodic re-election could not affect "men of real value"; in any event it was improper to name a second conductor for life. Lamoureux interrupted, angrily but wrongly, that he had been appointed with a contract that could not be broken. (No one thought to remind him of his own strident advocacy, a few years before, of periodic auditions for all.) The cellist Dufour observed the clear advantages, when it came to choosing successors, of having already been exposed to as many second conductors as possible—the very argument advanced by Charles Dancla in 1863. Taffanel responded that their knowing Deldevez did not seem to have improved his chances of defeating George-Hainl. And he reiterated how much he feared the disruption of frequent elections.[56]

On this occasion the proposal failed: 60 favored maintaining the statutes, 42 favored a change, with 2 blank ballots. The following season a proposal to limit the term of office for the conductor to four years, renewable, failed narrowly for lack of a two-thirds majority. This meant that conductors over the age of sixty—Deldevez was fifty-eight—were still expected to stand for periodic reaffirmation.

The 1876–77 season was the fiftieth for the Société des Concerts, its *noces d'or.* Discussions of a suitable commemoration carried on through the summer and fall of 1876. A plan to duplicate the first season was considered and abandoned both for material reasons and owing to the obsolescence of a good deal of the music. Beethoven would of course be featured, especially since political events had precluded celebrating the centenary of Beethoven's birth in December 1870. Habeneck, too, would honored. The venue would necessarily be the Salle des Concerts, however, which could not possibly accommodate the crowd of well-wishers and the curious who would appear for a highly publicized event. The society's golden anniversary, it was concluded, should be less a public spectacle than a family reunion of *sociétaires* and the subscribers "who have passed the right to hear us from father to son, and who have never abandoned us." [57] It was not meant for strangers.

Not, then, until the rehearsal of Saturday, 20 January 1877, did the committee unveil its anniversary project. The concerts of 4 and 11 February 1877, falling during the anniversary week of Habeneck's death, would be dedicated to his memory with the Ninth Symphony, the Rondeau and Bourrée from the Bach B-Minor Suite, a scene from Gluck's *Armide,* and the excerpts from the Beethoven Septet that Habeneck had made famous. For the public at large, and in collective memory of all who had gone before, a mass would be celebrated at the Église de la Trinité on Friday, 9 February.

Despite his delicate health, Deldevez was able to conduct the entire anniversary season, including his own Requiem for the ceremony at the Trinité. The archbishop's objection to women in the choirloft was, on this occasion, overcome with time to spare. Delphin Alard, retired since 1865, returned to play a work by Habeneck during the collection of an offering to benefit the Association des Artistes-Musiciens. But the contributions of 1,526.80 francs were disappointing, and the expenses— posting of handbills and printing and postage, transport, police, the *garçon d'orchestre*—considerable at 966.55 francs. This left only 560.25 francs for the Artistes-Musiciens. [58]

Later Taffanel assured his colleagues that February and March 1828, when Habeneck "laid the first stone in an edifice he saw reach beyond his dearest hopes," had been a turning point in French music history. He praised a philharmonic society that had survived without a penny of subvention, recruited the nation's musical elite, offered hospitality to the best virtuosi in the world, and propagated the taste for Beethoven and Mendelssohn and the best of the French repertoire. He saluted the "marvelous sagacity" of the statutes, which had held without fundamental change for a half century. Few founders remained, *hélas,* but they had left behind a beautiful work of art that their successors would surely conserve and perfect.[59]

Deldevez would brook no criticism of what he saw as a prevailingly conservative but consistent fifty-year policy of attention to "masterpieces of the classical school."[60] (His count of symphonies performed in the first half-century is of course led by Beethoven, with 287 performances, followed by Haydn with 66, Mendelssohn with 60, and Mozart with 36.) Nevertheless Deldevez and his committees brought the most aggressive programming the society had seen in decades. Table by table his book on the Société des Concerts proudly documents his advances. In the eight years between his accession to the podium and 1880, for instance, he introduced some sixty-five new works.[61] One particular focus was an effort to complete the Schumann and Mendelssohn repertoires. Schumann's First and Fourth were, we have noted, already in the repertoire, alongside *Manfred,* in Victor Wilder's translation, played nearly every season. The Third Symphony, in E♭ major ("Rhenish"), appeared in December 1876 and the Second, in C major, in December 1879. Mendelssohn's *Die schöne Melusine* overture was heard from 1876, a pair of unaccompanied choral works *(Le Départ, Le Chanteur des bois)* from 1872; excerpts from *Paulus* and *Elijah* suggest bigger projects in the making.

In those same years Alexandre Guilmant popularized the Handel organ concertos; the new solo oboist, Georges Gillet, recruited in 1877, did likewise for the Handel oboe concerto. At least one Haydn symphony, No. 95 in C Minor (Deldevez No. 41), may have been new. The 1879–80 season opened with a three-part suite from Spontini's *Fernand Cortez,* delayed for a year because of the deplorable state of the material borrowed from the Opéra. Louis Diémer introduced two movements of Chopin's First Piano Concerto, in E minor, in January 1879.

Another effort was to reclaim Berlioz from the Colonne concerts. The 1875–76 season included, after "long and patient study," parts I and II of *La Damnation de Faust.* It was, the secretary noted proudly, "a runaway success with the public, and doubtless better than anything Berlioz himself ever obtained." *Le Carnaval romain* was already popular, and *Le Corsaire,* first offered in the opening concerts of 1880–81, would soon become so. *Roméo et Juliette* was essentially complete by January 1879, lacking only the prologue and—curiously, since it would have been a good vehicle for the chorus—the "Convoi funèbre." At the Assemblée Générale of 1878, Lebouc went out of his way to defend the society's conduct toward Berlioz, responding to passages in Georges de Massougnes's *Berlioz: son œuvre* (1870) and Arthur Pougin's updating of the Fétis biographical dictionary (the first volume of which had just appeared, with its "Berlioz" entry). He enumerated thirty-eight performances since the ill-fated *Rob-Roy* in 1834. During Berlioz's lifetime the relationship had been cordial, he asserted, and the society had recognized from the outset the value of Berlioz's performance materials— which in fact they were using all the time. They took pride in recognizing that the music of Berlioz had since triumphed over public indifference and was acclaimed everywhere.[62] The remaining major works for orchestra and chorus, Lebouc promised, would be added to the repertoire as fast as opportunity allowed. He failed to mention the *Fantastique,* still conspicuously lacking from the society's programs.

Berlioz's most direct descendent, Ernest Reyer, had composed a single work that so far interested Deldevez, the opera *Sigurd;* from it he drew, between 1876 and 1881, the overture, act II finale ("Brunnhilde's Awakening"), and a long excerpt from act III—all before the work was first produced in 1884. (Garcin later conducted a scene from *Érostrate,* in 1891; the *Sigurd* overture was recorded in 1934.) Of the next generation, it was Saint-Saëns who achieved unrivaled dominance in the programs, in those years with *Le Rouet d'Omphale,* the Third Piano Concerto, and from 1880 his popular cantata *La Lyre et la harpe,* encored at its first performance. His contemporaries—Lalo, Massenet, Gounod—gained acceptance by the society at a slower but on the whole decent pace. Lalo's *Le Roi d'Ys* overture was introduced (by Ernest Altès, substituting for Deldevez) in 1878; the first portion of Massenet's *Ève* in the same year, and three movements of Gounod's *Messe solennelle de Sainte-Cécile* in 1879. Less prominent composers were cultivated as well, with movements from the Second Symphony of Alfred Holmes, Louis Lacombe's *Sapho,* Théodore Gouvy's overture to *Giaour,* and a reprise of Gouvy's F-Major Symphony, first played in 1869.

The 1877 reading of excerpts from Vaucorbeil's unperformed opera *Mahomet* extended an association begun with *La Mort de Diane* in 1869–

70. At the time Vaucorbeil was the government's *commissaire* for sub-ventioned theaters, on the verge of becoming inspector-general of fine arts. His subsequent appointment (1879) as administrative director at the Opéra led to a notable lessening of friction between the two insti-tutions. Having the view that they were "branches of the same house-hold," [63] Vaucorbeil was gracious in allowing use of materials from the library and actually encouraged his singers to appear with the Société des Concerts. His enthusiasm was central to the emergence of the great Gabrielle Krauss (who had sung the title role in *La Mort de Diane* and in the second-act duo from *Mahomet*) as the society's prima donna of her generation.

But Deldevez would have little to do with Liszt and Wagner and their followers. He scorned the "modern" element in works he thought were "made, in general, to sap all structure, destroy all form, and replace imagination with thematic transformation." [64]

Deldevez proudly claimed that the Société des Concerts was sole pro-prietor of a so-called *symphonie inédite* by Haydn, first performed at the opening concerts of the 1877–78 season and featured for many years af-terward. Like Girard, Deldevez fancied himself something of a Haydn specialist, and had attempted to reconcile the several numbering schemes then in use by building up the thematic index he published in his *Cu-riosités musicales* of 1873.[65] Sometime thereafter he came across manu-script parts for a C-major *"Symphonia del sig. Giu. Haydn"* for *"harmo-nie et double quatuor"* shelved with the orchestra's collection; based on his previous work he thought there was every reason to conclude that the society owned a priceless treasure. He went on to write a ten-page digression on the subject in his study of the Société des Concerts.[66]

The source manuscript parts, which Deldevez describes as copied on the cheap blue paper, can no longer be found. He gave them the date "about 1837," to match orchestra parts from the Opéra that had much the same look, and imagined they were acquired by Habeneck, possibly through the Siebers. In fact he appears to have been off by about a de-cade; Habeneck indeed mentioned wanting to acquire a *symphonie in-édite,* but not until 1848,[67] a year interrupted by revolution and his own decline. The copies were most probably made from a borrowed manu-script and then forgotten.

The manuscript full score Deldevez caused to be prepared from the old parts is, however, preserved. It lets us match the *symphonie inédite* with Hoboken's entry I.c3 (attributed in one source to Cartellieri).[68]

Adagio maestoso

Allegro Presto

Andante poco Adagio

Menuetto: Allegretto

Final: Allegro

Haydn: *Symphonie inédite*

The symphony consists of an opening Adagio maestoso in C minor followed by an unusually long Allegro presto in ¾ (561 measures), and an
Andante, minuet, and finale. The oboe solo in the second movement
and oboe and flute work in the minuet attracted notice in the reviews,
and the "Turkish percussion" of bass drum, cymbals, and triangle in the
finale was highly praised.

One reviewer contested the attribution to Haydn, which he considered an "unmerited honor." He wondered how the *symphonie inédite,* ornamented with "reminiscences" of *The Barber of Seville,* could be perceived as the genuine work of the composer of *The Creation.* The oboe parts were too high for Haydn (a point contested by Deldevez); it was a pleasant composition, he said, *"mais voilà tout."*[69]

The only thing unusual about such a *contretemps* is how much Deldevez and his followers, so anxious to establish their particular turf, made of the discovery. Haydn authenticity remained a conundrum in Paris, as it had always been, and the numbering of the symphonies reflects at least three different systems.[70] Altogether the society appears by the 1870s and 1880s to have been familiar with some twenty Haydn symphonies, though often we cannot tell which is which; by the time the program notes begin, with Taffanel in 1902, the symphonies were being performed much less frequently. From Gaubert onward there are fewer than a half dozen in the popular repertoire (notably "La Reine," No. 85 in B♭ major; the "Military," No. 93 in G major; and No. 101, in D major). As for the *symphonie inédite,* the Société des Concerts went on performing the work and billing it as their "exclusive" and essentially secret property, denying the Richault firm's 1879 request to publish it.[71] Gaubert is to be found conducting the *symphonie inédite* as late as 1939.

A quite similar story played out two decades later, this time regarding the "unpublished overture" of Mozart that Marty offered during his inaugural concerts of 24 November and 1 December 1901. Weckerlin apparently brought the society's attention to a set of printed parts in the Conservatoire library carrying the title *Ouverture à grand orchestre, par MOZART—Prix 9 ff.—A Paris, à l'Imprimerie du Conservatoire, faubourg Poissonnière, no. 152,* a work was not mentioned at the time in Köchel's catalogue. In his brief program note, Tiersot suggested that Mozart had composed it during his 1778 sojourn in Paris, and did not doubt the attribution. The modern Köchel dates the publication, from evidence of the plate number, to late August / early September 1778, asserting that the parts were found by Julien Tiersot and Léon Mathieu "in the archive of the Société des Concerts"; it assesses the authenticity as doubtful, assigning the K. number C 11.05.[72] There was little interest in adding the overture to the permanent repertoire, and it was played only the once. (A score and parts were published in 1937 by Litolff in Brunswick.)

Théophile Tilmant, third conductor in the lineage, and François Benoist, the first official *répétiteur de chant,* died in May 1878 with funerals a day apart. Two active members, the cellist Marx and the young French horn player Baneux, succumbed during the season as well. Deldevez missed eight concerts in the first quarter of 1878, the longest a conductor had been absent in anybody's memory. Ernest Altès, Lamoureux's successor as second conductor, earned lasting and markedly affectionate support for his substitutions that season, which included the premiere of the "Fête chez Capulet" from Berlioz's *Roméo et Juliette*. Altès conducted again on 16 February 1879, with no rehearsals, when Deldevez was suddenly taken ill,[73] and then for seven concerts in 1879–80. Deldevez offered his resignation for reasons of health, but the assembly, confident in the abilities of Altès, refused it with best wishes for the complete restoration of his health and his "tireless devotion" to them.[74]

Altogether during the life of the Société des Concerts, Paris hosted six major world's fairs: in 1855, 1867, 1878, 1889, 1900, and 1937. Each one charged the imagination and changed the cityscape. The focal point and architectural centerpiece of the 1878 exposition was the Trocadéro, an imposing faux-gothic edifice intended in part for music performances. Plans had begun during the 1860s, possibly in conjunction with Girard's project for a festival venue like the one in Lille, when Baron Haussmann invited the architect Gabriel Davioud to develop an assembly room for 10,000. Work began on a project of rather smaller scale in 1876; when finished, the room accommodated 400 performers and seating for 4,300 beneath a dome 45 meters in diameter. The stage area, being very wide and abnormally shallow, was problematic for conventional orchestra seating. The huge pipe organ by Cavaillé-Coll, on the other hand, was judged nearly perfect for the French repertoire. (The Trocadéro was destroyed in 1935 to make way for the Palais de Chaillot, built for the exposition of 1937.)

At the request of the council governing the 1878 Exposition Universelle, the committee of the Société des Concerts granted its members permission to participate in the orchestra and chorus of the Trocadéro concerts led by Édouard Colonne. Though this was a major exception to the rules, putting impediments in Colonne's way was not thought on this occasion to be in anyone's best interests.[75] For one thing, the society was smarting not to have been designated an official purveyor of music to the exposition; it was feared that their progress toward becoming a state orchestra had somehow been compromised. To compensate in some measure for what was in fact an unintended slight, the minister of fine arts, Bardoux, sponsored a gala summer concert by the

Société des Concerts on 11 July 1878—a splendid *soirée* in their own hall, with elite guests who mingled with the musicians at a post-concert reception that did much to assuage wounded egos. Nationalization was on everyone's mind, and we encounter little warning as to its obvious disadvantages, nor recollection of the many times a close relationship with the government had brought unwanted intrusion into the society's affairs.

Colonne's Trocadéro concerts featured works by contemporary composers and noted French soloists, exposing the society's participating musicians to a number of works they did not know. Deldevez observes that his own 1878–79 season purposefully followed suit by seeking the collaboration of living French artists in order to draw the sympathetic attention of the authorities.[76] Among these were two movements from the Second Symphony by Alfred Holmes, excerpts from a *Stabat mater* of Bourgault-Ducoudray, and an overture of Théodore Dubois. Two recent laureates of the Conservatoire were featured soloists, Martin Marsick in the Mendelssohn Violin Concerto and Léon Desjardins in a violin concerto by the orchestra's own Antoine Taudou.

On the whole, however, Deldevez took greater pride, in his account of the Exposition year and its aftermath, in the big chorus-and-orchestra works they had systematically prepared and now brought to the attention of the public: the first four movements of Mendelssohn's *Elijah* in December 1878; the near-complete *Roméo et Juliette* of Berlioz in January 1879; the major portion of Weber's *Euryanthe*, act III, later in the same month; and Beethoven's *The Ruins of Athens* in February. Deldevez reports a high level of audience satisfaction with these undertakings, though with the intriguing observation that the subscribers to the second series—the newer, less experienced patrons—were less attentive to long works, like the Berlioz, than their first-series counterparts.

The bitter winter of 1879–80 brought with it a round of illnesses that caused personnel shortages at every level of the organization. Housset, the committee's factotum, died in March and was succeeded by his son, who died less than a week later. The *sociétaires* found their attention forcibly drawn to the lack of any provision for sick leave; the practice had always been that absence for any reason entailed forfeiture of the *jeton* for that service, and the musicians who had been unable to work for an extended period had their income severely compromised just when they needed it most. The *aspirants* called as replacements received only a half-*jeton*, however, and under the circumstances it seemed socially conscious to establish a new policy whereby a *sociétaire* incapacitated by illness would receive the other half-*jeton* instead of having its value left in the general pool. To prevent cheating, a severe penalty was specified for "simulated illness." One member, offended by that provision, suggested that "no member of the Société des Concerts would stoop so low," to which the committee responded that while it shared that sentiment, they thought it "prudent to envisage the impossible." Some years later the cellist Marthe stooped precisely that low, attributing his absence from two concerts to sickness when in fact he had been seen playing elsewhere across town.[77]

Other changes in policy as the decade approached its end recognized the mutations of concert life in Paris and the proven fact that the committee could no longer manage all the production details by itself. This was the case, for instance, with publicity. Prevailing practice had long been for the committee to write and oversee the printing of weekly handbills, then to remit them to employees of the city of Paris for posting in the neighborhoods occupied by the concertgoing public. In theory 175 copies were posted on Thursdays and another 175 on the morning of the concerts, thus enabling announcement of any last-minute changes. But for years subscribers had been complaining either that no poster could be found where they lived—in St-Germain, for instance—or that the postings were so late as to cause them to miss works in which they were especially interested. (Or occasionally the contrary; one patron discovered a program not to his satisfaction, with *Israel in Egypt* and the Berlioz *Francs-Juges* overture, and to the committee's amusement asked for his money back.)[78] The committee understood this growing concern with a formerly routine practice for what it was: one direct effect of the new choice to be found in Sunday afternoon concerts. Patrons wanted to compare the offerings.

Investigation revealed that the city had granted a monopoly on theater posting to a private enterprise that was in the habit of relegating the society's small-format flyers to the outside corners of cluttered walls. That being the case, the committee's initial idea of posting seventy-five copies every morning from Thursday to Sunday seemed pointless. Meanwhile the Drouart news agency proposed to mount the handbills in frames on their kiosks, in exchange for complimentary tickets. This plan, entailing an annual reduction in expenses of 200 francs, was adopted, with the savings applied to the cost of mailing programs to the domiciles of subscribers, as was said to be the practice of many European orchestras. While these changes were thought "worthy of the dignity of the Society," overt paid advertising was not. Yet it was recognized that discrete promotional efforts would become the rule; by the end of the decade, for instance, we find handbills being delivered to the Jockey Club, the Cercle de l'Union Artistique and similar literary organizations, and the lobbies of the best hotels.[79]

In the spring of 1880 the Easter Sunday *concert spirituel,* having already been moved from afternoon until evening, was abandoned in favor of Holy Saturday. Each year the number of places returned by subscribers with holiday obligations had grown, and in the seasons just past the vacancy rate had reached one empty chair for every seven filled.[80]

With great reluctance, the committee began to discuss—for only the second time in their history—the possibility of increasing ticket prices. This became inevitable in June 1882, when the authorities sent word that more seats were to be removed from the Salle des Concerts in order to widen the fire escape corridors. As there was no longer any margin at all in the budget, the decision was to raise prices for the most popular seats, those of the *rez-de-chausée* and 1ères *loges,* just enough to make up for the value of the lost places. (To ease the blow, the society absorbed a new stamp tax on theater tickets.) Denying outright any move to market pricing, thought "speculation," the committee sought to maintain the appearance of a typical, conservative management: "If one of our duties is to defend the artistic interests of the Society, it is equally our duty to defend its material ones." In the event, but only after the ticketing was done that October, it turned out that only a few of the infamous corridor seats were removed, and only from the amphitheater. The result was a quite significant and altogether welcome augmentation in annual income. The disadvantage was that prices had already been raised, so that any later loss of seats would have to be absorbed, with what would by that time be perceived as a loss of income to the musicians.[81]

Brahms entered the repertoire with the Second Symphony, after "careful study," in December 1880. The performance was not a success;[82] found too severe, the music of Brahms was only reluctantly received in Paris for many years. Deldevez led the Second once more during his tenure, Garcin introduced the Fourth in 1890, and Taffanel the Third in 1895. Meanwhile Schubert's "Unfinished" Symphony first appeared on a program, without fanfare, in February 1883.

In fact the programming had begun its gradual but unstoppable mutation toward what would soon be identified as the New French School. We notice this less at first with symphonic music—the symphonies of

Bizet, Franck, and Saint-Saëns would be introduced by Garcin—than in the flood of opera and oratorio excerpts Deldevez tended to favor. There was Gounod in abundance: *Sapho* and *Polyeucte* and a very popular duo, *D'un cœur qui t'aime,* to a text of Racine. An *ode-symphonie* by Joncières, with the pregnant title *La Mer,* was presented in January 1881, scenes from Félicien David's *Herculanum* in December. Saint-Saëns's *La Lyre et la harpe* was completed; Franck's *Béatitudes* began to be programmed with no. 6 in January 1882.

Jules Garcin, having become second conductor when Altès resigned to become chief conductor at the Opéra, first conducted the Société des Concerts on 8 January 1882. He led the Franck premiere, but postponed Schumann's *Manfred* and portions of Handel's *Saul* until the next season. The society observed the tenth anniversary of Auber's death by dedicating the concert of 29 January 1882 to his memory, inserting the overture and prayer from *La Muette de Portici* and the elegy by Arthur Sullivan into a program dominated by Schumann and Berlioz. At the end of the season the musicians were allowed to lend their support to a *grand festival* benefit organized by the Société Française des Amis de la Paix.

Crisis with Deldevez, now entering his tenth year on the podium, erupted at the beginning of the 1882–83 season. He scolded the committee after the fall readings, annoyed at having prepared new works that they later declined to program. On 25 November 1882 he lectured the orchestra for unseemly deportment and caused a *précis* of his remarks to be entered in the record. Urging a return to the discipline and "perfect order" he imagined obtained in eras past, he reminded them of the necessity for technical accuracy, early arrival for tuning, silence in the ranks, no pre-concert warming-up on stage, no saluting one another before the public. "Rededicate yourselves," he exhorted, "to artistry, zeal, ardor, conviction, and faith."[83] The committee was annoyed by both incidents.

Deldevez's constitution had taken an obvious turn for the worse. In January he had been too crippled to mount the stairs to the committee room and had his advice carried up by a porter. After an onstage attack during the concert of 18 April 1883, he concluded that the "hour of retreat has definitively sounded." On 24 April, in a note to the committee canceling his appearance the next day, he announced his great regret at needing to retire definitively from the Société des Concerts, prompting what was recorded as a "profound *coup d'émotion*." The committee immediately adjourned their meeting and sent a commission—Garcin, the secretary Viguier, the chorusmaster Heyberger, and Tubeuf—to convey their distress. Deldevez was touched by the errand, and they left with some hope that he would reconsider.

The next day, though he was feeling better, Deldevez came in person to the committee to maintain a decision he said had been motivated by long and serious reflection. The *ordre du jour* calling the membership to its annual general assembly on 22 May 1883 used the word *définitive* to describe his retirement—as did the press reports—and reserved time to discuss options for the succession.

For this was by no means clear-cut, and Deldevez himself did not indicate a preference between his two experienced associates, Altès and Garcin. The composers Ernest Guiraud and Benjamin Godard announced their candidacies, leading to speculation in the press that the sainted repertoire was on the verge of passing into the hands of amateurs who had never even conducted their own work. Journalists suggested in their columns that the election should be delayed until the autumn.[84]

At the assembly Viguier delivered a heartfelt tribute to Deldevez, recalling his appointment as *aspirant* in 1831, *aspirant actif* in 1833 and *sociétaire* in 1839; then his rise to *2e chef* in 1863 and *1er chef/ vice-président* in 1872—a tenure of more than half a century. Deldevez had conserved intact the great traditions of the orchestra; as a member from its infancy, he could himself claim to be its living tradition. Under his direction the Société des Concerts had grown to a size and prosperity that, Viguier suggested, it was inconceivable to exceed.

Periods of adversity, Viguier went on in reference to the 1860s, had taught Deldevez the merits of patience and the value of time to invest in research. One could never know enough, Deldevez believed, hence his careful study of the repertoire, his passionate admiration of the great masters, his theories of how to lead even experienced musicians to ever greater perfection. In recent years he had devoted himself entirely to the Société des Concerts, and it had filled and fulfilled his life. It broke their hearts, said Viguier, to think of their separating, but Deldevez deserved many years of repose from a long and noble career. Viguier then cited article 62*bis,* adopted on Habeneck's retirement: that the society, in witness of its high esteem and admiration, might accord the title *président honoraire à vie* to a conductor who had served twenty years or more. Viguier so moved.[85]

At this point the general assembly of the Société des Concerts took one of the most dramatic turns in its history. Lebrun rose to suggest that Deldevez's resignation was a rash response to his failure to appear at the last concert; he was now, it was believed, happier and healthier, and the *sociétaires* might best confide themselves once more to their trusted leader. Lebouc called for a commission to go visit Deldevez while the meeting continued; probably he would relent, since his actions might just as well be interpreted as gestures of discretion and modesty. The vote indicated 78 of 104 electors favoring the return of their conductor and extending his mandate for two years. The deputation—Taffanel, Heyberger, Lebrun, and Jacquin—left on their mission, returning a half hour later with a positive response. Bravos erupted in the room. "All's well that ends well," they observed, and the optimistic imagined that the Société des Concerts would be for Deldevez a "veritable fountain of youth."[86] Ambroise Thomas, in the president's chair, was well pleased.

On 20 October 1883 Deldevez greeted the musicians at the next season's first rehearsal, apologizing for his involuntary absence and assuring them that he approached his new term with neither fear nor regret. He was happy, he said, to help the society sustain both "certain modern tendencies" and the classical traditions that were the source of its glory.[87]

While the visiting commission was on its errand in May, the assembly approved two resolutions. The first answered an invitation from the Institute to support a monument to Berlioz in the square by the rue de Calais and rue Vintimille, where he had lived and died. The committee proposed to vote a sum of 1,000 francs: "You are doubtless as certain as we are that the Société des Concerts could not fail to take part in a mission whose goal is to honor the memory of a composer long disputed but now recognized as one of the greatest musical lights of France." The vote to support was unanimous.[88]

A more controversial issue concerned the recruitment of new personnel. The society was losing the best young musicians to the rival orchestras because the half-*jeton* offered *aspirants* was less than they could make elsewhere, while full *sociétaires* made considerably more than senior members of the other orchestras. It was important to be able to compete at the entry level. The committee thus proposed to add to the statutes that "in case of necessity the committee can grant an *aspirant* three-quarters of a *jeton* per service from the first year." This language carried, 88 favoring, 14 opposed. Shortly afterward, as though to insure that this new investment would yield the desired results, it was decided that all new employees would sign a contract binding them to the principle of exclusive service to the Société des Concerts.[89]

Before the vote, however, the secretary was interrupted by Désiré Thibault with an ill-timed question as to why members of the committee who played no concerts at all continued to receive full payment. Though ruled out of order by the president, Viguier asked to address the matter—

> not because of the thinly veiled personal attack, since I give my *jetons* to the Caisse de Prévoyance anyway, but because it involves a question of common interest. The Société des Concerts, founded with a purely artistic goal, has become a commercial enterprise. Like all such enterprises it is directed by an administrative council, whose members earn certain privileges and a *jeton* at each meeting, the value varying according to the financial success of the society they direct. Since the season was extended the committee work has become much more onerous and difficult to accomplish, where before it was mostly routine. The only recompense the members get is two tickets for each concert and the maximum *droits de présence*. This system has been formally validated by the society more than once.
>
> The only members to have realized a payment under this system without actually playing were either indisposed or absent on the business of the society. And I will observe that M. Thibault himself profited from it very liberally when he was conductor of the matinees at the Théâtre de la Gaîté.

This was one of the noble Viguier's last stands, as he was forced to retire the following season owing to his failed eyesight. "We lose in him," remarked his successor, Taffanel, "one of the most zealous and capable administrators we've ever had."[90]

The committee made a conscious decision to return Wagner to the programs after a fourteen-year hiatus following the Franco-Prussian War. The marches from *Lohengrin* and *Tannhäuser* had been removed for reasons of "high propriety." Now they were exhumed, and the overture to *Tannhäuser* ended the *concerts spirituels* of April 1884 (and thus the season). All three selections stayed in the repertoire. Not everyone approved, though Wagnerism already had Paris intellectuals in its grasp. "They are essentially dramatic works," Taffanel complained, "of an often excessive sonority that doesn't lend itself to performance in our little hall."[91]

One of Habeneck's fond but unrealized dreams, we have had more than one occasion to note, was to find a way for the Société des Concerts to encourage beginning French composers. The traditional mechanism, especially once the experiment of playing Prix de Rome *envois* had failed, would have been a prize competition. Much later the violist Léopold Délidicque led a campaign for a more compelling system to achieve the same end. In 1873 he reminded his colleagues that at the close of the 1870 concerts, before the collapse, he and fourteen colleagues had petitioned to propose a 5,000-franc commission of a new symphony every three years. The committee apologized for the oversight and promised to study the question.[92] He returned to this question at the assembly of 16 May 1876, and this time was invited to come meet with the committee—again, without particular result.

Now, in the spring of 1884, the society was approached on behalf of the Académie des Beaux-Arts by Saint-Saëns, Gounod, and Ambroise Thomas, with an invitation to participate in the awarding of the Prix Rossini for young composers and librettists. (The Prix Rossini had been funded by a provision of the composer's will that took effect after the death of his widow in 1878; the inaugural prize had been won by the librettist Paul Collin and the composer Marie, Countess de Grandval, but the ceremonial performance in February 1881 had not been a success.)[93] First- and second-prize winners were to have prestigious renderings of their work. The academy offered funding of 7,500 francs in the first year and 6,000 francs biennially after that. Having presented their project, the dignitaries expressed their gratitude for being received and retired to allow the committee to reach its decision.

Ensuing discussion noted that the proposed fee was considerably less than the 9,000 francs the society was accustomed to receiving for other official duties, and that the expenses would be great. The Académie des Beaux-Arts alone would pre-empt 220 seats. But a brilliant strategy—built on the circumstance that Thomas was at once chief spokesperson for the academics, director of the Conservatoire, and the society's own president—was soon found, whereby responsibility for the Prix Rossini duties would be undertaken in exchange for the Conservatoire's according the Salle des Concerts to the society for eighteen consecutive Sundays, abandoning its claim to one Sunday a month. Thomas readily agreed.[94]

Thomas then strongly argued the case for the Prix Rossini to the general assembly. The secretary followed suit, noting that it would be an official event without a public ticket sale, that the 6,000 francs would be distributed among the members as usual, that it would take place two weeks after the final subscription concert. "Therefore," he concluded, "your committee asks you to approve our participating in the production of the Prix Rossini of the Académie des Beaux-Arts."[95] The members proceeded to vote unanimously on 20 May 1884 to accept the proposal, noting their desire to be associated with the memory of the illustrious composer of *William Tell*.

Subsequently the Prix Rossini cantatas were allocated a quite generous schedule of rehearsals, five for orchestra and six for chorus. The performance would be framed as a solemnity of the Institute, given in its own great hall on the Left Bank, and with tickets and programs headed *Institut de France / Académie des Beaux-Arts*. Since the fee was roughly what the Salle des Concerts might bring if sold out, and since the presenters and prizewinners would require much of the seating in any case, all the tickets went to the sponsors to distribute as they saw fit. The lyric scenes would be played in the order of their priority: first Lucien Lambert's first-prize *Prométhée enchaîné,* then Georges Matthias's. That all this came at the end of the year, on 19 April 1885, was found a "painful circumstance," but in summary the first year of the Prix Rossini seemed an excellent beginning.[96]

The experiences of 1885, notably the difficulty in arranging for soloists and the long delays while the composers copied out their parts, made it clear that a two-year cycle was overly optimistic, and it was later agreed to open the competition only once every three years.[97] In 1893 the prize ceremony moved from post-season to pre-season, two weeks before the opening concert. With Marcel Rousseau's *Le Roi Arthur* in 1903, where the expenses of copying alone came to 1,500 francs, it became necessary to renegotiate the fee, which rose to 9,000 francs inclusive of all expenses.[98]

Altogether the Société des Concerts appears to have given a half-dozen Prix Rossini concerts between 1885 and 1911. Every one of the prizewinning composers, in their twenties and thirties at the time, went on to successful careers in the profession: Will-Chaumet (1842–1903), Auguste Chapuis (1858–1933), Henri Hirschmann (1872–1961), Marcel [Samuel-]Rousseau (1882–1955), and Marc Delmas (1885–1931).[99] The Prix Rossini is still awarded.

Later on the Société des Concerts would from time to time undertake other prize concerts. In 1904, for instance, they premiered Charles Tournemire's *Le Sang de la Sirène,* winner of the Prix de la Ville de Paris; in 1906, a concert of works by Guy Ropartz featuring his Prix Cressent work, a Third Symphony for soloists, chorus, and orchestra. The Prix Cressent had been established in the will of the lawyer Anatole

Cressent (d. 28 May 1870), who wrote that "the cult of the fine arts, and of music in particular, was always the dearest of my predilections."[100] Accordingly, Cressent left a bond, later augmented by his heirs, that produced some 6,200 francs a year to support a triennial competition and public performance of a dramatic work, "with choruses and an overture." The prize was administered by the Société des Compositeurs de Musique.

Garcin conducted eleven concerts from 25 January 1885, as well as the Prix Rossini ceremony in April. Deldevez was overcome with a chill at the rehearsal on Saturday, 24 January, and the musicians watched with mounting alarm as the episode appeared to become life-threatening. Dr. Firmin was summoned and stayed in the Salle des Concerts with Deldevez until he stabilized.

It had been hoped that the concerts of 1884–85 would gather into a celebration of the Bach-and-Handel bicentennial, perhaps concluding with a large work by each composer. This project had to be abandoned with the loss of Deldevez, leaving only a concert partly devoted to Handel (excerpts of *Israel in Egypt* and *Judas Maccabaeus* already in the repertoire, and an organ concerto with Alexandre Guilmant) and at a later concert the standard excerpts from the Bach B-Minor Suite. Garcin did oversee the premiere of the third movement of *Les Argonautes,* an *ode-symphonie* by Augusta Holmès, characterized to the players as "a musician of the young French school." It may be significant that the secretary changed his draft remarks concerning its reception from "a very large success" to "a legitimate success."[101]

The Assemblée Générale on 23 May 1885 began with optimistic welcome of "their kind and valiant *chef* back to his family." But when Deldevez took the floor he announced "in the most elevated and touching terms" his irrevocable intent to step down. Thomas managed to quiet the hubbub with remarks along the lines of 1883, and Deldevez was (again) acclaimed *président honoraire à vie.*[102] The assembly adjourned until 2 June, giving the musicians just over a week to consider their options.

Deldevez appeared before them for the last time on 2 June 1885, saluted with a prolonged accolade and an embrace from Ambroise Thomas. Responding to his words of thanks and farewell, Thomas recalled their shared youth and long careers and spoke of himself as "your old comrade and friend." Later the *sociétaires* would present him a bust of Gluck, chosen by the new conductors, Garcin and Danbé; and after his retirement from the Conservatoire, the director of fine arts would orate grandly on his "kindness, simplicity, intelligence, and knowledge." Deldevez left behind him a healthy institution that was well positioned to go on without him, and he could claim a fair share of responsibility for "the music fever devouring Paris."[103] His public career with the Société des Concerts, from 1825 (violin recitals at the age of eight) to 1885, had spanned an unparalleled six decades.

The 1884–85 season closed on a note of unaccustomed merriment. To support the annual lottery of the Association des Artistes-Musiciens, the committee had taken ten tickets at its own risk and peril. The intent was to ask the assembly to approve their little expenditure retroactively. As it happened, they held the winning ticket in the first drawing. "So our problem [of disclosure] was resolved," confessed Taffanel. "But by then we were hooked, so we used the money to buy more than a hundred tickets. We can't promise to succeed so well on the second round, but we hope you won't disapprove of our *petite opération*."[104]

CHAPTER 8

Garcin, Taffanel, and Marty

(1885–1908)

While Jules Garcin, as incumbent second conductor to Deldevez and his substitute for more than a dozen concerts in the seasons just past, had good reason to expect the post of first conductor, that was on this occasion less than a foregone conclusion. Paul Taffanel, arguably the strongest figure in the administration, favored Bizet's disciple Ernest Guiraud, professor of composition at the Conservatoire. Some members still supported Ernest Altès, their former concertmaster and second conductor, who had left the Société des Concerts in 1881 pleading overwork after his inaugural season as 1er *chef* at the Opéra. The second-chair violinist, Jules Danbé, conductor at the Opéra-Comique, wanted the post, and the composer Benjamin Godard had again presented himself. All were affiliates or graduates of the Conservatoire.

The real question, in view of the many advances of the Deldevez years, was to ascertain something from each candidate of what entrusting the podium to him might bring. For the election of 5 June 1885 nominees were invited for the first time to amplify their thoughts as to the present and future of the Société des Concerts, to go beyond the usual formula of listing past accomplishments thought to "entitle" the nominee to the vacant post. Garcin and Danbé, as *sociétaires,* presented their statements in person, then left the room; communications from Guiraud and Godard were read aloud by the secretary. Opposition to Guiraud, the only candidate with a reputation that extended much past the theater district, was apparent from the outset. Aside from the fact that as a conductor he was unknown to them, there was the usual fear that a serious composer might foist unwanted works on the society. Garcin's supporters argued the obvious: that he had served well as second conductor and that his chair, the concertmaster's, had been seat of the heir apparent since Habeneck.

On the first ballot, however, Garcin had only 42 votes, well short of the 66 necessary to elect, followed by Guiraud with 28; Danbé, 15; Godard, 10; and Altès, 3. After a third inconclusive ballot, Danbé was consulted in the *foyer* and withdrew his candidacy in favor of Garcin, but even that failed to secure the necessary total in the fourth round. In the runoff Garcin won 59 votes to Guiraud's 39 and was thus proclaimed *1ᵉʳ chef*. A strong majority then elected Danbé *2ᵉ chef* on the first ballot, and the session ended with a unanimous confirmation of the new conductor as vice president, as though to assure him a mandate the close voting had not suggested.[1]

Garcin, at fifty-five, was prepared for his new duties by long experience with the Société des Concerts and as chief conductor at the Opéra. Descended from a family of professional musicians, he had enjoyed an uninterrupted if rather standard series of successes at the upper echelons of the Paris musical establishment: an 1853 *1ᵉʳ prix* in violin, simultaneous appointment to the Opéra orchestra and Société des Concerts in 1856 (his long apprenticeship as an *aspirant* waiting for a vacancy to open, 1856–63, has been noted), and rapid advance through the solo desks to the rank of concertmaster and second conductor of both orchestras. He had been a co-founder of the Société Nationale de Musique in 1871 and professor of violin at the Conservatoire since 1875. Like the majority of his colleagues he was a sometime composer, having appeared with the orchestra as soloist in his own violin concerto in 1868; in 1890 he would conduct a four-movement *Suite symphonique* of his composition, the only other time Garcin's work figured on a Sunday concert. Garcin succeeded Lamoureux and Altès as second conductor of the Société des Concerts in 1881, during a period of unusual opportunity for exposure as Deldevez canceled more and more often.

Considered alongside his literarily inclined predecessor Deldevez and his politically engaged successor Taffanel, each of whom exercised significant influence over the affairs of the Société des Concerts long before becoming its conductor, Garcin seems from the written record a musician of rather ill-defined personality. His tenure was short, the course of his seven seasons comparatively smooth. He seems content to have left the government to those who had already proved capable of it, hon-

ored to lead but not to dominate in a post he most likely considered
an altogether natural, and certainly final, step for a longtime concertmaster. His sense of himself thus epitomized what the musicians liked
to think of as their signal social identity, that of a "phalanx of virtuosi"
with a conductor "who reigns but does not govern." [2]

Given this fundamentally old-fashioned attitude toward the profession of conducting, Garcin's legacy in modernizing the Société des Concerts seems all the more substantial. However tempting it is to construe
him as the last of a dying breed of violinist-conductors in Habeneck's
mold, a perusal of his programs suggests a great deal more than ordinary craft. Garcin seems intellectually engaged, a broad-minded student
of the repertoire, unfailingly curious, eager to transmit discovery to the
public at large, as cognizant of advances in understanding music of the
past as of the accumulation of good works that would come to be identified as the first salvo of the New French School. He contributed hugely
to Wagnerism in France, introducing at the Conservatoire the Spinning
Chorus from *Der fliegende Holländer,* a scene from *Die Meistersinger,*
and the prelude to *Tristan et Isolde* (1886, 1890, and 1891); he also prepared a scene from *Parsifal,* conducted by Danbé in 1892. Garcin was
enough of a proponent of Brahms to have introduced the Fourth Symphony in 1890, overcoming by the end of the rehearsals his musicians'
distaste for music they found "severe," and—in a somewhat scornful
context—"German." [3] He returned the Second to the programs in 1891,
with better reception than Deldevez had had. This time Brahms arrived
at the Conservatoire to stay.

Overall Garcin's was an era of formidable expansion of the society's
horizons, with a half-dozen or more premieres each season: first performances at the Conservatoire, first performances in France, and a few
first-ever performances. Chief of these were the complete *Missa solemnis*
in 1888, the Franck D-Minor Symphony in 1889, and Bach's B-Minor
Mass in 1891. The generation of French composers by then in their sixties—Gounod, Franck, and Lalo, joined by Saint-Saëns, just entering
his fifties—commanded a prominent share of the repertoire. There was
a significant body of new music by decently established composers in
their forties—Charles Lenepveu, Massenet, Fauré, and Augusta Holmès
—and a few works by the very young. Still the tendency was to focus
on big texted works: Gounod's *Mors et vita* and *La Communion des
saints,* Saint-Saëns's *Le Déluge,* Schumann's *Paradise and the Peri* and
Faust. A symphony or overture of Beethoven was still to be heard on
nearly every program, as was a work of Mozart, Haydn, or Mendels-

sohn—sometimes all three. Weber begins to fade, as do, temporarily, the many short *a cappella* pieces for the chorus.

Star soloists became a major priority of the programming. The days were over when ticket holders would flock to the Conservatoire each Sunday in simple anticipation of whatever pleasures might be offered. In this period the Société des Concerts continued to rely primarily on resident soloists, those affiliated either with the Conservatoire or the Opéra. Of the pianists these included the prodigious Francis Planté, whose meteoric career was disrupted by his sudden vow circa 1900 never again to appear before the public; the still more colorful E.-M. Delaborde, natural son of Alkan and a wealthy mistress, professor of piano at the Conservatoire, collector of jungle wildlife, swimming partner of Bizet, lover (and eventually second husband) of Mme Bizet; and Louis Diémer, likewise professor of piano at the Conservatoire, a popular soloist with all the concert societies, and a pioneer in the Bach keyboard repertoire. Gabrielle Krauss, the Austrian soprano who had been a favorite of Paris audiences since her appearances in 1867 in Verdi's *Il Trovatore,* returned after the Franco-Prussian war and stayed, opening the Palais Garnier—the new Opéra—as Rachel in Halévy's *La Juive.* Her last appearance with the Société des Concerts was in January 1890, two years after her farewell to the stage in 1888. Of the *sociétaires* the favored soloists were Taffanel, the oboist Gillet, the violinist Édouard Nadaud, and perhaps more than any of the instrumentalists the bass Florentin Auguez, master of roles from *Roméo et Juliette* and *L'Enfance du Christ* through *Tannhäuser.*

Of the famous tourists Joachim returned to play Spohr in April 1887 and Sarasate to play Lalo's *Symphonie espagnole*—on a *concert spirituel*—in 1891. Paderewski, after launching his career in western Europe with a Paris recital in 1888, played the Schumann Piano Concerto in 1890, the first of four appearances with the Société des Concerts over four decades. Nellie Melba sang the soprano solos in Handel's St. Cecilia Ode in January 1890, then returned in 1891 for two more Handel arias.

Like his predecessors, Garcin built his early seasons largely of inherited fare. Beethoven's Ninth, the traditional measure of a new conductor's inaugural year, was sung in German, probably for the first time. In his second year Garcin began to put his stamp on the institution: a Raff symphony, Bruch's *Kol nidrei* with the rapidly advancing second-chair cellist Loëb, particular focus on the *concerts spirituels* as occasions of note,

with a major soloist engaged well in advance and a major sacred work—
the Mozart Requiem in 1887, for instance, not heard in many years.

The Société des Concerts presented the first Paris performances of
Saint-Saëns's C-Minor ("Organ") Symphony on 9 and 16 January 1887.
(The premiere had been in London in 1886.) The public reception was
unprecedented for a new work, and in a response of rare enthusiasm the
committee formally entered its satisfaction with the new symphony in
its minutes of 11 January 1887. (Both concerts, however, were compromised by the chorus. On 9 January they were late to take the stage for
their Palestrina *Gloria,* despite prior warning that the *Leonore* overture
at the opening of the concert was quite short, and on 16 January could
be heard talking in the *foyer* during the Saint-Saëns, resulting in several
audience complaints.) Ambroise Thomas came in person to the committee to promote a third hearing of the symphony: "It is powerful and
exceptionally noteworthy, and given the invasion of German music, it
would be well to offer another performance of this work that so honors
the French school." [4] Accordingly, a supplementary concert, with ticket
sales open to the public at large, was offered on 13 March 1887. Later the
committee sent a delegation to invite Saint-Saëns to compose a new
symphony for the Société des Concerts, [5] but he was instead to abandon
the genre altogether.

An unexpected highlight of the 1887–88 season was the first performance of a patriotic *ode-symphonie, Ludus pro patria,* by Augusta
Holmès, with the great tragedian Mounet-Sully offering the spoken
recitatives. *Ludus pro patria* earned a sustained ovation from a public
that, the secretary later reported, had grown to like Mlle Holmès—not
only for her patriotism but for a voluptuous style he called "by turns
sweet, then seductive." [6] There were failures, too, notably of the two
new works that closed the first concert of the season: Henri Litolff's
heroic overture, *Le Chant des Guelfes,* and Verdi's *Pater noster.* The severe judgment of the Litolff was thought unjust "toward a composer
who merits more enthusiasm." [7]

The second Prix Rossini concert, featuring *Les Jardins d'Armide* by
Auguste Chapuis, took place on Sunday night, 29 April 1888. A minor
fire in a light fixture threatened not only to end the concert but to become the last straw in the growing concern over theater security—since
the Opéra-Comique had burned to the ground the previous spring
(when the *sociétaires* had voted a 1,000-franc allocation from the Caisse
de Prévoyance to an emergency fund for the victims). Since the certain
administrative response to any fire would be to remove more seats and

therefore lower possible income, which had been substantial since the augmentation of ticket prices in 1881–82, the incident was hushed up.[8]

The first performance in France of Beethoven's *Missa solemnis* on 8 and 15 January 1888—a "colossal work, long awaited and often postponed for a variety of reasons; at last it triumphed in a performance of rare perfection"[9]—was almost certainly the high point of Garcin's tenure. He and his chorusmaster, Heyberger, had devoted "insistent effort and ardent study" to the project, and while there is some evidence of harried last rehearsals, the chorus was, unusually for this period, strongly praised.

The *Missa solemnis* was not born without struggle. Originally planned as the centerpiece of Garcin's second season, the traditional time for a new conductor to plot his own course, it had been abandoned after a series of setbacks. In late December 1886 during the pre-season rehearsals, there had been an outburst of hard feeling among the violinists owing to the choice of Martin Marsick for the solo in the Benedictus. Marsick, the prominent Belgian virtuoso who eventually succeeded to Sauzay's professorship at the Conservatoire, had been recruited to be a *sociétaire* after his *1er prix* but had declined to join; in 1879 he was featured in the Mendelssohn Violin Concerto. The players objected strongly to the suggestion that no *sociétaire* was capable of the passage. They urged Garcin and the committee to appoint one of their own, to which proposition the committee agreed in principle but preferred letting the violinists themselves choose their soloist. At a post-rehearsal audition in January the young violinist Henri Berthelier, who would succeed Danbé as concertmaster, earned the distinction. Then, after a difficult rehearsal in mid-February, both choral and orchestral musicians went away thinking that it would be impossible to present the mass that season in performances worthy of the society. Garcin was sharply opposed to the suggestion, but in a split vote it was decided to postpone the work.[10]

On 27 February Arthur Pougin published a notice of the postponement in *Le Ménestrel*.[11] Garcin returned to the committee to beg for a rescheduling. He foresaw "ominous consequences"—though did not say what they might be—if the work were not programmed before the close of the season, and proposed devoting the Holy Week concerts to the *Missa solemnis* alone. Joseph Joachim had already been booked. The committee, having just named Berthelier as soloist, bristled at the thought. "It's clearly unfortunate," they noted, "that the Mass in D won't be performed after having been so noisily announced, but it would be equally unfortunate to present such a masterpiece without sufficient preparation." The confrontation of conductor and musicians was in this case a major divisive incident. Taffanel, generally sympathetic to Garcin, went away to develop new guidelines for removing primarily artistic decisions from the committee's purview in order to prevent further episodes of this kind.[12]

In the end it was just as well to delay, since the musicians returned to their Beethoven with renewed energy during the fall 1887 preparatory rehearsals and had the *Missa solemnis* well polished in time for the second pair, in January 1888. By dramatic coincidence, the sculptor Eugène Guillaume, of the Institute (and formerly director of the Villa Médicis), came in person to a committee meeting on the 31 January to present the Société des Concerts with his magnificent bronze bust after the death mask of Beethoven. It had served as the model for a version in marble commissioned by a wealthy Russian aristocrat; the patron had asked specifically that the bronze be given to the orchestra. The committee reckoned the confluence of the *Missa solemnis* and Guillaume's statue as a symbol of rededication to the "insoluble link" between the Société des Concerts and Beethoven.[13] Today the bronze watches over the offices of the Orchestre de Paris.

In every orchestra a wave of retirements typically accompanies a change of conductor. Matters of personal loyalty are in play, and the senior generation is prone to take its cue from a retiring conductor. In some cases, too, musicians quietly depart out of nervousness at the thought of surviving changed standards. In June 1885, just after the departure of Deldevez and those who followed him, Taffanel, acting as secretary of the Caisse de Prévoyance, notified the committee that the high level of retirements was causing a run on the pension fund, which had started the year with an overall market value of about 300,000 francs. Withdrawals of more than 100,000 francs at the close of 1884–85 led him to predict a deficit in 1885–86 and failure of the account the year after. The fund had performed well since its placement in 1882 with a broker, or *agent de change;* that year the growth had been 3,658 francs, roughly 12 percent, whereas the passbook interest the previous year had been 700 francs, or 2½ percent.[14] (The *agent de change,* Rolland Gosselin, was still in the service of the Société des Concerts in the late 1920s.) By November 1885, the total to be invested in bonds had shrunk to 166,000 francs.

Audan, the *agent comptable* for the fund, resigned at the possibly well founded suggestion that he should have recognized the problem long before. Unable to sway him from this resolve, the committee was forced to call a general assembly for 8 March 1886 to designate a successor. There it was argued that an officer could not abandon his position without valid reason, still less without a final accounting. Audan replied with extended discourse in his own defense and after much persuasion agreed to return to his task long enough to close the books for the 1885–86 season. But when applause was heard after his address, another *sociétaire* rose to say that, on the contrary, he was far from approving a tenure that had threatened everyone with financial embarrassment and instead deserved a vote of censure. Garcin, presiding, quelled the dispute by adjourning the meeting; Audan, by telegram, quit his post definitively the moment the books were closed.[15]

The question of any particular *sociétaire*'s financial competence, however, was coincidental to the underlying problem of a primitive investment strategy managed largely by amateurs, its accounts reckoned in haste once a year and never audited or analyzed. The beneficiaries, meanwhile, were ignorant of truths of the marketplace, happy enough to take the risk when the growth was many times greater than could be found at a savings bank but prone to disgruntlement when the tide turned downward. The time was right to appoint a commission to redefine the society's approach to its pension fund: Taffanel, the new treasurer Lafitte, the notary, and the broker.

Their long report of May 1887 was heard with interest and audible expressions of approval, though since it was delivered orally the *sociétaires* could not have followed, as one member observed, the particulars.[16] And the first new measure proposed—to reckon the accounts according to their value as of the preceding 30 April, thus giving the commissioners sufficient time before the general assembly to balance the books —failed to win approval by the committee.

With the committee and the commissioners of the Caisse de Prévoyance very unusually at an impasse, "it was agreed to call on the wisdom of competent authority"—that is, a professional accountant. By the close of the 1887–88 season new bylaws for the Caisse de Prévoyance, articles 71 and following, had been drafted and in a special assembly of July 1888 were adopted unanimously, minus one vote. Technical amendments were passed in May 1889 after a year of experience.[17]

Less happy was the membership to sustain the cost of an independent accounting. M. Réaux, a personal friend of Taffanel, charged 250 francs or more annually for work that was thought by some "inessential." The arrangement was "often inconvenient," as Réaux lived in the distant suburb of Poissy and kept the ledgers at his residence. If the *sociétaire* they had elected *agent comptable* of the pension fund was incompetent to do the work himself, he should sell his complimentary tickets and use the proceeds to pay a qualified assistant. The new system, some continued to argue, followed "simple rules of arithmetic" that any number of members should be able to manage for themselves.[18] Taffanel, short-tempered throughout such discussions, briefly quit the Caisse de Prévoyance over this accusation of conflict of interest.

The principle of having an employee keep the accounts of the pension fund was nevertheless established. After the services of Réaux were discontinued, the committee's staff employee, Gesta, assumed the same duties in addition to assisting at the box office, and at half the cost; but the implication, on his death from a three-day case of flu in 1907, was that this praiseworthy but excessive measure of economy had hastened the end of a valuable colleague who was poorly paid and overcome with work. The committee then engaged a Monsieur Golaz, an "informed and wise" employee of the Banque Suisse et Française, to provide competence in accounting and independent audit at double the fee formerly paid to Réaux.[19]

In an attempt to guarantee ongoing quality of the personnel in a time of rapid turnover, the administration of the late 1880s began to monitor new appointments and the capabilities of aging personnel more closely than ever. The chorusmaster Joseph Heyberger, with the *Missa solemnis* and other big projects doubtless in mind, called for dozens of firings and as many new engagements. In the fall of 1885, for instance, nine women of the chorus were dismissed. Mme Méneray, the principal soprano II, and Mlle Touller, third seat in her section, both protested and appealed to the general assembly for a referendum on their cases. The lawyer was consulted, with a ruling soon issued that *sociétaires adjoints,* the title held by all the women, were not entitled to appeal to an assembly of which they were not full members.[20] This of course exacerbated the women's already strong discontent with the dubious nature of their appointments.

It also affected several men. The committee noted that in the rush to fill the chorus, the question of affiliation with the Conservatoire was being routinely overlooked. While some of the candidates could show certificates of having attended a class or two, six of the new choristers had no credentials at all. There was little particular attraction, or even opportunity (beyond the *classe d'ensemble vocal* devoted to sight-reading and repertoire), to study choral singing at the Conservatoire; graduates of other Paris music academies, notably the École Niedermeyer, could provide equally skilled candidates. In November 1885 it was decided to appoint the six singers in question, all of them *aspirants* expecting to become full members in due course, as *sociétaires adjoints*. This turn of events, combined with legitimate suspicion that the instrumentalists considered not just the women but singers in general as second citizens, "failed to give them entire satisfaction."[21] A petition of twenty-six singers placed the question on the agenda of the Assemblée Générale of 29 May 1886. The discussion was not productive, though the assembly inclined toward regarding the committee's decision as a "useful administrative measure"; at length a motion to table carried by a vote of 57 favoring, 41 opposed, 2 blank.

A subsequent committee, acting in October 1887, reversed the offending decision with the reasoning that the six *sociétaires adjoints* had entered as *aspirants* before the problem was identified and "that it was right that they should enjoy the advantages they had expected at the time of their admission." Four (Gilbert, Mesme, Gaby, and Périn) were named *sociétaires* that autumn, while two (Aubert and Delsart) were asked to await new vacancies—the whole circumstance to be considered, it was pointedly noted, a one-time exception to the statutes.[22]

What proved to be a much more sweeping change in recruitment strategies was the decision to require competitive auditions for every vacancy, thus extending to instrumentalists a condition to which the singers were long accustomed. The measure was proposed by a petition of thirty-three rank-and-file *sociétaires;* the committee, surprised by this substantial departure from tradition, nevertheless received it with enthusiasm and approved it unanimously.[23] At it happened this was just after two violinists and a violist (Schvartz, later the chorusmaster) had been selected as *aspirants en cas* from a written list, without audition; so in keeping with the spirit of the measure, all the candidates were called to audition. One refused to play alone before jurors, and was crossed off. After the formality was done, not surprisingly, the same three players headed the list. But the auditions had the positive result that three others were also found to be qualified for appointment *en cas.*[24]

In point of fact, auditions seldom turned up qualified candidates not already known to the musicians, but in the case of the strings they did help quell disputes between rival professors at the Conservatoire and, more significantly, became the method for establishing the order in which *aspirants* were elevated to *sociétaires*—generally in the priority they had been ranked in the most recent auditions. Overall the experiment was received well, as a useful check that tended to guarantee virtuosity throughout the ranks and prevent unpleasant surprises. It represented another time-consuming demand on the administrators, however, and an obvious stumbling block when it came to recruiting a senior player normally exempt from the indignities of a juried audition. Young graduates of the Conservatoire would answer the call to auditions; ranking players from the other orchestras would not.

This was precisely at issue in the retrenchment of the bassoon section when the principal, Adolphe Bourdeau, retired at the end of the 1886–87 season (simultaneously with the longtime principal clarinetist, Cyrille Rose). A single bassoonist appeared for the audition advertised in June 1887; meanwhile the preferred successor to Bourdeau, Léon Letellier, could not secure a quick release from his solo position with the Colonne orchestra. After lengthy discussion of the society's best interests, it was agreed to constitute a temporary section and hold the principal chair open until Letellier was free—which was not until 1891.[25] A little later no one at all answered the call to auditions for clarinet and horn vacancies, and they were filled with *externes*.

The full assembly also had to address the latest dispute over the use of the Salle des Concerts, because this time the challenge had come from a *sociétaire* within. The tenor Alphonse-Émile Granger asked to use the hall and presumably many of his colleagues for a springtime chorus concert and was refused; that he would ask at all was thought unusual enough that copies of the exclusivity statutes, articles 38 and 40, were printed and distributed anew to all the personnel.[26] In the particular context of the other "agitations" from the chorus, the committee felt that the matter should be reviewed by the membership at large. The secretary, Albert Ferrand, dutifully traced the history of their use of the hall from 1828—familiar to us by now, but being heard for the first time by many in the room—with particular reference to the astonishment of successive ministers at discovering the society's resolute opposition to any occupancy of the Salle des Concerts by outsiders. Since the end of the 1887–88 season, moreover, there had already been three extraneous events in the hall.

Ferrand went on to remind the members of their signed engagement not to appear in other concerts; their superiority, he remarked, was earned by their commitment to participate exclusively in the Société des

Concerts, where every member was a musician of the highest artistry and "intrinsic value. . . . If, in thoughtless division of our forces, each of us claims a freedom to participate in rival associations or random concerts given in the Salle des Concerts, the prestige of our society would be gravely diminished. If complete liberty were granted our artists, there would be neither society nor association." The musicians were free to leave the society and join lesser ensembles, but for *sociétaires* to be seen in other groups, especially on the stage of the Salle des Concerts, was certain to confuse the public. "When the doors are open, they imagine it's us inside." The committee signaled its intention to mete out severe penalties to those who would knowingly violate the rules.[27] Granger argued, rightly, that different standards of measure were being applied, since a group of prominent wind players—Taffanel's Société des Instruments à Vent, a chamber ensemble—had been excused to travel abroad the previous season. Too much was made, anyway, over random uses of an otherwise vacant hall.[28] Granger's particular case was lost, as he already knew, but he had engaged almost inadvertently a question— the right of orchestra and chorus to split apart for concerts on their own—that would dominate the society's business, and sorely try its interpersonal relations, for two decades more.

The programs for 1888–89, year of the first centenary of the French Republic, were elaborated with an eye toward putting the special character of the Société des Concerts on prominent display, for instance with the unlikely but imaginative pairing of the *Missa solemnis* and Saint-Saëns "Organ" Symphony on 17 March 1889. This event was a threefold success, allowing a new audience to hear central works of the signature repertoire, helping out the sorely pressed pension fund, and, most particularly, affording every journalist who desired it free admission—"for we couldn't really count as a proper *service de presse* the two miserable boxes we usually provide." This last gesture was one component of a new effort to "submit to and channel" the power of the press. "We need the press; that's undeniable—not just for satisfying our modest *amour-propre*, but so that our artistic superiority might be recognized, and universally so."[29] Nevertheless the secretary paused in his report to chuckle over a recent article in the *Journal des Débats* saluting the beautiful voice and stylistic precision of a singer who hadn't appeared.

Concerts earlier in the season featured the first performance of Gouvy's D-Major Symphony in January, the Fifth Brandenburg Concerto (Berthelier, Taffanel, Diémer at the piano), a more-or-less complete *Roméo et Juliette* of Berlioz with Auguez as Père Laurence, and the premiere of the Franck D-Minor Symphony. Not a great deal of enthusiasm for the Franck is to be found in the record, published or manuscript, though the *bon mot* of how it could not be a symphony because it had an English horn was recounted, variously ascribed, with glee. It would take Marty's performances in 1906 to earn the work its following. For his part, Franck said it sounded about like he thought it would.[30]

Sarasate, booked for the *concerts spirituels,* suggested the *Symphonie espagnole* Lalo had written for him. Discussion of his proposal was to the effect that the "very light character of the work is scarcely in keeping with our programs, especially for Holy Week," but Ambroise Thomas defended it, observing that the simple suppression of the last movement would overcome any objections, as had been the case for a similar sacred concert in Leipzig. Going to some trouble to record the feeling that it would be better to hear Sarasate in something more appropriate, and that M. Lalo was well enough regarded to survive the indignity of being postponed, the committee then voted to approve the program anyway.[31] "Prodigiously performed," the *Symphonie espagnole* was of course the hit of the ordinarily placid weekend, somewhat compromising the premiere of Gounod's new *"légende provençale," La Communion des saints,* as "deliciously sung" by Mlle Landi.[32]

Nobody had been happy about the modest role that the Société des Concerts had played in the Exposition Universelle of 1878: not the minister of fine arts, not the Conservatoire, not the subscribers, and certainly not the musicians. The Centennial Exhibition of 1889 was to be the most lavish ever seen, and in addition to the year-long fair there would be concerts and governmental solemnities requiring music. The minister went out of his way to assure the Société des Concerts that this time it would have an official role. The question was, as before, what and, more pressingly, where.

The exhibition authority proposed a series of concerts at the Trocadéro where each society, beginning with the Société des Concerts, would present its characteristic repertoire. But the Trocadéro was simply too big, as unfavorable to the better part of the repertoire as it had been in 1878; the delicate nuances of Beethoven and Mendelssohn would be demeaned in the enormous hall, even if played by an expanded cohort. The musicians would be away from their home, and—they touchingly put it—confused.[33] An alternative came from the composers on the centenary commission, who wanted exclusively French works to constitute their "exposition of fine arts." Several of these might survive the Trocadéro.

Learning of this, the Société des Concerts seized on the admirable notion that, as the first orchestra of France, it would undertake a concert of works by members of the Institute: Thomas, Gounod, Saint-Saëns, Massenet, Reyer, and Delibes. The program could be fashioned largely of works in the existing repertoire: excerpts from Thomas's *Psyché* and Gounod's *Mors et vita*, the Saint-Saëns Organ Symphony, and the overture to Massenet's *Phèdre*. They considered Reyer's *Madeleine au désert*—in the event returning to *Sigurd*—and the dance music "in the old style" from *Le Roi s'amuse* by Delibes. A performing force of more than two hundred could be assembled by drawing on students from the Conservatoire, thus overcoming the problem of the Trocadéro's size. The government would offer 10,000 francs to offset expenses.[34]

On 15 December 1888 the membership gathered to consider the Trocadéro project: "When the state asks," proclaimed Ferrand, "it is impossible to refuse." The members were less enthusiastic, and both Taffanel and Rabaud argued that the Salle des Concerts, "cradle of our society," would be the more appropriate venue. Ambroise Thomas, as both president of the Société des Concerts and a member of the Institute, urged uniting with the government in this expression of patriotism on behalf of the nation's composers. Indeed, he warned, it would be dangerous not to. The Société des Concerts, he concluded, had nothing to fear from anybody, anywhere. It was a moving address, and his perspective carried the day as the *sociétaires* voted to accept the enterprise.[35]

But by the end of the season the Trocadéro concert had not taken place. It appears to have been booked for late April or May 1889, after the *concerts spirituels,* and postponed at the last minute because of a poor pre-sale attributed variously to the program, the weather, and the rival attractions of the Exposition. Instead the committee began to plan a gala evening in the Salle des Concerts, offered without charge to the government so that the chief of state could invite prominent international guests to venerate the "cult of the beautiful" in an unforgettable surrounding—much the same formula as in 1878. This project was well advanced—the secretary had already written out his oration for the assembly—when it was suddenly withdrawn, presumably because the Trocadéro concert had been rescheduled.[36]

Meanwhile the society was summoned to provide music for the official centennial ceremony on 5 May 1889 at Versailles. They were able to arrange the details in three days, for this time the conditions were attractive indeed: a good room, a reasonable fee, favorable treatment by the railroad. It was, further, a perfect opportunity to consolidate their position with the government, as patriotism and artistic interests so neatly intersected. What was said the previous fall about the Trocadéro concert was still true; to be heard and seen participating in an event of historic importance was in their very best political interests.

This simple formulation was not enough for Ferrand, who felt it necessary to wax poetic in addressing his assembled colleagues: "History needs to register that when, a hundred years afterward, all France saluted the meeting where the Estates General proclaimed the emancipation of mankind, to which we owe our rights as citizens—at that moment the Société des Concerts du Conservatoire, first symphonic society of the world, lent the sparkle of its performance. . . . *Messieurs,* your committee solicits your vote, so as to present our society, without rival, to the nations who will bear witness to our glorious centenary." [37] A preliminary problem, Ferrand said, had been overcome; news reports originally had it that the Société des Concerts would be conducted by Édouard Colonne, already appointed and arranging for his personnel. The minister of fine arts had energetically intervened to say this was an official ceremony of state, and the government firmly desired the Société des Concerts under its own *chef,* and not a festival orchestra of hired hands. The program would consist of the *Marseillaise,* the Soldiers Chorus from Gounod's *Faust,* the duo prayer from Auber's *La Muette de Portici,* and the march from Thomas's *Hamlet.* It could be done with one short rehearsal on Saturday morning, 4 May. This proposal was adopted unanimously—and in less than an hour. The society's role in the ceremony indeed had "immense effect," noted the minister's letter of gratitude, read to the musicians at their end-of-year assembly. [38]

The Trocadéro concert finally took place on Thursday, 20 June 1889, at 2:15 in the afternoon. Some 220 performers affiliated with the society in one way or another had been assembled, despite the absence of many *sociétaires* who had already left Paris to join their summer spa orchestras. [39] To the repertoire developed long before, they added an aria from Cherubini's *Les Abencérages,* the Andantino from Reber's Third Symphony, and the prayer from Auber's *La Muette de Portici* as given at Versailles. The fear of "this vast space, so different from every point of view from our usual venue," proved unjustified; the program lent itself to the surroundings, and there was a full house. Just afterward both Garcin and Taffanel were granted the Légion d'Honneur. [40]

The long centennial year was not yet over. In October Garcin convened an urgent pre-season meeting of the committee to consider a request for two more concerts before the exposition closed on 6 November. Of the dates proposed, 27 October was out of the question at such short notice, leaving only 3 November. This would put the rehearsals in the week of All Saints, when most of the singers and many of the instrumentalists were engaged for church services. Francis Planté, the proposed soloist, did not reply to their invitation. But what concerned the committee most was that it might be impossible to detour a public directing itself toward the Champ de Mars one last time. It was a good idea that had come too late and, regrettably, would have to be abandoned.[41]

When César Franck died in November 1890, the Société des Concerts did not pause to look back on their long but on the whole antipathetical relationship—and there was no Franck on the programs between the D-Minor Symphony premiere in February 1889 and Taffanel's second season, 1893–94. The young César Franck, at sixteen, had been heard in 1839 in a Hummel Fantasy with Habeneck conducting; the society had quarreled over the use of the hall with the Francks, father and son, in 1846. Seven movements of *Ruth* were presented in 1872, and later in the year Franck had demonstrated the new pipe organ in the Salle des Concerts with a Bach Toccata and Fugue. The next season he proposed his hour-long *Rédemption*, a *poème-symphonie* for soloists, chorus, and orchestra; this was declined by the committee at the time but would soon have an important place both in the concert repertoire and, for the excerpted *morceau symphonique,* on record. Just before the end of the Deldevez regime the sixth of *Les Béatitudes* was heard, then nothing more until the symphony.

After Franck's death the pace of adoptions was marginally improved during the tenure of Taffanel, with Psalm 150, the great symphonic poem with chorus *Psyché,* and three more of the Beatitudes (1896, 1897, 1898). As late as the turn of the century the other works that would become central to the society's identity—*Le Chasseur maudit, Les Djinns,* the Symphonic Variations—remained unplayed. The disinclination of the Société des Concerts to adopt Franck until it was too late was as great a failing as its treatment, during his lifetime, of Berlioz.

Toward Gounod the society was considerably more attentive, largely on account of the very great success of *Près du fleuve étranger,* sung by the chorus countless times from 1860. (Charles Dancla describes Gounod's "openly expressed rapture" at the first performance.)[42] *Gallia,* Gounod's lament on the fall of Paris, had been the society's principal commentary on the siege and Commune. Once he returned to Paris in 1874, Gounod was "in the habit of dropping in" to committee meetings with his proposals, at least annually and sometimes more often, and these were customarily welcomed with the courtesy of at least a reading. In the 1880s and 1890s his works for voices and orchestra came in rapid succession: the St. Cecilia Mass, the popular duo *D'un cœur qui t'aime, Sapho, Polyeucte, Mors et vita*. In 1886 Gounod proposed a Suite for Pedal Piano and Orchestra, in which the committee at first evinced interest. But then the Pleyel-Wolff company said it would take forty minutes to install and twenty minutes to remove the piano, and though they later revised their estimate downward, the committee concluded that the instrument was too large and not in keeping with the logistics of the stage and *décor*.[43] While they did not cultivate excerpts from the operas during Gounod's lifetime, these would come in due course. The 1954 Aix-en-Provence production and recording of *Mireille*, with Janette Vivalda and Nicolai Gedda, was one of Cluytens's triumphs with the Société des Concerts.

Gounod's death in 1893 was, unusually for a non-member, commemorated in the secretary's oration of 1894: "He was, at heart, part of our society. He came nearly every Sunday. His Requiem is dedicated to us."[44] They programmed it for the *concerts spirituels* that March.

On 24 April 1890, ceding to pressure from several different quarters, the Société des Concerts lent itself most unusually to a *soirée* of the music of J.-B. Weckerlin, librarian of the Conservatoire: seven works, concluding with *Samson*, a *drame biblique* after Voltaire's text for Rameau. Weckerlin had been grumbling since the Deldevez years of being an employee of the Conservatoire ignored by its own concert society. Their participation in an exceptional event not to be repeated, the *sociétaires* were told, would even the score.[45] Largely this was a matter of assuring good rapport between the libraries of the Conservatoire and the Société des Concerts. Aside from the Prix Rossini ceremonies and occasional command performances, it was one of the first times the society consented to appear for an "external" sponsor—in exchange, that is, for a fee, usually some 8,000 or 9,000 francs. A petition of twenty members proposing a modification of the statutes to permit separate bookkeeping for external concerts—essentially allowing the musicians a concomitant fee for service—was killed in committee as simply too complicated.[46]

The decision that the Société des Concerts would undertake Bach's B-Minor Mass, reached during the planning for the 1889–90 season, indicates a confidence that the decade invested in discovering the Baroque oratorio repertoire had left the organization with the means and technique to master its capstone within the constraints of available rehearsal time. The orchestral personnel had acquired the hardware as well as experience in continuo work, usually with Alexandre Guilmant at the organ or piano. The oboists (Georges Gillet and Louis Bas) and trumpet trio (Teste, Lallement, possibly Lachanaud) were eager. After the *Missa solemnis* there was new confidence in the chorus, and Heyberger reminded his singers weekly that the Société des Concerts, alone of the Paris concert associations, had the wherewithal to produce the work. Players and singers alike began to consider it their artistic duty to brave the organizational challenges.

These were quite formidable. The chorus found itself at the outer limit of its endurance and musicianship, and the members did not always hide their impatience. It was exceptionally difficult to fix dates for two successive concerts with five major vocal soloists—let alone, in the case of success, a third performance.[47] Understudies had to be found in the chorus, since last-minute cancellations were unavoidable; one or more soloists were absent for most performances of both the *Missa solemnis* and B-Minor Mass. More than a few feared, too, that a work of such length and rigor would fail with the public.

But the committee held firm in the notion that their undertaking, though difficult, was one of glorious promise. They expressed confidence that the public would surely tolerate and might even appreciate the immense but stunning work.[48] After two years of preparation, then, the complete B-Minor Mass was announced for 22 February and 1 March 1891. Correctly heralded as a "veritable artistic event," it was presumably the first studied performance of the work in France.

And they feared its reception for nought. The public had rarely been so enthusiastic. When, with some reservations, the committee decided to add a third performance on 3 May 1891 for non-subscribers, the house was packed into the corridors, and the box office receipts were 9,635 francs, the largest recorded to date. The musicians, meanwhile, had succumbed to the work, struck by the grandeur of effects achieved with a "simple" force, by the sublimity of its pages, by the intellectual authority of the whole.[49] To their credit, they kept the B-Minor Mass in repertoire for many years, that it might secure a lasting place in the French culture. "To stage a conquest is difficult," it was later observed in summary; "to preserve a victory, even more so."[50]

Garcin and his musicians achieved an impressive stride throughout that season, premiering the prelude to *Tristan und Isolde,* two movements of

Bizet's Symphony in C (identified as an *envoi de Rome*), *Le Déluge* of Saint-Saëns, Gounod's *Saint François d'Assise,* Massenet's *Biblis,* the Epithalamium from Chabrier's *Gwendoline,* and scenes from Fauré's *Caligula.* The following season came eight new introductions, among them works of Reyer, Widor, Lalo, Godard, and Hüe, with a long excerpt from *Parsifal* in March and the Saint-Saëns Requiem in April. Garcin missed his first performances that spring, the Wagner concerts of 20 and 27 March 1892, where Jules Danbé—praised by Dancla as a capable conductor with a clear and precise beat—had his single opportunity to conduct the Société des Concerts in public.[51]

The income tax passed into law on 29 June 1872—3 percent on all interest, dividends, and revenues of societies, companies, and private enterprises, civil and commercial—was first levied on the Société des Concerts in 1891.[52] Until then the bureaucrats, at least one of them an ardent admirer, had quietly overlooked the society. A new administration now ruled that the society fell under the purview of the code, though the committee was quick to cite an 1875 measure exempting cooperatives. Having submitted a copy of the statutes and engaged a lawyer to handle this onerous confrontation, the committee began to consider structural changes that would assure a waiver in the future. An overall revision of the statutes would be drafted by Taffanel.

Taffanel was always cross when the good order of the Société des Concerts was challenged from outside agencies, which perhaps explains his short temper at the end of the season. He closed the 1890–91 general assembly with an unusually sharp lecture on the need for order and dignity in the ranks, noting troublesome examples of negligence and indifference. He reminded members of the principles of commonality and collectivity, and of the policy of shared and equal remuneration that had taken the quality of their performances well beyond those of their rivals. He asked pardon of "the great majority" for his remarks, but said he was moved by his love of the society to speak out.[53]

Joseph Heyberger's death in the spring of 1892 left the post of chorusmaster vacant and indirectly set the stage for a number of significant changes in administrative personnel that were to affect the orientation of the Société des Concerts over the next decades. For the emergency short term the administration simply appointed as interim director the young chorusmaster from the Opéra, Paul Vidal (1863–1931; chief conductor at the Opéra from 1906). But Vidal was unwilling to consider the position in the long run, perhaps because in April 1892 the membership all but unanimously declined an invitation from the Opéra to present a series of three evening concerts in the Palais Garnier. (The objection was on financial grounds; the fee offered was 4,000 francs, whereas the Société des Concerts could get twice that in their own hall.) Whatever concerts were organized by the Opéra would thus be in competition with those of the Société des Concerts, and the ambitious Vidal would most likely find himself in a conflict of interest; later it was regretted that he had not been pursued more aggressively.[54] It was in this context that the candidacy of Georges Marty, chorusmaster at the Opéra-Comique, was first suggested. It was thought likely that he would succeed Vidal as chorusmaster at the Opéra that fall.

Garcin, meanwhile, was approaching his sixty-second birthday and thus needing to stand for his first biennial reappointment according to the amendment of 1863. He was in declining health. He may well have found a petition of 1890, written by the violinist and aspiring conductor Désiré Thibault and signed by thirty-two colleagues, to constitute a gesture of no confidence; the petition would have required re-election of the first conductor every five years until he reached age sixty as well as the statutory ratifications after that.[55] It was, Garcin should have remembered, an old suggestion, already put and defeated in 1863, 1873, and 1889. But the discussion in 1890 made it clear that the issue of his succession was in the air.

There was also a none-too-subtle hint that Garcin's own election, and Hainl's, had been too hurried and ultimately disappointing; the petitioners worried that when the next vacancy "presented itself," they might not immediately find a candidate "possessing all the gifts required for the high direction of the Société des Concerts and its glorious history." Choices could be made too quickly, leaving them with a conductor for life who did not fulfill their expectations. The committee strongly opposed the petition, arguing as before that the required two-thirds majority mediated against hasty choice and that the first conductor of the Société des Concerts would be unable to make the difficult choices of artistic leadership if faced with recurring tests of his popularity.[56] Once again the amendment failed, but it cannot be simple coincidence that at the next Assemblée Générale, on 27 May 1892, Garcin announced that "for reasons of ill health" he would not be a candidate for re-election. As was by now the custom, he was named honorary president by acclamation, and a succession of orators praised his faithful devotion to their society and in particular the "new orientation" he had given both the orchestra and the chorus.[57]

Whatever conversations the *sociétaires* may have had about rushed decision making were forgotten as they proceeded in a week's time, on

3 June 1892, to elect a new conductor. The field was led by Paul Taffanel, longtime principal flutist and devoted administrator—and if anyone deserved the post based on record of service alone, it was he. But even after his two respectable seasons as conductor at the Opéra there remained those to whom the idea of a flutist-conductor was anathema. The other two candidates were Gabriel Marie (1852–1928), conductor of the orchestral concerts presented by the Société Nationale and before that chorusmaster for the Lamoureux concerts; and Jules Danbé, Garcin's successor as *2ᵉ chef* of the society and concertmaster and first conductor at the Opéra-Comique since 1876. Of these three Danbé was the best known to the musicians as a conductor, both as leader / impresario of the Grand Hôtel and summer casino concerts and because he had substituted for Garcin the previous spring.

After the presentation of statements, Taffanel and Danbé remained with their colleagues to answer questions. Taffanel was asked specifically if he expected to keep his post at the Opéra, since Ernest Altès had found the positions at the Opéra and Société des Concerts incompatible. Taffanel responded, diplomatically, that he would do whatever was necessary "to safeguard the dignity of the Société des Concerts," then left the room. Danbé, long in waiting for the position, lost his composure over the implication that his colleagues already considered Taffanel's election a *fait accompli.* He uttered a thoughtless remark and stormed out, as the president tried to excuse this expression of "quite legitimate" feelings. Taffanel held a comfortable lead through all four ballots but was unable to establish a two-thirds majority; in the runoff he defeated Danbé 49 to 36 with 1 blank and 1 *nul* ballot.[58] Thus his margin of victory was even narrower than his predecessor's (Garcin 59, Guiraud 39).

Hearing these results, Danbé angrily resigned his appointments as *2ᵉ chef* and *sociétaire* and left the *foyer.* Words of gratitude and regret were formulated by the president, and a commission was sent to visit Danbé and return him to the fold.

The meeting concluded with the election of Samuel-Alexandre Rousseau—called Samuel-Rousseau, and not to be confused with his son, a more famous composer of the same name—as chorusmaster to succeed the late Heyberger. Samuel-Rousseau was an excellent choice for the position: a former organ student of Franck and a successful young composer who could boast both a Prix de Rome (1878) and a Prix Cressent (1879); during the course of 1892 he also won the Prix de la Ville de Paris and was named conductor at the Théâtre-Lyrique. His collaborations with Taffanel were as ambitious and interesting as those of the Garcin–

Heyberger years, and he was a close runner-up in the election of Taffanel's successor.

Danbé not having relented, the assembly reconvened two weeks later,
on 17 June 1892, to choose a new second conductor. Over the course of
the several recent elections, the musicians had conceived a growing determination to build successors within the ranks. Now they decided to
elect a second conductor for a four-year term only, but to give him a
considerably greater responsibility for rehearsals than had been customary thus far. Again there were four *tours de scrutin,* with Désiré Thibault
eventually elected over Arthur Boisseau and Victor Gasser—all three of
them front-desk strings players. Before the runoff, Thibault was induced to promise to resign from his direction of "frivolous" masked
balls, and subsequently did so.[59] Nor was his tenure short, as he was twice
re-elected with comfortable margins. For the second time since Deldevez, the first conductor, second conductor, and chorusmaster—Garcin,
Danbé, Heyberger; now Taffanel, Thibault, and Samuel-Rousseau—
served their terms together.

What little we know of Paul Taffanel as a personality suggests a thoughtful, sometimes severe person, naturally attracted to neatness in his artistic and administrative pursuits and quick to become annoyed when
situations grew past his control. The Van Dyck beard and *pince-nez* that
characterize his photographs hint at a certain stylishness (a quality not
shared, so far as I can tell, by any of his predecessors). He was one of
the several conductors of the Société des Concerts—with Tilmant, Deldevez, Marty, and Messager—admired for the way sobriety of gesture
seemed to convey the most minute details of intention. He was said
to study and meditate on every score with the greatest diligence, arriving at the first rehearsal with his performance fully conceptualized.
Dandelot praises the nuance, expressiveness, and intensity of Taffanel's
performances.[60]

A successful flutist since childhood—from Bordeaux, as were his rivals Colonne and Lamoureux—Taffanel had studied with Dorus at the
Conservatoire and there mastered the Boehm flute, winning his 1er *prix*
in 1860. He soon established his place at the head of the French flute
school as it had coalesced around Tulou, Dorus, and Henri Altès, whom
he succeeded as principal flute at the Opéra (ca. 1868) and as professor
at the Conservatoire (1893). Though not especially active as a flute composer, Taffanel was the original author of the Taffanel–Gaubert *Méthode
complète* still in wide use today. His particular interest was in woodwind

chamber music, and his Société de Musique de Chambre pour Instruments à Vent, founded in 1879, had the effect of passing on the Paris tradition of virtuoso wind quintets, as established by Reicha and promoted by the principal wind players of the Société des Concerts, to such composers as Ibert and Bozza.

Since 1890 Taffanel had been a conductor at the Opéra. At forty-seven, and having begun with the Société des Concerts at age twenty, he was approaching three decades of service, including fifteen years of alternating terms as secretary. He arrived on the podium with a reputation for perfect musicianship and limitless energy, and there is every indication that he lived up to it. More than once he was described as "tradition's guardian," and it is true that he greatly enjoyed reviving the mainstays of his early years—the Beethoven Septet, for instance, and the Weber overtures. On the other hand, there are no huge undertakings like the *Missa solemnis* and B-Minor Mass. He did well by Brahms —introducing the First Symphony, the *Song of Destiny,* and the Requiem (apparently in German)—and by both Berlioz and Liszt. And in acceding, as a flutist, to the podium at all, he set the stage for one of the best of his successors, Philippe Gaubert.

Taffanel took his place as the popularity of live symphonic concerts, in Paris and beyond to the world at large, reached a level it never surpassed. The 1890s until World War I were the heyday of the post-Romantic philharmonic society. In Paris the "four associations"—the Société des Concerts, Concerts Pasdeloup, Concerts Colonne, and Concerts Lamoureux—were all thriving, all giving Sunday afternoon concerts, and all sharing to a greater or lesser degree the principles that had re-established concert life in France following the Napoleonic adventure. The Société Nationale, structured on different lines, was entering its third decade with some signs of decline but others of robust health, as in the case of the first performance of Debussy's *Prélude à l'après-midi d'un faune* (1894).

Four major orchestras playing similar music at the same time every week was, of course, a singular arrangement; neither London nor New York, with all their musical treasures, sustained as many. On the face of it the system seems a paradigm of over-supply, but it had some real advantages. Graduates of the Conservatoire found quick employment in a favorable job market. There was a marked shift by serious composers away from music for the stage in favor of music for the concert hall, as demand for orchestral music and opportunities for its performance multiplied several fold. The best soloists were very well paid. The public, drawn primarily by star billings, was pleased with the opportunity to pick and choose. And that brought into sharp focus the central challenge of the next four decades: how to pay the escalating price of first-quality art music with a static maximum income of some 10,000 francs per concert.

It was in keeping with Taffanel's predilection for tidy administration that he began by attempting to bring closure to the thorough modification of the statutes that had been at issue since financial irregularities in the Caisse de Prévoyance were uncovered in the late 1880s. In 1890 it was reported to the membership that the statutes had become incoherent as the result of frequent changes in response to temporary situations. Titles and admission policies were confused and confusing; rules and penalties were inconsistently set out and inconsistently applied. A simple sprucing-up would not do; the statutes would have to be rewritten entirely, though with "scrupulous respect for the general spirit of the originals." The membership agreed to the expense of preparing a printed document giving parallel texts of the old statutes and the proposed new ones, to be distributed in time for leisurely study in advance of the general assemblies that would be needed for ratification. An interim report had been presented in November 1891.[61]

In consequence a series of assemblies took place in the spring of 1893, toward the end of Taffanel's first season.[62] In April the musicians began to discuss and vote the new articles one by one. At article 4, which embraced a clause on mandatory retirement at age fifty-five for singers, the process began to disintegrate. The chorus thought that a differential in retirement age formally tore the society in two; in any case the committee, suggested the tenor Colombe, had acted on the issue without a mandate. Parliamentary maneuvering led to the decision to table that article for a week and move along, but by the end of the meeting the discussion had only reached article 6 out of more than eighty.

On 6 May 1893 the discussions again focused on retirement age. The committee assured the *sociétaires* that any new provision would affect only members not yet appointed, and that both Taffanel and the new chorusmaster, Samuel-Rousseau, supported the draft language. After several hours the general concept of separate retirement ages passed, but the members had only considered a total of thirteen articles before adjourning the second session. On 13 May Taffanel stunned the assembly by announcing that he was withdrawing the project altogether. A substantial minority of the musicians disapproved of it; word of the internal debate had reached the press and competing ensembles, and a negative effect on the recruitment of *aspirants* and *externes* was strongly feared. The *sociétaires* were confused by what had and had not been voted. At length they decided, with several members still stridently opposed to any changes in policy at all, to appoint yet another commission to examine and "reflect upon" the bylaws, proposing a new constitution some other time.

From this episode through the 1940s, the Société des Concerts was effectively governed by institutional memory of the addenda to its statutes of 1841, though the question of rules and penalties was solved in 1911 with the publication of a *règlement intérieur* and a new system of signed contracts. For the moment the most pressing issue was to add the words *"du Conservatoire"* to the legal title of the organization, mostly to secure its grip on the hall. But even this measure was tabled, out of the feeling that it was unwise to prompt the ministry to investigate a sensitive issue unless the outcome was a foregone conclusion; Ambroise Thomas was likely to oppose new concert societies claiming to be *du Conservatoire* anyway.[63]

When Thomas entered the room for the general assembly of 26 May 1894, he was greeted with a burst of applause and a speech:

> Illustrious Master and Dear President:
>
> The Société des Concerts du Conservatoire, glorious in having at its head the chief of the French School, cannot let pass unremarked the unforgettable day when we celebrated the one thousandth performance of *Mignon,* nor fail to bring you in tribute its enthusiastic admiration and deepest thanks.
>
> The committee, speaking for the entire society, hopes, *cher maître,* that you will be good enough to accept these sentiments of unfailing devotion and respectful affection.
>
> What else might we say of this memorable evening that you don't already know? No musician has ever before been elevated to the dignity of the Grande Croix of the Légion d'Honneur.
>
> The government wished to glorify the great artist that we all admire and the character of the man we all love.
>
> Thus we are especially pleased to be assembled today since, *cher président,* you wished to show us once again the paternal interest that you bring to the Société des Concerts by sharing in its work. The entire society hopes, *cher maître,* that you will accept its affectionate congratulations as from the depths of all our hearts.[64]

Thomas was eighty-three, approaching twenty-five years as president of the orchestra and director of the Conservatoire. Though the Société des Concerts routinely presented only excerpts from his *Psyché,* he had long been popular with the society, not least for the salon he and Mme Thomas held for guest soloists following the Sunday concerts. Few people in the room remembered any other president. It was clear that his days were numbered—he died in February 1896, in his office at the Conservatoire—and hence the time for ceremony.

The *sociétaires* took the opportunity to renew their commitment to having as president the director of the Conservatoire, partly owing to news that the government planned to offer a five-year term to Thomas's successor—a structure that might have left them with an elected president for life while administrations changed at the Conservatoire. The connection of the two offices had been critical on multiple occasions in the history of the Société des Concerts, since the director of the Conservatoire had always held particular sway with the government. It was good to have had this discussion well in advance of the change, for Thomas's successor, Théodore Dubois, was to be swept immediately into a crisis where that very connection was a key to averting disaster.

Also of note is that the citing of precedents on this occasion referred not to documents retrieved from the society's own archive but to passages in the books of Elwart and Lassabathie, read aloud.[65] The institutional memory no longer extended, with particular accuracy, to the foundation.

Counting every *centime* was a tradition that extended back to the foundation of the society, but an episode that spring showed just how creative its financial practice could be. The Société des Concerts had presented a concert in the Hôtel de Ville for the Municipal Council of Paris to honor representatives of the Russian navy. A Paris music publisher, miffed at not having been invited, subsequently telegraphed a bill for an unbudgeted 300 francs. Thibault, "always ready to do anything on behalf of the society," prevailed on a functionary in the city government to slip an additional 500 francs into the budget to cover the new expense, then succeeded in getting the publisher to back down and withdraw the charge entirely. The result was 800 supplementary francs to be divided among the players, giving each an extra few francs for his services—an almost unheard-of closure to a fee-for-service concert. A few weeks later Thibault scored another victory. Told by the percussionists that the Conservatoire's timpani were in need of repair, he went to visit Tournier, the noted *fabricant,* and returned with all-new percussion valued at 1,400 francs in exchange for granting the notice *"fournisseur des instruments de percussion de la Société des Concerts."*[66]

The 1893–94 season centered on Schumann's *Paradise and the Peri,*
now complete; parts III and IV of Émile Paladilhe's new oratorio, *Les
Saintes-Maries de la mer;* the Brahms *Song of Destiny (Chant des Parques);*
and, on the occasion of the composer's death, Gounod's Requiem. Summarizing the Brahms, the secretary spoke of "an elevated conception,
but very severe and less acclaimed by the public" than the other featured
works. Early in the season Taffanel conducted his first Ninth Symphony;
a week later, the Polovtsian Dances from Borodin's *Prince Igor* in a rendition with chorus that became a popular new standard. Raoul Pugno
introduced the Grieg Piano Concerto in December 1893. "My career as
a virtuoso," he later wrote, "dates from the day I played the Grieg concerto at the Conservatoire."[67]

That the seasons now extended a full month or more past Holy Week
was thought by several musicians to compromise opportunities for spring
and summer employment elsewhere, but their petition to begin in October and conclude with the *concerts spirituels* was set aside by the committee. The first two pairs of 1893–94 had had uncomfortably high subscriber turn-backs, and it was felt that in a choice between the habits of
the subscribers and the passing whims of the musicians, favor had to be
shown the patrons. Another reason the season extended past Lent was
that the Conservatoire was again using the hall once a month. In any
event, it made sense to get accustomed to the lengthening season, which
in Paris was regularly extending into mid-June.[68]

Nevertheless, the 1894–95 season was arranged to open the first week-
end in December and finish on Holy Saturday, which fell three weeks
later than in 1894. Activity actually began with a national ceremony: the
funeral for Sadi-Carnot, fourth president of the Third Republic, who
had been stabbed to death at the opening of a fair in Lyon in June 1894.
The formal season introduced Brahms's Third Symphony, Wagner's *Flying Dutchman* and Berlioz's *Benvenuto Cellini* overtures, and the Saint-
Saëns Second Symphony; featured large works were the B-Minor Mass
and Saint-Saëns's *Le Déluge,* both being led for the first time by Taffanel. Special pleasure was expressed over the first appearance in the Salle
des Concerts of Rose Caron, "our *grande tragédienne lyrique,*" in scenes
from act I of Gluck's *Alceste.*[69]

Already in both 1894 and 1895 there was concern over Taffanel's state
of health, but he missed no concerts and went on systematically cultivating the repertoire for which he would be remembered. He "tempted"
Saint-Saëns to open 1895–96 with the Mozart Piano Concerto K. 488
by programming *La Lyre et la harpe* for the same concert. Over the next
two seasons he introduced the Bach Cantata No. 21, d'Indy's Symphony

on a French Mountain Air, the Saint-Saëns Fifth Piano Concerto, portions of Dubois's *Le Paradis perdu* in salute to their new president, and Franck's *Psyché* complete with its chorus. The secretary, Pierre Chavy, did not hide his personal reservations with regard to the Franck, "which we like or not according to our personal taste and temperament, but the sincerity of which we must acknowledge."[70] Liszt's *Les Préludes* and Bizet's *Patrie* overture were late but conspicuously important entries to the repertoire. It was of Taffanel's 1896 performance of the Berlioz *Roméo et Juliette* that the press observed, "Only the Société des Concerts is capable of presenting so dangerous a work, and only at the Société des Concerts, so far, have you been able to admire the delicate Queen Mab scherzo."[71] For the Schubert centenary in January 1897 the orchestra played the "Great" C-Major Symphony for the first time in France.

It was brilliant programming, but also the kind that left the society open to assaults from both directions. An organized movement of the better music journalists was once again labeling the institution as retrogressive and had quoted *sociétaires* to the same effect. Édouard Nadaud offered the traditional defense, that "it isn't the society's role to welcome musicians who are not already classed among the masters." The new school had great value, but "over-advanced tendencies" offended a public "that comes here only to admire impeccable performance of masterpieces by recognized masters." Nadaud urged the musicians to keep their opinions within the walls of the Conservatoire so as not to compromise an appearance of unanimity.[72] There are indications that his assessment of the public was right on the mark, since a program for the 22 December 1895 performance of the Brahms Second Symphony notes *"nombreux chuts 2 sifflets"* ("lots of shushing [restless patrons], two hisses"), and one for d'Indy's symphony on 15 March 1896 says, likewise, *"très nombreux chuts, plusieurs sifflets!!"*

Pablo de Sarasate (1844–1908), who had made his debut with the Société des Concerts and played under every conductor from Tilmant to Marty, returned in December 1896 to offer the Mendelssohn Violin Concerto, following which he was recognized as an honorary *sociétaire*. No foreign soloist had appeared so frequently as he, nor was anyone higher on the first-choice list for the *concerts spirituels*.[73] Both Lalo's *Symphonie espagnole* and Saint-Saëns's Third Violin Concerto were written for and played by Sarasate with the Société des Concerts. It was fitting, too, that he should have introduced the practice of playing an encore from the Bach suites; solo encores after the concerto soon became the norm (in 1908, for instance, Busoni followed the Beethoven Third

Piano Concerto with six of Liszt's Transcendental Études). And it was especially poignant that Sarasate's last appearance with the Société des Concerts was in an all-Beethoven benefit for a new statue in Paris.

If Sarasate was the society's preferred foreign guest, Saint-Saëns was its favorite son. Their relationship began in April 1862, when Saint-Saëns introduced the Beethoven Choral Fantasy, still considered "his" piece well into the twentieth century. Beginning with what was presumably the Second Piano Concerto in December 1869, two movements of a new symphony (probably the Third) in 1872, and the First Cello Concerto in 1873, virtually Saint-Saëns's entire orchestral output was played during his lifetime, with some three dozen works—about a third more than Beethoven—in the active repertoire before 1900. Saint-Saëns opened many seasons as soloist or featured composer; the premiere of his Fifth Piano Concerto, with Louis Diémer, opened the 1896–97 season, followed later by the premiere of *La Nuit persane*. "They say that the Société des Concerts is becoming the Concert Saint-Saëns," the press muttered. But it was only proper, the secretary responded, "to bring the work of a countryman to light where it concerned an artist of such recognized value already well played abroad; the audience reception is the better measure."[74]

In his student days Saint-Saëns had been a somewhat furtive devotee:

> How many people have cherished all their lives the dream of a stall at the Conservatoire without being able to achieve it! . . . It was Paradise guarded by an angel with a gleaming sword in the person of Lescot, the doorkeeper in the rue Bergère whose duty it was to prevent the impious from entering the sanctuary. . . . He went on his rounds as slowly as possible so as not to have to throw me out until the very last minute. . . . I tiptoed through corridors, squatted low in boxes, and always managed to snatch a few shreds of music, taking back to class with me an odor of Beethoven and Mozart, a strong taint of heresy.[75]

Tilmant had conducted the eleven-year-old Saint-Saëns in his Paris debut, Mozart's Concerto K. 450, in 1846. Taffanel had been a partisan of his work since discovering the Romance for Flute and Orchestra. Their relationship became closer still when Saint-Saëns agreed to be godfather of Taffanel's daughter. Altogether Taffanel led thirty-one performances of works by Saint-Saëns during his tenure of nine seasons.

Welcoming Théodore Dubois to the president's chair in May 1897, Nadaud suggested that "to talk of your person is to offend your modesty; to enumerate your successes is merely to repeat the story of creations of which we were all, in our respective theaters and churches, a part." Referring to the loss of Ambroise Thomas, he said, "You occupy the seat of a deeply venerated master, and like him, you are a member of our glorious Institut de France. We wish you the same affection and a glorious and long career." [76]

Dubois, Prix de Rome laureate and *maître de chapelle* at the Madeleine, was already an ardent supporter of the Société des Concerts. In August 1871 he had sought and won election to the post of chorusmaster, and shortly thereafter had overseen the presentation of excerpts from *The Seven Last Words of Christ*.[77] Since then he had become a successful composer, decently represented on the society's programs with a motet, a *Mélodie provençale,* and *Le Paradis perdu.* Now, for obvious reasons, he would see his works billed routinely at the Salle des Concerts, beginning with the Second Piano Concerto in 1898, *Le Baptême de Clovis* in 1899, and the Violin Concerto in 1901. There would be Dubois premieres through 1920, and a last appearance on the programs in 1921.

Dubois was put to the test right away. Among the most elegant benefits frequented by the highest elements of Paris society was the annual Bazar de la Charité. The 1897 fair took place in a temporary structure at 17, rue Jean-Goujon near the Champs-Élysées—a series of picturesque stalls built of wood and covered with an immense awning. On 4 May 1897 a fire started by a *cinématographe* (a sort of magic lantern) and fanned by high winds swept through the market while 1,200 visitors were present. A panic ensued as the crowd tried to find its way out through insufficient exits, and 129 souls were lost, among them the duchess of Alençon, sister of the Austrian empress. With this fire coming so soon after the one that had destroyed the Opéra-Comique in 1887, the authorities could no longer turn a blind eye on crowded gathering places. The prefect of police launched an immediate investigation, and in the late spring of 1897 the Commission Supérieure des Théâtres informed the society of its findings. The Salle des Concerts—still less than one hundred years old— was ordered summarily closed and slated for immediate demolition.

Dubois and Taffanel reacted calmly, taking the summer to formulate their strategy. Within a few weeks they had secured provisional agreement from the Opéra to present the 1897–98 concert season there. Then they drafted a delicately expressed yet passionate approach to the director of fine arts at the Ministry of the Interior:

A Monsieur le Directeur des Beaux-Arts:
I have the honor to ask the courtesy of your attention to a new state of affairs that risks gravely compromising the normal operation of the Société des Concerts.
Following the catastrophe of the Bazar de la Charité, M. le Préfet de Po-

lice, properly preoccupied with measures necessary to assure public security in gathering places, inspected the great Salle du Conservatoire where for seventy years the Société has given its concerts.

Thoroughly cognizant of the necessity to remodel this room, we had hoped that its long history with not even the suggestion of an emergency, its reputation for exceptional acoustics, and the glorious memories that are attached to it would mediate in its favor—especially if one took into account our strict compliance with all the measures the Theater Commission required in 1882 for the security of the public. That was not to be, and M. le Préfet de Police ordered complete demolition.

If this room were to disappear, it would be impossible for us to count on rebuilding in the area anything similar to replace it, since reconstruction would be linked to that of the Conservatoire itself—a question still unresolved. There results a terrible embarrassment with regard to our concerts. M. le Préfet de Police has tolerated the provisional reopening of the present room, on the condition of major changes for which a credit balance is now being asked from the public authorities. But these changes imply the suppression of numerous seats (something like 16 percent of the capacity), and the number of disenfranchised would reach more than two hundred. For those who know the value that the subscribers attach to their seats, considering them virtually a property, it is easy to understand the kind of inextricable situation the administration of the Société des Concerts would be placed in.

And to these issues we add another: public opinion has been aroused in this moment to the danger of fire, and no effort has been spared to stir the public up. Thus we suspect that the administration, despite its good will toward us, will see itself in the impossibility of allowing us our concerts, whatever promise it has made.

I thus have the honor, Mr. le Directeur, to ask you to be so kind as to have us accorded, by the Minister of Public Instruction and Fine Arts, authorization to give sessions of the Société des Concerts in the auditorium of the Opéra, while waiting the reconstruction of the Salle du Conservatoire.[78]

The letter was signed by Dubois, Taffanel, and Albert Vernaelde, the secretary.

Ministerial reaction was swift, and on 31 July 1897 the necessary decree authorized concerts for 1897–98 at the Opéra:

Decreed by the Minister of Public Instruction, 31 July 1897:
In view of the decree of 13 December 1832 establishing the Société des Concerts du Conservatoire;
In view of the decision by the Minister of the Interior, 30 October 1850, reserving the Salle des Concerts of the Conservatoire National for teaching and for the Société des Concerts;
In view of the letter of [13] July 1897 of the director of the Conservatoire National and president of the Société des Concerts;
In view of the letter of 26 July 1897 from the directors of the Opéra;

In view of article 47 of the *cahier des charges* of the Théâtre National de l'Opéra;

It is therefore decreed:
    1. The Société des Concerts du Conservatoire is authorized to present its concerts for the season 1897–98 at the Théâtre National de l'Opéra;
    2. This decree serves to notify those whom it may concern.

Paris le 31 Juillet 1897
Signed: A. Rambaud[79]

The membership was notified of the situation and summoned to hear the plans for the season on 13 October 1897. The doublebassist Veyret wondered whether they might not essentially refuse to leave the Conservatoire, remodeling the hall at their own expense. One couldn't simply remodel someone else's property, Dubois replied, and besides, the building had been "irrevocably condemned." Taffanel meanwhile took great satisfaction in the minister's use of the terminology Société des Concerts *du Conservatoire,* which he thought was good for the future, and in the way the decree had suggested only a year in a temporary facility. It amounted, at least in his optimistic interpretation, to a governmental commitment to pay for any remodeling required. The *sociétaires* had little choice but to approve the measure, 90 favoring, 5 opposed, 10 blank.[80]

But there were problems with the Opéra, not least among them its own competing series of orchestral concerts. The cost of stagehands and machinists did not figure in the society's budget, nor did that of the auxiliary artists needed to constitute an orchestra large enough to fill the hall. Many thought the very existence of the organization was "gravely compromised," and that the loss of the Salle des Concerts would surely mean the disappearance of the society altogether, causing "a profound stupor throughout musical Europe."[81]

In fact the 1897–98 concerts, opening with Beethoven's Ninth, carried on much as they would have done at the Conservatoire, though there were only fourteen instead of the usual eighteen. The "irrevocable condemnation" of the hall was soon rescinded, and even during the year the society was away the Conservatoire was allowed to use it for the ordinary *concours* and end-of-year exercises. Meanwhile the committee engaged in every form of diplomacy it could think of to limit the loss of seats before the concerts resumed there.

The original plan drafted by a special commission charged with redesigning the Salle des Concerts envisaged removing the entire amphitheater at the top of the house, some 300 places. Little by little the commission yielded to pressures from the musicians, and in the end the loss was 147 places, mostly seats in the amphitheater and the *strapontins* in the corridors.[82] Additionally swinging doors were installed behind the *loges* to avoid accidental lock-ins, and new stairs to the stage permitted access to the exit routes used by the musicians. A huge reservoir of water was retained nearby.

Before the changes there were 921 paying seats and 71 complimentary; afterward, 771 paying and the same 71 house seats. The total possible receipt dropped by about 1,000 francs, to 8,600 francs. Dubois, in a symbolic gesture, gave up his seat, which was sold at 40 francs for the second series and given to the prefect of police for the first. Just before the seventy-third season (1899–1900), Vernaelde and Julien Gaillard, the new *archiviste-caissier,* convinced the inspector from the theater commission to let them reinstall some of the *strapontins*. Four years later they were allowed to reestablish 10 places in the amphitheater: 2 five-person benches on the third floor, bought at their own expense.[83]

The 1898–99 session was thus authorized, in November 1898, to take place in the Salle des Concerts. The season moved from nine to ten pairs, beginning in late November and ending in late April. If the extra concerts made up in some measure for lost total income, they did nothing to accommodate the 150 subscribers who had lost their seats to the new *sorties de secours.* Gaillard printed a form letter to these patrons sometime during the summer of 1898:

> I am pleased to inform you that the Société des Concerts has been authorized to resume its activities in the Salle du Conservatoire.
>
> During the 1898–1899 session, it will present two series of ten concerts each. The work on the exits imposed by the Commission Supérieure des Théâtres to assure the complete safety of the public having led to the suppression of a certain number of seats, among which are those you occupy, the committee will do everything possible on your behalf, either putting at your disposal vacant seats, or those that eventually become vacant, in the expectation that your seats will be returned to you in a new concert hall, construction of which is planned.
>
> I would be grateful if you would let me know, as soon as possible, which kinds of seats would best suit you, and I will go out of my way during the vacation to offer you satisfaction, or at least to file your request in such a way that the wait to honor it will be as short as possible.
>
> *L'Archiviste*
> Gaillard [84]

By the season opening, much of the demand had been met, and moreover every seat, without exception, was subscribed for the year.

The season opened with Beethoven's Fifth and a new setting by Saint-Saëns of the Rameau motet *Quam dilecta*. It introduced three works from the new school—Augusta Holmès's *Hymne à Apollon*, Fauré's *La Naissance de Vénus* (called a *scène mythologique*), and excerpts from Massenet's *La Vierge*—and an unaccompanied *Ave Maria* by Dubois. The musicians themselves most enjoyed the new Berlioz added to their repertoire: *Le Roi Lear*, the *Marche funèbre pour la dernière scène d'Hamlet* ("so moving, so poignant"), and scenes from *La Prise de Troie*. Featured large-scale works were the Saint-Saëns Requiem for the *concerts spirituels* and a concluding B-Minor Mass. Given the struggles of two years, it was an indisputably triumphant return to their historic home.

The Société des Concerts also provided music for two provocative government ceremonies, a centennial commemoration at the Panthéon of Jules Michelet (1798–1874), the great liberal historian and philosopher deprived of his post in the Second Empire, and the funeral services for Félix Faure (1841–99), president of the Republic. (In 1907 the orchestra was called to play for the state funeral of the chemist Marcellin Berthelot, 1827–1907.) These events had political significance in a nation torn asunder by disruptions, of which the Dreyfus Affair was only a part. The Michelet centenary celebrated, not subtly, the liberal anticlerical values supported by the minister of public instruction and fine arts, Léon Bourgeois. Bourgeois (1851–1921) was a distinguished public servant for the many governments of the Third Republic (and, later, a strong proponent of the League of Nations and winner of the 1920 Nobel Prize). His letter of thanks for "seconding my administration in the preparations for the ceremony" was read aloud to the *sociétaires;* it was followed by remarks from the rostrum concerning the manner in which the minister's work, especially his intention to create in Paris a Conservatoire "truly worthy of our country," had been paralyzed by "the crisis that has so painfully stricken the heart of France." [85]

For some the involvement of the society, however inadvertent, in partisan politics underscored the drawbacks of its determined march toward official status. Relationships described as patriotic could too easily turn political. It was a disadvantage of which the shrewder conductors—including both Deldevez and Gaubert—were enough aware to keep their distance. A look back at the uses of the orchestra by the government—to celebrate empire, as the plaything of wives of heads of state, and now for what could be interpreted as leftist purpose—is enough to suggest that their concerns were well founded.

But there were good reasons to celebrate in the spring of 1899, and Vernaelde, one of the secretaries who most enjoyed his opportunity to orate, rose to the occasion. His address praised a B-Minor Mass that "crowned the season as the *façade* crowns the temple," a work that "exhausts every laudatory epithet and before which the human spirit must remain awestruck." Bach he described as the composer "who conceived and built this glorious monument, . . . a god who wandered awhile among the crowd of mankind." At length approaching his close, he congratulated the musicians on their several victories and foretold a rich future as they shared faith in the power of art. He concluded: "Let us love our dear Society as a little colony of our great nation: love it, for it is the eldest daughter of our *belle école,* the Conservatoire, to which we all belong and to which we each owe our birth into the artist's life."[86]

It would have been welcome, after the stresses of moving to the Opéra and back, for the society to enjoy a few seasons of uninterrupted ordinariness. But Taffanel fell gravely ill with influenza in January 1900 and was absent for nearly two months. He canceled again in February 1901, during a wonderful season that began with the Brahms First Symphony and ended with the Fauré Requiem, *Missa solemnis,* and Organ Symphony. When he returned in March, he greeted the musicians with the announcement that he would retire at the end of the session. He tendered his official resignation on 7 May 1901, and the assembly to elect his successor was called for 12 June.

Taffanel had grown immeasurably in nine seasons on the podium of the Société des Concerts, not only as a conductor but also in the affection of the members. Vernaelde suggests that he was the best of the conductors of his era, and easily the most popular. (That assessment was to change with the passage of time, as we will have occasion to note.) He would enjoy a quiet retirement, profiting from the leisure to write a conducting treatise, *L'Art de diriger,* published posthumously in Lavignac's *Encyclopédie;* from time to time he would appear to conduct something on a benefit or festival concert. Losing Taffanel, who had run the Société des Concerts as long as most of the members had been in it, must have felt to the musicians of that epoch as disorienting as the loss of Deldevez to an earlier generation. Succeeding him would be difficult for anybody, and there was no heir apparent among the violins. Three fine violinist-conductors from the membership had stood to succeed Deldevez (Garcin, Danbé, and Altès); on this occasion there was only one.

Désiré Thibault, with nearly thirty years in the front desks of the violin section, had conducted the Société des Concerts a half-dozen times in Taffanel's stead and enjoyed a modest but solid reputation as a theater conductor. He was over sixty, however, and of delicate constitution, and little in the record suggests the kind of enthusiasm for his work that Deldevez or Garcin had garnered for their emergency appearances. His challengers were the greatly admired chorusmaster Samuel-Rousseau, chief conductor at the Théâtre-Lyrique and an architect of the society's B-Minor Mass; Georges Marty, chief conductor of the Opéra-Comique; André Messager, fast-rising musical director of the Opéra-Comique; and the unlikely prospects Eugène d'Harcourt, Gabriel Marie, and Widor. The principal violist Émile Schvartz initially posed his candidacy, then as the situation clarified withdrew to run for chorusmaster.

At the election assembly the letters of candidacy from the outside were read and the internal candidates spoke, Thibault trying hard to establish that he was the natural successor to Taffanel—and the only violinist. Backing this position, the great Charles Dancla, eighty-three, rose to read a long address reminding his colleagues that the quartet was the *base de l'orchestre,* and that the necessity of proper bowings and fingerings, indispensable to fine performance, demanded a conductor of Thibault's credentials. Not so, argued the secretary, Nadaud, though sorry to disagree with his mentor; new music required a pianist / composer for effective conducting—thus implying Naudaud's support for Samuel-Rousseau.

The conversation turned to Marty and Messager. Both were employees of the Opéra-Comique, which had Sunday *matinées* that would prevent their uninterrupted service to the society. That assertion was corrected by a member who was certain that the Opéra-Comique had guaranteed the necessary release to either candidate; one of the two, moreover, might well be moving to the Opéra. Nadaud worried that Messager was absent from Paris during May, June, and July to attend to his duties as music director at Covent Garden, the time of year the committee would require his presence for the Assemblée Générale and yearly attention to outgoing and incoming personnel. Nor had Messager been a student at the Conservatoire. Nadaud also thought Widor unacceptable, by virtue of the "lack of deference" revealed in his letter of candidacy. (Apparently he had said in his "profession of faith" that

"I'm an eclectic: I'll play all kinds of works but [referring to Franck] the music of savages.")

Gianini, a ranking violist soon to become principal and later 2^e *chef*, strongly supported Messager, contesting the idea that he would somehow be tied to London. A member spoke up regretting that Samuel-Rousseau's qualifications had yet to be mentioned; another observed that Marty and Messager were obviously the best conductors, but since both presented problems the members should rally around Thibault. When Gianini tried to return to Messager, Nadaud overruled him and tempers began to flare. "M. Nadaud," he shouted, "wants to take the whole society under his wing."

Dubois stopped this descent into personalities by inviting the members to return to order: "Discuss, don't dispute; then vote according to your personal convictions." A motion to suspend the meeting so the members could collect themselves did not pass.

Before the voting, the candidates were told not to leave the *foyer*, as in the previous election details of the ballots had reached the press, presumably from the disgruntled Danbé, before the meeting was over. In the first round Samuel-Rousseau had a narrow advantage with 30 votes to 23 for Marty, 17 for Messager, and 13 for Thibault. By the fourth ballot Marty was in the lead: Marty, 48; Samuel-Rousseau, 30; Messager, 11; Thibault, 5; other votes, 6. Returning to the chamber before the runoff, Désiré Thibault urged his supporters to vote for Samuel-Rousseau, which they seem to have done. But nevertheless Georges Marty was elected 1er *chef d'orchestre* in the runoff ballot by a vote of 54 to 37 for Samuel Rousseau, with 10 blank ballots.[87]

Both Thibault and Samuel-Rousseau submitted their resignations within the week. Delegations were sent to dissuade them, and while Thibault said he would consider the question over the summer, Samuel-Rousseau held firm. A second assembly was therefore called for 28 June 1901 to elect a new chorusmaster.

Debussy, at the end of his column of 1 July 1901, noted testily: "The Société des Concerts du Conservatoire had the chance to have M. André Messager as its conductor. Needless to say, they missed it. The subscribers to this music hall for the soft-headed can continue their sleep."[88]

On 28 June Théodore Dubois took the privilege of the chair in order to introduce Georges Marty to the *sociétaires:* "He is a man of talent and duty. He understands the importance of the high artistic mission with which you have honored him."[89] Under Marty's firm and intelligent leadership, the Société des Concerts would retain the great, well-earned reputation that it had always had; he would "keep it on the first rung." Marty responded in kind. He had wanted the job, he said, for its duties were noble and lovely. He would walk hand in hand with Taffanel and consider his predecessor's affectionate advice as precious. He had faith in the future, and in fulfilling his new duties he would spare neither time nor effort. Together, they would create beautiful music. Applause rang out, and his election as vice president passed by acclamation.

Marty, meanwhile, had convinced Thibault to remain as second conductor, so they proceeded to the election of the chorusmaster. Their colleague Émile Schvartz, principal violist in the orchestra and professor of *solfège* at the Conservatoire, was the easy winner. Victor Gasser moved into his seat in the viola section and in October, after Thibault decided to maintain his resignation after all, was elected second conductor.

Georges-Eugène Marty, forty-one, was born in Paris and raised in the shadow of the Opéra, where his father—presumably the tenor Baptiste-Pierre Marty, also a *sociétaire*—was a member of the chorus. At the Conservatoire his gifts were recognized as exceptional early on; he took a medal in *solfège* at age fifteen, *1ᵉʳ prix* in harmony at eighteen, and after composition studies with Massenet and Dubois the Prix de Rome in 1882, shared with Gabriel Pierné. (Debussy, the 1884 winner, describes Marty, Pierné, and the 1883 winner Paul Vidal as "running each other down" in Rome.)[90] After their Roman sojourn, Marty and Pierné traveled together in Germany, visiting among others Liszt, Richter, and Reinecke, and they remained steadfast friends afterward. Marty had occasionally accompanied chorus rehearsals of the Société des Concerts and had been considered for appointment as interim chorusmaster after Heyberger's death in 1892.

As *chef de chant* at the Opéra Marty shared duties with Paul Vidal for the concert series there, where he mastered the central repertoire and began to attract attention as a first-rate conductor. He moved to the Opéra-Comique in 1900. At the Conservatoire he was at first professor of the *classe d'ensemble vocal,* then professor of harmony. By the turn of the century composition had taken second place to conducting in his career, but two of Marty's works, the overture to his opera *Balthazar* and *Les Saisons,* a suite with chorus, had become reasonably well established.

Marty was a portly man given to informal dress—preferring a kerchief to a necktie—and agreeable disposition, though his frankness of expression was occasionally thought "coarse."[91] His vision was poor, aided by thick *pince-nez* spectacles, and it was one reason he memorized his scores—though he kept them on the music stand and might randomly turn a page or two. Mme Marty was an alto from the Opéra, first seen on the programs of the Société des Concerts as soloist in Beethoven's Ninth and the *duo-nocturne* from Berlioz's *Béatrice et Bénédict* in 1897. In 1900 she sang the title role in excerpts from act I of Charles Lefebvre's *Judith;* under her husband's direction she sang the alto solos in the Bach repertoire, Handel's *Saul,* Saint-Saëns's Christmas Oratorio, and the Ropartz Third Symphony.

Marty's tenure was short but impressive. There seems little question but that he was a gifted conductor, generally characterized as commanding and of limitless energy and patience in preparing difficult works. His technique was described as unctuous, precise, and without hint of useless exuberance; yet for all the talk of precision and grace, the word most commonly used to summarize his presence is *authority,* sometimes associated with the adjective *imperial.*[92] Over the years he became quite popular with the public, and greatly respected by the musicians. One internal salute described him as "a conductor of triple prestige: gifted in technique, professional virtuosity, and frankness—with a good faith that brings out everyone's confidence and kindness."[93] Arthur Pougin's review of the inaugural concert on 21 November 1901—Beethoven's Sixth, three opera choruses, the "unpublished overture of Mozart" (K. C 11.05), the first performance of Saint-Saëns's Orchestra Suite, op. 49, three *a cappella* choruses, and the *Freischütz* overture—observes much of the same in summarizing a technique that "surely inspires confidence" and goes on to note how at the close both audience and musicians rose in a swell of applause directed toward their new conductor. Pougin regarded the debut as auguring well for the future and looked forward to the renewed emphasis on the chorus Marty would surely bring.[94]

Marty's particular fondness was indeed for Baroque oratorio and opera. Of Bach he introduced the St. John Passion, Magnificat, Christmas Oratorio, three sacred and two secular cantatas, and two of the orchestral suites. "Bach," it was noted, "brings receipts!"[95] In 1905 Marty presented Handel's *Saul,* complete. He was an active partner in efforts to reconstruct the works of Rameau, programming new scenes from *Hippolyte et Aricie,* a suite from *Les Indes galantes* reorchestrated by Dubois and Saint-Saëns, and a first hearing of excerpts from *Platée* from the edition he prepared with Saint-Saëns. (The chorus from *Castor et Pollux* introduced by Girard in 1851—"Dans ces doux asiles"—had stayed in the repertoire through Taffanel's performances in January 1900.) He also returned both *The Creation* and *The Seasons* to the programs, for the first time since 1859 and 1869 respectively, with fresh translations by Paul Collin. Nor did he slight the post-Baroque oratorio repertoire, reviving the Mozart Requiem, *Missa solemnis,* and Saint-Saëns's *La Lyre et la harpe,* and premiering the complete *Les Béatitudes* of César Franck over two concert pairs.

A new generation of distinguished players advanced to the front desks in the Marty years, many of whom are to be heard on the early recordings. The principal strings were Alfred Brun and André Tracol, the great violist Maurice Vieux, and the cellist C.-E. Cros-Saint-Ange. In the winds there were Philippe Gaubert and the oboist Louis Bleuzet, the clarinetist Prosper Mimart, and the bassoonist Léon Letellier; behind them, the Opéra's entire horn section (Vuillermoz and later Reine, Delgrange, Pénable, Vialet), the trumpeters Lachanaud and Fauthoux, and the famous timpanist Joseph Baggers. The new century also brought the next generation of great guest soloists. Lasting and affectionate relationships developed with Ricardo Viñes, Édouard Risler, Alfred Cortot, Jacques Thibaud, and Pablo Casals. In 1908 Marty introduced Marguerite Long in the Fauré Ballade, a work she was still playing with the Société des Concerts in the 1950s.

Marty's seven seasons of programs show the Société des Concerts on the verge of completing its metamorphosis into a philharmonic orchestra fully engaged with the outside world. One by one the canon of masterpieces from civilizations to the north and east of the French began to appear on the programs: the *Siegfried-Idyl* and "Good Friday Spell," the *Bartered Bride* overture, Brahms's First Piano Concerto and Tragic Overture, Liszt's *Orphée,* the *Peer Gynt* Suite and, on receiving news of Grieg's death in 1907, the Holberg Suite. The *répétitions d'essai* of October 1903, for instance, were devoted to the Symphony in E♭ of Borodin, Schumann's *Julius Caesar,* the Brahms Tragic Overture, and Saint-Saëns's *Phaéton.* All but the Schumann were scheduled for premieres—though *Phaéton* was delayed for three seasons, until 1906.[96]

Past Saint-Saëns and Fauré (the lovely Pavane with chorus in 1905 and the *Pelléas et Mélisande* suite in 1906, of which it was said that only the society's violinists could manage the difficult spinning-wheel figure), Marty's attention to living French composers is modest to the point of reluctance—a return to the position that works needed to be well established before reaching the hall of the Conservatoire. Nevertheless there were some major steps forward, as for instance with *L'Apprenti sorcier,* d'Indy's *Le Camp de Wallenstein,* and the *Prélude à l'après-midi d'un faune.* Meanwhile Schvartz and the chorus considerably enhanced the *a cappella* repertoire, offering groups of four or five selections, notably the French composers Janequin and Costeley but also Palestrina and Lassus; Lotti, Corsi, and Nanini; and even Michael Haydn. Complimenting the singers for these advances, the secretary remembered a time when Dubois as chorusmaster had needed to reprimand choristers who objected to singing a Bach motet.[97]

The later popularity of most of these titles, as though the society had discovered some knack for finding crowd-pleasers, masks the bitterness of the ongoing struggles, both internal and external, over the programming. Within months of his appointment Marty was under attack by the conservatives for the "grievous multiplication" of new works he had fostered and by the progressives for his "lack of inertia." The society played Beethoven's Fifth only three times during his tenure, leading one secretary to remark that it had become "too rare."[98] The committee began to count again, finding for the 1904–05 season nine performances of living composers, thirty-five of the dead. In a different method of accounting, the same season numbered twenty-two performances of the "classical" repertoire—that is, Palestrina through Schumann and Mendelssohn—and twenty-two of the "modern," Berlioz to the present.

Berlioz was of course no longer a modern composer. His centenary was celebrated on 6 and 13 December 1903 with *Rob-Roy,* the first Berlioz work the society had played, and a complete *Roméo et Juliette.* His own materials were now *hors usage,* leading to a purchase of the new edition by Charles Malherbe and Felix Weingartner, published by Breitkopf & Härtel from 1900. Julien Tiersot, the society's program annotator, was just finishing his book on Berlioz, which they promoted in a published prospectus distributed with the programs for the centenary concerts—this despite a prolonged skirmish with Tiersot over his failure to deliver his notes on time, which eventually led to his giving up the chore altogether.[99] At the suggestion of the organizers of a ceremony at Berlioz's statue on 12 December, the Société des Concerts approved purchase of a floral offering for 100 francs.[100]

In 1907 Marty presented the first complete *Harold en Italie* with the violist Maurice Vieux; in 1908, a magnificent first performance of the complete *L'Enfance du Christ.* "If only Berlioz could have heard it, it might have consoled him for his life of artistic setbacks," summarized the secretary. Returning to the stage to conduct the last work on the program, Marty was greeted with a salvo of applause for the Berlioz, in which the orchestra joined; he turned to recognize their brilliant new chorusmaster, Jean Gallon (later teacher of Delannoy, Dutilleux, and Messiaen; brother of the composer Noël Gallon), and the applause went on and on. The trio for two flutes and harp (Hennebains, Lafleurance, Martenot) was memorable. "My God," a patron was heard to remark on the way out, "they played the flute well in the time of Jesus Christ." [101]

One by-product of flourishing concert life was an ongoing shortage of personnel. The 1903–04 season, for instance, was found lacking in concerto soloists "of the first rank," a situation exacerbated when Francis Planté declined to appear owing to an impending operation. A call of distress went out to Saint-Saëns, who agreed to have a festival performance built around him to close the season: the Organ Symphony with the composer at the console, the Mozart D-Minor Piano Concerto, and *Le Déluge*. It was the same formula Taffanel had used to induce Saint-Saëns to open the 1895–96 season. [102]

There was continuing dissatisfaction with the second conductors. Victor Gasser, the violist-violinist who had been elected in October 1901 to finish Thibault's term of office, failed to be ratified after seven rounds of balloting in May 1902; the concertmaster Nadaud was elected to the post, with Gasser moved to become principal second violinist. The incident became ugly when Chavy, the secretary and also a violist, snapped that incumbents must always be re-elected. Not only was that untrue, Vernaelde retorted, but his committee was unrepresentative, having "too many violists" (Chavy, Gasser, Gaillard)—an attack that led Chavy to quit his position. [103] But Nadaud was no more successful than Gasser had been and was pressured to quit in 1903, at which time the violist Gianini took the post, also without success. By November 1904 most of the members had signed a petition urging appointment of second conductors by competitive audition, and it was in this context that Philippe Gaubert emerged from a *concours* that month as the new *2ᵉ chef*—a position he filled with distinction and to the great relief of his colleagues, for fifteen years. [104] The violists, incidentally, were there to stay. The next distinguished secretary was the violist Albert Seitz, and Julien Gaillard served as *commissaire du matériel* and *archiviste-caissier* through 1927.

At the Assemblée Générale of 1905 it was announced that Théodore Dubois, after more than a half-century of affiliation with the Conservatoire as student, professor, and from 1895 its director, would retire at the end of his second five-year term. He had contributed significantly, and at critical junctures, to the work of the Société des Concerts. The secretary's salute cited his "high artistic probity" and tendered particular ap-

preciation for how he had made it a first priority to give aid and counsel to their members. Dubois was bid farewell to a sustained ovation.[105]

Gabriel Fauré, his successor, was neither a strong nor a particularly
sympathetic president of the Société des Concerts. His education had
been at the École Niedermeyer and in private study with Saint-Saëns; he
owed his appointment largely to his personal friendships with Dubois and
Saint-Saëns. In 1892, when the death of Ernest Guiraud vacated a chair
in composition, Ambroise Thomas blocked Fauré's advance ("Fauré, *jamais!* if he is named, I resign!").[106] On Thomas's death in 1896, Massenet took a similar position and resigned from the Conservatoire at the
inevitability of Fauré's advance; in the aftermath Dukas ended up in
Thomas's chair, and Fauré in Massenet's. Fauré then championed Ravel
through each of his failed Prix de Rome attempts in 1900–03 and 1905,
and it was the *affaire Ravel* that particularly led to Dubois's downfall.

As president of the Conservatoire, where they soon began to call him
Robespierre, Fauré immediately set about his long-threatened "tempest
of reforms" that changed the curriculum, professoriat, and bureaucracy.
Much of this—the class in orchestral performance, the chairs in conducting and music history—was to the good, but there was no denying
that Fauré's main interests lay elsewhere than with the Société des Concerts. He was, without a doubt, in the camp that found the society retrogressive. On the other hand, his legacy to the society was eventually
quite substantial, since it was Fauré who promoted Messager's career,
organized the movement to install him at the head of the Société des
Concerts, and convinced him in 1908 to take the job.

Fauré's attitude toward the Salle des Concerts was especially vexatious. He began by claiming the room for class activities during the chorus's traditional rehearsal time, leading the seventy-two chorus members on an odyssey about the courtyard to find a place to practice. The
first retreat was into a cramped cellar, dark at high noon and stifling
when the two gas jets were lit. Several fainted, and death by asphyxiation
was feared. The unheated vestibule of the Salle des Concerts was worse,
threatening death by pleurisy and exposing the rehearsals to passers-by
in the rue du Conservatoire. Only the coming of spring, they said, saved
several of them from enrollment on the list of martyrs to their art, and it
was hoped that the next season might begin in "hygienic conditions." [107]
Fauré further backed the letting of the hall to the Quatuor Capet for
two concerts in 1906.

Whether the Société des Concerts in the early years of the twentieth century had unwittingly tumbled into circumstances that really threatened

its continued existence, or simply found itself in one of the inevitable downswings of any institution's history, is, a century later, impossible to say. It is in the nature of things that bad times are not voluntarily made public; the secretarial reports of those years generally focused on the good times, and the businesslike minutes of committee meetings are without much by way of storm warnings.

Gaillard, as *archiviste-caissier,* first signaled disaster in the making when in November 1903 he announced numerous "defections" of the subscribers.[108] The committee meeting of 17 November was devoted to studying the problem. Gaillard reported that the first series had 49 non-subscribed seats and that so far 120 seats for the second series were not placed; he reckoned the value at 500 lost francs per concert in the first series and 1,200 in the second. There was little demand for the "bad seats," even those on the front row; the committee was soon to give up its prime seats to subscribers unhappy with their "execrable" locations. The box office had just barely managed to resell the vacant seats for the previous season, and would certainly not be able to sell the additional 200 places now vacant for every concert. Gaillard recommended a greatly enhanced publicity effort, including the purchase, for the first time, of space on the familiar green Morris columns about Paris. This idea was initially opposed by one member because added expenses would further compromise an already unhappy financial situation for the musicians. In a subsequent meeting Gaillard reported a total subscription income of 157,825 francs for 1903–04, down 16,000 francs from the previous season; the end-of-year report showed a slightly improved gross income of 161,923 francs, though still down about 12,000 francs.[109]

By another critical measure, the amount paid to a rank-and-file *sociétaire* at the end of the season, the society was in at least a perplexing environment:

1900–01	Fr. 176.13
1901–02	Fr. 321.00
1902–03	Fr. 176.03
1903–04	Fr. 174.90

It seemed to be a case of vacillating receipts and inexorably rising expenses, with figures so unstable as to be beyond prediction. "Not an agreeable situation," Seitz summarized, "but not as bad as some think."[110] (However that may be, a per capita income of 175 francs for a season of twenty concerts seems desultory by any measure.)

Every member had his particular explanation. The discomfort of the seats and their cost, now considerably more expensive than tickets for the other associations. Changing habits of the wealthier patrons, thought to be wintering over in Nice and Cannes. The national economic climate. The fees necessary to attract Planté or Casals. The silence of the critics.

"Our sympathizers, still numerous, come to our old association as to a tranquil port where storms cannot reach," said Seitz. "Others, and their number is getting bigger, prefer their freedom of choice and the dangerous life at large." It was critical that they make their programs more widely known. "The sacred confidence of the Golden Age has been replaced by circumspection and study of the poster. The listener who before paid well for the assurance of a reserved seat now inspects the Morris columns and goes where his taste leads him." And they had to act quickly, for the situation seemed to grow worse with each passing week. "We must find the formula that reconciles traditions of the past with the demands of the future. We must struggle as we did at the first, work in disciplined fashion, avoid assaults from without, and search for interior weaknesses. Only at that price will we keep the predominance that was, and that must remain, ours." [111]

Financial uncertainty brought stirrings of *malaise* within the ranks. There were public breaches of discipline, as for example an incident when one of the musicians—surely an *aspirant,* for a *sociétaire* would never have done such a thing—made percussive rattles in the last bars of the Schubert Great C-Major, then did it again a few days later at the end of another very long work. Rehearsals were being skipped, even performances. "At not a single concert," complained the secretary, "were you '*au grand complet.'* The young *aspirants en cas* are to be called only for illness. If the Société des Concerts comes after your other duties it will be our certain ruin. . . . We start two months after the other societies, we have only two rehearsals a week, you are free from Sunday night to Friday morning. And every fourth Sunday you have off. And that doesn't suffice? No other society offers its artists such liberty." [112]

Money was of course the central issue, and accordingly the Société des Concerts embarked, with gathering assurance, on an aggressive public relations program designed to increase single-ticket sales and improve the balance sheets. Beginning in 1903–04, at Marty's suggestion, the repertoire for the next concert appeared on every program. [113] The Morris column project was undertaken, with posters eight times larger than the old handbills. Flyers were sent to the first-class hotels; unclaimed tickets were deposited at Durand and Co., the great music publisher at the place de la Madeleine, for resale to clients and tourists. Advance notices were published in twenty of the most widely read Paris newspapers and magazines. "It's impossible not to know," the *sociétaires* were assured, "that the Société des Concerts plays on Sunday afternoon at the Conservatoire."[114]

"It is very important," said the new secretary, Théodore Heymann, "that each of us, in his sphere, create the propaganda necessary to produce new subscribers. Tell music lovers that there are places available for all our concerts, since, unfortunately, a large portion of the public who could be our clients still thinks that the society is unattainable, that it is impossible to get tickets. Say that owing to illnesses and deaths a few places are always available to the public and that your position with the society gives you priority in arranging for available places and subsequent subscriptions."[115]

Finally, on the advice of Heymann, an authentic press service was begun, whereby an initial 3,000 francs was allocated to offset the cost of ten attractive seats for the critics: Prod'homme of the *Messidor,* Samazeuilh of the *République française,* Bruneau of *Le Matin,* Lalo of *Le Temps*—to cite only the most influential. The system worked; for the first sixty tickets given away, at a value of 500 francs, there were thirty published reviews. The result was to lead the organization out of its "splendid isolation. . . . They're talking about us in the papers, and in an especially sympathetic and praising manner." The initial signs were good; the orchestra had, for instance, to turn away a large public from the second performance of Franck's *Rédemption* in March 1908; indeed Marty succeeded in popularizing Franck, notably the D-Minor Symphony—heard without response, they noted, in 1889, without interest in 1901, and in 1906 the object of ardent admiration and vigorous support. "If our resolve is not broken, my dear colleagues, everyone who has had confidence in the future of our glorious society, and stayed faithful to it, will be repaid: morally and materially."[116]

And that was the case. In 1907–08 there was 5,070 francs' worth of new subscriptions. Except for retrenchments of the old subscribers— holders of both series who renewed for only one, renters of an entire *loge* who kept only two or three seats—the worst was over.[117] Resales of empty seats augmented 40 percent, and once filled led to new subscriptions. Most spectacularly, the musicians' individual income more than tripled, to above 700 francs a year by the end of the decade.

In view of Marty's strong association with the chorus, it is all the more remarkable that the movement to separate the chorus from the or-

chestra began during his last years. The matter of the orchestra's desire
to travel alone had been the source of hard feelings since 1904, when a
vote of the general assembly had failed to reach the two-thirds majority
(49 favoring, 31 opposed) necessary to allow the committee to develop
viable responses to invitations from London, Brussels, Geneva, and provincial France—invitations the Colonne and Lamoureux orchestras had
been accepting for some time.[118] Instead they would submit an estimate based on fees and travel for nearly two hundred musicians, to
which the sponsors would invariably reply that the expected ticket income would not reach anything like the proposed fee.

In 1905 the situation—in some respects a personal confrontation between two powerful administrators, the violist Seitz and the singer Vernaelde—came to a head when organizers of an annual *solennité musicale* in Lyon invited the Société des Concerts for a concert that might
well be the first of an annual series. While the committee went through
its customarily time-consuming analyses, the sponsors approached the
Paris impresario Gabriel Astruc—a figure who will assume a prominent
role in our next chapter—to negotiate a way the orchestra could appear
without the chorus. "We can tell you in advance," they wrote him in
June 1905, "that [the society's] accounting of travel expenses surpasses
our means." Astruc's first tactic was to describe the problem in a letter
to Fauré, who passed it on to the committee without comment. The
record indicates that this unexpected intrusion of an impresario into the
society's affairs, almost surely with the collusion of some of the instrumentalists, "struck a nerve."[119]

While neither Fauré nor the committee discussed their deliberations
outside the committee room, Astruc approached the orchestral musicians directly. Some forty-four members organized themselves for battle,
submitting on 6 December 1905 a valid signed petition that required action of the general assembly: "We the undersigned desire to be granted
the right to give concerts in Paris, in the provinces, and abroad, without the participation of the chorus personnel, and still conserving our
title 'Société des Concerts.'"[120] The committee, charged by statute to
examine and develop a response to such petitions, agreed at the outset
that to consider the implication of the words "in Paris" was premature;
for the rest they were split along expected lines, with the instrumentalists inclined to follow through with it and the singers holding that the
title Société des Concerts belonged to the entire collective just as surely
as the title *membre de la Société des Concerts* belonged to each individual. The negotiated solution was to send Seitz to a chorus rehearsal to

find out what terms might induce the chorus to go along with a change of statutes.

Hoping to avoid the cost of a general assembly and to keep the negotiation "on friendly terms," since the chorus could not possibly prevail in a voted confrontation, the secretary wrote and published two versions of a convention: one to be signed by the chorus members allowing their colleagues in the orchestra to appear separately, and an essentially identical text where the orchestra granted the chorus the same opportunity. After the secretary read the text aloud at the chorus rehearsal of 15 December 1905, the majority present refused to sign—though a few approached him individually with compliments for his effort to avoid an abrasive full-scale encounter of the singers and instrumentalists. As a result he never presented the version intended for the instrumentalists but instead convoked the Assemblée Générale for 30 December.

Seitz began the meeting by saluting Fauré, occupying the president's chair for the first time—"for most of us, one of the most original minds of the French School." He continued:

> He doesn't come to us on a calm day. "So much the better," I'm tempted to say, for we can show him the vitality of our association from the start.
>
> By our calm attitude, by the courtesy of our debate, by the precision and concision of our orators, we will show him among other things that the traditions of the century just past are not incompatible with the aspirations of the one just arrived.

"*Messieurs,*" Seitz continued, "a proverb holds that 'travel is instructive for the young.'" It was time to leave Paris. The proposed new article *8bis* had six paragraphs, envisaging that either the orchestra or the chorus could travel separately under the appellation *Société des Concerts,* and that even in Paris the orchestra might occasionally be authorized to appear without the chorus for evenings of concertos with celebrated soloists.[121] Supporters argued that the enhanced financial results for the orchestra players would return the society to a competitive position in recruiting and go a certain distance toward stemming the recent wave of defections in their ranks.

Vernaelde, endeavoring to accommodate the orchestra, rose to rally the singers to the proposal by attaching three conditions: that in Paris the orchestra always appear with the chorus, that the title "Société des Concerts" never be used for a cohort of less than 50, and that the matter be deemed a *cas grave,* requiring a two-thirds vote to approve. When reminded that the players needed to be able to offer *concerts d'accom-*

pagnement in Paris, he insisted that it was beneath the dignity of the Société des Concerts to lower itself to the position of a vendor of accompaniments. His motion to establish a *cas grave,* where the block of 30 singers could effectively stop the 58 or so instrumentalists present (and had done exactly that in 1904), was not agreed to.

As each article was voted, all the choristers abstained, with a final vote on the overall article registered as 54 favoring, 4 opposed 2 blank, and 27 not voting.[122] Everyone left the meeting unhappy, with accusations of intimidation being hurled from camp to camp.

In fact the first out-of-town appearance was not to Lyon but to the Belgian city of Antwerp, for a concert on 9 April 1907 at the Théâtre Royal: the *Egmont* overture, d'Indy's Symphony on a French Mountain Air, the incidental music from Fauré's *Pelléas et Mélisande,* the Bach B-Minor Suite with Hennebains as solo flute, and the Franck D-Minor Symphony. At the outset the musicians thought it a gamble, since Antwerp boasted a sophisticated series of concerts by visiting orchestras and the reputation of having a severe public. The Société des Concerts had never really been measured outside the hallowed hall of the Conservatoire.

No one need have worried. The reception was thunderous, with Hennebains recalled to the stage three times and encoring the Badinerie. The effusive press, though it was of the sort that became standard for road appearances, must have after this first journey been thrilling indeed. Critics praised the orchestra's equilibrium, finesse, volume-but-never-noise, the *inoubliable pianissimo. "Le timbalier même était un virtuose,"* wrote one. "This orchestra is far the best we have heard," wrote another, who was apparently the first to coin the term "phalanx of virtuosi."[123] It was a bracing experience for them all, especially in view of the battle to get there. Despite the many imitators they had engendered, despite their tardiness in unveiling their wares away from home, nothing could hide the fundamental lesson: they could properly think of themselves as the best orchestra in the world.

Just over six months later, the orchestra of the Société des Concerts at last made its debut in Lyon, for a concert in the pump room of the casino to benefit a local Jesuit school. The program consisted of the *Flying Dutchman* overture, the "Eroica" Symphony, the March of the Three Magi from Liszt's *Christus,* the Haydn *symphonie inédite,* the *Bartered Bride* overture, the Bach D-Major Suite, and Lalo's *Rapsodie norvégienne.* The program, model for many to follow, proudly listed the members and their affiliations:

COMPOSITION DE L'ORCHESTRE

Chef: M. Georges Marty, grand prix de Rome, professeur d'harmonie au Conservatoire de Paris; *second chef:* M. Philippe Gaubert, prix de Rome, flûtiste de l'Opéra.

Premiers violons: MM. Brun, violon solo, soliste de l'Opéra, professeur au Conservatoire; Th. Heymann, violon solo, ex-soliste de l'Opéra; Gibier (Opéra); L. Heymann; Mâche; Villaume; Saïller (Opéra); Besnier (Opéra); Loiseau (Opéra); Luqin; Candéla (Opéra); Tourret.

Deuxièmes violons: MM. Tracol (Opéra); Gasser; Gilbert (Opéra); É. Debruille (Opéra); Naëgelin (Opéra); Austruy (Opéra); Leplat (Opéra); Aubert (Opéra); Giry (Opéra); Boffy (Opéra); Chédécal (Opéra); F. Debruille.

Altos: MM. Vieux, solo de l'Opéra; Gaillard (Opéra); Seitz (Opéra); Le Métayer (Opéra); Bailly (Opéra); Migard, soliste de l'Opéra-Comique; Michaux (Opéra); Marchet (Opéra).

Violoncelles: MM. Papin, solo de l'Opéra; Girod, solo de l'Opéra-Comique; Gauthier, de l'Opéra-Comique; Gurt (Opéra); Alard (Opéra); Dumoulin (Opéra); Fillastre; Barraine (Opéra).

Contrebasses: MM. Martin (Opéra); Bouter (Opéra-Comique); Doucet (Opéra-Comique); Soyer (Opéra); Pickett (Opéra); Nanny, solo de l'Opéra-Comique; Gasparini (Opéra); Charron fils (Opéra-Comique).

Flûtes: MM. Hennebains, solo de l'Opéra; Lafleurance (Opéra); Gaubert, prix de Rome (Opéra).

Hautbois: MM. Bleuzet, solo de l'Opéra; Leclercq, solo de l'Opéra-Comique.

Clarinettes: MM. Mimart, professeur au Conservatoire; Lebailly, ex-solo de l'Opéra-Comique.

Bassons: MM. Letellier, solo de l'Opéra; Jacot (Opéra-Comique); Bourdeau (Opéra); Couppas (Opéra).

Cors: MM. Delgrange (Opéra); Pénable (Opéra); Vialet (Opéra); Reine, solo de l'Opéra.

Trompettes: MM. Lachanaud, solo de l'Opéra; Fauthoux (Opéra).

Trombones: MM. Allard, professeur au Conservatoire, solo de l'Opéra-Comique; Bèle (Opéra); Bilbaut (Opéra).

Timbales: M. Baggers (Opéra-Comique).

Harpe: M. Martenot, solo de l'Opéra-Comique; Demarquette.

Cornets: MM. Laforgue (Opéra); Deprimoz (Opéra).

Tuba: M. Brousse (Opéra).

Batterie: M. Truc (Opéra).

The orchestra left Paris at 7:00 on the morning of 26 November 1907, arrived in Lyon at 5:00, rehearsed, presented the concert, and were on the midnight train back to Paris, arriving the next morning at 11:00 — "exhausted, but happy, *combien!*" The response of the Lyonnais was one of stupefaction, especially gratifying as the Berlin Philharmonic under Hans Richter, thought to be the best in Germany, had just passed through, and the Parisians were found superior. A return engagement was booked for the next season. Members of the committee were soon making site visits to Geneva and Lille.

Antwerp and Lyon, it was said, rebuilt the soul of the Société des Concerts. Among the players there was a real sense of rebirth: they said they felt the stirring of their old souls, the fire that had once burned within, a new confidence in themselves and in their conductor.

"Oui, mes chers collègues," boasted Heymann, *"nous remontons!"*[124]

But just as the committee was assembling to plan the new season, they learned of Marty's sudden death from liver failure, at forty-eight, on 12 October 1908 — in the force of his age and the plenitude of his talent, as an obituary had it. The only other conductor to have died in office was Narcisse Girard in 1860.

Postponing any activity for the new year, the committee turned instead to organizing a funeral worthy of a first conductor of the Société des Concerts. Fauré was asked to preside and to give the main eulogy, and Jules Garcin returned to conduct the selections for the ceremony in the Église de la Trinité.[125] The artists of Paris turned out in the many hundreds; both the Lamoureux and Colonne orchestras sent large floral offerings. At the cemetery the chorus sang a last *De profundis*.

Mme Marty, having been suddenly deprived of resources, was offered the proceeds of a benefit on Sunday, 15 November, a week before the opening of the season; the large organizational committee was headed by Saint-Saëns, Dubois, and Fauré. A fulsome obituary appeared in the printed program. The packed house listened in silence as the society presented Marty's *Balthazar* overture; incidental music from *Shylock* by his lifelong companion Fauré; excerpts from act I of Gluck's *Alceste;* Saint-Saëns in the C-Minor Piano Concerto of Mozart, K. 491; and the Ninth Symphony. At the end of the Ninth there was quiet, then a sustained standing ovation. The income, remitted to Mme Marty, was 13,068 francs[126]—the largest amount ever raised in a benefit concert.

The long applause at the end of the Ninth Symphony recognized another turning point as well. For Fauré had worked his magic and persuaded André Messager to accept the call to come conduct the Société des Concerts.

CHAPTER 9

Messager

(1908–19)

André Messager was elected during a thirty-minute assembly on 26 October 1908 without the taking of nominations, without candidates opposing, and for all intents and purposes without dissent. One member objected to the fact that Messager had not even composed the traditional letter of application, but in the same breath expressed his satisfaction at the certain outcome.[1] Time was pressing, since the season was to open on 22 and 29 November and preparations for it had been interrupted by Marty's sudden death. A concert scheduled for Lyon in December could not be left to a substitute. Messager had already been a viable candidate at the previous election, in 1901. Since then he had administered the Royal Opera at Covent Garden in London (1901–07), conducted the 1902 premiere of Debussy's *Pelléas et Mélisande,* and returned to Paris as conductor and co-director of the Opéra. He could well claim to be the most influential of the several French composer / conductor / administrators active at the time. It was said of his years abroad that he had "seen all, heard all, and remembered all."[2] Certainly he had acquired glamour and a glamorous following—in short, was a star.

Messager's appointment marked a sharp turn from both precedent and statute, since he had not attended the Conservatoire but rather the École Niedermeyer. This was also the case with Fauré, Messager's chief sponsor; both were *protégés* of Saint-Saëns, who was surely working in the background to smooth feathers ruffled by so formidable a break with the past. What seems significant at this point is how resolutely the society kept on clinging to the words *du Conservatoire* in its formal title at the very time the connection seemed to matter less and less. In any event, the academic institution was on the verge of moving across town to quarters that lacked any provision for public concerts.

Messager was born in December 1853 in Montluçon, south of Orléans and Bourges. He arrived in Paris at the age of fifteen to enroll at the École Niedermeyer, where his five-year affiliation (1869–74) included counterpoint lessons with Gigout and "wise counsel" from Saint-Saëns. (Messager remembered his education in terms of the *fracas incessant* of two dozen students practicing in the same room while the composers tried to do their counterpoint.)[3] He conducted briefly at the Éden Théâtre in Brussels, then returned to Paris as organist at the Church of St-Paul–St-Louis in the Marais and chapelmaster at Ste-Marie-des-Batignolles. By 1898 he had become music director at the Opéra-Comique, the post that opened the way for his appointments at Covent Garden and the Opéra.

Messager's compositional promise was recognized as early as 1876, when his first (and only) symphony won a prize competition of the Société des Auteurs et Compositeurs de Musique and a public performance by the Colonne Orchestra (1878); his cantata *Prométhée enchaîné* took second prize in a later competition. Messager's popular reputation came from his string of uninterrupted successes as a composer of light music for the stage, notably the ballet *Les Deux Pigeons* (1886) and the relatively famous orchestra suite drawn from it. This avenue of his career was launched when he completed a comic opera left unfinished by Firmin Bernicat (1841–83), *François les bas-bleus* (1883); the comic operas and operettas that followed included *La Fauvette du temple* (1885), *Le Bourgeois de Calais* (1887), *La Basoche* (1890), and *Véronique* (1898), and there was also the ballet *Scaramouche* (1891). "Now seductive in their charm or their poesy," the society's publicity tells us, "now touching or merry, André Messager's works have enjoyed the most flattering public reception."[4] Even at the height of his conducting career Messager was an assiduous composer, and it was a characteristic of his tenure that he insisted on the opportunity to take abrupt leaves to finish a work or oversee a premiere.

That Messager's compositional forte lay in the decorative genres— ballet and light opera—says a certain amount about his tastes. His appearance was elegant to the point of dandy, given to immaculately tailored suits emphasizing his thin frame, careful grooming with particular attention to his mustaches, fine jewelry, and spats. The *décor* of his apartments and offices reflected the latest fashion. He was a witty conversationalist with an inexhaustible store of anecdotes and *bon mots*—a way with words that carried into his criticism for *Le Figaro*. His many admirers found him youthful of appearance and young at heart. He seemed an epitome of the new century.

Both Messager's wives were beautiful women: Edith Clouet, a French woman he married in 1883 and who later divorced him and died young; and the Irish actress and sometime composer Hope Temple, pseudonym of Dotie Davies, whom he married in 1895. (Clouet was the mother of a son, Jean; Temple, of a daughter, Madeline.) His "irresistible seduction" of Marguerite Long dated from their joint performance, set in motion by the composer's widow, of Debussy's *Fantaisie* for Piano and Orchestra. "Messager was charm itself," wrote Long's biographer, "and Mme Long was not insensitive to it." Long herself writes of how he imagined that an *engagement sentimental* had transformed their long friendship, and that before leaving for South America in 1916 he issued an *invitation au voyage* that "did not accord with sovereign reason. . . . I told him that after so many brilliant conquests he was risking defeat with me. And, then, to overcome my resistance, how he cheapened those who had succumbed! *Oh! éternel masculin!*"[5] Much later, in 1923–24, Messager agreed to her invitation to rescore Chopin's F-Minor Concerto and conducted the premiere with the Colonne Orchestra. Her 1930 recording of the work with Gaubert and the Société des Concerts—her first recorded concerto—won the Grand Prix du Disque that year.

Lucid and fastidious though Messager's conducting was, it appears also to have had depth and breadth. During his tenure at the Opéra-Comique, he promoted Charpentier's *Louise* as a worthy successor to *Carmen*. He was thought clairvoyant in his approach to new scores, finding details that lesser conductors missed; his championing of *Pelléas et Mélisande* alone would have earned him his place in music history. But at the Opéra his reputation was built not on new music—there was a single important premiere during his tenure, Alfred Bachelet's *Scémo* (1914)—but on the Wagner repertoire, largely responsible for the institution's return to financial respectability. He programmed the *Meistersinger* prelude for his first concert with the society, and it became a trademark of his tenure. For many he was the quintessential French Wagnerian: his legendary five-hour *Parsifal* on 31 December 1913 was an audacious gesture in a world charging toward war.

Messager went out of his way to nourish the impression that a concert by the Société des Concerts was a matter of venerating the great masters. He had the musicians take the stage in order, without warming up or tuning before the public. He followed closely behind his players, without a formal *entrée*, then turned directly to them and began.

Attempting to keep his gestures "tactful," "rare," and for the most part unseen by the public, he cultivated a sense that the orchestra was largely independent of its conductor. When he took his bows the orchestra rose behind him. Some found the approach precious and "excessively *soigneuse*," [6] but there are many ways in which it was a natural outgrowth of institutional tradition.

Well before his appointment to the society, Messager was known to be a shrewd, powerful administrator, and dextrous in managing the multiplicity of appointments that came to characterize twentieth-century life. He presided personally over meetings of the committee, a responsibility that had fallen over the years largely to the secretary. (Fauré had by his own admission little interest in the routine governance of the society, and in any case the president's single traditional duty was to occupy the chair at the annual Assemblée Générale.) He demanded, and got, fierce loyalty from his associates; for most of his tenure nearly every committee vote was unanimous or nearly so, and the tenor of the minutes is one of concord and consensus, perhaps obedience. The press liked to imagine from his public persona that Messager saw himself as a friend and colleague of the musicians. That may have been partly true, but in the longer run he enjoyed being an autocrat. And autocracy was fast becoming the preferred mode of orchestra conductors in the world at large.

Philippe Gaubert had been comfortably ensconced as second conductor since 1904 and after Marty's death had succeeded to one of his posts, conductor of the summer concerts in Vichy. The relationship between Messager and Gaubert was formal to the point of coolness and in the end became overtly hostile, but between 1912 and 1918 Messager was happy enough to entrust the society to Gaubert's baton when he had outside engagements. The chorusmaster was Jean Gallon, who had succeeded Émile Schvartz in 1906 and was to occupy the post until the war. Gallon's work appears to have been outstanding, both with the big pieces and in the ongoing pursuit of the *a cappella* literature. But he must have sensed the chorus's increasingly marginal role—its declining size, the arguably make-work character of the little Renaissance pieces—in the organization, and probably came to see his responsibility as one of falling in behind Messager while quietly delaying for as long as possible the inevitable extinction of the singers.

Messager's chief legacy to the Société des Concerts lies in his unswerving determination to draw his orchestra out of its isolation in a fading neighborhood and into the international spotlight. The *sociétaires* themselves had long sought—and been sought—to travel, and Marty had led their first two ventures away from the city. The epoch of international orchestral touring was at hand, made possible by the railroad network and reliable steamship service; individual composer / conductors and big-name virtuosi had been globetrotting for more than five decades. At least two of the other three Parisian *associations symphoniques* had made successful and widely noted journeys by train. The major German orchestras were being heard in France and Belgium and Switzerland. (Mahler and the Vienna Philharmonic had come for the 1900 Paris Exposition, when they played to prevailingly poor houses at the Châtelet and Trocadéro and had to borrow a great deal of money to pay for their return passage.)[7] But it was Messager who had the influence to sell the concept of the Société des Concerts as a vehicle for broadcasting the glory of French music abroad. One or more out-of-town engagements each season now become the rule, and the Messager period concludes with a courageous journey past the front to Switzerland at the height of World War I and then a magnificent three-month progress through the United States and Canada in 1918–19.[8]

In his first season (1908–09), Messager led the orchestra on return visits to both Lyon and Antwerp, with the mid-December concert in Lyon coming just over a month after he had first taken up his duties. The programs mixed the society's traditional repertoire and some of its newer interests, each with a Beethoven symphony and concluding with Messager's signature *Meistersinger* prelude. The very long program in Lyon on 15 December 1908 also included Schumann's *Manfred* overture, a suite from Rameau's *Les Indes galantes, Les Préludes,* the Mozart G-Minor Symphony, and *Le Rouet d'Omphale.* In Antwerp on 6 April 1909 there were the Fifth, Fauré's *Shylock,* the Franck Symphonic Variations (just introduced in Paris), and d'Indy's *Le Camp de Wallenstein.*

These performances gave public and press the opportunity to compare Messager with their still vivid memories of Marty. The Lyon reviews drew attention to the difference in their temperaments, finding Messager less nervous, perhaps more "phlegmatic" (i.e., lacking in overt emotion), but with a precision of gesture and gentle, almost caressing movements that gave the music an extraordinary sweetness and charm. Beethoven's Seventh was found very grand (though one critic thought the first movement too slow), the *Meistersinger* exempt of heaviness. One journalist found the wind players superior to those of the Berlin Orchestra, which had just passed through, and concluded that the Société des Concerts was at least the equal of the first orchestras of Ger-

many. He reports a full house with every *strapontin* occupied, and prolonged ovations at the end of a concert that had to be reckoned the best
of the season to date.[9]

Much the same was said in Antwerp, the second of two successive triumphs there that suggested to a critic he was right to conclude that the
orchestra was becoming the most perfect ensemble that had ever existed. Messager was praised for his "infinitely eloquent and intelligent
gestures," those of "a master among masters." The contrabasses, bassoons, and horns in Beethoven's Fifth earned special praise, as they often would elsewhere, and the orchestra as a whole seemed to have "a
soul and sensitivity independent of the *maître* in charge." It was said,
curiously, that whereas Marty's program had been "prevailingly German," Messager's was the more sensitive to the orchestra's heritage.
Neither half of that proposition was true. Marty had played the Bach
B-Minor Suite to feature Hennebains, but no Beethoven symphony
(only the *Egmont* overture); and the works of d'Indy, Fauré, and Franck
chosen for that occasion had, in fact, much to say of the society's true
identity.[10]

The press was read with glee in Paris, of course, and thought important enough to have been assembled and reprinted for distribution to
the members and for later promotional purposes. Nevertheless it may
be useful at this point to issue a certain disclaimer about both the tone
and the particulars of the reviews the musicians liked to cite. There can
be no denying the uniformly rapturous response the Société des Concerts earned on the road. But much the same was said—allowing of
course for pre-existing bias, mostly on nationalistic grounds—of every
major orchestra as it passed through small and medium-sized cities.
That such sounds had never been heard before in thus-and-such a hall
stands to reason, and many of the assessments of a conductor's technique or an orchestra's specific sonority have more to do with the vocabulary at the writer's disposal than anything else. "Sobriety of gesture," for one. We read of this feature of the society's conductors often
enough to imagine it must have been the case, but then the same thing
was said of Mahler's conducting in Paris—the same Mahler later described by Romain Rolland as conducting "like an epileptic cat."[11]
"Rich sonority of the strings," for another. This cannot have been all
that true of the Société des Concerts, at least in comparison with the
German orchestras, on account of both the style of playing cultivated at
the Conservatoire—relatively thin, narrow of vibrato, and so far free of
the sentimental elements increasingly to be found in post-Romantic

technique—and the relatively small size of the sections, especially those taken on the road. It takes very close reading to ferret out the truly distinctive elements of the Paris style, and in the long run the effort only begins to pay real results with the dawn of recordings, now just around the corner.

Paul Taffanel died in late November 1908, a few weeks after the death of Marty and just as Messager's first season was getting under way. The committee's studiedly cool response was to send a floral offering. Likewise, in the secretary's report in 1909 Taffanel was mentioned only in the "roll call of the deceased," whereas Marty was the subject of poetic commentary. A member rose to suggest that the passage in memory of Taffanel was "a little short," and three senior *sociétaires*—Nadaud, Gaillard, and Vernaelde—spoke to concur with that sentiment and to object to the secretary's suggestions that Taffanel had abandoned his post. If he quit the society, Nadaud said, it was because he was ill. While Taffanel's duties at the Opéra seemed never to tire him, his work with the Société des Concerts so "filled him with emotion" that he could not continue without further detriment to his health. (Just the opposite was said of Habeneck: that whereas the Opéra fatigued him, the Société des Concerts always brought him to life. The point was the same; both were more engaged by the concerts than the humdrum of daily life at the theater.)

The secretary, Théodore Heymann, responded that there could be no doubt as to Taffanel's many qualities as flutist and conductor. He was, after all, a child of the Société des Concerts. "But you discover who your real friends are in time of adversity, and I hold it against him that he brusquely abandoned the society at a time when we were counting on him, provoking a crisis that had disastrous effects for several years." Hence the society owed Taffanel less its outright gratitude than the expressions required by courtesy and *politesse*.[12]

This post-mortem exchange, suggesting a long-standing grudge in several respects unique to the society's documented history, fails to reveal the true details of an animosity that would re-erupt in two years' time. Here the stated complaint was over Taffanel's leave-taking just as the nuanced question of the Conservatoire's real estate was reaching its head, and perhaps an implied discontent with Marty's subsequent stewardship. Heymann was eventually to be dismissed for elevating his charges to "defamation." The assembly's decision to expand the written record by recording objections to the terse obituary had, ironically, the opposite effect—since, rather than protecting Taffanel's posthumous reputation, it left an evidentiary trail of discontent that would otherwise have been forgotten.

In his first recorded remarks to the society, at the Assemblée Générale after the 1908–09 season, Messager outlined an ambitious agenda of broadened horizons. He promised to reunite the chorus and orchestra, a commitment that may, in view of subsequent developments, have been more political than real. Surprising some of his musicians, he took the opportunity to defend the system of paid performance rights, one of his principal interests. (His primary employment, after he left the Société des Concerts, was as president of SACEM.) He hinted of plans for a performance venue to be added to the new Conservatoire.[13]

Messager's first season was dazzling by every measure, as though overnight the Société des Concerts, in a new quest to be measured against the philharmonic societies of Berlin and Vienna, had shed any vestiges of the provincialism it might have acquired since Deldevez. The season was anchored around four big works: the B-Minor Mass, Berlioz's *Roméo et Juliette,* Franck's *Rédemption,* and a first complete performance of Bach's St. John Passion. Nor was it short of new additions to the repertoire, notably including the *Meistersinger* prelude, Rimsky-Korsakov's *Capriccio espagnol,* and on the same program Raoul Pugno, appearing for the last time with the society, in both the Schumann Introduction and Allegro and the Franck Symphonic Variations. Louise Grandjean triumphed in the Liebestod from *Tristan and Isolde*—and enjoyed her experience so much that she became a subscriber. Also from the German repertoire were the *Siegfried-Idyl* and the overture to Humperdinck's *Hansel and Gretel.*

In his essay "Wagner au concert," the French academician Adolphe Boschot argued that the vogue for Wagnerian excerpts, which he traced rightly to ca. 1890 (the period of Garcin's aggressive programming at the Conservatoire), was a good thing. The performances were usually of much higher quality than in the theater, he says, and above all there were no *longueurs.* "The Germans prolong their intermissions and devour *chockolades,* sausages, caviar on bread with raw onions, and other *delicatessen.* In the next act they can digest while sleeping, or sleep while digesting. But a Latin listener, clear of head and empty of stomach, returns to the seamless Wagnerian sublimity: '*C'est bien long,*' he says to himself." Further, Boschot notes, the overall sonority was better when there was no pit to separate the musicians from the audience. "The best performances of Wagner, and the most purely *musical,* are often given in Paris, notably by our *grandes associations symphoniques.*" [14]

It was not Wagner, however, who took the honors of the season but rather Bach. The B-Minor Mass sold out early with a large turn-away from the box office, bringing the best financial results of the year. The work was now closely identified with the society. It had prominent solo passages that featured distinguished artists: Lachanaud and Fauthoux on the high trumpet parts, Bleuzet as oboist. In the St. John Passion there was prominent viola d'amore and viola da gamba work for Vieux, Michaux, and Papin. (Papin had been engaged to succeed Cros-Saint-Ange, in part owing to his expertise on the viola da gamba.) The players took particular satisfaction that several Belgian visitors presented themselves at the box office for the Passion on 8 and 9 April after having first heard the orchestra in Antwerp on the sixth. [15]

Individual ticket sales rose sharply during the season, as in a few months did subscriptions for the following year. There were turn-aways from the final concert as well: the Saint-Saëns Organ Symphony and Franck's *Rédemption.* In view of the effort publicists had put into assuring patrons that tickets were always available (for instance, a note to that effect at the foot of every program), this could have been an embarrassing situation, with a large crowd declined admission at the box office yet empty places in the hall. But the *archiviste-caissier,* suspecting as much, had gone out of his way to solicit the return of ticket coupons from subscribers not expecting to attend. [16]

The enhanced Service de Presse, finally, began to have good results. "They are writing of us again, at last, in the papers, and in a manner particularly kind and praising," reported the secretary at the end of the year. He went on to compliment his colleagues for "leaving our Ivory Tower to contact the public at large. . . . All of you who have had confidence in our glorious society, and stayed faithful to it, are being repaid, morally and materially." [17]

Succeeding seasons followed much the same formula, organized around centerpiece works for orchestra and chorus (in 1909–10 the Ninth Symphony and *Missa solemnis,* Berlioz's *L'Enfance du Christ,* and the Fauré Requiem) and continuing an aggressive program of new acquisitions. First performances in 1909–10 included a Bach cantata, a lyric scene by Chabrier titled *La Sulamite,* Liszt's *Faust* Symphony, and Debussy's Prix de Rome cantata *La Damoiselle élue.* Schumann's *Faust,* the Verdi Requiem, and the *Nocturnes* of Debussy followed in the next season. The German and Russian repertoires grew, notably with systematic attention to the music of Richard Strauss and Rimsky-Korsakov.

The Lyon concerts continued annually; an invitation to appear in Lille was tendered and eventually accepted.

Messager cultivated the star system, of which he was so obviously a part, not only by featuring his best players (the concertmaster Alfred Brun, the violist Maurice Vieux, the flutist Adolphe Hennebains, the oboist Louis Bleuzet) and his best singers at the Opéra (Yvonne Gall, Claire Croiza) but also by insisting that guest artists be only those of the highest caliber. There was a *contretemps* with the committee when Messager objected to the qualifications of Georges de Lausnay to cover the piano solo part in d'Indy's Symphony on a French Mountain Air. Lausnay was engaged over his objection and acquitted himself, acceptably but no more, in concerts of January 1912; Messager regretted causing an incident, he told the committee afterward, but "the moral of the story is that, as I have always asked, we must only invite artists of the first order and international reputation." [18] Of these the most renowned were Emil von Sauer (March 1910, in the "Emperor" Concerto); Kreisler (the *concerts spirituels* of 13 and 14 April 1911, in the Beethoven Concerto); Harold Bauer (December 1912, in the Schumann Piano Concerto); Georges Enesco (November and December 1913, in the Lalo F-Minor Concerto); and Busoni (January 1914, in the Saint-Saëns Fifth Concerto). Leading all these in international prestige was the great Paderewski, who appearance in an evening benefit concert on 17 February 1910 —his second, after a *début* in 1890 —was of such triumph that thereafter he had the committee's standing invitation. He was announced for the 1911–12 season but had to postpone until 1913; after a number of other cancellations, he made a final appearance in February 1929 that was the event of the season.

The celebrities left *souvenirs* of their visits in the society's *livre d'or*— another indicator of how prevalent the star system was becoming. The cellist André Hekking, after the Saint-Saëns A-Minor Concerto in February 1911, wrote of "one of the most beautiful memories of my career as a virtuoso." Louis Diémer, who played the Saint-Saëns Fifth Piano Concerto in November 1911, thought there could be "no greater artistic joy" than to appear with the Société des Concerts, and recalled his debut in the Mendelssohn G-Minor Concerto twenty years before. Enesco complimented the "divine" orchestra, and Busoni wrote of his "unexpected acclaim." [19]

Overall Messager supported the society's progressive wing, completing the Berlioz, Wagner, and Brahms repertoires and popularizing Dukas and Debussy. Marty had introduced *L'Après-midi d'un faune;* Messager programmed it frequently, and added *La Damoiselle élue* in 1910, the *a cappella* songs to texts of Charles d'Orléans in 1912, and most significantly the *Nocturnes* in 1914. "Nuages" and "Fêtes" entered the orchestra's list of signature works.

Another sign that the Société des Concerts was evolving into a year-round primary engagement for the musicians was the relative ease with which they managed to assemble sufficient strength to appear in Brussels in high summer, on Saturday afternoon, 9 July 1910. The occasion was the once-a-decade Exposition de Bruxelles, for which they chose an all-French program of "refined good taste": the C-Major Symphony of Dukas, *L'Après-midi d'un faune,* Franck's *Rédemption,* Saint-Saëns's *Phaéton,* Fauré's *Shylock,* and the "Fête chez Capulet" from Berlioz's *Roméo et Juliette.*[20]

Elizabeth, queen of the Belgians and noted patroness of fine music, was among the large crowd drawn to hear a repertoire with which they were already somewhat familiar now played by the leading orchestra of its *pays d'origine.* The queen summoned Messager to her box after the Franck *Rédemption* and conversed with him for some time while the orchestra remained standing—a gesture, remarked one reviewer, of "remarkable chic." Charles van den Borren thought the concert a triumph for modern French music, for the players, and for their conductor. The French were often reproached, he says, for a certain dryness of approach; yet this was not *froideur* but rather distaste for excessive display. Messager was able to forge a perfect equilibrium between passion and good taste. Nothing was brutal, and there were few *fff*s or *ppp*s; one was drawn above all to the extreme delicacy of nuance and the overall sweetness of the sonority. Van den Borren liked the Berlioz and Franck but found *Phaéton* pale; he went on to rave about the Debussy, both the composition and its performance.[21]

Again the press clippings were assembled by the committee and later reprinted in leaflet form. In general the journalists shared van den Borren's views, especially about the ravishing performance of *L'Après-midi d'un faune* with Hennebains as the flute soloist. The Belgians had known of the reputation of the orchestra, but few had until then had the privilege of studying it. Neither the Colonne nor Lamoureux orchestras, though more experienced travelers, had impressed them to this degree. One especially interesting observation was to the effect that the works played seemed only a detail: one found oneself listening primarily to the orchestra.[22]

Withal Brussels was a memorable success and would be long remembered. The Société des Concerts appeared again for the Belgian expositions in 1920 and 1930, with two related visits to the Liège exposition of 1930 as well.

At the end of the general assembly of 26 May 1911, Messager took the floor to offer "several thoughts" on the overall situation of a society now firmly under his control, an analysis of programming, public tastes, and their particular venue that took as its first principle how the society's repertoire had definitively outgrown the Salle des Concerts. He was pleased with the direction his programs had taken, especially considering that "several years ago the society opened the door to compositions whose notoriety was insufficiently established." But, he hoped, "we can soon quit our hall, a *véritable tombeau* for the Société des Concerts." While its much-vaunted acoustic was still praised, it was in truth satisfactory only for Haydn, Mozart, and some Beethoven. It was impossible to play later music properly because of the hall's "excessive sonority," and a chorus of sufficient size simply would not fit. The public no longer tolerated its cramped provisions.

> Don't give up hope! Let us have a hall truly accessible to all definitively consecrated masterworks. We'll need to redo our statutes completely and modify our procedures. If we must make some monetary sacrifice, let's do it without complaining. Our compensation will be in the future. The day the public at large—those who ignore us because they think they can't get in—hears you [in a proper venue], it will recognize the overwhelming superiority of the Société des Concerts and the chorus that is unique to it. You may be sure, gentlemen, that, as in the past, I will employ all my goodwill and all my energy to find that very solution.[23]

The applause was recorded as warm, and prolonged.

The 1911–12 preseason included a concert in Lille and the ceremonial playing of the Prix Rossini, won by Marc Delmas for *Anne-Marie*. Delmas had taken both the Prix de Rome and the Prix Rossini in 1911; later he won the Prix Cressent—and went on to write respected books on Bizet and Charpentier. The Sunday concerts opened, after Beethoven's Fourth, with the *Cantique de Jean Racine* of Fauré (who used a novel new technology, the *pneumatique*, to assure the committee he would attend).[24] New works included a Bach Cantata for the Feast of St. John the Baptist (almost surely BWV 30: *Freue dich, erlöste Schar*) and an otherwise unidentified Rimsky-Korsakov *conte féerique*, both of which were purchased and added to the library, along with the Symphony in F♯ of Glazunov (not played).[25] A Tournemire psalm was brought to the attention of the committee, and on 4 November the composer came to play it. After he left, Messager examined the score attentively and concluded that such a difficult work could not be done on two rehearsals; it was thus scheduled for 28 January and 4 February, then postponed again in view of new plans for a monster concert at the Trocadéro, until early March.[26] The *Missa solemnis* in late March had impressive enough results that a third performance seemed necessary, but it could not be scheduled. A first performance of Chausson's Symphony in B♭ was slipped into the last concert pair, in late April.[27]

Owing to Messager's sudden indisposition the concerts of 18 and 25 February 1912 were conducted by Philippe Gaubert, making his unexpected debut in a program of the "Eroica," the first performance of Max Bruch's viola Romance, op. 85 (Maurice Vieux, soloist), Bach's *Phoebus and Pan* with Marcel Dupré at the harpsichord, and Rimsky-Korsakov's *Capriccio espagnol*. Gaubert's nervousness at the dress rehearsal—*"Je tremble, je frémis"*—faded as the musicians began to grasp the promise of their audacious colleague, an artistic triumph that was all the more remarkable in that he had never held a baton, he alleges, until that very week.[28] This last seems unlikely, as he had been conducting in Vichy since 1909.

Among those who sensed the momentous nature of the orchestra's tentative steps outside the faubourg Poissonnière was the impresario Gabriel Astruc, who foresaw capital opportunity in it. (He was not the only one. In 1907 the piano manufacturer Étienne Gaveau had tried to interest the society in moving to his new hall in the rue La Boétie, but they were not yet prepared to think carefully about renting a facility, and simply thanked him for the evidence of his esteem.)[29] Astruc was perhaps the most prominent of the new wave of concert organizer / managers, agents on whose services the society would rely increasingly as the century progressed. He had, among other accomplishments, produced the first *Salomé*. His negotiating tactics, not always subtle, had cleared the way for the recurring Lyon concerts. Sometime after the Brussels journey Astruc approached the Société des Concerts with a project for an impresario-produced concert of five hundred at the Salle des Fêtes of the Trocadéro, with its forty-five-hundred-seat capacity and pipe organ by Cavaillé-Coll. Their own forces would be augmented by a large chorus from the École de Chant Choral, led by the orpheonist and writer Henri Radiguer. Astruc argued that the society had "a duty to broaden its sphere of influence and occasionally to escape from its historic room, part temple, part prison." The performing force would be large enough to overcome the acoustic of the cavernous space, and, he asserted, the central heating would function admirably. This last was an ongoing problem at both the Trocadéro and its successor, the Palais de Chaillot; Astruc's subsequent publicity took care to observe that those who had been to the first rehearsal could testify to the perfect atmospheric conditions.

In part because it was now urgent to find some alternative to the Salle des Concerts, in part out of Messager's obsession with raising the orchestra's profile, the committee was at length convinced by the project. A *séance extraordinaire* was billed for Sunday, 11 February 1912, with Beethoven's Ninth, the Saint-Saëns Organ Symphony, and a French version of Richard Strauss's *Taillefer* for soloists, chorus, and orchestra (1903). The press release trumpeted "this little revolution in our austere habits." [30]

This new working arrangement brought with it inevitable problems, of which the most difficult was the scheduling of rehearsals. The choral society, consisting of volunteers with day work, was only available nights and Sunday mornings, precisely the time the professional singers among the *sociétaires* were engaged by their opera choruses and church choirs. There was of course no ready venue at the Conservatoire where hundreds of singers might rehearse. These questions were long negotiated and finally settled with a compromise plan that reserved the Trocadéro for a series of Thursday-night rehearsals. [31]

The Conservatoire, meanwhile, refused to authorize its box office to sell tickets for an impresario concert. As of the committee meeting on the Tuesday before the concert, gross proceeds amounted to only 5,349 francs. In the end, there was a reasonable sale and decent attendance, but then a round of disagreements with Astruc as to how to reckon the accounts for printing and advertising compromised whatever good feelings had so far been achieved. It is to Astruc's credit that he understood how these first-ever encounters of the society with the outside world would need patient and flexible administration if they were to survive at all. Tensions were gradually lowered in every case, with the books made to balance when Astruc reduced his own fee. With all accounts reconciled, the Société des Concerts took away 7,820.65 francs from the Trocadéro, something less than the 9,000 they usually got and the 10,000 they expected, but in view of the risks scarcely a poor result. [32]

In the months leading up to the Trocadéro concert Astruc met regularly with the committee, and in the end they reached a congenial working relationship and mutual respect. At nearly every meeting Astruc would have heard discussion of the crisis of venue that had dominated societal concerns since the announcement in 1908 that the Conservatoire would definitively relocate to the rue de Madrid, leaving the Société des Concerts the sole occupant of a dying property slated for demolition. (The move took place in the fall of 1911.) During the course of the Assemblée Générale of 1909, Théodore Heymann as secretary delivered an oration, *"Notes sur les origines de la Société,"* that documented the struggle for the hall by citing the decrees of 1828, 1832–33, 1850, and 1897–98. Then he unveiled—begging that the musicians keep it in their confidence—the committee's project for a new auditorium on the plot in the rue de Madrid, with construction costs reckoned at 250,000–300,000 francs. The hall would be reserved for the Société des Concerts. Prosperity would surely follow, and Messager would become the new Habeneck. The proposal, Heymann said, had been quietly circulated and had met with no objections.[33]

In fact the project had been met with little reaction at all. It was in this context that Astruc unveiled in turn his own plan for a complex of fabulous new halls in the avenue Montaigne: the Théâtre des Champs-Élysées.[34] He and his associate Gabriel Thomas had already constituted a *société immobilière* that would fund the building and guarantee the partners a twenty-year lease. For purposes of discussion, Astruc proposed to undertake the administrative direction of the Société des Concerts, gradually capitalizing the enterprise. The society would be the principal occupant of the new building. Whether the members were, in fact, especially interested in Astruc's vision is a matter for conjecture; I suspect they were not. But the plan at least recognized the possibility that the orchestra might flourish in an open market, divorced from the Conservatoire, and a copy of the proposal was thus sent to Fauré, along with a request from Messager for a meeting to discuss a strategy for delivering the society from its "menacing danger."[35]

At the Conservatoire, Gabriel Fauré was "quite vividly contrary" to learn that the Société des Concerts was even considering a separation from the Conservatoire. While admitting that he had failed to take an active part in the society's work, he also went on to maintain that everything that touched his institution interested him in the highest degree. He had properly pled the case, with the undersecretary for fine arts, for a hall "in greater rapport with the requirements of performing modern work and also greater correspondence with the comforts that today's public can find in others theaters and halls." But he was adamantly opposed to divorce. They could keep their name, he threatened, only if they remained a branch of the Conservatoire. Then he argued rather feebly that the solution to their problems was to hew faithfully to their tradition of impeccable performances of the *grands classiques*—he listed Bach, Mozart, Haydn, and Beethoven—in a fabled place. The public existed and would continue to exist; and if the society were to refuse its responsibility, someone else would come along to gather up the heritage they had abandoned.[36] This was, of course, the old Louvre-of-music argument.

In early February 1912 Messager and the secretary carefully drafted a letter summarizing the situation. As it was a critical manifesto, in fact a turning point, the text was reviewed and approved by each member of the committee before being submitted to Fauré:

M. Gabriel Fauré, member of the Institute
President of the Société des Concerts

Monsieur le Président:
In response to the request you honored me by tendering, I hasten to furnish you with the details of the crisis now facing the Société des Concerts. The Société des Concerts, originally established to enrich the public exercises of the Conservatoire's students, was never and has never become a commercial enterprise in the strictest sense. The profits realized were, and still are, considered as an honorarium reimbursing the *sociétaires* for the time they devote to the rehearsals and performances.

Last year each *sociétaire* earned, after the 20 percent deducted for the Caisse de Prévoyance, the sum of 633 francs. (The Société gives twenty concerts, which require forty rehearsals.) By contrast, the other main Paris orchestras enjoy the satisfaction of seeing their work well compensated.

For those honored to be members of this most elite of ensembles, the Société des Concerts is thus not about money. The interest of artists wishing to be part of the society lies in the very recognition of having been appointed by the administrative committee.

I just noted, Mr. President, the financial results of last year. Those were less than in 1910, which in turn were less than the profit realized in 1909.

We are thus led to a painful conclusion: the public, our subscribers, are leaving us.

To what may we attribute their dissatisfaction? Certainly not to our performances. Like our predecessors, we maintain the same care for perfection in our performances that earned the Société its worldwide reputation. And be assured, Mr. President, that all our efforts have but a single goal: to keep intact, and to transmit to our successors, the beautiful traditions and artistic probity that were left us by our predecessors.

Thus we have to look elsewhere for the causes of the precarious state in which the Société des Concerts finds itself. In my opinion these are:

1. The tiny hall in the faubourg Poissonnière. The limited dimensions of

this room prevent us from allowing into the repertoire the majority of contemporary works, despite their having been proven by their character and the standing of their composers; in a room built for the symphonies of Haydn and Mozart they explode with noise.

2. The high ticket prices we are obliged to charge in view of the small number of seats: only eight hundred. This tends to chase away a numerous, interested public.

3. The transfer of the Conservatoire to the rue de Madrid, which has dealt a near-fatal blow to the Société des Concerts. It is now isolated in a *quartier* that has definitively lost the musical excitement that the Conservatoire lent it.

Led to believe that this situation would not last forever, the society bravely undertook to endure these vicissitudes. But last year the powers that be did nothing at all about building a concert hall in the rue de Madrid. That is why I need to tell you, Mr. President, of the substantial unrest and great malaise that reigns in our group—discouragement, even, that has come to afflict even our most devoted *sociétaires*. I need scarcely add that our recruitment grows ever more difficult. The young artists of today—and, alas, can we hold it against them?—no longer separate questions of material satisfaction from purely artistic considerations.

Moreover the nature of the frenzy into which we have been plunged is far from unknown to others; we have received offers to give our concerts in another hall.

It is to be feared that the Assemblée Générale of our members will vote to oblige us to accept this proposition, too advantageous to be ignored in this crisis.

If the State were to agree to a temporary subvention of 30,000 francs per year, to last until we can occupy the rue de Madrid, this measure—thus restoring our receipts to the level of two or three years ago—would settle the *sociétaires'* concern over the future that awaits the Société des Concerts.

This arrangement, which I take the liberty to submit to you, would I think allow the Société to wait for the building of the hall in the rue de Madrid and our consequent reintegration with the school—soon enough, we hope, since we know how much you want it.

Finally, if this were to happen, we would continue to be what we have never ceased being: completely absorbed in the musical instruction given by the Conservatoire. For the Société des Concerts is the only orchestra in France where, in order to belong, you have to be French and to be part, or have been part, of the Conservatoire, as professor or student.

The Société des Concerts thus well merits the title often bestowed on it: affiliate of the Conservatoire.

Agréez, je vous prie, M. le Président, l'assurance de mes sentiments les plus respectueusement dévoués.

Messager[37]

The authorities read the essay not as a compelling case for a new building of semi-permanent subvention but as evidence of a passing fiscal embarrassment. In mid-March the undersecretary of fine arts responded with a grant of 1,000 francs, "most exceptionally, in encouragement." The formulation was as offensive as the money was trivial; it was the language of royal tipping now eight decades past—and half the sum. Fauré used a delaying tactic to dissuade the angry committee members from going to call on the government, promising to support the idea of a new hall at the new Conservatoire when it came before his *conseil supérieur* in a year's time; Messager should then, he said, take care to attend. By late April it was clear that the government had no intention of attaching the necessary appropriation to the annual budget submitted to the Chamber of Deputies. The minister of finance was heard to say, "If the Conservatoire wants a hall that badly, why don't they go to a loan company?"[38]

Meanwhile Astruc's Théâtre des Champs-Élysées was nearing completion, and it did not escape attention that "private initiative had resolved, with rare success, a problem that the State itself so conspicuously failed to resolve." The promotional materials boasted of an architectural union of "French taste with Anglo-Saxon technique"—elevators, hidden wiring, a designer salon-boudoir at the disposal of the *spectatrices* during the intervals, wide aisles, and comfortably large seats all with full visibility—in the *quartier* now recognized as the center of elegant Paris. In stark contrast to the Salle des Concerts (and the Trocadéro) the new theater would be "healthy"; modern heating with forced-air ventilation promised "absolute hygiene."[39]

The souvenir program for the gala opening in April 1913 listed patrons including eight royal highnesses and, among the Americans, J. Pierpont Morgan, Mrs. William K. Vanderbilt, Mrs. John Jacob Astor, and Mr. and Mrs. Otto Kahn.[40] (Kahn is shortly to play a role of immense importance in the society's fortunes.) The inaugural season at the Théâtre des Champs-Élysées saw the premieres of *Le Sacre du printemps* and *Jeux* and reprises of *Daphnis et Chloé* and *L'Après-midi d'un faune;* operas from *Khovantchina* and *Boris* to *Rosenkavalier* and *Elektra;* orchestras under Saint-Saëns, Debussy, Weingartner, Mengelberg, and Toscanini; Beethoven's Ninth and the Verdi Requiem. There was no participation by the Société des Concerts. Instead Astruc's season was their principal competition.

But by October Astruc was bankrupt. Within a few weeks a businessman named de Mortier, representing a new Société des Amis de la Musique, again approached the Société des Concerts to occupy the Théâtre des Champs-Élysées. The new consortium proposed a rent of 1,500 francs per concert (modified in the written proposal to 2,000 francs), inclusive of heat, electricity, and staff—noting that the large auditorium seated two thousand and was equipped with a pipe organ. Messager and the committee were now prepared to take the proposal a good deal more seriously than they had greeted Astruc's first initiatives, and indicated their readiness to occupy the house for the 1913–14 season, scheduled to open on 30 November. But the musicians, when consulted, thought otherwise. The rent was considerably too high, they said, and the new corporation had presented no proof of actually having the lease. Moreover Fauré sent word of his "strongest reservations," again reminding them that the cherished words *du Conservatoire* were at risk. It was agreed to postpone the decision until there was more time to think about it; the secretary left to tell Mortier immediately and would break the news to Messager that night at the Opéra.[41] Before the matter could be taken up again, war intervened.

The Théâtre des Champs-Élysées did, in fact, become the home of the Société des Concerts, but not until many years later. The orchestra played there for the first time during World War II, and adopted the theater as their permanent venue with the Liberation.   •

Théodore Heymann's distaste for Taffanel and his inability to control his own tongue led finally to his dismissal in August 1910. When the minutes of the 1909 assembly were read to membership—the meeting where several members had risen to suggest that the brief obituary remarks of 1908 reflected poorly on "a man of goodwill" and "an honest man"—Heymann insisted on continuing the fray. "Taffanel was not an honest man," he began. Then he accused his late colleague of having kept a fee remitted by the government for the society's participation in the funeral ceremonies for Sadi-Carnot as long ago as 1895, whereas the members had been told that the government had never paid it. Heymann alleged he had found evidence in the committee's records that Taffanel had called on the government to collect the money but had never recorded its receipt. "When one is acting honestly, why hide anything?" he asked. Heymann had since discussed his suspicions with a bureaucrat at the ministry, who had confirmed "a stain on the committee of 1895." He went on to blame Édouard Nadaud, secretary in 1895, for not having followed up on the matter, then Nadaud's successor, Vernaelde, who had also failed to act.[42]

"Violent protestations" erupted in the room. "These are very grave accusations," Messager observed from the chair, and went on to pay homage to Taffanel's memory and to the unfailing propriety of his behavior; Gaubert forcefully seconded his remarks. "Monsieur Heymann," he concluded, "has defamed him." The assembly applauded vigorously. Vernaelde and others insisted that Heymann either back his accusations with evidence or stand down; Heymann retorted that it was up to the committee to exonerate itself. But this would be difficult, it was asserted, since financial records were routinely destroyed after ten years in the archive. (Messager confirmed that this was the current practice, though certainly that had not always been the case.) Vernaelde said he expected to inform Nadaud, now retired, of these new accusations against a previous committee. Gaillard hoped that the "painful incident" would be left out of the minutes, then moved for Heymann's censure. Messager ruled the discussion closed before taking a vote.

In August, however, the committee went on to exercise its statutory right to dismiss Heymann, giving as its reason his "defamation of a *sociétaire*."[43] Heymann immediately appealed the decision to an Assemblée Générale *extraordinaire,* which was called for 19 November. Messager opened the meeting by reading two letters from the government, one from an auditor and one from the secretary-general of the minister's cabinet. Their records showed a parliamentary credit of 100,000 francs toward the expenses of the funeral, and a single charge from the Société des Concerts: 426 francs for the luthier, M. Bernadel. Nothing had been remitted to Taffanel.[44]

Heymann, without quite apologizing for his behavior, said that he was "prepared to associate himself" with Vernaelde's positive assessment of Taffanel's character as expressed at the previous assembly. A member inquired whether the committee meant to maintain its decision to dismiss; Heymann, at fifty-eight, was after all a doyen of the society and its committee. But Messager insisted on a vote. It would be up to the assembly to decide.

Now the venerable Nadaud took the floor. He had spoken with no member of the committee, he said, and even though Heymann sought to defame a dead man, he himself would say no ill of a fallen colleague. Nevertheless he needed to defend his committee. Several of them, he continued, had together visited the ministry to collect the money; Schvartz had duly recorded the errand in the minutes. Turning to the events of recent weeks, Nadaud objected to Heymann's having called for a commission of arbitration and then procrastinating for weeks without presenting his defense. As for Heymann's service to the society, it could hardly compare with Taffanel's thirty-seven years. For the rest, Nadaud urged the assembly to maintain the dismissal, since it would be difficult to recruit committee members for already grueling work if they could be subject to later recriminations of the kind that had just erupted.

The arbitration panel had ruled unanimously that there were no grounds to attack Taffanel's memory and that no suspicion remained on the committees of the era. It recommended that the incident be closed as things had stood before Heymann's dismissal. Now Heymann's brother, Léon, spoke to suggest that when an arbitration had been reached the society was obliged to heed it; moreover it was insensitive of the committee to continue to hold his brother accountable for utterances made in the heat of the moment. Messager, on the other hand, was strongly opposed to accepting an arbitration over a committee decision, feeling that it compromised the very basis of the society's structure. Couppas rose to complain that the day after Taffanel's death, while the committee was considering arrangements for the funeral, Heymann had already indicated his animosity (presumably by limiting the society's response to the floral offering). Now his odious words were in the record, calumnies that could be neither proved nor erased. "Today you beg for the pity of the Société des Concerts, but it's too late for apologies."[45]

Attempting to end a long and increasingly bitter confrontation, Messager commented that a member of parliament wished to convey his influence in suggesting that the society content itself with accepting Heymann's resignation, pure and simple. That being the case, Messager went on, he found it all the more astonishing that Heymann still refused to resign. He then renewed the motion for a censure that would have in effect put Heymann on involuntary leave for a year; that motion, too, failed to get support. Nor, after all that had gone on, would resignation be accepted by the assembly. A *cas grave* was proclaimed, requiring fifty-nine of the eighty-nine voting to approve the dismissal of their colleague. The final vote was sixty-one favoring dismissal, nineteen against, eight blank, and one void. The motion thus carried.

Even this was not the end of the dispute. At the end-of-year assembly, on 26 May 1911, Léon Heymann asked for the floor at the very start of the meeting. Though he wished to be done with this *triste affaire*, he said, he had to protest the content of the minutes, so short in recounting his brother's defense and so deliberate in recording the "veritable vendetta" against him. He objected, too, to the committee's threat to resign if his brother's dismissal were not upheld. The members began to quarrel over what had and had not happened; Vernaelde, who had composed the minutes, complained that not being a stenographer he was unable to record word for word what had been said. But he took offense at the suggestion of a vendetta; he was far from taking pleasure over a fallen comrade. Messager gaveled the discussion to its end and ruled the incident definitively closed.[46]

By 1912 the various measures to increase ticket sales, and the general excitement surrounding Messager's reign, had begun to take effect. At the close of the eighty-fifth season (1911–12), the committee noted its opinion of the financial results: that, in spite of losses in 1909 and 1910, "the society is not in as bad a posture as one is tempted to think. The other associations, especially as it regards [the season just past], might well envy their elder sister."[47] With the financial situation stabilizing, the officers could begin to address the next most severe problem, the recruitment of younger members and retention of their elders. In 1911 a new short contract (*engagement*) for new members had been drafted, along with a summary *règlement* that would be given them at the time of signing. It specified that *aspirants* were to play exclusively for the Société des Concerts during a three-year apprenticeship at three-quarters of a full *sociétaire*'s earnings. Breaking the agreement during the contract period would result in a fine of 1,000 francs.

The *règlement* reiterated the expectations of French citizenship and affiliation with the Conservatoire, though noting that urgent exceptions might be made. The interdiction of women remained: *"Les Femmes ne peuvent devenir Sociétaires."* Punctuality was required, and those not attending the rehearsals would not be allowed to play the concert. All season activities, including tours, were obligatory. No one could refuse to take the seat designated for him by the conductor, nor refuse to play particular works.

Later articles specified mandatory retirement at age sixty and tried to put teeth into the exclusivity clause:

> No one may, without authorization from the committee, participate in other societies or enterprises giving periodic orchestral or choral concerts, nor play or sing in public concerts and official ceremonies led by conductors of one of said societies and enterprises.
>
> This interdiction extends to concerts given outside of Paris; it extends equally to all musical solemnities not organized by the committee that might take place in the Salle du Conservatoire between 1 October and the Assemblée Générale for the reckoning of accounts.[48]

But the majority of the *aspirants actifs* had not signed the new *engagement* and *règlement* by the opening of the season, complaining that the proposed three years of apprenticeship was too long and the penalty for early resignation too high. In December they sent two representatives (Samson and Mayet) to the committee to plead their case. Anxious to resolve this matter, the committee quickly agreed to a two-year contract and 500-franc fine for violating it.[49]

The young people continued to take more remunerative work elsewhere. In October 1913 the personnel manager complained that there were no affiliates of the Conservatoire left to convoke for temporary employment, since all the musicians on the roster of supplementary players had found permanent work. The committee's suggestion, that he contact the professors at the Conservatoire to urge their 1er prix students to add themselves to the on-call list, was met with the reminder that the prizewinners were the very musicians noted for not taking orchestral work seriously and for ignoring suggestions of veteran sociétaires.[50] ("Don't leave them by themselves on a stand; surrounded by their elders, they'll be more serious.") The effort to secure long-term contracts with the substitutes failed miserably; two of the best had left by year's end.

The 1912–13 season began on 12 November 1912 with the society's third appearance in the Lille hippodrome, the program dedicated to the memory of Massenet, who had died in August. Anchoring the subscription season in Paris were L'Enfance du Christ in late December and Schumann's Faust in February. Faust was also selected to open 1913–14 in a pre-season non-subscription concert. The eighty-seventh season was structured around a "chronological audition" of the Beethoven symphonies, a successful formula to which the Société des Concerts would return after the war, complimented by the Verdi Requiem on the occasion of the composer's centenary. In January the musicians traveled to Belfort to inaugurate the new concert hall there in a program now typical of the road appearances: Beethoven's Fifth, L'Après-midi d'un faune, the Meistersinger prelude, the Roman Carnival overture, Saint-Saëns's Le Rouet d'Omphale, and the Capriccio espagnol. Such programming was to show the orchestra's best wares, of course, but was also a function of leaving town with minimal or no rehearsal. In April they went again to Antwerp, likewise a third appearance. To conclude the Paris season they chose the Missa solemnis for the concert spirituel and the St. John Passion for the closing concert pair. That these noble works, so closely associated with the Société des Concerts at the height of its superiority, were to be among the very the last appearances of the society's chorus was, at the time, suspected only by the insiders.

The end-of-year assembly in 1914 found itself preoccupied with law-suits filed by the violinist Louis Duttenhofer, over irregularities in a competitive audition to reseat the first violins, and the flutist Léo-pold Lafleurance,[51] presumably concerning the principal flute seat just vacated by Hennebains and assigned by Messager and his committee to Gaubert. The incident is symptomatic of a general unrest over seat-ing and rights of succession. It was also the first occasion for which the society had had to allocate funds for a court case; there had been, and would continue to be, many threats of litigation, but the society had seldom if ever actually been to court. Lafleurance eventually lost his case, and resigned in 1917. His 1954 obituary recalled "a certain blus-ter that tended to hide the man's good heart . . . and great artistic probity."[52]

Finally the committee had paused once more to draft yet another pe-tition to the ministry insisting on a modern, comfortable venue. The Salle des Concerts, they observed again, was no longer respectable in terms of either public comfort or public hygiene (central heating and elegant lavatories having been promoted, we have seen, as a primary drawing card of the new Théâtre des Champs-Élysées). Their distance from the new Conservatoire seemed to make their connection with the academic institution less and less clear. And the government's increas-ing tendency to authorize use of the hall for purposes "having little to do with art music considerably diminishes, at least in terms of public perception, the value of its concession to the Société des Concerts."[53] All this was true, and similar points had been made many times before, but in 1914 there was nothing to be done about the stalemate.

André Messager, having served five years and having turned sixty in December 1913, was now required to stand for re-election. Before pro-ceeding to the vote, Messager asked his colleagues to allow him the courtesy of reflecting on his changed situation, the result of his rather sudden departure from the Opéra when his administration had col-lapsed. It would be a great joy and signal honor, he said, to continue to lead the Société des Concerts, but mindful of the need to put the good standing of the association before his personal interests, he needed his colleagues to understand that he could no longer simply turn his back on offers from abroad—the possibility, for instance, of six weeks in Bos-ton in 1914–15. He urged that they consider themselves at liberty to take any action they desired; his *amour-propre* was not engaged.[54] Vernaelde, the reigning elder, pronounced the customary courtesies, including the sentiment that whatever the outcome of the vote, their leader enjoyed the sympathy and admiration of one and all. (In 1919, on hearing the five-year-old minutes read aloud after Messager had in fact quit his post, Vernaelde remarked that he was not the admirer of Messager suggested by that rendition of the proceedings; his later written and oral delight with the work of Messager's successor, Gaubert, seems to underscore the point.)[55] Responding to a question as to the possible lengths of his absences, Messager had nothing firm to say but hoped that they would be infrequent and as short as possible. He then left the room.

The tenor of the discussion plainly favored keeping Messager as chief conductor. By tradition the post was a lifetime appointment, after all, and so far every conductor had served until his retirement from public appearances or unexpected death. It was observed that Messager's name, in and of itself, was of a certain value. The vote showed 60 favoring continued appointment and 13 blank ballots, with the customary applause greeting Messager's reentry. Gaubert was reelected *2ᵉ chef* with a slightly narrower margin of approval (54 favoring, 20 blank), and the assembly moved to consider the delicate matter of a *répétiteur de chant* to succeed Jean Gallon—delicate since many of the players by then imagined, and all of the singers feared, that the incumbent would not be rehearsing a chorus at all, but rather presiding over its dismemberment. Félix Leroux was elected.

The Société des Concerts adjourned in June 1914 more than a little aware of its uncertain future. On the positive side of the ledger were its eighty-seven years of primacy and the solidarity of its support for Messager, a powerful commander and a musician of true substance. Any future that did not promise its survival was unthinkable; its very longevity seemed a real advantage. On the negative side were the unsolved problem of venue and the volatile financial picture, the one widely thought responsible for the other. By the summer everyone was aware, of course, of the grave political situation in Europe; the assassination in Sarajevo occurred on 28 June 1914. Mobilization, which would at the minimum affect the third of the members in their twenties and thirties, was expected at any time.

The society's written record defines 2 August 1914 to 29 May 1919 as the Période de Guerre.[56] Germany officially declared war on France on Monday, 3 August 1914; 29 May 1919 was the day before the first Assemblée Générale since 1914. The eighty-eighth, eighty-ninth, and most of the ninetieth seasons elapsed without a functioning society and without internal documentation; beginning in March 1917 the Société des Concerts returned gradually, and then dramatically, to life in the ninety-first and ninety-second.

Initially the falling dominoes had little effect on cultural life in Paris; it was the summer vacation, when each year music crept to a halt anyway (or, as Prod'homme writes, "Paris took refuge in the casinos at the watering places").[57] But as the young men were called up and sent to the front, as the parliament adjourned and the government fled to Bordeaux, as the cinemas and *cafés* closed their doors, the *rentrée* was to eerie silence in a Paris deprived of its entertainments.

The Société des Concerts was forced to contemplate suspending its activities as it saw the ranks depleted by conscription of the younger members—two of whom later died in the trenches—and the impossibility of replacing the retirees. As in 1870, the musicians with country houses simply stayed away from Paris in the hope of waiting out the hostilities. In September and October 1914, working artists could only stand by and watch as their resources dwindled and their employment opportunities disappeared entirely. Once the military conflict had begun to settle into the trenches to the north and east, the prefecture of police encouraged the resumption of normal leisure activities; some two hundred establishments—mostly *cafés*, movie theaters, and music halls—reopened on 1 January 1915, though the Opéra did not resume productions until December.

At the Office of Fine Arts, Alfred Cortot helped organize an Œuvre Fraternelle des Artistes to find work opportunities for unemployed actors and artists and an Association des Anciens Élèves du Conservatoire that amounted in those years to a relief agency. For classical music it was agreed that the remaining members of the Société des Concerts would join together with their counterparts from the Colonne and Lamoureux orchestras, supplemented by retirees and external nonmembers —everyone, in short, who was still around—for the Sunday "symphony concerts, which have long been the very heart of our musical life."[58] Messager and his colleagues from the other orchestras, Pierné and Chevillard, would share conducting responsibilities with Rabaud and Henri Büsser, chief conductor at the Opéra. These *matinées nationales,* under the high patronage of the minister of public instruction and the undersecretary of state for the fine arts, were to take place (since the theaters remained closed) in the amphitheater of the Sorbonne— the splendid room decorated with celebrated frescoes by Puvis de Chavannes, "The Sacred Wood." Any proceeds past expenses would go to the war wounded.

The first *matinée* at the Sorbonne was on Sunday, 29 November 1914. In keeping with the venue and the political circumstance, the dean of the faculty of letters at the Sorbonne delivered a stirring patriotic oration. Subsequent programs included remarks by the undersecretary, members of the National Assembly, the university faculty, and the bar—among them Adolphe Brisson, Tristan Bernard, Paul Painlevé, and the publisher Flammarion. The typical program also featured scenes and monologues by noted actors of the era and would conclude with the *Marseillaise*. Already by the end of 1914, however, the orchestral partnership broke apart when the members of the other two symphonic associations formed a Colonne-Lamoureux orchestra that carried on through the war years independently.

In all there were twenty-six public events in 1914–15: twenty-two at the Sorbonne, three at the Trocadéro, and, on 11 July 1915 in the courtyard of the Sorbonne, Sophocles' *Oedipus Rex* with Mounet-Sully. Additionally the company was on hand when, on Bastille Day 1915, the remains of Rouget de Lisle were transferred to the Invalides to rest alongside those of Napoléon and his generals. The concert repertoire was limited to the art of the Allies—France, Russia, and England—and, given both the politics and the somewhat miscellaneous program content, tended toward short compositions of patriotic bent: Bizet's *Patrie* overture, a *Symphonie funéraire* of Théodore Dubois, and Henry Février's *Hymne aux morts pour la patrie* to a text of Charles Péguy.[59] Péguy had written the poem in 1913, then volunteered for service. In the aftermath of the battle of the Marne, though standing alone, he was shot to death in the forehead by retreating Germans (5 September 1914). The musical composition thus seemed a mystic premonition of the poet's heroic death, concluding:

> Heureux ceux qui sont morts dans une juste guerre!
> Heureux les épis mûrs et les blés moissonnés!
>
> Blessed are those who died in a just war!
> Blessed is the wheat that is ripe and the wheat that is gathered in sheaves![60]

The ovation that followed the first performance of Février's work, saluting the memory of a poet now read as the literature of one who had died for his country, was a high point in Février's career. "The *Hymne aux morts* followed me [through the war]," he writes, "until the day in 1918 when Clemenceau called for its singing, on a given day and hour, by the children of every elementary school in France."[61]

Major works performed at the national *matinées* included the *Fan-*

tastique, Scheherazade, Antar, and *Petrushka.* The nation's most celebrated living composers—Saint-Saëns, d'Indy, Fauré—participated by
appearing at the piano. Not everyone was impressed by the nationalistic display of a correct repertoire. "A most unfortunate consequence of
the great war," wrote the *Mercure de France,* for instance, "is that for a
long time we shall be deprived of the masterpieces that simply cannot
be replaced by the music of the Allies."[62]

In fact the "Eroica" Symphony managed to find its way onto a concert in the second season of the wartime *matinées,* which ran for twenty-
four programs from October 1915. These, it appears, consisted mostly of
classical music conducted by Henri Rabaud, soon to become a major
figure in the life of the Société des Concerts. Prod'homme suggests that
the repertoire was largely French: works of Chabrier, Franck, Lalo, Massenet, and the works cited above. Saint-Saëns appeared as concerto soloist, as did, in his uniform, the great pianist Alfred Cortot.[63]

Cortot was the most influential musical personality in the government,
and apparently the chief architect of an organized national propaganda,
where classical music had a key role. He had advanced to become chief
of staff in the Office of Fine Arts. When Clemenceau, in a wartime reorganization, suppressed the historic Bureau des Beaux-Arts, Cortot
moved to head the branch of the Ministry of Public Instruction and
Fine Arts that had as its mission harnessing the nation's art on behalf of
the war effort. This became the Section d'Action Artistique à l'Étranger, overseeing concerts, dance and theater productions, expositions,
and lectures abroad. The Action Artistique, as it was widely called, established social precedents noted by Franklin Roosevelt's Works Progress Administration and political precedents absorbed into the United
States Information Service. (Today the organization is called the AFAA:
Association Française d'Action Artistique.) Cortot's overall aims were
in perfect concord with Messager's program for rebuilding the Société
des Concerts, and together they were well positioned to recall musicians from their disarray into the service of the nation. A *soirée* with the
Société des Concerts, it was reasoned, was worth more than a dozen
volumes of published polemic.

So it was that players were assembled in early March 1917 to prepare
for a concert tour of Switzerland at the end of the month. Geographi-
cally, the plan was audacious and somewhat dangerous, for it involved
traveling south beyond the military front, then more or less beneath and
behind it; in Neuchâtel and Basel the musicians were within earshot of

artillery fire.[64] Strategically, the Swiss tour involved organization on a scale with which they had little if any prior experience: preparations for a week on the road, exchange of currency, questions of taxation and performing rights in a foreign country. Artistically, it posed, in addition to the obvious challenge of assembling adequate personnel and re-building a dormant repertoire, the delicate question of the society's merit as measured against major competitors, for not only had the Colonne and Lamoureux orchestras both visited Switzerland already but German conductors and orchestras would be appearing there si-multaneously with the French.

Responsibility for organizing the concerts was assigned to the firm of René Jean in Bern, who subcontracted the work to local music pub-lishers and theater enterprises. Posters and newspaper ads were readied, promotional articles placed with the press, and a printed prospectus widely distributed to known music lovers. In the French-speaking parts of Switzerland nearly all the tickets were sold in advance.

Meanwhile, in Paris, the committee deliberated on the choice of a repertoire suitable to attain their several goals. In the end it consisted of seventeen works arranged in programs of about 150 minutes in length:

Beethoven	*Egmont* overture, Third and Fifth Symphonies
Berlioz	*Benvenuto Cellini* and *Roman Carnival* overtures, *Symphonie fantastique*
Franck	*Rédemption* excerpt
Saint-Saëns	*Le Rouet d'Omphale*
Lalo	*Rapsodie norvégienne*
d'Indy	*Le Camp de Wallenstein*
Fauré	Nocturne (op. 57, no. 5), "Fileuse" from *Pelléas et Mélisande*
Dukas	*L'Apprenti sorcier*
Rimsky-Korsakov	*Scheherazade, Capriccio espagnol*
Debussy	*Nocturnes* ("Nuages," "Fêtes"), *L'Après-midi d'un faune*

There were eight concerts in as many days, beginning and ending in French-speaking Geneva and Lausanne:

Geneva	26 March 1917	Victoria Hall
Lausanne	27 March 1917	Cathedral
Bern	28 March 1917	Casino municipal
Basel	29 March 1917	Sankt Martins Kirche
Zurich	30 March 1917	Tonhalle
Neuchâtel	31 March 1917	Temple du Bas

| Lausanne | 1 April 1917 | Cathedral |
| Geneva | 2 April 1917 | Victoria Hall |

The contingent numbered eighty-three: Messager, eighty players, and two *garçons d'orchestre* (MM. Giboin and Nicet).[65]

The tour began well in Geneva, where the Victoria Hall was filled to its capacity of 1,700, and gathered further momentum in Lausanne, where a crowd of 2,600 packed the cathedral. This was not entirely unexpected, for the orchestra was in French-speaking and presumably sympathetic territory. The unknown began in Bern, where the musicians offered their wares to a primarily German-speaking public for the first time. Moreover, Felix Weingartner and the Darmstadt Orchestra had played Beethoven's Fifth, already announced for the society's own program, in Bern the night before. As it happened, the two orchestras, German and French, crossed paths in the Bern train station. ("Since that was neutral territory," a journalist noted, "the weapons stayed in their cases.")[66] The public of Bern turned out in greater number than for the Germans, and the victorious progress continued.

But it was in Zurich that an international triumph was confirmed. Again the hall was full: "full to bursting," said the newspaper, "and itching with enthusiasm." There was frenetic applause after each piece. Messager was called back to the podium ten times. In Basel, the profound meaning of an "Eroica" played by the Parisians at the door to Germany was lost on no one. All this paled by comparison with the delirium surrounding the orchestra's return to Geneva for their closing concert— "an unforgettable *soirée*, to be retained in the memory forever." More than two thousand tried to gain admission, with hundreds of turn-aways. Above the orchestra there hung the flags of Geneva, Switzerland, and France; afterward, at a diplomatic reception, government officials would speak at length to express the same sentiments that the flags so simply and elegantly conveyed. At the end there were incessant curtain calls, and when a crown of flowers mingling Swiss and French colors was presented to Messager, pandemonium broke out. One journalist wryly noted that the public response passed the limits of neutrality and became a patriotic demonstration: "Indeed no one will ever say again that the people of Geneva are proverbially cool and restrained."[67] On hearing of all this, it was rumored, Nikisch canceled scheduled appearances in Geneva and Lausanne.

More than fifty reviews appeared in the Swiss press. As they had done after concerts in Antwerp, Lyon, and Brussels, the committee extracted the best clippings to publish in a promotional leaflet. This time the brochure ran to twenty pages, in which the journalists seem to vie with each other to find superlatives, or to tremble at the necessity of rendering the magnitude of the effect in prose. Several admit to their inability to describe perfection.

"Those who maintain there is no such thing as perfection have never heard the Société des Concerts," for instance, as one review concludes.[68] Another describes *"distinction sans snobisme, sobriété sans sécheresse, sensibilité sans nervosité, esprit et rondeur sans vulgarité, pittoresque sans afféterie, exacte mise en place sans méticulosité."*[69]

The Swiss press booklet as published by the Société des Concerts is itself a work of propaganda, to be sure, and most of the journalists had their own pro-French politics to uphold. Nevertheless it affords an overview of how things were in those years that is, in many ways, unlike any other. One can hardly fail to sense the overflow of emotions prompted by the grand old orchestra offering its art on behalf of a nation overrun, and it seems reasonable here to give considerable excerpts from what was written. One, for instance, speaks of

> a ninety-year tradition of virtuosity of the purist and interpretation of the most authentic sort. . . . You have no idea of the prodigious unity of their performance: each musician from the same school, all with the same goal—that of glorifying music with all their might and all their talent. The secrets of virtuosity are transmitted from generation to generation. When one disappears his role is given by election to the most worthy successor, someone who has already lived in the *atmosphère de la maison*, hoping someday to earn the coveted title *sociétaire*. Their modesty equals their talent: at concert time they enter in order and silently take their places without tuning on stage. The *chef* follows them on without a wait, not soliciting applause. He is a member of the orchestra, their respected director, but also their friend and collaborator. . . .
>
> *Quelle admirable qualité de son, quelle grâce, quelle souplesse, quelles nuances subtiles!* Have you ever heard such balance of violins I and II, such perfect unity of timbre from violas, such bowing of cellos, contrabasses so in tune, so vigorous, and with such full sonority?[70]

Messager, for his part, was praised for the elegance of his gestures, absolute simplicity, respect of the musical text, and utter scorn of excess. The orchestra was held to be the greatest legacy of the Paris Conservatoire, almost without exception ranked at the head of the world's philharmonic societies. "Paris is the only city of the world to possess such an instrument" wrote one reviewer; another suggested in the same vein that "if the orchestras of Berlin, Leipzig, and Vienna are not strictly speaking inferior, . . . only this orchestra is capable of the subtlety and finesse it takes to propagate the modern French school."[71] A Lausanne paper summarized, it is worth repeating from chapter 1:

> In Germany you can easily enough find conductors who surpass in genius and personal magnetism the best French *chefs*, but nowhere else will you find an orchestra that even distantly approaches the orchestra of the Conservatoire of Paris. It has a unique gift, the result of the individual merit and artistry of its members. Everybody knows that what they do and possess to do it with far surpasses what even the better orchestras beyond the Rhine can offer. It gives the performances of this unique company a final polish, of an order and perfection that no other conductor will ever obtain—not a Nikisch, not a Richard Strauss, not a Weingartner.[72]

"People like to make comparisons," wrote another, who believed that the performance in Neuchâtel "surpassed that of the Berlin Philharmonic 10,000-fold. It expressed the genius of a people. Musicians in a German orchestra count for nothing, only the personality of the conductor. The Société des Concerts is a group where everybody is somebody—yet with a cohesion and discipline that unites the individualities." French art music was seen, as the presenters had intended, as worth the effort of learning it and able to hold its own with that of Berlin, Leipzig, and Vienna. "*C'est Paris qui est maintenant le vrai centre de la musique.*"[73]

"The essential difference between the German and the French orchestras," wrote another, "is that in the former the virtuoso is the conductor, the interpretation stamped with his personality and his temperament. With the French the orchestra is itself the virtuoso, and the conductor assumes a secondary position. . . . In fact it seems like this orchestra is independent of its *chef*; he conducted with such restraint that he would have got nothing had it not been for the tradition, innate so to speak." It was also a matter of subtlety—"latent rhythm," for example, "not the massive, hammered rhythms of the Germans."[74]

As always, the society's Beethoven was found especially revealing. Technically educated writers noted the detail of the bowing and other advanced nuances of the string ensemble. They would salute the famous wind players by name, then turn to the delicate sonority of the woodwinds, the suave color of the horns, the richness of the bassoons (which in Switzerland, curiously, were said to lack nasality; the early recordings suggest that this was hardly the case), the ability of the brass to sound

TABLE 10. Accounts, in French Francs, for Swiss Tour,
26 March–2 April 1917

Income	
Receipts	57,703.20[a]
Subvention	20,000.00
Profit on exchange	2,016.75
TOTAL	79,719.95
Expenses	
Per diem (82 travelers × Fr. 300)	24,600.00
Messager's fee	2,000.00
Travel	6,214.30
Luthier	444.00
Soc. des Musiciens suisses	1,000.00
Misc. bills	20,679.35
TOTAL	54,937.65
NET PROFIT	24,782.30
Distribution	
To musicians (80 × Fr. 300 + 200 to each *garçon*)	24,400.00
CARRYOVER	382.30

SOURCE: Swiss tour 1917: D17263 (5).
[a]See breakdown in table 11.

brilliant without covering. Here Beethoven seemed effortless, unnaturally natural.

It took time to reconcile the figures everyone knew would be favorable. There was the problem of mixed currencies, and a mild dispute over whether the *droit des pauvres* for Geneva should have been levied at 5 percent or 10 percent. (The police had come to the second concert to double the poor tax, observing that this was what the Colonne and Lamoureux orchestras had paid in Geneva, and threatened fines and cancellation if it were not remitted on the spot.) The final accounting reckoned a profit of 24,782.30 French francs, dispersed directly to the travelers, with each *sociétaire* given 300 francs and the two *garçons d'orchestre* offered 200 francs. The remaining 382.30 francs were, symbolically, placed in a new fund for future tours (table 10). The subaccounting of receipts shows the paid attendance at each concert (table 11). Artistically, financially, and politically, Switzerland could only be reckoned a major success.

The Action Artistique, like everybody else, sensed the significance of

TABLE II. Sub-Accounts for Swiss Tour, 1917

City	Number of Tickets Sold	Net Receipts (French Francs)
Geneva	1,681	8,087.85
Lausanne	2,394 [a]	8,835.25
Bern	1,533	6,102.80
Basel	923	5,055.60
Zurich	1,705	7,015.25
Neuchâtel	?	5,000.00
Lausanne	2,527 [a]	9,589.20
Geneva	1,662	8,017.25
TOTAL		57,703.20

SOURCE: Swiss tour 1917: D17263 (5).

[a] In addition, 146 gratis tickets were given for the first Lausanne performance and 145 for the second.

the accomplishment and set immediately about organizing new ventures abroad. Obvious destinations were Spain, England, and Italy; the Swiss journalists, meanwhile, had overheard talk of forthcoming visits to Argentina (in imitation of Messager's successful trip there in 1916 — alone, though it is held in the literature that the society went with him)[75] and the United States. By February 1918 plans for a visit to England in the fall were well advanced; a tour to Spain was organized for early summer, but this had to be abandoned at the last moment because of the internal civil unrest there and what turned out to be the concluding campaigns of the war.

Meanwhile a ninety-first season (1917–18) had been undertaken with a formula of ten concerts in the Salle des Concerts, eventually extended to twelve concerts between 2 December 1917 and 10 March 1918. In spring the rehearsals carried on despite the worst of the overhead bombings and stray shrapnel, though the minutes acknowledge in unusual understatement the "*influence fâcheuse*" of these on the music.[76] The season included first performances of *Souvenirs*, a symphonic poem by d'Indy; a Ukrainian Rhapsody for piano and orchestra by Sergei Liapunov with Ricardo Viñes as soloist; and two comments on the war by Théodore Dubois, *In memoriam mortuorum (chant élégiaque)* and *Évocation (1915!)*. The cellist Fernand Pollain played the Haydn concerto in his military uniform.

The plan for an extended tour of the United States took shape gradually during winter 1917–18 and spring 1918, its general outline drafted in

Paris by Messager and Cortot and in New York by Walter Damrosch and, increasingly, the American philanthropist and Francophile, Otto Kahn (1867–1934). The earliest date for which there is evidence of planning in full swing is 21 April 1918, when Cortot designated Édouard Risler to accompany the society to America as piano soloist.[77] But Kahn wanted Cortot himself as the soloist, and Damrosch had the notion that Cortot would premiere the Rachmaninov Third Piano Concerto in New York. (He eventually played the second performance, in January 1920.) The authorities would "find some money" to attract him—at least $5,000, plus first-class steamship passage across the Atlantic and first-class railroad accommodations in the United States.[78] Risler, serving the military in the rail yards near Chartres, had fallen from a train and was severely injured. Cortot, who had not played in public in four years, yielded to the pressure; and renting a house in Brittany for the summer, he mastered the Saint-Saëns Fourth Concerto, Franck Symphonic Variations, Schumann Piano Concerto, and d'Indy's Symphony on a French Mountain Air to take to America.[79]

The strongest pillar of the Franco-American relationship, however, was Otto Kahn. A Jew born in Mannheim, where he served in the German army, Kahn had learned his banking in London and there become ardently Anglo- and Francophile. His New York firm—Kuhn, Loeb & Co.—having been widely suspected of pro-German leanings, Kahn took it upon himself to become an inexhaustible orator and pamphleteer on behalf of the Allied cause and in favor of American involvement in the world war. His opinions were taken seriously by President Wilson and the cabinet.

Kahn was a firm believer in the power of the arts to win supporters to his cause. Having been in the audience at the 1909 Paris premiere of the Ballets Russes and perhaps present for the opening of the Théâtre des Champs-Élysées (in which he had taken a major financial position),[80] he had used his position as principal stockholder of the Metropolitan Opera to assure the New York visit of the Ballets Russes in January 1916. For the return visit of the ballet company that October, he convinced the French authorities to grant Pierre Monteux leave to abandon the trenches for the pit. (This particular tour cost Kahn personally $500,000. "I must atone for my wealth," he often said.)[81] At the Met he went on to promote *Pelléas et Mélisande,* Dukas's *Ariane et Barbe-bleue,* and Rabaud's *Mârouf.*

Anxious to see the Anglo-French alliance firsthand, Kahn sailed for England in early May 1918. (The submarine menace was at its height, and there would still be danger when the Société des Concerts sailed later in the year. Kahn said he was frightened but exhilarated.) He brought personal greetings from Wilson to Lloyd George and was carrying a letter from Theodore Roosevelt to Clemenceau. He crossed the channel to France on 27 May.

The arrival of the legendary American *"grand ami de la France"* was much heralded. On reaching Paris he presented the Société des Auteurs Dramatiques a gift of 10,000 francs and a widely publicized note: "Only a great poet could find the words needed to express what I feel, as a man and an American, toward France, that nation so noble and proud, whose territory is *la Terre Sainte de l'humanité.*" [82] Kahn saw the effects of the spring bombardment of Paris by the "big Berthas" and "Gotas," then visited General Pershing at the front during the Battle of the Aisne (27 May–5 June 1918).

On 6 June 1918 Otto Kahn and André Messager co-signed a contract for a fifty-concert tour of the United States by the Société des Concerts. [83] The sponsors were Kahn's own French-American Association for Musical Art; the French legation in New York (Haut-Commissaire de la République Française aux États-Unis) and its cultural attaché, Henri Casadesus, the United States government, and eventually local American agencies, usually the War Council of the local Chamber of Commerce. The general manager of the tour would be the impresario Richard G. Herndon, with Max Hirsch assigned as tour director to accompany the musicians.

Walter Damrosch, for his part, arrived in Paris to continue the negotiations insofar as they concerned New York, and to conduct a Bastille Day 1918 festival concert, supported by the New York YMCA, at the Conservatoire. The all-French program included the Saint-Saëns Organ Symphony with Nadia Boulanger at the organ and the Franck Symphonic Variations with Cortot. The national anthems preceded and concluded the program; proceeds went to the Red Cross.

The American itinerary as announced circled from New York north to Boston and back, then south, then westward to California, and back through the Midwest, Chicago, Toronto, and Montreal. This underwent considerable change as events unfolded. [84] The repertoire as first drafted was substantial:

Beethoven	Symphonies 3, 5, and 7; Piano Concertos 4 and 5; *Egmont* and *Leonore* No. 3 overtures
Berlioz	"Fête chez Capulet," from *Roméo et Juliette; Benvenuto Cellini* and *Roman Carnival* overtures

Bizet	*Patrie* overture
Chabrier	*Gwendoline* prelude
Chausson	Symphony
Chopin	Andante Spianato and Polonaise (Cortot)
Debussy	*L'Après-midi d'un faune, Nocturnes* ("Nuages," "Fêtes"), *La Mer*
D'Indy	*Symphonie sur un chant montagnard français, Le Camp de Wallenstein*
Dubois	*Frithjof* overture
Dukas	Symphony, *L'Apprenti sorcier*
Fauré	Nocturne de *Shylock;* "Fileuse," "Ballade" from *Pelléas et Mélisande*
Franck	Symphony; *Rédemption;* Symphonic Variations (Cortot)
Lalo	*Rapsodie norvégienne; Symphonie espagnole*
Liszt	*Les Préludes*
Rabaud	*Procession nocturne*
Rimsky-Korsakov	*Capriccio espagnol*
Saint-Saëns	Symphony No. 2 in A Minor; *Le Rouet d'Omphale; Danse macabre; Le Déluge,* prelude; Piano Concertos 2, 3, 4, 5 (Cortot); Violin Concerto No. 3
Schumann	Piano Concerto (Cortot)

These were arranged into six sample programs submitted to the local presenters.[85] In fact the customary concert played on the tour began with Bizet's *Patrie,* then continued with Beethoven's Fifth or Third, *L'Après-midi d'un faune* or *L'Apprenti sorcier,* the Saint-Saëns Fourth Piano Concerto with Cortot, and for a finale the *Roman Carnival* overture—much the same, that is, as the concerts the orchestra had played on the road for many years.

The contract called for a minimum of fifty and a maximum of sixty concerts to be presented by the Société des Concerts, comprising all its eighty-two musicians *titulaires* with all their necessary instruments, conducted by Messager himself or, if he was prevented by reason of *force majeure,* Philippe Gaubert. Cortot was expected to play in the major cities, perhaps twenty or thirty times. (In the event he did rather less than this with the society, but appeared nine times on his own, then extended his stay with four recitals for Steinway and recording sessions for Columbia. America opened a whole new life for him, and afterward he returned to the United States for six further concert tours.) These concerts, the contract noted pointedly, were not to exceed two hours. A global fee of $60,000 would be guaranteed the Société: $30,000 to be

TABLE 12. Budget, in Dollars, for American Tour, 1918–19

Travel Paris / New York / Paris	15,000
Hotel, 70 days (× $4 × 82 musicians)	22,960
Ground travel U.S. and Canada	35,000
Guarantee to Société des Concerts	60,000
Ten extra concerts (at $600)	6,000
Management, publicity	10,000
TOTAL	148,960

SOURCE: Contract: D 17263 (36).

deposited in Paris one month before departure, the other $30,000 to be paid at the rate of $600 per concert at the end of each week; with an additional $600 for each concert over the minimum of fifty up to the maximum of sixty concerts. Additionally each member would receive a $4 per diem to a maximum of seventy days. The sponsors likewise undertook to pay first-class steamer passage for all the musicians, and ground travel in the United States by *wagon-lit* (Pullman), or touring-car (bus). The overall budget, which was finalized during the summer of 1918 in conference with Henri Casadesus, was just short of $150,000 (table 12).

Profits in excess of the guarantee were to be split between the Société des Concerts and the French-American Association, with the hope of garnering at least $5,000 or $6,000 for the work of the Red Cross. The draft contract was written in New York by an attorney at the French mission (a former member of the Société, it was later noted) and was sent to the musicians in France with Casadesus and by American consular mail pouch to Otto Kahn, also in Paris. A somewhat different final text was signed by Kahn and Messager; already there were hints of discrepancy between the French *manière de voir* and that of the Americans. Kahn then proceeded from Paris to Spain, returning home in July to report to President Wilson; he deposited the first $30,000 at the Crédit Lyonnais in August, with one paper reporting (doubtless correctly) that he had personally guaranteed the entire budget. Kahn's efforts on behalf of Franco-American relations were recognized later that year with his appointment as *chevalier* of the Légion d'Honneur.

Meanwhile a telegram from Columbia Records (USA) arrived at the Conservatoire, inviting the Société des Concerts to record for Columbia on an advance of $7,500 against a 15 percent royalty. The records would be sold on tour. The committee agreed that the orchestra spend the time between their arrival in America on 2 October and the first concert, scheduled for the 8 October, recording six works chosen from their tour repertoire.[86] Soon afterward Howard Wurlitzer of the Rudolph Wurlitzer Company in Cincinnati wrote of his excitement at the impending visit and to express his firm's willingness to provide instruments (cellos, doublebasses, harps, and percussion), assistance at any of the twenty-four Wurlitzer outlets, and considerable corporate influence—"for it is our duty as an ally of France to help propagate the reputation of French artistry in our country." The Wurlitzers asked only to be recognized as official purveyors to the tour and to be allowed to send one of their own technicians along.[87] Their offer in fact solved a major technical problem: the transport of the large instruments and a piano for Cortot.

For an ensemble of eighty whose total experience on the road had so far been day trips and the week in Switzerland, the American tour was an undertaking of positively Yankee proportions—a high drama with the threat of German torpedoes and epidemic disease, three months of sudden absence from whatever work the musicians had in Paris, and the inevitable confrontations, not only with the unexpected but also with business and finance on an unprecedented scale. It was also certain to take a good deal of raw courage. More than a few of the musicians were at first reluctant, and Messager was disinclined to force the issue except to say that it was all or nothing; everybody went, or there would be no tour. "In his place," wrote Cortot, "I harangued the musicians. I argued that the dangers of a wartime crossing were little enough compared with those faced by the soldier in the battlefield. Was not the orchestra, moreover, on a governmental assignment? It was impossible to retreat, in these conditions. It would be shameful, both in the eyes of France and of its ally, America."[88]

There was a particular problem with the players who also served in the military band of the Garde Républicaine, some four or five, including Louis Costes, the principal clarinetist; Louis Bas, English horn; and Emmanuel Chaine, the principal trumpet. Their director refused to consider granting them leave in high wartime; Messager wrote in their behalf, arguing the essentially patriotic "goal of introducing and promoting our music teaching and our music traditions."[89] The commanding colonel responded that despite the society's admittedly noble purpose, an absence for that long of his best players would cause him real damage in the event of equally important public ceremonies at home. The military governor-general of Paris, not wanting to create a precedent, refused to receive Messager to hear his appeal.[90] The issue remained unresolved for weeks, with Messager insisting that he would not leave without the players from the military band and the ministry insisting the tour not be canceled. Finally the orchestra got the upper hand, and all but one (Bas) actually made the trip.

The Société des Concerts at last assembled on 17 September 1918 for the first of four days of rehearsals, expecting then to sail from Bordeaux on the twenty-first. Of the eighty-two musicians on the published roster, more than two dozen were not, in fact, *sociétaires* but rather *aspirants* or substitutes. Just before they were to leave, two more—the violinist Eugène Lestringant and the principal cellist, Marcel Magard—were called to active duty and had to be replaced. The harpist Pierre Jamet contracted influenza and had to cancel as well. Each of these changes of personnel was in its own way a critical problem, but none so grave as the transportation crisis that emerged in the last week of September.

The musicians were booked to sail from Bordeaux on 21 September 1918 aboard the luxury liner *Rochambeau,* but this voyage was canceled when an examination of the hull revealed that it had been too badly damaged by Axis submarines to take on passengers. An alternative booking was found with the steamer *Aeolus,* scheduled to sail from Brest on 29 September. (The first concert in New York was to be on 8 October 1918; as a crossing took between eight and ten days, the orchestra was already in danger of compromising its schedule.) The Société des Concerts traveled from Paris to Brest by special train on 27 September, expecting to board the next day and cast away the following dawn.[91]

But on 28 September, with the orchestra on board, the sailing of the *Aeolus* was also forbidden (for unspecified reasons—perhaps it was needed for a military purpose). Late that afternoon, the United States Army's supply depot issued an order to board the musicians on the "first available transport" to the United States.[92] The passage would be free, if crowded and ordinary of accommodation; meals were to be billed to the passengers. At least the arrangement afforded some hope of meeting the American itinerary. Accommodation was found on the American ship *Louisville,* and the orchestra and its baggage were offloaded from the *Aeolus* to the *Louisville.* Baggage and equipment were lost in the shuffle, it was later discovered, and the hornist Delgrange was diagnosed with tuberculosis by the American ship's doctor and forbidden to board. The military order lists eighty-two passengers altogether, including Messager, Cortot, the concertmaster's wife (Marie-Louise Brun), and at least one *garçon d'orchestre.*

This meant that the orchestra was leaving France short four of the eighty-two contracted players, which was to cause repercussions when they came to reconcile accounts the following spring. The roster already being published in the United States by concert promoters and the manifest for passage on the *Louisville,* then, differ in many particulars.[93] Among the substitutes were the young conductors Robert Siohan and Vladimir Golschmann in the strings and possibly the composer Léon Moreau covering fourth trumpet.[94] The orchestra appears to have traveled with only three horns, two trombones, and one harpist.

The *Louisville* finally embarked on 2 October and arrived in New York harbor on the morning of 12 October—four days after the announced beginning of the concerts, twelve days after the agreed-upon week in advance. On the East Coast the influenza epidemic was at its peak, and health authorities had forbidden public assemblies in many of the cities where the orchestra was to play. For Herndon and his management staff this added a new complication to the already herculean task of rescheduling fifty concerts across the country. While the musicians were still in New York, the flu claimed one of their number, the violinist Eduardo Fernandez, an *externe* from the Opéra; it was necessary to arrange services and transportation of the body back to France. Also during the first week in New York the *garçon d'orchestre* abandoned them, apparently to seek a new, if undocumented, life in America. His duties were added to the other chores overseen by the committee and largely performed by the *commissaire du matériel,* Julien Gaillard.

The New York debut was on 15 October 1918 at the Metropolitan Opera. The program was, by American standards, far too long: the Franck D-Minor Symphony, *L'Apprenti sorcier, Le Rouet d'Omphale* of Saint-Saëns, Berlioz's *Benvenuto Cellini* overture, Lalo's *Rapsodie norvégienne,* and "Nuages" and "Fêtes" from Debussy's *Nocturnes. Le Rouet d'Omphale* and *L'Apprenti sorcier*—that is, the storytelling music—gave particular pleasure; the "amplitude and quality" of the winds was noted. At the end Kahn presented Messager a magnificent golden crown—and was himself decorated with his Légion d'Honneur.

The second concert, on 20 October, was received with equal enthusiasm, though in the large house the sonority seemed small, and a reviewer remarked that French music remained "little liked and misunderstood" in the United States. He meant that as a compliment and a salute to the "first-order propaganda effort," but it can be read either way.[95] It was another very long program: Bizet's *Patrie*, *L'Après-midi d'un faune*, excerpts from Franck's *Rédemption*, the *Roman Carnival*, Beethoven's Fifth, and the Saint-Saëns Fourth Concerto with Cortot.

It seems certain that the recording sessions with Columbia took place between the two New York concerts—that is, during the third week in October 1918. (The matrix dates, which probably indicate the day the master was shipped for production, run from 17 to 24 October.) The orchestra recorded, and Columbia subsequently released, eight four-and-a-half-minute sides (thus in most cases abbreviating the musical text). Five of the eight selections were outside the concert repertoire, suggesting that the musicians had brought along a good deal of music for encores.

Saint-Saëns: Prélude to *Le Déluge* and *Le Rouet d'Omphale*
Columbia A 6087

Delibes: "Les Chasseresses" and "Cortège de Bacchus," from *Sylvia*
Columbia A 6090

Charpentier: "Sérénade" and "À Mules," from *Impressions d'Italie*
Columbia A 6101

Rimsky-Korsakov: *Capriccio espagnol*
Saint-Saëns: "Bacchanale," from *Samson et Dalila*
Columbia A 6122[96]

The recordings were advertised in the printed programs on a full page taken by Columbia: "the *only* phonograph records on which you can hear the exquisite music of the French Symphony Orchestra (La Société des Concerts du Conservatoire de Paris)." (The designation "French Symphony Orchestra" also appears on the disc labels.) A second full page went on:

> The Paris Symphony Orchestra makes records exclusively for Columbia.
>
> To those who know the exquisite tone, the smooth, rich volume and the absolute fidelity of reproduction for which Columbia Records are famous, this is no surprise. It is natural that this great ensemble of master-musicians should select such a medium to carry their wonderful artistry to the music-lovers of America.
>
> And, long after the musicians themselves have returned to la belle France, you may still have the joy of hearing in your own home their wondrous music, exactly as you have heard it today, on Columbia Records.

> The profits of the French Orchestra are being turned over to French War Relief Work.[97]

It seems likely that the manufactured products caught up with the orchestra as they proceeded southward.

The orchestra also recorded a number of other faces never released, apparently because Messager did not approve of their quality. These included excerpts from *L'Arlésienne,* Messager's own *Les Deux Pigeons,* and *Coppélia;* and very probably the orchestral accompaniment—since the matrix number falls squarely in the series—for Hulda Lashanska and Hipolito Lazaro in "O terra addio" from *Aida* ("vocal duet with orchestra").[98]

By the time the Société des Concerts reached Washington, D.C., on 8 November 1918, airplanes overhead were showering down newspapers proclaiming "War Is Over"—and news of Caruso's divorce. The hall was decked with tricolored bouquets, and revolver shots rang out during the concert. A woman approached Messager and suggested that, as a result of the victory, "You will make a great lot of dollars."[99] The armistice, on 11 November 1918, came while the orchestra was in Richmond, Virginia, and the concert there turned into a civic celebration, with a long, loud ovation that gathered into general havoc. Richmond was remembered by the musicians as the turning point of the journey, from a plagued wartime campaign into a euphoric transcontinental progress. (Richmond is also remembered in the annals of the Société des Concerts for a decidedly less happy turn of events, since it was there, during the first tour of the new Orchestre de Paris in 1968, that Charles Münch was found to have died in his sleep.)

The multicolored programs and souvenir brochures for these "patriotic symphony concerts," headed by crossed flags and concluding with notice that "*The Star-spangled Banner* and *The Marseillaise* will be rendered during the evening," went out of their way to underscore the overt political aims of the visit. Short program notes did their best, given the language barrier, to explain the French repertoire. In the case of *The Sorcerer's Apprentice,* for instance:

> This symphonic poem, in Scherzo form, illustrates musically Goethe's Ballad which ironically depicts the adventure of an old magician's indocile (intractable) servitor, who, thinking he retains the words with which his master actuates the evil spirits, unchains a liquid tempest which he is powerless to control. It requires the return of the magician to restore all things to order.[100]

Post-concert receptions—a memorably elegant party at the San Antonio Country Club, for instance—afforded at least the opportunity for the two cultures to mix more personally, though at such affairs the rank and file generally amounted to onlookers, and there was always the problem of language. For the rest it was the decidedly mundane business of three hundred miles a day on buses and trains—"always too hot or too cold," said Charles Münch of a later American tour, and "always dirty."[101] Always behind schedule, too, with the musicians always tired, invariably short on changing rooms, and generally short on cigarettes and coffee. For much of the tour the musicians traveled by special train and would often dine and change for the concert onboard, then return to their compartments to sleep as the train made its way by night to the next destination.

In El Paso, on the Mexican border, they heard the fusillade of partisans fighting a few kilometers away, across the Juarez bridge—much as they had heard the German artillery from Basel in 1917.[102] Before the San Diego concert there was an error in the itinerary and transportation, and a portion of the orchestra missed the performance. The contingents had been reunited by the time of the Los Angeles concert on 3 December in the (original) Shrine Auditorium, days after a civic orchestra concert had been canceled by the public health authorities during the flu epidemic. The reviewer, Jeanne Redman, was taken above all by the choice of Beethoven's Fifth at the very moment of victory over Germany: "To have given us the greatest work of the greatest composer, was a piece of French subtlety hard to surpass." But it was not a German performance, and Fate stayed away from the door: "There was no knocking here, but a suave and smoothly presented work of art." Nor was there tremendous volume (in a legendarily tremendous venue of some six thousand places), "but the unison of the veterans, some of whom, notably one of the 'cellists, played with a serene indifference to the printed page, gave breadth to the tone." Messager conducted without a score, she noted. Cortot earned the honors of the second half in the Saint-Saëns concerto, with such prolonged applause that Messager "took on the air of the Frenchman who wished he were at home"; Cortot then offered Liszt's Second Hungarian Rhapsody as an encore. ("The French dress [it] up too much.") The piano and orchestra were out of tune with each other, which must have been a frequent occurrence with the European-built wind instruments and a lower pitch-standard than was customary in the United States; but overall the review found the quality "beyond dispute," and the horn playing, in particular, "outstanding."[103]

In San Francisco, more than eight thousand—one estimate had the crowd at ten thousand—turned out to hear the Société des Concerts in the Civic Auditorium, the largest public, said Max Hirsch, that had ever heard the orchestra. San Francisco, with its substantial Franco-American populace, offered a natural venue for a patriotic event, and 4 December 1918 was proclaimed "tricolor day" in the city. Some half the members of the San Francisco Symphony (Alfred Hertz, conductor) were either French or spoke French well enough to "fraternize with the artists of the Paris orchestra and make them feel at home," or at the very least offer them "a typically warm and hearty Western welcome"[104] during the day-long festivities that had been planned. But the train from Los Angeles was delayed, and a ceremonial luncheon had to go on without them. The train pulled in at 2:30 in the afternoon, and after brief remarks from the mayor, Hertz, and representatives of the sponsoring Musical Association of San Francisco, the musicians were loaded into a caravan of forty automobiles, each hosted by a French-speaking Symphony musician, for sightseeing to Golden Gate Park, the Presidio, and the beach. The musicians were returned to their train to dine and dress for the concert that evening—a standard program with the standard glowing response for Messager, Cortot, and the players. A similar scenario was played out in Oakland the next night.

But by the time the orchestra reached Sacramento on 6 December, the influenza had spread to the west coast—the headline in the *Sacramento Bee* read "San Francisco Remasks"[105]—and a decision was made, there at the junction of the north-south and east-west rail lines, to abandon the leg that was to have taken the group to Portland, Seattle, Spokane, and Boise (then Denver and north toward Fargo) in favor of the direct rail line via Denver to Oklahoma City / Tulsa and north to Kansas City. From Kansas City on 15 December they continued north to Sioux City and Minneapolis / St. Paul, then back down to Chicago via Milwaukee.

In the American west the promoters had successfully sold the notion that hearing the Société des Concerts was "a privilege that but few of the French can boast of"—or, as the *Bee* had it, "Sacramento Given Opportunity to Hear Concerts That Is Denied Majority of French." "The tickets are not sold, as they are in this country," said the story, "but are handed down as treasured heirlooms from father to son; in short, the admittance to the concert hall is hereditary."[106] In Chicago, by contrast, there was apathy, partly because the concert pair came on the Sunday before Christmas (22 December 1918 at 3:30 and 8:15 P.M.) and partly out of the American equivalent of chauvinism; the reviewer thought the performance made clear that "the Chicago Symphony is, as intimated in earlier issues of the *Daily Tribune,* the First Orchestra."

The papers suggest a few dozen patrons for the *matinée* and a few hundred for the evening. "So sparse was the gathering that André Messager, still tall and straight and handsome with his sixty-fifth birthday a bare week off, inspected it, in the frequent intervals of warm and real applause, with wide-eyed incredulity."[107]

After Christmas the crowds and spirits improved as the orchestra carried on to Indianapolis, Louisville, Cincinnati / Dayton, and Detroit. Indianapolis, for instance, held a parade in their honor led by the mounted police, and there were receptions at both the city hall and the state capitol.[108] From Detroit the journey continued to Cleveland and Pittsburgh, then northeast along the bottom of the great lakes to Rochester and Syracuse and finally Montreal.

Once the momentum of the tour had been established, the committee's principal concern turned to getting home again. This was a sensitive issue back in Paris, where leaves had been reluctantly granted to begin with and, as it turned out, postwar nightlife was re-establishing itself. The players from the Opéra were expected back on 1 January 1919; several of the churches were threatening to replace their missing employees. En route to Louisiana the committee had written Herndon, their New York impresario, that steamship passage had been assured for 2 January and that it would be impossible to continue past that date. Envisaging dispute on this point, since all fifty contracted concerts would not have been played by then (owing, the committee held, to *force majeure*), they caused a copy of the contract to be prepared and notarized in New Orleans on 18 November. From Kansas City on 15 December, Messager dispatched a strong letter to the effect that the tour must reach its definitive conclusion on 28 December, by which time the orchestra would have played about forty-five concerts.[109]

Herndon telegraphed, in response, that he and Cortot had completed a revised itinerary, in which a fifty-second concert in Burlington, Vermont, would conclude the tour on 6 January 1919, with return passage booked on the steamship *Espagne,* departing on 8 or 9 January. The per diem would of course be continued. From Chicago on 22 December the committee wrote to Messager, who had left the tour to conduct in New York (at the invitation of Walter Damrosch), that in view of the problem of appearances canceled by the epidemic, the players would consent to play fifty concerts through 4 January. But to account for fees lost to the musicians for engagements they already had in Paris, the price for concerts in the new year would double to $1,200. The disappointment of the players not to be relieved after their contracted eleven weeks on the road is made very clear; they had indicated that they would refuse to work if not entirely satisfied on the question of fee, and they demanded an immediate response by telegram.

"We take pleasure," Herndon replied, "in honoring the terms of our contract, including those clauses to which your committee has repeatedly drawn attention." At the same time he objected to Messager's appearances in New York, since the chambers of commerce in Dayton, Cleveland, and Youngstown had threatened to cancel their commitments in the event that Messager stayed in New York and turned the remaining concerts over to Gaubert.[110] It appears that Messager yielded on this point, for on 26 and 27 December he confirmed general approval of Herndon's plan and a departure on 7 January. Concerts already announced for 8 January at Carnegie Hall and 9 January in New Haven were thus canceled.

In Montreal on 4 and 5 January 1919, the orchestra had to appear at midnight because the Loew's Theatre ran its scheduled movies earlier in the evening. The orchestra played a good half of its repertoire during their stay in the city: four symphonies (Franck, Dukas, Chausson, d'Indy); three overtures (Bizet's *Patrie* and the two Berlioz overtures); the Franck Symphonic Variations; fragments of Franck's *Rédemption;* Rabaud's *Procession nocturne;* and seven symphonic poems, including two foreign works: *Les Préludes* and the *Capriccio espagnol.* The absence of Beethoven was not noticed, but the reviewer lamented that Fauré and Ravel had not been heard.[111]

On 6 January the group traveled by bus for the 100-mile trip south to Burlington, on Lake Champlain, and immediately after the fifty-second concert that evening reboarded for the overnight journey of 350 miles to New York Harbor, where they met the *Espagne* for the morning departure on 7 January 1919. The crossing took ten days, and the players were in Bordeaux on the morning of the seventeenth, reaching Paris on the nineteenth and twentieth.

The Société des Concerts went on to offer nine Sunday concerts in their own hall—but without the chorus—from 23 February through 27 April. In early April they traveled again to Bordeaux for a concert,[112] then on 11 May 1919 presented their particular celebration of peace, a gala at the Trocadéro with Beethoven's Ninth and the Saint-Saëns Organ Symphony.[113]

Messager had stayed in New York to join the Franco-American Association (Herndon and possibly Kahn) and the French High Commission

TABLE 13. Disputed Accounting, in Dollars, for American Tour, 1918–19

Debit Société des Concerts	
Losses due to change of itinerary, additional printing, etc.	2,700.00
Four missing *sociétaires* (× $731.70)	2,926.80
Two extra concerts (doubletime disputed)	1,200.00
Funeral for Fernandez	285.00
Hotel New York (recording sessions)	2,184.00
TOTAL	9,295.80
Credit Société des Concerts	
Meals, transportation France / New York	ca. 1,800.00
TOTAL OWED FRANCO-AMERICAN ASSOCIATION	ca. 7,496.00

SOURCE: Mémoire-Rapport: D 17263 (36).

(Cortot, Henri Casadesus, and career diplomats, including the brilliant young André Tardieu, soon to be prime minister of France) in clarifying the contested points of the accounting. His capacity for such negotiations was already well established, and both he and the committee assumed that final settlement would be simple enough. That was not the case. The parties reached an impasse almost immediately, and according to one account Messager cried *"inutile de causer plus longtemps"* ("no use chatting any longer") and left saying he would resolve the matter privately with Otto Kahn. (He later denied this version of the story.)[114] He sailed for France three weeks afterward, believing that matters had been resolved to the satisfaction of his committee. As the exhausted conductor boarded his ship, Herndon passed him an envelope Messager assumed to contain the final payment.

What was in the envelope, instead, was Herndon's controversial reckoning of accounts, which showed the Société des Concerts owing nearly $7,500 to the Franco-American Association. Herdon had charged the final ledger with nearly $3,000 for the four players the society had been short from the contracted eighty-two, a part of the hotel bill in New York that he thought the responsibility of Columbia Records (USA), $1,200 for the two concerts he had paid at double fee, and various other losses having to do with the changed itinerary (table 13).

Additionally there was a strong disagreement with Columbia Gramophone Association, which had advanced the society $10,000 against royalties and was now demanding a refund of $3,924. Much of what was recorded had not been approved for release, the advanced amount was not reached in royalties due, and sales in any great number stopped, Columbia said, with the end of the concert tour.[115] (In fact the firm kept the titles in print for some time, and later appears to have recouped and rereleased some of the selections.)

Herndon, for his part, had never grasped the governing structure of the Société des Concerts, especially the concept that final authority lay not with Messager or Cortot but with the committee. He rationalized the standoff as a labor dispute: "It seems that a committee of three of the orchestra met almost daily on trains and rendered certain decisions coupled with telegraphed threats to refuse continuing unless their interpretations of the various clauses were immediately accepted." It was, he recalled, a "very disagreeable time."[116] Nor did Herndon understand the society's practice of dividing up global proceeds as opposed to player-by-player fees—a critical issue, in that the orchestra was short players to start with and had incurred the death of another during the tour. This made no difference to the committee, expecting to divide the global amount promised. It was particularly vexing to Herndon that the committee insisted on counting the fee for the "dead artist" in their version of the accounts; he thought it should go instead to the widow.

The society reckoned all the changed circumstances for which Herndon sought to deduct expenses—the lateness of their arrival in New York and resulting need to restructure the schedule, the shortage of four players, the two concluding concerts played under duress, and the per diem for the Columbia recording sessions—to be cases of *force majeure*. Far from incurring increased expense, they argued, the promoters had realized savings on the ship passage from France to the United States, the per diems not required for the missing musicians, and so forth. The dispute dragged on into late spring 1919; Herndon visited France in early June but failed to appear for his appointments with the committee.[117] A few days later Messager was enlisted to intervene directly with Otto Kahn, who responded in July with his customary grace but without giving satisfaction:

> I must tell you how much I regret that the American tour of your great orchestra, which was a considerable success from the artistic and emotional points of view, has ended up, as a secondary result, in a misunderstanding in financial matters. As I told you when I had the pleasure of seeing you in New York before your departure, I was not personally familiar with the monetary details, but I insisted that the affair be arranged in a spirit of complete liberality from our point of view. . . . I had hoped that the points where the Société des Concerts and Mr. Herndon failed to see eye to eye could be resolved before the orchestra left New York, and if not, certainly during

Mr. Herndon's visit to Paris. I am greatly disappointed to discover that agreement has not been reached. . . .

I know Mr. Herndon to be an honorable man, highly motivated and conscientious. I am equally convinced that the Société des Concerts would not want to accuse him of anything unjust or inappropriate. You understand that it is impossible for me to ignore Mr. Herndon pure and simple, and to put his objections aside: this would be unfair to him and would reduce his authority and his responsibility as manager of the French Association. Thus I suggest that you submit this controversy for mediation to the consul general of France in New York or to the chair of the French High Commission. It would be entirely satisfactory to us to concur with the decision of either of these men. We hope that the society will also find this satisfactory, and that in so doing we could find, with mutual trust and good will, the solution to this most regrettable incident.[118]

Kahn's response was an undeniable setback for the committee, and their determination to emerge victorious from the fray hardened considerably. They referred their side of the case to the American Federation of Musicians for arbitration, arguing now that the compensation was poor in any case, to which Herndon replied that no other touring orchestra had ever reached the salaries attained by the orchestra during the tour.[119] Meanwhile the French-American Association dissolved in the wake of failed projects (notably a tour proposed by the Société des Instruments Anciens, founded in 1901 by Saint-Saëns and Henri Casadesus) and the consequent fading of commitment by its principal French participant, Casadesus—owing also to the illness of his wife and his return to Paris to conduct at the Opéra-Comique.

Not until 1921, after intervention from both the Ministry of Foreign Affairs and the Office of Fine Arts, was the account for the American tour of 1918–19 liquidated. The final resolution was signed after a meeting of 12 March 1921 at the Ministry of Foreign Affairs. The document paid homage to Otto Kahn, who had already covered much of the disputed amount; he may also have covered the $3,924 still contested over the Columbia recordings.[120]

André Messager resigned in April 1919, a decision he probably reached on his way home from the United States to France. The letter he submitted to the committee cited "various incidents which took place during the tour," and concluded that "the attitude and state of morale of a certain number of the orchestral artists do not permit me to solicit the Assemblée Générale for the renewal of my mandate, which expired at the end of 1915."[121] Friction with Gaubert had intensified as the American tour progressed, and Messager must have been keenly vexed that his right to accept guest conducting engagements—thus, perhaps, establishing an ongoing relationship with Damrosch and the New York Symphony Society—was challenged by both the tour organizers and the *sociétaires*. He quickly resurfaced as conductor at the Opéra-Comique (1919–20) but by then had already begun to suffer from the kidney disease to which he succumbed in 1929. Philippe Gaubert, who had served as second conductor for fifteen years, was elected to succeed him at the Assemblée Générale of 30 May 1919.

Henri Grévedon (1776–1860):
Portrait of Beethoven,
after Ferdinand Schimon,
*"propriété de la Société des
Concerts du Conservatoire,"*
1841

Eugène Guillaume (1822–1905):
Bust of Beethoven, 1888

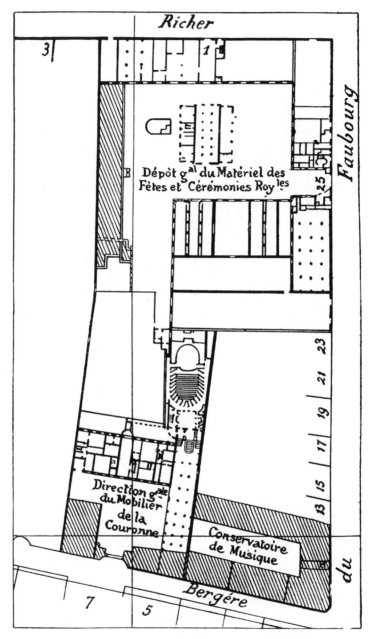

Site plan, the old Menus-Plaisirs and the Conservatoire, 1836

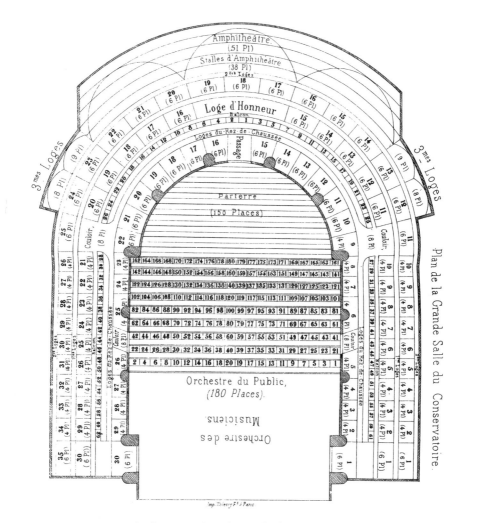

Audience seating plan, Salle des Concerts

A concert at the Conservatoire, 1843

Entry to the Concerts du Conservatoire, 1848

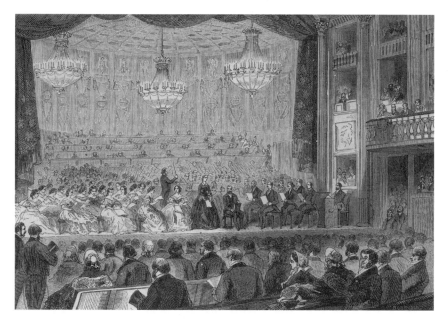

A concert of the Société des Concerts du Conservatoire, 1861

Gaubert and the orchestra, Salle des Concerts, 1937

ÉCOLE ROYALE

De Musique et de Déclamation Lyrique.

2me. CONCERT

CONSACRÉ A LA MÉMOIRE DE V. BEETHOVEN,

MORT LE 26 MARS 1827;

Le Dimanche 23 *Mars* 1828.

Programme.

Nota. Tous les morceaux qui seront exécutés sont des productions de ce Compositeur célèbre.

PREMIÈRE PARTIE.

1°. Symphonie héroïque (*généralement redemandée*).

2°. *Benedictus* avec chœurs et récits chantés par Mme. CINTI-DAMOREAU, Mlle. NÉLIA-MAILLARD, et M^{rs}. ALEXIS DUPONT et LEVASSEUR.

3°. Premier morceau de concerto de piano en *ut mineur*, exécuté par Mme. BROD.

4°. Quatuor de l'opéra de *Fidelio*, chanté par Mme. CINTI-DAMOREAU, Mlle. NÉLIA-MAILLARD, et MM. ALEXIS-DUPONT et LEVASSEUR.

5°. Concerto de violon, exécuté par M. BAILLOT (*Ce concerto n'a jamais été entendu à Paris*).

DEUXIÈME PARTIE.

6°. *Le Christ au Mont des Olives* (Oratorio avec chœurs). Les parties récitantes seront chantées par Mme. CINTI-DAMOREAU, et MM. ADOLPHE NOURRIT et LEVASSEUR.

L'orchestre sera dirigé par M. HABENECK.

Ve. BALLARD , Imprimeur, rue J.-J. Rousseau, No. 8.

Program for all-Beethoven concert, 23 March 1828

GRANDE SALLE DES CONCERTS, RUE BERGÈRE, 2.

Conservatoire National de Musique.

SOCIÉTÉ DES CONCERTS.

21ᵐᵉ ANNÉE.

CONCERT EXTRAORDINAIRE

DONNÉ

AU PROFIT DES BLESSÉS

Aujourd'hui DIMANCHE 5 Mars 1848, à 2 heures.

PROGRAMME.

1° *La Marseillaise*;
2° Symphonie en *ut mineur*,　　　　de BEETHOVEN;
3° Affranchissons notre patrie,
　(chœur d'*Euryante*),　　　　de WEBER;
Les solos seront chantés
Par Mᵐᵉˢ GUEYMARD, BALANQUÉ et GÉNIBREL.

4° Septuor,　　　　　　de BEETHOVEN;
5° Chœur de HÆNDEL (Chantons victoire.)
Les solos seront chantés par Mᵐᵉˢ GRIMM et POINSOT.

L'orchestre sera dirigé par M. HABENECK.

AVIS.

Le 5ᵐᵉ Concert, dû aux Abonnés, est remis au Dimanche suivant 12 Mars.

Le Bureau de Location sera ouvert de 11 h. à 2.

Le Public est prévenu qu'il y trouvera encore des Places.

PRIX DES PLACES :

Premières et Galeries 8 fr.; Secondes, Rez-de-Chaussée et Orchestre 6 fr.; Stalles d'Amphithéâtre et Troisièmes Loges 5 fr. 50 c.; Parterre 5 fr.; Amphithéâtre 2 fr.

Paris. — Imprimerie de Vinchon, rue J.-J. Rousseau, 8.

Handbill for concert of 5 March 1848, following the
revolution in February

AMERICAN TOUR

AUSPICES OF THE FRENCH GOVERNMENT

Société des Concerts du Conservatoire de Paris

ANDRE MESSAGER, Chef d'Orchestre

DIRECTION OF THE FRENCH AMERICAN ASSOCIATION
FOR MUSICAL ART

OTTO H. KAHN, Chairman

LIBERTY HALL

EL PASO, TEXAS

Friday, 8:15 p. m., November Twenty-ninth

Nineteen Eighteen

Auspices of the El Paso Chamber of Commerce

Program for concert of 29 November 1918, El Paso

Marcel Landowski, André Malraux, Charles Münch,
Orchestre de Paris, 14 November 1967

Lucien Thévet, *horn;*
Robert Casier, *oboe:*
Salle Pleyel, 22 March 2002

Robert Doisneau (1912–94): place du Marché St-Honoré, 1948

PART FOUR

1919–1967

Three major developments define our last era: recording, broadcasting, and the hegemony of the star system. Of these the first has obviously proved most consequential to our understanding of the "modern" Société des Concerts. But at the time, by far the greatest impact on the orchestra was that registered by the maestro and star concerto soloist—fostered, to be sure, by the radio and records. We enter the period of "the great conductors," Toscanini and Stokowski and Koussevitzky in the United States, but still more significantly the Weimar-Republic Berliners, then at the height of their powers: Furtwängler, Klemperer, Erich Kleiber, and Walter. All were known, from tour appearances or the mass media, in Paris. Walter's identification from 1928 with Paris and the Société des Concerts, coming close on the heels of the Concerts Koussevitzky (which Virgil Thomson thought the best by some distance of the Paris orchestral offerings), taught the French what impact a great conductor could have on orchestral performance.

These are only the most palpable indicators of a substantially increased pace of change. After World War I it became necessary to experiment with solutions that would allow the major step of engaging guest conductors, eventually those of foreign birth. The demise of the resident chorus posed both a programming void and the budgetary issue of how (and who) to pay on an ad hoc basis. Admission of a ticketed public to the Saturday morning dress rehearsals delivered a new kind of audience and, unexpectedly, a major new source of income. The impresario-sponsored concert became commonplace, leading to multiple experiments with venues beyond the Salle des Concerts. The outside concerts, too, brought the musicians a significant new income, as did the recordings: a landmark series of early electric-microphone 78s conducted by Piero Coppola through the justly celebrated stereophonic recordings of the mid-1960s. Before the outbreak of World War II most of the components of year-round, exclusive employment of the musicians were in place. This was in part the result of a hostile but successful takeover of the administration, and thus the agenda, by young radicals of the administration—the proximate cause of Gaubert's resignation.

It seems reasonable to identify, from the several parallels between the years following 1870–71 and those after 1914–18, a kind of cycle in the affairs of the Société des Concerts. On the one hand, the history and principles that bound it together enabled it to negotiate even the harshest of crises with some dignity and to re-emerge on Sunday afternoons in an almost relentless permanence. On the other, the very same institutional givens consistently allowed the inevitable mutations of politics, taste, and culture to take the Société des Concerts by surprise. The goal in time of trouble was always to reopen the temple for the worship of artifacts from a more perfect past. That the radically changed circumstances of all the society's constituencies—the public, the musicians both internal and external, and the composers whose work was the only thing that could promise a real future—demanded something more aggressive than reaction seems to have occurred to too few of the members, and too seldom. Their unbridled euphoria over the new opportunities brought by the impresarios, broadcasters, and the recording companies was doubtless merited at the beginning. In hindsight they seem terribly late in recognizing the true costs: the astounding inflation in artist fees, the erosion of their loyal public, the formidable size of the stay-at-home audience.

Charles Münch and his secretary-general, Jean Savoye, negotiated the Société des Concerts through World War II with what was, under the circumstances, remarkable grace. An active concert life was assured throughout the Occupation by various clever tactics and rationales: the emergence, for instance, of a significant program of educational concerts for young people. Münch himself nourished, though there was considerable objection from Savoye, his particular interest in new music, especially that of Ropartz and Honegger—imbuing in turn such works as *Jeanne au bûcher* ("Joan of Arc at the Stake") with patriotic nuance in a nation overrun. The often fraught business of living out the war masked the emergence of a quite substantial involvement in contemporary, if prevailingly conservative, music. Immediately after the war, cultivation of such a repertoire became an ever more strident condition of the *cahiers des charges* attached to government subventions.

Both Münch and Cluytens sought to become maestros. In both their cases, success in that ambition meant breaking contracts based on the old rules that bound them to the Société des Concerts, thus restricting their artistic choices and limiting their opportunity to access the vast audiences abroad. Both ruptures were harsh, and after Cluytens the post of chief conductor was left unfilled. By the 1960s it was held in many quarters that the Société des Concerts was underfunded and second rate, no longer able to represent the best of French culture to the outside world. The first of these propositions was undeniably true; the second may well have been true of the orchestra's live concerts (though not, I think, of the best records). Since it was a point of André Malraux's ambitious cultural agenda that Paris compete effectively with Berlin, London, and Vienna, it was thus necessary to constitute, one way or another, a modern, fully funded Orchestre de Paris. It was just as necessary to bring Charles Münch home to conduct it.

CHAPTER 10

Gaubert

(1919–38)

At the close of the 1918–19 season the Société des Concerts had its first assembly in five years: 30 May 1919. The secretary's report pointed with natural pride to the wartime activities: the Sorbonne concerts, two foreign tours, and the successful, if admittedly ad hoc, sessions of 1917–18 and 1919. Decisions were made to enable the governing committee to be reconstituted in an orderly re-election pattern. Toward the end of the meeting came the first controversial item of business—tactfully described in the published agenda as "letter from twenty *sociétaires* on the present and future of the society"—to address the thoroughgoing organizational changes that would characterize the postwar era.[1]

The letter, dated 5 May 1919, was the work of the violist Albert Seitz, emerging from the war years as one of the society's most powerful administrators. It began by noting the substantial rise in postwar cost of living and the dramatic decline in each *sociétaire*'s earnings: about half, in 1919, of what it had been before the war. Had there been a chorus for the nine concerts that season, the value of the *jeton* would have been still less. If both orchestra and chorus were to be used for the forthcoming 1919–20 season, Seitz continued, the value of the *jeton* would be some 5 or 6 francs, down from 10 or more francs in the first decade of the century.

Further, Seitz and his orchestral colleagues argued, public taste for the big chorus-and-orchestra works, opera excerpts, and *a cappella* vocal repertoire had evaporated in favor of the popular vogue for "no matter which" suite or symphony. This point was dubious, even in the context of the wreckage of 1914–18, and subsequent events proved it quite wrong indeed. Chorus-and-orchestra works continued to draw a large public whenever they were programmed; and later the Orchestre de Paris was constituted from the first with a large affiliated chorus, much as the original society had been.

In any event, an annual income of a few hundred francs per *sociétaire*, it was reasoned, would mean the certain death of the organization, since it would no longer be a competitive recruiter of young musicians. "Paris has long counted on us to have the very best of the performers. From here on, no one will come to us but those who didn't get accepted into the other societies." The current members would watch helplessly as the Société des Concerts became "old and decrepit."[2]

Of the three options for financial reorganization advanced to the musicians, two—moving to a modern, spacious hall in a better location, thus promising enhanced ticket sales; and commercialization of the society by an impresario or commission of prominent donor-executives—presented formidable, and time-consuming, obstacles. The Lamoureux and Colonne orchestras, already capitalized, were known to be dissatisfied with their own arrangements, and neither had a full resident chorus. Major donors were, as has nearly always been the case with orchestras, in shorter supply than the musicians generally imagined. The only viable solution appeared to be the separation of the orchestra and chorus, thus allowing the orchestra to seek its own fortune unencumbered by the singers. Four scenarios were presented to the membership:

- A divorce, pure and simple, along amicable lines recognized to be in the best interest of the association
- A dissolution of the society as envisaged in the existing statutes, followed by the reorganization of the chorus into a powerful association that might be engaged by any of the Paris orchestras
- The "extinction" of the chorus by attrition, with each remaining chorus member receiving full rights until retirement (a solution proposed, and defeated, some years earlier)
- If none of the above, a mass resignation of the instrumentalists, who would then reconstitute their orchestra on other lines.[3]

This final measure, though acknowledged as a desperate last resort lacking all social conscience, was nevertheless an effective threat.

After reading the prepared text, Seitz went on to develop his thoughts, apologizing to his colleagues of the chorus for their bluntness but certain of the need for an awakening, however rude. Julien Gaillard, who would serve as *archiviste-caissier* for the next eight years, observed that the committee's good will toward comrades of the chorus had been shown by its decision to consider the post-season Trocadéro concert (11 May 1919: Beethoven's Ninth and the Saint-Saëns Organ Symphony, the first official appearance of the chorus since before the war) a component of the session, thus qualifying the singers for stipends. But the Trocadéro concert had yielded only 320 francs for division among nearly one hundred members, a "ridiculously small amount" per *sociétaire*. Adding that modest sum to the overall season income and distributing the whole among all the members was, under the circumstances, only fitting. The choristers had thus, however, effectively drawn on the orchestra's earning power—a practice that could not be sustained for long.

At this juncture the assembly was suspended to allow the singers time to caucus. It is no great surprise that they returned with a less-than-enthusiastic preference for their demise by attrition. An agreement was soon reached whereby each vocalist—there were perhaps a dozen left, all men—would continue as a full *sociétaire* until his mandatory retirement date plus one year of *sursis*. He would earn his *jetons* by attending general assemblies, supplementing any outside chorus that might be engaged, and appearing at the Sunday concerts in some production capacity, most often as ticket taker. For an institution that took considerable pride in the fraternal care its members had traditionally extended to each other, this solution was just barely dignified. And it was thoroughly undignified with regard to the women singers, who were simply dismissed.

Nevertheless, the players went on to complain about the 20 percent withheld from each member's earnings for the communal Caisse de Prévoyance, since this resulted in redistributing income earned by the players into the retirement accounts of the remaining singers. Vernaelde, a singer, rose with the noble thought that assuring the life of the society was worth more than the comfort of one's own old age; he would donate his own account, if necessary, back to the Caisse de Prévoyance that the Société des Concerts might not die. With that not-so-empty gesture, followed by a "great salvo" of applause, the matter was decided. The dissolution-by-attrition plan carried with 56 in favor, 8—most of the singers, that is—opposed.[4]

A number of problems stood in the way of an orderly transition to concert life without *sociétaires du chant:* where, for instance, a competent chorus might from time to time be found, and how it might be financed. There was the particular question of the *répétiteur du chant*, who was by statute a member of the governing committee, and a good deal of alarm over how to replace the repertoire just lost. But the arrival at a crossroads had been generally acknowledged, and a fundamental decision had been reached as to the new order of things. The number of *sociétaires* now stabilized at 80, down from a high of 120.

Only then did the assembly proceed to what would have been in any other context the central decision of the era: electing a first conductor. Here, however, the decision had in essence already been made. Philippe Gaubert was the committee's single nominee (though Francis Casadesus had proposed his own candidacy by letter), and he carried a two-thirds majority on the first ballot: 49 favoring Gaubert, 1 in favor of Cortot, and 12—again, surely, the singers—blank. André Tracol, the popular principal second violinist, was elected second conductor by acclamation. In the same manner Seitz became the new secretary, succeeding Tracol, and the other members of a new committee were ratified. The post-war governance of the Société des Concerts was at last in place.

In the year following the armistice Philippe Gaubert thus claimed his rightful place at the head of the French orchestral establishment, appointed 1er *chef* at the Société des Concerts in 1919, then professor (of flute, succeeding Hennebains) at the Conservatoire in October 1919, and finally 1er *chef* at the Opéra in 1920. Born in Cahors on or about 5 July 1879, he had enrolled at the Conservatoire as a pupil of Taffanel, whose favorite and heir apparent he soon became. In 1894, at the age of fifteen, he garnered the 1er *prix* in flute, and three years later had settled comfortably into the flute section at the Opéra. Meanwhile he followed the traditional curriculum in counterpoint and composition with Xavier Leroux, Georges Caussade, and Charles Lenepveu, taking in due course the prize for fugue and a Second Grand Prix de Rome (1905).

Observers were quick to remark on the closeness with which Gaubert's career seemed to follow, twenty-five years later, that of Paul Taffanel. Certainly the mentor left his disciple a strong sense of the multiple opportunities open to a virtuoso flutist / conductor / composer. Taffanel and Gaubert enjoyed a long and collegial friendship, publishing together, for instance, an edition of the Mozart concertos. Gaubert's influence on the French flute school is arguably as great as that of

Taffanel and Hennebains; his *Méthode de flûte* (1923) and compositions for the instrument are still studied. Among his first students was Marcel Moyse, who succeeded him in the flute section of the Société des Concerts and as professor at the Conservatoire.

Named *sociétaire* in 1901, Gaubert spent virtually the whole of his career, more than thirty-five years, with the Société des Concerts, nineteen of them as its chief conductor—a record surpassed only by Habeneck and only by a year. Gaubert was twenty-five when elected *2ᵉ chef* in 1904, thirty-four when he succeeded Hennebains as principal flutist. His military service in World War I was closely followed in the press, and his celebrity was by then well enough established for him to have been the first to be given leave to travel to the United States with the orchestra in 1918. He returned, if there were ever much doubt about it, as designated successor to Messager.

After the war Gaubert's careers as flute soloist and conductor, and arguably as composer, became international in scope and presented a not inconsiderable challenge to his loyalty to the orchestra he had served for so long. For one thing, the fees he commanded away from the Société des Concerts were greatly in excess of his (lion's) share of the *répartition,* even in good years. It is thus to his substantial credit that he never fully abandoned his Paris colleagues. Although he disappeared with growing frequency as the years passed and became irritable about having to fulfill his obligations as *1ᵉʳ chef,* his final separation amounted to a legitimate retirement.

Gaubert was well recognized for his work, appointed to the Légion d'Honneur in 1921 and elevated to the rank of *grand officier* in 1929. He was in failing health by the time he retired in March 1938, and if the support of his musicians was by that time conspicuously eroding, they nevertheless acclaimed him honorary vice president for life as they bid him farewell. He died a little over three years afterward, on 8 July 1941.

Like Deldevez and Messager, Gaubert was an accomplished composer. By the measure of frequency his works were programmed by the Société des Concerts, with something over two dozen performances, he was greatly more successful than either of them. Nor was this an overt case of a conductor programming his own compositions, as had been feared in the case of Berlioz's candidacy in 1863. Gaubert's committees appear to have been genuinely fond of his music—though after his death it quickly disappeared from the repertoire, unlike, say, the music of Henri Rabaud. Gaubert's orchestral music, strongly influenced by the Debussy "sound," was also popular with the Lamoureux and Colonne orchestras. His opera *Sonia* had been produced in Nantes (1913); the ballet *Philotis* (1914) reached the Paris stage. *Naïla,* a *conte oriental* considered the major work of his middle age (1927), was staged at the Opéra, where Gaubert was first conductor.

Gaubert's most successful orchestra work was the *Cortège d'Amphitrite,* a *tableau musical* after the poem by Albert Samain, composed in early 1911 and read by Messager and the orchestra that April—though it does not appear to have been heard on a Sunday concert before March 1918. With Gaubert's accession to the podium of the Société des Concerts came the routine introduction of his music, often songs to round out a vocal soloist's set: for instance *Soir païen,* sung by the soprano Julia Nessy from 1922, with the flute solo work by Marcel Moyse. The F-major *Fantaisie* for Violin and Orchestra was played by both Claude Lévy and Firmin Touche (1925, 1927) on its way to becoming part of a full-fledged concerto; similarly the *Concert en fa* for orchestra premiered in 1932 appears to have been the predecessor of an F-major Symphony first performed in February 1937. *Les Chants de la mer,* three symphonic *tableaux,* was first performed by the Société des Concerts at a festival concert in Vevey in September 1930, then offered on a subscription concert that November; *Les Chants de la terre* followed in March 1932. In the meantime the two-part symphonic poem *Au pays basque* had been given its first Conservatoire performance in February 1931. In 1936 Gaubert recorded both *Les Chants de la mer* and *Les Inscriptions pour les portes de la ville* (four scenes, 1933; first performed at the Sunday concert of 3 February 1935) with the Société des Concerts. The orchestra also premiered Gaubert's *Divertissements sur un choral* on 20 February 1938, during his final season.

From Taffanel's conducting class at the Conservatoire Gaubert absorbed the ideals of the citizen-*chef:* disciplined rehearsal technique, discretion of public gesture, a wide repertoire anchored by Beethoven and extending into the best of the contemporary literature. He gained the bulk of his podium experience on succeeding Georges Marty in 1909 as conductor of the summer casino concerts in Vichy, where he had been Marty's assistant. His nervous public debut with the Société des Concerts, substituting for Messager, was followed by appearances in January 1913 and December 1913–January 1914. It is likely that Gaubert conducted some of the concerts during the American tour of 1918–19; certainly he did at least a part of the preparatory work.

The press habitually called Gaubert a "great conductor," and a colleague remarked that "no one equals him in the speed with which he perfects even the most complex works. [He rehearses] without the slightest hesitation, in minimum time, with precise indication of what he wants and the way to get it."[5] More than one observer mentions his unfailing seriousness of purpose in the mission of conducting. Following Messager's lead, he clearly enjoyed the growing celebrity accorded star conductors and appears to have stamped the orchestra's traditional performances with his own personality; the one-among-equals theory of conducting was fading fast away. One also has the impression that Gaubert's earthy, almost peasant-like orientation toward his life and work were a welcome counterfoil to Messager's studied elegance—some would have said pretentiousness.

It was thought at the time that Gaubert's taste ran to "big, noisy works like the *Fantastique*."[6] Certainly he was fond of Berlioz, and his *Les Troyens* at the Opéra was much admired, but on the whole there is rather less Berlioz than in the heady years of discovery led by Deldevez and Taffanel. After Beethoven, the non-French composer most frequently programmed continued to be Wagner, with half a dozen or more performances every season. Gaubert's other passions were for the Russian repertoire and Ravel, and he introduced a healthy and on the whole laudable corpus of new or unfamiliar music by French composers of both the old and new generations: Widor, Chausson, Duparc; Caplet, Schmitt, Honegger, Hahn, Milhaud. His curiosity extended to Stravinsky *(Fireworks)* and Prokofiev (the Third Piano Concerto, *The Love for Three Oranges* suite), Richard Strauss *(Taillefer),* and a little Liszt.

But one does not sense the thirst for discovery or the much-vaunted zeal to bring foreign works to Paris that had characterized the work of Garcin and his successors. Gaubert's mission, to the extent that it can be isolated from the general spirit of the epoch, seems to have centered on perfecting the French virtuoso repertoire since 1880 and assuring that masterpieces premiered or promoted by others reached the Société des Concerts in due course. During Gaubert's tenure the shift in focus from a primarily Classical and Romantic literature, more often than not by foreigners, to one dominated by late-century French masters, Wagner, and the Russians—the opulent style of post-Romanticism—is manifest. On the road, where the Société des Concerts increasingly identified itself as a representative of the nation's best art, the programs always included two or three of the orchestra's "new" signature works:

in Lyon in 1928, for instance, *Mother Goose,* Honegger's *Pacific 231,* and Ibert's *Escales.*

The repertoire of the Gaubert years is as noteworthy for what it does not contain as for what it does. While the Beethoven symphonies and piano concertos continued at the core of each season, and the Ninth Symphony and *Missa solemnis* were frequent centerpiece works, Mendelssohn all but disappeared entirely and there was very little Haydn. A few great Mozart symphonies and concertos remained; of Schubert there was the Great C-Major, the "Unfinished," and a performance or two of an orchestrated *Erlkönig.* There was virtually no Brahms, and no Tchaikovsky at all.

The mutations of an orchestra's repertoire are only partly the result of conductor decisions, and certainly at the Société des Concerts the committee remained at least theoretically in charge of programming. What was of course most conspicuously absent from the repertoire during Gaubert's tenure was that portion that a resident chorus had made possible. A good deal of what had made the character of a Sunday concert at the Conservatoire distinct from the other Sunday concerts simply evaporated. A dozen or so central orchestra-and-chorus works remained—the Ninth, the B-Minor Mass and St. John Passion, the Fauré Requiem, sung not by *sociétaires* but by hired choruses—vestiges of a distinguished repertoire that had included Renaissance *a cappella* works, a great deal of Bach and Handel, incidental music and operatic excerpts in abundance, the full *Roméo et Juliette* and *Damnation de Faust* of Berlioz, and some of the greatest works of Franck, Gounod, Saint-Saëns, and Dubois.

A growing proportion of the repertoire was suggested by the soloists of note who now appeared on nearly every program—or by their managers acting for them. Germaine Lubin, a favorite of those years, often sang Wagner, sometimes, from 1931, with the popular tenor de Trévi. Ricardo Viñes played *Nights in the Gardens of Spain;* Marguerite Long's Chopin was all the rage. Such "early music" as was heard was often brought by the Casadesus family and Marguerite Roesgen-Champion, a pioneer of the harpsichord revival. And many of the first performances of music by younger composers were scheduled largely in order to qualify for the government subventions that came with a *cahier des charges.*

It was said of Gaubert that beneath his veneer of good humor and peasant charm there lay a cold, enigmatic person whom one could encounter for decades without really knowing. Gaubert's moments of irascibility, as preserved in the written record, are somewhat reminiscent of Habeneck's. Several of his most fetching photographs have in common a bemused, perhaps mischievous glint of the eye; more often than not the stub of a cigarette dangles from his mouth in what was a fashionable look of the time. One has the impression of a no-nonsense, verbally terse artist-craftsman more devoted to *métier* than to the taking of a long-considered philosophical stance. Certainly Gaubert enjoyed his stardom as much as Messager had. This led to his willingness to be away and in turn to the very gradual but unstoppable motion toward relying on guest conductors, even foreigners. But on the whole what most characterizes his tenure is the way his approach was rooted in institutional traditions extending back to 1828. He was the last of the conductors raised in the true spirit of the "old" Conservatoire.

In retrospect Gaubert's era seems the period of the most sweeping changes of all: the replacement of the "classical" canon with the post-Romantic, mostly French repertoire, the often controlling influences of celebrity soloists and conductors and their managers, the increasing capitalization of the society in terms of fee-driven appearances both in Paris and on the road, broadcasting and recording—all to be considered part of a now-venerable institution's struggle to maintain stature in a modernist climate where old age alone had few advantages. It was under Gaubert that the Société des Concerts confirmed its international standing, now measured less by comparison with the rival Paris societies than with what was to be heard from Berlin and Vienna and New York. Yet cosmopolitan listeners seldom anymore placed the Conservatoire concerts on a plane with the highly promoted concerts of the visitors and immigrants. The society was seen as a reliable, indeed essential component of Parisian art, but the thrill was to be found elsewhere. In fact Paris was generally perceived as an eccentric place to do orchestral business.

Another fundamental change in French musical life took place when Gabriel Fauré was retired from the Conservatoire in 1919 after fifteen years as director, to be replaced by Henri Rabaud. After two full five-year terms of office (1905–09, 1910–14), Fauré's mandate, like the mandates of nearly everyone else in authority, had been extended until the end of the war. In September 1919 it was renewed for a single year—the traditional signal that one should seek one's retirement. Fauré's health had been deteriorating for some time; indeed he was taking a cure at Bad Ems when the war broke out. He was in the habit of wintering in the Midi, thus missing a good deal of the Paris season, and since 1918 had been unable to shake a severe bronchitis. His deafness had reached a "deplorable state." Since he was worried about his financial circumstance in retirement, the government paved his way with various inducements and indemnities: a stipend as honorary life director of the Conservatory, and, on 26 April 1920, elevation to the rank of Grand Officier of the Légion d'Honneur, virtually unknown in musical circles.

Fauré's successor, Henri Rabaud (1873–1949), was already a staunch admirer of the Société des Concerts, in a way Fauré had never been. For one thing, Rabaud had literally grown up in its shadow; he was the son of the cellist and faithful servant of the orchestra Hippolyte Rabaud, the grandson of the flutist Dorus, and the great-nephew of the violinist Victor Gras and Mme Gras-Dorus, the celebrated opera star. He was a respected composer of works the players already knew, notably *La Procession nocturne* (op. 6, 1899), and a capable conductor who had served a season with the Boston Symphony Orchestra. He often covered Pierné's absences at the Colonne concerts and led performances at both the Opéra and Opéra-Comique. Rabaud was to serve nearly two decades as director of the Conservatoire and president of the Société des Concerts.

Following the precedent established during the wartime concerts, Rabaud was often to be seen on the podium of the Société des Concerts. Both Gaubert and the titular second conductor disliked this practice, Gaubert remarking on one occasion that while Rabaud "might be an illustrious musician, he's a mediocre personality."[7] But Rabaud and the players seem to have exchanged a real affection. When asked in 1948 to inscribe the society's *livre d'or*, he remarked that he had not missed a single concert between 1884 and 1894, when he would have just been turning twenty-one. "It was [the Société des Concerts] that made me love music, that made music the cult of my entire life. Having had the honor to be its president for twenty years, how would I not sense the most faithful attachment and the most fervent gratitude?"[8]

Postwar adjustments, even more than the aftermath of 1870, changed everything about the Société des Concerts—its economy, its aesthetic, its daily life. Vernaelde thought its physiognomy profoundly modified.[9] Yet he described the ninety-third season (1919–20) as the best in his memory, consisting of a dazzling juxtaposition of the old—the Beethoven symphonies in chronological order—and the new: Fauré's *Masques et bergamasques,* Dukas's *La Péri,* Debussy's *Ibéria* and *Petite Suite* (orch. Büsser), works of Hüe and LeBorne, a septet by Théodore Dubois. Nadia Boulanger appeared as organ soloist in a Handel concerto, seeing to it also that the lovely song-cycle *Clairières dans le ciel* composed by her late sister, Lili Boulanger, was added to the program.

The five years from 1919 also saw the largest influx of new members since 1828, as Gaubert and his committee struggled to rebuild an orchestra that had nearly died out during the war and that had, in any event, existed for some time largely on the questionable strengths of the very young and the very old. Most of Messager's principals had retired, and Gaubert himself, of course, had vacated a principal seat to take the podium. In an effort to lessen an inadvertent reliance on temporary players of "novice musicality," the best of the substitutes from the war years were elevated to the rank of *aspirant* with the promise of full membership a year later—and the stern reminder that being a *sociétaire* included the obligation to travel with the orchestra and the implicit liberty so to do. There were particular problems along these lines with the brass players from the military band; the Brussels trip of May 1920, for instance, conflicted with the band's appearances in Switzerland.[10]

Nearly three dozen new *sociétaires* were elected during the Gaubert's first three seasons, and another two dozen just afterward. Auditions for the winds were held on 2 October 1919, after which there began to emerge a stunning ensemble led by Marcel Moyse as solo flute, with Jean Boulze and Albert Manouvrier as his seconds. (Moyse's career was short and tempestuous—strongly reminiscent of Lamoureux's; Manouvrier's lasted over thirty-five years. Boulze soon resigned to become principal with the Lamoureux orchestra and was replaced in 1922 by Lucien Lavaillotte, whose distinguished career lasted until 1960.) There was a new clarinetist, Duquès, and three new bassoonists, all superb: François Oubradous *père*, Lucien Jacot, and Maurice Guilloteau—a formidable trio soon to be joined by Fernand Oubradous *fils*. The hornist Émile Épinoux came as fourth horn and moved to second in 1924. Two new trumpet players, Pierre Vignal and René Voisin, came to fill the vacancies caused by the postwar "defection" of Emmanuel Chaine (who was denied his pension as a result) and the long overdue exit of his cover Jean Lachanaud, who had formally retired in 1912 and was now approaching seventy years of age. (Voisin was the father of Roger Voisin, longtime principal trumpet player of the Boston Symphony Orchestra.)

By 1921 the strings sections and their leadership were also beginning to take shape: a dozen new violins, a half-dozen cellos, and two new principals of substantial merit—the violist Pierre Villain and the brilliant, provocatively attractive young cellist Maurice Maréchal. Villain was chosen in a competitive audition; Maréchal was directly recruited, in the course of which the incumbent soloist, Papin, was asked to vacate his seat in favor of the young "career virtuoso." Papin, who was just short of sixty, replied in affectionate terms with his decision to resign altogether so as to leave the committee a free hand in its negotiations.[11] Meanwhile the other three senior cellists, Barraine, Furet, and Rabatel, objected to the process by which Papin was seemingly encouraged to leave and Maréchal appointed without audition, so resigned *en masse.*

Maréchal proved a superb hire until his solo career took its inevitable course. During his four seasons with the Société des Concerts he was featured as soloist a half-dozen times: in the Schumann Concerto in 1920—substituting for André Hekking—and 1924, a Tartini concerto and the Fauré *Élégie* in 1922, the Lalo concerto in January 1923, and what must have been a stunning Brahms Double Concerto with Firmin Touche in October 1923. After leaving the society Maréchal returned as soloist for Sunday concerts in 1943 and 1944 and occasionally hired the orchestra for his own concerto nights. He is to be heard in several recordings of the Société des Concerts, notably a 1943 reading of the Andante from Honegger's Cello Concerto, Charles Münch conducting.

The timpanist Alphonse Lafitte and percussionist Leteneur preferred neither election nor registry as *externes,* but rather to be called as needed and paid according to the union scale. Lafitte attributed his unusual gesture of declining election as *sociétaire* to past history. In cordial conversations with committee members, he reminded them that at the end of 1905 he was named timpanist of the Société des Concerts with the informal promise of an election that had never been forthcoming. If he had been asked before the war, he would have been happy to become a *sociétaire* and accumulate a good pension. Fifteen years later, the proposal was of little interest.[12]

What was left of the chorus appeared officially for the last time in the 25 January / 8 February 1920 pairing of the Fauré Requiem and Beethoven's Ninth; thereafter a "women's chorus" or "men's chorus," usually backing an opera excerpt, is occasionally to be seen in the program. The name of the *répétiteur du chant,* Félix Leroux, continues on the committee list through 1924, though he was never elected a *sociétaire.* The few remaining choristers continued to claim their stipends and tried to make themselves useful in a variety of management capacities. In 1928 an effort to force the retirement of the last seven singers came close to a lawsuit but ended in a more or less amicable buyout.[13] The bass Marc David, who retired in 1934, continued to come to the general assemblies until 1958, the year of his death; Jean Saraillé did not retire until 1941,

and even then continued to serve as *inspecteur de la salle* until the illness
of his wife forced him to relinquish the duty in 1954, at age seventy-five.

Works with full chorus resumed with the engagement for the 1924–
25 season of the sixty-voice Chœur Mixte de Paris, supplemented by the
eight or so remaining male *sociétaires,* under the direction of Marc de
Ranse. Three programs were announced for late March and early April,
including the Fauré Requiem and Ninth Symphony and Franck's *Béatitudes.* For 1925–26 the Chœur Mixte was engaged for Schumann's *Faust*
and the B-Minor Mass on successive Sundays in January. De Ranse complained that he was not certain he could go on assuring that large a repertoire in that tight a time period, but for the moment the solution met
everyone's needs well enough. Inevitably the women of the old Société
chorus asked to be included, as were their male counterparts, but De
Ranse preferred not to risk it; they were unlikely to come to more than
one rehearsal, and all but one was already past retirement age.

Meanwhile the city's professional and semi-professional choristers—
the victims, as it were, of 1920—tried to reorganize themselves into a
hundred-voice organization meant to be available to all the professional
orchestras of Paris. The committee responded to their approach by noting that the Société des Concerts could never use a chorus of that size,
for lack of space, and that M. de Ranse and his ensemble of sixty were
for the moment offering good satisfaction.[14]

In May 1920, just at the close of the ninety-third season, the New York
Symphony Society with Walter Damrosch arrived in Paris in the next
phase of the ongoing Franco-American cultural exchange promoted
largely by Otto Kahn. An assembly had been called to discuss the appropriate manner of returning the hospitality extended by the American musicians in New York in 1918, resulting in an invitation to the New
Yorkers for a morning ceremony at the Conservatoire and a mid-day
banquet. There was the inevitable squabble over responsibility for the
expense, since the *sociétaires* who had not gone abroad in 1918 objected
to any scheme that foresaw their contributing to the return of a *politesse* from which they had not profited in the first place.[15] But Franco-
American relations seemed to demand a gesture, and at length it was
decided to proceed on the assumption that voluntary private donations
would somehow cover the cost. Any gesture at all was noble and self-
effacing, since the society was still in litigation with Kahn's representatives over the contested accounts from 1918–19, and there were still very
hard feelings in Paris as to the American way of doing business.

As it turned out, the Gallic welcome provoked a series of events that finally led to the closure of the disputed books. For Otto Kahn was greatly moved that, after all was said and done, the French players would have invited their Americans counterparts to lunch. On the night of 7 May 1920, in that frame of mind, he received Messager and the past and present secretaries André Tracol and Albert Seitz to review the state of the litigation between the Société des Concerts and the French-American Association, managed by Richard Herndon; also on the table was a draft arbitration proposed by Paul Léon, the director of fine arts.[16] Kahn had studied Seitz's long memoir on the matter, praising it as worthy of a fine barrister or even a member of parliament, and proclaimed himself entirely convinced by the French *manière de voir*—objecting only to the lumping together of the accounts for services rendered, reckoned in French francs, and the bill for repayment of royalties advanced by Columbia Records, reckoned in dollars. (Messager responded that this was because Herndon's own accounts were so ordered.) Kahn added once again that he had no reason to doubt good faith from the American side, to which Tracol responded that Herndon's recent trip to Paris had only made matters worse. As the airing of views approached an amiable end, Kahn took Seitz aside and presented his personal checks for 11,859 francs and $1,475.77—essentially the entire contested amount.

Quite apart from the French francs, which would allow the disgruntled musicians to claim their back pay, Kahn's *"cheque-dollars"* amounted to a financial windfall owing to the 50 percent increase in the value of American currency since the accounting had been prepared. As it happened, the difference was enough to pay for the morrow's banquet, and a proposition to that effect, couched in compliments for the "excellent social spirit" shown by all, carried by acclamation at a quick caucus of the membership the next day.[17]

The historic formal reception of the New York Symphony by the Paris Conservatory Orchestra thus took place in the Salle des Concerts on Saturday, 8 May 1920, beginning at 10:15 A.M. Paul Léon, who, because he was a noted specialist in civic art and public monuments, was particularly pleased to be in the venue, presided. Seitz, as secretary, offered the formal and almost certainly very long welcome, presumably then translated into English. André Messager presented Walter Damrosch the society's portrait of Beethoven and proclaimed him an honorary member of the Société des Concerts. Then the 175 French and American musicians retired for an "intimate lunch" at a tavern in the boulevard St-Denis, where toasts and speeches were offered by Léon, Damrosch, Seitz, André Tracol (who, as secretary during the war years, had been the most visible of the musicians in America), and Otto Kahn. Gaubert, on a concert tour in provincial France, sent his regrets.[18]

Though a number of loose ends remained to be tied up, the luncheon in May 1920 effectively marks the conclusion of the society's involvement in the war and its aftermath. A final resolution with Herndon was signed in March 1921.[19] As opposed to the climate after 1870, there were few calls for benefit concerts. Much later the orchestra would be asked to appear on behalf of, or contribute to, various memorials, including one for the first infantry regiment to have been victims of poison gas. Eventually the musicians would place a simple plaque commemorating their own war dead at the entry to the Salle des Concerts.[20]

Altogether the concert societies now shared a potential public estimated at about ten thousand. Prod'homme described the orchestral situation of 1918 in the following terms:

> Each of our large societies has its exclusive clientele, jealous of its habitual programs. The subscriber to the Conservatoire is classical and likes Beethoven; the Colonne audience is for Berlioz, that of Lamoureux for Wagner. Franck seems more at home at the Châtelet under the direction of his pupil, M. Pierné, than at the Salle Gaveau, where M. Chevillard displays all his tenderness for Schumann, the Russian school and Richard Strauss, while at the Conservatoire every novelty, no matter where it comes from, appears suspect and is never warmly received.[21]

By 1920 a general free-for-all in programming and competition for audience share had broken out. There was precious little, now, by way of "exclusive clientele" (and in fact Prod'homme's remark more aptly describes the situation in 1900 than in 1918). Moreover, new concert seasons, arranged by independent impresarios after the model of Astruc and Diaghilev, were springing up everywhere.

Among these were the festival concerts led by Serge Koussevitzky in those years. Koussevitzky had made his Paris debut in May 1909 in an all-Beethoven program with the Colonne orchestra. On his decision to leave Russia permanently in 1920 he and his wife relocated themselves and their fortune to Paris. His first Russian Music Festival took place in spring 1921 at the Salle Gaveau, featuring local premieres of music by Scriabin and Prokofiev. Two more seasons followed, well attended and well reviewed, and by the end he had popularized among others, Prokofiev's Classical Symphony and Third Piano Concerto, Wanda Landowska and her harpsichord, and of course *Pictures at an Exhibition*, which had been his idea to begin with. Paris was "at his feet," a *socié-taire* noted with some envy, suggesting that there had emerged nothing less than a "new orchestral tradition for us."[22] Koussevitzky's ability to make music pay, and pay well, seemed both a promise and a threat.

The Concerts Koussevitzky were followed by a string of other entrepreneurial successes, among them the Orchestre Walter Straram, Concerts Robert Siohan, Orchestre Symphonique de Paris (OSP), and Orchestre Philharmonique de Paris (OPP). There was considerable overlap between these enterprises and the established associations: Robert Siohan (1894–1985), for instance, was an *aspirant* in viola at the Société des Concerts, 1921–22, before establishing his series in 1929; later he was conductor of the Concerts Pasdeloup (1942–44) and professor of conducting at the Conservatoire (from 1948). At both ends of the spectrum—the celebrity soloists and the young *aspirants*—the players were caught between the monetary attractions of the new marketplace and the expectation of loyalty to their primary employer.

At the Société des Concerts, season subscriptions continued their downward trend. As of 9 November 1920 there were only 75,096 francs in subscription revenue for 1920–21, averaging roughly 3,750 francs per concert, or about half the house. A "modest" augmentation in ticket prices for the less expensive side seating, from 6 to 7 francs, was announced for the 1921–22 season along with a surcharge for resale of unused subscription seats.[23] Paid advertising occupied more and more space in the Sunday program booklets. Érard and Pleyel were induced to remit 500 francs each time one of their instruments was used for a concerto; later Steinway agreed to the same arrangement.[24]

Once having taken to the road, the Société des Concerts found its own niche in the celebrity marketplace, at least to the extent that such appearances could be worked into the schedule. Generally these were booked for just before or just after the season of Sunday concerts. The 1919–20 calendar, for instance, included a late-March appearance in Rouen and a post-season public dress rehearsal and concert, 30 May 1920, at the Théâtre de la Monnaie in Brussels. For this latter event the financial arrangements were particularly attractive, with the musicians given a good fee, transportation (a grueling eight and a half hours by train), three meals, and a contribution toward their night in a hotel; the theater was lent to them without charge. From the profits of this and similar trips the society opened a *"caisse de voyages,"* which was used largely to purchase percussion and keyboard instruments. (In October 1920 it contained 1,710 francs.)[25] During the 1920–21 season the committee discussed possibilities for trips to Antwerp and Brussels, Ghent and Liège (February 1921), a tour embracing Rouen–Le Havre–Lille, a proposal from a British impresario for fourteen concerts over seventeen days in England, and a trip to Spain. In April 1921 the orchestra traveled to Marseille for two days of concerts that garnered a press response reminiscent of the first journeys to Antwerp and Lyon.[26]

A natural outgrowth of the impresario-sponsored road trips was to try the same formula at home. After the war, more for simple enhancement of the purse than out of any considered change of perspective, the Société des Concerts willingly undertook engagements that before the players had considered beneath their dignity. The unwieldy billing "with the participation of the artists of the Orchestra of the Société des Concerts under the direction of M. Ph. Gaubert" began to be seen around Paris on announcements of celebrity concerts, festival events, and theatricals of every sort—especially concerto recitals by major soloists. These were typically arranged by the concert management bureaus with which the committee was working more often, anyway, in its efforts to contract major soloists for the Sunday concerts. Among the first of this genre were concerts for the violinist Serge Tenenbaum, apparently in late April 1920, and for the great violinist Bronislaw Huberman and the singer Julia Nessy the next season. The 1921–22 minutes record ten such enterprises, now in their own separate category. (We will call these events "independent concerts"; the French documentation calls them *concerts particuliers* and *concerts hors session*.)

A pair of appearances to accompany Isadora Duncan's *matinées* at the Théâtre des Champs-Élysées (19, 20 June 1920) was successful enough that the engagement was prolonged with another pair (26, 27 June). During intermission of the performance on twenty-sixth, Gaubert brought the committee word that the theater management was prepared to offer the Société des Concerts "the hospitality of the hall" at an attractive price. At a conference during intermission the next day, the impresario, Édouard Roze, confessed that he had not envisaged the possibility of Sunday afternoons, the only time that really interested the Société des Concerts. His projections of the probable receipt, however, could not be ignored. Roze retreated to consult his directors and the committee went its way, both intending to elaborate a project in due course.[27] Here was born, it appears, the series of Thursday evening concerts at the Théâtre des Champs-Élysées that began in January 1923.

Arranging soloists for the Sunday concerts was now a central activity of the committee, occupying as much space in the minutes of the 1920s as any other topic. For instance, under the rubric "Negro Soloist" appears, on 17 January 1922, a note to the effect that an agent had proposed engaging Roland Hayes, a celebrated "black English tenor"— actually from Mississippi and Tennessee. The committee regretted its decision not to pursue the possibility: "Despite the absence of all racial prejudice," it wrote, "the committee cannot expose the society to the thoughtless joking that this choice would cause."[28] (Hayes appeared with a rival orchestra in Paris; within a very few years, the vogue having changed, the society was itself seeking to introduce black American singers.) In June 1921 the committee declined to have Fritz Kreisler, on the grounds that he was still an Austrian officer.[29] Deliberations such as these drew the committee into ever closer involvement with the artist management agencies—the very enterprises that now promised to assure the society's own financial health by organizing the independent concerts and tours. The Société des Concerts had become an active, if inadvertent, buyer and seller in the commercial marketplace.

In another remarkable change of policy the committee encouraged, "with great sympathy," the oboist Bleuzet and nine of his colleagues to constitute a spinoff chamber ensemble: the Dixtuor à Vent de la Société des Concerts du Conservatoire.[30]

At 9:45 on Saturday morning, 6 November 1920, the doors of the Salle des Concerts were opened for the first time to anyone who cared to pay 5 francs for admission to the *répétition générale* at 10:00. Young people were especially encouraged, via letters to their teachers and schools, to avail themselves of this new opportunity. M. and Mme Giboin, the *garçon d'orchestre* and his wife, served as ushers. Those accustomed to free admission to the final rehearsals—the blind, notably—were quick to protest the new change, but in every other quarter the scheme was popular from the first and wildly successful within the year. There were 6 paid admissions on 6 November, 14 the following week, and 23 for the third week, rising quickly to more than 60 in January and well over 100 by the end of the ninety-fourth season. The rehearsal of 12 February 1921 saw 132 paid admissions, presumably attracted by the appearance of Georges Enesco in the Bach A-Minor Violin Concerto. (There was a correspondingly large ticket income for the formal concert.) The income from the public dress rehearsals in the first season amounted to nearly 7,000 francs.[31]

In 1921–22 between 500 and 600 listeners ordinarily came to the Saturday morning *répétition générale publique*, requiring from the *socié-*

taires formerly of the chorus five new ticket takers and five new ushers and, from the fire department, one corporal and one common fireman.[32] At one rehearsal the crowd numbered over 950, well in excess of the proper capacity of the hall. Ticket prices were soon increased to 6 francs (5 francs plus 1 franc of unexplained "tax"); Gaubert favored a price of 8 francs because he thought the market would stand for it.[33]

The 1920–21 season, following the precedent of the Beethoven cycle of 1919–20, included a chronological hearing of the symphonies of Schumann as well as numerous first performances at the Conservatoire: works of Guy Ropartz, Gabriel Grovlez, Roger Ducasse, Rabaud, Duparc, Gustave Samazeuilh, Max d'Ollone, Giovanni Sgambati, Ravel *(Shéhérazade)*, Chevillard, Maurice Emmanuel, and André Gédalge— not to mention a first-ever Second Brandenburg (with Brun, Moyse, Bleuzet, and Vignal). The next season's unexpected triumph was the success of a Franck–Wagner concert on 26 February 1922, which broke all records for ticket income, at 9,646 francs. Moreover, it was noted, the true income, including the promotional fee for the piano, the paid advertising, and the rental of the presidential box, came to a breathtaking 13,353 francs, plus another 3,040 francs from the public rehearsal. The following week a Beethoven–Wagner pairing on 5 March 1922 broke the previous Sunday's record with 9,720 francs in ticket sales and 3,075 francs for the Saturday rehearsal. In the next season a Franck centenary concert on 26 November 1922 broke the record yet again, earning 10,251.50 francs for the Sunday concert and 4,657 francs for the Saturday rehearsal.

In July 1921 Gaubert and his committee listed more than a dozen major works they meant to add to the repertoire as soon as possible.[34] Most of these were acknowledged French masterpieces, including both *La Mer* and *Daphnis et Chloé*. Three works central to the Russian repertoire—the *Caucasian Sketches* of Ippolitov-Ivanov, the *Russian Easter* overture of Rimsky-Korsakov, and Mussorgsky's *Night on Bald Mountain*—appear on the list, as well as Stravinsky's *Fireworks;* also the Vivaldi Concerto for Four Violins in the edition of Charles Bouvet, a Mozart serenade, and Liszt's *Die Ideale* (called *Les Idéals*). Additionally, a decision was recorded to accept an organ symphony of Fernand LeBorne. It was not possible to schedule all these in a single season: *La Mer* and the *Night on Bald Mountain* had to wait for a year until 1922–23 (when *La Valse* was also premiered), d'Indy's *Istar* for three (when it was premiered alongside *Petrushka*). *Les Idéals* was not heard until 1927.

But with the 1921–22 season the orchestra had fully established its postwar rhythm, with twenty or more Sunday subscription concerts paired with Saturday morning public rehearsals, out-of-town appearances, independent concerts in Paris, and official ceremonies and events. That year alone there were more than a dozen independent concerts, including evenings with the Rumanian conductor Georges Georgescu, Mischa Elman, and the society's own Claude Lévy, a fast-rising violin virtuoso. Two concerts planned for the spring of 1922 with Stokowski had to be canceled owing to his illness. Additionally there were government ceremonies at the Sorbonne in May and June, the latter honoring Fauré on the occasion of his seventy-fifth birthday.

Not everyone was pleased with the new profile. In Paris a subscriber complained about the sudden disappearance of the chorus-and-orchestra repertoire and (unsuccessfully) urged a referendum where subscribers might agree to a 50 percent increase in price in order to have the chorus back.[35] In Lille there was serious opposition to a series of three concerts announced by a local promoter at the very time the resident professional orchestra was regaining its postwar strength. A pseudonymic "Jules Casadesus" placed blistering commentary in the press, noting that indigenous orchestra concerts were a long tradition in northern France, that the Fédération de Musique du Nord et du Pas-de-Calais (sponsor of the Lille Hippodrome concerts) had had fifty thousand members before the war, and that the Lille Société des Concerts Populaires had just managed to assemble the elements of a good professional orchestra—and a small government subvention—that might help "repair the moral and material loss" caused by the war and German occupation. The writer could not understand how a Paris association "of worldwide reputation, considered everywhere as the very safeguard of our musical traditions" might even consider coming to Lille to mount a "dishonest competition." Why not, instead, send Gaubert to conduct the resident orchestra for free?[36]

Meanwhile the director of the Lille Conservatoire appealed to Paul Léon with his belief that three outside concerts would constitute "moral prejudice" to the local society. Léon summoned the committee to the ministry to discuss the question but did not insist on any particular solution. The Société des Concerts was inclined to the position that a contract was a contract, and that the concerts scheduled for 2 October 1921, 19 February 1922, and 9 April 1922 must go forward, and they proceeded to give the October concert in Lille. The municipal authorities responded by forbidding use of the theater for February and April. Meeting during the rehearsal of 20 January 1922, the musicians declared their belief in the right of the society to appear wherever it might be called. A dossier was prepared for presentation to the mediation service of the musicians' union (which declined the case, holding that the Société des Concerts, as a civil entity, must represent its own interests at its own expense; with regard to the individual members represented by the Société des Artistes-Musiciens de Paris, the union reasoned conversely that having done one concert in Lille, the musicians must still be under contract for the remaining two).[37] During the winter the furor subsided; the Société des Concerts abandoned the February engagement and played the April one—which seems on the whole a sensible course of action for everyone concerned.

Camille Saint-Saëns died in Algiers on 16 December 1921. Immediately on receiving the news Paul Léon summoned Gaubert to the Office of Fine Arts to discuss the funeral arrangements, and shortly the orchestra and a chorus were convoked for the state ceremony. (The women formerly of the chorus were forgotten in the rush, and they subsequently wrote of their astonishment at being left out, receiving in return the committee's abject apology.)[38] The succeeding Sunday concert, on 8 January 1922, began with Saint-Saëns's *Marche héroïque,* the program headed with the simple legend *"à la mémoire de Saint-Saëns."* For a more suitable memorial tribute by the Société des Concerts, the publisher Durand promoted the idea of a performance of *Le Déluge,* saying that he would pay for a chorus.[39] This plan was abandoned in favor of the orchestral program offered on 12 February 1922: the Organ Symphony with Georges Jacob, the Third Violin Concerto with Enesco, the symphonic poem *La Jeunesse d'Hercule,* two songs from *La Nuit persane* with David Devriès, and the *Suite algérienne.* A second memorial concert was offered on the Sunday of the first anniversary of the composer's death, 17 December 1922, with the Organ Symphony and *Danse macabre* (the concertmaster Alfred Brun, violin). *Le Carnaval des animaux,* publication of which was forbidden by Saint-Saëns until after his death, was added to the repertoire in February 1925.

Five days after the Saint-Saëns commemorative concert, on 17 February 1922 at the Church of St-Roch, the Société des Concerts participated in an unusual event: a solemn Requiem Mass for the playwright Molière. This event was sponsored by the Comédie-Française as an occasion of professional and national atonement for Molière's having been summarily buried, because he was an actor, without the funeral both he and his wife expressly desired. When the question of the "Molière Requiem" was put to the full orchestra, the players had been quick to associate themselves with this reparation, as it would "reflect well on the entire profession of acting."[40]

Gaubert's increasing over-extension, part and parcel of the thriving market in impresario-sponsored touring, now forced the issue of how substitute conductors were selected and kept on the rolls. Both tradition and statute called for the substitute to come from the orchestra: usually the concertmaster or principal second violinist, or, as in the case of Gaubert himself, the heir apparent. Questions as to the validity of this system had been posed from time to time, but mostly the position of second conductor had been important only during periods of a first conductor's illness—frequent, in the case of Deldevez and for Habeneck's last years, but otherwise inconsequential. Lamoureux and Garcin had arguably seen their careers launched from the second conductorship, but the violist Victor Gasser, for instance, never conducted at all.

André Tracol, principal second violinist and influential administrator of the society, had become second conductor on Gaubert's accession to the podium. He seems first to have conducted publicly at the Trocadéro benefit concert of 20 December 1921, when Gaubert was forced to stay at the Opéra for the final rehearsal of Massenet's *Hérodiade*. At the start of a rehearsal on 20 January 1922 the orchestra was told that Gaubert, still overwhelmed with work, was "leaving the baton to M. Tracol for the eleventh concert" two days later and that the committee was counting on the musicians to support their excellent comrade in the arduous task that had somewhat capriciously presented itself. This was an unusual formulation, since the program, with Marguerite Long, consisted but for the Debussy *Fantaisie* for Piano and Orchestra of works they already knew well. In short, the secretarial address suggests trouble was known to be in the offing. And while the minutes record applause at the announcement, the next entry notes the secretary's intent to reprove the orchestra for the "regrettable incidents" of the public dress rehearsal on the twenty-first, which apparently included misbehavior and audible disrespect.[41]

More than a year later, at the annual general assembly on 24 April 1923, Tracol was suddenly defeated for re-election as second conductor by a vote of 26 favoring and 46 opposed. Few of the players supporting Tracol's re-election were quite certain what had happened or why—in fact Seitz and Bleuzet, the outgoing and incoming secretaries, were working behind the scenes to assure that the post would remain vacant and ultimately be dissolved, thereby clearing the way for guest conductors, perhaps even foreigners. On 18 May 1923 the disgruntled musicians assembled again to "examine the situation created by the non–re-election of the second conductor."[42]

Drawing on their long tradition of particular civility when a comrade had suffered professional reverse, the speakers took care to compliment Tracol for his distinguished service to the society and his unfailing artistry. After the long-winded preliminaries, Tracol took the floor to present his account of the events that had brought them together, though professing ignorance as to the underlying cause for his defeat. He numbered his calls to conduct the Société des Concerts as fourteen: two subscription concerts and twelve independent events. Both the Trocadéro concert of December 1921 and a February 1922 recital of the pianist Mlle Demisgian had been done without rehearsal—the latter with only two hours' notice. (This was the very situation of which Deldevez had so strenuously complained sixty years before.) "To that obvious demonstration of a second conductor's usefulness," Tracol said, "it's worth adding that he is required to play in the orchestra and thus already knows the repertoire." He also recalled a public dress rehearsal before a full house on only a moment's notice. He doubted he had compromised his colleagues on any of these occasions. On the contrary, he was willing to undertake this kind of sudden substitution (*"à l'improviste"* and *"au pied levé"*) only because they had all played together for so long. He would not attempt such a thing with any other ensemble.

The problem, he reasoned, must lie elsewhere, and so he would disclose the true details of his dispute with the committee. This amounted to their preference for calling Messager to substitute for Gaubert—which, however sensible that must have seemed in the overall context of good management, was nevertheless a violation of the statute that passed the baton to the second conductor in the absence of the first. What had in fact occurred was that in mid-April 1923 the Propaganda Service had asked the committee to arrange a tour to Switzerland for late May. Gaubert would be unavailable. On 15 April, Tracol said, he was told of the committee's intention of inviting André Messager to lead the tour. This constituted, he felt, a triple violation of the statutes: he had not been invited to the meeting, though he was a statutory member of the committee; the committee had no mandate regarding outside conductors; and the right of replacing a first conductor was the second conductor's alone. He had tried without success to establish these points with the committee during their train journey back from Lyon on 20 April.

Tracol claimed to have no real objection to Messager's conducting in

Switzerland; he recognized the first principle of maintaining the best interests of the society. But the blatant violation of his entitlements could not go unnoticed. He also acknowledged the gossip that he had bypassed the committee and Rabaud to protest the incident to the director of fine arts. This he categorically denied.[43]

Vernaelde confirmed that it was precisely the gossip about going to the ministry that had cost Tracol his mandate; this, in view of his abilities and devotion, was deplorable. Moyse said that his own blank ballot was meant simply to challenge Tracol's expectation of conducting every time Gaubert was absent—though that was clearly the statutory provision—since Tracol lacked Gaubert's "authoritative personality." Bleuzet, the secretary, said that the committee had made no decision, only considered an idea; Gaillard observed that, far from hiding their intent from Tracol, they had told him at their first opportunity, and Tracol himself first mentioned it to Messager. In any case the whole issue was moot, since the Swiss journey had been postponed. (It finally took place in January 1924.)

Messager, attending the assembly in his capacity as *membre honoraire,* confirmed his conversation with Tracol, then took the opportunity of having the floor to suggest it would be a grave error not to have a second conductor. The needed improvement was to give him something serious to do: perhaps two or three guaranteed concerts a year. Gaubert, who almost certainly would have preferred any arrangement to one where the committee turned to Messager, was asked point-blank whether he would agree to such an arrangement; he responded that the question was out of order and that he had no idea how to answer it.

Rabaud now tried to close the debate with a vote on the question "Does the Assembly desire to continue to have a second (in the old-fashioned sense of the word) conductor?" Instead the committee moved a hastily drafted amendment: "When the first conductor cannot go to the provinces or abroad, the committee has the right to call on an outside 'artistic personality.'" Messager thought this illogical, implying that there would be a second conductor qualified to conduct in Paris but not beyond. That was precisely the point, they replied; Paris regulars could understand the occasional appearance of a substitute, while audiences on the road expected the first conductor or someone of equivalent name recognition. (This very matter had been at issue in America, when Messager had wanted to leave Gaubert in charge so as to accept Walter Damrosch's invitation to conduct in New York.)

Still trying to reach closure, Rabaud asked candidates for the post of second conductor to present themselves for election, and no one stood. Tracol, asked if he would run, replied only that the situation was untenable. The debate resumed, touching on the need to promise a second conductor something to do, the financial disadvantage of paying a substitute conductor from the outside, and the possibility of retracting the vote that had defeated Tracol to begin with. Seitz looked once again to Tracol, who nodded affirmatively, then announced that on the basis of all the discussion he had heard he was now willing to cast his vote for Tracol.

With this solution apparently agreed to, Rabaud now asked the assembly to take its position on the key question, "Can the committee call a 'French artistic personality' from the outside to conduct?" Tracol sat in stone-faced silence. On unanimous vote, minus Tracol's, the committee was sent to draft such a text for future consideration. Rabaud then asked Tracol, "In view of the devotion you have always shown the society, will you be a candidate even if the second conductor no longer has the automatic right to replace the first—if the committee is given the right to invite someone else?" Tracol remained silent.[44]

The members reassembled to consider the new text on 5 June 1923, with neither Rabaud nor Gaubert attending. The principle clauses proposed:

- A second conductor, who could be drawn either from among the active members of the society or from the outside, after submitting a letter of candidacy. The ordinary rules (French nationality, affiliation with the Conservatoire) would apply;
- A term of two years, renewable; and that
- A second conductor from the outside, not re-elected, would be considered to have resigned, thus retaining his right to his pension account.[45]

On the whole the document was not especially well written, primarily because no one could foresee what might happen next. The provision that an outside conductor who lost his mandate would be considered to have resigned, for instance, represents a fundamental shift in the very definition of *sociétaire*.

One member spoke against the text, observing that the society had never before called an outside conductor and that it seemed especially unreasonable "now that we are prospering more than ever." After a vote nevertheless tentatively approving the draft, a member rose to move what for many was the main point of the unwritten agenda: to delete the word "French" from the adopted text. Gaillard vigorously defended it. Neither the government nor the Conservatoire looked well on the notion of a foreigner leading the Société des Concerts, he insisted. Gaubert was himself not opposed, since the Opéra routinely had foreign guests; Rabaud, on the other hand, would be adamant on the point.

What was certain was that deleting the one word would lead to a flood of international exchanges and almost as certainly reduce the role of the second conductor to naught. Tracol protested any further altering of statutes that day (there was a maneuver on the floor to annul the 1919 article on the choristers, so as to edge the remaining ones out altogether) and was answered with the cry, "The assembly is sovereign!" Nothing the members did that day would take effect for another year, anyway, and the draft articles finally carried with 68 favoring, 2 opposed, 2 blank. The presiding officer, noting that Tracol had not approached the balloting urn, asked if he was thus intending to reserve his right to pursue the case in court. That was not at all his intent, he replied, raising his hand "in acquiescence"—and obvious surrender. He grumbled that he didn't see what a second conductor might be under the guidelines they had just adopted, to which the presiding officer replied, "Whatever he makes of it."[46]

In the aftermath, to no one's surprise, Tracol resigned as second conductor (though he continued to lead his section until 1931, when he was sixty-three). Typically, Seitz and his circle had a solution in mind, which they now submitted in the form of a petition: to leave the post vacant for a year and call on Henri Rabaud in any emergencies, while the independent concerts, not subject to the statutes, could be led by outside "personalities." In the interim the committee would be instructed to develop a proposal to do away with the second conductorship altogether and, several dozen hoped, incorporate language that would allow the regular engagement of guest conductors, including foreigners, as was growingly the habit around the world. Atypically, for such a debate, the committee took no stance, preferring instead to hear the assembly out. Ultimately it was decided that a true second conductor was indeed essential to the orderly operation of the Société des Concerts. A vacancy would be announced, and the new second conductor would be chosen by competitive audition.

To this end a listing was placed in the union newsletter announcing auditions for 15 and 16 October 1923 (subsequently changed to 12 and

13 October) at 9:00 A.M.[47] Candidates were required to be French, to have satisfied their military obligations, and to have "passed through" the Conservatoire. The elimination round on the twelfth saw some fifteen candidates conduct the first movement of Beethoven's Fifth; on the thirteenth three candidates led the *danse finale* from *Daphnis et Chloé* and, with violinists also competing for solo slots that season, a work for violin soloist and orchestra. (These were Pascal in the Saint-Saëns Havanaise, Hardy in the Chausson *Poème*, and Calvet in the first movement of Lalo's *Symphonie espagnole;* Hardy and Calvet were selected.)

The winner was Eugène Bigot, who carried the competition handily and was elected by acclamation.[48] He conducted the orchestra a single time, in December 1923, and was not reelected at the end of his two-year mandate. Subsequently he became conductor of the Lamoureux orchestra and principal conductor at the Opéra-Comique and conducted the Radio Orchestra (Orchestre National de la Radiodiffusion Française) from 1947 until his death in 1965. In the 1930s and 1940s Bigot made several good recordings with the Société des Concerts.

The first classical music was broadcast in Europe from England in November 1922. A few months later regular programming in France was being broadcast from the Eiffel Tower by the Radiola Company, while the government sought to exert national control by the PTT. The vogue for wireless radio, or TSF *(télégraphe sans fil),* was quick to take hold. Appliances sold rapidly, and listeners organized themselves into special-interest clubs. Columns on *la musique mécanique* began to appear in the music press—Pierre Blois's column in the *Chronique musicale,* for instance, which always ended with a promotion: "Programs received with the Superhétérodyne Radio LL, Philips bulbs, Phoebus batteries, and Dary aerial." The musicians' union filed an official complaint against the use of such devices just as high authorities were inviting the Paris orchestras to have microphones hung in their concert halls. As early as November 1923 a bureaucrat from the Office of Fine Arts suggested that the society consider installing a transmitting device in the Salle des Concerts. Both to the government and to a radio listener's association the secretary responded that this was forbidden by the union on pain of blacklisting (being "put on the index"). But by the spring of 1924 there was no turning back the march of progress, and the union directed the Société des Concerts to propose an appropriate fee for broadcast rights. Marcel Moyse was sent to the other associations in the hope of developing a common policy.[49]

In the same epoch the society was approached, somewhat more stridently, with the notion of installing equipment for short-range broadcast by Théâtrophone, a device that provided "the opportunity to hear, through your telephone line, the main plays and concerts of Paris. Its new T-31 amplifier is unmatched by any other device." [50] The society apparently agreed to the Théâtrophone equipment in spring 1926 and sent a contract to that effect for approval by the government. Rabaud objected to the society's arranging on its own for anything that would require alteration of the Salle des Concerts, and the government thus responded that "for any installation, electric or otherwise," authorization would have to come from the architect of the Conservatoire. [51] This was a curious tactic for administrators who must by then have been keenly aware of the orchestra's interest in leaving the hall in search of more modern conveniences; the government, after all, had already invited the society's interest in broadcasting. In the end, the Théâtrophone did not come to the Salle des Concerts. Not until March 1928 was the Société des Concerts first broadcast, and then it was from the Salle Pleyel, where the equipment had long been in place. Shortly thereafter the committee declined a proposal to advertise on the Radio-Journal de France, finding the suggested price of 1,000 francs a month *"un peu cher!"* [52] And not until 1930 did a member of the orchestra have the occasion to stay home and listen to what they sounded like over the air.

The explosion of what would come to be considered the entertainment industry caused the Société des Concerts as many problems as opportunities. In the early 1920s it was not so much a question of losing audience members to the other concert associations as of keeping the best musicians in Paris at all. Maréchal, the popular cellist, soon took to the road as a star; his successor, Alfred Zighéra, lasted only a season before going to America. Joseph Calvet's greatly successful string quartet, which included one and sometimes two other *sociétaires,* needed to be away as often as it could, and indeed most of the better strings players were part of one or more independent chamber formations. Marcel Moyse was earning 2,000 francs for a Mozart concerto versus 75 or 100 francs for even the best-paid independent concert with the Société des Concerts. Gaubert, quietly at first and then bluntly, let it be known that his fee was much too low.

The growing world economic crisis—manifest in an unstable franc and galloping inflation—began to touch them all. The *prix des places* was now increased every year. The market value of one of the society's bonds fell below book value, an eventuality that even their growing financial *savoir faire* had not foreseen, and the bonds at a fixed rate of 6 percent were losing money owing to an inflation rate that far exceeded that figure. This and other factors led eventually, in 1934, to the liquidation of the Caisse de Prévoyance and its re-emergence as a retirement fund with a more modern fiscal structure, called the Caisse d'Allocation de Post-Activité.[53]

New and more onerous taxes began to be proposed by the government. The most threatening of these was a new 5 percent tax on earnings of industrial and commercial enterprises. For a time the Société des Concerts was successful in securing exemption by establishing a not-for-profit status, but the annoyance of declaring their financial position and explaining their antiquated monetary traditions was nonetheless real. A new rubric, *"fisc.,"* begins to appear in the minutes.

No long-term financial stability for the Société des Concerts was likely until some workable arrangement for an alternative venue had been found. This was no secret in art music circles, and beginning in the early 1920s competing offers began to reach the committee in promising number. Often the response was to procrastinate the opportunity away; sometimes an experimental series would be essayed. Ever present in the minds of the musicians was (and for that matter still is) the thought that sooner or later the national government would step in and build its "first" orchestra a proper concert hall.

In 1921, for instance, the Opéra proposed the use of the Salle Garnier for Thursday night orchestra concerts. The principal disadvantage was what it had always been: the cavernous dimensions of the room. On the other hand there was at least the possibility that collaborating with the Opéra would enable the society to have a standing chorus and to count on the big-name singers associated with the house. When the offer was renewed a year later, in September 1922, the committee agreed to pursue it on the condition that *"grandes auditions"*—the B-Minor Mass, the *Missa solemnis,* the Ninth—would be forthcoming.[54] Negotiations stumbled thereafter to a halt.

Simultaneously the Théâtre Mogador—which became home to the Orchestre de Paris in 2002—offered the kind of long lease the Société des Concerts was hoping for,[55] and they discussed with the administration of the Salle Gaveau the possibility of three post-season concerts in April 1923, to be marketed as a new subscription series. At the end of 1922 an impresario from the Pleyel firm of piano manufacturers approached the society with a prospectus for a new Salle Pleyel, to be constructed either near the Champs-Élysées or St-Philippe-du-Roule. (It was actually built at 252, rue du Faubourg-St-Honoré.) He proposed that the committee sign a memorandum of understanding destined to bring the Société des Concerts there as principal resident.[56] The document noted that the committee had examined plans for a building to be constructed beginning in the fall of 1924, and that it intended to offer forty-eight concerts there (i.e., twenty-four Sunday concerts and the corresponding Saturday public rehearsals) at a rent of 2,500 francs for each use, or 120,000 francs annually. If the orchestra moved to a season of thirty-six pairs in successive weeks, the rent would drop to 2,250 francs for a season total of 162,000 francs. This was an attractive but financially dubious proposal from the orchestra's point of view, since the figures suggested a quantum leap upward from their annual budget of some 220,000 francs total, with no rent at all. They would be gambling on a hall that so far had no address, let alone a faithful clientele. The committee played its usual card—to delay, pending an assembly to consult the full membership—and the opportunity lapsed.

In a more promising development, the new director of the Théâtre des Champs-Élysées, Hébertot, came again to discuss the series of Thursday concerts that had first been proposed during the Isadora Duncan recitals of 1920.[57] The Société des Concerts would play relatively informal afternoon concerts to include at least portions of the previous Sunday's repertoire. The risks, and the profits, would be the impresario's, but the musicians would be engaged at an assured fee: 35 francs for the rank and file, 45 francs for the principals. The committee, intrigued, countered with a demand of 40 and 50 francs and reminded Hébertot of the stumbling block of the high fees for star soloists. The proposal was agreed to at an assembly on 19 December 1922, and the series began on 18 January 1923 and continued until at least the following 8 March.

Though welcomed by the press *("beaucoup de monde, grand succès pour l'orchestre et son chef, . . . dans des œuvres souvent jouées"),*[58] the concerts were unpopular with the players, who found their Thursdays too cramped. In February 1923, twenty-eight musicians petitioned for a strict ending time of 5:00, and several wrote that they could no longer assure the increased services.[59] Then Hébertot came at last with the long-sought offer of the Théâtre des Champs-Élysées for Saturday mornings and Sunday afternoons. He would require a fixed rent instead of a percentage of the box office, and would not have concerts in January, when, he recommended, the orchestra should go on the road. The production staffs would be commingled. This was the plan that eventually took hold, but not for a very long time.

Yet the problem of venue grew more urgent every month. The historic acreage of the Menus-Plaisirs du Roi was being divided once again, this time to build a large, unattractive building (still in place) to house the PTT telephone switchboards. Complaints over construction (and a new flower stall belonging to the Vilmorin Company) that hindered the orderly flow of the public were filed weekly with the prefecture in the spring of 1924. Often the rue du Conservatoire was blocked completely.[60]

If Parisian concert life seemed to be facing insurmountable odds, the climate for foreign travel had never been better. Preparations for a week-long Swiss tour positioned between the subscription concerts of 13 and 27 January 1924 suddenly escalated when the society's Swiss agent, M. Fouilloux, suggested extending the itinerary with performances in Vienna, Prague, and Budapest—new venues all.[61] The idea rapidly developed into a plan for a formal state exchange between the Vienna Opera and the Société des Concerts, with both governments examining the possibility of covering a share of the deficits, first projected at 70,000 francs for the Paris orchestra and 100,000 francs for the Vienna Opera. The committee even developed a list of French operas they might be able to produce in Vienna: *Pelléas et Mélisande, Ariane et Barbe-bleue* of Dukas, Alfred Bruneau's *Le Rêve,* Charpentier's *Louise,* Alfred Bachelet's *Quand la cloche sonnera,* Ravel's *L'Heure espagnole,* and Gluck's *Orphée.* The expectation was to offer one of these, possibly stretched to two, with a mix of French and Austrian singers.

In November the agent traveled to Paris to complete the negotiations, noting that while there remained problems in booking the Viennese halls, "the atmosphere has never been more favorable." On 13 December 1923, astonishingly late for the musicians to clear their calendars, the draft itinerary was released:

M, 14 January	Geneva (cathedral or Salle de la Réformation)
T, 15 January	Lausanne (cathedral)
W, 16 January	Bern (cathedral or casino)
Th, 17 January	Zurich (Tonhalle)
F, 18 January	Basel (cathedral or casino)
Su, 20 January	Vienna Opera matinee
M, 21 January	Prague (Smetana hall) or Lucerne
T, 22 January	Vienna Grosse Musikvereinsaal

The orchestra would report directly to the train station from the concert on Sunday, 13 January 1924, and would arrive again in Paris on Friday, 25 January, in time for the public dress rehearsal the next morning. The contract embraced fees of 125,000 francs for the orchestra and conductor, 50,000 francs in transportation, and 30,000 francs in per diem for the ensemble. A total deficit of 130,000 French francs was envisaged. Even that was the most general of estimates, since the foreign exchange markets were fluctuating wildly, and the cost of postage and telephone calls was changing every week.

In early January the Prague concert was abandoned and a Brussels appearance substituted; then Vienna fell by the wayside.[62] Despite these disappointments—the Société des Concerts never appeared in either Vienna or Berlin—the orchestra was as successful in Switzerland as it had been in 1917, and the government wrote that it was well pleased with this new demonstration of the power of French musical art.

Just following the conclusion of the 1923–24 season of Sunday concerts, the society appeared with Walter Damrosch in a cycle of six all-Beethoven concerts billed as commemorating the centenary of Beethoven's Ninth (7 May 1824); these were Tuesday nights, 29 April to 3 June 1924, at 9:00 P.M.: all nine symphonies, the piano concertos, and the Scottish songs. The Beethoven / Damrosch cycle was a daring enterprise, since the Concertgebouw Orchestra under Mengelberg was in town, the Koussevitzky concerts were in session, and Jan Kubelík was offering recitals at the Opéra. If there was a financial loss, it was the impresario's, and was not noted in the record.

After the Damrosch concerts came a five-day trip to Barcelona, three days of concerts and two of travel. The committee had set the fee at 11,740 francs per concert in Barcelona (something just over what they typically made in Paris for independent concerts) and about 10,000 francs for *en route* events. The budget included 10,000 francs each way in transportation expense, 1,000 francs in on-location instrument rental in Spain, a per diem, and a clause exonerating the society from fluctuations in the rate of exchange between francs and pesetas. Meanwhile the Spanish representatives—not surprisingly, in view of the monetary instability—insisted on a fixed price in pesetas. The vice president of the Barcelona Chamber Music Society came to Paris to complete the arrangements, managing in due course to reduce the per diem from 28 pesetas to 20 (40 for Gaubert) on the promise of superb accommodations in both food and lodging at the Vittoria Hotel. The Parisians signed a contract on 8 May 1924 that required a deposit to be paid to a French bank in Barcelona, an advance on the rail fare, and the promise that the per diem in pesetas would be presented to the artists on their arrival.[63]

(The rail line Paris-Lyon-Marseille, PLM, provided "perfect" service, and on being warmly thanked by the society offered their every disposition for the future.)[64]

The Barcelona journey might have been remembered as routine, perhaps even pleasant, had it not been that Moyse and Vignal—the flute and trumpet soloists in the Second Brandenburg—as well as Lamouret, the principal horn player, had a prior engagement in Paris with the Robert Siohan concerts. Moyse was to be featured in Spain, as well, in the *Midsummer Night's Dream* music and Bach B-Minor Suite. Told of this conflict, the impresario responded that the programs had already been printed, and that the concerts would be canceled if Moyse failed to appear. After the committee dispatched a stern telegram reminding Moyse of his obligations, and just as the Beethoven / Damrosch cycle was getting under way, the matter blew overnight into a full-fledged crisis of principle. As it happened, both the Société des Concerts and the Siohan orchestra were rehearsing at the Théâtre des Champs-Élysées. The society's second conductor, Eugène Bigot, was sent downstairs from one rehearsal to the other to dissuade Moyse from continuing with Siohan. For one thing, Moyse was the *membre-adjoint* of the committee and was thus morally, if not quite statutorily, bound to travel with the Société des Concerts. Barcelona sent word by telegram that so long as the celebrated Moyse came along, the others could stay behind.

On Thursday morning, 5 June 1924, Moyse showed up at the rehearsal for the tour (being held, unusually, at the new Conservatoire in the rue de Madrid) to say that if the Barcelona enterprise was truly threatened, he would cancel his concerto with Siohan. But a few moments later he beckoned his colleagues of the committee aside and rebuked them for the tone of their telegram. Seitz took offense at this tactic; it was Moyse himself, after all, who had recently provoked a general assembly to insist on more discipline and a fraternal commitment to the independent concerts.[65] If the tour collapsed, it would clearly be his fault. Moyse then threatened to play no independent concerts at all so long as Seitz remained on the committee.

There was further unhappiness when Gaubert arranged with Jean Boulze, flute soloist at the Opéra and former *sociétaire,* to substitute for Moyse in lieu of the statutory second flutist, Manouvrier. In the aftermath Gaubert reversed his course by indicating that he had no objection at all to Manouvrier as first flute so long as Moyse would be assured a warm welcome whenever he deigned to appear. For a substitute second flute he suggested relying on one of his own past or present students from the Conservatoire—noting tersely that Moyse had never been a student there.[66] It was in this charged environment that the orchestra's visit to Spain took place, apparently with Moyse in his customary spot, and the long 1923–24 season came to its end.

The succeeding seasons were longer still, as the independent concerts and series essayed in other halls became more and more common. At the Conservatoire, where the twenty-two seasonal concerts now ran from mid-October to mid-April, the traditional programming continued to be inflected with first performances of some interest: in the ninety-eighth season (1924–25), d'Indy's *Istar, Petrushka,* Falla's *Nights in the Gardens of Spain* (published in 1922, and a runaway success in Paris), Chausson's symphonic poem *Viviane,* Debussy's ballet *Khamma,* Chabrier's *Bourrée fantasque* in the orchestration of Charles Koechlin, the prelude to the third act of Büsser's *Les Noces corinthiennes,* excerpts from Max d'Ollone's *Le Retour,* Pierné's *Ramuntcho* overture—and, as noted above, the Société's first public performance of *Le Carnaval des animaux.* In the ninety-ninth season (1925–26), there were Roussel's *Pour une fête de printemps,* Bloch's *Schelomo,* Ibert's *Escales, The Love for Three Oranges* suite, four orchestra dances by Louis Vuillemin, *The Pines of Rome* (a first performance in France, for which Ricordi offered the material free of charge),[67] Louis Aubert's *Dryade,* Florent Schmitt's *Antoine et Cléopâtre,* and a number of works by lesser composers.

This kind of programming represents a formidable exposure on the modernist front, and whether reflecting Gaubert's personal tastes, those of his committees, or governmental pressure, it could not be said that the society's role in contemporary culture was now anything but substantial. Yet one has the impression that their true interest and expertise was still focused on acknowledged masterpieces. In 1924, for instance, an impresario asked the committee to suggest a price and a program for a concert of the most signal and representative works of the *école française.* These were held to be the Chausson Symphony, Debussy's *L'Après-midi d'un faune,* Florent Schmitt's *Tragédie de Salomé,* Ravel's *Daphnis et Chloé,* suite 2, and the *España* Rhapsody of Chabrier. (The price was 10,000 francs.)[68] A Paris concert in conjunction with an international trade fair on modern decorative art the following summer featured works of the same composers, along with Roger Ducasse, Rabaud, Ropartz, and Pierné.

Of the independent concerts the most interesting was a Polish festival concert, largely of works by Szymanowski, at the Salle Gaveau on

23 June 1925; Gregor Fitelberg conducted, with Artur Rubinstein in the Chopin F-Minor Concerto. The following season the society self-produced two supplementary non-subscription concerts in their own hall: a program by the Brazilian virtuosa Magdalena Tagliaferro in *Nights in the Gardens of Spain* and Debussy's *Fantaisie* on 31 December 1925 (a New Year's *réveillon*); and, after several years of negotiating, a concert on Sunday, 21 February 1926, with Jascha Heifetz featuring the Beethoven Violin Concerto and Lalo's *Symphonie espagnole*. The week with Heifetz was for most of the players the highlight of the season. After the concert Gaubert gathered the orchestra in the lobby and offered unusually warm thanks to all the participants; Julien Gaillard presented the society's medal, and Seitz read a speech proclaiming Heifetz an honorary *sociétaire*, joining a roll that now included Planté, Busoni, and Paderewski. (Planté, who in principle no longer appeared in public, joined the orchestra once more in 1927, for a recording-and-technology festival concert.)[69] Paderewski canceled again, this time by telegram pleading extremely important personal business in California; the ten-year-old "Yeuudi" Menuhin was invited to substitute but did not appear.[70]

For its independent contracts the Société des Concerts now quoted fees that began at 40 and 50 francs (rank and file, soloists) for a rehearsal and 80 and 90 francs for a concert, with a 1,500-franc fee for Gaubert. A rank-and-file player would thus earn 160 francs for two rehearsals and a performance, and Gaubert nearly ten times that amount. Put another way, five or so independent concerts would pay a *sociétaire* roughly what the twenty-two Sunday concerts did in a year. Global prices for the orchestra ran from 5,200 francs for a chamber group of about two dozen with one rehearsal; to 9,000 francs for a typical symphonic complement and two rehearsals; to 18,300 francs for a large-sized concert with three rehearsals and Gaubert conducting. A fee of nearly 30,000 francs was asked for Bruno Walter's inaugural concert in May 1928; for the inauguration of the Salle Pleyel in 1927 the quoted fee was so high as to cause the promoters to threaten to go elsewhere for an orchestra.[71]

Impresarios typically found the society's asking price "highly exaggerated," and possible trips to England, central Europe, and the United States failed on account of it. In some cases the price was negotiable. To maintain the Bruno Walter engagement, the Société des Concerts had to lower its price to the 20,000 francs bid by Walter Straram and his pick-up orchestra. The musicians objected to this sudden drop in their fees and submitted a petition signed by twenty-four members urging the committee not to accept lower rates. The committee replied with its essentially capitalistic theory of confronting "orchestras on the side." They noted that Gaston Poulet's orchestra had already captured much of the market for concerto accompanying, and that Straram had done two lucrative concerts for Stravinsky and was to have his orchestra assimilated into Walter's Mozart cycle. The committee could only bid low. "We do not intend to prevent our colleagues from gleaning some extra income, but our interest must be to avoid prejudice to the society. This is only the beginning. Before events run their course and overtake us, we urge you, gentlemen, to take the measures necessary to stamp out the competition from a fire we must not be feeding." [72]

Such modern business ventures required upgraded business practices. Gaillard's successor as *archiviste-caissier*, Deblauwe, secured permission to open a societal bank account and, for the first time, write checks (to be countersigned by two other officers), thus ending the cash-and-bonds system that for a century had centered on the strongbox in the office. Deblauwe also insisted on having access to a telephone, but it was several more years before there was one in close proximity. [73]

Henri Rabaud, well in control at the Conservatoire, generally followed much the same policy toward the Société des Concerts as had his predecessor, Fauré: *laissez-faire* where it came to the orchestra's routine business, ongoing willingness to be of service in mediating conflicts ("finding a solution," he usually said) or intervening with the government authorities, and regular appearance on the rostrum to preside over the annual general assemblies. Unlike Fauré he attended many committee meetings. He was recognized as an eminent composer; if today Fauré has the greater reputation, in the 1920s that was not so obvious. Rabaud's relationship with the musicians, in spite of his imposing appearance and manner of expression, was more natural and consistently smoother than Fauré's. In part that was a matter of his impeccable pedigree; he was as much *chez lui* at the Salle des Concerts as any *sociétaire*. In part it was his skill, and willing availability, as a backup conductor during a period when it was becoming apparent to everyone that modern trends no longer favored holding a single conductor captive at the Opéra and Salle des Concerts for thirty-six weeks or more each year.

Gaubert's crises of over-commitment were now predictable for December and the end of season. To Rabaud, arguably the senior figure in the French music bureaucracy, appearing on the podium on these occasions seemed not only fitting but in its own way thrilling. The orchestra thought it an ideal solution; for one thing, his services were free. But the practice was not without troublesome implications for all the parties involved. Rabaud was, after all, the president of the Société des Concerts, and backing up Gaubert in what was perceived as the role of the second conductor tended to complicate the orderly chain of authority. And there continued to be the unavoidable (and probably correct) impression that the orchestra's own second conductors were second rate.

Extending an invitation to Rabaud to conduct his Second Symphony in December 1926 thus seemed to the society's management altogether routine. But on this occasion gossip began to circulate that Rabaud was turning into Gaubert's second conductor. A petition floated around the new patron association, called the Amis de la Société des Concerts, urging Gaubert and Rabaud to return to their proper roles. Gaubert and the committee caught wind of the document and hurried to arrange a meeting with its signatories, but an over-excited subscriber released it a few hours before the meeting, and copies reached the ministry and such theoretically disinterested parties as the concert promoter Dandelot.[74] Rabaud, with every reason to be vexed, convened the committee and announced that they should not count on him in December. Gaubert personally intervened to soothe him, and at length Rabaud succumbed to the committee's formal insistence that he accept the charge to lead his own composition.

Gaubert, in turn, was sorely aggravated when the plans for an official Beethoven centenary commemoration were unveiled by the government. The ceremony, featuring the Société des Concerts, would take place at the Sorbonne on 22 March 1927, with Gaubert invited to conduct "the overture and concerto"; Rabaud the Fifth Symphony; and Vincent d'Indy, the Conservatoire's professor of conducting, the Ninth. When the committee fired off a sharp letter refusing to participate unless the Ninth were reserved for their own conductor, Rabaud summoned them to "explain how this ceremony came to be organized—by me." He begged their support. *"Eh bien,"* Gaubert grumbled, "I'll do the overture and concerto, but only so as not to make waves."[75] Thereafter the tension between Gaubert and Rabaud became palpable, and certainly contributed to the Conservatoire's intransigent stance that the society must stay in its hall to keep its name. Except for Rabaud's strident opposition, the orchestra would probably have worked out a successful contractual arrangement with either the Salle Pleyel or the Théâtre des Champs-Élysées in the late 1920s.

The one hundredth season of the Société des Concerts (1926–27) thus coincided with the centenary of Beethoven's death. The 1927 concerts were headed, when appropriate, "Centenaire de Beethoven," beginning on 9 January with a Ninth Symphony as sung by the Chœur Mixte de Paris. (This was repeated in April, when it was paired with the Fauré Requiem.) On 27 January Rabaud conducted the *Missa solemnis,* and the state observance of the Beethoven centenary that had been at issue with Rabaud took place at the Sorbonne on 22 March 1927. Almost unbelievably, the hundredth anniversary of the Société des Concerts itself appears to have passed without a formal ceremony.

This may well have been because the organization was simply too busy to think about such things. On Tuesday, 18 October 1927, for instance, the Société des Concerts inaugurated the new Salle Pleyel at 252, rue du Faubourg-St-Honoré. (They were also present for a public open house with tea on 17 October.) Surely this was the most fabulous season opening in the history of the organization, with Ravel and Stravinsky each conducting, a glistening new *art déco* edifice, and the orchestra's best repertoire:

Nouvelle Salle Pleyel
Inauguration
MARDI 18 OCTOBRE 1927
Concert de Bienfaisance:
Association des Anciens Élèves du Conservatoire
Association des Artistes et Musiciens (fondation Taylor)

PREMIÈRE PARTIE

1. Ouverture des *Maîtres Chanteurs*	Wagner
2. Variations symphoniques	César Franck
M. Robert CASADESUS	
3. Deux *Nocturnes*	Debussy
"Nuages" – "Fêtes"	

DEUXIÈME PARTIE

4. *Nuits dans les Jardins d'Espagne*	de Falla
M. Robert CASADESUS	
5. Suite de l'*Oiseau de feu*	Igor Strawinsky
Sous la direction de l'auteur	
6. *L'Apprenti sorcier*	Paul Dukas
7. *La Valse*	Ravel
Sous la direction de l'auteur	

The orchestra continued in the Salle Pleyel for a series of concerts drawn from their spring repertoire on the eight Saturdays in January and February 1928 at 3:30 in the afternoon. This was a noble experiment toward achieving a long-term solution to the problem of venue, but after a few weeks—the Saturday mornings and Sunday afternoons at the Conservatoire carried on uninterrupted—the musicians were simply too exhausted to continue, and the contract was not renewed.

On 9 March 1928 the Société des Concerts appeared again in the Salle Pleyel for their first complete St. Matthew Passion, conducted by Fritz Münch (1890–1970), the older brother of Charles. Münch had succeeded his father, Ernst, as director of the famed St-Guillaume Chorus of Strasbourg in 1924. (Fritz Münch and his chorus were soon to create, in 1925, then make a historic recording of, in 1929, Honegger's *Le Roi David,* with the Strasbourg orchestra—thus preceding by more than a decade his younger brother's celebrated Honegger recordings with the Société des Concerts.) It was Fritz's habit once a year to bring the chorus to Paris, where he would engage one of the local orchestral associations. For the Bach passion the society proposed to him a complement of 14–14–9–9–7 strings with 8 oboes and 8 flutes, two rehearsals and the concert, at a fee of 9,300 francs. (Münch removed the cello solo and oboe d'amour from the manifest, presumably intending to bring his own, and agreed to double fees for the soloists: one violin, one oboe, one flute, and two English horns.) The proceeds were designated to support summer holidays for working women (the Œuvre de Villégiatures du Travail Féminin), a project of Baroness de Watteville.[76]

The St. Matthew Passion was the first performance of the Société des Concerts to be broadcast over the radio, and thus the first time the management had to discover what the financial implications of broadcasting might be. On this occasion the musicians' union required a gift of 400 francs to its emergency fund and a 25 percent supplement to the musicians' fees. The surcharge could, in the case of a benefit concert, be waived by a vote of the members, thus favoring the proceeds to the benefit cause; the orchestra subsequently voted so to do.[77]

Three days later, close on their own centenary, the *sociétaires* participated in a ceremonial dedication of the new organ studio at the Conservatoire in the rue de Madrid. In April they were engaged for concerts with Thomas Beecham, and just afterward, in early May, were to have traveled to Turin for a week. It is not clear from the documentation whether they actually made the trip. Certainly the plans were well advanced, but the trip may have fallen victim—as did the possibility of a third Beecham concert—to the much larger undertaking that engulfed the society that summer and fall.

Bruno Walter's ambitious Mozart Festival consisted of fifteen public

events at the Théâtre des Champs-Élysées in May and June 1928: an inaugural concert on 19 May, then at least four of the Mozart operas *(Entführung, Don Giovanni, Così, Zauberflöte)* in three performances each,
then a repeat of the festival in Geneva for two weeks in July. The "Mozart Festival Orchestra" was constituted primarily of members of the
Société des Concerts supplemented by members of the Robert Siohan
orchestra. For the musicians the Mozart Festival was a financial windfall, with continuous work for a month paid at a high fee; in all there
were twenty-one rehearsals, from 10:00 A.M. to 1:00 P.M. with thirty
minutes for lunch, paid at 50 francs per service and including the mid-
day meal.[78] The festival was historic for another reason, since on 14 and
18 June Walter and his orchestra recorded both the *Magic Flute* overture
and Schumann's Fourth Symphony, op. 120, for Columbia France.[79]
The Schumann symphony was their first four-disc set.

The furious pace continued in the fall and winter of 1928–29. The long-
delayed Paderewski gala concert finally occurred on 25 February 1929 at
the Théâtre des Champs-Élysées, with two works by Paderewski himself—a symphony and a concerto—along with the Saint-Saëns Fourth
Piano Concerto and *Roman Carnival* overture. It was a splendid but
also melancholy occasion, for in the musicians' *foyer* of the hall that
night, just before the concert, Gaubert told the orchestra of André
Messager's death the night before, and of the wish Messager had expressed to have the Société des Concerts play at his funeral. He himself
had specified the program: the *marche funèbre* from the "Eroica" Symphony, a Bach aria, the Debussy "Sarabande" from *Pour le piano* as arranged by Ravel, the finale ("Death of Mélisande") from Fauré's *Pelléas
et Mélisande,* and the adagio from his own *Hélène* suite. The funeral was
at noon on Friday, 1 March 1929, in the Church of St-François-de-Sales,
the parish church of the elegant quarter in the XVIIᵉ Arrondissement
where Messager lived.[80] He was buried in the Cimetière de Passy, near
Fauré and Debussy. On Sunday, 3 March, there was a concert at the
Conservatoire; on Monday the orchestra was off to Antwerp.

As circumstance would have it, Messager's funeral was followed on
26 March 1929 by a full-blown state funeral for Marshal Ferdinand Foch
at Notre Dame, with an orchestra and chorus of 140. The program included the "Eroica" funeral march and excerpts from the Fauré Requiem, concluding with military tattoos and the *Marche héroïque* of
Saint-Saëns. In April the musicians traveled to Strasbourg for a concert organized by Guy Ropartz, new conductor of the orchestra there

and director of its Conservatoire, featuring one of his works. In August 1930, at the last minute, negotiations were completed for another journey to Switzerland, and the members were notified on 1 September. Many of the musicians were still on their summer holiday, and the dates (Vevey on 27 September, Neuchâtel on 28 September, and six subsequent services for a theater festival in Geneva) conflicted directly with opening night at the Opéra. There was considerable ill will among the musicians as to the lateness of the call. Gaubert made the trip; his concertmaster did not.[81] At length a band of eighty-four traveled, raggle-taggle, to Switzerland on three trains.

Journeys like these became excessively grueling when the organizers and musicians would agree, in order to economize on per-diem costs, to outbound travel, the concert, and a late-night return all on the same day. The concert of 28 April 1929 for Guy Ropartz in Strasbourg saw the orchestra leave Paris at 7:00 A.M., arrive in Strasbourg at 2:00, play the concert at 4:00, and return later that night. After the second concert of a Lyon–St-Étienne pair on 11–12 March 1930, the musicians were bused from St-Étienne to Lyon to meet the 1:20 A.M. train back to Paris. For their return from Liège that June, the railway company added carriages to the 11:45 P.M. train for Paris. In this case there was supposed to have been provision for the musicians to stay overnight, but owing to the crowds at the exposition there ("we're even preparing the barges on the Meuse," wrote the organizer),[82] only fifty rooms could be found for the eighty-two musicians.

The resignation of Émile Loiseau, *1er violon solo*, at the end of 1928–29 was formally attributed to his overextension as professor at the Conservatoire. In fact he was angry at having been rebuked for skipping the Paderewski concert and embarrassed over inadvertently creating an incident when his substitute failed to provide satisfaction during a recording session for Rimsky-Korsakov's *Scheherazade* (Columbia, 1929; Gaubert, cond.). Loiseau had simply had enough of the frenzied pace: "My duty to my students at the Conservatoire, and too often to my own peace of mind, prevents my participation in all this outside activity."[83] The incident suggests, again, the growing pressures of the schedule on all the musicians, especially the celebrities; however attractive the new income was to the rank and file, the sharply increased pace led to more conflicts than ever for those who were in independent demand. For the stars, every extra concert risked keeping them from an engagement where they could make even more.

An open competition was announced for 18 May 1929 to fill the solo slot. Most of the younger *sociétaires* presented themselves: Carembat, Hardy, Lepetit, Pascal, André Le Métayer, Lespine, and Blareau. The non-members included two acknowledged virtuosi, Henri Merckel and Roland Charmy, and that year's stock of prizewinners from the Conservatoire, notably René Chédécal and André Huot. The 10-member jury cast 5 votes for Merckel, 2 each for Pascal and Chédécal, and 1 for Charmy—one vote short of the majority. On the second round, Merckel took the deciding sixth vote (Chédécal 2, Pascal 1, Charmy 1) and was announced the winner, while Chédécal and Huot were engaged as *aspirants* on the spot.[84] (Huot served the Société des Concerts long and well; Chédécal soon left to become director of the Perpignan Conservatoire.) Merckel played five seasons, taking a sudden unexplained leave in 1934 and then disappearing altogether. Roland Charmy would be designated his successor in May 1935.

Merckel was unpopular with the orchestra from the beginning. Already in June 1930 the committee received a petition complaining of his supercilious attitude at a concert with Jascha Heifetz, the first recorded incident in a long series.[85] More significantly, perhaps, his stand partner, Luquin, as *2ᵉ violon solo*, insisted on changing desks and no longer having their names appear contiguously on the program. Subsequently Luquin tried to resign altogether but was convinced instead to become *chef d'attaque* of the second violins.

In the same general reorganization of the string ensemble two of the elder players were edged back in favor of younger musicians. Debruille, in the violin fifth seat, was asked to move to the violins II, and the assistant principal cellist, Dumont, was directed from the front desk into the ranks. Both protested, Debruille "with emotion"; both decisions were upheld on appeal; both players soon took their retirement. There was also unhappiness about the involuntary retirement of the noted violinist and sometime *2ᵉ chef* André Tracol, but again the decisions stood. This prompted resignations from all the violinists on the committee in October 1931 and the need for an Assemblée Générale *extraordinaire* to fill the void.[86]

Eventually the combination of Roland Charmy as concertmaster from 1934 and the spectacular Paul Tortelier as principal cellist offered the promise of a string ensemble anchored by virtuosi of real distinction. But Tortelier played only two seasons: his *aspirant* year in 1934–35 and a year in 1946–47 as *1ᵉʳ violoncelle solo*.

It may not be entirely coincidental that during these personnel shifts,

Gaubert informed the committee in mid-October 1931 that his doctors thought it best he limit his duties to sixteen concerts per year. Hence, he insisted, there would need to be at least one assisting conductor of distinction.[87] Gaubert's position was not taken especially seriously, even though it was already known that he needed to be away for much of 1932–33. To cover his absence in October 1931 the committee had already appointed Gustave Cloëz, but this was soon perceived as an unsatisfactory arrangement. Eugène Bigot, having failed to have his mandate renewed in 1925, would not set foot in the Conservatoire. Robert Siohan initially indicated his interest in the post, but then learned that he would be expected at all performances, all rehearsals, and all meetings whether or not his services were needed; and faced with those conditions, he withdrew his candidacy. Given this circumstance, the assembly finally voted on 21 May 1932 to dissolve the post of second conductor (41 favoring dissolution, 25 opposed).[88] Henri Rabaud conducted most of the 1933 concerts.

From Berlin in the fall of 1929 there had arrived news of a stunning subvention scheme for the Philharmonic there, with joint major contributions from the Reich, the state of Prussia, and the city of Berlin to the tune of 436,000 DM, reckoned by the Parisians as nearly 3 million francs. "What," asked Jean Chantavoine in *Le Ménestrel*, "are the French state and the city of Paris doing for the Société des Concerts?"[89]

State subventions had begun to reach the concert societies in 1897. After the war, as a foil to inflation and a by-product of the theory of music as propaganda, subventions increased dramatically. By the mid-1920s the subvention accorded the Société des Concerts was some 25,000 francs annually. Receipts had risen substantially as well, mostly as a result of annual increases in ticket price. Average per-concert income for 1925–26 was 10,329 francs (14,593 francs, counting the public rehearsal), and in 1928–29 it was 13,326 francs (17,870 francs with rehearsal). The passing of 100,000 francs in subscriptions was recorded in 1924. Yet operating expenses, especially the new web of postwar taxes, were rising still faster, and by some measures the society was fast losing ground. Invited by a legislator to provide figures for hearings on the fine arts subventions for 1929–30, the committee submitted a sobering account:

	RECEIPTS	EXPENSES
1878	Fr. 160,000.55	Fr. 20,648.40
1928	Fr. 284,931.00	Fr. 133,093.00

That is, the society's income had not quite doubled in fifty years, but its expenses had more than sextupled. The tax situation was onerous:

TAXES

1924–25	Fr. 229.20
1925–26	Fr. 385.90
1926–27	Fr. 9,918.50
1927–28	Fr. 12,075.55
1928–29	Fr. 12,246.48

The same documentation shows per-concert expenses for the 875-seat venue to have been stable at roughly 950 francs:

Heating and lighting (set payment to Conservatoire): Fr. 600
Personnel, hall, and box office: Fr. 348[90]

(At the Théâtre du Châtelet, which seated 2,500, the Colonne Orchestra paid 1,000 francs in weekly rent.) The cost of publicity, the committee noted in a later communication to the Prefecture of Police, continued its inexorable rise:

POSTERS

1927–28, per concert	Fr. 500
1–13 October 1928	Fr. 554
14 October 1928	Fr. 675[91]

This particular round of negotiations was successful. The Société des Concerts saw its subvention increased from 25,000 francs to 36,000 francs per annum and an epochal doubling of the fee for the presidential box from the 2,000 francs established by the government of Louis-Philippe to 4,000 francs—a Pyrrhic victory, it was noted, since the same seats on the open market were worth 4,200 francs. But the overall subvention program rankled considerably (though it was probably fair enough by the measure of audience size):

SUBVENTIONS 1929

Concerts Colonne	Fr. 75,000
Concerts Lamoureux	Fr. 75,000
Société des Concerts	Fr. 36,000
Concerts Pasdeloup	Fr. 20,000
Soc. pour le développement du chant choral	Fr. 15,000
Société Nationale de Musique	Fr. 6,000[92]

In another financial reverse, during the winter of 1928–29, the Assistance Publique stepped in to claim the *droit des pauvres* on complimentary tickets, including those for the presidential box. Despite the many historic documents provided by the committee to the agency, it was ruled that the society's exemption was limited to the seats for the physician in attendance, the representative of the police, and critics holding a valid pass—and four places for the society itself.[93] This represented 36 francs in added new expense per concert, or 792 francs per season.

Nevertheless, some of the financial figures were superb. The overall budget for the subscription concerts soon reached 300,000 francs. Record companies and impresarios competed to pay the orchestra 10,000 francs per service; from Columbia in 1928 the orchestra earned over 150,000 francs. The Paderewski gala brought 145,000 francs—nearly as much in one festival performance as half a year's Sunday concerts earned. Not infrequently the society encountered the underworld of arts management. After the state funeral for Marshal Foch, for instance, the curate of Notre Dame indicated that he required a gratuity of 25 percent of the fee allocated the Société des Concerts by the government: 5,000 francs, that is, on a payment of 20,000. The committee succeeded in retroactively raising its fee to 25,000 francs, then passed the clergy its expected amount "hand to hand, and not to be written down."[94]

Meanwhile the committee members began to flag beneath the staggering workload. The 1930 end-of-year assembly digressed into general grumbling about the administrative structure—though they were able to reach the happy decision to make the stenographic, typed transcripts of the minutes, essentially verbatim, that are preserved from 23 May 1930 forward.[95] The administrative secretary had emerged as essentially the managing director of the Société des Concerts, and the authority of the *archiviste-caissier* had dwindled to practically nothing. (For one thing, now that there were more than enough subscriptions to go around, the *archiviste-caissier* was no longer the arbiter of the society's favor at the box office.) This state of things was fine by the generation of aggressive young musicians now trying to frame a modern agenda, since the *archiviste-caissier* was by tradition the eldest of the long-term servants of the society. The violinist Jean Savoye, soon to emerge in a position of unrivaled authority, moved the abolishment of the office.

Its incumbent, Émile Deblauwe, complained that "there's only one employee who counts with the public, and that's the secretary. . . . Which is wrong." His own work lasted all summer. "It's the young woman who does all the work," muttered Candéla. "In the ticket office, perhaps, but not in mine," he replied.

"Messieurs, Messieurs," urged Rabaud from the president's chair to quell the disturbance. But Deblauwe would not be silenced: "M. Candéla's interruption disgusts me. He ought to be happy, the toad" *("espèce de crapaud")*. The committee later recorded its approval of Deblauwe's stewardship—though that was not to last—and condemned Candéla's outburst.[96]

As the 1930s dawned, Paris seemed more than ever the world's center of good music, gripped in as "fantastic and fatal" a dervish's dance—to use Ravel's description of *La Valse*—as in the decade or so leading up to 1914. Visitors and newcomers were seduced by the Sunday offerings of the orchestral societies, and enjoyed the embarrassment of the choice. Boschot, citing figures published in the *Courrier musical,* counted 1,344 concerts in Paris during the 1929–30 season, 400 of them given by the four associations. There had been 184 first performances of the work of 132 composers.[97]

Ravel fever gripped the capital. The 1930–31 season of the Société des Concerts began with a gala Mozart–Ravel program, featuring three first performances at the Conservatoire that went a long way toward completing the Ravel repertoire: the *Pavane pour une infante défunte;* the *Chansons madécasses* with Madeleine Grey, Ravel at the keyboard, and Moyse and Cruque as flute and cello soloists; and the *Boléro* as conducted by its composer. French music and French musicians, with Ravel at their forefront, had claimed a major piece of modern culture.

"Paris was still," wrote one observer, "a marvelous city of artistic industry and aesthetic fervor."[98] In retrospect critics would trace the decline of public interest in the concert societies to the spectator and participant sports—tennis, soccer, cycling, and skiing—and "automobile mania" that detracted the populace from its long-standing Sunday pursuit of art music. But for the moment the musical enterprise seemed stronger than ever, supported by another industrial revolution, that of radio broadcast and electronic recording.

That very autumn, for instance, Radio Paris began to broadcast the Saturday morning public rehearsals of the Société des Concerts, setting in motion a fundamental change in professional and public habits that would take decades to resolve. There was little doubt about the sound quality. Deblauwe skipped the rehearsal on 25 October 1930 to listen to Beethoven's Fifth on the radio, later assuring his colleagues that "it's marvelous what a listener can tell of the performance. The room lends itself well to the microphone."[99]

But therein lay a real danger. Listeners would hear the concerts broadcast on Saturday mornings and stay away from Sunday afternoons—or, worse, listen to the Société des Concerts for free and then buy tickets for Colonne or Pasdeloup. One of the society's chief benefactors began to stay home to listen to the radio broadcast, as did the musicians' students and their families. By 1932, when the committee reconsidered the problem, they could note that not once, when they were broadcast, was the Salle des Concerts full to capacity. In any event the 10,000-franc fee paid by the radio for each concert, from which the union required its proration, was little enough income from what was proving to be a major headache. Despite the fact that the year's receipts were low (or, from one point of view, because of it), the decision was made to take a year off from broadcasting and to demand a considerably higher fee when a new contract came to be negotiated.[100]

Apart from the eight sides recorded in New York in 1918, the Société des Concerts did not make recordings during the "acoustic" period—or at least did not have its name identified with them. Many of the *sociétaires* must have been called for the hundreds of discs, mostly of light fare and opera excerpts, recorded *"avec orchestre."*

"Then came the miracle," writes one of its architects, the conductor Piero Coppola, in his memoirs, *Dix-sept ans de musique à Paris, 1922–39*.[101] News reached Paris from Camden, New Jersey, of the success achieved in recording a full orchestra with an electric microphone, and Coppola soon heard the April 1925 recording of Saint-Saëns's *Danse macabre* with Stokowski and the Philadelphia Orchestra. "I was flabbergasted. Here, finally, was real music. . . . It was the end of the sound of penny whistles and the nasal meowing of unrecognizable instruments, the end of nails scraping on blackboards that would make you gnash your teeth. The sound that came from a spinning disc on a good machine with the top down seemed to me miraculous in fidelity and warmth—and we were only at the beginning."[102] Coppola convinced the London Gramophone Company (HMV: His Master's Voice) to send him the Western Electric equipment, which he connected from a studio to the old Salle Pleyel, several hundred meters away, by means of a special line run for the purpose by the PTT. The first HMV France electronic recording was released in late 1926.

Within months the phonograph had come to rival the radio in quality of sound. By the turn of the decade both the technology and the ultra-modern design of the equipment ("in perfect taste," said the publicity) made it suitable for even the most fastidious music lover's salon. For the fall of 1929 the French Gramophone Company promoted an automatic player that could change up to twenty discs, "non-stop."

The French firms of Columbia, Gramophone, Pathé, and Odéon embarked on a spirited rivalry in the race to capture the orchestral repertoire on disc and to secure exclusive contracts with the leading soloists, conductors, and ensembles. Columbia France won a first two-year contract with Gaubert and the Société des Concerts that extended from 1 January 1927 to 30 December 1928, covering six sessions a year. Some nine titles were released with Gaubert conducting, a repertoire that included *The Marriage of Figaro* overture and the *Meistersinger* prelude but focused on the Russian and French moderns (Mussorgsky, Borodin, Fauré, Debussy, Dukas, Ravel), notably including historic renditions of *La Valse* and two of the Debussy *Nocturnes*. Additionally there were the two Mozart and Schumann recordings of 1928 by Bruno Walter and the Mozart Festival Orchestra described earlier in this chapter. The succeeding two-year contract period, 1929 and 1930, saw the publication of several greatly more substantial works, including the Franck D-Minor Symphony, Tchaikovsky's Pathétique Symphony, and Rimsky-Korsakov's *Scheherazade*. It culminated in the great recordings of Marguerite Long with Gaubert and the Société des Concerts: the Fauré Ballade and Chopin F-Minor Concerto. Long's Chopin Concerto, which took the Grand Prix du Disque of 1930, was welcomed in the press by Janine Weill (later her biographer) with wonder: "The supple and precise playing of Marguerite Long is essentially phonogenic. . . . The music is there, palpitating, at our doorstep."[103] (Long herself later observed that she was "always more nervous in front of the microphone than in front of the public.")[104]

On 13 February 1930 a new contract was concluded by a vote of 72 to 1 with the nation's oldest recording company, the Compagnie Française du Gramophone (est. October 1899)—by then allied with HMV England and Victor U.S.; this was later renewed for two two-year terms, thus forming an exclusive relationship with Gramophone that lasted from 1930 to October 1935. Columbia France meanwhile had reached an exclusivity arrangement with the Straram Orchestra. Gaubert's exclusive contract was also with Columbia—as was Stravinsky's.

It was for these reasons that the formidable series of recordings made by the Société des Concerts between February 1930 and October 1935—

virtually the whole of the "Impressionist" repertoire, and a good deal more—was led not by Philippe Gaubert but by Piero Coppola (1888– 1971), artistic director of the Compagnie Française du Gramophone / La Voix de Son Maître and thus chief French liaison to the British parent company, His Master's Voice.

Much of Coppola's work with the Société des Concerts was reissued on compact discs in 1998 and 1999 (and a good sampling issued much earlier on a commemorative set published by the Orchestre de Paris, 1990). The orchestra is undeniably fine, especially when at full strength, and Coppola seems a sensitive and capable musical executive. His Debussy cycle, including his own transcriptions of *La Soirée dans Grenade* and *Cloches à travers les feuilles* (1935: three months after the first performances by the Pasdeloup Orchestra), is without rival for the period. *La Mer* in 1932 established Coppola's credentials as a major exponent of Debussy; the twenty-three-minute *Nocturnes* of 1938, including "Sirènes" with a small chorus, is his masterpiece. Coppola's Ravel is equally impressive: *Le Tombeau de Couperin* won the Grand Prix du Disque in 1932. Here the listener is seduced in equal measure by the matchless ensemble of the strings and the remarkable flute and oboe solo work by Moyse and Bleuzet.

A characteristic of all the early recordings, and a long tradition at the Conservatoire, is the excellence and prominence of the harp work, here probably tendered by Victor Cœur and Alys Lautemann. For his part, Gaubert seems to favor uncommonly fast tempi, as though to emphasize the orchestra's capabilities in that arena: note, for instance, the breathtaking speed of the 1927 *Marriage of Figaro*. Note, too, with both conductors and especially in Ravel's *La Valse,* the strong dose of violin portamento, now long gone from the style.

By the mid-1930s the fortunes of the Compagnie Française du Gramophone were in decline, as French recording companies proliferated without a corresponding growth in the number of discophiles. Coppola resigned his position in 1934 in the wake of the industry consolidations taking place in London. When he returned to record the Debussy *Nocturnes* in May 1938, he was approached concerning his willingness to succeed Gaubert if the matter of his foreign nationality could be resolved.[105]

The reorganization of the industry, followed in March 1936 by the expiration of the society's exclusive contract, made it possible for Gaubert to return with the Société des Concerts to the studio for two discs of his own music, *Les Chants de la mer* and *Les Inscriptions pour les portes de la ville.* There appears to have been a last successful session with Gaubert in 1938, devoted to excerpts from Berlioz's *La Damnation de Faust*. Finally in May 1939 Gaubert and the orchestra recorded the Saint-Saëns Second Piano Concerto with Artur Rubinstein, who, feeling that the orchestra had made "too many mistakes," vetoed its release. (A compact disc of this session was first published in 1999.)[106] The orchestra for the July 1935 recording of the Saint-Saëns Fourth Piano Concerto, with Alfred Cortot and—in his first known recording session—Charles Münch, is unidentified but may have consisted in part or even mostly of *sociétaires;* it may indeed be the source of player enthusiasm that soon led Münch to be elected Gaubert's successor. Interestingly, the best of the records between Coppola and the start of the world war are those conducted by two foreigners, Bruno Walter and Felix Weingartner.

Altogether the Société des Concerts recorded some 650 four-and-one-half-minute faces during the 78 era, some three thousand minutes, or fifty hours of music. One could not argue that preparing this remarkable discography much changed its repertoire, now an essentially stable mix of acknowledged traditions (Beethoven, Wagner, the Russians, the French Romantics and post-Romantics) and a modest commitment to living French composers. But it added a new, and central, pillar to the orchestra's mission: to record aggressively, both for the income and for the prestige of the institution and the nation. Without a doubt, the recordings elevated the stature of the orchestra in the estimation of a far larger public than it would ever have reached in Paris or on the road. The discs renewed international perception of the Paris Conservatoire as an eminent locus of orchestral activity. Few record buyers outside greater Paris could have known what little connection remained between the academic institution and the professional orchestra that carried its name.

The effects of the frenzied marketplace in art music—the astounding inflation in fees, the erosion of loyal publics, the size of the stay-at-home audience—weighed heavily on Gaubert. The evidence suggests that he came to think of the Conservatoire concerts as an imposition. He no longer considered himself an equal with the *sociétaires* of the rank and file. When challenged to correct the stasis that many felt settling in, he would instead become hostile and uncooperative.

Much of this was less a matter of art than of economics. But whatever the causes, the effect was a general unrest in the ranks that fomented a revolution (a chapter rather less well documented that we would like, owing to the loss of the committee records between November 1931 and March 1935). A new generation of warriors essentially seized power from their elders and went on to develop a progressive, sometimes radical agenda to secure real primacy among the associations and ultimately formal recognition as the single national orchestra of France. Later they looked back with satisfaction at having been the *jeunes révolutionnaires du moment.* "I was one of them," remarked a secretary of the mid-1960s, Manuel Recassens, with a certain delight.[107]

The young radicals found reasons for dissatisfaction at every turn— in May 1932, for instance, when the society was not called for the funeral of Paul Doumer, the assassinated president of the Republic, after a long monopoly on such events. Their inability to arrange a long-term relationship (or for that matter a single concert) with Toscanini rankled them; their forced alliance with Coppola stifled, they believed, the growth of a massive program of recordings. The new Orchestre Symphonique de Paris (OSP, established 1928) seemed particularly threatening, while talk of an Orchestre National at Radio France implied that broadcast contracts might soon be eliminated altogether.

The *sociétaires* began, almost abruptly, to characterize their repertoire as stale and uninteresting. Ravel's G-Major Piano Concerto, played everywhere else by Marguerite Long, was not to be found on their programs. They read Roussel's Fourth Symphony at a single Tuesday rehearsal and never returned to it. Their renditions of Debussy's *Children's Corner* (March 1931) and even *Pictures at an Exhibition* (October 1932) were ridiculed in the press.[108]

Gaubert, who had good reason to be proud of his contributions to the repertoire, was particularly sensitive over this line of attack. "The listeners only want consecrated works," he complained, sounding just like Deldevez. "We can play Saint-Saëns without fear, but then things heated up when we tried *L'Apprenti sorcier* for the first time [on 5 March 1933]: the subscribers demanded their money back. When we tried Pierné's *L'An mil,* three-quarters of the subscribers didn't show up at all. One of our main subscribers, M. Risler, begins to read his newspaper whenever we play Debussy. Our faithful clients want the classics, a little modern music, and never a first performance—never something by young men just out of the Conservatoire who have not earned the right to be played here. For sixty or seventy or eighty years the Société des Concerts has scrupulously avoided being *avant garde.*"

"Ravel is not an *avant-garde* composer," the young André Huot shouted back. "The Société must renew itself."[109]

In another episode of the rebellion the *archiviste-caissier* Deblauwe, arguably the society's senior statesman, was removed from office when it was discovered he was paying his maid from the society's accounts. Though the verifiable discrepancy was a mere 69 francs diverted between October 1933 and February 1934, it was concluded that "where there's smoke there's fire," and Deblauwe was expelled.[110]

The radicals selected as their leader Marcel Moyse, fresh from his nomination to the Légion d'Honneur and as stridently expressed as ever. Standing for the office of secretary at the Assemblée Générale of 16 May 1936, he proposed a smaller, more active committee, and a much higher public profile. "It's high time, gentlemen, to defend ourselves better than we do against all sorts of musicians, composers, critics: all sorts of people who associate to drown the Société des Concerts." He was particularly harsh on the critics, who preferred the visiting foreign orchestras and accused the Société des Concerts of not rehearsing. Yet Moyse, too, feared that their reputation was of a band of "musicians who didn't want to rehearse and didn't want to do much. . . . If M. Gaubert wanted it, and the Société supported him, he could be not just the first conductor of France, but of the whole world."

Gaubert responded crossly that all this was simply a matter of the French taste for novelty; crossing the Alps or the Rhine gave visiting orchestras a certain cachet. If the visitors stayed in Paris for six months, they would seem the same as all the others. *"Que voulez-vous?"* he said: *"C'est là une question psychologique."*

But Moyse continued: "I have the impression that the Pasdeloup and Colonne orchestras are more successful with the public than we are." He went on through his litany of woes: a ministry that on the whole was doing less for the society in 1936 than La Rochefoucauld had done in 1828, the problem of the hall, the lack of public education in music, the uncertain progress toward official recognition as the state orchestra.

"Enfin," Gaubert cried with impatience, "what do you really want to make of the Société des Concerts?" A voice replied: "An orchestra that works and makes money."

"How?" Gaubert asked. "Appointed by the state? As if we were in Berlin? You'll never separate Colonne and Lamoureux from their subventions. You are a hundred years old. You are famous, you are the greatest orchestra in France, even the world. And you're afraid to leave the Conservatoire! What will you do as the state orchestra: command performances at the Élysée Palace? Like the Garde Nationale?"

But something along those lines was indeed their goal. "Fine," said Gaubert. "I'll go tend my sheep."[111]

The conflict of tradition and progress reach a head in 1936, when the committee recommended to the general assembly its plan to split the twenty concerts each year into fall and spring seasons of six programs at the Conservatoire and four in the Salle Pleyel. The Conservatoire concerts would be every two weeks, once begun, and the Salle Pleyel concerts fitted in between. Programs in the old hall would be "in harmony with the room"; the bigger repertoire, works with chorus, and big-name soloists would be reserved for the larger venue, with the hope of breaking even but no more. The report to the membership began, as usual, with a sober statement of the facts: the descendents of 1828 had not only not multiplied but were increasingly drawn to the elegant and spacious halls of their competitors; the maximum receipt for the Salle des Concerts, 12,000 francs (800 seats × 15 francs average ticket price), was a figure their competitors were paying for concerto soloists alone. Bach's B-Minor Mass, in January 1936, had sold out but barely made expenses; if, for that event, they had sold out a 2,000-seat hall twice, with two public rehearsals, they would have had a remarkable year.[112]

Subsequent discussion made it clear that giving only twelve concerts annually in the Salle des Concerts risked its rental to a competing organization, possibly a new orchestra composed exclusively of former students of the Conservatoire. At length the society embarked on a riskier project still: a very slightly reduced series at the Salle des Concerts (eighteen concerts in lieu of twenty, plus a benefit concert for the retirement fund) and a total of five concerts at the Salle Pleyel—25 October, 19 November, and 17 December 1936, and 4 February and 4 March 1937. The first of these was a memorial concert for the Marxist composer Albert Doyen (1882–1935), founder of the Chorale des Fêtes du Peuple, and featuring his masterpiece for orchestra, chorus, and organ, *Le Chant d'Esaïe le prophète.*

The season concept proved greatly more optimistic than circumstances were to allow. For one thing, Hitler's remilitarization of the left bank of the Rhine stopped subscription fulfillment in its tracks; another war was increasingly certain. "Owing to the ongoing deficit for the [first] three concerts in the Salle Pleyel," the other two were canceled. The hall's directors insisted that the orchestra keep the 1937 dates, but the committee could only offer a conciliation payment of 1,500 francs, noting that the musicians could not "play to lose money: we aren't yet that rich." The first concerts had been veritably "disastrous to our *caisse.*"[113]

Partly as a result, Marcel Moyse abruptly resigned as secretary, and an emergency election was held on 9 January 1937 to choose his successor. The young violinist Jean Savoye, another of the radicals, stood for the post. *"Messieurs,"* he began, "I do not hesitate to say that our society is on the verge of disappearing. If we don't react, we can close our operation. Our enterprise is dying because it has nothing to offer." Though the potential public was great, "we present programs chosen so that nobody comes." They had virtually no more subscribers left. "I deplore the way we work. We have no administration, and we don't adapt to the new formulas. We can't run the society as we did even ten years ago." He outlined an ambitious platform: staying on the road at premium price, chorus concerts using local professional ensembles (almost immediately the Chorale Yvonne Gouverné began to appear with the society, in what became over the years a major partnership), young people's concerts, returning to radio broadcasts, aggressive recording of their entire repertoire, and moving to the 5:00 time slot on Sunday afternoons.

Savoye was willing to accept the condition imposed by the government of three hours annually of new music as a condition for subvention; here, grumbling was heard from the ranks. He would willingly promote independent concerts of the highest quality to the musicians' financial advantage: in 1937–38, for instance, appearances by Feuermann and Adolph Busch, also Bruno Walter in a "Jupiter" Symphony and a Verdi Requiem with 250 performers, with ticket prices rising to 100 francs. Savoye was elected secretary by a vote of forty-six out of only fifty voting; André Huot was elected *agent comptable*. This put into place the extraordinary administrative constellation that achieved the radical agenda and, no less importantly, led the Société des Concerts to survive World War II.[114]

It was, however, too much for Gaubert. In September 1937 he wrote to secure leave for the entire 1937–38 season. Gustave Cloëz, conductor at the Opéra-Comique, regarded for a time as Gaubert's probable successor, led the fall concerts, succeeded by Roger Désormière (a prophet of the *"Jeune-France"* composers: Daniel-Lesur, Delannoy, Jolivet, and Messiaen), Rabaud, Jean Morel, and Jean Clergue. Morel was apparently Gaubert's *protégé*. But in February 1938 the committee began to look past Morel to Charles Münch, who within a few weeks came to be regarded by both the musicians and the public as the obvious solution. In March, Gaubert submitted his resignation.

From the president's chair on 31 March 1938, Henri Rabaud observed that Gaubert's decision, though "legitimate and natural, was regretted";

Rabaud promised to "walk forward with the Société" into its next chapters. Gaubert bid his *adieux,* calling the musicians his comrades and saluting a society "that has been all my life, all my joy as an artist, and to which I have given the best of myself. I wish it long life, glory, and prosperity." [115] Together he and Messager had overseen the orchestra for three decades, during a period of thorough transformation; he himself had been conducting his colleagues since 1904, and had been a *sociétaire* for forty-one years.

By now everyone perceived the magnitude of the turning point they had reached. No one knew what to make of the darkening international environment.

CHAPTER 11

Münch and Cluytens

(1938–60)

Gaubert had no successor waiting in the orchestra. Henri Rabaud, presiding at the Assemblée Générale on 31 March 1938, made clear his commitment to a full and public search, yet in the same breath went on to attach considerable importance to the clause in the statutes that required the conductor to have been affiliated somehow with the Conservatoire. He reminded the members that the Conservatoire had long produced celebrated violinists and flutists—the traditional field of search in the world—and that for fifteen years the institution had sponsored a class in orchestral conducting. To the institution's alumni, he believed, the *sociétaires* must look first of all. It was agreed to publish the vacancy, audition certain candidates, and consult the assembly for its decision before the musicians left for the summer.[1]

Rabaud's passing over "certain points"—the movement to include foreign artists in the field of candidates—was purposeful. What was necessary at the momentous occasion of Gaubert's retirement was unity, by which Rabaud meant having the orchestra and the Conservatoire go together into the uncertain but obviously threatening future. The assembly was over in an hour.

It was the last peaceful meeting of the Société des Concerts for many months. By the time the musicians gathered again on 10 May 1938, Rabaud had sensed there was no turning the tide of opinion favoring a foreign conductor and skipped the meeting, pleading lamely that he had not received the published agenda in time. (It was on this occasion that Raphaël Delbos cited "the sad privilege of age" as he took the chair.)[2]

At issue on 27 May 1938 was clearing the way for official concerts (as opposed to impresario-sponsored events) with a foreign national, Bruno Walter, who had fled the Austrian Anschluss in March 1938 and established himself in Paris. After considerable maneuvering, language was adopted (64 favoring, 12 opposed) that allowed the committee to invite guest conductors for as many as four concerts in a row.[3] Walter's concerts wound up under the auspices of the Opéra, but he did lead an ambitious series of recordings with the Société des Concerts, including a Handel concerto grosso and Haydn's "Oxford" Symphony recorded in May 1938, and in May 1939 the historic six-disc *Fantastique.*[4]

At the same assembly the members approached an even more critical question: whether or not the first conductor might come from the outside and, on election to the post, become a *sociétaire.* Here the point was not so much to allow for foreign nationals—the grave international situation of the moment virtually demanded a French citizen at the helm of the Société des Concerts—as to permit a conductor who had never been affiliated with the Conservatoire. Despite the fact that there was precedent in the case of André Messager for this very course of action, it was still thought a radical departure from the rules, certain to offend the senior musicians. Rather than support the inevitable decision with the weight of his own presence, Henri Rabaud—in an unprecedented gesture that was remembered and often recounted in later years—resigned his presidency of the Société des Concerts altogether and left the room. Likewise Georges Guérin, the *commissaire du personnel,* was deeply opposed to the motion, perhaps because he hoped to be a viable candidate in a field of non-celebrity conductors.

As they approached the moment of truth, Guérin, too, stormed from the room, and the membership grew unruly. Amid cries of *"Ordre! Calme!"* it was observed that every member had a right to express his thoughts—to which came the response that "a member of the committee does not have the right, even if his name is Guérin and he is, I repeat, one of my closest friends, to leave the room slamming the door." (*"Exclamations!"* reports the transcript.)[5] Of the candidates who presented themselves—Clergue, Cloëz, Louis Fourestier, François Gaillard, Morel, Münch, Szifer, Henri Tomasi (Bozza had retired his candidacy)—all were French, all were over twenty-one, and all had completed their military service.

The matter of Münch's Alsatian heritage and of his strong ties with Germany had already been discussed at length. His father was born before 1870, and was therefore French; his mother was a Parisian; a grand-father, moreover, had been pastor at the Oratoire in Paris—but these were, to be sure, delicate nuances, and to some degree rationalizations of a decision already made. What few opponents there were pointed to Münch's failure to take French citizenry and come to Paris after World War I. Instead he chose to play for Furtwängler in Leipzig, and had only assumed full citizenship when his brother was under consideration, in 1929, to succeed Ropartz as director of the Strasbourg Conservatory. The law held, on the other hand, that Alsatians were French unless they had formally opted for German citizenship. Moreover professors at the Strasbourg Conservatory, as Münch was briefly from 1919, had been named by an official commission sitting in Paris. Alsatians had never had to be naturalized.

After long discussion of the pros and cons, it was decided to invite Charles Münch to assume the podium of the Société des Concerts with a contract of five years, to be ratified by absolute majority of the general assembly after one year. The motion carried with 64 favoring, 2 opposed, and the most entrenched of the old guard having already abandoned the proceedings. A year later, on 26 April 1939, Charles Münch was formally elected 1er *chef* and vice president to prolonged applause. The radicals congratulated themselves, for good reason, and decades later enjoyed reflecting on having had the courage to establish a new "strength and dynamism, which we have kept ever since."[6]

Shortly afterward, with the upheavals of war masking the gravity of the changes, Rabaud retired from the Conservatoire just as Münch announced his discontent with the title of vice president. For the duration of his tenure, then, Münch served as the official president of the Société des Concerts, while the new Conservatoire director, Claude Delvincourt, was called the honorary president. Jean Savoye assumed the title of secretary-general and would eventually name himself vice president. Old Raphaël Delbos became treasurer when the office of *archiviste-caissier* was abolished (this had been a central plank in the radical platform for some time). Savoye's comrade André Huot became assistant treasurer, certain to be elevated to the rank of treasurer as soon as Delbos retired.

Charles Münch, at forty-seven and just toward mid-career as a conductor, was a worthy successor to Messager and Gaubert and ended up with a much higher international profile than either. Certainly he emerged from his years with the Société des Concerts as a "great" conductor, surrounded during the last twenty years of his life with all the trappings of stardom: elegant apartments in the XVIe Arrondissement, a country house, a devoted domestic staff who traveled with him. Such little time as he had to himself he spent seeking out treasures from antiquarians and second-hand shops. He owned fine prints and engravings (Breughel to Delacroix, Monet, Pissaro, and Sisley) and Ysaÿe's Stradivarius. The admiring young women who surrounded him came to be known as the *münchettes*—Munchkins. His family and a few intimate friends called him "Charry."[7]

It appears, too, that Münch encouraged Raoul Dufy (1877–1953) in his passion for music and musicians by allowing him to come to rehearsals and sketch from a seat next to the timpanist, Félix Passerone—thus at the top center of the scaffold, looking outward into the house. The acquaintance of Dufy and Münch, and the sketches themselves, date back to the early 1930s—before, that is, Münch and Passerone were affiliated with the Société des Concerts. The best of Dufy's orchestra paintings, ca. 1941–48, appear, from the placement of the doublebasses behind the first violins and the bespectacled likeness of Louis Fourestier, largely to represent the Colonne Orchestra in the Châtelet Theater. Nevertheless, several paintings, notably *Red Orchestra / L'Orchestre rouge* (ca. 1946), evoke the character of the Salle des Concerts and its suspended horseshoe balcony, and the overall corpus affords a memorable look at orchestral practice of the era. (To Dufy Casals remarked, "I can't tell what piece your orchestra is playing, but I know what key it is.")[8] *Intermission / L'Intervalle,* where a single player sits cross-legged in a sea of empty chairs and instruments left behind, is especially fine.[9]

We know more about Charles Münch than about any other *sociétaire,* in part because of his era's obsession with public relations and stardom, in part because of the more complete documentary record. His autobiography of 1954, *Je suis chef d'orchestre*—in the *Mon Métier . . .* series—affords an excellent view of what he himself thought of the profession. He was an idealist and philosopher, promoting the values of hard work, discipline, and experience in the making of a well-formed musician. He believed in giving himself totally and often spontaneously to the work at hand, and in particular enjoyed the notion of revealing new aspects of familiar works to the public. He was from the beginning to the end a great public draw. Audiences flocked to hear him.

Born in Strasbourg in 1891, Münch had been raised in the elevated musical atmosphere surrounding the Strasbourg Conservatory, where his father was a professor. The family had long been associated with the

Protestant ministry and sacred music. Münch heard and played the fabulous Silbermann organ in Strasbourg (his uncle, Albert Schweitzer, played the same instrument) and listened as his father led Bach and Berlioz; he heard Nikisch and Richard Strauss and Mahler conduct in Strasbourg. After a flirtation with medical study, he chose a career as an orchestral player and violin teacher. He had come briefly to Paris to study violin with Lucien Capet and composition with d'Indy, playing some concerts during that period with the Colonne Orchestra, but was drafted into the German army in 1914. On his discharge he found work in Strasbourg as an agent for the Rhine and Moselle Insurance Company and in a few months had been appointed assistant concertmaster of the Strasbourg orchestra and violin professor at the Conservatoire. Both these were led by Guy Ropartz, who is to be considered Münch's most significant mentor, especially in matters of new music.

Münch would have liked to find a post in Paris, but instead won a competition to become concertmaster of the Leipzig Gewandhaus Orchestra under Furtwängler—the historic seat once occupied by Mendelssohn's concertmaster Ferdinand David, who had premiered the Mendelssohn Concerto and played *Harold en Italie* with Berlioz. This was a formidable apprenticeship in any event; it was given particular direction when Münch was asked to substitute as conductor of the Thomanerchor for a Sunday morning Bach cantata and later when he led a historical concert, in the long-standing local tradition, from his seat at the head of the violins.

There seems little reason to question Münch's assertion that his departure from Leipzig in 1932 was the result of growing personal distress over the political climate; the National Socialist movement surely ran counter to everything he believed about his own cultural roots. He was anxious to reassert his French citizenship in any case, and was by then equipped both monetarily and artistically to achieve a professional stature that would have been impossible two decades before. He set down at the Gare de l'Est, he says, burning with desire to conquer Paris.[10]

In addition to the four venerable societies, Paris in that year boasted the young Orchestre Symphonique de Paris (OSP) as well as the for-hire orchestra organized by Walter Straram (where Koussevitzky had had his start). Münch engaged the Straram orchestra for his conducting debut on 1 November 1932, deemed an immense triumph despite his debutant's terror. In a subsequent engagement with the Lamoureux orchestra he demonstrated "galvanic power" as a conductor, and it was soon enough clear that a new star had dawned on the Paris orchestral scene. Finding his engagements with the old societies constrained by their classical repertoire, he helped establish from 1935 still another new ensemble, the Orchestre Philharmonique de Paris (OPP), and took the lead in developing its reputation for adventuresome programming: from the Brahms Requiem and Bruckner Te Deum to the work of living composers in whom he was most interested, notably Ropartz and Honegger but also Roussel, Poulenc, and increasingly Messiaen. He was active as a Paris liaison for the ISCM (International Society for Contemporary Music, established in Salzburg in 1922) and took the lead in bringing the 1937 ISCM festival to Paris.

Charles Münch became a champion of the French orchestral repertoire, which he saw as extending forward seamlessly from Berlioz to Honegger and Messiaen. He was a strong partisan of Berlioz, whose music he admired and whose prose work he knew and often cited; eventually he accrued the most substantial Berlioz discography before the Colin Davis Berlioz cycle.[11] He also took the centrality of Beethoven as a matter of faith, and thus was in perfect accord with the orchestra's history and mission. His recorded work with the Société des Concerts includes important readings of Berlioz, Franck, Fauré, Debussy, Ravel, and Honegger—also Tchaikovsky and Prokofiev. Münch saw thoughtful programming as central to the conductor's craft, and his determination to be personally involved in choosing the programs came to cause considerable friction with his governing committees.

The spectrum of experience Münch brought to the podium of the Société des Concerts was unusually broad. From Strasbourg he had his thorough-going love of Bach; from Leipzig, a full command of the classical canon from Mozart and Haydn through, notably, Schumann and Mendelssohn and Liszt. He knew the workings of the German orchestras from the inside out; moreover he sensed just how far he could push his progressive inclinations into the staid practice of the Société without compromising its identity. He knew the personal costs of a conductor's public exposure, which he likened to St. Sebastian exposed to the Roman arrows and to Joan of Arc waiting to be burned, but was nevertheless gifted with courage to risk the unknown. He was acutely conscious of Berlioz's admonition that conductors are the most dangerous of all a composer's interpreters.[12]

Münch worked hard at being a conductor and over the years developed a professional ethic that put the daily well-being of his players and electrifying live performance at the head of his priorities. His working method was rooted in diligent personal score study, frequently through the night before a first rehearsal, so as to keep the rehearsals as efficient as possible. With new music, that of Messiaen for instance, he would spend considerable time with the composer before first reading a work with the orchestra, again in the hope of preventing the waste of precious rehearsal time. (Like most conductors of his ilk and era, he was not averse to adjusting scores—making cuts, for instance, in the Bizet and Dukas symphonies to render them "more palatable" to the public.) He also tried to keep pace with the other major conductors; when Toscanini came to Paris to conduct the Straram orchestra in 1934, Münch brought his violin to the rehearsal and quietly took a seat at the back of the section.[13]

While virtually all the conductors of the Société des Concerts rose to the podium from the ranks, Münch showed an uncommonly good understanding of people who make their living as orchestral musicians: "a hundred human beings, each one of whom knows joy and pain and suffering." He understood the "almost philanthropic act" that membership in an orchestra implies. He was acutely cognizant of the profession's physical, intellectual, and spiritual demands. Prior to taking the stage at a rehearsal, he would pause in the wings to listen to the musicians warm up, trying to gauge their feeling of the day. He sensed that over-rehearsing professional ensembles, particularly the Société des Concerts, was ill advised, and he often preferred to rely on their "receptivity and spontaneity" in the concert environment.[14] In a widely distributed videotape you can see and hear an obviously spontaneous 1962 performance where Münch leads the Boston Symphony Orchestra in the last movement of the *Fantastique,* driving them into a frenzy of speed and volume as if the idea had occurred to him on the spur of the moment. The musical results make little enough sense analytically but are undeniably thrilling. Note in this clip, too, the other evidence of his style: the long baton, the delicate gestures, the rapt concentration, the engaging personal warmth.[15]

Münch enjoyed being with the musicians in his charge—or at least acted like he did—and was given to calling them by pet names. Often in rehearsals he would acknowledge and pass over a player's error in what amounted to an unspoken but mutually understood contract that it would not recur. Knowing full well that orchestral musicians led a life of hard physical labor exerted for modest pay, he would still be taken aback to see his players standing around a movie set hoping for work or when a taxi driver told him he had been a 1er *prix* at the Conservatoire.[16]

The documents suggest an unusual compassion in his manner of expression around the players, a far cry from Gaubert's terse confrontations with his stars. One senses in Münch something of the amateur psychologist—something more, I think, than the average conductor acquires by osmosis.

He understood, too, the thing that separated him from the rank and file: "Musicians are generally not intellectuals." And who it was that paid his salary: "In the end," he observed, "it is the public who writes our history, who names the masterpieces and the great interpreters— and it is hard to please. There is only one valid, certain, effective way to keep its favor: to practice our art with frankness and joy, and to live for music more than for anything else in the world."[17]

Münch's salary was, to be sure, substantial from the first. In 1944–45 his income was 139,968 francs, compared with a typical rank-and-file stipend of 19,000 francs. Put another way, an average musician's share of the proceeds that year was 135 *jetons,* while Münch accrued 972. In 1945–46 he earned 660 *jetons,* while the players made 100; his share of the overall proceeds was 145,200 francs.[18]

This narrative will soon reach a point where Münch becomes an obstacle to the prosperity of the Société des Concerts, when the musicians begin to perceive his outside activities as treachery and the complexities of his character to be little short of villainous. To say that it was "nothing personal"—the French manner of debate always assumes a colleague's dignity, even when subjecting it to the most vigorous attack— begs the issue, for the disruptions of 1947–48 surrounding Charles Münch were among the most dramatic in the ensemble's history (and the folders documenting *l'affaire Münch* among the thickest in the archive).[19] But even if, as the *sociétaires* saw it, Münch quit them and their enterprise without so much as a by-your-leave, it says a great deal about both the worth of the man and the spirit of his players that they were always ready to have him back. It also bespeaks the tautness with which the once-suspect Alsatian had forged personal and artistic links to the very heart of the French nation.

The other central character in the history of the Société des Concerts during World War II and its aftermath was the violinist Jean Savoye. He was thirty-five when elected secretary in 1937 to oversee the program of modernization the radicals so vocally pursued, and he served in the post until his dismissal in 1948. Unlike many of the society's officers, Savoye had been interested in its leadership from the first. In several respects he was gifted for it: a superb office manager, unfazed by the mountain of paperwork required to administer a well-ordered symphony orchestra.

Like most of the other strong leaders of the Sociéte des Concerts, Savoye had a way with words that usually allowed him to get what he wanted. His contentiousness, especially when he felt the primacy of the society threatened from without, was unparalleled. He was all too well known and on the whole rather feared at the ministry, the union, and the rights organizations. Savoye was also the senior member of the administration; his policies had been governing the organization for more than a year before Münch appeared on the scene. That they never got along especially well, and at length became bitter enemies, was in the nature of their joint thirst for uncontested dominance of the Société des Concerts and its affairs.

Charles Münch inaugurated the 1938–39 season of twenty concerts— his first, the society's 112th—with Beethoven's Seventh Symphony, followed by the "Emperor" Concerto with Marguerite Long (recorded in 1944, at the end of the Occupation),[20] the premiere of a *Nocturne* for orchestra by Guy Ropartz, and *Daphnis et Chloé*, suite 2. The season continued in that vein, rich with orchestral showpieces (*La Valse* and *La Mer; Don Juan* and *Till Eulenspiegel; Scheherazade* and *Capriccio espagnol*) and a strong dose of the classical canon (the B-Minor Mass and Brandenburg Concertos; a good deal of Mozart and Haydn and a great deal of Beethoven; Schubert's A♭ Mass and "Unfinished" Symphony). Special events included a Bizet centenary concert in October, an all-Schubert concert in November, and a Fauré festival at the Palais de Chaillot in March. Walter, Monteux, and Nadia Boulanger appeared as guest conductors; among the soloists were Szigeti, Francescatti, Rubinstein, Alfredo Casella, André Navarra, and Feuermann. Fernand Oubradous played the Mozart bassoon concerto at a Mozart–Beethoven festival in January 1939 ("carrying me," wrote Oubradous, "to a privileged level until then reserved for Marcel Moyse alone");[21] Marcel Mule premiered a saxophone concertino by Eugène Bozza in February, the composer conducting. Other first performances included the Szymanowski *Stabat mater, Le Diable boiteux* of Jean Françaix, and Florent Schmitt's *Stèle pour le tombeau de Paul Dukas*. From almost any point of view this represents a season of uncommon interest, certainly on a par with the prevailing norms and practices of the best orchestras anywhere.

Marguerite Long played twice that season: the "Emperor" Concerto for the season opener and the Fauré Ballade toward the end of the year. Long was now more closely associated with her "glorious triad"— Fauré, Debussy, and Ravel—than even with Chopin. She saw it as a matter of nationalism, pure and simple: "All three, of diverse temperaments, are nonetheless essentially and uniquely French. They reflect the face of our art, the features that belong only to us: distinctiveness, elegance, profound emotion soberly expressed—that technical perfection and perfect taste that in every domain assures first place to the French, whether it be in fashion, in literature, or in art. And finally that incomparable thing: clarity. Fauréen, Debussyste, and Ravélien art is a thing of light, the light that is France. It lives without excess and without meaningless noise, lifted to the spiritual realm by an interior flame!"[22]

The French nation now had ample reason to draw on that flame, as world war came again. The younger musicians were mobilized in early 1939 and assigned to "passive defense" in the hospitals, armories, and *abattoirs* of the Paris region. France and its European allies declared war on Germany on 3 September 1939; in the minutes of the Société des Concerts the new *période de guerre* was reckoned from 1 November 1939. Some dozen musicians went to the front, a loss that exacerbated the personnel problems always faced by a new administration. Many of the senior members had elected to retire with Gaubert, among them the principal second violinist Luquin, Moyse, and the great oboist Bleuzet. As the 1939–40 season approached, Münch wrote the government attempting to secure special privileges for his "artists of the first order, irreplaceable members of our orchestra," naming Charon (doublebass), Dechesne (cello), Girard (*aspirant* in violin), Ladoux (cello), Lepetit (violin), Logerot (doublebass), and Oubradous. Savoye, not named by Münch, had also been called up. It was hoped that they could be stationed nearby and secure leave for Thursday, Saturday, and Sunday services of the Société des Concerts.[23]

But the 1939–40 season had for all intents and purposes to be abandoned. The musicians still in Paris offered benefit concerts for such worthy but unusual causes as Christmas trees for military units (the "Eroica," Ravel and Roussel, *L'Apprenti sorcier;* 17 December 1939), and, on 3 March 1940, a Journée Nationale de l'Œuvre du Vin Chaud de Soldat, where the proceeds supported the hot wine offered to the soldiers at the front—some 560,000 quarts per day, distributed by the French Red Cross and veterans' agencies from thirty-three centers across the country. During the French retreat from the east, the orchestra sustained a major loss when a truck containing Savoye's instruments, music, and personal papers was waylaid and apparently destroyed near Metz. It was perhaps on this occasion that the register of minutes for the mid-1930s was lost.

Overt military operations in France ended in the nation's defeat after the winter of 1939–40, and Paris was occupied on 14 June 1940. Now began, starting with the preparations for the 1940–41 season, the four-year saga of living with the enemy, of finding ways to carry on some semblance of ordinary artistic life. The Société des Concerts lived through the Nazi occupation the way the rest of Paris did—by ignoring it when possible, cooperating when necessary, and either bargaining with or cheating the Germans as often as they could. Mozart and Beethoven would be traded for heating in the Salle des Concerts; invitations to appear in festival performances touted by the propagandists —thus suggesting to the public that civilized life was possible under the Germans—would be accepted with the condition that the orchestra's prisoners of war be returned. When the Conservatoire's entire graduating classes of 1941 and 1942 were threatened with conscription for forced labor in Germany, Claude Delvincourt—Rabaud's successor as director—counter-attacked by forming an Orchestre des Cadets du Conservatoire (Conservatoire Youth Orchestra) that required them to stay in Paris.[24] This was the cleverest of strokes at the time; but almost immediately after the war the organization would be nipping at the rights and privileges of the original Conservatoire orchestra, as had always been feared. (In the early 1950s the Cadets du Conservatoire were reabsorbed into the academic institution as the senior student orchestra.)

Savoye planned and executed the society's week-by-week survival. Münch stayed as far above politics as possible but was also able to show whichever side of his heritage needed to be on display; both the Germans and the French knew that having him at the helm of the Parisian musical establishment was in their best interests. Münch himself reasoned that "my role was to help saddened souls escape to happier worlds."[25] It was later said that his country house in Marly served as a way station for escaped prisoners being smuggled to England and that he had directed a great deal of his personal wealth to financing the Resistance.

As the newspapers disappeared and assemblies came to be forbidden, communication with the public and the musicians took place mostly by postings in and around the Conservatoire. In October 1940 the musicians' union posted a plea for discipline and calm in the ranks and an orderly return to work so that the concert season could begin.[26] In November Savoye was notified that Jews were not allowed as administrators, directors, or secretaries-general of organizations receiving state subvention and was directed to attest to the society's compliance.[27] The documents of this period suggest that from the 1940 – 41 season the Société des Concerts managed tolerably well despite the shortages of personnel, fuel, and paper. Two weeks before each concert Savoye and the secretary submitted typescripts of the poster and program to censors at the Gruppe Cultur, along with a Visumantrag / Demande de Visa for printing that asked of the printer, *"Ist diese Firma jüdisch?"* It went on to warn that granting of a visa did not assure the rationing of enough paper to print and that no printer was to begin work before the visa was granted (a stipulation routinely ignored). The program leaflets from this period, incidentally, are half the dimension of the traditional booklets, some 11 × 14 centimeters.

Astonishingly, in view of the circumstances, the Société des Concerts was able to offer thirty Sunday concerts in 1940 – 41 and an additional end-of-season festival of three concerts at the Palais de Chaillot in June; Beethoven's Ninth concluded the year on 27 June 1941. The absence of foreign soloists that season had the effect of bringing the French establishment to the fore in a parade of talent reminiscent of earlier times: Pierre Bernac, Jean Doyen, Marcelle Meyer, Jacques Février, Lucette Descaves, René Benedetti, Marguerite Roesgen-Champion, Marcel Mule, Janine Micheau, Poulenc, and—again and again—Marguerite Long. Stravinsky conducted *Les Noces*.

Münch continued his aggressive promotion of new music with major performances that season of works by Honegger, Schmitt, and others. The program of 26 January 1941 featured Honegger's *Danse des morts* with narration by Jean-Louis Barrault, repeated on 2 February and then 23 March at the Palais de Chaillot, and soon issued in a deluxe recording. In May 1941 Münch and Marcelle Meyer introduced Conservatoire audiences to Honegger's Piano Concerto. Honegger himself was booked to conduct two concerts the following season. On 8 February 1942 he led the Prelude to *La Tempête*, the Concerto, *Pacific 231*, and another performance of the *Danse des morts;* on 25 June 1942, in the new "Spring Season," he gave the first Paris performances of the *Symphonie* [No. 2] *pour cordes*, composed 1941, and of a second dramatic work with Barrault, *Jeanne au bûcher* ("Joan of Arc at the Stake"). Münch thereupon learned and programmed the String Symphony on several occasions before recording it in March 1944. Honegger's *Chant de la libéra-tion* was featured on the first concert after the Liberation, on 22 October 1944.

Arthur Honegger's work had entered the repertoire of the Société des Concerts more than a decade before with the *Pastorale d'été* under Gaubert (17 January 1926). *Pacific 231* was featured in a number of concerts in 1928 and 1929, including two out-of-town appearances in Lyon. *Rugby* concluded the opening concert of the 1929–30 season; Maurice Maréchal offered the first Conservatoire performance of the Cello Concerto toward the beginning of the following season, 26 October 1930, and recorded the Andante in 1943. In addition to the recordings with Münch from the 1940s, the Société des Concerts left an important Honegger discography in LP (long-playing) format, including the 1957 suites from the films *Mermoz* and *Les Visiteurs du soir,* Georges Tzipine conducting.

In October 1941 the administration was called to the Reich Propaganda Ministry and told to ready gala concerts for the 150th anniversary of Mozart's death. The first of these, an all-Mozart concert on 30 November 1941 in the Salle des Concerts, featured Münch conducting and Jacques Thibaud in the Mozart A-Major Violin Concerto, K. 219, which they had recorded for Gramophone the previous June. At the Palais de Chaillot on 7 December 1941 the German conductor Hermann Abendroth (Furtwängler's successor at the Gewandhaus) appeared on the podium with the Leipzig pianist Hans Beltz. Here the bizarre program consisted of the Franck Symphonic Variations and Mozart C-Minor Piano Concerto, K. 491, and Max Reger's Mozart Variations—recorded two days later for Odéon.[28] The bilingual programs are headed "Orchester der Konservatoriums-Gesellschaft."

Minutes of the general assembly called for 16 November 1941 to discuss the command performances appear beneath the bold rubric "Concerts de Collaboration." There was no choice but to agree to appear, though the proposal caused *"une certaine émotion,"* and the Germans were warned in a bilingual written response that the atmosphere for such events was scarcely ideal. Conditions were set: the four *sociétaires* still prisoners of war had to be returned before the concert, and the forty tons of coal already promised for the season would need to be delivered in full, since only fourteen had so far arrived. What the committee might do if the prisoners were not returned was the most delicate of the questions posed, to which Savoye replied that if such were the case he would present himself to the military governor and threaten to sabotage the concerts; the proposal was consciable only insofar as it produced the missing colleagues.[29]

The 1941–42 season also included a memorial performance on 26 October 1941 of the Concerto for Orchestra by Philippe Gaubert, who had died in Paris on 8 July.

Another important mechanism by which the Société des Concerts assured its livelihood during the 1940s was through its involvement in the music-education movement, an exploding network of enterprises that embraced as much pragmaticism as social theory. Youth concerts began in late 1941 under the rubrics "Concerts Jeune France" (ten concerts, 1941–42) and "Concerts Éducatifs," later "Jeunesse et Musiques" (Youth and Music), and quickly developed into full-fledged series administered by enthusiastic lay and professional organizations.

On 31 January 1942, for instance, the orchestra devoted a program at the Palais de Chaillot exclusively to students (Étudiants-Scolaires / Centres de Jeunesse), but the room was so cold that the orchestra stayed only to avoid the negative publicity that abandoning the young people would have caused. (Photographs of concerts in the Palais de Chaillot during the war show the public, including German military officers, bundled in overcoats.) By 1943 the program called Évolution Musicale de la Jeunesse (EMJ) was well established, with fifteen pairs of brief concerts on Thursday afternoons. On Thursday, 14 January 1943, for example, Mme Germaine Arbeau-Bonnefoy presented the fifth program in that year's series. At 2:15 P.M. she lectured on "Rhythm: Its Diversity," with illustrations from the music of Bach, Mozart, Beethoven, Weber, Ravel, and an unspecified Strauss. At 4:45 she focused on J. S. Bach, answering the question "What is Imitation? Canon, Fugue," with "explanations made concrete by dance examples choreographed by Janine Solane and performed by three students from her class." Jean Constantinesco conducted the pianist Geneviève Joy in the first movement of the F-Minor Harpsichord Concerto, BWV 1056, and Pierre Nérini in the first movement of the E-Major Violin Concerto, BWV 1043.[30]

In 1944 the remarkable organization called Jeunesses Musicales de France (JMF) was created by René Nicoly and extended to Brussels in July 1945 by Marcel Cuvelier as the Jeunesses Musicales Internationales (JMI), in order to build an organization that "would actively work against the causes of international conflict through the universal language of music."[31] (Today the annual audience in France of live concerts sponsored by the JMF is estimated to be in excess of one million listeners, and the JMI is the world's largest network for youth-and-music activities.) The Société des Concerts played twenty-five JMF concerts in the 1944–45 season, generally in three- or four-day sessions. Among the prominent soloists associated with the movement were Marguerite Long and Jacques Thibaud, Samson-François, Lily Pons, Jacques Février and Francis Poulenc, and Janine Micheau; the orchestra was conducted by Münch, Cluytens, Martinon, Cloëz, and many others.

Another important development along these lines was the emergence, from June 1942, of the Chorale de l'Université de Paris under the direction of Jean Gitton, a violinist in the orchestra. The university chorus appeared in many of the student concerts during the war, then was gradually replaced in its functions by the Société des Chanteurs de St-Eustache, established in 1944 by the Reverend Père Émile Martin and frequently conducted by Gitton. By the 1950s Gitton had essentially become an associate conductor of the orchestra, specializing in choral works and ballets.

The student concerts helped the society establish and keep a wartime rhythm and what rapidly approached full employment for the *sociétaires*. In 1941–42 in addition to twenty-four major concerts there were eleven youth concerts, a tour to the provinces, about a dozen independent bookings, some thirty radio broadcasts, and more than two dozen recording sessions; the following season consisted of twenty-five major concerts and nearly twice as much activity on the other fronts. Savoye had succeeded in establishing what he liked to call an administration in perfect order. The Société des Concerts was, at least in outer appearance, a model of social well-being in an occupied land.

Marguerite Long continued to play a major professional and personal role in using her art to quell political tension. On 14 February 1941 she and Jacques Thibaud joined Münch for an afternoon concert sponsored by the Red Cross to benefit French prisoners of war. In March she agreed to premier Ernesto Halffter's *Rapsodie portugaise* for piano and orchestra, in several respects the most direct descendent of *Nights in the Gardens of Spain;* this was first performed 23 March 1941 at the Palais de Chaillot. Halffter had wanted a first performance in France since his work was dedicated to Ravel, so Long learned it directly from the manuscript score;[32] a recording was made in October 1946 and March 1947. On 4 June 1942 Long was the featured soloist in a Festival Fauré–Debussy—where the Debussy *Fantaisie,* so closely associated with her, was identified as by Fauré.[33]

In what was perhaps a less astute decision on her part, Marguerite Long joined the Société des Concerts when it traveled to Vichy on 20 October 1942 with Mozart, Beethoven's Third Piano Concerto, Ravel's *Rapsodie espagnole,* and Roussel's Third Symphony. The program for the season-opening concert in Paris on 13 October, billed "to benefit the Marshal's winter relief effort and the Association des Anciens Élèves du Conservatoire de Paris," proudly announced the Vichy concert beneath the heading "Activité de la Société des Concerts" as "in honor of Marshal Pétain, chief of the French state." The press released by government officials after the concert oozed with contrived patriotism:

HOMMAGE
of the Société des Concerts du Conservatoire
to Marshal PÉTAIN, chief of state

The Société des Concerts du Conservatoire, "the musical expression of France," presented its official artistic homage to the chief of state at his residence in Vichy.

A full house, among whom one could note Madame la Maréchale Pétain, M. Hautecœur the director of Fine Arts, the most eminent personalities of the diplomatic corps from all the countries in Europe, as well as *le tout Paris* of the provisional capital, offered a grandiose ovation at the end of the concert, to the great conductor of such elevated musical soul who is Charles Münch.

Mozart, Beethoven, and two composers of our own were on the program: Ravel, with his dramatic, fairylike and colorful *Rapsodie espagnole,* and Albert Roussel (former officer of our navy, whose works are too rarely performed at the Sunday concerts), with his splendid and very French Symphony in G.

"Là, tout n'est qu'ordre, beauté, clarté, équilibre, esprit, joie." Never, perhaps, has our Charles Münch, so admired and so beloved, conducted with more fervor or enthusiasm. This exceptional man is touched by the grace of music. He knows its secrets, and has the genius to put each musical thought in plain light, practically on stage.

There was not a note without intention, without emotion; not a measure without interest. Everything sang, everything palpitated, everything was human, laughing, or suffering. The meaning of music is thus illuminated as life is by faith. We thank Münch once again for the total gift of himself that he makes to our art.

Our countrywoman Marguerite Long covered herself in glory in interpreting, through her infinite mastery of the keyboard, the exquisite charm and incomparable pearl that is Beethoven's Concerto in C Minor. Finally, let us praise the magnificently "sonorous and human" instrument on which Münch plays, from its percussionist to its concertmaster (a prince of violinistic genius)—an ensemble admirable in sonority and subtlety that senses, imagines, and understands in an instant the unbelievable nuances of a prestigious baton.

The Société des Concerts du Conservatoire needs to become, without delay, the national orchestra of our great land, in order to travel the world as ambassador of French musical thought.[34]

(The allusion of the lines given in French, above, is to Baudelaire's "L'Invitation au voyage": *"Là, tout n'est qu'ordre et beauté, / Luxe, calme et volupté."*)

This flirtation with the Vichy government was followed by an equally nuanced event on 12 December 1942, a "Gala of Works by Prisoners, organized by the Office of Fine Arts of the City of Paris and by the Société des Concerts, Ambassador Georges Scapini and General Commissioner for Prisoners Maurice Pinot, honorary presidents." (Scapini, blinded in the first world war, was the Vichy government's chief envoy to Berlin for issues involving military prisoners, and a frequent visitor to the camps; Pinot ran the office of repatriation in Vichy and oversaw a certain amount of the propaganda effort.)[35] The program consisted of works by four French composers, two of them (Émile Goué and Émile Damais) still in captivity in Poland; the two former prisoners of war, Maurice Thiriet and Henri Challan, were able to attend the concert, conducted by yet another former prisoner, Jean Gitton. What made the "prisoners concert" historic—"a unique event in the history of music and war"—was that it was broadcast to central Europe, with special arrangements made to provide radio receivers in the camps. The propaganda machine again provided the publicity: "We can never do too much, we can never think too much, of our friends spending their slow and dull lives, all these months, behind the barbed wire."[36]

Two *sociétaires*, the violinist François Lovisolo and the violist Jacques Boucher, were released to rejoin the orchestra in February 1943. Boucher, having lost a finger, spent a couple of seasons in the percussion battery, then moved permanently to the doublebass section—he had earned the *1er prix* in both viola and doublebass—where he served until 1963. The concertmaster Roland Charmy was returned to France in March 1943. The other members recorded as having have been away at war were André Pascal, René Chédécal, Louis Franquin, Albert Charon *fils*, Ulysse Delécluse, and Arthur Pavoni. There appear to have been no war-related deaths.

In February 1943 Münch declined an order to conduct Wagner in the Palais de Chaillot, a *"Hommage français à Wagner à l'occasion du 60e anniversaire de sa mort"* on 9 and 16 March, and turned the podium over to Alfred Cortot. The committee took care to note in the official minutes why it had "decided to agree to participate in these concerts, believing it essential that no artist of the Société des Concerts should be swept away" [into the forced labor pool].[37] All the major celebrities in French music were by the 1942–43 season faced with difficult decisions as to their participation in events that might be seen—and soon enough were indeed seen—as collaborationist. All had imagined until about then that their only option as artists was high visibility, preferably in the French repertoire. Cortot, meanwhile, was known to believe in the musical superiority of Austro-German composers and genres and had concertized widely in Germany after the fall of France.[38] His particular solution to the question of living with the Germans cost him dearly after the war, and was at the root of the famous incident of 19 January 1947: when Cortot took the stage for the Schumann Piano Concerto in his first appearance at the Conservatoire after the Liberation, the *sociétaires* rose *en masse* and left him to face the public alone.

Another activity open to charges of collaboration was a series of five Beethoven concerts in July 1943 with Hermann Abendroth at the Palais de Chaillot. The soloists were Cortot, Ginette Neveu, Wilhelm Kempff, and Elly Ney. These were listed in the minutes simply as "*5 concerts Beethoven*," without further specifics.

A subtler political gesture of Münch and the Société des Concerts was their engagement to provide the soundtrack for Marcel Carné's great film *Les Enfants du paradis*. The music was by the Jewish composer Joseph Kosma, who composed in hiding under the pseudonym Georges Mouqué. (Maurice Thiriet's name was used for the credits). Shot during the Occupation, *Les Enfants du paradis* was, and is, viewed by the French as one of the greatest statements of resistance among professional artists. It release was purposefully delayed until 9 March 1945, to celebrate the Liberation.[39]

During the war Charles Münch rose to unrivaled and on the whole well merited pre-eminence as the nation's finest conductor. It was a position he meant to retain after the war was over, and to that end he kept a careful eye on competitors emerging from the provinces. At the same time, it was no longer possible for him to conduct everything, or even all the Sunday concerts, and attractive invitations were being extended to him from abroad even before the end of the war was in sight. It was in that context that André Cluytens was first called by the committee from his post at the Lyon Opéra to conduct the concert of 20 December 1942 (Beethoven's Fourth and one of the *Leonore* overtures, the Liszt E♭ Piano Concerto, and *The Pines of Rome*).[40] Cluytens was unusually successful with the public and—more unusually still—popular with the musicians, and the committee indicated at once its interest in having him back as often as possible. He appeared regularly with the Société des Concerts beginning with the 1943–44 season.

Münch strenuously objected to Cluytens; if a Lyon conductor were to be engaged it should be Jean Witkowski (a cellist, son of the composer / conductor Georges Martin Witkowski, director of the Lyon Conservatoire). But Witkowski's April 1943 appearance showed him to be "notoriously incompetent," and Savoye and the committee counted him as one of a series of poor conductors purposefully engaged by Münch.[41] Münch also went to some lengths to move Cluytens's 1943–44 concerts from the Palais de Chaillot to the Salle des Concerts, then accused Savoye of "betrayal" in the matter of contracting Cluytens for the forthcoming season. Both Savoye and Münch tried, at the Assemblée Générale of June 1943, to put the best face on their differences, and the minutes note a decision to leave them to their *"tête-à-tête."*[42] Yet there was more than the usual degree of unrest among the musicians; Münch had moved the popular principal cellist, Auguste Cruque, into the ranks, holding that he "no longer retained his former powers, once used with such *brio*," and the committee had dismissed Fernand Oubradous for absences caused by his work as artistic director of Taffanel's venerable Société des Instruments à Vent, now evolved into a rival enterprise, the Concerts F. Oubradous / Association des Concerts de Chambre de Paris.[43]

By spring 1944 optimism over the end of the war was full blown. The official season was suspended in March, and all the musicians released from their obligations at the end of April, though some independent concerts carried on through May. The invasion in Normandy began on 6 June 1944; by mid-August the Allies were reaching Paris, from Mantes to the northwest and Orléans to the south. The general assembly of 10 June 1944, with the invasion in full swing, began in high exaltation but was soon interrupted by an air-raid alert and a long delay while members trickled back from having taken shelter in a Métro tunnel. Münch's entry, late as usual, was greeted with a salvo of applause; he went on to thank the musicians for their loyalty during the war years and asserted with confidence that they were gathered for the last assembly ever to open in wartime.[44]

The Resistance took the streets of Paris on 19 August 1944; on 24 and 25 August 1944 General Leclerc and French military personnel, through prior agreement with General Eisenhower, officially liberated the city. Münch, whose patriotic activities during the Occupation now left him comfortably above suspicion, took the lead in conducting the Liberation concerts. The 1944–45 season opened with a carefully chosen festive program: Ibert's *Ouverture pour une fête,* Roussel's *Le Bardit des Francs,* Honegger's new *Chant de la libération,* and Debussy's *Le Martyre de Saint Sébastien.* As the season went on there was a good deal of Bach, Mozart, and Beethoven, but not a note of Wagner, who would not be heard again until late 1946. In January and February there were concerts honoring, and entitled, "Alsace-Lorraine," "URSS," "Commandos," and "Armée Rouge." The Allies crossed the Rhine in late March 1945; on 4 April in Paris there was a gala performance at the Théâtre des Champs-Élysées sponsored by "Special Service, Seine Section—United States of America, by special courtesy of l'Association Française d'Action Artistique." The souvenir program has Münch's picture placed directly opposite General de Gaulle's and indicates in English that "the services of the artists have been donated of [*sic*] the Allied Armies."[45] In Berlin on 30 April 1945 Hitler and Eva Braun married and committed suicide in the ruins of the Chancellery.

The postwar years were to bring a new round of uncontrolled inflation, governmental disarray, and difficulties for the musicians in feeding their families that most of them had been spared during the war itself. Real socialist thinking would permeate the society, and struggles between labor and management were soon to become routine and fierce. The Paris musical establishment would be fundamentally rebuilt around the radio and television stations. For the moment, however, there were grounds only for celebration, and for expecting that the Société des Concerts was on the verge of becoming the national orchestra of France, with a year-round program of concerts, tours, and recordings and a roster of the world's best conductors and soloists.

In the summer and fall of 1945, Savoye sought to discover which of the *sociétaires* meant to rejoin the orchestra, releasing in turn the wartime substitutes, who were sent on their way with the society's warm thanks. The postwar adjustments in personnel went on for many months; the pay records for spring 1946, for instance, still show nearly forty nonmembers, and the manifests for the following season show about fifteen substitute musicians at every service. The concertmaster, Roland Charmy, left in June 1945; Pierre Nérini was elected (over Dumont and Huot) to succeed him.[46] Münch, too, was anxious to leave, having had to abandon his first attempt to go to the United States when the war broke out. For 1946 he accepted engagements in New York, Los Angeles, Chicago, and Houston, among other American cities, as well as London, Prague, and Israel. He was also being pursued by London Decca to record a sizeable repertoire in England.

The Société des Concerts at last transferred the bulk of its activities to the Théâtre des Champs-Élysées. The four associations—the Société des Concerts and the Colonne, Lamoureux, and Pasdeloup orchestras—quickly regained their hegemony over Paris concert life. Each now played every Sunday at 5:45 between October and April, with the Colonne at the Théâtre du Châtelet, Lamoureux in the Salle Pleyel, and Pasdeloup in the Palais de Chaillot. Delvincourt's Cadets du Conservatoire appeared in the Salle des Concerts and were successful in securing governmental subventions to meet their deficits; it was observed that in some respects the Société des Concerts had become the *"parent pauvre."*[47] Much of the rest of the Paris season was presented by the impresarios, now calling themselves Organisateurs de Concerts: members of the Dandelot and Valmalète families and the new agency of Charles Kiesgen. Savoye and his successors, administering a year-round full-service orchestra from a minimal office, relied on the agencies as much as they could. The business arrangements were tidier when the bulk of the contractual paperwork and long-range planning for soloists and guest conductors was left to the agents.

The seasons grew more and more ambitious: twenty-four Sunday concerts in 1944–45 and almost exactly one hundred other services; 1945–46 saw only twenty subscription concerts (and in the spring numerous schedule changes owing to Münch's "indisposition"), but even more ancillary services and a return to out-of-town appearances: a week in England in November (in exchange with the London Philharmonic Orchestra, which played Sunday concerts in Paris under Münch and Thomas Beecham) and dates in Lyon and Le Mans. In October 1946 the Société des Concerts spent a week in the Walthamstow Town Hall preparing a major series of recordings with Münch for Decca: Berlioz's *Le Corsaire,* the Franck D-Minor Symphony and Symphonic Variations, *Boléro* and *Daphnis et Chloé,* the Roussel suites, and *Le Rouet d'Omphale.* There was a corresponding decline in new music undertaken, with many fewer first performances than during the war. This was very much to Savoye's liking, and very much disapproved of by Charles Münch.

None of the musicians could participate in anything approaching the totality of their engagements as *sociétaires,* let alone properly assure their service as theater and chamber players. The Radio Orchestra, in which a number of the *sociétaires* played, demanded that their musicians be on call whenever air time was available, thus sharply increasing the number of conflicts for all. Motion toward exclusivity of appointment was now inexorable, and for his part Savoye tried to insist that *sociétaires* owed their first allegiance to the Société des Concerts by levying monetary penalties on his colleagues when they missed engagements in order to play for competing organizations.

Belonging as it did directly to the state, the RDF (Radiodiffusion Française) had unusual powers that it did not hesitate to wield, threatening the concert associations in a number of heavy-handed ways. In the postwar years the battles of that campaign often seem to dominate the activities of the Société des Concerts and its administrators. To consider in detail how the Radio Orchestra forced reshaping of the national orchestral enterprise in the 1940s and 1950s would be to take this chapter well beyond its established boundaries. Suffice it to observe here that the society's name is engraved in the annals of European jurisprudence on account of it, in the opinion called Conseil d'État 9 Mars 1951: Société des Concerts du Conservatoire.[48]

This particular incident began no differently than many another. The committee refused permission for *sociétaires* to play in a radio concert of 15 January 1947, presumably because the Société des Concerts had two engagements for (lesser paying) youth concerts that day. Two players ignored the injunction and played for the RDF, thus incurring sharp fines from the committee. The RDF responded by suspending broadcasts of the Société des Concerts (and hence the income) until the minister of fine arts had ruled on a complaint brought against Savoye by the affected players. In February 1947 the society filed a case for damages and interest against the radio service with the Conseil des Ministres. Subsequently the Conseil d'État, the nation's highest appellate court on administrative matters, ruled in favor of the Société des Concerts du Conservatoire on 9 March 1951, awarding it 50,000 francs plus interest from February 1947. It held that the RDF's motive in suspending the society's broadcasts had no foundation that could be construed as in the public interest; that it had misused its power, prejudicially treating the Société des Concerts differently than the other *grandes associations symphoniques;* and that responsibility for the error must be borne by the state.

"Conseil d'État 9 Mars 1951: Société des Concerts du Conservatoire" today is regarded as a landmark decision establishing that a public service must treat all its constituents equally *("principe d'égalité devant les services publiques")*. This is one of the three legal conditions—the so-called *lois Rolland:* continuity (thus limiting the right to strike), equality, and mutability (the requirement to adapt to changing circumstance)—now incumbent on all public services in France, from the gas company to the pharmacies. French notions of the public interest, in turn, strongly shape the emerging field of European Union public law.

All this did little, of course, to remedy the root cause of the institutional unrest brought by the advent of radio orchestras and of broadcasting in general. On the contrary, and even after the principal of exclusivity of appointments was established, the rivalry between the Orchestre National de la Radiodiffusion Française and the Société des Concerts—and its successor, the Orchestre de Paris—continued strong, often ferocious. The word *national* raised particular hackles.

Internally, the first post-war crisis may be said to have begun in March 1946, when an Assemblée Générale *extraordinaire* was called in response to a circulated petition of some of the musicians to the effect that "a *malaise* exists at the heart of the society" that demanded immediate correction. It was alleged that the orchestra had separated into clans, that the secretary-general, Savoye, was behaving like a dictator in hiring and firing, that the standoff with the national radio service was unnecessary, and, finally, that relations with the government and other societies had reached a nadir.[49]

At the meeting on 28 March 1946 Savoye read a long, imperial response to the petition, noting particularly how his *amour-propre* was wounded by overhearing the names he was being called behind his back and even to his face. (The most common of these was *salaud*, "bastard.") He had not in fact fired *sociétaires* who wanted to work for the Radio Orchestra, even though both Lamoureux and Pasdeloup had done precisely that, and even though the radio service had forbidden some of his *sociétaires* to travel to England the previous November. While it was true that in 1939 Savoye had fired the bass clarinetist Loterie for a "lack of talent prejudicial to the interests of the Société des Concerts" and the oboist Boudard for deafness (about which Bruno Walter had complained), otherwise every single member of the Société des Concerts had kept his place during the war. Any problems with extramural relations Savoye attributed to jealousy: "An institution on the move makes enemies." As far as the government was concerned, "we've been on good terms with them and we've been on bad, but we never get anything out of them anyway."

At the conclusion of his remarks there was not the customary round of polite applause, but rather, the minutes indicate, a *"silence absolu."* Questioners moved quickly to the matter of the unwelcome dictatorship that had emerged during the war. It was suggested that Savoye had edged the popular personnel officer Georges Guérin out of office. The orchestra had lost a valued contract with the Comédie-Française, in effect for the 1943–44 season, owing to Savoye's manner of behavior. Lucien Thévet, the hornist who with the trumpeter Geneste appears to have led the opposition, noted (rightly) that "the society doesn't really exist at all anymore. The committee doesn't run it. Only M. Savoye is in charge." A partisan of Savoye called out: "But Thévet never goes to the committee meetings. If all the committee members were like he is, Savoye really would be governing alone."

Robert Benedetti suggested, in written remarks, that the source of the *malaise* was simple; the *camarades stagiaires,* on whom they were more reliant than ever, had little if any security of employment. In one of the wiser contributions to that day's gathering he urged calm, a return to government by the statutes, morality, discipline, and a steadfast belief in the talent of the young people. A vote of confidence in the committee (and thus in Savoye's stewardship) yielded results of 32 in favor, 14 opposed, and 4 abstentions. The bloc of nay-sayers was, nevertheless, alarmingly large.[50]

A few weeks later, at the year-end assembly of 30 June 1946, Münch took the chair and cited the friction with Savoye as an excuse for his own release. He began by noting that the confidence a conductor and an administrator must share was no longer to be found, and that under those circumstances he could not continue to conduct their concerts and take responsibility for the results. "All that said, *messieurs,* it's obvious that you must choose between M. Savoye and me. If you name another secretary-general, I'll stay as your president-conductor and do the next season. If you choose to keep M. Savoye, I would need to ask you, for now, to give me a year's leave. My decision is irreversible, and it would be useless to ask me to go back on what I've just said."

During the discussion that followed his prepared remarks, Münch held his ground: "Savoye has his good points, and I like him fine. But he does what he wants. I'm sorry, *messieurs,* but I can't go on. I can't. I'm no longer young. Give me a leave of absence. You did it for others, for Gaubert." Cries of "Never!" rang out in the hall.

"Don't deny me that," he replied. "I want you to know how happy I would be to conduct an orchestra like that of the society, where there are so many fine artists. But now let me leave: you choose, vote, decide. Let me know the outcome." He made ready to go but was dissuaded by Benedetti's observation that in order to make any progress, the members needed to hear both sides of the story.

Savoye, said Münch, considered him merely a commodity; Savoye talked quite openly in those terms, and Münch resented it. Savoye revealed that their differences had come to a head only a few weeks earlier, as they were planning for the triumphant return to Paris of Zino Francescatti in late spring 1946. Münch had insisted on programming Messiaen's *Offrandes oubliées* and the first performance of a new Suite for Violin by Milhaud, and in addition had wedged Pierre Bernac and the St-Eustache singers onto the program in excerpts from Monteverdi's *Orfeo*. Savoye, thinking the program too elevated for the public, had put the Beethoven Violin Concerto at the front of the program without consulting Münch. Then Münch had rearranged the dates, with the result that Francescatti appeared (on 2 June 1946) back to back with another legendary violinist, Szigeti (on 12 June).

For the forthcoming trip to Nancy and Strasbourg (July 1947) Münch was insisting on a program with Beethoven's Eighth Symphony and Roussel's *Bacchus and Ariadne*—certain, thought Savoye, to lose money. Furthermore Münch was now in the habit of summoning the secretary-general to his country house instead of coming to committee meetings; Savoye said he was made to feel like a groundskeeper or butler.

Münch now turned to his discontent with the favors routinely being accorded André Cluytens, so obviously being groomed to succeed him. He had voiced his disapproval as early as the first engagement of Cluytens in 1942, which Delvincourt had solved by "taking everyone to dinner." Jean Gitton tried to inject some compassion into the debate: "Everybody in the orchestra knows that M. Münch is irreplaceable" (*"Pas du tout,"* interjected Münch. "No one is irreplaceable.") "M. Münch knows very well," continued Gitton, "that the orchestra loves him. But we all know, too, how hard Savoye works to make the administrative and artistic areas function. For those of us who have to making a living, who have to support families, this [making of a choice between Savoye and Münch] is an impossible situation, a terrible blow, one that strikes at the renown of the Société. All the effort of the last six or seven years will be lost."

"*Merci,* my dear Gitton," replied Münch. "What you say is very sweet. But . . . "

As courage to confront Münch began to gather, Elissalde asked him whether he would conduct all the Sunday concerts if he stayed on. "Not all," he replied. But he would engage first-rate conductors to replace him while he was in Boston.

"We're forced to ask," said Benedetti, "if you are still giving the Société des Concerts as much as when you took the position."

"I've always put it in first place," he answered.

"You had us gather at the Café de Madrid to tell us how deeply you loved the Société and that you would never abandon it. Today you change your mind. It's a difficult situation. Nobody wants to see you go; the entire committee would resign if it would make you stay. But you have your own ideas. You want your particular programs. Imagine if we did exclusively what you wanted: the programs would interest the public less, and the receipts would fall."

Münch replied: "Have you had anything to complain about monetarily since I've been at the head?"

Now André Huot, a partisan of Cluytens and so far Savoye's trusted collaborator, suggested that Münch's out-of-town engagements left him in unpredictable humor. He had come back to Paris for the 1945–46 concerts from an engagement in Prague, for instance, transformed and fresh. But in the spring he went to Egypt and on his return things were altogether different, culminating in the disagreements over the Francescatti concert.

"I'm always fine," Münch replied, "when I don't have to see M. Savoye and yourself." Yet Huot was routinely summoned to join Savoye on the missions to visit Münch at his country house. "I'm in the bathtub with them," Huot noted; if Savoye were to lose his mandate, he himself would have to resign, too.

"Keep Savoye," Münch shouted. "I'm leaving."

"You aren't allowed to," cried Huot.

"*Alors,* I'm going anyway. Send the police after me. . . . I'll be back on the sixth. Make of it what you will."

Here the stenographer gave up trying to transcribe the conversation, writing simply "*brouhaha.*" Huot tried to make progress on the matter of who would conduct in 1946–47, since the candidates Münch had proposed—among others, Pierre Sancan and Franz André—were not of sufficient stature. Huot now asked Münch point-blank, "Would you accept Cluytens?"

To which came the terse reply "*Non!* . . . Take Martinon."

Münch's favorite *protégé* had played two seasons as a violin *aspirant* toward the end of the war and had served as unofficial *2ᵉ chef*—he was never made a *sociétaire*—from 1945. The committee agreed that Martinon had considerable talent, but he did not sell out the house, while Cluytens did. Martinon was also a composer of not inconsiderable ambition, which always frightened the membership. The orchestra's poll on the question of what amounted to the designation for 1946–47 of a principal guest conductor showed Cluytens with 40 votes and no more than 5 for anyone else.

There matters stood. There was no swaying Münch from either his opposition to Cluytens or his intent to go to Boston. The musicians thought the latter a flagrant breach of contract. In a single meeting the very structure of the Société des Concerts, suggested the violinist Fontalirand, had unraveled. In truth it had been unraveling for some time, largely through the routine ignoring of the statutes that wartime had engendered, and the resultant transfer of administrative and artistic power from the musicians to the conductor and general manager. Münch had no intention of recognizing a contractual obligation to the Société des Concerts. (His second five-year mandate would have been in effect through 1947–48.) "Now it's up to the lawyers," he shouted to the committee as the society retreated for the summer vacation.[51]

But the next day, 1 July 1946, the committee met and officially refused him his leave of absence.

An Assemblée Générale *extraordinaire* was convened on Sunday, 29 September 1946, to examine the implications of the stalemate. Münch send a conciliatory note:

Chers messieurs:

I greatly regret not being able to be with you today to tell you personally of the chagrin I've had to withstand over not conducting the six concerts that I had planned for the first half of the season.

You know why, and it would wound me to have you think that I wouldn't conduct these concerts simply because I preferred to be away.

Forgive me for having asked for leave, during our last general assembly, in such a brusque fashion, without having brought you up to date about what had come before. I had returned from a trip the night before, and I didn't know that a leave request had to be filed three weeks before the meeting. The statutes don't say so. I must tell you, further, that the situation that led to my request had been going on for three months.

I have the fondest memory of the years we worked together and I thank you from the bottom of my heart for the effort you made. I would be most pleased, if the future allows, to conduct you again.[52]

Münch was not expected back in Paris until October 1947, though he had unilaterally committed the society to travel to England for the recording sessions with Decca in October 1946. There were few workable provisions in the statutes for the governance of the Société des Concerts without a president, and the need for checks and balances to Savoye was now apparent to everybody. Both sides had engaged lawyers; the society retained Me Roger Hauert, and Münch first engaged Me Jacques Charpentier, then—after Charpentier and Hauert had begun to forge a compromise—Mme Pillot, with whom Münch was rumored to have a romantic attachment. The committee had virtually no contact with their president, but instead read about his peregrinations to South America, then New York, Boston, and Chicago, then Palestine, in the *Figaro.*

Savoye now read a long address on how things stood. The committee had hoped for a reconciliation with Münch over the summer, perhaps delegating his administrative responsibilities to Delvincourt at the Conservatoire. But Münch had refused this plan, then failed to appear for any committee meetings. Viola and contrabass auditions had been scheduled for the second of the two days Münch was in Paris, but at the last minute he canceled his participation, pleading an early-morning flight that he must have known about in advance. The society had yet to announce its 1946–47 season, traditionally unveiled on the first of September.

Earlier in the month (September 1946) Savoye and the violinist Marcel Larue, as *commissaire du personnel,* had needed to go all the way to London to consult with their conductor. They lacked details on the London concerts and Decca recordings Münch had arranged on his own and meant, among other things, to dissuade him from a new Nielsen symphony for which there was insufficient rehearsal time. Every effort to agree to the programs failed; Münch would suggest them, then refuse to initial the typewritten drafts. "One day was white," complained Savoye, "and the next one black."(Münch would then deny having had conversations with the committee at all. "No one has spoken to me about anything," he later complained.) Given an ultimatum, he agreed to conduct two London concerts and the Decca recording sessions in October, but declined to appear in Paris at all during 1946–47.[53]

By an overwhelming majority, the general assembly proceeded to approve a lawsuit against Münch for breach of contract (53 favoring, 9 opposed) and to continue an "orderly operation" of the society as ad-ministered by Savoye and his committee, largely through engaging the guest conductors of their choice (58 favoring, 4 opposed). Yet the as-sembly declined to name a formal successor, preferring instead to force a compromise that would retain Münch on the podium. They would withdraw the suit the minute there was positive response from anyone in Münch's camp.

On 25 October 1946 a mediation was attempted at the Beaux-Arts, chaired by its director-general, Jacques Jaujard. By prior arrangement no lawyers were present; Münch came with his assistant, Mlle Laurent, and the Société des Concerts was represented by Savoye, Huot, and La-rue. Jaujard indicated his objectives: that Münch should retain his place as *président-chef* of the Société des Concerts, that he would abandon his recently announced November appearance with the rival Orchestre Na-tional, that he would conduct a series of UNESCO-sponsored benefits in November and December, and that he would appear, at a minimum, for the closing Sunday concerts of the season, 16 and 23 March 1947, and perhaps two or three more. He would preside until the end of 1947–48, the conclusion of two five-year terms of office. The atmosphere was con-ciliatory and generally respectful, and the representatives of the society shook hands and left thinking they had obtained an *accord complet*.[54]

Münch told his brother a different story: "*They* had me today. I was summoned to the director-general at the Beaux-Arts, Jaujard, in the company of these gentlemen, not to say gangsters, and faced with pro-testations of affection and calls on my patriotism, I had to yield—until fall 1948."[55]

It was under these ground rules that the 1946–47 season finally took shape. Münch appeared only minimally thereafter; Cluytens led twenty concerts, with the rest covered by guest conductors, including Nicolaï Malko, Eduard van Beinum, and Bruno Walter. As had long been en-visaged for the era when the society finally moved away from it, the Salle des Concerts became the chief venue for a new series of Tuesday eve-ning concerts of the Bach-through-Beethoven repertoire. The conduc-tor was Arthur Goldschmidt, with whom the musicians later recorded *Eine kleine Nachtmusik* and other Mozart favorites (as "Chamber Or-chestra of the Paris Conservatoire"); a recital with the tenor Charles Hol-land; Haydn and C. P. E. Bach with Marguerite Roesgen-Champion; and a rather good recording of the Haydn "Farewell" and "La Reine" symphonies.

By 1946–47 it was politically acceptable to resume contact with the least suspect Austro-German conductors. Bruno Walter appeared in a special concert in the Salle Pleyel on 26 November 1946 (Haydn's "Oxford" Symphony, the *Siegfried-Idyl*, the Schubert "Great" C-Major) and a regular Sunday concert on 1 December, thereby continuing his long association with the orchestra. Later he shared the podium with André Cluytens when the society appeared at the Edinburgh Festival in September 1949.[56] Furtwängler, who despite a correspondence dating back to the early 1940s had not been able to appear with the society, at last visited in January 1948 with a program that returned Strauss and Wagner to the repertoire; he came again in November 1948 (Strauss, Schumann, Beethoven) and February 1949 (Mozart, Wagner, Brahms). In June 1947 Leopold Stokowski conducted his trademark Bach Toccata and Fugue in D Minor, a work of Paul Creston, and Beethoven and Wagner. Herbert von Karajan first appeared with the orchestra in the spring of 1950. The big-name soloists began to return: Edwin Fischer (who found *"le vrai esprit de la grande musique européenne"*), Rubinstein, Kempff (*"une joie olympique"*).[57]

The administrative arrangement was unprecedented but by some measures operable: Charles Münch, the official president, was exercising no role at all and was largely out of the country. André Cluytens, without a title, was for all intents and purposes the resident chief conductor. Jean Savoye imagined his authority to be essentially unchallenged. How very much he was wrong became clear at the Assemblée Générale of 8 June 1947. Savoye's *rapport moral* summarized the status of the Münch affair, the situation with the radio service, and the society's standing with the government. None of these was especially promising: the Radio Orchestra now insisted its players give it priority over the activities of the Société des Concerts, Opéra, and Opéra-Comique; the global state subvention for the associations had declined from 8 million francs to 6 million (with a bonus promised to whichever of the four did the best by living French composers and French soloists). The authorities had seen the full houses at the November and December 1946 concerts with Bruno Walter and at the Lily Pons / André Kostelanetz recital in May 1947 and imagined that the Société des Concerts was thriving in the status quo. Of Münch Savoye suggested that the time was at hand to say, "Enough! It's over." He ended with a defiant refusal for the orchestra to be dominated by politics, and cried, *"Vive la Société!"* But when the ordinarily pro forma vote on approving the secretary's report was taken, it revealed, of 64 voting, 34 in favor and 26 opposed, with four abstentions—reasonably close to a vote of no confidence.

Savoye, stung, lost his composure. "I'm leaving with my head held high. My successor will have to do the best he can. I've finished, I've read my report, I thank you, and I bid you goodbye." Protestations were heard from the floor, but he would not be swayed: "I'm leaving; I have that right. I said what I had to say. The time has come that I don't need to be here." And he strode from the room.

The treasurer's report, by Huot, began by noting that every member in the room had earned at least 1,950 francs per concert. (The 200 percent increase in fees since the 1930s was largely the result of inflation.) At the Concerts Colonne, Huot noted, the year-end figures were as follows:

Soloists	Fr. 56,629, or Fr. 1,654 per concert
Seconds	Fr. 46,949, or Fr. 1,380 per concert
Thirds	Fr. 42,294, or Fr. 1,243 per concert
Fourths	Fr. 34,180, or Fr. 1,002 per concert

Thus even the rank and file of the Société des Concerts got 390 francs more per concert than did the soloists of the Colonne orchestra. Huot concluded by threatening to resign himself if his report were not approved, and got the desired results: 52 favoring, 7 opposed.

The wiser members now tried to restore a measure of composure to the proceedings. The sixty-year-old violinist Louis Serret, who had been recalled from retirement during the war, suggested that their jealousy of the Radio Orchestra and anger over the subventions were passing annoyances; the Société des Concerts remained the best in the land, and it was not unreasonable of the government to imagine that with financial self-sufficiency the subventions might naturally come to an end. But anger was the order of the day; Robert Benedetti, for instance, announced his probable resignation over the large fines levied when *sociétaires* skipped an activity of the society to play for the Radio Orchestra. With at least four "sensational" resignations now on the floor, it was decided to proceed to a vote on renewing Savoye's mandate; this showed a sharply divided constituency, with 29 in favor and 21 blank ballots. The committee thence resigned *en masse,* and the assembly adjourned with no government at all, engaging to return a week later to resolve the difficulty.[58]

The following week, on 15 June 1947, the director of the Conservatoire, Claude Delvincourt, was once again to be seen in the president's chair. He pledged to help lead the orchestra out of its difficulties if he were so allowed, and within a few minutes a government had been reconstituted: Delvincourt as president, Savoye as vice president and secretary-general, and Huot as treasurer. Cluytens would be acting chief conductor.[59]

In April 1948 Münch was once again in Paris, and Savoye induced Delvincourt to offer him lunch. "I myself put a hand in the dough," Delvincourt later reported. "I had him drink a lot, because that kind of argument, too, is not without value."

"This state of things cannot go on," he began, then asked Münch directly: "Will you return as president and conductor of the Société des Concerts?"

"*Impossible,*" Münch replied. He had been named music director of the Boston Symphony Orchestra beginning in 1949. That being the case, Delvincourt asked, would Münch agree to appear as guest conductor in Paris from time to time? When Münch responded in the affirmative, they concluded an agreement for six "great springtide manifestations" some with chorus, from 1 May to 15 June 1949. The Société des Concerts would drop its lawsuit. The committee readily agreed to Delvincourt's plan, which was soon leaked to the press as the promise of an all-Debussy concert featuring the pianist Nicole Henriot (Nicole Henriot-Schweitzer, Münch's niece-in-law and to some degree his *protégée*). Another of his favorites, the violinist Ginette Neveu, would also appear.

The arrangement immediately began to go astray. In October and November 1948, over the strenuous objection of all four societies, Münch led the Orchestre National de la Radiodiffusion Française—the Radio Orchestra—on a tour of the United States and Canada. Neither of the resident conductors, Roger Désormière and Manuel Rosenthal, would risk the consequences of leaving town at the head of an orchestra that still considerably overlapped the membership of the concert associations; Münch simply refused to see their secretaries-general and argued that "the renown of France had been put into play." A major incident threatened to erupt that season when he joined the Société des Concerts for some last Decca recordings: Beethoven's Eighth, the Ravel G-Major Concerto with Henriot, Tchaikovsky's *Romeo and Juliet,* and a "Berlioz Program" of excerpts from *Roméo et Juliette* and the Royal Hunt and Storm from *Les Troyens.* The producers concluded that the orchestra was poor and the project would have to be abandoned, a message Münch delivered the next day. But good feeling and artistry were somehow restored, and at the last of the sessions, on 1 June 1949, Münch congratulated the players with a promise that "I shall return to you; you

can count on me, and soon." The Debussy concert had meanwhile succumbed to an unreturned telephone call, but Münch appeared three
last times with the Société des Concerts that spring as planned: 27 May
1949, 3 June (with Neveu), and 10 June (with Henriot).

By now it was clear Münch would never really return, despite some talk
of an exclusive agreement for ten Paris appearances annually for ten
years, during which he would preside over the society. Gitton's attempt
to woo him back with a petition failed when it was signed by only 45
of the 100 players; even Gitton was now convinced of Münch's "perfect
inconsistency. It's impossible to get him to say yes or no. . . . It's impossible get anything from him at all."

"Münch is a great man," Gitton went on, "and a great conductor,
but you can't pin him down. He sees only his personal interest, and he
puts it in front of the interests of those who paved his way into the fir-
mament of stars. As an artist, I much admire what he has done, but as
a man, I admit to feeling knocked around."

"Every time you get to something precise," added Delvincourt, "he
marches away. It's like a ghost evaporating."

The wise Fontalirand now led the assembly to the obvious conclusion: "It's tomorrow that counts."[60] On 20 November 1949 the members finally elected André Cluytens to the traditional position of 1er chef /
vice-président—well over three years after he had first been registered as
a sociétaire. The vote was 49 favoring and 5 abstaining; 11 members had
been excused from the meeting.[61]

But that is to jump ahead of the other major turning point of 1948: the
dismissal of Jean Savoye from the Société des Concerts. Savoye's final
chapter probably begins in 1946–47 with his grossly overextending the
orchestra's commitments in a postwar drive to secure year-round employment for the rank and file. It reaches its climax in a road trip run
amok—that of 10–20 October 1948 to Rome, Naples, Palermo, Aquila,
and Milan. The repertoire included the *Firebird* suite, the *Fantastique,*
Franck's D-Minor Symphony, the Ravel G-Major Piano Concerto with
Marcelle Meyer, and for one concert the Schumann Cello Concerto
with Enrico Mainardi.

Planning for an overly ambitious 1948–49 season, including three
foreign journeys, had fallen behind by mid-summer. Savoye showed
profound disinterest in the Italian tour, leaving most of the travel arrangements to the Italian impresario De Vietto and referring most of

the monetary questions to Huot. The Franco-Italian tuba player Pavoni was preparing to make an advance visit to Italy when Savoye and his wife suddenly went themselves, as though taking a late-summer vacation on the society's budget.[62] It appears that the Savoyes waited in Italy for the arrival of the orchestra, while Huot was left to organize the last-minute details at home.

The journey was troubled from the outset. Wives showed up to accompany their husbands in considerably greater number than had been foreseen, causing shortages of seats on the trains and buses, of hotel rooms and food, and of cash. Italian lire were in short supply, since the orchestra needed some million lire in cash just to feed everyone and had left Paris with only about 350,000. The train to Italy was filthy and overcrowded; the hotel accommodations were poor. On the overnight boat to Palermo, the musicians were given third-class accommodations while Savoye and his party went in first class. Nor had provision been made for Savoye's personal entourage, including Mme Savoye, Mᶜ Hauert, the French cultural attaché in Italy and his wife, and the impresario and his wife—a total of seven. There were not enough seats on the buses from Rome to Aquila, and when Savoye tried to eject musicians to accommodate his party, they refused to budge.

Sharp words were exchanged in front of the players, when at one point Huot shouted, "You lie, and have been lying for a decade." Savoye cried, "That's one word too many. . . . It will only be for three more days. I quit."[63]

"*Eh bien,*" replied Huot, "*tant mieux.*" In Avila Savoye refused to sign for a cash advance from the impresario—leaving the musicians without a way to pay for their dinner—on the grounds that he was no longer in charge. The ship was sinking, Huot later said, and the captain tried to save his own neck: "'I have resigned,' he seemed to say. 'Work your way out of it, and I'll sign after you admit the mistake.' . . . I found this attitude *pas très fair-play.*" Moreover, Mᶜ Hauert observed, there was no one to resign to, and they had a concert to give. On the quay after the concert Savoye persisted in his refusal to sign for the cash until the full committee was there to witness it. It was 2:00 in the morning, with one of the committee members sleeping and two others still packing trunks.

The orchestra made the long train journey home in utter disarray. A suddenly scrupulous accounting showed that Savoye had taken a large sum of money advanced by the promoter of the two independent concerts that fall with the conductor Richard Korn, and suggested that the

Savoyes were in the habit of paying personal expenses with societal funds. Huot attributed Savoye's belligerence, which (unlike his colleagues) he found atypical, to the committee's decision the previous summer to dismiss Mme Savoye from the office staff as a cost-cutting measure. That would explain the Savoyes' abrupt departure for Italy, purposefully leaving the office unattended just as subscriptions were being filled. Mme Savoye had also failed, Huot noted, to return the society's typewriter.[64]

Savoye submitted his formal letter of resignation the day the orchestra arrived back in Paris, 22 October 1948. In view, he wrote, of the incident provoked by Huot in Italy and the ongoing discontent in the ranks, he found it impossible to continue. Among the intolerable conditions, he listed a part-time committee obliged to earn its principal livelihood elsewhere, a situation he found manifestly incompatible with orderly administration. He complained of the committee's false sense of thrift (presumably alluding to his wife's circumstance), always looking for corners to cut and objecting to necessary expenditures on publicity, soloists, and front-line conductors. The officers had conspired to abandon the student concerts and the chorus. They had been elected without a thought of their competence for office.

He complained, too, about the smug self-satisfaction of the *"artistes de l'orchestre"*—sloppy in rehearsal, unwilling to undertake extra events and tours. At the general assemblies their behavior toward him was insupportable. Nor was the financial situation promising. Economic conditions continued to deteriorate, with expenses well in excess of receipts and ticket prices unable to keep pace. High government officials, far from supporting the Société des Concerts, opposed it with a negative inertia he termed *quasi totale*. Reform was impossible under the present circumstances.

"For fifteen years," he said, "the Société des Concerts has been all my activity, all my leisure." He had entered as a violinist and would depart as one; but his resignation as vice president / secretary-general was effective at once, and he asked leave for 1948–49—that is, for the remainder of the season.[65]

On 25 October 1948 the committee with Delvincourt presiding unanimously accepted the resignation. Further, in view of the grave fiscal irregularities surrounding the Korn concerts, Savoye's name was stricken from the records and a fine of 35,000 francs, roughly what he had paid himself so far that season, was levied. The committee demanded the return of its register of minutes and arranged for the Savoyes' personal property to be delivered to their home. Savoye immediately appealed to the general assembly, and an extraordinary meeting was called for Sunday, 7 November 1948, to hear his case.

André Huot had always before come to Savoye's defense in public meetings; they had been allies from the beginning of the new era. Now he led the attack, acknowledging a profound and total change in their relationship as he catalogued the events of recent weeks and closed with the committee's recommendation for dismissal (*radiation*). Savoye had wanted to be master of the house, but the house had always been a democracy. His dictatorship was over.

Savoye, angrily reading from a typewritten text, reviewed the events of the unpleasant tour. Much of what Huot had said was true, he acknowledged, but incomplete. The Savoyes had gone to Italy, not on a vacation, but to verify the arrangements personally; the Rome hotels worked out well precisely because Savoye had checked them out in advance, while Naples was a disaster because there the arrangements had been left to the impresario. Huot should have known before they left that he was more than a million lire short of cash; in the event, Savoye himself had found the money to tide the musicians over during the crisis. The impresario was patently dishonest. In Aquila, for example, they had been billed 650 lire per person for dinner, whereas the hotel was advertising the same meal for 550. After the incident with the buses, the committee had negotiated on behalf of the Société des Concerts and, that being the case, Savoye had properly refused to sign the financial documents. "I knew we were in the process of being bilked in colossal fashion," and he very much regretted seeing the committee thank the impresario so warmly at the end of the tour.

Savoye closed by reminding the members that for more than a decade he had managed successful tours. This one, despite the incidents, was "one of the most beautiful we've ever done; . . . it will rest engraved in our thoughts as one of our great souvenirs." He demanded a formal audit of his accounts and an administrative review of his correspondence, engagements, and dealings, perhaps by the financial service of the Action Artistique. Finally he asked that his dismissal be changed into a simple resignation, allowing him to keep his pension.

The violist Emmanuel Elissalde, Huot's assistant, tried to smooth things over, observing that Huot, being a kind person, was easily offended, and that Savoye might be well advised to modify his "incessant wiliness." But the majority of the musicians were more concerned about the Savoyes' financial malfeasance, now shown to include payments for transporting a personal piano, for several kilograms of coffee, and for automobile insurance, a total of some 10,000 francs. Mme Savoye, who had paid these bills, refused to respond to inquiries from the lawyers. Dismissal was the inevitable consequence of what amounted to embezzlement: "Savoye knows the statutes perfectly," a member remarked. "He certainly changed them enough." There was little support for clemency: "We're all adults." Approval of the secretary's report, including the dismissal of Savoye, was moved, and a secret ballot called. The vote was 59 favoring dismissal, 1 opposed, and 5 abstaining.[66] The news was reported to the public in a gossipy article titled "Gâteau de Savoye" (a pun on "Gâteau de Savoie," poundcake).[67]

In part because of the press coverage, the parties retreated somewhat in the weeks that followed. Delvincourt arranged for an arbitration of the case consistent with labor laws of the era. The lawyers negotiated a settlement whereby Savoye discharged any legal complaints against the society in exchange for a payment of 42,988 francs (roughly 115,000 francs owed him in earnings, from which roughly 66,000 francs in fines and disallowed expenses was subtracted). The case reached its essential conclusion in May 1949,[68] soon after which the Société des Concerts regained its equilibrium under André Huot and André Cluytens.

André Cluytens was born in 1905 to a musical family of Antwerp in Belgium and naturalized a French citizen as a child. He graduated from the Antwerp Conservatory at nineteen, with first prizes in piano, harmony, and counterpoint and fugue. His father, conductor of the Antwerp Opera (the Théâtre Royal d'Anvers), engaged him as chorusmaster and coach, and there he began to conduct full productions from 1927, including the first Antwerp production of *Salomé*. In 1932 Cluytens was called to the Théâtre du Capitole of Toulouse primarily to conduct the orchestra concerts, then in 1935, at the age of thirty, as first conductor at the Opéra of Lyon, where he became musical director in 1942.

During the war he led the Vichy summer concerts, which may have been behind the brief period he was blacklisted by the musicians' union in Bordeaux. In the 1940s he commuted frequently from Lyon to Paris for engagements at the Opéra and with the Société des Concerts; in 1947 he became musical director of the Opéra-Comique. During his four years of guest-conducting the society without a contract, there had been petitions for and against his continuance. By 1949 he had the musicians solidly behind him, in part owing to his great triumph with them at the Edinburgh Festival that September. Their only concerns were his tendency, at the Opéra-Comique, to lead dry and uninspiring rehearsals (squinting, said a player, at his miniature scores) and that he might be wooed away to the Radio Orchestra or one of the foreign orchestras. Cluytens himself was moderately concerned with the provisions in his contract that required him to conduct half of all their concerts and that reasserted the committee's control of programming, but was willing to take the risk in order to forward the relationship.[69]

Cluytens was as capable a musician as Münch. If he lacked some of his predecessor's personal magnetism, he was relatively untouched by the less attractive characteristics of celebrity. Where Münch favored Berlioz and Debussy, Cluytens was a strong and gifted partisan of Ravel. He also had particular credentials in the Russian repertoire—*Pictures at an Exhibition* was one of his trademark works—that led the Société des Concerts to reestablish that niche in the repertoire wars. Cluytens's Beethoven was widely admired (though his recorded Beethoven cycle is not with the Société des Concerts but rather the Berlin Philharmonic). Unlike Münch, Cluytens was a wonderful opera conductor and left a major operatic discography, some of it—*Don Giovanni,* Gounod's *Mireille,* and a historic *Boris Godunov*—with the Société des Concerts. He was as peripatetic as any of the modern conductors, and particularly enjoyed appearing on the road with the *sociétaires.* Cluytens oversaw the re-emergence of a major touring program, with visits to the major French cities, London, the Edinburgh Festival, Brussels, Holland, and Italy; the eagerness of the Société des Concerts to displace itself was once again widely known.

Indeed the most sweeping change to be introduced during the early tenure of André Cluytens began in July 1949, when the Société des Concerts consented to serve as resident orchestra for the second summer festival in Aix-en-Provence. The following summer they added the Besançon Festival, and for a decade assured an orchestral presence at both.[70] This, effectively, secured the year-round employment the society had long sought for its musicians: September in Besançon; fall season concerts from October through December; winter season from January through March or April; spring season in May and June; July in Aix; and August for vacation.

The Aix festival each July was (and is) anchored by Mozart opera—nearly always including *Don Giovanni*—in the courtyard of the archbishop's palace, with related concerts, recitals, and church music in the cloister of the St-Sauveur Cathedral and the courtyard of the Maynier d'Oppède house. The festival had been established in 1948 by Gabriel Dussurget (1904–96, "the magician of Aix") in collaboration with the casino management, major stage and costume designers, and Hans Rosbaud, popular conductor of the Südwestfunkorchester of Baden-Baden. From 1949 through 1961, the second to fourteenth years of the festival, the Société des Concerts was the primary of two resident orchestras, guaranteeing an ensemble of some 43 musicians (10–8–6–6–4 strings and 9 winds), plus necessary supplemental players. The resident vocal star was the American soprano Teresa Stich-Randall, surrounded by virtually all of the better French-oriented opera artists of the era—Janine Micheau, Michel Dens, Nicolai Gedda, Michel Sénéchal, André Vessières—and many superb foreigners. The musicologist Marc Pincherle (1888–1974) served as secretary-general (and simultaneously president of the Société Française de Musicologie), helping extend the repertoire to Gluck and, most notably, the charming 1956 production of Rameau's *Platée*—for many years the only recording of a Rameau opera in wide circulation.

The repertoire of the orchestral concerts was limited by the complement of players to works no larger than Schubert's Ninth (recorded 1956). Additionally there were masses in the cathedral and black-tie galas for the opening and closing concerts, usually all-Mozart. Baden-Baden radio (SWR: Südwestrundfunk) would often broadcast Rosbaud's performances.

The musicians loved summering in Aix. "Here, all is well," wrote one musician home to Paris: "sun, music, relaxation."[71] Not a few of the musicians the Parisians first encountered in Aix were subsequently invited to appear with the Société des Concerts in Paris, notably Stich-Randall herself and the young German conductor Michael Gielen.[72]

The Aix festivals are especially well documented in sound recordings and even in film and videotape.[73] Pathé-Marconi (EMI) issued an important series of recordings, among which *Mireille* (1954) and *Platée* (1956) are pillars of the orchestra's discography. Additionally Rosbaud's 1954 *Entführung*, 1957 *Così*, and 1958 *Don Giovanni* have become available in CDs made from broadcast tapes, along with the 1956 performance of Schubert's Great C-Major Symphony and a Stich-Randall recital with Rosbaud at the piano. The orchestral players were not particularly fond of these recordings, owing to the unusually small number of players in the cohort,[74] but they give an excellent sense of the festival spirit afoot each summer.

The Besançon Festival, also founded in 1948, takes place in early September—close to the annual *rentrée* and reopening of the Paris theaters but by the same token a civilized way to end the vacation period. Situated beneath a rocky citadel a short distance from Switzerland and Italy, Besançon focused from the outset on assembling international casts. The formula consisted primarily of symphonic concerts in the Municipal Theater by two visiting orchestras, one in the first week and one in the second, a sacred concert the Sunday morning in between at the Church of the Ste-Madeleine, and a concluding *spectacle chorégraphique* by visiting ballet companies (those, for example, of the Paris Opéra and La Scala). An important competition for young conductors was added in 1951 by Émile Vuillermoz, introducing in due course Sergiu Comissiona, Seiji Ozawa, Michel Plasson, Jesús López-Corbos, and Sylvain Cambreling.

The Besançon Festival was closely associated with André Cluytens, who conducted there annually from 1948. Carl Schuricht lived just across the Swiss border in Vevey, and it was in Besançon that the Société des Concerts forged the rich relationship with him that resulted in their great Beethoven cycle of 1958; it was there, too, that they grew fond of Schuricht's gifted student Ataulfo Argenta (1913–58). Félix Raugel, the noted early-music authority, conducted the sacred repertoire. Among the international celebrity conductors who appeared were Josef Krips, Eugen Jochum, and Georg Solti, who led them in 1959, the last year the orchestra went to Besançon. The star soloists were of the caliber with which the Société generally worked in Paris: Elisabeth Schwarzkopf, Pierre Fournier, Wilhelm Kempff, Clara Haskil.

Together, Aix-en-Provence and Besançon brought the Société des Concerts interesting new work, important new audiences, and the opportunity to make a certain amount of money in pleasant and relatively informal surroundings. Their presence lent the festivals considerable prestige, and went a long way to assuring the present success of both. The festivals were a good business proposition all around.

André Huot brought a refreshing calm to the daily operations of the Société des Concerts. In 1956, when they encountered their next crisis, it was noted that not for eight years had they had to have an extraordinary meeting; things had become routine. Huot's good humor and businesslike efficiency were appreciated by everyone.

There was immediate improvement in the orchestra's relations with the government, as they complied scrupulously with the *cahier des charges* (favoring French conductors and soloists and contemporary French composers) accompanying the subventions. For 1948–49 the Société des Concerts was pleased to report 21 French and 19 foreign conductors in 39 concerts, with 11 French and 23 foreign soloists. (One of the guest conductors was Roberto Benzi, a *protégé* of André Cluytens, said in the program to be *"9 ans et demi"*; actually he was two years older.) Of music by living composers the society noted Rivier's Symphony No. 3 (31 October 1948, 22 minutes); Schmitt's *Psaume XLVII* (idem, 25 minutes); Milhaud's Violin Concerto (first performance 7 November, 25 minutes); Louis Aubert's *Le Tombeau de Chateaubriand* (13 March 1949, 14 minutes); Messager's Symphony (idem, 30 minutes); Poulenc's *Les Biches* (20 March, 15 minutes); Landowski's *Rythmes du monde* (27 March, 35 minutes); and Honegger's *Symphonie liturgique* (27 May, 30 minutes). The pace was similar in the following two seasons.[75]

Among the few negative financial indicators was the growing deficit record of the young people's concerts. These worsened considerably in the early 1950s, and the activity was gradually abandoned. The frenzy of independent concerts slackened noticeably under Huot; the tours were fewer and further between, but a great deal more carefully planned.

With Carl Schuricht the orchestra recorded Beethoven's Fifth in June 1949; in November they collaborated again in a triumphant Beethoven's Ninth (Hélène Bouvier, Madeleine Dubuis, Georges Jouatte, Heinz Rehfuss; Chorale Élisabeth Brasseur). Schuricht found their growing symbiosis exalting, and wrote Huot with heartfelt compliments to an "incomparable orchestra of spirit, overwhelming power, and prodigiously great emotion," which, he felt, always shared his sentiments. He asked Huot to convey his thanks to the orchestra for "a state of unparalleled happiness and the kind of powerful inspiration that, truly, one senses only rarely."[76]

The orchestra traveled to Spain in early March 1951, presenting a total of seven concerts in San Sebastián, Madrid, Saragossa, and Barcelona. They took an enormous repertoire, including Vivaldi, Weber, Mendelssohn, and Wagner as well as their standard Beethoven and French showpieces; one of the Madrid concerts closed with Falla's *Le Tricorne*. It was a leisurely trip, planned to give time for sightseeing and, after the Italian debacle of 1948, to restore the players' confidence in the pleasures of foreign travel. A full complement made the journey, accompanied by numerous wives and dependents, a total of 120. Ataulfo Argenta conducted at least one of the concerts owing to an indisposition of Cluytens. In April the orchestra made a two-day trip to Antwerp and Ghent, again featuring *Le Tricorne*.

As Cluytens's international career blossomed, especially in conjunction with the European music festivals, his availability to the Société des Concerts waned. Huot tried, without notable success, to cultivate a roster of middle-aged and younger conductors: Pierre Dervaux (1917–92), the Polish-Swiss Paul Klecki (Pavel Kletzki, 1900–73), the Hungarian Georges Sebastian (György Sebestyén, 1903–89), even Cluytens's *protégé* Roberto Benzi (b. 1937). Generally the guests were either unsuccessful in drawing the public or unpopular with the players. Two exceptions to that rule were Argenta (1913–58), whose early death, by carbon monoxide poisoning in an automobile, interrupted a fruitful collaboration, and André Vandernoot (1927–91), conductor of the Royal Flemish Opera in Antwerp and later the major companies in Brussels. Both left a significant legacy of recordings with the Société des Concerts, perhaps most importantly Argenta's excited, bizarre *Symphonie fantastique,* released a few weeks before his death.

Cluytens first notified the committee of his intention to resign in the spring of 1952. His personal circumstances required a change, he wrote. He especially disliked the Saturday morning public dress rehearsals before a famously unruly public and the other tedious duties of a house conductor. He appears to have been jealous of Bruno Walter's wild success in a pair of concerts that April. The maneuver took the committee by surprise, but they adopted the good-sense approach of begging him to continue through December 1952, then take a leave for the 1953 winter and spring seasons. The concert of 22 December 1952—Respighi's *Gli uccelli,* the Prokofiev Third Piano Concerto with Magda Tagliaferro, a new work of Rivier, and a stunning *Pictures,* one of Cluytens's specialties—was supposed to be his last, but afterward Huot called on him to review the artistic success, high morale, and excellent financial receipts of 1952, and Cluytens withdrew his resignation. The committee noted its great satisfaction in this "happy decision."[77]

During 1952–53, both oboists, Lamorelette and Claro, left the orchestra, one to retire and the other owing to ill health. Jules Goetgheluck was designated principal oboist in March 1953 without competitive audition; a heated playoff for the other seat in April was won by Robert Casier, who had held the second chair that season while covering for Claro's illness. (Casier is the principal oboist for most of the great LP recordings with Cluytens.) The involuntary retirement, at age sixty-two, of the principal cellist, Auguste Cruque, met with the vivid protest of his colleagues, since the mandatory age in the theaters had increased from sixty to sixty-five. Cruque had been principal since 1926. The committee sustained their position, though in terms couched "out of deference and friendship." By contrast, in the case of the violinist Louis Franquin, the committee reversed itself on learning that his retirement benefits would be compromised by his not having been employed long enough to be fully vested in the system.[78]

Cruque's successor, Robert Albin, served as principal cellist for only a year, 1953–54. He had been announced as concerto soloist for the concert of 17 January 1954 under Artur Rodzinski. Owing both to a poor pre-sale and Rodzinksi's preference for a more famous soloist, Albin was replaced by at the last minute by the pianist Lucette Descaves, then in protest failed to appear for the rest of the season. The committee dismissed him in May for unexcused absence, a decision upheld by the assembly after a long debate.[79] (In later years, Albin conducted the Orchestre Radio-Symphonique of Strasbourg, with which he made recordings.) Albin's replacement, Robert Cordier, had begun his career with the Société des Concerts at the age of nineteen, in 1935; he served as principal cellist until the dissolution, by which time, still only fifty-one, he could look back on a career of thirty-two seasons.

In April 1954 Claude Delvincourt, the director of the Conservatoire and president of the Société des Concerts, was killed in an automobile accident near Grosseto on his way home from a music festival in Rome. Aside from the forced closeness Delvincourt and the society shared during the war and *l'affaire Münch*, they had developed a solid mutual respect on musical grounds, with the orchestra having played both his *Le Bal vénitien* and *Pamir* on Sunday concerts. The concert of 19 December 1954, with *Pamir*, was dedicated to his memory. Delvincourt was succeeded briefly in 1954–55 by Marcel Dupré as interim director of the Conservatoire, then by Raymond Loucheur (1899–1979). Loucheur's name had first appeared on Société programs as early as 1936; during his years as their president they played his Symphony No. 2 and popular *Hop-Frog* ballet suites, later premiering his Violin Concerto (February 1965). By the time Loucheur reached his highest offices, however, the Conservatoire and the Société des Concerts had essentially gone their separate ways. Having studied the statutes, he concluded that his only responsibility to the society was his largely ceremonial appearance once annually to preside over their general assembly.

At the concert of 17 October 1954, an all-Fauré festival commemorating the thirtieth anniversary of the composer's death, the eighty-year-old Marguerite Long appeared with the Société des Concerts, for the last time, playing the op. 19 Ballade. (They had recorded the work together, she for the second time, two years earlier.) The public, in standing ovation, demanded an encore. Cluytens, knowing she was ill, tried to dissuade her. *"Alors,"* she told him sharply, "fifty years ago in this very place they found this music obscure. Now they cheer it—and you want me to refuse?" Then she took her seat and played it again.[80]

The same concert featured, for Fauré's Requiem, the remarkable pairing of the black American soprano Mattiwilda Dobbs with the French baritone Gérard Souzay. Both sang Fauré *mélodies* earlier in the program. (Souzay's landmark recording with the society, *Souzay chante Ravel,* comes from 1958.) Long postponed her official farewells until the 1959–60 season, at the conclusion of which she was honored with orchestral *Variations sur le nom de Marguerite Long* by Françaix, Dutilleux, Milhaud, Poulenc, Daniel-Lesur, Rivier, Sauget, and Auric. (There was also a *Cap Canaveral* on the program, 2 April 1960.) Long had made her debut with the Société des Concerts fifty-two years before, in 1908, and had been a *membre honoraire* since 1937. In the *livre d'or* she used the vocabulary of the Gaubert years as she remembered "so many artistic joys shared with this glorious phalanx."[81]

Paul Hindemith appeared as conductor in November 1955, with the Bach Magnificat and his own Psalm XVII, presented in memory of the great French poet-ambassador Paul Claudel (1868–1955). In December 1955 the young pianist Daniel Barenboim, aged thirteen, made the first of his two appearances with the Société des Concerts, in the Mozart E♭-Major Piano Concerto, K. 482; two decades later he was to begin his magical tenure at the head of the Orchestre de Paris. Later in the season, on 22 January 1956, Cluytens led a major all-Ravel program—one of the most prominent way-stations toward the society's epochal Ravel *intégrale* recording project of 1961 and 1962. Simultaneously they were advancing their affinity with the brilliant pianist Samson-François (1924–70), who would record the Ravel piano concertos with them in a still-admired recording of 1959. He first appeared with the orchestra in 1944, at the age of twenty, and first played Ravel with them in March 1953.

The 1955–56 season concluded early to allow a tour to Switzerland, with concerts in Zurich, Geneva, Lausanne, Bern, and Basel, much along the lines of the society's first major multi-city tour in 1917. This time a contingent of eighty-five musicians, each earning 5,000 francs, made the trip with Pierre Dervaux, since Cluytens's fee of 10,000 Swiss francs was deemed too high. Huot, working from his seaside retreat at Denis d'Oléron the previous August, had negotiated the program and soloists. The promoters wanted the Swiss pianist Hedy Salquin and the black American singer Lucretia West (who was to appear with them in Paris on 18 March 1956 in Mahler's *Kindertotenlieder*); in the end Monique Haas went with the Ravel G-Major Concerto, the programs completed with Beethoven's Second, *La Valse,* two of the Debussy *Nocturnes,* excerpts from *La Damnation de Faust,* and Florent Schmitt's *La Tragédie de Salomé.* A subvention of 2,500,000 French francs was forthcoming against expenses very slightly in excess; as these budgets went, the Swiss tour was a financial success.[82]

In succeeding months ongoing inflation and unstable exchange rates—two factors that led both to currency reform (100 francs = 1 new franc) and, taking the long view, to the concept of the euro—combined to block other major tour initiatives. A complex project to have the Société des Concerts appear in *semaines françaises* being organized for October 1959 in Munich and Italy failed in the summer of 1956. So, too, did the orchestra's plan to travel to Vienna with Cluytens in conjunction with an international festival scheduled there for June 1959.[83]

A fierce struggle broke out when Jean-Pierre Rampal was engaged by the management in Besançon to appear with Eugen Jochum in a concerto scheduled for September 1956, thus usurping the statutory privilege of the incumbent principal, Lucien Lavaillotte. Lavaillotte's complaint noted his considerable seniority in French flute circles (he was fifty-eight; Rampal, thirty-four) and especially that he was principal flutist at the Opéra, where Rampal sat in the third chair.[84] Within the year Lavaillotte had been edged out at the Opéra to create a seat for Rampal, who served as principal flutist there for five seasons before leaving to devote full time to his solo career. At the Société Lavaillotte was succeeded in 1958 by Henri Lebon and in 1964 by Michel Debost.

On 1 December 1957, Maurice Le Roux (1923–92) made his debut with the Société des Concerts, conducting a program that included Webern's Variations for Orchestra. "Webern *à la Société des Concerts!*" wrote one reviewer. "You couldn't believe your eyes or your ears. But you couldn't help admiring Le Roux's courage. Let's hope that the applause, well merited by his authority and *souplesse,* compensated for the indignant—and predictable—protests by the Saturday morning ladies."[85] Le Roux was invited back in 1959 for a concert that included the Berg Three Pieces for Orchestra, and twice in 1960 with more traditional programs. In 1959 he was appointed first conductor of the Orchestre National de l'ORTF (Orchestre National de l'Office de Radiodiffusion-Télévision Française, formerly the Radio Orchestra). Cluytens greeted the arrival of a serialist composer / conductor on the podium of the Société des Concerts with considerable alarm, and within a few weeks was using the occurrence to engineer his own release.

The dawn of the unbreakable vinyl microgroove LP in 1948 first introduced by Columbia USA made possible fifty-minute records that were attractively priced (typically $5.95 in the United States) and easy to store. The new technologies allowed another quantum leap in quality of sound, first through Decca / London's *ffrr* ("full frequency range recording") system of high fidelity, then with stereophonic sound from 1956 (called by London *ffss*, "full frequency stereophonic sound"). Many collectors and audio enthusiasts think the Decca / London *ffss* recordings of classical symphonic music represent the highest point of the stereophonic age.

For the Société des Concerts the beginning of a major legacy in LP recordings came, perhaps, with Rimsky-Korsakov's *Scheherazade* with Ernest Ansermet, recorded 1948 as six 78s and released in early 1951 as a single LP (London LLP 6); likewise Tchaikovsky's Sixth with Münch, 1948, was transferred from six 78s published in 1950 to one LP published in 1952. Another milestone was organized by Westminster in London, when Hermann Scherchen recorded a *Les Troyens à Carthage* (2– 9 May 1952) for a three-record set, followed by a live festival concert performance on 10 May 1952 at the Palais de Chaillot. In the early 1950s the publication rhythm for LPs quickly reached a dozen or more a year.

Engagements for recording were now contracted with both Decca / London and Columbia UK / Pathé (EMI), and occasionally some smaller enterprises, in agreements that established a minimum number of sessions a year. The repertoire chosen was dictated primarily by market forces in western Europe, especially London, cultivating in turn a vogue for the light classics and ballet music—for instance Roger Désormière's 1952–53 Decca series that included suites from *Les Sylphides, Coppélia, Sylvia, The Sleeping Beauty,* and *Les Biches.* In the same period and for the same label Anatole Fistoulari recorded ballets and light classics by Gounod, Ponchielli, Thomas, and Tchaikovsky. There were also vocal recitals by star singers (Souzay, Mado Robin, Janine Micheau, Charles Holland), and later a fierce competition among the record producers in studio recordings of operas, first engaged by the Société des Concerts with the Pathé recordings of the Aix festival performances.

For many of the recordings of this period, the identity of the orchestra was all but coincidental. Any competent group would suffice, and the job of the producers was merely to concoct marketable alliances of orchestras, conductors, repertoire, studios, and engineering teams. Grand projects were not the order of the day. One conspicuous exception to this rule is the 1953 Columbia two-disc recording titled *Le Groupe des Six,* where the six composers' works are introduced by Jean Cocteau, concluding with Milhaud's Second Symphony. The public concert was on 4 November 1953, with the recording sessions on 6–10 November.

In other cases, commercial affinities grew into remarkable discographies, notably in the case of the four recordings with Argenta, the Honegger recordings with Georges Tzipine, and the major Mozart cycle developed with André Vandernoot in the late 1950s and early 1960s. For their brilliant engineering and orchestral virtuosity, the recordings with Albert Wolff in the Decca SXL series are particularly valued by connoisseurs: Glazunov's *The Seasons* (1956), a record of Spanish-themed music by Falla and Ravel (1958), and perhaps above all the famous *Overtures in Hi-Fi* (1959: *Zampa, Donna Diana,* and others). Wolff had previously made significant recordings of the Auber and Berlioz overtures.

With the society's own chief conductor André Cluytens and such major house conductors as Schuricht and Georges Prêtre, there developed a much more thoughtful and coherent synthesis of the recording industry and the orchestra's long traditions. We will treat these projects of the 1960s in chapter 12.

Cluytens's career progressed rapidly during the 1950s, owing not least to his international exposure at the head of the Société des Concerts. His festival work soon included appearances in Edinburgh, Lucern, Berlin, Vienna, and the Maggio Musicale of Florence in addition to his standing commitments to Aix and Besançon. He had triumphed as guest conductor of the Berlin and Vienna orchestras and made recordings with both. In 1955 he conducted *Tannhäuser* in Bayreuth, followed by *Die Meistersinger* and *Lohengrin*—thus was the first French conductor to appear there. In 1956 he not only became a house conductor at the Vienna State Opera, but also led (with Carl Schuricht) the Vienna Philharmonic on a greatly successful American tour. Concurrently he began to try to disengage himself from Paris.

As Münch had used Cluytens as an excuse to escape from the Société des Concerts, Cluytens now used Maurice Le Roux. Gossip had reached his ears that Le Roux was circulating malicious assessments of his musical abilities. Le Roux had been engaged, Cluytens said, without his approval, and he sternly reminded the committee of its obligation to clear such appointments with him. The committee proceeded to decline his request to annul existing contracts with Le Roux, reasoning that personal antagonisms could not be allowed to affect their planning. Nor had Cluytens raised any objection to Le Roux's appointment for the 1957–58 season or the one that followed. "I couldn't predict," said Huot, "that suddenly in 1960 Cluytens would have it in for him." [86]

On New Year's Day 1960 — coincidentally, the day France adopted its new currency — Cluytens telephoned Huot to say that if Maurice Le Roux were to be engaged in 1961 he meant to quit. Huot decided to force the issue by inquiring what his own 1960–61 dates might be; Cluytens in turn submitted his verbal resignation followed by a letter to that effect. The committee summoned the attorney. "The interest of the Société des Concerts," Huot later remarked of the dispute, "is to have a *président-chef* who participates fully in its activities." [87] A meeting of Cluytens, the committee, and the lawyers on 16 April 1960, resulted in his agreement to conduct 30 October and 6 and 13 November 1960 but, *sans ambiguïté*, these would be his last appearances. Mme Cluytens discovered this news in a telephone conversation with Huot, whom she called a liar. *"Madame,"* he responded, *"les affaires de la Société des Concerts ne vous regardent pas."*[88]

So far all this was much in keeping with the circumstances that had led to the rupture with Münch. Cluytens was rarely, now, in Paris, and he had failed to keep the committee informed as to developments in his career, especially his appointment as president and conductor of the Berlin Philharmonic. It particularly annoyed them that he was willing to conduct the Orchestre National de l'ORTF in gala events and concerts, so that it was not uncommon to see posters in front of the Théâtre des Champs-Élysées billing Cluytens at the head of two different orchestras. Unlike Münch, Cluytens did his best to be civil about the period of transition — and indeed later appeared as often as he could with the orchestra. But in fact he had "confused his schedule," and in the event conducted only on 30 October and 13 November in the 1960–61 season.

The musicians were hardly surprised when they assembled on 8 January 1961 to consider the problem. Thévet noted that Cluytens had sought to make an incident, and Lebon confirmed that he had been "most disagreeable" at his last concert. "It's finished with M. Cluytens," remarked another. "He has never concerned himself with the business of the society, except with his baton." Cluytens indicated his willingness to remain as vice president while the society identified "a *dauphin*," but would not consent to any minimum number of appearances thereafter, however small: "Don't count on me a single instant."[89] On the vote to accept his resignation, of 64 voting, 58 favored, with 6 opposed.

The two options remaining were to choose a new conductor / vice president or to leave the post vacant. The possibility of attracting Münch back was dismissed by management as quickly as it was broached by the players. "What we need," said Manuel Recassens, "is moral sustenance and effectiveness of action. If it's a handicap not to have a true resident conductor, it's a catastrophe to have one who is actively hostile to the institution. We need someone to take care of us."[90]

One viable candidate was proposed: Pierre Dervaux, who had just re-signed from the Colonne orchestra. Huot strongly supported Dervaux as a solution to the society's particular array of needs; he was highly placed with Pathé-Marconi, with the lyric theaters, and with the festi-val in Aix-en-Provence. He had independent wealth, which the record showed he was willing to spend on his orchestras. Moreover, he was principled; in defense of his players at the Colonne, he had quit his post over the resale of an unauthorized tape to foreign broadcasting con-cerns. A conversation had indicated his excitement over moving to the Société des Concerts. His only condition was that of an eventual presi-dency, the better to bolster his international reputation.

The musicians were uncertain. Dervaux's personality was less than dynamic, and he had little work elsewhere. Where they feared Cluytens would conduct too little, with Dervaux they were afraid he would con-duct too much. How would they break a contract, if things proved un-satisfactory? The vote showed 17 favoring Dervaux, and 41 for no con-ductor at all.[91] Loucheur, in the president's chair, observed that that result spoke eloquently; he pled only that the specifics be kept within the walls of the room. The post of first conductor was declared officially vacant and would remain so for the rest of the history of the Société des Concerts.

CHAPTER 12

Endings

(1960–67)

In view of the original mission of the Société des Concerts, it is curious how little Beethoven they recorded with their own conductors: none at all with Messager or Gaubert (or Coppola); with Münch only the "Emperor" Concerto in 1944 and an Eighth Symphony in 1949—though the "Emperor" with Marguerite Long is one of their great recordings. With André Cluytens there is a *Prometheus* overture in 1951 and a Third Piano Concerto with Emil Gilels in 1954. Cluytens's cycle of Beethoven symphonies and concertos was with the Berlin Philharmonic (EMI, 1957–60). The society's own historic Beethoven cycle was recorded with Carl Schuricht in 1957 and 1958 for Pathé; earlier Schuricht had led a 1949 Decca / London recording of the Fifth Symphony. The 1958 project remains the only complete symphonies of Beethoven recorded by a Paris orchestra.

Abandoning Germany in 1944, Carl Schuricht (1880–1967) had established himself in Vevey on the north shore of Lake Geneva and within commuting distance of the summer festival in Besançon. He first conducted the Société des Concerts in February 1949 in a program that included Brahms's Fourth and Beethoven's Third Piano Concerto with Marguerite Long; thereafter he appeared annually with the society until their last concert together, the Ninth Symphony in October 1961. Schuricht and Cluytens enjoyed a warm personal friendship, and they had shared conducting responsibilities for the 1956 Vienna Philharmonic tour of the United States. With Cluytens contracted for the Berlin Philharmonic's cycle of Beethoven symphonies, it was a natural step to assign the Paris project to Schuricht.

Except for the Decca / London engagements, the major recordings of the late 1950s and 1960s, including Schuricht's Beethoven cycle, were produced and published by Pathé-Marconi / EMI —formally Les Industries Musicales et Électriques Pathé Marconi SA (France)—which owned the labels La Voix de Son Maître (VSM and HMV, and the famous "Nipper" logo); Columbia UK; Pathé; and the budget label Collection Plaisir Musical (Music for Pleasure, Classics for Pleasure). EMI had been formed in 1931 in England as a merger, to avoid bankruptcy, of the rival British Columbia Graphophone Company and the Gramophone Company. In England the staff and studios remained separate for many years; in France, they were shared, such that all three labels— Gramophone, Pathé, and Columbia—produced their recordings of that period in the rue Albert studio. By the mid-1950s, EMI had acquired companies in Germany, Italy, Japan (Toshiba-EMI), Australia, and the Capitol label in the United States and Canada. By 1965 EMI was the proprietor of most of the labels with which the Société des Concerts had ever been associated: Pathé and Pathé-Marconi, La Voix de Son Maître (VSM), His Master's Voice (HMV), Columbia UK, Angel (the export label Americans associate most closely with the Société des Concerts), Capitol, Discophiles Français, Ducretet-Thomson, Plaisir Musical, and so on. EMI's remaining competitors in France were Decca (London), Disques Véga, and the Compagnie Générale de Disques (Orphée, Pacific, and distributors for Vox).

Most of the Pathé-Marconi / EMI recordings were made in the Salle Wagram, a huge ballroom in the avenue Wagram first built in 1812 that had over the years served as the venue for major congresses, political manifestations, fashion shows, historic tango competitions, and *soirées* of every sort. Its studio capacities were unparalleled in France, and it remains today a major venue for state-of-the-art broadcasts and recordings. (The August 2000 *La Traviata from Paris* with Zubin Mehta and the Italian Radio Orchestra was taped with the singers on location across Paris while the orchestra and conductor were in the Salle Wagram.) EMI's chief French producer was Norbert Gamsohn, who in addition to his close personal affiliation with Cluytens and the Société des Concerts also managed the French concerns of the Greek composer-singer–political hero Mikis Theodorakis and, among several other major pop groups, Pink Floyd. (In a 1973 interview, Pink Floyd's drummer, Nick Mason, said of the band's visits to France: "The food, the wine, Norbert Gamsohn, the producer we usually work with, are all good reasons to go there often.")[1] The sound engineer was typically Paul Vavasseur.

Schuricht and the Société des Concerts began recording their Beethoven cycle in late April and early May 1957 with the Fifth, Sixth, and Eighth Symphonies; the Seventh was prepared in June, and the "Eroica" in late December. The Ninth was recorded in the last week of May 1958, and the First, Second, and Fourth in the last week of September 1958. (Curiously, Schuricht's public performances with the orchestra during this period included a single Beethoven symphony: the First, in January 1959.) The recordings were released in 1959–60 both as a set and individually. A remastering for compact discs was issued by EMI in 1989.

To reflect adequately on the artistic stance taken by these artifacts of the late 1950s, let alone on the central question of how they might reflect a performance tradition of 125 years' standing, would require a volume of its own. One needs to locate such an analysis in the prevailing norms and expectations of Europe in the 1950s; it would even be well to try to filter out the particulars of the conducting, since Schuricht was to some degree an alien. A summary finding would surely begin with the relative smallness of the sound; the Société des Concerts was never a particularly large orchestra and never cultivated a massive sonority. The dominant stylistic concept embraces a clipped, almost matter-of-fact perfection of the pitch content; staccati, for instance, are unusually short, and there appears to be a scrupulous avoidance of *bel canto* phrasing. Vibrato is kept at a minimum, both in the wind and string playing, and is seldom used to enrich single pitches. (This approach changes dramatically in later recordings.) The result, however counter it runs to modern ideals of lushness, seems less a matter of sterility than a kind of purity of expression. This may be part of the historic refinement that had always governed the society's approach to canonic works. *Le goût français* was not an idle concept.

The flute, clarinet, horn, and trumpet playing seem on the whole well within international norms of the era for the major-orchestra sound—though always with a hint of understatement. Oboes and bassoons cultivate the reedy and somewhat nasal sound associated with the French instruments, as for instance in the lovely oboe cadenza in the recapitulation of the Fifth Symphony, first movement. The narrow envelope and somewhat muted volume of the French-system bassoon—the features that Berlioz felt demanded four players in a section—should by all rights be a prominent feature of the society's recordings, but in fact the use of the French models declines quickly in this era in favor of the darker, more rounded sound and technically superior mechanics of the German bassoon. Lucien Thévet reminded me that the more the Société des Concerts played for guest conductors, the more it would be insisted that their habits of bowing, vibrato, and overall sonority be the same as every other orchestra's.

The strings, in the Beethoven symphonies, are generally dominated by the first violins, whose astonishing ensemble quite confirms the notion that they played like a single individual. In the cellos and basses, it is the equilibrium that most attracts the ear, and the way the octave doubling of the bass line is always sensed. The inner strings are seldom the equal of the outer, perhaps owing to engineering practices of the era. Hints of portamento creep into the slow movement of the Ninth.

The performances are substantially free of technical error, though in a few cases there are separations in the ensemble that would not have passed muster in the 1960s. Tempi are brisk. Perhaps the most interesting single movement is the stylish Allegretto scherzando of the Eighth Symphony, where these and other character attributes of the orchestra coalesce into an especially provocative reading.

During 1961–62 the Société des Concerts spent more than three hundred hours in the "miraculous acoustic" of the Salle Wagram as titular first orchestra for Pathé-Marconi, not a great deal less than they would have spent together at the Sunday concerts. Here, away from the public, they developed not only the performances by which they are most permanently remembered, but also treasured personal and artistic friendships: with Victoria de Los Angeles and Dietrich Fischer-Dieskau for the Fauré Requiem of February 1962 in the Church of St-Roch; Poulenc and Jacques Février playing Poulenc's Concerto for Two Pianos in January; and Henri Dutilleux, who watched from the control booth as they recorded *Le Loup* in October 1961. The resulting *Trois Ballets français contemporains* (with *Le Loup,* Poulenc's *Les Biches,* and Milhaud's *La Création du monde,* Prêtre conducting) became a best-seller in France, England, and North America. Nicolai Gedda taped his contribution to Gluck's *Iphigénie en Tauride* between two long airplane journeys; the success of Rosanna Carteri in Gilbert Bécaud's *Opéra d'Aran* in the fall of 1961 resulted in her engagement for a live Verdi Requiem in February 1962. Georges Prêtre, who was quietly succeeding Cluytens as conductor of the best recordings, is included in the register of special "new friends" for 1961–62.[2]

With André Cluytens these years saw the Société des Concerts reach the summit of its recording history and as a result the maximum international exposure it ever had. In 1962 alone there were three incontestably great recordings: the Fauré Requiem, *Boris Godunov,* and the still-influential Ravel *intégrale.* Of these the project remembered with greatest affection in both the written documents and the recollections of the participants was *Boris,* which occupied the entire month of September 1962—more than two dozen recording sessions. The Bulgarian bass Boris Christoff, the bulk of whose career was spent in Italy, was at the peak of his vocal capabilities, and here leaves the only modern stereo recording of a role in which many connoisseurs say he had no peers. (He had made an earlier recording in Paris with the Orchestre National de l'ORTF, Issay Dobrowen conducting; in both he also sings the roles of Pimen and Varlaam.) The supporting cast, including Dimitri Ouzounov and "the ravishing" Evelyn Lear, was also popular with the Parisians. The chorus of the National Opera of Sofia traveled to Paris for the sessions, "encircling Christoff like a lost brother found."[3] At the end of the project, the musicians each contributed 10 francs to offer the Russians a farewell gift.

If a single recording project of the Société des Concerts were to be identified as the best, or most significant, it would surely be the complete Ravel orchestral works as recorded from April 1961 to October 1962 and released in early 1963: four LP discs, including the complete *Daphnis et Chloé,* produced by the French composer René Challan. The CD remastering of 1987 has been more or less continuously in print. One particular attraction of these recordings is that the three featured *sociétaires*—the trombonist Marcel Galiègue in *Boléro,* Lucien Thévet in the *Pavane,* and Robert Casier in *Le Tombeau de Couperin*—are identified. Another is that the orchestra is at its fullest complement and playing at its very best.

Also to be counted in Cluytens's Ravel cycle is his *Pictures at an Exhibition,* which won the Grand Prix du Disque of 1959, and the two piano concertos with Samson-François, which earned the same distinction in 1960. By the 1960s Ravel was as strong a pillar of the society's traditions as Beethoven had been; the liner notes of the complete Ravel speak to his assimilation into the repertoire as a mark of "the society's dedication to . . . works which merit being performed alongside Beethoven."[4] Since Messager and Gaubert the Société des Concerts had featured the French post-Romantic orchestral masterworks, especially when traveling, as though they were at the core of its repertoire. In that respect these particular discs from the golden age of stereophonic recording are the best evidence we have of the society in all its splendor.

Cluytens left many another recorded artifact of the richness of his work with the Société des Concerts: a Roussel cycle in 1964 and 1965; a charming *Les Contes d'Hoffmann* of 1965 with Nicolai Gedda, Gianna d'Angelo, Elisabeth Schwarzkopf, and Victoria de Los Angeles; and at the very end, in 1967, an *Enfance du Christ* with Gedda and de Los Angeles, Roger Soyer, and Ernest Blanc. Of equivalent musical merit is the wonderful series of 1963–64 recordings with Rafael Frühbeck de Burgos: the thrilling *Cantos de España* with de Los Angeles, the best of the *Nuits dans les jardins d'Espagne* (with Gonzalo Soriano), and a disc of Spanish orchestral music featuring Turina's *Danzas fantásticas*. The orchestra's friendship with Frühbeck de Burgos was established uniquely through their recordings; despite several campaigns to engage him, he never appeared in a live concert of the Société des Concerts.

Among the curious streaks of the Pathé / EMI repertoire is the series of French-language operettas for which the society provided, sometimes unacknowledged, the orchestra—part of the headlong competition among the recording companies in both serious and light opera. In 1961 the players laughed uproariously during the recording sessions for Ralph Benatzky's *L'Auberge du cheval blanc,* the French version of *Im Weissen Rössl* (Berlin, 1930; called in English *White Horse Inn*), conducted by Félix Nuvolone.[5] With Franck Pourcel they recorded *Les Cloches de Corneville* (1961), *Paganini* (1962), and *La Chauve-Souris* (*Die Fledermaus,* 1965). Also in 1965 Prêtre recorded the historic *Tosca* with Maria Callas, following up on their celebrated *Callas à Paris* of 1963. (Callas had also made three famous discs in 1964 with Nicola Rescigno conducting, as well as a number of takes that were not released until after her death.) With Jean-Claude Hartemann they recorded Chabrier's *Une Éducation manquée* (1965) and *La Maison des trois jeunes filles,* to music after Schubert (1967); Offenbach's *La Grande Duchesse de Gérolstein* also appeared in 1967, Jean-Pierre Marty conducting; *La Veuve joyeuse* ("The Merry Widow") was apparently released in 1972 after recording sessions preceding the dissolution of the society. One final Pathé curiosity that must be mentioned is the delightful recording of *Babar, le petit éléphant,* narrated in French by Peter Ustinov, the music by Poulenc arranged by Françaix and conducted by Prêtre (1966).

Two recordings with the Roger Wagner Chorale—the Fauré Requiem and Vivaldi Gloria—were released in 1961 on the Capitol label, an American subsidiary of EMI. For the French Teppaz label, the Société des Concerts recorded a major budget series called Collection Concert, which included a reading of the Pierné *Concertstück* for harp with Lily Laskine (1962). Milhaud's Third Symphony and Concerto for Two Pianos were first recorded in 1962 on the Vega / Westminster label. This recording was an outgrowth of the festival concert of 1 April 1962 celebrating Milhaud's seventieth anniversary; he had been a *habitué* of the orchestra, he says, since 1909.[6] By 1967 the orchestra's Milhaud discography numbered eleven titles.

The furious pace and ongoing fascination of the recordings were counterbalanced by the relentless routine of the live concerts. The Sunday concerts were nothing if not predictable: eighty-five minutes or less, without intermission and with minimal rehearsal time. Out-of-town touring had nearly disappeared, just as international tours by air were becoming the rage—package deals that included star conductors, big-name soloists, souvenir programs, and aggressive lobby marketing of records. The Lamoureux and Colonne orchestras likewise found touring beyond their capabilities, and Paris was thus eclipsed by New York, London, and Berlin, whose orchestras undertook ambitious journeys every other year or so. A problem particular to the Société des Concerts was how difficult it was, beyond Paris, to understand the name. Even when the English-language equivalent—the Paris Conservatory Orchestra—was used, the public suspected it might be buying tickets to hear a student ensemble. It was in this context that the name Orchestre de Paris / Société des Concerts du Conservatoire first came to be considered.

In one sense, life without a *1er chef* was not so much different than it had been for the previous decade. The secretary-general, working with the artists' agencies, booked conductors the same way he booked soloists, and the most successful would be invited back annually. The repertoire would be fashioned by exchange of letters, with the secretary-general trying to push it into some coherence, balance the dates, and keep the fees in check. The committee's role in programming grew insignificant: instead it was almost uniquely concerned with internal personnel issues and the mechanics of concert production. The main cost of not having a senior music director was thus the shapelessness of the seasons. This does not seem to have much bothered the musicians, who were greatly more engaged by the recordings than by the Sunday concerts. They went on regarding Cluytens as de facto first conductor until the dissolution. In my conversations with Casier and Thévet, neither seemed to remember the formal decision to dispense with a first conductor.

Nearly all the guest conductors first proposed much longer programs and many more rehearsals than were accorded them. (The exception was Boulez, who asked for and got eight rehearsals for a concert pair in

1966.) The conductors had to agree to conduct the Saturday morning *répétition générale publique,* and they were not to appear with the other concert associations in and around Paris during the calendar quarter they conducted the Société des Concerts. The secretary-general matched soloist and conductor, and often overrode their preferences in programming. Fees for both conductors and soloists were quite modest: around 2,000 [new] francs on the average, plus 25 percent when a concert was broadcast. A few of the most desirable artists earned more, while young artists beginning their careers got considerably less. Rafael Kubelík said his fee for 1963–64 was $1,000, reckoned to be 5,000 francs, and for that reason was not engaged; in 1961 Wilhelm Kempff quoted a fee of 250 guineas, some 3,500 francs, plus first-class airfare round trip from London, and Huot scrawled the words *"trop cher"* in the margin of his letter. By far the highest-paid soloists were Arthur Rubinstein (8,000, then 10,000 and 12,500 francs) and Isaac Stern (8,000 francs). Van Cliburn, in 1961, was paid the unusually high fee of 7,500 francs; Segovia, in 1965, commanded 5,000. Arturo Benedetti Michelangeli was the first soloist to be paid 10,000 francs, for his concert of 5 December 1965.[7]

André Huot worked assiduously at these tasks, earning over the passing years the implicit trust of artists and co-workers and developing a real knack for the work. To Marie-Anne Corre de Valmalète, he writes, with his accustomed jollity: "I hope you are, like me, taking the necessary vacation [after the birth of her son Hervé], and I hope that some true rest puts you in good health, along with the heir to the crown."[8] In a single letter from Aix in July 1960 he goes through a dozen items of business:

- Understanding Michèle Boegner's disinclination to appear with a lesser conductor, replaced Gitton on 11 December with Prêtre. "Prêtre has a greater reputation here and abroad. But with Prêtre she can't do two concertos: I only proposed that because Gitton was conducting. Keep the Chopin."
- Kempe: His concerto goes to Gitton.
- Wayenberg: Signed his contract in the wrong place: "I can't play the Gershwin, even if he can run the Société des Concerts."
- Celidibache: Out of the question at that price [6,000 francs], especially from somebody who has never conducted in Paris.
- Pennario: Ferras has 8 January and Biret 29, thus Pennario has 15 January. So Gamsohn must press him to abandon his engagement in England.

- Dorati: "Where are we with him?"
- Silvestri: Can't have an extra rehearsal, which would cost 2,000 francs. "He must content himself with two rehearsals for the Jolivet work. M. Cluytens often presented excellent performances of new works and never had more than two rehearsals. Silvestri needs to talk less and work faster. But he can have an extra forty-five minutes at the Saturday dress rehearsal."
- Kogan: Please send the contract.[9]

Huot writes with the gusto of a person enjoying his power and using it well.

There were the inevitable squabbles. Samson-François required an exception to the rule requiring exclusivity for his appearances in the two Ravel piano concertos in February 1962, since he was playing with the Colonne orchestra in October and meant to give two solo recitals in Paris; but he would lower his fee, "tit for tat," wrote his agent, "and this is your fault, by the way, because you wouldn't have him in October, and you can't ask Samson-François to stay around in Paris for eight months just to give you priority."[10] The pianist also insisted on prior approval of his conductor (who turned out to be Antal Dorati), the sort of privilege the society only accorded its particular friends.

There was a long correspondence with Valmalète over the appearances of Rafael Kubelík envisaged for January 1961, first as to the fee (finally settled at 4,000 francs, including the public dress rehearsal), then over the soloist, where Kubelík preferred Cziffra to Idil Biret and said he would not appear with soloists he did not know. Huot responded testily: "If M. Kubelík only accepts soloists he knows, he'd better get to know some. Certainly Mme Biret will give satisfaction. I don't understand Kubelík's obstinacy, and our committee doesn't pay much attention to conductors' wishes with regard to soloists, anyway, having the exclusive right to determine that matter. And he can't do Mahler, because the Société des Concerts will do *Das Lied von der Erde* on 4 December [with Oralia Dominguez and Waldemar Kmentt, Richard Kraus, conducting], and think we will have done our duty toward this composer, so little known in France."[11]

Dorati was addicted to "endless" correspondence and did not understand the principle of their programming, routinely suggesting enormous programs and asking for extra rehearsals. From the first he had wanted to do the Bartók Concerto for Orchestra. He was "hardly pleased" with the notion of doing two concertos with Brailowsky

(11 March 1962), but he was appeased with the Bartók and an extra rehearsal. His 24 February 1963 concert, with Nicholas Nabokov's *Solitudes,* was particularly interesting, but he began to want much higher fees and soon disappeared from the roster of frequent visitors.[12]

The Romanian conductor Constantin Silvestri (1913–69) forced the issue of rehearsal time for the November 1960 performance of Jolivet's Second Symphony, and after a long negotiation he was given an extra rehearsal with full percussion; to his reply that for a performance of the same work on Eurovision five days later he had been given four rehearsals, the officers observed simply how pleased they were for him— and how very satisfied by the thought that they had set the premiere in motion to begin with.[13] (The Société des Concerts had made a half-dozen major recordings with Silvestri, several featuring the violinist Leonid Kogan, and including a rather good *Polovtsian Dances* marred by shockingly aberrant percussion.)

Always the musicians were on the lookout for a potential first conductor. The leading candidate was Jean Martinon (1910–76). After two years as a prisoner of war Martinon had briefly been an *aspirant* with the orchestra, 1943–45, and had served as second conductor in 1945–46 to Münch, who strongly favored him as a successor. In October 1950 Martinon returned with a potent Verdi Requiem, but this led instead to an engagement with the Lamoureux orchestra. Honegger said of Martinon: "He conquers not only the public, but also—and this is the hard part—the musicians." [14]

In 1960 Martinon became music director in Düsseldorf, an appointment widely noted as a turning point in post-war relations. Almost immediately he approached the Société des Concerts with the notion of regularly bringing the Düsseldorf Chorale to Paris, listing program possibilities from the Pergolesi *Stabat mater,* St. John Passion, and Mozart Requiem to Ravel's *L'Enfant et les sortilèges* and Stravinsky's *Symphony of Psalms.* This proposal was at first declined, but Huot was pleased to invite Martinon himself to conduct in November 1961. In accepting, Martinon proposed Bartók's *Miraculous Mandarin* or *La Mer* or the Brahms Second along with a modern concerto; in any event, since it was his first appearance with them in eleven years, he wanted a brilliant program. Martinon's concert of 28 November 1961—Handel's *Berenice* overture, Schumann's First Symphony, the Prokofiev Third Piano Concerto with Wayenberg, and Stravinsky's *Firebird*—made a strong impression on the orchestra. Huot, using the familiar *"tu"* form, congratulated him warmly and took the obvious next step of suggesting multiple engagements for the following season.[15]

Within a few weeks Martinon and Huot were negotiating toward four concerts in the 1962–63 season—the very same arrangement already suggested to Cluytens. These would include both a program of contemporary French music with a major first performance in France, and as featured season centerpiece the Brahms Requiem with the Düsseldorf Chorale, later changed to Haydn's *The Seasons* owing to a conflict with the Lamoureux's season. At length Martinon appeared three times in 1962–63. The concert of 4 November with Bruno-Leonardo Gelber in the Chopin E-Minor Concerto was broadcast on both radio and television. The contemporary program on 11 November, titled *Musique européenne,* was easily the most interesting of the season: Frank Martin's Concerto for Seven Instruments and Orchestra featuring the section principals, Jean-Louis Martinet's Symphonic Movement for String Orchestra, the Berg Violin Concerto with Gérard Jarry, and *The Miraculous Mandarin.* The relationship with Martinon remained close thereafter, with some implicit understandings that he could be named first conductor whenever he was ready. At the dissolution in 1967 Martinon and Georges Tessier, the secretary-general, were discussing a 1968 French premiere of the Shostakovich Second Cello Concerto with its dedicatee, Rostropovich, and the possibility that Martinon would lead the twenty-concert tour of Germany in 1969 if Münch were not to be available.[16] In the end Martinon went to the competition, appointed first conductor of the rival Orchestre National de l'ORTF in 1968.

While the Korean conductor Eaktay Ahn (or Ahn Eaktay, 1900–65, composer of the Korean national anthem) created a sensation at a private concert of 2 February 1961 with the Société des Concerts, a major effort to engage him for 1962–63 failed owing to the cost of his fee and air travel.[17] Zubin Mehta was introduced by Mme Valmalète in April 1961 as "a young conductor of Hindu origin, developing a brilliant career: he's greeted with stentorian success wherever he conducts. . . . I'm certain his Paris debut will be a sensation."[18] Mehta appeared in March 1964—his choice of the Kodály *Dances of Galánta* was at first overruled, then accepted—with enough success that he was invited back the following fall. On this second occasion, in November 1964, Mehta arranged to have one of his circle of intimates, Daniel Barenboim, as piano soloist, forming the next stage of the relationship that eventually made Barenboim's appointment to the podium seem natural.

The brilliant David Zinman, who had been Monteux's student and his assistant conductor at the London Symphony Orchestra, was booked to appear with Byron Janis in October 1965. His particular interests were the French masters—Berlioz, Debussy, Ravel—but he was also anxious to do Dvořák, "which he conducts remarkably."[19] There was confusion over the Dvořák numbering system—by Eighth Symphony Zinman meant the G-Major, op. 88, which the orchestra thought of as the Fourth—then a crisis in the summer, when the musicians in Aix heard that Janis was canceling concerts owing to grave illness. This was a rumor; Janis had had a minor operation for a calcium deposit in his shoulder, and was ready for the season opener on 10 October 1965 in the Tchaikovsky Piano Concerto. Zinman returned in December 1966 in a program featuring the orchestral excerpts from Berlioz's *Roméo et Juliette* and *La Mer.*

The major administrative concern of the early 1960s was the growing hegemony of the radio-television orchestra. For the 1961–62 season the Orchestre National de l'ORTF meant unilaterally to apply a contract that embraced greatly improved salaries, more services, and—in what was the single most significant turning point of postwar musical life in Paris—the requirement of exclusivity of commitment, since the ORTF players would not be allowed to continue in the Sunday concert associations. Protests from all four associations were to no avail, and the affected *sociétaires* were finally put into the position of having to make a choice once and for all. Two, the violist Lemaire and the bassoonist Moulinié, resigned from the Société des Concerts outright; five, including the doublebassist Roland Ergo and the harpist Mme Lautemann, vowed to defy the provision and struggle to play in both orchestras. (Mari, the tuba player, left to head the committee of the Lamoureux orchestra, also in crisis over the exclusivity clause.)[20] A few musicians postponed the decision for a year, taking advantage of a no-questions-asked offer of leave from either group for 1962–63. Six new musicians were engaged to cover the vacancies.

In a signal indication of modern practice, a support group of *membres bienfaiteurs* emerged in 1961–62, offshoot of the 1926 friends group. It required an initial donation of 1,000 francs and annual dues of 100 francs; some 150 patrons responded.[21] The funds were used primarily to sustain the money-losing contemporary music programs but also to underwrite such opportunities as bringing the Düsseldorf Chorale for Haydn's *The Seasons* and engaging expensive soloists—for instance, the quartet for the February 1963 Verdi Requiem with Georges Prêtre: Rosanna Carteri, Consuelo Rubio, James King, and Nicolas Giaurov. A portion of the support went to the development of a "public for tomorrow," increasing the subvention of student tickets and hoping to reestablish free student concerts. This new circle of friends was made an official category of membership in the Société des Concerts by a statute of 1962. Among other privileges, the *membres bienfaiteurs* were invited to the annual Assemblée Générale as non-voting observers.

Such conspicuously modern budgetary approaches had by the 1960s become an integral part of administering symphony orchestras all over the world. So, too, were the stereophonic recordings and the color subscription brochures filled with portraits and candid photographs and the now-obligatory promotional prose. But these outward signs of success—described by the press agents as "lovely halls, famous soloists, prestigious conductors, fine programs"—masked the certainty of a financial reckoning that, without a program of massive government subvention modeled on London and Berlin, would, sooner rather than later, unleash the society's apocalyptic end. Public opinion was purposefully brought into play, notably in Bernard Gavoty's series of one-page essays in the season brochures. His winter season 1962–63 contribution begins with the salty observation of Marshal Foch: "My left flank weakens, my right surrenders, my center collapses: I attack." It goes on to describe a faithful public, sunk into their accustomed seats, hardly aware of the magnitude of financial stress at the Société des Concerts, imagining they each are paying their fair share of the orchestra's cost. In fact the receipts of a concert were less than a soloist took in a simple recital.[22] Gavoty advances the long campaign of convincing the orchestra's core subscribers that major change was the order of the day, and that it had to include a new approach to government funding.

The Assemblée Générale closing the 1962–63 season, on 12 May 1963, marked the last official appearance of the venerable secretary-general, André Huot. His thirty-five years of service had embraced a tenure as principal second violinist and distinction in managing the orchestra's finances; since the war he had steered the Société des Concerts out of one of its most difficult periods into an era of relative tranquility and aggressive modernization. It was a good time to step back into the ranks; the society had survived and was, by some measures, prospering. But Huot knew better than any that the next chapter would require more than he could give. Sad to leave a post he could no longer manage, he warned his colleagues to avoid internal division and march forward in a united front, then assured them all of his perpetual affection. In 1965, on reaching the mandatory retirement age of sixty, he sent a typed letter to be read to the Assemblée Générale, notifying them of his firm decision to leave the "great family of *sociétaires* to take my place among the old."[23] Instead the members elected him honorary vice president, to be kept on the pay registers for the two years of customary *sursis;* he was thus officially retired as of the dissolution in 1967. Few had done so much for the Société des Concerts in the twentieth century as André Huot.

The change of watch was all the more emphatic that morning owing to the new occupant of the president's seat, Raymond Gallois-Montbrun (1918–94), who had been named director of the Conservatoire on Loucheur's retirement in 1962. Gallois-Montbrun had first heard the orchestra under Gaubert at the old Conservatoire and perhaps played some concerts as a substitute violinist; he had won the Prix de Rome in 1944 and subsequently risen to the directorship of the École Nationale de Musique at Versailles. Saluting his arrival at the Conservatoire, the orchestra played Gallois-Montbrun's *Symphonie japonaise* in March 1963. He professed delight to be returning to the fold, and said he meant to be an activist, not the kind of president who dropped in to bid them *"bonjour"* once a year—and subsequent events proved how serious that intention was. The relationship, he thought, should be symbiotic, for in serving the Société the musicians served the Conservatoire and its reputation as well. Extraordinary luck seemed to have brought them together, just as deliberations on the "complete reform" of organized music in France were beginning to take shape.[24]

"Complete reform" was hardly to overstate the case. Though André Malraux, as Charles de Gaulle's minister of cultural affairs, was not especially interested in art music and had more urgent priorities for his infant administration, he gradually yielded to mounting nationwide pressure from professional musicians to address a governmental neglect of fifty years' standing: "It's time to be done with that," he told the National Assembly.[25] In December 1962 he appointed a blue-ribbon commission, chaired by Robert Siohan and including among its several luminaries Gallois-Montbrun, "to study the problems of music in France and elaborate a course of action." It now seems clear, from documentation that began to accumulate in the 1990s, that the notion of forming a prestigious, handsomely subventioned new orchestra in Paris was the first proposal to gain consensus within the commission, apparently as early as spring 1963.[26]

If subsequent forward motion toward this end proved painfully slow, that was largely a function of the way budgets were established in those years, complicated by profound disagreement in intellectual circles as to what might come afterward. By 1965, when tempers were flaring and patience with what had become a national debate reached its breaking point, Malraux told the National Assembly, in his typical arch-Gaullist manner: "After all, you weren't waiting for me to do nothing." [27]

Concurrently the composer Marcel Landowski (1915–99) was emerging, quietly at first, as the chief architect of the new policies and, without a doubt, as the single most influential figure in the mutation of the Société des Concerts into today's Orchestre de Paris. The report of the Siohan Commission, well-meaning but tame, was drafted in early November 1964 and formally submitted in December; already on 5 December Landowski was named to succeed Siohan as inspector-general of music education in Malraux's cabinet. Finding himself "walled in" at the ministry, largely owing to the unwillingness of the two senior figures, Gaëtan Picon (as director-general of arts and letters) and especially Émile Biasini (as director of theater, music, and cultural programming) to let music find its own way, Landowski developed a circle of intimates that soon realized they were theorizing nothing less that a new *politique musicale*. One turning point was reached in March 1965, when a Comité National de la Musique chaired by Jacques Chailley, professor of musicology at the Sorbonne, submitted a memorandum demanding that the elements of a new *politique* be left in care of a professional musician. From there Landowski gained his dominance in policy making, first as chief of a separate Music Service (1966), then as the nation's first director of music, opera, and dance (1970–75)—formally "Directeur de la Musique, de l'Art Lyrique et de la Danse au Ministère de la Culture."

He famously carried the "Landowski Plan," or "Plan de 10 ans pour l'organisation des structure musicales françaises," in his mind for many months before it was first put to paper in July 1969: a pyramid with the Orchestre de Paris and Paris Opéra at its point and, at its base, a conservatory, orchestra, opera house, and local program for each region in France. As perpetual secretary of the Académie des Beaux-Arts, 1986–93, and chancellor of the Institute from 1994 until his death in 1999, Landowski lived to see much of his vision come true, even such impressive projects of brick and mortar as the Opéra Bastille (1989) and the new Cité de la Musique at La Villette (1995).

Nothing in France is so noisy as a new *politique*. Landowski's endeavor was buffeted on all fronts, and not only by assaults from the other arts. Among musicians there were objections both from organized syndicates, who feared government intervention in general and the loss of some obviously wasteful privileges in particular, and from radicals like Boulez, who held that little short of a national turn away from the centrality of opera and symphony orchestras would do. "To want to make such an ensemble these days is folly," Boulez wrote of the orchestra that topped Landowski's pyramid.[28] He held that recordings and radio / television had put fine art music at everyone's disposal, and that the foreign orchestras did well enough at bringing front-line classical music to Paris. The acidic groans of the *tam-tam boulézien,* wrote Landowski in his absorbing memoirs, *Batailles pour la musique* (1979), "gave [my] score its spice."[29]

The tam-tam was an apt metaphor for the Boulezian pronouncements. Boulez, during these critical years for French classical music, was racing about the international stage as a self-exiled expatriate and just reaching his maximum stride as an aging *enfant terrible.* His own sweeping plans for a French resurgence in music, voiced to anyone who would listen, were thought by ordinary working musicians arrogant and laughable. Intellectuals wondered whether he was a national treasure or something of an embarrassment. And everything about the new official *politique* galled him. "A total absence of ideas," he thought; the policy was "as sad as the Maginot Line and about as effective," the work of "amateurs incapable of taking the long view: mediocre squanderers." He appeared jealous that others were doing the work. He found their strategy a *"bric-à-brac,"* Landowski's long-term plan "an abortion . . . destined to sterilize music in France for twenty or thirty years."[30] It is generally believed that Malraux's decision to put Landowski in charge of the nation's music is what caused Boulez to leave Paris, "saying," reported the *New York Times,* "he could never again live in a city where music was in the hands of incompetent functionaries."[31]

The aftermath of these celebrated confrontations is still taking place. The debate was at its most electrifying after the Orchestre de Paris was already a *fait accompli.* What is important at this point in our chronicle is that consensus for action had been reached by 1964. Landowski's alliance with Gallois-Montbrun and, increasingly, the capital's best orchestral players succeeded. Soon they had established the foundation for widespread agreement on the look and feel of a new national orchestra.

Huot was succeeded by the cellist Manuel Recassens (or Recasens),[32] who for two years as Huot's assistant had been called *le dauphin.* In his inaugural remarks Recassens urged his colleagues to continue making sacrifices for a little while longer, certain as he was that the corner was soon to be turned.[33] His hot temper was reckoned a token of his will to succeed, a force that might be harnessed in the skirmishes certain to come. And his program was indeed imaginative—for instance in 1964 the launch of a series of five Thursday night concerts in the Church of St-Louis-des-Invalides, featuring the celebrity organists Marie-Claire Alain, Pierre Cochereau, and Bernard Gavoty. At the second of these Jean Gitton led a Bach cantata at the beginning and Honegger's *Le Roi David* at the end, surrounding a Handel organ concerto. At the fifth Serge Baudo, a potential candidate for the podium, led an all-French program of Delalande, Charpentier, and the Poulenc *Stabat mater.* (Pathé recorded a program of Charpentier, Lully, and Delalande with Roger Blanchard in June 1965.) The Invalides concerts, however, incurred a substantial deficit and were not resumed.

Chamber orchestras and the Baroque repertoire were nevertheless gaining an important following. People liked Bach and Vivaldi who didn't like Wagner, it was observed, and a new public was there to cultivate. While a chamber formation originating from within the Société des Concerts would have to be subventioned to make it competitive with leading German ensembles, countless engagements, Recassens and his committee believed, would surely be forthcoming. But the rank and file feared the extra work, and it was thought a new emphasis on Baroque music might detract from the true mission of the Société des Concerts. The players were already notorious for failing to appear at concerts devoted to "unusual" music. Lespine remarked, however, that such extra duty "puts butter on your spinach."[34]

Another plank in the Recassens platform was to return the Société des Concerts to its former prestige as a touring orchestra, to which end he successfully negotiated the packaging of a major journey to Japan. André Cluytens was quick to accept the assignment, and went on to program a dazzling repertoire of the society's best works. With a gala farewell concert on 19 April 1964 (the "Eroica," *Siegfried-Idyl,* and *La Mer,* Cluytens conducting) the society adjourned its 1963–64 season early to allow for a week of intense rehearsals.

The Société des Concerts played nine concerts in Japan over a two-week period, 28 April–11 May 1964: three in Osaka, one in Fukuoka, and five in Tokyo. There were five separate programs in all, including an all-Ravel concert, *Pictures at an Exhibition,* two Beethoven symphonies, and most of the pillars of the French repertoire.[35] The party numbered ninety-six, including two harpists, a saxophonist, four trumpets, and six percussionists. A few last-minute defections had to be covered, but otherwise the tour was short on reverses and thoroughgoing in its triumph.

The musicians remember the Japan journey as a highlight of the 1960s. In Tokyo there had been a major civic face-lift—and the inauguration of the Tokyo–Osaka bullet train—for the summer Olympic Games. Long lines stretched to see the Venus de Milo, which André Malraux had shipped for the games. (Malraux had also sent the Mona Lisa to the New York World's Fair, and the pope had shipped Michelangelo's *Pietà*, in a confluence that provoked outraged response from conservative art critics. "Whatever will they do next?" asked E. H. Gombrich: "Take out the windows of Chartres and send them to a show? Lend the caves of Lascaux to Egypt for the promise of one of their pyramids? It would cost a lot, but it could be done, and would it not further understanding among men or at least among transport contractors?")[36] Fernand Lelong, the tuba player, fondly recalled the meal he and other wind players enjoyed in a geisha house.

Both the audience reception and critical response to the orchestra ran toward the ecstatic, and the musicians—many of whom were too young to have taken a major road trip with the Société des Concerts—repeatedly heard that they were competitive with anybody anywhere. Still today the Paris Conservatory Orchestra and André Cluytens are remembered enthusiastically in Tokyo, and a Cluytens retrospective collection, available only in Japan, continues in print.

There was no question but that the triumph in Japan could be seen as a step in restoring the Société des Concerts to the prestige enjoyed by the Vienna and Berlin orchestras. Recassens was bitter, however, that on their return to France there was no semblance of governmental interest—no mark of recognition from the foreign minister or minister of cultural affairs, nor much by way of thanks from anybody else. Three articles had appeared in the press, but these had all been placed by publicists. The orchestra was made to wait for the last part of its subvention—some 18 million francs—despite the fact that the treasury was as exhausted as the musicians were. Recassens was quite simply indignant; it was not fair to urge the players to do more and more on the basis of promises unkept, and if he failed to deliver a higher level of subvention and better working conditions by the next season, he meant to resign. Meanwhile, the society had no choice but to carry on as "a *grande maison*, which must maintain its quality and its dignity at all costs."[37]

Recassens and his committee, meanwhile, began to plan for a tour of the United States in 1965–66: some two dozen concerts spread over a month abroad. The full schedule met with some resistance in the ranks, and the inevitable observation: *"vingt-quatre concerts en un mois, c'est fatigant."* The musicians, who had been pressed for leisure time in Japan, wanted more time off on the road; one even suggested a tour of six months. Above all they refused to travel eight hundred kilometers during the day by bus and be deposited at the hall just before concert time. The money needed looking out for; American impresarios, they had heard it said of 1918, were not especially scrupulous.[38]

At the Assemblée Générale in 1964, meanwhile, Gallois-Montbrun unveiled ideas for a new Conservatoire to be built at La Défense as part of a comprehensive *centre culturel*—with the École Nationale d'Architecture, the École Supérieure du Cinéma, and the Musée d'Art Moderne—designed by Le Corbusier. There would be residence space for five hundred students supported with the kind of state scholarships Gallois-Montbrun had just learned about in Russia. Foreigners would at last be welcome to finish their music studies in Paris. At the very least there would be a rehearsal facility for the Société des Concerts, and quite possibly a public concert hall. La Défense would host the best orchestra in the world—"and that would be you."

But there was more. The national commission had agreed to the principle of a state orchestra. "That, too, must be you: nobody thinks otherwise." There would be inevitable changes; exclusivity would be required, and the new orchestra might have to work with student conductors once a week. Sooner or later the offer would come, he promised, and then the difficult decisions could be made. Recassens thanked Gallois-Montbrun for taking the long view and voiced the hope, as though not entirely convinced, that their years of sacrifice were on the verge of paying off.[39]

Over the next six months the *sociétaires* heard little that could be construed as progress toward any of these goals. To allay their growing impatience and almost certainly to exert pressure on the authorities, Recassens called an Assemblée Générale *extraordinaire* for 31 January 1965 to discuss the state of play. Here Gallois-Montbrun reported that the commission had finished its work and that a multi-volume report would be released in a matter of weeks. In May he confessed that the process was taking longer than expected—in fact the budget provisions were proving more difficult to conclude than anybody had imagined—but that there was no reason for pessimism. ("People say I make it rain or shine at the Conservatoire; if that were the case, I'd make it shine always. Some just say I'm the fifth wheel.") In six months, a year at most, there would be details to discuss.[40]

When pressed on the rumors of a 20-million-franc subvention to come to the orchestra from the state, Gallois-Montbrun responded that the notion of state funding of that magnitude had been agreed to, though its sources had yet to be identified. Without it, the musicians reminded him, further touring was impossible. A trip to Spain and Portugal, in planning since 1962, had repeatedly foundered over the question of projected deficits; at length the Portuguese leg of the tour was announced for October 1965, supported by the Gulbenkian Foundation, only to fail for budgetary reasons at the last minute.[41]

Since the rival societies were no longer being considered for elevation as the new national orchestra, Gallois-Montbrun hinted, the most nuanced diplomacy—and not a little secrecy—was the order of the day. So, too, were good manners. Suddenly raising every eyebrow, he launched into as stern a warning as the members ever heard from their president.

He found their behavior, especially at engagements outside their Sunday concerts, disgraceful. "You have, I'm sorry to say, the fault of the French race, which is a frightful tendency to grouse." Their manners, from which he himself had suffered, were to be deplored. Their artistic merit was generally understood, but it needed accompanying with proper dress and seemly stage presence.

> When a less good conductor is with you, you play badly. The back stands just pretend to play. The sonority is catastrophic, as is the public result. People say, "The Société des Concerts, when it doesn't want to play, is awful." They hear an abominable orchestra, they check the program, they see "Société des Concerts du Conservatoire." Possibly you really are the best orchestra in the world. But you will have to correct yourselves. The price is small. And it would be unthinkable to confer this prestigious honor on those not worth it. . . .
>
> Your *métier* is *agréable:* you make music. The work is hard, but decently paid. And hard work is required everywhere. The postal employee has to be at his window; the diplomat must practice diplomacy even when he is tired. In every *métier* you have to have the courage to overcome difficulties. *Tant pis* if you don't. . . .
>
> You see how important it is to reaffirm your artistic superiority, to be perfect everywhere and all the time. Affect public opinion. You'll be closely scrutinized by the agents of government who will make the decision. Don't produce merely a good concert but instead a little theatric spectacle: a majestic taking of the stage, and an irreproachable conduct. It's important. When the hall is occupied, it's indispensable that the public think you are the most beautiful association of the world.

> I tell you this with friendship, commitment, and respect. If you don't
> change, I will be annoyed. But you yourselves will be the victims."[42]

Recassens thanked Gallois-Montbrun for his seductive vision and
suggested that despite moments of internal discord they were well along
the road to full partnership in the project. The musicians then began to
grouse, as if on cue; Gallois-Montbrun hadn't been asked for his opinion, and he seldom came to the concerts anyway. And whatever his optimism, the months continued to pass by with nothing new to report.

Otherwise 1964–65 was deemed an excellent season, owing largely to a
very successful Beethoven cycle with Cluytens. Zubin Mehta and Lorin
Maazel had both appeared, as had, under a three-year exclusivity contract, Arturo Benedetti Michelangeli. The secretary's report lamented
the loss of the popular doublebass player Roland Ergo, who had finally
resigned to join the Orchestre National; this was troublesome not only
for what it seemed to symbolize but because Ergo was a hard-working
and effective assistant treasurer. ("Triple applause," the minutes read.)
Members were cautioned as to their deportment during the forthcoming concerts under Boulez, who had "quite particular ideas about work
and how to prepare a concert, and who accepted our invitation with
particular conditions."[43] There would be sectionals for all, a rehearsal
of danger points, and two general rehearsals for each of the pair: a grueling but necessary agenda. Everyone, they were assured, would delight
in working with him. Pathé-Marconi was to record the concerts.

The Boulez concerts of 23 and 30 January 1966 featured works of Debussy, Bartók, Stravinsky, Webern, Berg, and Boulez himself; Jean-
Pierre Rampal played a Mozart concerto. The second was recorded but
not released until 1987, when it was published as a CD in the series Les
Grands Concerts Inédits du Théâtre des Champs-Elysées. It consists of
Jeux, the Bartók Second Piano Concerto with Jean-Bernard Pommier,
and Berg's Three Pieces, op. 6.

Recassens grew decidedly morose over the orchestra's financial standing
and the lack of signals from the government. At the public rehearsal of
Saturday, 27 November 1965, and the Sunday concert the next day, he
took it upon himself to read aloud a manifesto on the untenable nature
of the circumstances. To force the attention of the public, the press, and
most of all the government, he announced his intention to defy the *cahier des charges.* Effective immediately, the Société des Concerts would
decline to engage French conductors and soloists, and the orchestra

would play no French music until a solution had been reached. (A look at the fall programming—all foreigners, except for Cluytens and one appearance by Baudo—suggests that this tactic had been envisaged for some time.) Further, the orchestra would not return at all in January unless the government responded in some fashion.

Recassens had successfully vetted his remarks, written in consultation with two conspirators not affiliated with the society, to the membership at the break from the rehearsal on Friday, then had a copy delivered to the Conservatoire at 5:45 in the afternoon. Otherwise he did not consult the committee. The ensuing ruckus spun fast out of his control. The committee, incensed at not having been forewarned, resigned *en masse,* and Gallois-Montbrun severed his relationship with the orchestra. In turn Recassens resigned and was replaced by Lucien Thévet as interim secretary-general. The professors at the Conservatoire submitted a scathing attack by mail.

At a heated emergency assembly before the concert on 9 January 1966, Recassens complained that the committee's angry response was insulting; well accustomed to attacks from the outside, he was appalled to be insulted by and in front of his own colleagues. The *boycottage* he had announced was not really about French music in general, but rather a reaction to the government's meddlesome insistence on too much contemporary repertoire and on soloists and conductors of lesser quality. As for acting without the committee, he had done that for five years while his colleagues slacked. Thévet himself remarked, at the end of the concert, "Bravo, that's exactly what needed saying." [44] The measures announced were blunt but necessary to write the problem large. The Strasbourg orchestra had sent congratulations.

Recassens had believed in the promise of the Société des Concerts as a world-class player: protected, subventioned, nationalized: "I was living only for that." His colleagues had made the sacrifices necessary to establish their good intentions—for instance, staying together over the summer, when individually they could have made more elsewhere. The musical results for the last three years, he said, had been magnificent. Everyone's heart had been in it.

And what, Recassens asked, had they got for it? Nothing at all. For 1965–66 they had seen 4.5 million old francs (450,000 new) in subvention and paid 6 million in tax, then watched helplessly as the tax bill rose to 8 million. Gallois-Montbrun had refused to go with him to the ministry to plead for help. October came, and with the last-minute cancellation of the Portugal trip for lack of government subvention it became clear that he was doing no more than plugging the dike. He decided to hurl his thunderbolt, and the committee was at first in his camp. Afterward they turned on him, then following a meeting with Gallois-Montbrun in December went back to supporting him. "It isn't easy to work with a weather-vane committee," he complained.[45] A full five years earlier he had meant to break the stalemate or resign; now his decision not to return as secretary was irreversible.

The musicians, who had of course heard the speech when it was first read to the public, were firmly behind the threatened strike. But there was some confusion about what to do next. On the question of dismissing the committee it was urged not to put the cart before the horse—rather to deal with the concert cancellations first of all. The vote for canceling the spring concerts sustained strongly: 45 yes, 13 no, 4 abstentions. The motion to engage an adjunct secretary-general, as Recassens had wanted in order to carry on without a strong committee, was narrowly defeated. Georges Tessier stood to propose himself as Recassens's successor; by the second ballot he had the absolute majority: 37 votes, to 16 for Casier, 1 for Wesmaël, and 6 abstentions. Tessier was the principal of the second violins, where he had served with distinction since 1949.

The executive body that would oversee the transition now consisted of Gallois-Montbrun as president, Tessier as secretary-general, Lucien Wesmaël as treasurer, and Jacques Balout in the delicate role of personnel manager. At the ministry Landowski had given himself a fiscal year, 1966–67, to activate the new orchestra—the cornerstone of his plan. He was fond of all four members of the transition team, especially Tessier, whom he considered "the soul of the operation."[46]

A first negotiated principle was to assure automatic advancement to the second round of auditions for "a certain number," in recognition of the service the elder members had provided. Opponents talked of the patchwork of mediocrity this measure would cause, but Landowski held firm in the decision: "It seemed to me beneficial to have veteran musicians cohabiting with the mass of young people I knew we were about to recruit."[47] The rest would have to be elaborated, point by point.

One last upheaval at the Société des Concerts prior to the dissolution was a major dispute with Pathé-Marconi. This began in January 1966 when Pathé, pleading that the market for classical music was saturated, proposed to renew a three-year contract without an increase to the existing fee schedule—and thus to pay the musicians at lower than union scale. But Pathé would guarantee the typical number of services by using the full Société des Concerts as the accompanying orchestra for operetta projects already on the agenda.[48] During the statutory six-week delay between the offer and its expiration the musicians' union, fearing the precedent about to be established, called a general strike against all recording companies for 29 March–1 April 1966. This was purposefully set to conflict with already scheduled recording sessions, possibly for *The Merry Widow,* so that Pathé would be obliged to pay the contracted singers anyway. Pathé-Marconi responded that in such an eventuality it would seek reimbursement of expenses, a penalty, and interest from the Société des Concerts, to the tune of 20 million old francs.

The committee edged its way out of the dilemma in unilateral talks with the union, SAMUP (Syndicat des Artistes-Musiciens de Paris).[49] The Société des Concerts agreed to respect the union's mandated minimum wage in every other circumstance but for the arrangements with Pathé; in turn the society was given autonomy to negotiate whatever terms it could get for the new recording contract. This was scarcely a victory for anyone involved, but it did spare the society the embarrassment and expense of going to court, and Tessier imagined that the outcome made the most of an untenable circumstance.

The Assemblée Générale called for 24 April 1966 to ratify the solution was thus the occasion for Gallois-Montbrun's first appearance among the musicians since the incident of Recassens's mutiny. Gallois-Montbrun asked to review the *fort mauvais souvenirs* of the situation that had led to his resignation, then draw some lessons vital to the health of the Société. It would be naive, he suggested, to think that the situation was as neat as it had been a year before. The incident had damaged both the Société des Concerts and the Conservatoire. He had had sleepless nights, bombardments of mail, and feelings of bitterness that the confidence, friendship, and esteem he held for the Société des Concerts were not returned.

Nevertheless one could not turn back the clock. Gallois-Montbrun had seen Landowski and the other government personalities and minimized the damage. They were making progress. He begged the *sociétaires* to hold steady; their noble and ancient origin was clearly cultural capital to be invested. Above all they must make no more *faux-pas.*

Tessier boasted of an administration in perfect health, and everything seemed amiable until Recassens stood to observe that for all the rhetoric there had not been the slightest motion forward. It was time to get serious; otherwise the government would go on reducing the Société des Concerts to an orchestra of second quality. "We must try everything to keep from sinking into mediocrity. It's to you to decide. As for me, my decision was made long ago." [50]

The ideas of Boulez, who was now promoting alternate plans for the new orchestra based on his own success at getting extensive rehearsal time in Vienna and London, were held to be pure fantasy. If he had had twelve rehearsals with the Vienna Philharmonic, as he told the press, that was an exception to the rule; he was known to have led *Parsifal* and *Rosenkavalier* in Vienna on no rehearsal at all. The London Philharmonic had been bankrupt since the beginning of the year owing to overtime billings; the Vienna orchestra ordinarily refused to come to any extra rehearsals. They hoped indeed that Boulez would someday become their conductor, for he deserved it, and they would be honored. But his world view needed controlling. "Things just aren't perfect that way," Tessier said, "except in the United States." [51]

On 23 September 1966 the committee at last had an informational meeting, where Marcel Landowski presented the details of his proposal and the committee first heard the term "ten-year plan." A subsequent vote of the full membership, only three short of unanimity, approved continuing along the established lines. Tessier begged them to keep the news strictly private, "between associates, between friends." On a previous occasion when he had told the rank and file all he knew, idle gossip had leaked and within a few days the whole profession was talking about what the *sociétaires* alone should have known. Opponents of the scheme quickly mobilized, and it had taken all Landowski's skill with the newspaper editors to keep the story off the front pages. Since then, the negotiations had been held in secret. Tessier's first experience with frankness had its serious repercussions, so he tried to remember the proverb Once burned, twice shy—in French, "A scalded cat fears even cold water" *("Le chat échaudé craint l'eau froide").* [52]

The draft statutes of the new association were made public in April 1967. The Orchestre de Paris would be sponsored by the state, the city of Paris, and the Department of the Seine. There would be a council of fifty-one directors serving four years, meeting once each year in a general assembly chaired by the director of the Conservatoire as *président d'honneur.* Directors included such ex officio members as the minister of cultural affairs, the director of music and dance, the prefect of the Paris region, and so on. Fourteen members would be appointed by the ministry, fourteen by the Council of Paris, eight by a patron organization. An administrative board of seven would be chosen from the council.

The management committee would consist of the conductor, the chief administrator, and the personnel officer. Later a *chef du matériel* and others would be engaged as functionaries. The conductor would be appointed for three years by the minister of culture, but could be terminated by the administrative board before the end of his contract. He might engage one or more assistant conductors. The chief administrator would serve for four years, and come at least initially from within the orchestra—thereby guaranteeing yet another link with the practice of the associations.

The initial staffing plan envisaged engaging twenty new members by general audition, then filling the rest of the seats with *sociétaires* and *stagiaires* of the Société des Concerts du Conservatoire, with any vacancies at the end of the process open to applicants from the Colonne, Lamoureux, and Pasdeloup orchestras.[53]

At the close of the 1966–67 season, the subscribers were not sent a season brochure. Meanwhile, on 3 June 1967, Cluytens died in Paris, and it was indicative of the general upheaval that his passing went uncommemorated at the orchestra.

André Malraux decreed music to be the first priority of his 1968 budget, while Landowski sequestered enough funds to guarantee the subvention from October 1967 to the end of the year. In the long run the national government would provide 50 percent of the subvention, the city of Paris 33 percent, and the Conseil Général of the Seine 17 percent. The text read to the musicians included three controversial points: juried reauditions for each member every four years, with a salary increase for those who were deemed worthy of continuing; individual accounting of services, largely to allow for small rehearsals; and exclusivity except for teaching and mitigating circumstance—the better to prevent the old arguments of "fatigue" and "extenuation" that so pepper French music history.[54]

The move toward exclusivity was strongly opposed by the unions, especially representatives of the theater orchestras and—in an interesting reversal of circumstances—the ORTF. Together, with Georges Auric at their head, these agencies launched an offensive to kill the project. Malraux was momentarily alarmed but soon calmed; it took longer with Auric, who was genuinely persuaded that the unwritten goal was to destroy the Opéra orchestra. At length he was brought around in the classical

French manner, over a "sumptuous poached turbot."[55] The confrontation reached its head when the union placed an interdiction on auditioning for the new orchestra, but in the event, a sufficient number ignored the decree to render that tactic moot. Landowski had lobbied the union stewards for a year: "One constant of the French *esprit*," he remarked, "is to contest, protest, complain, and demand, but . . . in the end the whiners aren't that unhappy with their lot."[56] Their opposition was indefensible; the plan did after all propose 110 better jobs, a much-improved salary schedule—and the promise that these ameliorations, in due course, would invigorate and restore Parisian art music across the board.

The Société des Concerts du Conservatoire was dissolved on 21 June 1967.[57] That day its members met for their final Assemblée Générale in the Salle de Danse at the Conservatoire in the rue de Madrid. The *ordre du jour* called for the usual approvals of minutes and reports from the secretary-general and treasurer, then presented the dramatic item "Transformation de la Société des Concerts en Orchestre Officiel sous le Titre: ORCHESTRE DE PARIS."[58]

Sixty-six *sociétaires* were present for the meeting. Lucien Wesmaël, as treasurer, was elected to be the official liquidator of the Société des Concerts. At 12:45 the assembly moved into extraordinary session, with Gallois-Montbrun in the chair and Marcel Landowski observing. Gallois-Montbrun's oration recognized Landowski's signal contribution to their having at last reached the moment of victory. He had understood the necessity for France to boast an orchestra of national dimension, having at its core "those who carry the true and purest flame of French symphonic art, the Société des Concerts du Conservatoire."

"We are at the summit of French musical art, thus in the highest realm of education, elegance, and courtesy. You can say anything, so long as you remember that position. For my part I will rule out of order anyone who allows himself to stray."

Tessier apologized for the secrecy, and the sudden call to the meeting. But the result was nothing less than a miracle. He praised Landowski and Gallois-Montbrun: "It would take me hours to tell you how much we owe to this heaven-sent man and to our president." He went on to provide details of the final proposal: of 111 new jobs, 52 would be reserved for members of the Société des Concerts. There had been about 300 outside candidates auditioned by Charles Münch and representatives of the union, and their quality had been very high. The "new

Société des Concerts," with its ideal working conditions, would certainly be competitive with the best orchestras anywhere.

The questions from the floor were largely technical: Would the musicians be fully employed or *stagiaires* in their first year? Only the new players, it was answered, would have to serve apprenticeships, while the players from the Société des Concerts, Opéra, or ORTF orchestras would be exempt.

What would happen to players who choose not to belong? Gallois-Montbrun answered that the resultant upheaval in Parisian musical life would leave many vacancies, and they could seek them.

What about those who did not pass the audition? "That," said Gallois-Montbrun, "is the only sad part of what we did. But it also justifies what we did; those who didn't pass the audition proved that auditions were needed. I know that's a little harsh, but what else was there to do? If they were not engaged, it did not signify that they lacked talent, but simply that others were better. The blow of losing an audition is cruel, that's true. But I know they will find a satisfactory position, perhaps at a higher level than they were."

Would the title Société des Concerts du Conservatoire disappear entirely? Landowski responded: "We intend to keep the title. If the Société des Concerts du Conservatoire was chosen as the kernel of the new orchestra, it was because of its glorious past and all it represents. If the new orchestra is called 'de Paris,' it is because the City of Paris is making an important financial contribution and also offering us the theater of the Opéra-Comique. The complete title will be Orchestre de Paris / Société des Concerts du Conservatoire." That remains the case today.

The pension fund, or Caisse de Post-Activité, was a more delicate matter, having, as it turned out, no legal standing. Landowski said that it was obvious that those who had paid into it would get their investment and interest back at retirement. For the rest, he said, "We'll see." But under no circumstance would pensions be lost: "I give my most formal pledge to that effect."

Manuel Recassens, the fallen secretary-general whose courageous threat to close the society down had finally set this dénouement into play, took the floor and spoke at length. "No one would think," he said, "of opposing the realization of a plan that, from the point of view of the development and defense of French music, is exceptional." But he was concerned about the old *sociétaires* and those who would not belong to the Orchestre de Paris—heirs to more than a century of tradition, who gave it their care and talent that it might continue to exist. Some of them had personal reasons not to belong to the new orchestra; others, to benefit a cause certainly worth the effort, were rather more brutally separated and sent away. There must be something to do for those *sociétaires* and the recent *membres honoraires*. Perhaps an association of the former members could guard something of the old society, the moral and artistic patrimony—not as performers, perhaps, but as curators. It was a moral issue: not to forget completely those who were about to be totally cut off from all they had built.

Landowski replied that particular effort would be made to keep in contact with those who had spent a great portion of their lives as *sociétaires*. (An association of retired *sociétaires* continues to exist.) The more delicate point, the one that, he admitted, had much preoccupied him, was that of the active musicians who for one reason or another would not be part of the new orchestra. Clearly they could not be suddenly cut off from symphonic life. Perhaps the solution lay with the three other associations; the twenty-five or thirty musicians about to be laid off could find a place there. Certainly there was to be a reclassification of the musicians of Paris, and certainly the following season would be kinder.

"What about foreigners?" asked Debost. Three had been engaged; a maximum of 10 percent was allowed by existing immigration statutes. Many French musicians, observed Landowski, worked abroad, and it was certainly good for everyone to have foreigners in their midst. Some of the French expatriates, in fact, were returning to the Orchestre de Paris (from Germany, Belgium, Switzerland, and one from the United States), not to mention the musicians from the provinces.

Then the discussion settled into the details: conditions for accepting outside engagements, recording contracts, trips, tours, leaves, days off. The players would be off on Saturday afternoons, all day Sundays, and most of Monday, giving them, for the first time, *"un vrai week-end."* They would ordinarily have a month's paid vacation. Disputes would be settled by a tribune of ten principal players, selected by the members.

Robert Casier, not continuing, rose to speak on behalf of the departing members, "wishing to yesterday's colleagues and tomorrow's happy heirs all the success they deserve. Long live the Orchestre de Paris / Société des Concerts du Conservatoire!"

With that a vote was taken of the 65 remaining in the room, requiring a two-thirds majority of 43. The result was 51 favoring, 13 opposed, 1 abstention.

Gallois-Montbrun proclaimed the Société des Concerts dissolved. In closing he addressed in particular "our *sociétaires* who are entering the magnificent orchestra just created. I ask them never to forget that if they had the luck to accede to such a fine situation and to exercise such a luminous activity, they owe it above all to the existence of the magnificent orchestra to which you have so contributed. I beg you never to forget your elders, and especially those who won't be with us any more." The meeting was adjourned at 1:30 P.M.[59]

To the subscribers Tessier summarized what had happened in a mimeographed circular: "The State, City of Paris, and Department of the Seine have joined together to create and administer a full orchestra, which, by its exceptional quality, will have as its mission to give concerts in Paris, in the Paris region, and throughout the nation, and to broadcast the musical prestige of Paris throughout France and foreign lands." The work group had recommended that the oldest of the societies be converted into the Orchestre de Paris / Société des Concerts du Conservatoire, with its forces strongly augmented to 110 musicians. Gallois-Montbrun would serve as *président d'honneur* and Charles Münch would be permanent conductor. Executive and artistic committees, including some of the greatest names in French music, would oversee the organization. "The return of Charles Münch as permanent conductor at the head of such a formation is already, by itself, an event," Tessier rightly observed.

Tessier's next paragraph says much about the reasons for the change: "All our artists are henceforth bound by an exclusivity clause, and the preparation for each concert will consist of several full and sectional rehearsals, our ambition being that an Orchestre de Paris / Société des Concerts du Conservatoire will bring it, thanks to its work and its ability, to the first rank of the world's orchestras." The traditional Saturday morning open rehearsal at the Théâtre des Champs-Élysées would be retained for a time as a concert reserved for subscribers. The Sunday afternoon concerts would be replaced by *manifestations de gala* during the week, twice a month, and for which the subscription system would be retained.[60]

Their inventory, made the following 22 September, was surprisingly small: 4 four-stringed doublebasses and 3 five-stringed, harp, celesta, keyboard glockenspiel, chimes, tam-tam, gong, mandolin, American and German timpani, and old hand-tuned timpani, the total valued at 59,134 francs. There were traveling cases for the instruments valued at 21,500 francs, and miscellaneous material, including the doublebass stools, stands, and bass drum stands, valued at 1,100 francs. The library numbered 407 works valued at 40,700 francs. The total value of the inventory was estimated at 122,434 francs. Funds in that amount were deposited in the Caisse de Prévoyance and distributed to the living members by their years of service. (Later there would be a dispute with the tax collectors over whether or not that should be taxed.) The books were balanced and closed for the last time on 30 September 1967.[61]

Naturally it had fallen to Landowski to persuade Charles Münch to undertake leading the new orchestra. Münch was known to harbor ill feelings about the circumstances of his dismissal in 1946. Having enlisted the "delicious and great" pianist Nicole Henriot to prepare the way, he traveled to Münch's sumptuous estate at Louvenciennes, in the Forêt de Marly near Versailles. Landowski offered the appropriate flatteries, including the observation, doubtless a fact, that Münch was the only figure in France who could accomplish the task. Münch smiled "that adorable smile" and after a long silence, "doubtless rich with malicious reflections," responded: "Let's have a little whisky." The deal was thus concluded.[62]

Münch went right to work on the new season. Among his first moves was to invite Seiji Ozawa to an engagement in March or April 1969 with his new Paris *orchestre de prestige.* Ozawa's agent declined in May, citing his 1968–69 commitments in Toronto and Japan—"his native country, where he has not been able to give much time during the past three or four years. . . . As you can imagine, Mr. Ozawa is extremely touched by the kindness of Maestro Münch, who discovered Mr. Ozawa. He would do anything in his power for Maestro Münch, but he does not want to cancel an existing contract, for he does not feel that would be the right thing to do."

"Mr. Ozawa hopes that at a later date Maestro Münch will still wish to invite him to conduct his orchestra, for nothing would give Mr. Ozawa greater pleasure."[63]

As late as the festival in Aix that summer the chatter was that the Orchestre de Paris would never see the light of day. Münch was too old, they said. He would not be able to get them to work. There was still no decent hall. Failure was not an option, however, especially since the rest of Landowski's strategy, with new orchestras in Lyon, Angers, and Nantes, and the new regional conservatories, depended on the repercussions of the first salvo. Defeat for the new orchestra would mean defeat for all the rest.

In fact the Orchestre de Paris was born more or less on schedule on 14 November 1967. The program alone said a good deal: *La Mer,* Stravinsky's *Canticum sacrum,* and the *Symphonie fantastique.* Münch's own self-doubts—that it would be too much money wasted on an old, spent conductor—were quickly overcome. Karajan was later heard to remark, *"Orchestre fabuleux."* Malraux, who never went out at night, was persuaded to attend the dress rehearsal. "You are going to be a great, prestigious orchestra," he said. "On behalf of France, I thank you." [64]

Afterword

In 1998 there were some twenty living *sociétaires*. As the dozen or so years of work on this project were coming to a close, I enjoyed several afternoons with former members of the Société des Concerts.

Lucien Thévet, first horn *solo* at the Opéra and Société des Concerts, was president of the Association Amicale d'Anciens Sociétaires; Robert Casier, first oboe *solo* at the Opéra and Société des Concerts, was its secretary. Thévet was eighty-four, and had been appointed more than sixty years before, in 1938; Casier was seventy-five. Both were fit and elegantly turned out, both with decorations in their lapels. They were talkative and factually precise about events that had taken place four and five decades before—though at one point Thévet paused for a time to search his memory, then remarked with a smile: "Well, that was a long time ago." Both were in general agreement on the points we discussed: the atmosphere of the institution during its last decades; the festivals, tours, and recordings; the orchestra's sound and general performance practice.

What was especially interesting was how they seemed to exude the same spirit the documents record, of camaraderie and the honor they felt to be a part of a historic society. They focused on their pleasure at creating concerts "of the first order," on the friendliness of the artists, the solidarity, and on the relative lack of conflict in the affairs of the institution. "We ourselves were the society; there was no boss." Neither seemed to have any doubt that the Société des Concerts of the 1950s and 1960s was without rival. Proof of that, said Casier, was that Rubinstein would always insist on engaging the Société des Concerts for his Paris concerts.

Each had his anecdotes: Casier, of being recruited in his twenties in conjunction with the second Aix-en-Provence festival, to which Lamorlette could not go, after having appeared in the first festival as a member of the Cadets du Conservatoire; Thévet of a concert at the Palais de Chaillot where a horn player, arriving late from a previous engagement, was motioned onstage by Münch during the first measures of Beethoven's Ninth, only to drop his horn as he climbed the risers. Mostly they remembered how busy they were beyond the Sunday concerts and their theater engagements, with the recordings, films, chamber groups, teaching, and the hundreds of concerts for young people in Paris and the provinces. Especially during the periods of intense recording, it was exhausting. It was not uncommon, they said, to have recording sessions in the morning, after lunch, and in the late afternoon, just finishing in time to be in the pit at the Opéra that night.

In retrospect they had a strong sense of how thoroughly the world of orchestral music changed after the war, when rapid travel by air and rail challenged and then defeated the notion of a repertoire company with its own conductor and stable of soloists. Audiences followed suit, expecting new conductors and soloists in each season. They focused for a few moments on the problems of new music: that the house was empty when they built, as they preferred to do, full concerts of new music. Instead, to meet the conditions of their modest subvention, they had to slip new works into the middle of concerts of familiar fare. Both were quite proud of their role in having created particular twentieth-century masterworks. Though they were on their best behavior, I had the impression that they considered the dissolution a natural step in the march of history. They seemed more pleased to have been a part of the society than saddened by its end.[1]

I met Fernand Lelong, tuba, and Joseph Ponticelli, violin, during a lunch break between rehearsals of the Orchestre de Paris as it prepared for a tour of Japan in November 1998. (A third *sociétaire* still with the Paris orchestra, Tassin, horn, was not going to Japan and so missed these rehearsals and our interview.) Lelong had been engaged by the Société des Concerts as *aspirant* in 1962, shortly after winning his *1er prix*, to fill the vacancy created when Jean-Baptiste Mari left to run the committee of the Concerts Lamoureux. He was twenty-two, and advanced to *titulaire* two years later. Ponticelli was a member of the last class elected as *sociétaires* on 17 March 1966; in 1998 he was one of two *chefs d'attaque* of the first violins.

Both in chronological age and in manner of expression, Lelong and Ponticelli were from a different generation than Casier and Thévet, but in many ways their recollections of the last years of the Société des Concerts were identical to those of their elder colleagues. They too recalled the particular satisfactions of a self-governing society—again I heard the formulation "We were our own boss"—and reflected with nostalgia on the loss of the "more precise, more specific" orchestral colors that resulted as Paris began to absorb, through visiting conductors and the market in recordings, the ideals of London, Berlin, Vienna, and the American ensembles. Lelong spoke as enthusiastically of Aix-en-Provence as Casier had; the combination of good weather, good music, and excited crowds was clearly unparalleled in his experience.

Lelong also recalled the charged calendars of the 1960s, from what he remembered as twenty-eight recording sessions for *Boris Godunov* with Boris Christoff and the Sofia chorus to the annual spate of end-of-season ballets. Turning to the 1964 tour of Japan, they described a twenty-odd-hour airline journey with stops in Amsterdam and Anchorage before arriving in Tokyo; then what they called an "odyssey of discovery," as night after night they encountered a culture ravenous for art music, audiences who would applaud their *Fantastique* and *Pictures at an Exhibition* with half-hour ovations in sharp contrast to the Paris response—what Bernard Gavoty described as "hands pensively folded, immobile, lost in satisfied silence." By day they would venture into the streets and a tea-house or two; in Tokyo they marveled at the queues of more than a kilometer waiting to see the Venus de Milo.

Earlier that week I had heard from a wise, elderly (and quite famous) concertgoer that "ultimately the Société des Concerts [of the 1960s] was not a very good orchestra"—the first such formulation I had encountered. Lelong and Ponticelli were quick in their response, with the now-familiar observation that there were no rivals in Paris and nothing in their own experience to compare. I asked them for a more detailed evocation of Cluytens as conductor than the documentation seemed to allow. "For me," said one, "he was like a god." His patterns were somewhat circular and now and then hard to interpret. "But when you knew what he wanted, as in Ravel, the performances seemed definitive." Of all the records they seemed proudest of, beyond the Ravel cycle, *Boris Godunov,* the Fauré Requiem, and the Roussel recordings of 1964 and 1965.

The *sociétaires* gave me programs and other souvenirs of their tenures. Lelong showed me his letter of appointment, signed by Recassens, as a treasured souvenir, and he seemed pleased when I told him that it was the 844th such letter of record.[2]

As it happened, the 1998–99 season of the Orchestre de Paris opened in the Salle Pleyel with a mostly Ravel program that ended with the wild, terrifying collapse of *La Valse*. Ravel had conducted the work here; the Société des Concerts had inaugurated this very room. It is oversized for a concert hall, and in midweek, there were some empty seats. The seats are unpleasantly cramped, less spacious than those in the tourist-class of an airplane. A woman who appeared to be in her sixties, in street clothes of modest quality, edged her way down into the better seats reserved for invited guests: board members, bankers in the sponsoring guild, representatives of the government and the ORTF, a few musicologists. It felt—authentic.

The Orchestre de Paris now looks like any other, with women musicians (including principal players), a mix of young and old, surnames from all over Europe, and a strong representation of Asian faces. Most of them would not have been able to identify the Société des Concerts, let alone remember how it sounded. Yet among the group were three former *sociétaires*—Messieurs Ponticelli, violin; Tassin, horn; Lelong, tuba—and a number of others who had once played with the parent orchestra. There was little doubt in my mind that at least some of its traditions were still alive.

The rival societies continue as well, and indeed guard the old Sunday afternoon time slot. The Orchestre Colonne offers eleven concerts on Mondays and Tuesdays at 8:30 P.M. in the Salle Pleyel, with subsidiary events on Saturday and Sunday at 10:45 A.M. The Orchestre Pasdeloup, conducted by the former *sociétaire* Jean-Pierre Wallez, plays Saturdays at 5:30, again about a dozen concerts. The Lamoureux orchestra plays Sundays at 5:45.

The Orchestre de Paris of the present is, at its best, a vibrant ensemble as comfortable in its artistic and financial situation as its predecessor ever was. It took the lead in reclaiming Berlioz as French patrimony, just as the two hundredth anniversary of his birth came into view. *La Mer* and *La Valse* are as thrilling as ever; Messiaen is better than ever. Not a few artifacts of the old society are still to be found in the administrative offices, still watched over by Guillaume's bronze bust of Beethoven.

Governments of France

FIRST EMPIRE

Napoléon I, emperor	1804–14
The Hundred Days	1815

BOURBON RESTORATION

Louis XVIII	1814–24
Charles X	1824–30

JULY MONARCHY

Louis-Philippe	1830–48

SECOND REPUBLIC

Louis-Napoléon Bonaparte	1848–52

SECOND EMPIRE

[Idem,] Napoléon III, emperor	1852–70

THIRD REPUBLIC (PRESIDENTS)

Adolphe Thiers	1871–73
Mac-Mahon	1873–79
Jules Grévy	1879–87
Sadi-Carnot	1887–94
Casimir-Perier	1894–95

Félix Faure	1895–99
Émile Loubet	1899–1906
Armand Fallières	1906–13
Raymond Poincaré	1913–20
Paul Deschanel	1920
Alexandre Millerand	1920–24
Gaston Doumergue	1924–31
Paul Doumer	1931–32
Albert Lebrun	1932–40

VICHY GOVERNMENT

| Philippe Pétain | 1940–44 |

PROVISIONAL GOVERNMENT OF THE REPUBLIC

| Charles de Gaulle | 1944–46 |
| Félix Gouin, Georges Bidault, Léon Blum | 1946–47 |

FOURTH REPUBLIC

| Vincent Auriol | 1947–54 |
| René Coty | 1954–59 |

FIFTH REPUBLIC

| Charles de Gaulle | 1959–69 |

Administration of the Société des Concerts

I^{ERS} *CHEFS D'ORCHESTRE*/VICE PRESIDENTS
OF THE SOCIÉTÉ DES CONCERTS

François-Antoine Habeneck	1828–48
Narcisse Girard	1849–60
Théophile Tilmant, *aîné*	1860–63
François George-Hainl	1864–72
E.-M.-E. Deldevez	1872–85
Jules Garcin	1885–92
Paul Taffanel	1893–1901
Georges Marty	1901–08
André Messager	1908–19
Philippe Gaubert	1919–38
Charles Münch	1938–46
André Cluytens	1946–60

PRESIDENTS OF THE SOCIÉTÉ DES CONCERTS/
DIRECTORS OF THE CONSERVATOIRE

Luigi Cherubini	[1828]–42
Daniel F.-E. Auber	1842–71
Ambroise Thomas	1871–96
Théodore Dubois	1896–1905
Gabriel Fauré	1905–20
Henri Rabaud	1920–41
Charles Münch, *president;* Claude Delvincourt, *honorary president*	1941–46
Claude Delvincourt	1946–54
Marcel Dupré	1954–56
Raymond Loucheur	1956–62
Raymond Gallois-Montbrun	1962–67

Seasons and Conductors, 1828–1967

FRANÇOIS-ANTOINE HABENECK

1ᵉ année: 1828	12ᵉ année: 1839
2ᵉ année: 1829	13ᵉ année: 1840
3ᵉ année: 1830	14ᵉ année: 1841
4ᵉ année: 1831	15ᵉ année: 1842
5ᵉ année: 1832	16ᵉ année: 1843
6ᵉ année: 1833	17ᵉ année: 1844
7ᵉ année: 1834	18ᵉ année: 1845
8ᵉ année: 1835	19ᵉ année: 1846
9ᵉ année: 1836	20ᵉ année: 1847
10ᵉ année: 1837	21ᵉ année: 1848
11ᵉ année: 1838	

NARCISSE GIRARD

22ᵉ année: 1849	28ᵉ année: 1855
23ᵉ année: 1850	29ᵉ année: 1856
24ᵉ année: 1851	30ᵉ année: 1857
25ᵉ année: 1852	31ᵉ année: 1858
26ᵉ année: 1853	32ᵉ année: 1859
27ᵉ année: 1854	

THÉOPHILE TILMANT, *AÎNÉ*

33ᵉ année: 1860	35ᵉ année: 1862
34ᵉ année: 1861	36ᵉ année: 1863

FRANÇOIS GEORGE-HAINL

37e année: 1863–64	42e année: 1868–69
38e année: 1864–65	43e année: 1869–70
39e année: 1865–66	44e année: 1871
40e année: 1866–67	45e année: 1872
41e année: 1867–68	

E.-M.-E. DELDEVEZ

46e année: 1872–73	53e année: 1879–80
47e année: 1873–74	54e année: 1880–81
48e année: 1874–75	55e année: 1881–82
49e année: 1875–76	56e année: 1882–83
50e année: 1876–77	57e année: 1883–84
51e année: 1877–78	58e année: 1884–85
52e année: 1878–79	

JULES GARCIN

59e année: 1885–86	63e année: 1889–90
60e année: 1886–87	64e année: 1890–91
61e année: 1887–88	65e année: 1891–92
62e année: 1888–89	

PAUL TAFFANEL

66e année: 1892–93	71e année: 1897–98
67e année: 1893–94	72e année: 1898–99
68e année: 1894–95	73e année: 1899–1900
69e année: 1895–96	74e année: 1900–01
70e année: 1896–97	

GEORGES MARTY

75e année: 1901–02	79e année: 1905–06
76e année: 1902–03	80e année: 1906–07
77e année: 1903–04	81e année: 1907–08
78e année: 1904–05	

ANDRÉ MESSAGER

82e année: 1908–09	85e année: 1911–12
83e année: 1909–10	86e année: 1912–13
84e année: 1910–11	87e année: 1913–14

88e année: 1914–15   91e année: 1917–18
89e année: 1915–16   92e année: 1918–19
90e année: 1916–17

PHILIPPE GAUBERT

93e année: 1919–20   103e année: 1929–30
94e année: 1920–21   104e année: 1930–31
95e année: 1921–22   105e année: 1931–32
96e année: 1922–23   106e année: 1932–33
97e année: 1923–24   107e année: 1933–34
98e année: 1924–25   108e année: 1934–35
99e année: 1925–26   109e année: 1935–36
100e année: 1926–27   110e année: 1936–37
101e année: 1927–28   111e année: 1937–38
102e année: 1928–29

CHARLES MÜNCH

112e année: 1938–39   116e année: 1942–43
113e année: 1939–40   117e année: 1943–44
114e année: 1940–41   118e année: 1944–45
115e année: 1941–42   119e année: 1945–46

ANDRÉ CLUYTENS

120e année: 1946–47   127e année: 1953–54
121e année: 1947–48   128e année: 1954–55
122e année: 1948–49   129e année: 1955–56
123e année: 1949–50   130e année: 1956–57
124e année: 1950–51   131e année: 1957–58
125e année: 1951–52   132e année: 1958–59
126e année: 1952–53   133e année: 1959–60

NO PRINCIPAL CONDUCTOR

134e année: 1960–61   138e année: 1964–65
135e année: 1961–62   139e année: 1965–66
136e année: 1962–63   140e année: 1966–67
137e année: 1963–64

Notes

ABBREVIATIONS

AG	Assemblée Générale (minutes)
Arch. nat.	Archives Nationales de France
Bnf	Bibliothèque Nationale de France
Com.	Comité d'Administration (minutes)

The Bibliography of Works Cited and Consulted, on the website
(www.ucpress.edu/holoman), includes publishers' names.

PART ONE

Chapter 1

1. François-Joseph Fétis, in *Revue musicale* 3 (1828): 145–53, the lead article of no. 13. For French text, see the website.

2. Joseph d'Ortigue, "Société des Concerts," in *Le Balcon de l'Opéra* (Paris, 1833), p. 333. D'Ortigue's chapter consists largely of his reviews of the concerts of 1833.

3. Antoine Elwart, *Histoire de la Société des Concerts du Conservatoire Impérial de Musique* (Paris, 1860; 2d edn., 1864), p. 3 (hereafter cited as Elwart).

4. I am grateful to Michael H. Gray for alerting me to the existence of the 1964 film clip, included in a six-hour documentary of celebrated companies and virtuosi on tour in Japan, broadcast on NHK Educational Television 9, 17, and 24 January 1999; and to Jean-Michel Molkhou for notice of the EMI release: *Henryk Szeryng,* Classic Archive DVD, EMI DVD 490 4399 (2003). In my interview with them in Paris on 21 October 1998, Lucien Thévet and Robert Casier recalled cameras being present at Versailles, with a child conductor. This was

the young Roberto Benzi, a protégé of Cluytens, in 1949 or 1950, when Benzi would have been about twelve years old. Possibly they were remembering a shoot for the first of two films of Georges Lacombe featuring Benzi: *Prélude à la gloire* (1950; not to be confused with the nearly identical British film of the same year, *Prelude to Fame,* directed by Fergus McDonell) and *L'Appel du destin* (1952, with Jean Marais). It appears from still photographs that the Société des Concerts was used in scenes in the first and possibly also the second film. See Bernard Gavoty, *Roberto Benzi* (Geneva, 1955; photographs by Roger Hauert).

5. D'Ortigue, "Société des Concerts," p. 345.

6. Dominique Sordet, *Douze Chefs d'orchestre* (Paris, 1924), p. 26.

7. Cited in a published booklet of press clippings from the 1917 "Tournée de Suisse," p. 14. Bnf Musique (hereafter cited as Bnf Mus.), Programmes Société des Concerts (hereafter cited as "boxed programs").

8. Rapport moral 13 May 1866, 12 May 1867 (Gautier): D 17341.

9. Théodore Heymann, "Note sur les origines de la Société des Concerts," address delivered 26 May 1909: D 17264 (18), pièce 1; see also AG 26 May 1909: D 17432 (1).

10. Jean Mongrédien, "Les Premiers Exercices publics d'élèves (1800–15) d'après la presse contemporaine," in *Le Conservatoire de Paris: des Menus-Plaisirs à la Cité de la Musique, 1795–1995,* ed. Anne Bongrain et al. (Paris, 1996), pp. 15–37; see p. 16. The programs are given in Constant Pierre, *Le Conservatoire National de Musique et de Déclamation: Documents historiques et administratifs* (Paris, 1900), pp. 476–97.

11. Mongrédien, "Exercices," p. 23, after a document citing the orchestra's makeup in 1813–14, Arch. nat. AJ^{37} 87.

12. Ibid., pp. 35, 34, and 31–32, citing respectively *Journal de Paris,* 28 May 1807; *Allgemeine musikalische Zeitung,* 30 October 1811; ibid., 21 June 1809.

13. Cherubini, ca. 1824 (veterans of the Conservatoire): Arch. nat. O^3 1809; Cherubini to La Rochefoucauld, 7 March 1827 (a lot of trouble): Arch. nat. O^3 1811; La Rochefoucauld to the minister, 29 December 1827 (I have thought it necessary). All cited in Anik Devriès-Lesure, "Cherubini directeur du Conservatoire de Musique et de Déclamation," in *Le Conservatoire . . . des Menus-Plaisirs,* pp. 39–96; see pp. 91–92. Article 1 of the *règlement* of 5 June 1822 (to populate the ranks), given in Pierre, *Conservatoire,* p. 245; cited by Devriès-Lesure, p. 44. Decree of 15 February 1828: D 17338 et al., given in full on the website.

14. Elwart gives names of some of the guests, p. 61; "in the name of a grateful Beethoven," p. 62. The "*à table*" anecdote is told in most accounts of the foundation.

15. A Select Bibliography of central resources for the study of the Société des Concerts can be found at the end of the book. The complete Bibliography of Works Cited and Consulted is given on the website.

16. Maurice Cristal, "Les Concerts du Conservatoire," *Le Ménestrel* 37/14 (6 March 1870): 107–09; 15 (13 March 1870): 117–18; 16 (20 March 1870): 124–25.

17. Typescript of Cordey's address: D 17264 (18), pièce 2; the pamphlet appeared as *La Société des Concerts du Conservatoire: Notice historique par Jean Cordey, conservateur de la Bibliothèque et du Musée de l'Opéra* (Paris, July 1941).

18. Jean-Michel Nectoux, *Association pour le 150ᵉ Anniversaire de la Société des Concerts du Conservatoire* (Paris, 1978), catalogue in the form of a brochure accompanying the exposition. See also the souvenir program for the anniversary concert, Orchestre de Paris, 14 January 1979.

19. Heymann: D 17264 (18), pièce 1.

20. Com. 30 May 1911: D 17345 (18).

21. [Sauzay], "La Vie musicale à Paris à travers les mémoires d'Eugène Sauzay (1809–1901)," ed. Brigitte François-Sappey, *Revue de musicologie* 60 (1974): 159–210. A list of books by *sociétaires* is given on the website.

22. Corresp. Berlioz to the Société des Concerts, 25 March 1853: Berlioz, *Correspondance générale* 6, ed. Hugh Macdonald and François Lesure (Paris, 1995), no. 2702. This paragraph is drawn from my study "Orchestral Material from the Library of the Société des Concerts," *19th-Century Music* 7 (1983): 106–18.

23. See series D, vol. 8 of *The Symphony, 1720–1840*, ed. David Charlton (New York, 1982). The recording by the Orchestra of the Gulbenkian Foundation, Michel Swierczewski conducting, of *The Complete Symphonies* is Nimbus 5184–85 (1989), with notes by Charlton; it was recorded 19–23 December 1988 in Lisbon.

24. Deposition copy: Bnf Mus.

25. The bulk of the archive at Bnf Mus. is found with the series of shelfmarks D 17257–67 and 17329–53. A summary description appears in the Select Bibliography at the end of the book, with more details on the website.

26. Meifred's register: D 17344.

27. Dossier "Carrière chefs d'orchestre / Élection de Hainl (1863) / Succession de Tilmant": D 17330.

28. AG 3 June 1902: D 17345 (15).

29. Bnf Mus. ms. 17668 (hereafter cited as ms. 17668, *livre d'or*).

30. Pictured in *Guide du Musée de la Musique* (Paris, 1997), pp. 150 (Romagnesi) and 155 (Dantan). The more extensive collection of Dantan *jeune*'s work at the Musée Carnavalet is treated and pictured in H. Robert Cohen, "The Musical World of Dantan *jeune*: Subtle Distortions and Giants Reduced," in *Music in Paris in the Eighteen-Thirties / La Musique à Paris dans les années mil huit cent trente*, ed. Peter Bloom (Stuyvesant, N.Y., 1987), pp. 135–208.

31. Elisabeth Dunan, *Inventaire de la série AJ³⁷*, etc. (Paris, 1971). Access to the other catalogues, mostly typescripts often by Brigitte Labat-Poussin, is most efficient by Internet: <www.archivesnationales.culture.gouv.fr/> (*link* Centre Historique des Archives Nationales).

32. *La Vie musicale sous Vichy*, ed. Myriam Chimènes (Paris, 2001); *Les Affaires Culturelles au temps d'André Malraux, 1959–1969*, ed. Augustin Girard and Geneviève Gentil (Paris, 1996); *Le Conservatoire de Musique de Paris: Regards sur une institution et son histoire*, ed. Emmanuel Hondré (Paris, 1995); *Le Conservatoire. . . des Menus-Plaisirs; Le Conservatoire de Paris: Deux Cents Ans de pédagogie, 1795–1995*, ed. Anne Bongrain and Alain Poirier (Paris, 1999). See also Laetitia Chassain-Dolliou, *Le Conservatoire de Paris, ou les voies de la création* (Paris, 1995).

33. See Jeffrey Cooper, *The Rise of Instrumental Music and Concert Series in*

Paris, 1828–1871 (Ann Arbor, 1983; from Ph.D. diss., Cornell, 1981); Katharine El-lis, *Music Criticism in Nineteenth-Century France:* La Revue et gazette musicale de Paris, *1834–80* (Cambridge, 1995); Jane F. Fulcher, *French Cultural Politics and Music: From the Dreyfus Affair to the First World War* (Oxford, 1999); Jann Pasler, *Useful Music, or Why Music Mattered in Third Republic France* (Berke-ley, forthcoming); William Weber, *Music and the Middle Class: The Social Struc-ture of Concert Life in London, Paris, and Vienna* (London, 1975; 2nd edn. Aldershot, 2003).

34. Here I follow, and acknowledge with special thanks, the unsigned report on my manuscript to the Editorial Committee of the University of California Press, December 2001.

35. Projet de modification aux statuts, 18 May 1890, article 15 (length of con-ductor's tenure): D 17340.

Chapter 2

1. Com. 1 February 1848 (Lecointe): D 17345 (4). Com. 4 November 1884 (Jacquin and insurance company); see also 6 October 1885 (discussing his leave of absence), 19 October 1886 (his resignation accepted), 4 June 1889 (fire insur-ance): D 17345 (11).

2. Hector Berlioz, "Concert de Mlle Mazel à l'Hôtel de Ville," *Revue et ga-zette musicale,* 10 July 1836; in *Hector Berlioz: Critique musicale II, 1835–1836,* ed. Yves Gérard et al. (Paris 1998; hereafter cited as Berlioz, *Critique musicale* 2), pp. 491–95; see p. 495.

3. Com. 14 October, 27 November, 11 and 18 December 1839; 20 January, 23 and 30 November 1840 (Masset's change of profession and resulting problems): D 17345 (2).

4. In 1929, for instance, Saraillé made 3,226 francs out of a maximum pos-sible 3,770: D 17329 (2).

5. Rapport moral 29 May 1908 (Heymann): D 17341.

6. Com. 23 December 1844: D 17345 (3).

7. Corresp. A. Rignault to committee, n.d. ca. 20 October 1868: D 17330. A year later, Rignault expresses gratitude in similarly gracious terms for being named *membre honoraire:* D 17330.

8. Corresp. Juette to committee, 23 May 1885: D 17330.

9. Com. 18 June 1929: D 17345 (20).

10. Com. 30 March 1886: D 17345 (11).

11. Corresp. Garcin to committee, n.d. ca. 1856: ms. 17668, *livre d'or,* no. 5b. Corresp. Lamoureux to committee, 14 November 1859: ms. 17668, *livre d'or,* no. 5a.

12. Corresp. Conte to committee, 3 December 1871: D 17330.

13. AG 13 May 1838: D 17345 (2).

14. Com. 11, 20 November 1845: D 17345 (4).

15. A list of solo and honorary *sociétaires* is given on the website.

16. Com. 30 March 1835 *(sociétaire solo),* 6 April (Baillot's visit), 18 May (the medal): D 17345 (2).

17. Com. 25 January 1841 (Viardot going to London); see also 6 December 1842 (Viardot reserves her calendar for 1843): D 17345 (3).

18. Com. 8 March 1841 (Dérivis): D 17345 (3). Com. 4 February 1851 (Lefebvre): D 17345 (5).

19. Com. 9 June 1944 (Lautemann): D 17345 (21).

20. Attendance and payment records: D 17329 (2). Charles Münch, *Je suis chef d'orchestre* (Paris, 1954), ed. (with treatises of Berlioz, Wagner, et al.) Georges Liébert (Paris, 1988); pp. 689–90; Engl. transl. as *I Am a Conductor*, transl. Leonard Burkat (New York, 1955), p. 80. AG 8 June 1947 (Huot): D 17342 (3).

21. Rapport moral 24 May 1907 (Seitz, thanking Couppas): D 17341.

22. E.-M.-E. Deldevez, *Mes Mémoires* (Le Puy, 1890; hereafter cited as Deldevez, *Mémoires*), p. 201.

23. Projet de modification aux statuts, art. 15, 18 May 1890 (an exemplary case): D 17340. Election of 21 December 1863 (humiliating): D 17330, dossier "Carrière chefs d'orchestre / Élection de Hainl (1863) / Succession de Tilmant," outlining the committee's reasons for opposing the measure.

24. Salaries 1938*ff.*: D 17329 (2).

25. Some of these "secretarial analyses" are in D 17337 (1), a miscellany that appears to consist, in part, of documents deemed precedent setting by the secretaries. Others are folded into the annual secretarial report (rapport moral): D 17341.

26. D 17337 (1). The archive of annotated programs mentioned here does not appear to be preserved.

27. E.-M.-E. Deldevez, *La Société des Concerts, 1860–1885* (Paris, 1887; hereafter cited as Deldevez, *Société des Concerts*), p. 263; modern edn. ed. and annotated Gérard Streletski (Heilbronn, 1998).

28. AG 30 May 1965: D 17342 (6).

29. Com. 6 September, 11 October 1839: D 17345 (2).

30. Com. 13 March 1837: D 17345 (2).

31. Rapport moral 12 May 1844 (Meifred): D 17341.

32. AG 18 May 1845: D 17345 (3).

33. AG 28 May 1902: D 17345 (15).

34. Com. 4 June 1872: D 17345 (8).

35. Com. [entry just before] 20 April 1841: D 17345 (3).

36. Com. 20 and 27 November 1928: D 17345 (20).

37. Com. 16 January 1844: D 17345 (3).

38. Com. 13 April 1886: D 17345 (11).

39. Corresp. sec. to Andrade, Sauzay, Cuvillon, 16 February 1833: D 17344 (nos. 46–48 for 1833).

40. Com. 13 January 1845 (Mlle Dellanoy): D 17345 (3). Com. 14 January 1873 (Garry stunned), 26 March (fired): D 17345 (8). Com. 14 March 1843 (another *aspirant* dismissed); 13 January 1845 (three sopranos): D 17345 (3).

41. Com. 8 May 1844 (Triébert, Chevillard); 1 and 8 March 1841 (Franchomme chastised, apologizes): D 17345 (3).

42. Com. 16 January 1835: D 17345 (2).

43. Com. 5 February 1846: D 17345 (4).

44. Com. 17 November, 15, 23, and 27 December 1844: D 17345 (3).

45. Com. 17 November 1844: D 17345 (3).

46. Corresp. sec. to Servais (the famous cellist), 5 February 1834: D 17344 (no. 151 for 1834).

47. Corresp. sec. to Legros, 14 February 1833 (the necessity of replacing you): D 17344 (no. 45 for 1833); ibid., Goblin, 18 February 1833 (know of my regret): D 17344 (no. 49 for 1833).

48. Corresp. sec. to Devise and Bénard (two letters), 7 January 1835: D 17344 (unnumbered).

49. Corresp. sec. to Francilla Pixis, 1 November 1834: D 17344 (unnumbered).

50. Com. 27 May 1951: D 17345 (22).

51. On Gand and one violin used at the Société des Concerts, see Charles Dancla, *Notes et souvenirs* (Paris, 1893), pp. 27–28; Eng. transl. as *Notes and Souvenirs,* transl. Samuel Wolf (Linthicum Heights, Md., 1981), pp. 18–19. A facsimile of Gand's bill to Berlioz on the occasion of the first performance of the *Symphonie fantastique* in 1830 appears in Thomas Kelly, *First Nights: Five Musical Premieres* (New Haven, 2000), p. 219.

52. Com. 18 March, 14 October 1873: D 17345 (8).

53. Hauert's candid photographs appear in over two dozen celebrity biographies, notably those of the series Les Grands Interprètes published in Geneva by Éditions René Kister in the mid-1950s and largely written by Bernard Gavoty (*Ataulfo Argenta, Alfred Cortot, Carl Schuricht,* etc.), including *André Cluytens* (1955).

54. Janine Weill, *Marguerite Long: Une Vie fascinante* (Paris, 1969), pp. 214–15.

55. Com. 31 December 1872 (first warning), 21 January (second warning), 28 January (doctor invoked), 4 February 1873 (doctor's report): D 17345 (8).

56. Com. 19 November 1912: D 17345 (18).

57. Rapport moral 10 May 1868 (Lebouc): D 17341.

58. AG 8 January 1961: D 17343 (6).

59. Rapport moral 12 May 1844 (Meifred; on guard against indifference): D 17341. AG 8 May 1836 (on Meifred's remarks: redouble our zeal): D 17345 (2). Rapport moral 18 May 1862 (Gautier: no victory without struggle): D 17341.

60. AG 11 May 1851 (Dancla): D 17345 (5). AG 20 May 1841 (Tulou): D 17345 (3).

61. Remarks by sec. (Lebouc) at AG 21 December 1863: D 17330, dossier "Carrière chefs d'orchestre / Élection de Hainl (1863) / Succession de Tilmant," on a loose leaf.

62. AG 4 March 1828: D 17338 (3). Elwart, p. 68, gives a date of 24 March 1828, almost certainly in error; and he also changes "en 50 articles" of the source to "en 52 articles." This latter figure represents the number of articles in the best source of the original statutes: D 17338 (5). See the website.

63. Elwart, p. 82.

64. Com. 27 February 1872: D 17345 (8).

65. Habeneck's *livret:* Bnf Mus. lettres aut. Habeneck.

66. Com. 20 January 1845: D 17345 (3).

67. Elwart, p. 101 (flower of his youth). Com. 20 November (Javault's illness acknowledged; *congé*), 27 November 1845 (*secours* 300 francs), 20 October 1846 (almost no hope; retired): D 17345 (4).

68. Rapport moral 29 May 1908 (Heymann): D 17341.

69. Com. 27 March 1928: D 17345 (20).

70. Com. 7 April 1874: D 17345 (9).

71. Com. 6 December 1835: D 17345 (2)

72. Com. 10 February 1874, 20 October 1874, 30 March 1875 (leaves of absence for J. White), 19 October 1875 (leave prolonged until 30 January 1876, with ultimatum to return), 14 March 1876 (leave extended until 15 October 1876): D 17345 (9). Rapport moral 15 May 1877 (Taffanel: noting regret): D 17341.

73. Com. 26 November 1838 (Seligmann applies), 27 January 1840 (asks for solo), 23 December 1840 (named *sociétaire*, but decision withheld from him until his intentions were clearer): D 17345 (2). Com. 14 February, 1, 8, 15 November 1842; 27 April, 27 November 1843 (subsequent developments): D 17345 (3).

74. The lineages are traced in a website by José Sánchez-Penzo, "The Way Famous String Instruments Went," with documentation: <www.jose-sanchez-penzo.net>. The "Messiah" instrument is so called after Alard's remark to its boasting but secretive owner to the effect that, like the Messiah, you were always hearing about it but never seeing it. In his early years Charles Dancla preferred his Gand violin to a Stradivari instrument: see *Notes et souvenirs*, p. 28 and note.

75. *L'Express* of Lyon, 16 December 1908; quoted in pressbook published after Lyon concert of 15 December 1908: boxed programs.

76. F.-J. Fétis, "Tulou," in *Biographie universelle des musiciens*, etc. (Brussels, 1835–44, and subsequent edns.), vol. 8, p. 267.

77. Münch, *I Am a Conductor*, p. 86.

78. Rapport moral 26 May 1905 (Seitz: obituary remarks): D 17341.

79. Berlioz, "Sixième concert du Conservatoire," *Journal des Débats*, 18 April 1835; in Berlioz, *Critique musicale* 2, pp. 124–25. The sixteen horns were used, for instance, in the concert of 18 April 1847: see website (programs).

80. Com. 10 January 1832: D 17345 (1).

81. Rapport moral 29 May 1891 (Taffanel: fearless trumpet): D 17341. Rapport moral 30 May 1896 (Chavy: the trumpet's renown): D 17341.

82. Deldevez, *Société des Concerts*, p. 255.

83. Rapport moral 18 May 1862 (Gautier): D 17341.

84. See Christian Gendron, *Auguste Tolbecque: Luthier et musicien* (Niort, 1997), a lavishly illustrated and copiously documented catalogue / source book published in conjunction with a major exhibition at the Musée Municipal Bernard d'Agesci, Niort.

85. Rapport moral 24 May 1907 (Seitz): D 17341.

86. Com. 4 March 1873: D 17345 (8).

87. Com. 16 December 1871 (notice of Vogt's gift), 21 May 1872 (thanks to his family): D 17345 (8).

88. Rapport moral 12 May 1844 (Meifred: Demouy): D 17341. Com. 29 April

1893 (Wacquez): D 17345 (12). Rapport moral 10 May 1868 (Lebouc: Triébert and Barthélemy): D 17341.

89. Com. 5 October 1936 (Michaux): D 17345 (21); reported by Savoye in corresp. with Seitz, 13 February 1937: D 17263 (10). The firing of Boudard was at issue as late as AG 28 March 1946: D 17342 (3).

90. Com. 6 January 1874 (Cras): D 17345 (8). Com. 31 March and 7 April 1874 (Lejeune and Jolivet): D 17345 (9).

91. Com. 20, 27 February, 20 March 1838: D 17345 (2).

92. Fétis, "Verroust," in *Biographie universelle,* vol. 8, p. 331 (invincible passion for wine). The *affaire Verroust* is at issue through much of 1853, notably 12, 15, and 19 January 1853: D 17345 (5).

93. Fétis, ibid.

94. Com. 16 January 1844 (*huissier*'s visit): D 17345 (3). Com. 4 May 1847 (recurrence, com. discusses dismissal), 2 November 1847 (statement): D 17345 (4).

95. Com. 28 January 1873, 4 and 11 February (Vicini's checkered career): D 17345 (8). Com. 7, 28 July 1874 (his arrest): D 17345 (9).

96. Note on nomination of aspiring singers, ca. 1865: D 17337 (1).

97. Münch, *I Am a Conductor,* p. 84.

Chapter 3

1. Henri de Curzon, *L'Histoire et la gloire de l'ancienne salle du Conservatoire de Paris (1811–1911)* (Paris, 1917); Eng. transl. as "History and Glory of the Concert-Hall of the Paris Conservatory," *Musical Quarterly* 3 (1917), 304–18; see p. 309. Curzon cites *Le Moniteur universel* of 9 July 1811. See also "Plan de la grande salle et de l'orchestre du Conservatoire Impérial de Musique," Elwart, pp. 108–19, with two plates (including the audience seating plan, which follows p. 378 above); and J.-G. Prod'homme and E. de Crauzat, *Les Menus Plaisirs du Roi: L'École Royale et le Conservatoire de Musique* (Paris, 1929), with its site plans (one of which also follows p. 378 above).

2. Precise measurements (in French feet = 12.8 inches) for the components of the structure are given by Alexis Donnet (see n. 3, below), cited by Prod'homme and Crauzat, *Menus Plaisirs,* pp. 119–24. Dimensions of the existing room are given in *Lieux de spectacle à Paris: Abris et édifices,* ed. Michel Seban, the catalogue of an exhibition at the Pavillon de l'Arsenal, June–September 1998 (Paris, 1998), p. 39.

3. A 1:50 scale model of the original ivory-and-green Salle des Concerts, built by Patrick Guillou in 1995, is on display at the Musée de la Musique, Cité de la Musique, Paris. It follows the accounts by Alexis Donnet, "Théâtre du Conservatoire," *Architectonographie des théâtres de Paris,* etc. (Paris, 1821), pp. 247–52 and pl. XVII; and [François-Jacques Delannoy], *Souvenirs de la vie et des ouvrages de Delannoy* (Paris, 1839).

4. Elwart, p. 113.

5. Rapport moral 28 May 1890 (Taffanel): D 17341.

6. Elwart, pp. 114–15.

7. Ibid., p. 113.

8. Com. 13, 22 February 1883: D 17345 (10).

9. Curzon, "History and Glory," p. 310, citing *Le Courrier de l'Europe* and *Les Tablettes de Polymnie.*

10. The paintings now hang in the Musée de la Musique, Cité de la Musique (i.e., the present Conservatoire), Paris. They were moved from the old Conservatoire to the rehearsal hall of the new Conservatoire in the rue de Madrid ca. 1911. [Gioacchin] Giuseppe Serangeli (1768–1852) was a student of Jacques-Louis David.

11. See, for instance, com. 30 April 1921: D 17345 (19).

12. Com. 21 January 1851: D 17345 (5).

13. Com. 2 and 23 December 1851 and 1 December 1853: D 17345 (5).

14. Com. 3 November 1874 (king of Hanover): D 17345 (9). Com. 12 December 1871 (emperor of Brazil): D 17345 (8).

15. These were listed in the register as *Artiste, Charivari, Constitutionnel, Corsaire, Courrier français, Entr'acte, Figaro, Gazette de France, Indépendante, Journal du commerce, Journal des Débats, Journal de Paris, Monde dramatique, Moniteur, National, Quotidienne, Revue de Paris, Temps.* Corresp. com. to editors, 1833–35: 9 February 1833 (nos. 24–39), 7 and 20 January 1834 (nos. 108–19 and 123–33), 1 January 1835 (to fifteen papers, unnumbered): D 17344.

16. Corresp. com. to the editor of *Le Charivari,* 19 February 1833; idem, to *Gazette musicale,* 20 February 1834 (no. 161); idem., to Galignani, 16 March 1834 (no. 164): D 17344.

17. For instance, an 1837 request from the *Revue des théâtres,* com. 9 January 1837: D 17345 (2).

18. Com. 27 January 1845: D 17345 (3).

19. Com. 24 December 1872: D 17345 (8).

20. Com. 7 August 1844 (waiting list), 11 November 1844 (*parterre* privileges withdrawn): D 17345 (3).

21. Corresp. Institution des Jeunes Aveugles to com., 27 January, 13 February 1830, 18 January 1832 (annotated "accordé pour cette année et les années suivantes"), 8 April 1833: D 17337 (1). Berlioz, "Premier concert du Conservatoire," *Revue et gazette musicale,* 31 January 1836; in *Critique musicale* 2: 391–95; see p. 395 and note. Com. 9 November 1920 (blind patron and his guide): D 17245 (19).

22. Com. 16 January 1837: D 13745 (2).

23. The definitive study of the site and its history is Prod'homme and Crauzat, *Menus Plaisirs.*

24. Curzon, "History and Glory," p. 308, citing an official decree.

25. Curzon, "History and Glory," p. 310, citing *Le Courrier de l'Europe* and *Les Tablettes de Polymnie.*

26. Corresp. Cherubini to Montalivet, 25 November 1833 (inquiring when construction will begin): D 17344 (no. 94 for 1833). Com. 18 March 1835 (construction in the courtyard), 21 December 1836 (upholstery): D 17345 (2). Com. 30 October 1845 (plan for converting *parterre*): D 17345 (4).

27. Com. 18 May 1876 (widow Habeneck approaches Deldevez), 3 October

1876 (proposal submitted), 10 October 1876 (widow thanks); 5 February 1878 (no forward motion): D 17345 (9). Com. 28 January 1879 (letter to prefect of Seine), 11 March 1879 (his response): D 17345 (10).

28. Com. 7 May 1865: D 17345 (6).

29. Com. 10 December 1872 (Cavaillé-Coll), 17 December (Franck): D 17345 (8).

30. Com. 13 May 1873: D 17345 (8).

31. Com. 1 November 1881 (new organ *buffet*), 13, 20 February 1883 (hemicycle): D 17345 (10).

32. Project de loi 14 November 1881, in Pierre, *Conservatoire,* pp. 326–27; citing *Journal officiel,* 14 November 1881, p. 1719. The quotation abstracts longer remarks; full French text is at website.

33. Ibid.

34. Com. 18 December 1877 (architects consulted): D 17345 (9). Com. 1 November 1881 (increased seating), 25 April, 6 June, 4 July, 3 October 1882 (fire issues, increased ticket prices): D 17345 (10).

35. Com. 12 February 1884 (electrification proposed): D 17345 (10). Com. 24 February 1885 (*sonnette* installed; delayed use), 21 October 1885 (used for fall concerts), 7 May 1889 (repair): D 17345 (11).

36. Rapport moral 14 May 1907 (Seitz): D 17341.

37. Deldevez, *Société des Concerts,* p. 62.

38. Curzon, "History and Glory," p. 305, evokes this frequently heard construction.

39. Elwart, pp. 115–16 (1828), 114 (1860). Rapport moral 30 May 1899 (Vernaelde, for 1897 and 1899): D 17341. Com. 6 Nov. 1928: D 17345 (20).

40. *Lieux de spectacle à Paris,* pp. 38–39.

41. Berlioz, *Symphonie fantastique,* Orchestre Révolutionnaire et Romantique, John Eliot Gardiner conducting, Philips video 440 070 254–1 (laser disc), . . . 254–3 (VHS cassette), 1991; recorded September 1991.

42. Many of the letters requesting authorization to use the hall are found in D 17337 (1).

43. See table "Governmental Oversight of Hall and Orchestra" on the website. See also Mathilde Catz, "Instances de décisions à travers la législation organique du Conservatoire," in *Le Conservatoire . . . Regards sur une institution,* pp. 255–70 and charts pp. 271–75.

44. Hector Berlioz, *Mémoires de Hector Berlioz, comprenant ses voyages en Italie, en Allemagne, en Russie et en Angleterre, 1803–1865* (Paris, 1870, and many later edns. and translations), ch. 18 (. . . "Mon premier concert—Opposition comique de Cherubini").

45. Rapport moral 19 May 1833 (Plantade), 4 May 1834 (Plantade): D 17341. Com. 20 October 1837 (Cherubini's plan for exclusive use of hall discussed): D 17345 (2).

46. Decree of Conseil d'État, 25 April 1850, conceding the Salle des Concerts and its dependencies to the Conservatoire: transcribed in Pierre, *Conservatoire,* p. 325.

47. Rapport moral 19 May 1833 (Plantade, enumerating D 17341 (1833). The apparent *liste d'entrées* figures in Société des Concerts / Liste du Personnel / 1864–1865 (Commisre. de Personnel / G. Baneux): D 17331 (1). Corresp. com. to Rossini, 7 March 1833; to Sarrette and Auber, 14 January 1834; sec. (Gautier) to Rossini, n.d. ca. December 1861: D 17344 (nos. 65, 138, 139, unnumbered).

48. Corresp. Delavigne to Cherubini, 11 January 1837: ms. 17668, *livre d'or*, no. 2.

49. Com. 4 November 1851: D 17345 (5).

50. Com. 31 October 1871 (Boussagol): D 17345 (8). Com. 30 January 1837 (Aulagnier): D 18345 (2). Com. 31 December 1872 (Wilder): D 17345 (8).

51. Com. 6 November 1928: D 17345 (20).

52. Astruc's interactions with the committee form an ongoing thread in the minutes for 1911–12 and 1912–13: D 17345 (18). See also Gabriel Astruc, *Le Pavillon des fantômes* (Paris, 1929; modern edn. Paris, 1987).

53. Com. 15, 22, 26 June 1920 (Duncan), 28 November 1922 through February 1923 (Thursday afternoon concerts): D 17345 (19).

Chapter 4

1. Karl Baedeker, *Paris and Environs* (Leipzig, [etc.], 1910), p. 44.

2. *Musical World*, 28 February 1852. I am grateful to David Cairns for drawing this article to my attention.

3. Ibid., 31 January 1852.

4. Jean Cocteau, *Portraits-Souvenir: 1900–1914,* illus. by the author (Paris, 1935), pp. 23–24.

5. See, for instance, a printed announcement of the 1886–87 season, inviting subscribers to claim their places at the box office from 12 to 14 November 1886: boxed programs.

6. Elwart, p. 114.

7. Com. 12 November 1872 (Schoelcher), 26 November 1872 (Brandus and Heugel): D 17345 (8). Corresp. Cherubini's son to com., 4 September 1856; Gounod to com., n.d.: Ms. 17668, *livre d'or*, nos. 41, 9b.

8. Com. 30 October 1845 (piracy): D 17345 (4). Com. 14 January 1839 (strangers smuggled onstage), 20 January 1840 (extra child): D 17345 (2). Com. 21 December 1869 (woman enters box office): D 17345 (7).

9. Com. 12 March 1844 (employees charged with preventing invasion): D 17345 (3). Corresp. com. to Lambert, 2 April 1833 (the woman Fallague): D 17344 (no. 80 for 1833). Corresp. Lambert to com., 9 April 1833 (his response): D 17337 (1). Com. 16 February 1835 (Mmes Fallague and Grosset), 4 April 1836 *(une personne étrangère):* D 17345 (2).

10. Com. 20 May 1873 (Mme Labadens): D 17345 (8). Com. 17, 31 October 1882 (Mme Habeneck's will): D 17345 (10). Com. 28 October 1884, 13 January 1885 (id.): D 17345 (11). Com. 1 July 1873 (Vogt's daughter), 24 October 1871 (Mme Lassabathie): D 17345 (8).

11. *Liste des abonnés*, 1837–1935, 80 vols.: D 17257. See also Élisabeth Bernard,

"Les Abonnés à la Société des Concerts du Conservatoire en 1837," *Music in Paris in the Eighteen-Thirties / La Musique à Paris dans les années mil huit cent trente,* ed. Peter Bloom (Stuyvesant, N.Y., 1987), pp. 41–54.

12. D'Ortigue, "Société des Concerts," pp. 343–44.

13. Outdoor: *L'Illustration,* 15 January 1848, signed A. B. L.; indoor: *L'Illustration,* 15 April 1843, signed A. E. P., after P. S. Germain.

14. Elwart, plate betw. pp. 114–15 *(plan de l'orchestre).*

15. On Berlioz's preferred disposition of forces, see n. 17, below. Roundtable "Conducting Berlioz" (Norrington, Holoman, Hugh Macdonald, David Cairns; London, October 1995), transcribed as "Performing Berlioz's Music," *Berlioz Society Bulletin* 155 (Spring / Summer 1996): 27–50; also treated by Holoman, "Performing Berlioz," in *The Cambridge Companion to Berlioz,* ed. Peter Bloom (Cambridge, 2000), pp. 173–93.

16. Com. 8 December 1874 *(robes de Mousseline):* D 17345 (9). Com. 20 and 27 April 1840 *(spencers):* D 17345 (2).

17. Berlioz, "Observations" for performing *Roméo et Juliette,* NBE vol. 18, ed. Holoman (Kassel, etc., 1990), p. 383. Berlioz, *Grand Traité d'instrumentation et d'orchestration modernes* (2nd edn. Paris, 1855; incl. "Le Chef d'orchestre: Théorie de son art"), p. 310.

18. Press release, 1998, concerts by the Chœurs Élisabeth Brasseur: collection of the author.

19. Com. 1 February 1848: D 17345 (4).

20. In the end, the benefit for the Pas de Calais victims was presented by the Opéra.

21. Com. 14 January 1839: D 17345 (2).

22. Com. 20 April, 12 October 1920: D 17345 (19).

23. Schonenberger's *Répertoire* is enumerated on the website; see also citations there of the Alkan and Dancla works. Com. 11 February 1851 (Aulagnier): D 17345 (5).

24. Rapport moral 8 May 1864 (Lebouc): D 17341.

25. Deldevez, *Mémoires,* p. 202 (Old Masters). Deldevez, *Société des Concerts,* p. 275 (Girard's analogy; Deldevez does not specify the source for this citation). Deldevez, *Mémoires,* p. 201 (never change).

26. Com. 6 April, 4 November 1835 *(Egmont):* D 17345 (2). Com. 8 February 1841 (Schubert): D 17345 (3).

27. Com. 30 January 1838: D 17345 (2).

28. Com. 9 January 1837 (Rousselot), 20 February 1837 (thanking Täglichsbeck): D 17345 (2). Com. 11 February 1851 (Czerny): D 17345 (5). In the latter, Louise Farrenc's husband writes that he has found and purchased two manuscript copies of a symphony composed for the Société des Concerts by Czerny and given to Habeneck; he says he gave one to library of the Conservatoire and kept one for himself. I have not been able to locate either copy.

29. Com. 13 March 1837 (Credo rehearsed); 24 December 1838 (engraved copy); 25 February 1839 (*La Reine de Saba* essayed, approved); 13 November 1839, 17, 22 February 1840 (badgering); 27 April 1840 *(membre honoraire):* D 17345 (2).

30. Com. 14 March 1843 (*Ave verum*); 11 February 1845 *(Le Déluge):* D 17345 (3). Com. 11 December 1845 (oratorio); 30 December 1846 (symphony); 14 and 21 December 1847 (Mendelssohn elegy); 14 November 1848 (symphonies); 27 November 1849 (another proposal): all D 17345 (4). Com. 16 January 1844 (new year's greetings): D 17345 (3).

31. Corresp. Massé to Hainl, 28 December 1868: ms. 17668, *livre d'or,* no. 6b.

32. Com. 3, 22 February and 13 April 1840 (Mme Lesueur): D 17345 (2). Com. 14 November 1871 (Mme Charlot): D 17345 (8). Com. 28 March, 26 December 1876, 20 February 1877, 5 March 1878 (Mme Alfred Holmes): D 17345 (9); and 2 October 1878, 17 December 1878, 25 November 1879: D 17345 (10)— among many others; on 25 November 1879, the committee's response is quite testy. Corresp. from and to Mme Alfred Bruneau, 19 January, 13 February, 30 October 1937: D 17263 (10). Corresp. Nadia Boulanger to com., 31 October 1937: D 17263 (10).

33. Com. 17, 24 December 1912: D 17345 (18); also a later complaint by Emmanuel on the same matter, com. 6 September 1921: D 17345 (19).

34. Corresp. Charles Constantin to com., 12 November 1871 (Mendelssohn): D 17337 (1). Com. 31 December 1838 (economy), 22 April 1839 (disappearance): D 17345 (2). Com. 2 July 1872 (poor state of library): D 17345 (8); Deldevez gives a complete transcription of his remarks on that occasion, *Mémoires,* pp. 219–23.

35. AG 15 May 1863: D 17345 (6).

36. Corresp. Reyer (and Amb. Thomas) to com., n.d. ca. January 1870: D 17337 (1).

37. Com. 1 March, 16 November 1841 (Méhul): D 17345 (3).

38. Rapport moral 15 May 1870 (Viguier: fire insurance): D 17341.

39. Rapport moral 24 May 1907 (Seitz): D 17341.

40. Com. 26 December 1837: D 17345 (2).

41. Com. 21 and 27 October, 3 November 1885 (Besson): D 17345 (11). Rapport moral 16 May 1894 (Nadaud: percussion): D 17341. Com. 15 April 1924 *(caisse de voyages):* D 17345 (19).

42. Com. 22 June 1920: D 17345 (19).

43. Com. 20 February 1837: D 17345 (2).

44. Com. 6 November 1928: D 17345 (20).

45. Author's interview with Lucien Thévet and Robert Casier, Paris, 21 October 1998.

46. Com. 20 December 1859 (universal pitch standard): D 17345 (6). Com. 15 April 1924 (reinvited): D 17345 (19).

47. Interview, Robert Casier and Lucien Thévet, 21 October 1998.

48. Corresp. com. to Cherubini, 12 February 1832: D 17337 (1).

49. Rapport moral 13 May 1832 and 19 May 1833 (both Tajan-Rogé): D 17341. I have corrected the arithmetic.

50. Documents concerning arrangements for the hall are found, arranged somewhat haphazardly, in D 17337 (1); the cited list (four patrolmen, etc.) appears to come from 1911. Corresp. com to prefect of police, 19 March 1834 (theft): D 17344 (no. 171 for 1834). Com. 31 March 1879 (complaint from women of the chorus): D 17345 (10).

51. Com. 22 December 1841: D 17345 (3).

52. Citations for each increase in the poor tax will be given at the appropriate points in the chronological narrative. To summarize the situation of the early years:

In D 17344: Corresp. com. to Locré de St. Julien, 9 January 1833 (no. 20); to Administrateurs des Hospices Civils de la Ville de Paris, 28 December 1833 (no. 103); to the same, citing Berlioz and Hiller, 13 January 1834 (no. 121); to Mantou, referring to the 160 artists, 15 December 1834 (unnumbered).

In D 17337 (1): Corresp. from Conseil Général des Hospices, granting 200 francs / concert for 1835, signed Mantou, 24 December 1834; ibid., demanding 12½ percent, 1 January 1836; ibid., returning to 200 francs, signed Mantou, 20 January 1836; ibid., for 1837, 24 November 1836.

53. Citations for each increase in fees for performance rights will be given at the appropriate points in the chronological narrative. In summary here, see Rapport moral 28 May 1890 (Taffanel): D 17341. Com. 26 October and 9 November 1920, 21 November 1924: D 17345 (19).

54. Com. 3 December 1843 (Meifred), 25 November 1842 (Saint-Laurent): D 17345 (3). Com. 30 September, 7, 21, 28 October 1913 (telephone): D 17345 (18).

55. Com. 20 April 1920: D 17345 (19).

56. Com. 15 June 1920: D 17345 (19).

57. Com. 20 March to 12 April 1921: D 17345 (19).

58. Com. 30 April 1921: D 17345 (19). From 1920 financial results are methodically included in the committee's minutes; these are given on the website.

59. Corresp. com. to and from organizers 8 September (estimate), 10 September (accord), 23 September 1937 (bill): D 17263 (10).

60. Com. 14 October 1913: D 17345 (18).

PART TWO

1. Ellis, *Music Criticism,* pp. 104-12 ("Berlioz on Beethoven"). See also my introduction to a recent edition of Berlioz, *A Critical Study of Beethoven's Nine Symphonies* (Urbana, Ill., 2000), pp. v-xxii.

2. Fulcher, *French Cultural Politics,* p. 27.

Chapter 5

1. Léon Escudier, in *La France musicale,* 11 February 1849 (Habeneck's obituary).

2. Berlioz, *Mémoires,* ch. 20. The story of the snuffbox is in ch. 46; of Habeneck's ineptitude with *Benvenuto Cellini,* in ch. 48. Habeneck is the addressee of the eighth letter (Berlin) in "Premier Voyage en Allemagne" (following ch. 51).

3. Charles, baron de Boigne, *Petites Mémoires de l'Opéra* (Paris, 1857), p. 298; cited by Kelly, *First Nights,* pp. 198-99.

4. Camille Saint-Saëns, *École buissonnière* (Paris, 1913), p. 35; cited by Jean-

Michel Nectoux, "Trois Orchestres parisiens en 1830," in Bloom, *Music in Paris,* pp. 471–507; see p. 487.

5. *La France musicale,* 18 February 1849.

6. Generally these paragraphs follow Elwart, pp. 321–30: "Biographie d'Habeneck aîné." See also Élisabeth Delafon-Bernard, "Habeneck et la Société des Concerts du Conservatoire: Un Destin exemplaire," in *Le Conservatoire . . . des Menus-Plaisirs,* 97–116.

7. I am grateful to André Leplus-Habeneck for the genealogy of his family.

8. Draft decree, 11 February 1828; corresp. La Rochefoucauld to Cherubini transmitting decree, 15 February 1828: D 17337 (1).

9. There are two manuscript copies of the decree of 15 February 1828: D 17338 (1–2); transcribed by Pierre, *Conservatoire,* p. 332; and Elwart, pp. 64–66. The agreement of former students to participate, circulated 15–22 February, is D 17338 (4); see Elwart, p. 67. (Corresp. La Rochefoucauld to Cherubini approving this document, 22 February 1828, is in D 17337 (1).) Contents of D 17338, *actes de fondation,* transcribed on the website.

10. AG 4 March 1828 (ratification of the fifty statutes read aloud): D 17338 (3); transcribed on the website and, with errors, by Elwart, pp. 68–69. There is apparently no copy of the original fifty statutes read that day, but the fifty-two statutes of ca. 1832 are presumably all but identical.

11. Corresp. La Rochefoucauld to com., 21 March, 18 April, 20 June 1828: D 17337 (1).

12. Corresp. La Rochefoucauld to Lubbert, 25 April 1829: D 17337 (1).

13. Elwart, pp. 98–101.

14. Sauzay, *Mémoires,* p. 184.

15. Corresp. prefect to com., 8 October 1828 (will receive them); corresp. La Rochefoucauld to sec., 17 December 1828 (authorizing concert): D 17337 (1).

16. Com. 14 November 1828: D 17345 (1).

17. H. C. Robbins Landon, *Haydn: Chronicle and Works* (Bloomington, Ind., 1977), V, 329, citing C. F. Pohl.

18. Elwart, p. 149.

19. Quoted in corresp. com. to Cherubini, 12 February 1832: D 13337 (1).

20. Corresp. Mendelssohn to his sister, Fanny, 28 December 1831: in Mendelssohn, *Letters from Italy and Switzerland,* Eng. transl. Lady Wallace (3rd edn. London, 1864), pp. 307–13; see p. 307.

21. AG 8 February 1832: D 17345 (1). Corresp. com. to Cherubini, 12 February 1832: D 17337 (1).

22. Corresp. Cavé to Duc de Choiseuil, 28 February 1832; Cavé to com. 1 March 1832: D 17337 (1).

23. AG 8 February 1832 (ministerial charge read aloud); com. 10, 14 February, 9 March, 23 April 1832 (preparations for benefit); 11 May 1832 (proceeds deposited): D 17345 (1). Rapport moral 13 May 1832 (Tajan-Rogé, on financial results): D 17341.

24. D 17337 (1); presumably a draft of the secretary's report on the matter for the AG of 13 May 1832.

25. Provisional approval for 1833 signed Montalivet and Delavigne, 1 December 1832: D 17337 (1). Decree, "Arrêté du 13 Décembre 1832 sur l'Organization de la Société des Concerts," transcribed by Lassabathie, in *Histoire du Conservatoire Impériale de Musique et de Déclamation suivi de documents recueillis et mis en ordre* (Paris, 1860), pp. 486–87; also Pierre, *Conservatoire,* p. 332. See the website.

26. Corresp. Montalivet to Louis-Philippe (copy transmitted to com. via Delavigne), 24 December 1832; Delavigne to com. (confirming and enclosing same), 28 December 1832: D 17337 (1). Corresp. Cherubini to Montalivet, 24 February 1834 (acknowledging receipt of increased subvention): D 17344 (no. 163 for 1834).

27. Draft of sec. report on the situation for the AG of 6 January 1833: D 17337 (1).

28. Rapport moral 19 May 1833 (Plantade): D 17341.

29. Corresp. Thiers to Société des Concerts, 3 June 1833: D 17337 (1).

30. Rapport moral 4 May 1834 (Plantade): D 17341.

31. Corresp. Mendelssohn to his sister, Fanny, 21 January 1832 (seven or eight rehearsals); to his father, 21 February 1832 (it went admirably); to his mother, 15–17 March 1832 (ebullient); to his father, 31 March 1832 (the queen): *Letters from Italy and Switzerland,* pp. 323–41; see pp. 325, 332, 337–38, 340. See also Mendelssohn's long letter from Paris to Zelter, 15 February 1832: *Felix Mendelssohn: A Life in Letters,* ed. Rudolf Elvers, Eng. transl. Craig Tomlinson (New York, 1986), pp. 170–81.

32. Corresp. ministry to com., 16 March 1832: D 17337 (1).

33. D'Ortigue, "Société des Concerts," p. 362.

34. Kelly, *First Nights,* p. 201; citing Chopin to Joseph Nowakowski, 15 April 1832, in *Correspondance de Frédéric Chopin,* ed. Bronislas Édouard Sydow, etc., 3 vols. (Paris, 1953–60), v. 2, p. 69.

35. Com. 6 April 1835 *(Egmont):* D 17345 (2); the performance was 25 February 1855. Com. 22 April 1839 *(La Bataille);* 11 October 1839 (overture): D 17345 (2).

36. Berlioz, "Dernières séances du Conservatoire," *Journal des Débats,* 23 June 1835; in *Critique musicale* 2: 189–96; see pp. 190–91.

37. Berlioz, *Mémoires,* ch. 16 (in a footnote). Dancla, *Notes et souvenirs,* pp. 108–09 (the redundant measures); the issue is re-engaged in material added to Dancla's 2nd edn. in 1898, see Eng. transl., p. 70. On conductors conducting better than composer-conductors, see Dancla, *Les Compositeurs chefs d'orchestre: Réponse à M. Charles Gounod* (Paris, 1874), pp. 4–5 (of 7 pages).

38. Com. 30 March 1832: D 17345 (1).

39. Rapport moral, 13 May 1832 (Tajan-Rogé): D 17341.

40. Com. 20 March 1832 (Girard), 31 January 1832 (*aspirants:* zeal, etc.): D 17345 (1). Com. 5 and 18 October 1836 (Révial): D 17345 (2).

41. Com. 17 January 1832 (Labadens); 21 February, 3 March 1832 (Doineau): D 17345 (1). Com. 28 December 1835 (Halma): D 17345 (2).

42. Rapport moral, 13 May 1832 (Tajan-Rogé): D 17341.

43. Com. 14 September 1836 (Dupont welcomed back): D 17345 (2). Com. 21 March 1842 (Holy Week): D 17345 (3).

44. Com. 3 December 1838, 14 October 1839: D 17345 (2).

45. Corresp. com. to Réty, 5 February 1833: D 17344 (no. 5 for 1833).

46. Com. 27 March 1832: D 17345 (1).

47. Com. 27 February 1835: D 17345.

48. Com. 22 and 29 February; 2, 7, and 11 March 1836 (Lagarin): D 17345 (2).

49. Rapport moral 15 May 1837 (Dérivis): D 17341.

50. AG 1 December 1831: D 17345 (1).

51. Elwart, pp. 69–82; on p. 83 he talks of the *"règlement de 1832."* AG 30 December 1829 (appointment of a commission to "print" the *règlement*), AG 24 June 1830 (discussion of process for adopting statutes), AG 1 December 1831 (vote on *règlement*), AG 13 May 1832 (adopting *règlement,* with language of article 52 changed to accommodate AG at end, not beginning, of season): D 17345 (1). Elwart's transcription is essentially equivalent to D 17338 (5), presumably its manuscript source.

52. Decree of 13 December 1832: see n. 24, above. AG 7 November 1833: D 17345 (1). Corresp. com. to Cherubini, 8 November 1833: D 17344 (no. 93 for 1833).

53. AG 5 January, 4 April, 4 May 1834: D 17345 (1). Rapport moral 4 May 1834 (Plantade): D 17341. The *règlement* of 5 January 1834 is D 17338 (6). A document headed "Société des Concerts / Note: des changements que le Comité a jugé nécessaires d'apporter . . . " may represent the transformation of the edition of 1832 for January 1834, or it may possibly represent language changed between January and May 1834: D 17340.

54. Com. 18 March, 1 April 1839 (Easter concerts): D 17345 (2). This decision was not implemented until 1842.

55. Com. 1 December 1833: D 17345 (1).

56. Com. 6 January 1835: D 17345 (2).

57. Com. 6 January 1835 (decision), 9 January (response), 10 January (Habeneck's explanation, Bénard's response, Vogt's advice), 14 January (decision maintained), 22 October (purge): D 17345 (2).

58. Corresp. Chopin to com., 13 March 1832: ms. 17668, *livre d'or,* no. 3. Published in *Correspondance de Frédéric Chopin,* vol. 2, pp. 66–67.

59. Berlioz, "Concerts," *Le Rénovateur,* 29 April 1835; in *Critique musicale* 2: 135–37; see p. 137.

60. Com. 16 April 1835: D 17345 (2).

61. Com. 25 May 1835 (petition and response): D 17345 (2).

62. Com. 27 May 1835: D 17345 (2). Habeneck's direct involvement with the chorus continues to be a prominent theme in the minutes through 1836, e.g., 28 December 1836 (rearranging the chorus benches), 13 March 1837 (chorus parts): D 17345 (2).

63. Com. 26 January 1835 (Kuhn's absences): D 17345 (2).

64. Corresp. com. to Benoist, 12 December 1834: D 17344. Corresp. Kuhn to com., 3 May 1837 (letter of resignation, in notes for *rapport moral* by Dérivis, 15 May): D 17341. Com. 1 June 1836 (something to be desired): D 17345 (2).

65. Com. 5 November 1838 (Moreau moved from tenor to accompanist), 26 November (unreimbursed rehearsals to be accompanied by Moreau), 3 December 1838 (rehearsals for 6 and 9 December): D 17345 (2).

66. AG 27 October 1835 (Tulou); com. 4 November (archbishop), 5 November (press, king), 9 November 1835 (letter to king signed); AG 6 November 1836 (matter comes up again): D 17345 (2).

67. Corresp. com. to Habeneck, 29 November 1836: D 17344. Com. 29 November 1836 (id.): D 17345 (2).

68. Com. 2 December 1836 (Habeneck's response; com. resigns); AG 4 December 1836: D 17345 (2). Corresp. com. to Cherubini, 2 December 1836 (resigning *en masse*): D 17344.

69. AG 4 December 1836: D 17345 (2). Corresp. com. to Habeneck, 4 December 1836: D 17344. Both give the language of the new statute.

70. Rapport moral 15 May 1837 (Dérivis): D 17341.

71. Com. 17, 24 April 1837: D 17345 (2).

72. Com. 20 February 1837 (thanking Täglichsbeck): D 17345 (2). Berlioz, "Premier Concert du Conservatoire," *Revue et gazette musicale,* 31 January 1836; in *Critique musicale* 2: 391–95; see p. 393. The incident of the out-of-tune piano is reported by Berlioz in "Cinquième Concert du Conservatoire," id., 27 March 1836; in *Critique musicale* 2: 439–41; on Gluck: "Sixième Concert du Conservatoire, id., 24 April 1836; in *Critique musicale* 2: 451–54.

73. Elwart, p. 189, n. 2.

74. Com. 30 January 1838 (Habeneck's proposal); AG 1 February 1838 (objections to, amendments, adoption of same): D 17345 (2).

75. Com. 1 April 1838 (reading): D 17345 (2).

76. Com. 16 April (Turcas's many services), 19 April 1838 (new reading): D 17345 (2).

77. Com. 30 March 1840 (Turcas, again): D 17345 (2).

78. Com. 24 April 1838 (four possibilities); AG 13 May 1838 (new wording adopted): D 17345 (2).

79. Com. 2 December 1838, 19 January, 28 February, 16 March 1839 (readings of works listed in Table 8): D 17345 (2).

80. Wagner, *Mein Leben* (1881, etc.), ed. Martin Gregor-Dellin as *erste authentische Veröffentlichung* (Munich, 1963), pp. 206, 209–10 (*Columbus,* the Ninth), pp. 228–29 (Berlioz and *Roméo et Juliette*); as *My Life,* ed. Mary Whitall, transl. Andrew Gray (Cambridge, 1983), pp. 172, 174–75, 191–92. The remark about the scales falling from his eyes comes from Wagner's essay "Über das Dirigieren" (1869), *Gesammelte Schriften und Dichtungen* I/8 (edn. Leipzig, 1898), pp. 261–337; see pp. 271–72. Eng. transl. as "On Conducting," in *Three Wagner Essays,* transl. Robert L. Jacobs (London, 1979), pp. 55–56. Wagner probably attended the performance of Beethoven's Ninth on 8 March 1840. The Ninth was also given, during Wagner's Paris residency, on 21 March 1841 and 9 January 1842.

81. Com. 3 December 1838; 8, 16, 30 January 1839 (Mainzer's concert): D 17345 (2)

82. Com. 4 December 1838 (Habeneck's ideas for state subvention): D 17345 (2); also 26 November 1838, 5 May 1839 (efforts to regularize arrangements with the state). Deldevez, wrongly, takes issue with Elwart's account of Habeneck's desire, saying "Ces paroles . . . n'ont jamais été, bien certainement, prononcées

par Habeneck" (Deldevez, *Société des Concerts,* p. 255, referring to Elwart, p. 390; see also p. 330).

83. Com. 2, 4, 10 May 1838; AG 13 May, 5 June 1838 (Caisse de Prévoyance): D 17345 (2).

84. Com. 16 February, 4 March 1846; AG 10 March 1846 (Association des Artistes-Musiciens): D 17345 (4). Com. 14 May 1872 (interest paid to account no. 167,810 sér. 7, as of 11 May: 10,495 francs): D 17345 (8).

85. Com. 6 and 26 April 1839: D 17345 (2).

86. AG 5 May 1839: D 17345 (2).

87. Com. 16 August 1839: D 17345 (2).

88. Com. 11, 19 May and 13 October 1840 (Barbier): D 17345 (2).

89. Com. 26 November 1838: D 17345 (2).

90. Com. 21 February 1843 (Mocker), 27 November 1843 (Kilian), 28 December 1843 (Charpentier): D 17345 (3).

91. Com. 24 December 1838, 25 February 1839 (Franck): D 17345 (2).

92. Com. 25 January 1841 (Viardot at their disposal), 4 April 1842 (named *soc. solo*), 6 December 1842 (customary grace), 15 December 1844 (Habeneck's nominations of Roger and Hermann-Léon as *soc. solo*): D 17345 (3).

93. Com. 3, 8, 13, and 27 January 1840: D 17345 (2).

94. Com. 6 February 1838 (inviting Louise Farrenc), 10 February 1840 (her response): D 17345 (2).

95. AG 26 October 1845: D 17345 (4).

96. The lithographed version contained in Habeneck's *livret* (Bnf Mus. lettres aut. Habeneck) gives the range of dates; the notarized copy, D 17338 (8), gives the date the document was recorded: "Enregistré à Paris le trente un Décembre mil huit cent quarante un: folio 109, verso, cases 5, 6, et 7, reçu cinq francs cinquante centimes décime compris. Signé Doneaud."

97. AG 29 January 1842: D 17345 (3).

98. AG 1 May 1842: D 17345 (3).

99. Com. 28 April, 13 and 20 May 1841 (arrangements for printing), 16 November 1841 (copies to founders), 17 January 1842 (Pierret), 31 January 1842 (copy to Schindler), 11 October 1842 (further circulation prevented): D 17345 (3).

100. For instance, Com. 2, 4 May 1838 (Alard, Chevillard, Tilmant bros.): D 17345 (2). Com. 14, 21, 28 February, 4 March 1842 (outside concerts), 11 April 1842 (Franchomme and Dorus apologize; Mme Bouvenne's daughter), 13 February 1844 (Veny), 17 November 1844 (Berlioz): D 71345 (3).

101. Com. 17 January, 14 and 21 February, 4 March 1842: D 17345 (3)

102. Com. 26 April 1842; 1, 17, 28 December 1843: D 17345 (3).

103. Com. 16 November 1841 (Mme Garaudé's demand), 8 November 1842 (new title for women proposed), 13 December 1842 (draft of article on women), 3 January 1843 (Garaudé threatens to resign); AG 13 May 1843 (revised language adopted): D 17345 (3).

104. Com. 12 December 1841 and 24 January 1842: D 17345 (3).

105. Com. 21 March 1842: D 17345 (3).

106. AG 1 May 1842: D 17345 (3). Rapport moral 12 May 1844 (Meifred): D 17341.

107. Com. 28 February 1842 (Henry's illness), 30 March (members convoked to funeral), 4 April (aftermath): D 17345 (3).

108. Com. 28 December 1843: D 17345 (3).

109. Rapport moral 12 May 1844 (Meifred): D 17341.

110. Com. 13 March 1844: D 17345 (3).

111. Rapport moral 12 May 1844 (Meifred): D 17341.

112. Com. 13 December 1842 (language drafted): D 17345 (3); record of the contentious process of revising and trying to adopt this statute continues in this volume through 30 October 1843.

113. AGs 6, 13, 21, 27 May, 30 October 1843: D 17345 (3).

114. AG 21 May 1843: D 17345 (3).

115. Ibid.

116. AG 27 May 1843: D 17345 (3).

117. Com. 17 January, 21 February 1843: D 17345 (3).

118. Com. 8 May 1844: D 17345 (3).

119. Rapport moral 12 May 1844 (Meifred): D 17341.

120. Bnf Mus. ms. 17476 (260 × 332 mm., 101 pp.).

121. Com. 13, 20, 29 February 1844: D 17345 (3).

122. Com. 3, 11, 18/19, and 29 December 1845: D 17345 (4).

123. Com. 3 January 1846 (program), 4, 11 April, 5 May (honorarium): D 17345 (4).

124. Com. 15, 30 December 1846: D 17345 (4).

125. Com. 20 December 1839 *(homme de lettres):* D 17345 (3). Com. 1 December 1844 (id., identifying Bourges), 29 December 1845 (Beethoven): D 17345 (4).

126. Com. 30 December 1846, 2 March 1847 (Beethoven): D 17345 (4).

127. Com. 15 December 1846 (Halévy), 2 March, 6 April (delays), 14 April 1847 (citation): D 17345 (4).

128. Com. 29 February 1848 (hall sequestered; concert planned), 7, 14, 21 March (details); AG 7 May 1848: D 17345 (4).

129. Habeneck's obituary, in Escudier (see n. 1 above).

130. Com. 12 May 1845 (statute on honorary president): D 17345 (3). Com. 30 October, 6 and 11 November 1845 (Habeneck's illness; com. meets in his home); Com. 1 May 1848 (new committee), AG 7 September 1848 (draft article): D 17345 (4).

131. AG 7 September 1848: D 17345 (4).

132. Com. 27 April 1843: D 17345 (3).

133. Com. 10, 11 September 1848: D 17345 (4).

134. Com. 16 October 1848: D 17345 (4).

135. AG 18 October 1848: D 17345 (4).

Chapter 6

1. AG 18 October 1848: D 17345 (4). Details of the balloting appear on the website.

2. See Berlioz, *Mémoires,* ch. 45.

3. Elwart, p. 174n.

4. *La France musicale*, 11 (pale, suffering), 18 February (phantom) 1849. *Le Ménestrel*, 11 February 1849 (rupture).

5. *Le Ménestrel*, 18 February 1849.

6. Habeneck's *livret:* Bnf Mus. lettres aut. Habeneck.

7. Com. 17 and 24 April 1849 (project for a monument); AG 3 March 1849 (funds allocated for monument): D 17345 (4).

8. Com. 13 January 1852 (Habeneck's box): D 17345 (5). Mme Habeneck died in 1882, leading to a dispute with her lawyer over the disposal of her seats: com. 17, 31 October 1882: D 17345 (10); com. 28 October 1884: D 17345 (11).

9. Reported in *La France musicale,* 25 February 1849.

10. Published as no. 73 in Schonenberger's 1850 *Répertoire;* see the website.

11. *La France musicale,* 25 February 1849.

12. Elwart, p. 245.

13. Com. 21 November 1848 (schedules reading of Farrenc symphony), 20 February 1849 (accepting symphony), 27 March 1849 (scheduling its performance, 22 April 1849), 31 October 1849 (declining second symphony): D 17345 (4).

14. Com. 30 June 1849 (struck so young), 11 July 1849 (solicitation for widow Renouf; widow Saint-Laurent returns money found in cashbox); AG 22 July 1849 (joint memorial service to be held later); Com. 10 June 1850 (service set for 15 June 1850): D 17345 (4).

15. AG 2 February 1850: D 17345 (4)

16. Text of the decree of 30 October 1850 remains untraced, but it is cited as precedent in the decree of 31 July 1897, recorded in AG 13 October 1897: D 17345 (13). Documents relating to the transfer of authority for the Salle des Concerts to the administration of the Conservatoire are transcribed in Pierre, *Conservatoire,* pp. 324–35.

17. *Le Temps,* 26 December 1830 (transl. after Kelly, *First Nights,* p. 181).

18. Corresp. com. to Berlioz, 15 March 1833: D 17344 (no. 75 for 1833). This is a response to corresp. Berlioz to com., 13 March 1833: Berlioz, *Correspondance générale* 2, ed. Frédéric Robert (Paris, 1975), no. 328.

19. See Berlioz, *Mémoires,* ch. 39 (long and diffuse). *Séance publique annuelle,* 12 October 1833, Bnf Mus.; cited by Adolphe Boschot, *Un Romantique sous Louis-Philippe: Hector Berlioz, 1831–1842* (Paris, 1908), p. 201.

20. Corresp. com. to Berlioz, 12 April 1837: D 17344.

21. Berlioz, "Concerts de M. Liszt" [of 9 April 1835], *Journal des Débats,* 25 April 1835; in *Critique musicale* 2: 127–33; see p. 132.

22. Corresp. Berlioz to Janin, 21 April 1849; and to his sister Nanci, 25 April 1849 (a difficult public, waiting backstage): *Correspondance générale* 3, ed. Pierre Citron (Paris, 1978), nos. 1256, 1258. Berlioz, *Mémoires,* ch. 59 (Girard's refusal to grant an encore).

23. Jules Janin, "Berlioz au Conservatoire, enfin!" *Journal des Débats,* 23 April 1849. Beginning with "Both the movements," these two paragraphs come from D. Kern Holoman, *Berlioz* (Cambridge, Mass., 1989), p. 408.

24. Com. 31 October 1848 (Molet and Gouvy), 31 October 1849 (repertoire), 6 November 1849 (applications from pianists suspended), 20 November 1839 (three reading sessions), 11 December 1849 (essay system made everyone unhappy): D 17345 (4).

25. Elwart, p. 263, n. 1; p. 288, n. 1; pp. 389–96.

26. Ibid., p. 287.

27. Com. 11 November 1851 (pre-season readings); 16 November, 8 December 1852 (Girard's summer study, Marmontel's collection): D 17345 (5). A concordance of numbering schemes for the Haydn symphonies is given on the website.

28. Com. 13 January 1851 (Härtel in Leipzig): D 17345 (5). Dancla, *Les Compositeurs chefs d'orchestre*, p. 7 (perfect performance).

29. Com. 8 December 1852 (material for *Songe*): D 17345 (5).

30. Com. 29 December 1852 (Girard to Bélanger): D 17345 (5). Bélanger's *Egmont* translation for Habeneck in 1849, though not performed, was published: *Entr'actes du comte d'Egmont, musique de Beethoven, poème-résumé de la tragédie de Goethe; traduit de l'allemand par Bélanger* (Paris, [1849]). Bnf Tolbiac 4 YTH 1434.

31. Trianon's *Egmont* translation was published in a fifteen-page libretto for the 1855 premiere and reprinted for later performances: *Ouverture et entr'actes d'Egmont, par Beethoven; paroles de M. Henry Trianon, d'après le drame de Goethe* (Paris, [1855]). Bnf Tolbiac YF 13021 (dated 1861).

32. Adolphe Adam, *Derniers Souvenirs d'un musicien* (Paris, 1859), pp. 63–67; cited by Tiersot in his program note for the concert of 19 January 1900.

33. Com. 17 July 1851 (Panthéon): D 17345 (5).

34. Com. 17 July 1851 (manifestation of musical art), 30 July 1851 (everything necessary), 7 August 1851 (Lazard): D 17345 (5).

35. Com. 2, 9 December 1851: D 17345 (5).

36. Com. 2 December 1851: D 17345 (5).

37. Com. 21 December 1853, 3 January, 4 February 1854 (loans of imperial property suspended): D 17345 (5).

38. Com. 1 December 1852; 9, 16 March 1853; 16 November 1853: D 17345 (5).

39. Com. 13 January 1852: D 17345 (5)

40. Com. 20 January 1852 (text of warning), 3 February 1852 (incognito), 17 February 1852 (Nargeot and Girard), 24 February 1852 (Nargeot's letter): D 17345 (5).

41. AG 19 April 1854: D 17345 (5).

42. Com. 19 April 1854 (delegation to Girard), 16, 30 April and 5 May 1852 (engraved medal): D 17345 (5).

43. Com. 26 April 1839: D 17345 (2). Young Vauthrot was given twice his usual share of the proceeds.

44. Original language: Statutes 30 December 1841, art. 38; see website. AG 6 June 1855 (revision): D 17345 (5).

45. AG 6 June 1855: D 17345 (5).

46. Com. 23, 25 August 1855 (command performance, convoy), 4 September 1855 (Cerclier): D 17345 (5).

47. Elwart, p. 294.

48. Com. 13 February 1856: D 17345 (5).

49. AG 21 November 1857 (membership at 118): D 17345 (6). The two sopranos, Mme Archaimbaud and Mlle Méneray, were confirmed later in the winter.

50. Albert Vernaelde, "La Société des Concerts et les grandes associations symphoniques," in *Encyclopédie de la musique et dictionnaire du Conservatoire,* ed. Albert Lavignac and Lionel de La Laurencie (Paris, 1913–31), II/6 (ca. 1930), pp. 3684–714.

51. Deldevez, *Société des Concerts,* pp. 256–59; Scudo cited p. 256, n. 1.

52. AG 26 December 1858: D 17345 (6).

53. Com. 15 November 1859: D 17345 (6).

54. Elwart, p. 306n (a).

55. Com. 17 January 1860 (funeral repertoire, allocation, etc.); the rehearsal the next day, 18 January 1860, at 9:00 A.M. was followed by a committee meeting: D 17345 (6). Copy of the *faire-part:* Bnf Mus. lettres aut. Girard.

56. Corresp. 24 March 1860 (Minister of State to A. Thomas, authorizing concert), 9 April 1860 (Mme *veuve* Girard to com.): D 17337 (1).

57. AG 5 May 1860 (election of Tilmant): D 17345 (6).

58. AG 22 May 1860: D 17345 (6).

59. Elwart, pp. 406–07.

60. Rapport moral 15 May 1878 (Lebouc): D 17341.

61. Corresp. [undated] (Lebouc to Count Walewski nominating Tilmant): D 17330; rapport moral 18 May 1862 (Gautier; reporting the award): D 17341.

62. Elwart, p. 407, n. 1.

63. Text transcribed on website.

64. Com. 21 May 1861 (pledge to Cherubini monument), 1 October 1861 (Rossini's offer): D 17345 (6).

65. Corresp. Rossini to Alphonse Royer, 15 October 1861: Giuseppe Radiciotti, *Gioacchino Rossini,* vol. 2 (Tivoli, 1928), pp. 430–31. The score is published as Gioacchino Rossini, *Le Chant des Titans,* pref. Alfredo Bonaccorsi, rev. Lino Liviabella, *Quaderni Rossiniani* 8 (Pesaro, 1959), pp. vi–vii, 66–89. At the end of the autograph: *Laus Deo / G. Rossini, Passy, 15 Sept. 1861.*

66. The version given in *Le Ménestrel* (see n. 67, below) gives a slightly different version and implied date: "Rossini écrivit, l'été dernier, à la veuve de l'éminent directeur du Conservatoire: 'Voici le portrait de Cherubini, resté aussi jeune dans mon souvenir que dans votre cœur.'"

67. "Causerie musicale / Conservatoire Impérial de Musique / Concert à la mémoire de L. Cherubini," *Le Ménestrel,* 29 December 1861.

68. P[aul] S[mith], in *Revue et gazette musicale,* 17 November 1861.

69. P[aul] S[mith], in *Revue et gazette musicale,* 31 November 1861.

70. Rapport moral 18 May 1862 (Gautier): D 17341.

71. AG 31 May 1862, 28 June 1862: D 17345 (6). Elwart, p. 404, n. 2.

72. Charles Dancla, *Notes et souvenirs,* p. 23.

73. Deldevez, *Société des Concerts,* pp. 77–86: p. 78 (Mendelssohn), p. 80

(Zampa), p. 81 (counterpoint), p. 85 (Mendelssohn concerto, Battaille, Wagner), p. 86 (summary). The amateur's ultimate mark of praise, used throughout this section, is *"toujours"*—meaning "play it as often as possible."

74. AG 15 November 1863 (Marin's voice); com. 17 November 1863 (appeal retired): D 17345 (6).

75. Deldevez, *Mémoires,* p. 209.

76. Ibid., p. 210.

77. AG 21 November 1863 (Tilmant's resignation accepted): D 17345 (6).

78. Berlioz's letter of candidacy, 19 December 1863: *Correspondance générale* 6, ed. Hugh Macdonald and François Lesure (Paris, 1995), no. 2812; ms. 17668, *livre d'or,* no. 4b.

79. AG 21 November 1863: D 17345 (6).

80. AG 21 December 1863: D 17345 (6). Further documentation in dossier "Élection de Hainl (1863) / Succession de Tilmant": D 17330. A table of the results appears on the website.

81. Deldevez, *Mémoires,* p. 30.

82. Berlioz, "Voyages en France: Correspondance académique, Deuxième Lettre" [Lyon], *Les Grotesques de la musique* (Paris, 1859), ed. Léon Guichard (Paris, 1969), pp. 283–96 (see 287–91).

83. Rapport moral 8 May 1864 (Lebouc, on separations), 7 May 1865 (Lebouc, on Leborne), 13 May 1866 (Gautier, on Dancla's retirement and Leborne's death): D 17341.

84. Com. 26 December 1865: D 17345 (6).

85. AG 28 October 1866: D 17345 (7). Details of the balloting appear on the website.

86. Com. 8 December 1864: D 17345 (6). See also Berlioz, *Correspondance générale* 2932 (Hainl to B., 15 November 1864), 2933 (B. to Hainl, ca. 15 November 1864), 2936–37 (B. to Lebouc, 6 December 1864), and following letters regarding the cancellation.

87. Rapport moral 8 May 1864 (Lebouc): D 17341.

88. AG 7 May 1865 (both petitions considered): D 17345 (6).

89. Rapport moral 13 May 1866 (Gautier): D 17341.

90. Elwart had proposed a plan along these lines: Elwart, p. 393.

91. Rapport moral 12 May 1867 (Gautier): D 17341.

92. See corresp. Berlioz to Hainl, 22 June 1867, *Correspondance générale* 7, ed. Hugh Macdonald (Paris, 2001), no. 3247 and note, suggesting postponements until 11 July 1867.

93. Alan Walker, *Liszt* [vol. 3]: *The Final Years, 1861–1886* (New York, 1996), p. 99; Walker cites Lille de Hegermann-Lindencrone, *In the Courts of Memory, 1858–1875* (New York, 1925).

94. Rapport moral 15 May 1869 (Lebouc): D 17341.

95. Ibid.

96. AG 21 November 1863: D 17345 (6).

97. Com. 14 April 1868 (Hainl's re-election discussed; H. will not attend AG), 21 April 1868 (two-thirds vote with nominations from floor); AG 10 May 1868

(Hainl re-elected): D 17345 (7). Rapport moral 15 May 1869 (Lebouc: negative assessment of Hainl in newspaper): D 17341.

98. Rapport moral 10 May 1868 (Lebouc): D 17341.

99. Com. 22 December 1868: D 17345 (7).

100. Com. 6 November 1868 (Lebourlier dismissed), 10 November (Lebourlier refused *sursis*), 17 November (Lebaron dismissed), 24 November (Lebaron appeals to AG); AG 27 November 1868 (Lebaron ill), 18 December (another postponement), 8 and 9 January 1869 (dismissal reversed): D 17345 (7).

101. AG 18 December 1868: D 17345 (7).

102. AG 9 January 1869 (committee resigns; meeting adjourned), 19 January 1869 (aftermath): D 17345 (7).

103. Corresp. members to and from com.: D 17330 (dossier 1870–71).

104. Philippe Ricord and Jean Nicolas Demarquay, *Les Ambulances de la Presse annexes du Ministère de la Guerre pendant le Siège et sous la Commune 1870–1871. Cet ouvrage est vendu au profit de la caisse de la Société de Secours aux Blessés* (Paris, 1872).

105. Com., entry after meeting of 31 January 1871: D 17345 (7), transcribed in full at website.

106. Corresp. Blanc (in Geneva) to com., 24 February 1871: D 17330 (dossier 1870–71).

107. Corresp. members to and from com.: D 17330 (dossier 1870–71).

108. Corresp. Jolivet to com., 15 November 1871 (need to be heard): D 17330 (dossier 1870–71). Com. 17 October 1871, 24 November, 26 December (requests for leave; insufficient supply of musicians): D 17345 (8). Corresp. Conte to com., 26 March 1871: D 17330 (dossier 1870–71).

109. AG 4 October 1871: D 17345 (8).

110. Ms. 17668, *livre d'or*, no. 8; Thomas's letter of application for the presidency, dated 1 August 1871, is no. 7a.

111. Com. 7 October 1871 (adopting *Gallia*), 10 October (Choudens: 300 francs), 21 October (the four seats): D 17345 (8).

112. Com. 10 October 1871 (Dubois proposes piano readings); 29 November, 12, 20 December 1871, 19 January 1872, 9 February 1872 *(rép. d'essai);* 23 January 1872 (piano auditions; Hainl and Michiels): D 17345 (8).

113. Com. 26 January 1872 (Hainl's proposal), 27 January 1872 (letter from prefect): D 17345 (8).

114. Com. 30 January 1872 (benefit concert discussed), 6 February (scheduled), 13 February (ticket prices, collection), 16 February (patronage of president of France), 20 February (Mme Viardot invited), 27 February (com. *loge*), 2 March (canceled): D 17345 (8).

115. Com. 21 and 28 May 1872, 4 June (Femmes de France), 22 October 1872 (government acceptance in question), 25 October 1872 (national treasury will take; accounting): D 17345 (8). For accounting see website.

116. Com. 23 April 1872 (Hainl and Dubois: conflict of interest), 30 April 1872 (further conversations): D 17345 (8).

117. Deldevez, *Mémoires,* p. 117.

PART THREE

1. This is the primary subject matter of Fulcher, *French Cultural Politics*.

Chapter 7

1. Rapport moral 26 May 1874 (Viguier): D 17341.
2. Deldevez, *Mémoires*, pp. 113–15.
3. Ibid., pp. 117–18.
4. Additionally Deldevez wrote *La Notation de la musique classsique comparée à celle de la musique moderne, ou de l'exécution des petites notes en général* (Paris, 1867); *Principes de la formation des accords d'après le système de la tonalité moderne* (1868); *De l'exécution d'ensemble* (1888); and *Le Passé, à propos du présent, suite à Mes Mémoires* (1892). Three of these are published in modern, annotated editions: *L'Art du chef d'orchestre*, ed. Jean-Philippe Navarre (Paris, 1998); *La Société des Concerts*, ed. Gérard Streletski (Heilbronn, 1998); and *De l'exécution d'ensemble*, ed. Jean-Philippe Navarre (Paris, 1998).
5. Com. 2 July 1872 *(mauvais état,* Jancourt), 9 July (loans suspended), 22 October 1872 (Jancourt thanked): D 17345 (8).
6. Com. 2, 16 December 1873 (Gluck), 12 November 1872 (Handel): D 17345 (8). Com. 2 September 1874 (embarrassment of riches): D 17345 (9). Rapport moral 26 May 1874 (Viguier, on loss of access to Opéra and chapel libraries): D 17341.
7. Com. 29 October 1872: D 17345 (8).
8. Com. 3 September 1872 (Dubois resignation), 26 October 1872 (Dubois profoundly pained; Fétis as Belgian; Lafitte election): D 17345 (8).
9. Com. 24 September 1872 (chorus rosters), 1 October 1872 (organize music, patrons): D 17345 (8).
10. Com. 11 June 1872: D 17345 (8).
11. Com. 10 December 1872 (Cavaillé-Coll's request); see also 23 December 1873 (repairs needed): D 17345 (8). This thread continues: Com. 10 February 1874 (invoking A. Thomas's help), 17 March 1874 (C.-C. responds that the organ will be ready for Handel choruses later in the month): D 17345 (9).
12. Com. 21 January 1873 (extra perf. of Ninth envisaged), 25 February 1873 (extra perf. scheduled for 16 March): D 17345 (8).
13. Com. 19 March 1873: D 17345 (8).
14. Com. 29 October 1872; 2, 6, 12, 19 November; 10 December 1872 *(réps. d'essai),* 8 October 1872 (com. to listen to all works submitted): D 17345 (8).
15. Com. 1 and 5 March 1872 (musicians excused), 2 April 1872 (Miséricorde denied), 30 April 1872 (Orphelins denied), 10 December 1872 (Alsaciens-Lorrains denied): D 17345 (8).
16. Com. 7 February 1873 (proposal for amputees benefit), 14 February (conditions), 15 February (notification of musicians), 18 February (program done), 22 February (slow sales), 11 March (accounts); 5 August 1873 (financial result of Alsaciens-Lorrains benefit): D 17345 (8).

17. Accounts: D 17337 (1). This event was planned for Sunday, 26 April 1874, with prices from 3 to 25 francs.

18. Com. 6 July 1875 (flood victims; archbishop): D 17345 (9).

19. Com. 20 May 1873 (petition for twenty concerts), 27 May (discussion of number), 3 June (objection of A. Thomas), 5 August (ministerial approval): D 17345 (8).

20. Rapport moral 26 May 1874 (Viguier): D 17341.

21. Rapport moral for each year during the crisis, 15 January 1872 (Garcin), 26 May 1874 (Viguier), 18 May 1875 (Viguier), 16 May 1876 (Taffanel): D 17341. Also com. minutes during this period: D 17345 (8-9).

22. Com. 29 October 1871 (tax collector at concert that day), 7 November 1871 (threat to cancel season), 14 November 1871 (Assistance Pub. abandons its pretensions): D 17345 (8). Rapport moral 15 January 1872 (Garcin): D 17341.

23. Com. 3 December 1872 (arrangement to hold firm): D 17345 (8).

24. Com. 21 October 1873 (notified of 8 percent), 28 October (Lamoureux), 25 November (the violent article), 9 December (call to thank him), 16 December 1873 (ministers to work out): D 17345 (8).

25. Com. 15 September 1874 (notified of 12½ percent): D 17345 (9).

26. AG 25 November 1874: D 17345 (9).

27. Rapport moral 18 May 1875 (Viguier): D 17341.

28. Rapport moral 16 May 1876 (Taffanel): D 17341.

29. Com. 7 September 1875 (work action pre-empted): D 17345 (9). Rapport moral 16 May 1876 (Taffanel: privilege at its end): D 17341.

30. W. C. Handy, *Father of the Blues* (New York, 1941; and subsequent rpts.), p. 262.

31. E.g., the case of the tenor, Paul de Soros, considered at AG 15 January 1872; com. 12 November 1872 (Teste), 21 October 1873 (de Bailly): D 17345 (8).

32. Com. 11 November 1873 (Mac-Mahon, Thiers), 18 November 1873 (Mac-Mahons requisition both series), 10 December 1872 (faithful listeners): D 17345 (8).

33. Com. 3 February 1874 (Beethoven's Ninth, *Midsummer Night's Dream*); 17, 24 March (deaf-mutes), 31 March (orphans); 21 April (leftover tickets), 24 April (canceled): D 17345 (9).

34. Com. 23 and 26 January 1875 (Davidov): D 17345 (9). Programs 21 and 28 February 1875: see website.

35. Com. 17 September 1872 (artistic and patriotic): D 17345 (8). Scudo cited by Deldevez, *Société des Concerts,* p. 242. Com. 12 November 1872 (Schoelcher donates his edition); 12 December 1871 (magnificent chorus): D 17345 (8).

36. Com. 27 May 1873 (Lamoureux renews his proposal), 3 June (Deldevez's objections), 1 July (discussion of excessive fatigue; symphonic element; inconvenience; Lamoureux's response): D 17345 (8). Deldevez gives verbatim text of each in *Société des Concerts,* pp. 243-50.

37. Com. 5 August 1873 (record decision and Lamoureux's response in the minutes): D 17345 (8). See also Deldevez, *Société des Concerts,* pp. 243-50.

38. Com. 1 July 1873: D 17345 (8).

39. Corresp. Sarasate to com., 9 March 1868 (offering Spohr concerto): ms. 17668, *livre d'or,* no. 6a. Com. 9 December 1873 (inviting Sarasate), 13 December (substituting Bruch for Beethoven): D 17345 (8).

40. Com. 6 January 1874 (Cras), 14 January (impatience): D 17345 (8). Cras had been reprimanded for lax standards on 20 January 1872: D 17345 (8).

41. Com. 28 October 1873 (readings scheduled), 31 December 1873 (result of orch. readings), 13 January 1874 (chorus readings delayed): D 17345 (8). The vote on the Nyevelt overture was tied at ten to ten, then broken by Thomas in its favor. Rapport moral 26 May 1874 (Viguier): D 17341.

42. AG 25 November 1874 (partisan gesture), AG 18 May 1875 (apology): D 17345 (9).

43. Com. 23 February 1875: D 17345 (9).

44. Rapport moral 18 May 1875 (Viguier): D 17341.

45. Com. 2 November 1872 (costs of the system): D 17345 (8).

46. Rapport moral 18 May 1881: (Taffanel): D 17341.

47. Com. 2 September 1874 (no longer accepts), 10 November 1874 (a recent decision): D 17345 (9).

48. Com. 26 October 1875: D 17345 (9). The measure was discussed com. 3 August, 7 September, 5 October 1875 before being adopted.

49. AG 31 October 1877: D 17345 (9).

50. Rapport moral 18 May 1875 (Viguier): D 17341.

51. Com. 5, 12, 18 May 1874; AG 26 May 1874; com. 2 June, 7 July 1874 (salaried employee): D 17345 (9).

52. Com. 4 January 1873 (Bourgault-Ducoudray's project), 7 January (draft of Thomas's letter read), 1 April (Danbé, Grand Hôtel orchestra to assist B-D for Handel's *Acis and Galatea;* sociétaires authorized on condition), 30 December (Danbé excused for another B-D concert): D 17345 (8). The committee's memoir on the matter, dated 7 January 1873, is in D 17337 (1).

53. Com. 15, 29 April 1873 (Heugel, Thomas): D 17345 (8).

54. Com. 2, 3, 7, 9 and 16 February 1875 (St. Vincent de Paul): D 17345 (9). Rapport moral 18 May 1875 (Viguier, summarizing the incident): D 17341.

55. Rapport moral 18 May 1875 (Viguier), 15 May 1878 (Lebouc): D 17341.

56. Com. 2 November 1875 (petition received), AG 26 November 1875 (debate): D 17345 (9).

57. Rapport moral 15 May 1877 (Taffanel): D 17341.

58. Com. 27 February 1877 (accounting): D 17345 (9).

59. Rapport moral 15 May 1877 (Taffanel): D 17341.

60. Deldevez, *Société des Concerts,* p. 283.

61. The analytic tables in Deldevez, *Société des Concerts,* pp. 196–238, with a long digression on Haydn.

62. Rapport moral 16 May 1876 (Taffanel, long and patient study); 15 May 1878 (Lebouc, defending society's treatment of Berlioz): D 17341. Georges de Massougnes, *Berlioz: Son Œuvre* (Paris, 1870), pp. 46–47; cited by Deldevez, pp. 272–73.

63. Rapport moral 19 May 1880 (Taffanel): D 17341.

64. Deldevez, *Mémoires,* p. 202.

65. Ibid., *Curiosités,* pp. 29–53.

66. Ibid., *Société des Concerts,* pp. 201–10.

67. Com. 15 February 1848: D 17345 (4).

68. F. J. Haydn, *Symphonie (inédite) en ut majeur (op. 82);* Deldevez's conducting score with his assessment of the work's provenance bound in the front: D 17593.

69. *Le Ménestrel,* 9 December 1877. Reviews of later performances in *Le Ménestrel,* 14 August 1878, 6 April 1879, 17 February 1884. See also rapport moral 29 May 1908 (Heymann, performances in Lyon, November 1907, and Paris, January 1908): D 17341; these performances referenced by Michel Brenet (pseud. of Marie Bobillier) in *Haydn* (Paris, 1909).

70. A concordance of numbering schemes for the Haydn symphonies is given at the website. H. C. Robbins Landon frequently reminds us that a dozen or more pre- and post-Revolutionary publishing concerns listed Haydn symphonies, works they had sometimes gullibly acquired from travelers unauthorized to offer them and with no profit to Haydn. But the six "Paris" symphonies (nos. 82–87) were in fact composed for the Concert de la Loge Olympique, and Haydn had himself given the autograph of the "Drum Roll," no. 103, to Cherubini in 1805. See Landon *passim,* notably "France," in *Haydn Chronicle and Works,* vol. 2 (Bloomington, Indiana, 1978), pp. 590–95.

71. Com. 15 April 1879: D 17345 (10).

72. K. C 11.05. See also M. L. P[ereyra], "A propos de *Ouverture en Si bémol* de Mozart," *Revue de musicologie* 18 (1937), p. 55.

73. Rapport moral 14 May 1879 (Lebouc): D 17341.

74. Rapport moral 19 May 1880 (Taffanel): D 17341.

75. Rapport moral 14 May 1879 (Lebouc): D 17341. Further on the Trocadéro concerts for 1878, see Deldevez, *Mémoires,* pp. 230–35.

76. Deldevez, *Société des Concerts,* p. 266.

77. Com. 2, 9 March 1880 (death of Housset *père, fils*), 6 April (sick leave); AG 19 May 1880 (simulated illness, envisage the impossible): D 17345 (10). Com. 10 April, 1, 5 May 1888 (Marthe): D 17345 (11).

78. Com. 12 January 1875 (complaints, theory of posting 175 copies): D 17345 (9). Com. 16, 23 January 1872 (complaints, St-Germain): D 17345 (8). Com. 24 November, 8, 15 December 1874 (money back): D 17345 (9). Rapport moral 19 May 1880 (Taffanel: postings): D 17341.

79. Com. 12 February 1889: D 17345 (11).

80. Rapport moral 19 May 1880 (Taffanel): D 17341.

81. Rapport moral 22 May 1883 (Viguier): D 17341.

82. Rapport moral 18 May 1881 (Taffanel): D 17341.

83. Com. 14 October 1882 (new works not programmed): D 17345 (10). Speech Deldevez to orchestra, 25 November 1882: Deldevez, *Mémoires,* pp. 245–46.

84. Com. 16 January 1883 (crippled): D 17345 (10). Corresp. Deldevez to com., 24 April 1883: Deldevez, *Mémoires,* p. 247 (also press coverage of his retirement, pp. 247–50). Com. 24 April, 1 May, 8 May (reactions to resignation): D 17345 (10). Rapport moral 22 May 1883 (Viguier): D 17341.

85. Rapport moral 22 May 1883 (Viguier): D 17341.

86. AG 22 May 1883: D 17345 (10). Rapport moral 20 May 1884 (Taffanel: all's well): D 17341.

87. Deldevez, *Mémoires,* p. 250.

88. Rapport moral 22 May 1883 (Viguier: resolution on Berlioz monument): D 17341. AG 22 May 1883 (unanimous vote): D 17345 (10).

89. AG 22 May 1883 (resolution; vote): D 17345 (10). Rapport moral 20 May 1884 (Taffanel, re contracts): D 17341.

90. AG 22 May 1883 (Viguier's response to Thibault): D 17345 (10). Rapport moral 20 May 1884 (Taffanel: V.'s retirement): D 17341.

91. Rapport moral 23 May 1885 (Taffanel): D 17341.

92. Com. 24 May 1870 (petition of fifteen members): D 17345 (7). Com. 20 May 1873, AG 24 May 1873: D 17345 (8). AG 16 May 1876: D 17345 (9). The petition is preserved in D 17337 (1).

93. See Radiciotti, *Rossini,* vol. 2, pp. 532 (language of the will), 540–42 (first competition and award), and 554 (French text, in the oration of the prefect of the Seine, Poubelle, on the occasion of the exhumation of Rossini's remains at Père Lachaise cemetery, 30 April 1887, before re-interment at the Church of Santa Croce in Florence). According to the critic of the *Gazzetta di Milano,* the prize cantata by Grandval and Colin—*La Fille de Jaïre*—failed at a performance in the Salle des Concerts owing both to the simultaneous opening that night of Offenbach's *Tales of Hoffmann* and to inadequate playing by the orchestra, doubtless of students.

94. Com. 4, 18, 25 March, 18 April 1884; AG 20 May 1884: D 17345 (10).

95. Report of the secretary (Taffanel): D 17337 (1).

96. Com. 10 March 1885 (preparations, date, character), 17 March (date approved), 7 April (rehearsals), 14 April (order): D 17345 (11).

97. See also corresp. 31 January 1888, 24 February, 1 and 5 May, 2 July 1889: D 17345 (11).

98. Com. 23 June 1903 (6,000 francs insufficient; also 7,000; copy exceeds 1,500), 27 June (enlist help of Dubois to ascertain precise conditions), 13 October (M. Rousseau offers thanks and some other seats), 17 October (Institute sends 9,000 francs), 10 November (Rousseau thanks for performance), 17 November (Rousseau thanks for reimbursement of copy).

99. See table of Prix Rossini compositions premiered by the Société des Concerts on the website. Lucien Lambert was the son of Charles Lucien Lambert, ca. 1828–96, of the New Orleans dynasty of musicians.

100. Société des Compositeurs de Musique, "Rapport au Ministère de l'Instruction Publique, des Cultes et des Beaux-Arts. Extrait [offprint] du *Journal officiel* du 29 Janvier 1873." Copy in Bnf Mus. Vmc 4293, vol. 1867–88.

101. Rapport moral 23 May 1885 (Taffanel): D 17341.

102. AG 23 May 1885: D 17345 (11).

103. AG 2 June 1885 (continued from 23 May): D 17345 (11). Deldevez transcribes his remarks on 2 June in *Mémoires,* pp. 255–57. Corresp. Thomas to Deldevez, 20 November 1885 (responding to D.'s resignation from the Conservatoire): cited by Deldevez, *Mémoires,* p. 258. Com. 9 June 1885 (bust of Gluck):

D 17345 (11). Albert Kaempfen, speaking at the *distribution des prix,* 6 August 1886 (kindness, simplicity): cited by Deldevez, *Mémoires,* p. 259. Rapport moral 23 May 1885 (Taffanel: music fever): D 17341.

104. Rapport moral 23 May 1885 (Taffanel): D 17341.

Chapter 8

1. AG 2 June 1885: D 17345 (11).
2. Deldevez, *Mémoires,* p. 201 (reigns but does not govern).
3. Rapport moral 28 May 1890 (Taffanel): D 17341.
4. Com. 25 January 1887: D 17345 (11).
5. Com. 12 May 1888: D 17345 (11).
6. Rapport moral 31 May 1888 (Ferrand): D 17341.
7. Ibid.
8. Ibid. The text mentions a "particularity" of the concert that reinforced the members' collective concern about fire and caused them to begin to consider electrifying the lighting system.
9. Rapport moral 31 May 1888 (Ferrand): D 17341.
10. Com. 28 December 1886, 4, 7 January 1887 (Marsick, Berthelier); 15 February 1887 (*Missa solemnis* canceled at musicians' request): D 17345 (11).
11. *Le Ménestrel,* 27 February 1887 (Pougin's notice).
12. Com. 1 March 1887 (Garcin overruled, again): D 17345 (11).
13. Rapport moral 31 May 1888 (Ferrand): D 17341.
14. Rapport moral 20 May 1882 (Viguier): D 17341.
15. Com. 5 January 1886 (Audan resigns), 12 January (he maintains his stance), 26 January (com. declines resignation), 2 February (cont'd.); AG 9 March 1886; com. 11 May 1886 (telegram): D 17345 (11).
16. AG 31 May 1887: D 17345 (11).
17. AG 28 May 1889: D 17345 (11).
18. Com. 18 May 1888 (Réaux's first visit), 2 April 1889 (inessential, simple rules); AG 29 May 1889 (Poissy): D 17345 (11).
19. Rapport moral 24 May 1907 (Seitz): D 17341.
20. Com. 27 October (dismissals), 3 November (protests), 10 November (ruling) 1885: D 17345 (11).
21. Rapport moral 31 May 1888 (Ferrand): D 17341.
22. Com. 17 November 1885 (lack of credentials noted; six named *adjoints*), 2 March 1886 (they protest), 13 April 1886 (petition of twenty-six demands discussion at AG); AG 2 May 1886 (motion defeated); com. 25 October 1887 (admitted through exception to rule): D 17345 (11). Summarized in rapport moral 31 May 1888 (Ferrand): D 17341.
23. Rapport moral 29 May 1889 (Ferrand): D 17341.
24. Com. 27, 30 October, 13, 27 November 1888: D 17345 (11).
25. Com. 7, 14, 21 June 1887: D 17345 (11).
26. Com. 5 May 1888 (Granger's petition; circular distributed): D 17345 (11).
27. Rapport moral 31 May 1888 (Ferrand): D 17341.

28. AG 31 May 1888: D 17345 (11).

29. Rapport moral 29 May 1889 (Ferrand): D 17341.

30. The English horn anecdote goes at least as far back as Vincent d'Indy, *César Franck* (Paris, 1906); Eng. transl. Rosa Newmarch (London, 1909).

31. Com. 9 April 1889: D 17345 (11).

32. Rapport moral 29 May 1889 (Ferrand): D 17341.

33. Rapport moral 15 December 1888 (Ferrand): D 17341.

34. Ibid. AG 15 December 1888: D 17345 (11).

35. AG 15 December 1888: D 17345 (11).

36. Proposition d'un Concert de Gala à offrir au Gouvernement pour les Fêtes de l'Exposition, folded into rapport moral for AG 29 May 1889 (Ferrand) and marked *"projet retiré"*: D 17341. Com. 14, 28 May: D 17345 (11).

37. Rapport moral 26 April 1889 (Ferrand): D 17341.

38. AG 26 April 1889; com. 14 May 1889 (letter from minister): D 17345 (11).

39. Com. 25 June 1889 (absences): D 17345 (11).

40. Rapport moral 28 May 1890 (Taffanel): D 17341.

41. Com. 22 October 1889: D 17345 (11).

42. Dancla, *Les Compositeurs chefs d'orchestre,* p. 5. The pamphlet objects to Gounod's campaign for composers to be allowed to conduct their own operas. The motet, says Dancla, could not have been better performed had Gounod led it himself.

43. Com. 29 January 1889 (on dropping in); 5 October 1886, 16, 23 November (the pedal piano); 22 February 1887 (*Mors et vita*): D 17345 (11).

44. Rapport moral 26 May 1894 (Nadaud): D 17341.

45. Rapport moral 28 May 1890 (Taffanel): D 17341.

46. Ibid.

47. Rapport moral 29 May 1891 (Taffanel): D 17341.

48. Rapport moral 28 May 1890 (Taffanel): D 17341.

49. Rapport moral 29 May 1891 (Taffanel): D 17341.

50. Rapport moral 30 May 1896 (Chavy): D 17341.

51. Dancla, *Notes et souvenirs* [added to 2nd edn.], p. 26; see Eng. transl. p. 18.

52. Rapport moral 29 May 1891 (Taffanel): D 17341.

53. Ibid.

54. AG 17 February 1892: D 17345 (12).

55. Projet de Modification aux Statuts, 28 May 1890 (written by Thibaut; report by Taffanel): D 17340.

56. Ibid.

57. AG 27 May 1892: D 17345 (12).

58. AG 3 June 1892: D 17345 (12). The record of the balloting is found on the website.

59. AG 17 June 1892: D 17345 (12).

60. Dandelot, *Société des Concerts,* p. 144. The acknowledged authority on Taffanel is the English scholar Edward Graham Blakeman, whose documentary biography, *Paul Taffanel and His Significance to French Musical Life,* is forthcoming.

61. AG 21 November 1891: D 17345 (12).

62. AG 19 April, 6 May, 13 May, 24 May 1893: D 17345 (12).

63. Rapport moral 26 May 1894 (Nadaud, use of *"du Conservatoire"*): D 17341.

64. Rapport moral 26 May 1894 (Nadaud): D 17341.

65. Rapport du Secrétaire sur un Projet de Modification à l'Article 15 des Statuts, 30 May 1896 (Chavy): D 17340.

66. Rapport moral 26 May 1894 (Nadaud): D 17341.

67. Raoul Pugno, 2 January 1909: ms. 17668, *livre d'or,* no. 13.

68. Rapport moral 26 May 1894 (Nadaud): D 17341.

69. Rapport moral 26 May 1895 (Nadaud): D 17341.

70. Rapport moral 24 May 1897 (Chavy): found erroneously in D 17340.

71. Cited in rapport moral 30 May 1896 (Chavy): D 17341.

72. Rapport moral 26 May 1895 (Nadaud): D 17341.

73. A table of appearances of Sarasate appears on the website.

74. Rapport moral 24 May 1897 (Chavy): found erroneously in D 17340.

75. I follow the version of the (uncited) text given by James Harding, *Saint-Saëns and His Circle* (London, 1965), p. 40: from Saint-Saëns, *École buissonnière: Notes et souvenirs* (Paris, 1913), Eng. transl. (abridged) as *Musical Memories* (London and Boston, 1919; rpt. New York, 1969); see "La Salle de la rue Bergère" and "Le Vieux Conservatoire," pp. 33–47.

76. Rapport moral 24 May 1897 (Chavy): found erroneously in D 17340.

77. Théodore Dubois, 1 August 1871: ms. 17668, *livre d'or,* no. 7a. No. 7b is a note of 10 November 1912 assuring the committee that he hopes to attend the opening of the eighty-sixth season.

78. Com. 13 July 1897: D 17345 (13).

79. Decree 31 July 1897, in com. 5 October 1897: D 17345 (13).

80. AG 13 October 1897: D 17345 (13).

81. Ibid.

82. Rapport moral 30 May 1899 (Vernaelde): D 17341. Vernaelde refers to his report of 25 May 1898, not preserved.

83. Com. 10 November 1903 (convinced inspector), 24 November (installed at own expense): D 17345 (16).

84. Printed form letter, in boxed programs, 72^c Année.

85. Corresp. Léon Bourgeois to Taffanel, transcribed in rapport moral 30 May 1899 (Vernaelde): D 17341.

86. Rapport moral 30 May 1899 (Vernaelde): D 17341.

87. AG 12 June 1901: D 17345 (14). Rapport moral 29 May 1908 (Heymann, music of savages): D 17341. See also dossier "Candidatures aux successions de Taffanel et de Samuel Rousseau, 1901": D 17261 (4). The record of the balloting is found on the website.

88. Debussy, *La Revue blanche,* 1 July 1901; in Debussy, *Monsieur Croche et autres écrits,* ed. François Lesure (Paris, 1971; rev. edn. 1987), p. 53; Eng. transl. Richard Langham Smith as *Debussy on Music* (New York, 1977; paperback Ithaca, 1988), p. 49.

89. AG 28 June 1901: D 17345 (14).

90. Corresp. Debussy to Eugène Vasnier, early February 1885: in *Claude Debussy: Lettres 1884–1918,* ed. François Lesure (Paris, 1980), p. 7; Eng. transl. Roger Nichols as *Debussy Letters* (London and Cambridge, Mass., 1987), p. 5.

91. Maurice Emmanuel, Marty obituary included in the program printed for his funeral: boxed programs.

92. Extracts of the press from Antwerp for concert of 9 April 1907: boxed programs.

93. Rapport moral 26 May 1907 (Seitz): D 17341.

94. *Le Ménestrel,* 1 December 1901, p. 380.

95. Rapport moral 29 May 1908 (Heymann): D 17341.

96. Com. 13 October 1903 (works to read), 24 October (works adopted): D 17345 (16).

97. Rapport moral 22 May 1906 (Seitz): D 17341.

98. Rapport moral 26 May 1905 (Seitz): D 17341.

99. Com. 13 October 1903 (Marty proposes Berlioz concert), 3 November (acquire new material), 24 November (Tiersot's book): D 17345 (16).

100. Com. 1 December 1903: D 17345 (16).

101. Rapport moral 29 May 1908 (Heymann): D 17341.

102. Com. 17 October 1903 (short soloists, ask Planté), 3 November (he declines), 17 November (approach Saint-Saëns): D 17345 (16).

103. AG 28 May, 3 June 1902: D 17345 (15).

104. Rapport moral 26 May 1905 (Seitz): D 17341.

105. Ibid.

106. Jean-Michel Nectoux, *Gabriel Fauré: Les Voix du clair-obscur* (Paris, 1990), p. 228.

107. Rapport moral 22 May 1906 (Seitz): D 17341.

108. Com. 10 November 1903: D 17345 (16).

109. Com. 17 November 1903 (discussion of defections), 24 November (first results), 1 December (revised result): D 17345 (16).

110. Rapport moral 26 May 1905 (Seitz, incl. figures): D 17341.

111. Rapport moral 22 May 1906 (Seitz): D 17341.

112. Rapport moral 29 May 1908 (Heymann): D 17341.

113. Com. 1, 8 December 1903: D 17345 (16).

114. Rapport moral 26 May 1905 (Seitz, impossible not to know), 24 May 1907 (Seitz, on promotional activities): D 17341.

115. Rapport moral 29 May 1908 (Heymann): D 17341.

116. Rapport moral 22 May 1906 (Seitz, popularizing Franck); 24 May 1907 (Seitz, splendid isolation); 29 May 1908 (Heymann, resolve): D 17341.

117. Rapport moral 29 May 1908 (Heymann): D 17341.

118. Secretary's report for AG 30 December 1905: D 17340.

119. Ibid.

120. Petition 6 December 1905, in secretary's report for AG 30 December 1905: D 17340.

121. Secretary's report for AG 30 December 1905: D 17340.

122. AG 30 December 1905: D 17342 (1).

123. Extracts of the press from Antwerp for concert of 9 April 1907: boxed programs.

124. Rapport moral 29 May 1908 (Heymann): D 17341.

125. The program, as reported in the daily press, included the funeral march from Beethoven's "Eroica" Symphony, the "Pie Jesu" from Fauré's Requiem, an Offertoire by Théodore Dubois, and the Saint-Saëns *Marche héroïque*.

126. Rapport moral 26 May 1909 (Heymann): D 17341.

Chapter 9

1. AG 26 October 1908: D 17342 (1).

2. Ladislas Rohozinski et al., "Les Chefs d'orchestre," *Cinquante Ans de musique française de 1874 à 1924* (Paris, 1925), vol. 1, pp. 271–316; see p. 301.

3. Rohozinski, *Cinquante Ans,* pp. 300–01.

4. Program 17 February 1914, Lyon: boxed programs.

5. Janine Weill, *Marguerite Long: Une Vie fascinante* (Paris, 1969), p. 95.

6. *La Gazette* (Brussels), [10] July 1910 (tactful, rare); *Courrier d'Anvers,* 9 April 1909 (an orchestra independent of its conductor); *Journal d'Anvers,* 9 April 1909 (excessively *soigneuse*): printed extracts of the press from Antwerp, 1909, and Brussels, 1910: boxed programs.

7. Henry-Louis de La Grange: *Gustav Mahler* [vol. 2]: *Vienna: The Years of Challenge (1897–1904)* (Oxford, 1995), pp. 255–68.

8. A table of out-of-town appearances, 1907–31, appears on the website.

9. Extracts of the press from Lyon, 1908: boxed programs.

10. Extracts of the press from Antwerp, 1909: boxed programs.

11. Alfred Bruneau, writing in *Le Figaro,* refers to Mahler's "sober gestures" in Paris in June 1900; cited by La Grange, *Gustav Mahler* [vol. 2], p. 260. Other critical responses cited by La Grange, pp. 258–60, focus on Mahler's "excess of arabesques" and "overabundant nuances." Romain Rolland, in *Richard Strauss et Romain Rolland: Correspondance, fragments de journal* (Paris, 1951), p. 209 *(sa mimique de chat convulsé);* Eng. transl. ed. Rollo Meyers (London, 1968), p. 205 (as "a scalded cat").

12. AG 26 May 1909: D 17342 (1).

13. Ibid.

14. Adolphe Boschot, "Wagner au concert," *Le Mystère musical* (Paris, 1929), pp. 181–85; also in Boschot, *Portraits de musiciens,* vol. 2 (Paris, 1947), pp. 148–51.

15. Rapport moral, 29 Mai 1908 (Heymann): D 17341.

16. Ibid.

17. Ibid.

18. Corresp. Messager to Mimart, 19 October 1911: ms. 17668, *livre d'or,* no. 19a.

19. Ms. 17668, the *livre d'or:* Galston (14), 13 March 1909; Sauer (15), 24–25 March 1910; Hekking (17), 19 February 1911; Kreisler (18), 14 April (Vendredi Saint) 1911; Diémer (20), 25 November 1911; De Greef (21), 10 March 1912; Thibaud (22), 4, 5 April 1912; Capet (23), 28 April 1912; Bauer (25), 8, 15 December

1912; Paderewski (26), January, February 1913; Enesco (27), 1913; Busoni (28), 17 May 1913, January 1914.

20. There is an ornate souvenir program for the concert in Brussels, 9 July 1910: boxed programs.

21. Charles van den Borren, in *L'Indépendance belge,* extracts of the press from Brussels: boxed programs.

22. Extracts of the press from Brussels, incl. citations from *L'Indépendance belge* (van den Borren), *La Chronique, Le National, Le Soir, L'Étoile belge,* and *La Gazette:* boxed programs.

23. AG 26 May 1911: D 17342 (1).

24. Ms. 17668, *livre d'or,* no. 19b.

25. Com. 26 December 1911: D 17345 (18).

26. Com. 4 November 1911: D 17345 (18).

27. Com. 26 March 1912: D 17345 (18).

28. Philippe Gaubert, "Comment je suis devenu chef d'orchestre," *Le Monde musical* 48 (1938), 281; cited in Penelope Peterson Fischer, *Philippe Gaubert (1879–1941): His Life and Contributions as a Flutist, Editor, Teacher, Conductor, and Composer* (DMA diss., University of Maryland, 1982), p. 23.

29. Rapport moral 24 May 1907 (Seitz): D 17341.

30. Corresp. undersecretary of fine arts to com., 17 November 1911 (authorizing Trocadéro); [Astruc], press release Trocadéro concert, late January 1912: D 17337 (2).

31. Com. 5 December 1911: D 17345 (18).

32. Corresp. Astruc to Mimart, 6, 22 February 1912: D 17337 (1). Com. 12, 19 March 1912 (reduction in Astruc's fee): D 17345 (18).

33. Th. Heymann, "Notes sur l'origines de la Société": D 17264 (18).

34. See Gabriel Astruc, *Le Pavillon des fantômes* (Paris, 1929; modern edn. Paris, 1987). Com. 23 January 1912 (proposal unveiled): D 17345 (18).

35. Com. 23, 30 January 1912: D 17345 (18).

36. Com. 30 January 1912 (Mimart's account of his interview with Fauré): D 17345 (18).

37. Com. 6 February 1912: D 17345 (18).

38. Com. 19 March 1912 (1,000 francs), 23 April 1912 (loan company): D 17345 (18).

39. Prospectus and souvenir materials for opening of Théâtre des Champs-Élysées, April 1913: boxed programs ("Programmes Théâtre des Champs-Élysées").

40. Boxed programs Th. Champs-Élysées.

41. Com. 25, 28 November 1913: D 17345 (18).

42. AG 13 May 1910: D 17342 (1).

43. Com. 25 August 1910: D 17345 (17).

44. AG 19 November 1910: D 17342 (1).

45. Ibid.

46. AG 16 April 1911: D 17342 (1)

47. Com. 26 March 1912: D 17345 (18).

48. Com. 13 June 1911: D 17345 (18); transcribed in full on the website.

49. Com. 5 December 1911: D 17345 (18).

50. Com. 28 October 1913: D 17345 (18).

51. AG 2 May, 5 June 1914: D 17342 (1).

52. Rapport moral 30 May 1954 (Huot): D 17342 (3).

53. AG 5 June 1914: D 17342 (1).

54. Ibid.

55. AG 30 May 1919: D 17342 (1). See also Vernaelde, "Société des Concerts," p. 3705.

56. Com. ca. 30 May 1919 (brief retrospective of the society's wartime activities): D 17345 (18).

57. J.-G. Prod'homme, "Music and Musicians in Paris During the First Two Seasons of the War," *Musical Quarterly* 4 (1918): 135–50; see p. 135.

58. Julien Tiersot, "Souvenirs de cinq années" [1914–18], in *Le Ménestrel* 1920.

59. Henry Février, in *André Messager, mon maître, mon ami* (Paris, 1948), pp. 169–71, gives Péguy's text and suggests the date of the first performance as "toward the end of winter 1914–15," thus establishing a date considerably earlier than the date often given for the work, 1918.

60. Translation after *Encyclopædia Britannica*, 15th edn. (1978), vol. 7, p. 834.

61. Février, *Messager*, p. 171.

62. Joséphin Péladan, in *Mercure de France*, August 1915, p. 685; cited by Prod'homme, "Music . . . During the First Two Seasons of the War," p. 143.

63. Prod'homme, ibid., p. 141.

64. "Lettre de Bâle," in *Gazette de Lausanne,* 4 April 1917, cited in press booklet: boxed programs.

65. Financial documents and correspondence for Swiss tour 1917: D 17263 (5).

66. *Le Courrier musical,* April 1917, p. 209.

67. These quotations assembled from the Swiss press, notably *Le Courrier de Genève,* 8 April 1917; cited in press booklet: boxed programs.

68. *Le Démocrate* (Basel), 30 March 1917; cited in press booklet: boxed programs.

69. *La Tribune de Genève,* 24 March 1917; cited in press booklet: boxed programs.

70. *Le Journal de Genève,* 4 April 1917; cited in press booklet: boxed programs.

71. These quotations assembled from the Swiss press, notably *Le Courrier de Genève,* 8 April 1917; cited in press booklet: boxed programs.

72. *Tribune de Lausanne,* 3 April 1917; cited in press booklet: boxed programs.

73. *La Tribune de Lausanne,* 3 April 1917; cited in press booklet: boxed programs.

74. *Gazette de Lausanne,* 29 March 1917; cited in press booklet: boxed programs.

75. E.g., Andrew Lamb, "Messager, André," *The New Grove Dictionary of Music and Musicians,* 6th edn. (London, 1980), vol. 12, p. 202.

76. Com. summary of 91ᵉ Année, 1917–18: D 17345 (18).

77. Bernard Gavoty, *Alfred Cortot* (Paris, 1977), p. 130n., citing a letter in the archive of the Action Artistique.

78. Corresp. Otto Kahn to Cortot: 6 June 1918: D 17337 (2).

79. Gavoty, *Cortot,* p. 130.

80. Astruc, *Le Pavillon des fantômes,* p. 176.

81. John Kobler, *Otto the Magnificent: The Life of Otto Kahn* (New York, 1988), p. 27; citing *The Mirrors of Wall Street* (New York, 1933), p. 170.

82. French citation Kobler, *Otto Kahn,* p. 106. See also Mary Jane Matz, *The Many Lives of Otto Kahn* (New York, 1963; rpt. New York, 1984), pp. 188–89. Neither biography mentions Kahn's role in the American tour of the Société des Concerts. Kahn also underwrote many other Franco-American exchanges, some of which are treated by Matz and Kobler. Otto Kahn's papers are in the William Seymour Theater Collection at Princeton University (relevant corresp. filed by year under "French American Association" and "Herndon, R. G.") and the Metropolitan Opera Archive.

83. Notarized copy of the contract, prepared in New Orleans on 18 November 1918: D 17263 (36).

84. An attempt to match the announced itinerary with the one that actually took place appears on the website.

85. Draft repertoire list and sample programs: D 17263 (36). The six sample programs are given on the website. See also Messager's copious correspondence on the programming: Bnf Mus. lettres aut. Messager.

86. Telegram Columbia USA to Société des Concerts, noted 23 August 1918: D 17337 (2).

87. Corresp. Wurlitzer Co. to Conservatoire (carbon copy), ca. August 1918: D 17337 (2).

88. Gavoty, *Cortot,* p. 131.

89. Corresp. ministry of War to Commission for Franco-American Affairs, 14 August 1918, a long memorandum including Messager's arguments: D 17337 (2).

90. Corresp. August 1918, including memorandum cited in previous note: D 17337 (2).

91. "Historique et pièces," summary table at head of the long typescript Mémoire-Rapport documenting the later dispute over accounting: D 17263 (36).

92. General order "Headquarters Base Section No. 5 / Services of Supply / US ARMY Post Office no. 716 / 28 September 1918 (Subject: Transportation to the United States)": D 17337 (2).

93. An attempt to reconcile these two rosters appears on the website.

94. General order 28 September 1918. One unfamiliar name, Thibaud, may have been that of the *garçon d'orchestre.*

95. E. Nergy, in *Le Courrier musical,* 1 December 1918, p. 363.

96. Brian Rust and Tim Brooks, *The Columbia Master Book Discography,* vol. 4: *U.S.* (Westport, Conn., 1999), p. 175.

97. Advertisement in souvenir program book for American tour: boxed programs.

98. Rust / Brooks, *Columbia Discography,* p. 175.

99. Gavoty, *Cortot,* p. 131.

100. Program for concert of 29 November 1918, Liberty Hall, El Paso, Texas: boxed programs.

101. Münch, *I Am a Conductor*, p. 82.

102. Vernaelde, "Société des Concerts," p. 3703.

103. Jeanne Redman, in the *Los Angeles Daily Times*, 4 December 1918, part 2, p. 3.

104. *San Francisco Chronicle*, 1 December (fraternize, hearty Western welcome), 3 December, 4 December 1918 (review by Walter Anthony).

105. *Sacramento Bee*, 4 December 1918.

106. Ibid., 6 December 1918.

107. Frederick Donaghey, in the *Chicago Daily Tribune*, 23 December 1918.

108. Vernaelde, "Société des Concerts," p. 3703.

109. Corresp. Messager to Herndon, 15 December 1918: cited as pièce 5 in Mémoire-Rapport: D 17263 (36).

110. Corresp. Herndon to Messager in Dayton, Ohio, 26 December 1918: pièce 8 in Mémoire-Rapport: D 17263 (36).

111. In *Le Canada musical*, reported in *Le Courrier musical*, December 1920.

112. AG 30 May 1919: D 17342 (1). Vernaelde, "Société des Concerts, p. 3703, says the Bordeaux concert was in May 1919.

113. Vernaelde, "Société des Concerts," p. 3703.

114. Corresp. Herndon to Kahn (in Fr. transl.), 8 July 1919: pièce 13A in Mémoire-Rapport: D 17263 (36). A footnote reads: "M. Messager formally contests this recounting of the interview, where moreover M. Casadesus wasn't there. M. Messager deplores that a stenographer wasn't present to record the true face of the meeting."

115. Corresp. Herdon to Maurice Casenave at Action Artistique, New York, 11 January 1921: D 17263 (36).

116. Ibid.

117. Com. 3 June 1919 Société des Concerts: cited as pièce 11B/12 in Mémoire-Rapport: D 17263 (36).

118. Corresp. Kahn to Messager, 15 July 1919: D 17263 (36).

119. Corresp. Herndon to Kahn (in Fr. transl.), 8 July 1919: pièce 13A in Mémoire-Rapport: D 17263 (36).

120. Notice of resolution, "Palais Royal 14 Mars 1921 / Entretien avec M. SEITZ, au Service d'Études le 12 mars 1921": D 17263 (36).

121. John Wagstaff, *André Messager: A Bio-Bibliography* (New York, 1991), p. 28.

Chapter 10

1. Ordre du jour for AG 30 May 1919: D 17342 (1).

2. Petition of twenty *sociétaires*, 5 May 1919, in materials for AG 30 May 1919: D 17342 (1).

3. Ibid.

4. AG 30 May 1919: D 17342 (1).

5. Auguste Mangeot, "Philippe Gaubert," *Le Monde musical*, 31 July 1926; cited by Fischer, *Gaubert*, p. 45.

6. Follows Dominique Sordet, "Gaubert," in *Douze Chefs d'orchestre* (Paris, 1924), pp. 32–36.

7. Com. 2 November 1920: D 17345 (19). The occasion was a benefit concert of 9 December 1920 for the Conservatoire; Gaubert had favored Paul Vidal to conduct in his place.

8. Henri Rabaud, [21 February] 1948: ms. 17668, *livre d'or*, no. 38.

9. Vernaelde, "Société des Concerts," p. 3705.

10. Com. 24 April 1920 (Switzerland), 29 May 1920 (novice musicality), 18 April 1921 (sec. instructed to include stern reminder in his rapport moral): D 17345 (19).

11. Com. 29 May 1920 (decision on cello solo), 8 June 1920 (cordial resignation): D 17345 (19).

12. Com. 8 June 1920 (Lafitte's response): D 17345 (19).

13. Com. 27 March 1928 and following: D 17345 (20). The last seven, not counting Saraillé, were Barutel, Clamer, David, Delmont, Mallet, Manson, and Mille. Marc David served as their spokesman.

14. Com. 13 June 1925: D 17345 (19).

15. Com. 24 April 1920: D 17345 (19).

16. Com. 20 April 1920: D 17345 (19).

17. Com. 8, 11 May 1920: D 17345 (19).

18. Com. 8 May 1920: D 17345 (19).

19. Corresp. Paul Léon (minister) to New York consulate (copy), 17 March 1921, sent 19 March 1921: D 17263 (36).

20. AG 24 April 1923: D 17342 (1), with copy of Deblauwe's letter tipped in.

21. Prod'homme, "Music . . . During the First Two Seasons of the War," pp. 135-60; see p. 143.

22. AG 27 May 1921: D 17342 (1).

23. Com. 5 July 1921: D 17345 (19).

24. Com. 2 November 1920 (Érard and Pleyel asked), 16 November (Érard accepts): D 17345 (19).

25. Com. 20 April 1920 (accounting, Rouen); 20, 24, 27 April, 4, 29 May (Brussels); 6 October 1920 *(caisse):* D 17345 (19).

26. Com. 10 May 1921: D 17345 (19). The review, by the conductor Gabriel Marie for the Marseille *Spectator,* was read aloud to the committee, and a letter of thanks dispatched.

27. Com. 26, 27 June 1920: D 17345 (19).

28. Com. 17 January 1922: D 17345 (19).

29. Com. 14 June 1921: D 17345 (19).

30. Com. 15 February 1921: D 17345 (19).

31. Com. 20 April 1920 (proposal), 8 October (decision), 12 October (Insp. Salle convoked), 30 April 1921 (Giboin), receipts for each public rehearsal and concert: D 17345 (19). A tally of financial results for the season appears on the website.

32. Com. 24 January 1922 (firemen), 10 October 1922 (ushers, ticket takers): D 17345 (19).

33. Com. 7 July 1922: D 17345 (19).

34. Com. 5 July 1921: D 17345 (19).

35. Com. 27 March 1923: D 17345 (19).

36. Jules Casadesus, in *La Presse*, 24 October 1921, and *Journal des mutilés et reformés*, 19 November 1921, clippings pasted in minutes at Com. 18 October 1921: D 17345 (19).

37. Com. 4 October 1921 (moral prejudice), 11 October (Léon), 30 December (maintain dates); 20 January 1922 (right to appear), 31 January, 3 February (union invoked), 7 February (union's response): D 17345 (19).

38. Com. 10, 17 January 1922: D 17345 (19).

39. Com. 30 December 1921: D 173435 (19).

40. Com. 31 January, 3, 7, 28 February 1922: D 17345 (19).

41. Com. 24 January 1922: D 17345 (19).

42. AG 24 April, 18 May 1923: D 17342 (2).

43. AG 18 May 1923: D 17342 (2).

44. Ibid.

45. AG 5 June 1923: D 17342 (2).

46. Ibid.

47. Com. 29 June 1923: D 17345 (19).

48. Com. 9, 16 October 1923: D 17345 (19).

49. Com. 17 November 1923 (index), 5 February 1924 (syndicate opposed), 1 May 1924 (Moyse): D 17345 (19).

50. Théâtrophone publicity, concert programs 1926–27: boxed programs.

51. Com. 26 October 1926 (Rabaud's objection), 2 November 1926 (Fine Arts response): D 17345 (20).

52. Com. 6 November 1928: D 17345 (20).

53. AG 24 May 1924 (study of liquidation plans agreed to), AG 19 May 1925 (report presented; adopted): D 17342 (2). Com. 18 March 1926 (gradual liquidation approved): D 17345 (19).

54. Com. 13 September 1921 (invited), 4 October 1921 (name soloists), 26 September 1922 (renewed): D 17345 (19).

55. Com. 26 September 1922: D 17345 (19).

56. Com. 14 November 1922: D 17345 (19).

57. Com. 5, 12, 26 December 1922, 9 January 1923: D 17345 (19). AG 19 December 1922: D 17342 (1).

58. Pierre de Lapommeraye, in *Le Ménestrel,* 26 January 1923.

59. Com. 20 February 1923: D 17345 (19).

60. Com. 9, 30 October 1923 and frequently thereafter: D 17345 (19).

61. Corresp. to and from Fouilloux and Gaubert, July 1923: D 17263 (37, dossier 3).

62. Dossier of corresp.: D 17263 (37, dossier 3).

63. Com. 4 March 1924 (budget), 8 April (firm figures), 15 April (vice president arrives), 8 May (contract): D 17345 (19).

64. Com. 31 May, 24 June 1924 (PLM railroad): D 17345 (19).

65. Com. 17 June 1924 (note on "incident" read into the record): D 17345 (19).

66. Com. 17 June 1924: D 17345 (19).

67. Com. 19 January 1926: D 17345 (19)

68. Com. 8 April 1924: D 17345 (19).

69. Com. 13 September 1921 (Planté no longer appearing in public): D 17345 (19).

70. Com. 2 November 1926 (Paderewski cancels), 15 February 1927 (Menuhin proposed by Dandelot): D 17345 (20).

71. Com. January–February 1928 (fees quoted to various promoters); 27 February (5,200 francs); 5, 14 February (9,000 francs); 3 February 1928 (18,300 francs; 27,760 francs bill for Walter's inaugural concert); 3, 15 November 1927 (Salle Pleyel): D 17345 (20).

72. Com. 3 February 1926 (20,000 francs), 26 February (petition, "orchestras on the side"), 28 February (a fire we must not be feeding): D 17345 (20).

73. Com. 8 April 1924 (telephone in principle): D 17345 (19). Com. 12 July 1927 (banking), 3 November 1927 (install telephone without delay): D 17345 (20).

74. Com. 7 December 1926: D 17345 (20).

75. Com. 1 February 1927: D 17345 (20).

76. Com. 4 February 1928, 25, 26 February 1928: D 17345 (20).

77. Ibid.

78. Dossier of materials on the Mozart Festival: D 17263 (6).

79. Details on recording dates and CD rpts. are given on the website.

80. Com. [25] February 1929 [sec.'s diary entry]: D 17345 (20).

81. Dossier "Voyages à Frankfurt et à Génève," notably corresp. Société des Concerts to Action Artistique, drafted 31 August, typed 15 September 1930: D 17263 (7). Planning for this journey occupied the committee from February 1928: D 17345 (20).

82. Com. 24 April 1930: D 17345 (20).

83. Com. 20 April 1929 (quoting Loiseau's letter of 19 April): D 17345 (20).

84. Com. 18 May 1929: D 17345 (20).

85. Com. 5 June 1930: D 17345 (20).

86. Com. 11, 18, 23 June, 7 July 1931: D 17345 (20). AG 20 October 1931: D 17342 (2).

87. Com. 13 October 1931: D 17345 (20).

88. AG 21 May 1932: D 17343.

89. Jean Chantavoine, Le Ménestrel, 4 October 1929.

90. Com. 6 November 1928: D 17345 (20).

91. Com. 27 November 1928: D 17345 (20).

92. Com. 18 December 1928: D 17345 (20).

93. Com. 20 November 1928: D 17345 (20).

94. Com. 5 April 1929: D 17345 (20).

95. AG 23 May 1930: D 17343.

96. Ibid.

97. Boschot, Adolphe, "L'Action moderne de la musique," in Portraits de musiciens, vol. 2 (Paris, 1947), pp. 197–216; see p. 198n.

98. Piero Coppola, Dix-sept Ans de musique à Paris, 1922–1939 (Lausanne, 1944; rpt. Paris, 1982), p. 230.

99. AG 21 May 1932: D 17343.

100. Ibid.

101. Coppola, *Dix-sept Ans,* p. 60.

102. Ibid., p. 61.

103. Weill, *Marguerite Long,* pp. 118–19; the review appeared in *Le Petit Parisien,* 16 July 1930.

104. Weill, *Marguerite Long,* p. 118.

105. Coppola, *Dix-sept Ans,* p. 219.

106. *Arthur Rubinstein Collection,* vol. 82: BMG Classics (RCA Red Seal) (USA, 1999), CD 1, tr. 1–3.

107. Rapport moral 12 May 1963 (Recassens): D 17343.

108. AG 27 May 1933: D 17343.

109. Ibid.

110. AG 17 May 1934: D 17343.

111. AG 16 May 1936: D 17343.

112. "Nouvelle Proposition / Concerts Salle Pleyel," AG 16 May 1936: D 17342 (2).

113. Corresp. Savoye to Salle Pleyel Co., 4 January 1937 (ongoing deficit), 26 April 1937 (disastrous), 16 August (cannot play to lose money): D 17263 (10).

114. Savoye to Antwerp impresarios: 12 December 1937: D 17263 (10). AG 9 January 1937 (Savoye's remarks): D 17343.

115. AG 31 March 1938: D 17343.

Chapter 11

1. AG 31 March 1938: D 17343.

2. AG 10 May 1938: D 17343.

3. AG 27 May 1938: D 17343.

4. See website Discography, with citations of rpt. CDs.

5. AG 27 May 1938: D 17343.

6. Rapport moral (Recassens), in AG 12 May 1963: D 17343.

7. See Geneviève Honegger, *Charles Munch: Un Chef d'orchestre dans le siècle (Correspondance)* (Strasbourg, 1992).

8. Jules Lassaigne, transl. James Emmons, *Dufy* ([Lausanne], 1954), p. 82.

9. Lassaigne, *Dufy,* p. 81. See also Alfred Werner, *Raoul Dufy* (New York, 1973), p. 156. Good samples of Dufy's work on orchestral subject matter are given in Pierre Courthion, *Raoul Dufy* (Geneva, 1951) and Fanny Guillon-Laffaille, *Raoul Dufy: Catalogue raisonné des aquarelles, gouaches et pastels,* vol. 2 (Paris, 1982).

10. Münch, *I Am a Conductor,* p. 23.

11. The Berlioz cycle with the Boston Symphony Orchestra and Harvard/ Radcliffe / New England Conservatory choruses rpt. as an eight-CD set (New York: RCA Victor Gold Seal, 1996). Discography with the Société des Concerts appears on the website.

12. Münch, *I Am a Conductor,* pp. 73–74.

13. Ibid., pp. 35–36. See also Honegger, *Munch,* p. 84, and n.

14. Münch, *I Am a Conductor,* pp. 65 (receptivity and spontaneity), 77 (a hundred human beings), 79 (almost philanthropic act).

15. *The Art of Conducting: Legendary Conductors of a Golden Era,* VHS videotape, Teldec 95710–3 (1997). The film was made on 17 April 1962, Sanders Theater in Memorial Hall, Harvard University. Also included on the videotape are movt. II of *La Mer* ("Jeux de vagues"), *Daphnis et Chloé,* suite 2, and movt. IV of the *Fantastique* ("Marche au supplice").

16. Münch, *I Am a Conductor,* pp. 83–84.

17. Ibid., pp. 64 (intellectuals), 94 (the public).

18. Pay records for 1944–45, 1945–46: D 17239 (2).

19. Notably in AGs of 1946 and 1947 under the rubric "Affaire Münch": D 17342 (3), typescripts D 17343 (3). See also "Dossier Münch": D 17330 (7).

20. Weill, *Marguerite Long,* pp. 153–54, incorrectly places this concert at the season opening in 1939.

21. Jean-Pierre Séguin, "Fernand Oubradous: A Half-Century of Woodwind History" (interview), trans. Philip Gottling, *Journal of the International Double Reed Society* 14 (1986), pp. 36–40. Transl. from *Le Basson* 6 (1980). Online at <www.idrs.org>.

22. Weill, *Marguerite Long,* pp. 160–61.

23. Corresp. Münch to Beaux-Arts, 7 November 1939, in dossier "Guerre, 1939–45": D 17264 (7).

24. See Marguerite Sablonnière, "Claude Delvincourt et les Cadets du Conservatoire: Une Politique d'orchestre (1943–54)," *Le Conservatoire . . . des Menus-Plaisirs à la Cité,* pp. 261–81. For further information on the Conservatoire during World War II, see the articles of Agnès Callu and Jean Gribenski in Chimènes, *La Vie musicale sous Vichy.*

25. Münch, *I Am a Conductor,* p. 25.

26. Mimeographed bulletin from SAMUP, 4 October 1940: D 17264 (7).

27. Corresp. ministry to Société des Concerts, 27 November 1940: D 17264 (7). On the parallel exclusion of Jews from the Conservatoire, see the article of Jean Gribenski in Chimènes, *La Vie musicale sous Vichy.*

28. I am grateful to Eric de Rom for clarifying details of the Abendroth concert and recording.

29. AG 16 November 1941: D 17343.

30. Handbill, 14 January 1943: boxed programs.

31. JMI mission statement; see, for instance, the various national websites. See also Yannick Simon, "Les Jeunesses Musicales de France," in Chimènes, *La Vie musicale sous Vichy,* pp. 203–15.

32. Weill, *Marguerite Long,* p. 161.

33. Weill, *Marguerite Long,* pp. 165–66.

34. Leaflet presumably published by governmental agencies after the Vichy concert of 20 October 1942 for distribution at the Paris concerts, 27 October 1942 and following: boxed programs. Full French text on the website.

35. There are a number of references to Scapini in the transcripts of the 1946 Nuremberg trials, since he was an "official" witness to conditions in the camps.

Both Scapini and Pinot survived postwar loyalty hearings. Among Pinot's employees in Vichy, incidentally, was the young François Mitterrand. See also Leslie Sprout, "Les Commandes de Vichy," in Chimènes, *La Vie musicale sous Vichy,* pp. 157–78 (notably pp. 160–61).

36. Program 12 December 1942: boxed programs. This concert may have been postponed to, or repeated on, 17 December 1942.

37. Com. 25 March 1943: D 17345 (21).

38. On Cortot's stance toward Germany and German music, and on his activities during World War II, see Gavoty, *Cortot,* pp. 153–71.

39. I am grateful to Mark E. Brill for the essence of this paragraph.

40. Com. 9 December 1942 (the day of the public rehearsal): D 17345 (21).

41. Com. 15 January 1943 (Münch prefers Witkowski to Cluytens), 19 February 1943 (Witkowski engaged for 11 April): D 17345 (21).

42. AG 26 June 1943: D 17343.

43. AG 27 December 1942 (Oubradous dismissed), 26 June 1943 (aftermath): D 17343.

44. AG 10 June 1944: D 17343.

45. Boxed programs.

46. Com. 1 October 1945: D 17345 (22).

47. Recassens, welcoming Gallois-Montbrun in remarks reflecting on his predecessors, AG 12 May 1963: D 17343.

48. Marceau Long et al., *Les Grands Arrêts de la jurisprudence administrative,* 12th edn. (Paris, 1996), pp. 448–54.

49. Petition 20 March 1946, in materials for AG 28 March 1946: D 17343.

50. AG 28 March 1946: D 17343.

51. AG 30 June 1946: D 17343. See also Honegger, *Munch,* pp. 174–175.

52. Honegger, *Munch,* pp. 175–76.

53. AG 29 September 1946: D 17343.

54. "Compte-rendu de la Réunion du 25 October 1946" in "Dossier Münch": D 17330.

55. Corresp. Charles Münch to Fritz Münch, 25 October 1946: Honegger, *Munch,* p. 177.

56. Ms. 17668, *livre d'or,* no. 40, dated 24 November 1949.

57. All these signed the *livre d'or,* ms. 17668: Furtwängler, 25 January 1948 (no. 36); Stokowski, June 1947 (no. 32); Karajan, May 1950 (no. 42); Fischer, 30 November 1947 (no. 33); Rubinstein, 4 December 1947 (no. 34); Kempff, 22 November and 9 December 1946 (no. 39).

58. AG 8 June 1947: D 17342 (3) [no typescript].

59. AG 15 June 1947: D 17343.

60. AG 6 June 1948, a discussion of the "Évolution de l'Affaire Charles Münch": D 17343.

61. AG 20 November 1949: D 17343.

62. AG 8 November 1948: D 17343.

63. The details of this incident can be gleaned from the dossier "Affaire Savoye," D 17330, and the verbatim transcript of the AG 7 November 1948 called to consider the affair: D 17343. I have conflated the two sources in trying to re-

construct the conversations. The dossier D 17330 also includes Savoye's typewritten defense as presented at the AG.

64. AG 6 June 1948: D 17343.

65. Corresp. Savoye to com. 22 October 1948 (resigning): D 17330.

66. Typewritten text: D 17330.

67. "Gâteau de Savoye," *Arts*, 3, 10 December 1948.

68. Accounts, 2 May 1949: D 17330.

69. AG 20 November 1949: D 17343.

70. A table of the summer festivals appears on the website.

71. Corresp. Recassens to Valmalète agency, 9 July 1963: D 17337 (4).

72. Corresp. Huot to Valmalète agency, 16 August 1960: D 17337 (4).

73. Films and video conserved at Videothèque Internationale d'Art Lyrique et de Musique, Aix-en-Provence.

74. For instance, corresp. Huot to Bigonnet, 31 March, 23 August 1954: D 17337 (10).

75. Reports to the ministry on new French repertoire, 1948–51, are given on the website.

76. Schuricht to Huot, 7 December 1949: ms. 17668, *livre d'or*, no. 41 (conflated).

77. Com. 27 April, 20 May, 23 December 1952: D 17345 (22).

78. Com. 14 February 1953: D 17345 (22).

79. Com. 11 May 1954 (Albin dismissed): D 17345 (22). AG 30 May 1954, rubric "Affaire Albin": D 17343.

80. Weill, *Marguerite Long*, p. 192.

81. Marguerite Long, February 1960: ms. 17668, *livre d'or*, no. 45. She notes her appointment as *membre honoraire* on 5 August 1937.

82. Dossier "Suisse 1956": D 17337 (7).

83. Dossiers "Munich," "Vienne": D 17337 (7).

84. Corresp. Huot to admin. Besançon, 30 May 1956: D 17337 (9).

85. Suzanne Demarquez, *Guide de concert*, 13 December 1957.

86. Rapport moral (Huot), typescript in dossier for AG 8 January 1961: D 17343.

87. Corresp. Huot to Cluytens, 30 December 1960, cited in AG 8 January 1961: D 17343.

88. AG 8 January 1961: D 17343.

89. Ibid.

90. Ibid.

91. Ibid.

Chapter 12

1. Jean-Marie Leduc, interview with Nick Mason, March 1973, in *Pink Floyd* (Paris, 1977); transcribed on several Internet fan sites.

2. "La Société des Concerts et le disque," in season brochure Winter 1962–63: boxed programs.

3. Ibid.

4. Notes transl. from the Fr. of Maurice Delage and Jean Cotté, accompanying recording *Maurice Ravel: The Complete Orchestra Works*, Angel set 3636D, 1963.

5. "La Société des Concerts et le disque."

6. Milhaud, 1 April 1962: ms 17668, *livre d'or*, no. 46.

7. Fee amounts specified in the correspondence with the arts management agencies: D 17337 (4–6). A comprehensive table of fees paid to conductors and soloists in the early 1960s is given on the website.

8. Corresp. Huot in Aix to Mme Corre de Valmalète, 8 August 1961: D 17337 (4).

9. Corresp. Huot in Aix to Valmalète agency, 25 July 1960: D 17337 (4).

10. Corresp. Valmalète agency to Huot, 20 July 1961: D 17337 (4).

11. Corresp. Huot to Valmalète agency, 1 June 1960: D 17337 (4).

12. The corresp. to and from the Valmalète agency concerning Dorati includes more than three dozen references from August 1960 through February 1963. Huot complains of Dorati's endless letters on 12 October 1960; Dorati's disenchantment is recorded 5 May 1961: D 17337 (4).

13. The corresp. to and from the Valmalète agency concerning Silvestri and Jolivet's work runs from April to August 1960. The televised concert is at issue on 18 August 1960: D 17337 (4).

14. Honegger on Martinon, cited in a promotional note in *Le Guide du concert*, 28 January 1949.

15. Corresp. Huot to Martinon, 28 November 1961: D 17337 (4). The corresp. with Martinon is summarized in the next note.

16. Corresp. to and from the Valmalète agency concerning Martinon (a good example of the genre, with some thirty documents preserved): 20 April 1960 (proposals for 1961), 7 March 1961 (booking for 12 November), 31 March (fee), 4 April (program), 3 May (biographical note), 1 June (contract), 24 October (availability in 1962), 27 October (summary of conductors needed in 1962), 6 November (programs for 1962), 28 November (congratulations on concert; programs for 1962), 6 December (Gelber to solo), 11 December (meeting in Paris); 4 January 1962 (conflict with Lamoureux), 13 January (annoyance over conflicting Brahms), 13, 14 February (programs for three concerts), 20 February (contract), 5 March (meeting in Paris), 12 March (contract), 20 March (contract), 7 April (program), 8 November (accounts for concerts of November); 18 January 1963 (fee for radio broadcast), 4 April 1967 (dates for 1968, 1969), 6 May (Shostakovich / Rostropovich): D 17337 (4).

17. Corresp. to and from the Valmalète agency concerning Eaktay Ahn: 21 January 1961, 1 June, 5 July; 13 March 1962: D 17337 (4)

18. Corresp. Valmalète agency to Huot, 5 April 1961: D 17337 (4).

19. Corresp. Valmalète agency to Huot, 12 February 1965: D 17337 (4).

20. Rapport moral 26 May 1962 (Huot): D 17341, D 17342 (5).

21. "Bienfaits d'un mécenat," in season brochure, Winter 1962–63: boxed programs.

22. Bernard Gavoty, "Soyons tous solidaires!" in season brochure, Winter 1962–63: boxed programs.

23. AG 12 May 1963: D 17343. Corresp. Huot to com., in materials for AG 30 May 1965: D 17342 (5).

24. AG 12 May 1963: D 17343.

25. Malraux to the Assemblée Nationale, 18 January 1963: cited in Girard, *Malraux*, p. 497.

26. See notably Girard, *Malraux*; and Landowski's two volumes of memoirs.

27. Malraux to the Assemblée Nationale, 14 October 1965: cited in Girard, *Malraux*, p. 498.

28. Pierre Boulez interviewed by Louis Dandrel, *Le Monde*, 14 September 1970; cited (in an appendix of Boulez's outbursts) by Marcel Landowski, *Batailles pour la musique*, after interviews with Édith Walter (Paris, 1979), p. 166.

29. Landowski, *Batailles*, p. 12.

30. Boulez, in *Le Monde*, 14 September 1970 (total absence of ideas); *Le Figaro littéraire*, 22 January 1972 (as sad as the Maginot line, amateurs); *Sud-Ouest*, 7 April 1972 (bric-à-brac, abortion, sterilize). Cited in Landowski, *Batailles*, pp. 166−68.

31. *New York Times*, 9 November 1973; cited in Landowski, *Batailles*, p. 168. See also Boulez's famous essay "Pourquoi je dis non à Malraux," *Le Nouvel Observateur*, 25 May 1966; rpt. in *Points de repère* (Paris, 1981; rev. edn. 1985), pp. 481−84; Eng. transl. as *Observations*, ed. Jean-Jacques Nattiez, trans. Martin Cooper (London, 1986), pp. 441−43.

32. His name is spelled Recassens in much of the internal paperwork of the Société des Concerts and on record jackets; Recasens, in several of the orchestra's publications.

33. Rapport moral (Recassens), in materials for AG 7 June 1964: D 17343.

34. AG 30 May 1965: D 17343.

35. I am grateful to Yukihiro Okitsu of Tokyo for the text of the souvenir program, lacking from the Paris archive. It has been incorporated in the listing of programs on the website; see also Okitsu's website: <www.geocities.co.jp/MusicHall/1921/> (*link* Lucien Thévet).

36. Ernst H. Gombrich, "Exhibitionship," *Atlantic Monthly*, February 1964, p. 77−78; see p. 77.

37. Rapport moral (Recassens), in materials for AG 7 June 1964: D 17343.

38. AG 7 June 1964: D 17343.

39. Ibid.

40. AG 31 January 1965, 30 May 1965 (rain or shine): D 17343.

41. Corresp. Recassens to and from Valmalète, July−September 1962: D 17337 (4). AG 30 May 1965 (Portuguese journey announced); AG 9 January 1966 (last-minute failure): D 17343.

42. AG 31 January 1965 (Gallois-Montbrun's warning): D 17343.

43. AG 30 May 1965: D 17343.

44. AG 9 January 1966: D 17343.

45. Ibid.

46. Landowski, *Batailles*, p. 38.

47. Ibid., p. 39.

48. The Cluytens dossier at EMI-France confirms that the orchestra's classical recordings were not selling especially well. I am grateful to Michael Gray for this observation.

49. Memorandum of understanding, 13 April 1966, in AG 24 April 1966: D 17343.

50. AG 24 April 1966: D 17343.

51. Ibid.

52. Rapport moral 21 June 1967 (Tessier), in dossier "Actes de dissolution": D 17339.

53. Orchestre de Paris: Statuts, date-stamped 5 April 1967, in dossier "Actes de dissolution": D 17339.

54. Rapport moral 21 June 1967 (Tessier), in dossier "Actes de dissolution": D 17339.

55. Landowski, *Batailles,* p. 43.

56. Ibid., p. 42.

57. AG 21 June 1967, in dossier "Actes de dissolution": D 17339.

58. Ordre du Jour 21 June 1967, in dossier "Actes de dissolution": D 17339.

59. Feuilles de Présence du 21 Juin 1967 à 12h, in dossier "Actes de dissolution": D 17339. The account follows the verbatim minutes of AG 21 June 1967 in the same folder

60. Mimeographed circular, Tessier to subscribers, 8 July 1967, in dossier "Actes de dissolution": D 17339.

61. Inventory 22 September 1967, in dossier "Actes de dissolution": D 17339.

62. Landowski, *Batailles,* p. 43. Landowski recounts a slightly different version in "L'Orchestre de Paris," *La Musique n'adoucit pas,* pp. 56–59. See also Honegger, *Charles Munch,* pp. 353–58.

63. Corresp. Münch to Ozawa, 26 April 1967; Valmalète agency to Tessier, 8 May 1967: D 17337 (4).

64. Address André Malraux to Orchestre de Paris, 13 November 1967: cited in *Orchestre de Paris,* ed. Nicole Salinger (Paris, 1987), p. 22. Also quoted in Landowski, *Batailles,* p. 45.

Afterword

1. Author's interview with Lucien Thévet and Robert Casier, Paris, 21 October 1998.

2. Author's interview with Fernand Lelong and Joseph Ponticelli, Paris, 24 October 1998.

Select Bibliography

A full bibliography of works cited and consulted, including publishers' names and music publications related to the Société des Concerts, appears on the Internet at <www.ucpress.edu/holoman>.

THE ARCHIVE

Département de la Musique ("site Richelieu"), Bibliothèque Nationale de France, Paris. A detailed inventory appears on the website.

D 17257. Liste des abonnés, 1837–1935, 80 vols.

D 17258. Comptabilité, factures, recettes, grands livres, 1843–1935, 8 vols.

D 17259. États des droits des sociétaires, 1863–1967, 8 vols.

D 17260. Cahier des sursis des sociétaires, 1872–1883.

D 17261. Correspondance sociétaires; candidats à la direction, 1885–1941, 9 vols.

D 17262. Sociétaires. Two ms. notebooks listing *sociétaires* from 1828 through 1926, with matriculation numbers to just over 700. The last register, copied from D 17262 and used through the dissolution in 1967, remains at the Orchestre de Paris. See also D 17331.

D 17263. Organization de concerts, 1885–1950: lettres de solistes, compositeurs, agences, correspondance diverse, 37 vols. Note especially (5) Tournée en Suisse, 1917; (19) Programmes soumis à la censure, 1940–44; (36) Tournée USA, 1918.

D 17264. Dossiers divers, 19 vols. Note especially (5) Subventions; (7) Guerre, 1939–45; (17) Radiodiffusion, 1931–67; (18) Note sur l'origine de la Société.

D 17267. Catalogue de la bibliothèque (S–Z). Apparently the only preserved volume of the library catalogue prepared by Eugène Jancourt in 1872.

D 17329. Sociétaires: feuilles de présence et rétributions, 1828–1967, 3 vols.

D 17330. Sociétaires: correspondance relative à leur carrière, 1830–1948 (focusing on election of George-Hainl, 1863, and administrative difficulties with Charles Münch and Jean Savoye, 1946).

D 17331. Sociétaires: registres d'inscriptions, 1828–1924, 5 vols. See also D 17262.

D 17332. Comptabilité: journal, 1889–1967, 6 vols.

D 17333. Comptabilité: 1828–1967, 13 vols.

D 17334. Comptabilité: brouillard, 1939–67, 6 vols.

D 17335. Comptabilité: grand livre, 1945–67, 8 vols.

D 17336. Caisse de Prévoyance, 1842–1924, 6 vols.

D 17337. Organisation des concerts, 1828–1967, 10 vols. Note especially: (3) Correspondance Arts et Lettres, 1947–67; (4) Correspondance Valmalète, 1960–67; (7) Tournées à l'étranger, 1951–59; (9) Festival Besançon; (10) Festival Aix-en-Provence.

D 17338. Actes des fondation, 1828, 8 pieces.

D 17339. Actes de dissolution, 1967.

D 17340. Statuts: questions statutaires et syndicales, 1829–1966.

D 17341. Secretary's reports, 1830–1960, 44 pieces. Most are ms.; some printed, the last typescript.

D 17342. Assemblées Générales: procès-verbaux, 1903–67, 6 ms. vols. See also D 17343, the typed verbatim (thus more complete) transcripts, which began as of AG 23 May 1930. Prior to 1903 the minutes of general assemblies are included in the committee's minutes, D 17345.

D 17343. Assemblées Générales: procès-verbaux 1932–67, 51 typed fasc. See also D 17342.

D 17344. Comité: correspondance.

D 17345. Comité et Assemblées Générales: procès-verbaux des séances du Comité, 1828–1966, et des Assemblées Générales, 1828–1906, 24 vols. Volume [20+], 1931–34, lost in the 1940s. See also D 17342–43.

D 17346. Concerts hors série, 1948–67, 3 vols.

D 17347. Musique de film, 1936–66.

D 17348. Enregistrements, 1927–67.

D 17350. Association des Amis de la Société des Concerts du Conservatoire: statuts et procès-verbaux des Assemblées Générales et des réunions de 1943 à 1947.

D 17351. Correspondance d'abonnés, 1848–71 and ca. 1912–13, 57 pieces.

D 17352. Sociétaires: sécurité sociale, 1938–67, 9 vols.

D 17353. Comptabilité, divers, 1945–67, 8 vols.

D 17500s. Berlioz's orchestral library, presented in 1863. See Holoman, *Catalogue of the Works of Berlioz,* New Berlioz Edition, vol. 25 (Kassel, etc., 1987), *passim,* incl. sets identified there as F-Psoc.

D 17593. Haydn: *Symphonie (inédite) en ut majeur (op. 82).* Deldevez's conducting score with his assessment of the work's provenance bound in the front.

Ms. 17668. *Livre d'or.*

Programmes Société des Concerts. 4 boxes, including a near-complete run of programs for the Sunday concerts and, for later years, handbills, posters, and concerts for other concert activities.

See also music manuscripts Bnf Mus. ms. 17463*ff.*, itemized on the website, including works of Berlioz, Gluck (copied by Deldevez), Carl Schwenke, Friedrich Schneider, Conradin Kreutzer, and Louis Vierne. A number of the ms. *lettres autographes* to and from the most celebrated figures in the society's history have been moved to bound miscellanies arranged by the individual's name— e.g.: Bnf Mus. lettres aut. Habeneck.

SOURCE STUDIES OF THE SOCIÉTÉ DES CONCERTS

Bernard, Élisabeth. "Les Abonnnés à la Société des Concerts du Conservatoire en 1837," in *Music in Paris in the Eighteen-Thirties / La Musique à Paris dans les années mil huit cent trente,* ed. Peter Bloom (Stuyvesant, N.Y., 1987), pp. 41–54.

———. "A Glance at the Archives of Some Parisian Orchestral Societies." *19th-Century Music* 7 (1983): 104–06 (trans. D. Kern Holoman).

——— [as Delafon-Bernard]. "Habeneck et la Société des Concerts du Conservatoire: Un Destin exemplaire," in *Le Conservatoire de Paris: Des Menus-Plaisirs à la Cité de la Musique, 1795–1995,* ed. Anne Bongrain et al. (Paris, 1996), pp. 97–116.

Cordey, Jean. *La Société des Concerts du Conservatoire: Notice historique par Jean Cordey, conservateur de la Bibliothèque et du Musée de l'Opéra* (Paris, July 1941).

Cristal, Maurice. "Les Concerts du Conservatoire," *Le Ménestrel* 37 (6, 13, 20 March 1870): 107–09, 117–18, 124–25.

Curzon, Henri de. *L'Histoire et la gloire de l'ancienne salle du Conservatoire de Paris (1811–1911)* (Paris, 1917). Eng. transl. as "History and Glory of the Concert-Hall of the Paris Conservatory," *Musical Quarterly* 3 (1917): 304–18.

Daines, Matthew. "The Société des Concerts, 1980–1918: The Salle des Concerts and the State" (M.A. thesis, University of California, Davis, 1992).

Dandelot, Arthur. *La Société des Concerts du Conservatoire de 1828 à 1897; les grands concerts symphoniques de Paris* (Paris, 1898); 2d edn. titled *La Société des Concerts du Conservatoire (1828–1923) avec une étude historique sur les grands concerts symphoniques avant et depuis 1828* (Paris, 1923).

Deldevez, E.-M.-E. *La Société des Concerts, 1860–1885* (Paris, 1887); modern edn. ed. and annotated Gérard Streletski (Hilbronn, 1998). See also Deldevez, under "Memoirs of the Principals," below.

Devriès-Lesure, Anik. "Cherubini directeur du Conservatoire de Musique et de Déclamation," in *Le Conservatoire de Paris: Des Menus-Plaisirs à la Cité de la Musique, 1795–1995,* ed. Anne Bongrain et al. (Paris, 1996), pp. 39–96.

Elwart, Antoine. *Histoire de la Société des Concerts du Conservatoire Impérial de Musique* (Paris, 1860; 2d edn., 1864).

Holoman, D. Kern. "Orchestral Material from the Library of the Société des Concerts," *19th-Century Music* 7 (1983): 106–18.

———. "Orchestre de Paris," in *Symphony Orchestras of the World: Selected*

Profiles, ed. Robert R. Craven (Westport, Conn.: Greenwood Press, 1987), pp. 100–07.

Hommage à la Société des Concerts (Paris, 1979). Copy: Bnf Mus. 4° Vm, pièce 618.

Kelly, Thomas Forrest. "Hector Berlioz, Symphonie fantastique," in *First Nights: Five Musical Premieres* (New Haven, 2000), pp. 180–255 (includes considerable documentation of the first years of the Société des Concerts).

Lassabathie, Théodore. *Histoire du Conservatoire Impérial de Musique et de Déclamation, suivie de documents recueillis et mis en ordre* (Paris, 1860).

Mary, Annie. *La Société des Concerts du Conservatoire: Étude historique, 1919–339,* 6 vols. (Mémoire, musicologie, Conservatoire National Supérieur de Musique, 1977).

Nectoux, Jean-Michel. *Association pour le 150ᵉ Anniversaire de la Société des Concerts du Conservatoire* (Paris, 1978), an exhibition catalogue in the form of a brochure. See also the souvenir program for the anniversary concert, Orchestre de Paris, 14 January 1979.

———. "Trois Orchestres parisiens en 1830: L'Académie Royale de Musique, le Théâtre-Italien et la Société des Concerts du Conservatoire," in *Music in Paris in the Eighteen-Thirties / La Musique à Paris dans les années mil huit cent trente,* ed. Peter Bloom (Stuyvesant, N.Y., 1987), pp. 471–507.

Pierre, Constant. *Le Conservatoire National de Musique et de Déclamation: Documents historiques et administratifs* (Paris, 1900).

Prod'homme, J.-G. "Music and Musicians in Paris during the First Two Seasons of the War," *Musical Quarterly* 4 (1918): 135–60.

Prod'homme, J.-G., and E. de Crauzat. *Les Menus Plaisirs du Roi: L'École Royale et le Conservatoire de Musique* (Paris, 1929).

Salinger, Nicole, ed. *Orchestre de Paris* (Paris, 1987).

Vernaelde, Albert. "La Société des Concerts et les grandes associations symphoniques," in *Encyclopédie de la musique et dictionnaire du Conservatoire,* ed. Albert Lavignac and Lionel de La Laurencie (Paris, 1913–31), II/6 (ca. 1930), pp. 3684–714.

MEMOIRS OF THE PRINCIPALS

Astruc, Gabriel. *Le Pavillon des fantômes* (Paris, 1929; modern edn. Paris, 1987).

Berlioz, Hector. *La Critique musicale,* ed. Yves Gérard et al., 4 vols. to date (Paris, 1996–).

———. *Mémoires de Hector Berlioz,* etc. (Paris, 1870, and many later edns. and translations).

Coppola, Piero. *Dix-sept Ans de musique à Paris, 1922–1939* (Lausanne, 1944; rpt. Paris, 1982).

Dancla, Charles. *Notes et souvenirs, suivie du catalogue de ses œuvres et de la liste des violonistes célèbres dont les œuvres sont intéressantes et utiles à travailler* (Paris, 1893; 2d edn. Paris, 1898). Eng. transl. as *Notes and Souvenirs,* trans. Samuel Wolf (Linthicum Heights, Md., 1981).

Deldevez, E.-M.-E. *L'Art du chef d'orchestre* (Paris, 1878); modern edn. ed. and ann. Jean-Philippe Navarre (Paris, 1998).

———. *Curiosités musicales: Notes, analyses, interprétation de certaines particu-
larités contenues dans les œuvres des grands maîtres* (Paris, 1873). See especially
"Catalogue des symphonies de J. Haydn," pp. 30–51.

———. *De l'exécution d'ensemble* (Paris, 1888); modern edn. ed. and ann. Jean-
Philippe Navarre (Paris, 1998).

———. *Mes Mémoires* (Le Puy, 1890). Also *Le Passé à propos du présent: Suite à
Mes Mémoires* (Paris, 1892).

d'Ortigue, Joseph. "Société des Concerts," in *Le Balcon de l'Opéra* (Paris, 1833),
pp. [333]–76 (reviews of concerts of 1831–33, largely Beethoven).

Gautier, Eugène. *Un musicien en vacances: Études et souvenirs* (Paris, 1873).

Landowski, Marcel. *Batailles pour la musique* (Paris, 1979).

———. *La Musique n'adoucit pas les mœurs* (Paris, 1990).

Münch, Charles. *Je suis chef d'orchestre* (Paris, 1954); modern edn. with treatises
and related texts of Berlioz, Wagner, Weingartner, and Walter, ed. Georges
Liébert as *L'Art du chef d'orchestre* (Paris, 1988). Transl. Leonard Burkat as *I
Am a Conductor* (New York, 1955).

Saint-Saëns, Camille. "La Salle de la rue Bergère" and "Le Vieux Conservatoire,"
in *École buissonnière: Notes et souvenirs* (Paris, 1913), pp. 33–47. Eng. transl.
(abridged) as *Musical Memories* (London and Boston, 1919; rpt. New York,
1969).

———. "Société des Concerts," in *Harmonie et mélodie* (Paris, 1923), pp. 189–
98.

Sauzay, Eugène. "La Vie musicale à Paris à travers les mémoires d'Eugène Sauzay
(1809–1901)," ed. Brigitte François-Sappey, *Revue de musicologie* 60 (1974):
159–210.

Taffanel, Paul. "L'Art de diriger," in *Encyclopédie de la musique et dictionnaire du Conservatoire*, ed. Albert Lavignac and Lionel de La Laurencie
(Paris, 1913–31), II, 4, pp. 2129–34. Modern edn. included in Deldevez,
L'Art du chef d'orchestre, ed. and ann. Jean-Philippe Navarre (Paris, 1998),
pp. 142–51.

Tolbecque, Auguste. *Souvenirs d'un musicien en province* (Niort, 1896).

SELECT LIST OF MUSIC PUBLICATIONS ASSOCIATED
WITH THE SOCIÉTÉ DES CONCERTS

Alkan, Charles Valentin. *Souvenirs des Concerts du Conservatoire: Partitions pour
piano seul* (Paris, 1847). Also *Souvenirs . . . 2ᵉ série* (Paris, 1861).

Beethoven, Ludwig van. *Collection des symphonies,* symphonies 1–8 in 2 vols, "édi-
tion dediée à la Société des Concerts du Conservatoire et Musique, et revue
par Fétis" (Paris, 1841).

———. *La Délivrance de Vienne, par Jean Sobieski (12 7ᵇʳᵉ 1683) [Der Glorreiche
Augenblick]: Cantate dramatique avec chœur, exécutée pour la 1ʳᵉ fois à Paris
au concert du Conservatoire par la Société des Concerts, le 27 janvier 1850*
(Paris, 1850).

———. 7ᵉ Symphonie en la nat. majeur, arr. piano four-hands Renaud de Vil-
bac, "Hommage à la Société des Concerts du Conservatoire" (Paris, 1859).

Dancla, Charles. *Souvenir de la Société des Concerts du Conservatoire: 6 Duos pour piano et violon, op. 91* (Leipzig, 1859).

Expert, Henry, ed. *Répertoire de la Société des Concerts du Conservatoire de Paris extrait des* Maîtres Musiciens de la Renaissance française, ed. Henry Expert (Paris, 1906).

Gounod, Charles. *Répertoire des Concerts du Conservatoire,* etc.: Quatorze Grands Chœurs à quatre voix avec accompagnment de piano (Paris, ca. 1884).

Onslow, George. *1re Symphonie à grand orchestre, dédiée à la Société des Concerts du Conservatoire de Musique de Paris, op. 41* (Paris, 1830).

Répertoire des morceaux d'ensemble exécutés par la Société des Concerts du Conservatoire, arrangés très soigneusement pour piano seul (Paris, 1850); 170 volumes, including most of the central repertoire of the orchestra and chorus, notably the symphonies of Haydn, Mozart, Beethoven, and Mendelssohn in piano score.

Illustration Credits

1. François-Antoine Habeneck. Engraving by Massard, c. 1840. Bibliothèque Nationale de France, Paris.
2. Narcisse Girard. Photograph from A. Dandelot, *La Société des Concerts de 1828 à 1897* (Paris, 1898). Bibliothèque Nationale de France, Paris.
3. François George-Hainl. Photo provenance unknown. Bibliothèque Nationale de France, Paris.
4. E.-M.-E. Deldevez. Photo Disdéri, Paris, c. 1870. Bibliothèque Nationale de France, Paris.
5. Jules Garcin. Photo Pierre Petit (1832–1909). Bibliothèque Nationale de France, Paris.
6. Paul Taffanel. Photo provenance unknown. Bibliothèque Nationale de France, Paris.
7. Georges Marty. Photo provenance unknown. Bibliothèque Nationale de France, Paris.
8. André Messager. Photo Henri Manuel. Bibliothèque Nationale de France, Paris.
9. Philippe Gaubert. Photo Hulton, Roger Viollet, Paris / Getty Images.
10. Charles Münch. Getty Images.
11. André Cluytens. Sabine Weiss / Rapho.
12. Joseph Meifred. Lith. David. Bibliothèque Nationale de France, Paris.
13. Charles Lebouc. Photo provenance unknown. Bibliothèque Nationale de France, Paris.
14. Joseph White. Lith. Lemercier on *papier de chine*. Bibliothèque Nationale de France, Paris.
15. Albert Vernaelde. Photo provenance unknown. Bibliothèque Nationale de France, Paris.
16. André Boutard, Michel Debost, Robert Casier. Sabine Weiss / Rapho.
17. Henri Grévedon, Portrait of Beethoven. Bibliothèque Nationale de France, Paris.

18. Eugène Guillaume, Bust of Beethoven. Photo Frédéric Désaphi.
19. Site plan. J.-G. Prod'homme and E. de Crauzat, *Les Menus Plaisirs du Roi: L'École Royale et le Conservatoire de Musique* (Paris, 1929). Library of the University of California.
20. Audience seating plan. In Antoine Elwart, *Histoire de la Société des Concerts du Conservatoire Impérial de Musique* (Paris, 1860; 2nd edn., 1864). Library of the University of California.
21. A concert at the Conservatoire. Engraving on wood signed A. E. P., after P. S. Germain, *L'Illustration,* 15 April 1843. Bibliothèque Nationale de France, Paris.
22. Entry to the Concerts du Conservatoire. Engraving on wood signed A.B.L. *L'Illustration,* 15 January 1848. Bibliothèque Nationale de France, Paris.
23. A concert of the Société des Concerts du Conservatoire. Engraving on wood by Bourcier after Édouard Riou, from an unidentified publication, 23 February 1861. Bibliothèque Nationale de France, Paris.
24. Gaubert and the orchestra. Bibliothèque Nationale de France, Paris.
25. Program for all-Beethoven concert. Bibliothèque Nationale de France, Paris.
26. Handbill for concert. Bibliothèque Nationale de France, Paris.
27. Program for concert in El Paso. Bibliothèque Nationale de France, Paris.
28. Marcel Landowski, André Malraux, Charles Münch. Orchestre de Paris.
29. Lucien Thévet, Robert Casier. Photo by author.
30. Place du Marché St-Honoré. Robert Doisneau / Rapho.

Index

Abendroth, Hermann, 452, 457

Abneck, Adam, 140

Académie des Beaux-Arts. *See* Institut de France

accounting, accountants, 20, 44, 56, 283–84, 420, 519. See also *agent comptable*

Action Artistique, 131, 355, 360–61, 475

Adam, Adolphe, 190; arrangements, 189, 199; *Reine d'un jour, La,* 26

admission: day of concert, 75–76, 91–92; *parterre,* 157–58; price, 39, 56, 122–24, 143, 173, 214, 245, 267, 319, 344, 400, 412–13, 501; proceeds, 161, 320–21, 336, 349, 403

admission, complimentary, 88, 175, 248, 429; blind and war-wounded, 78; Conservatoire employees, students, 78, 98, 107, 248; dignitaries, 56, 86–88, 143, 149–52; press, 77–78; publishers, 88; service providers, 88

Aeolus (ship), 367

agent comptable, 43, 200

agent de change, 52, 282–83

Ahn, Eaktay, 499

Aix-en-Provence, festival of, 7, 292, 477–78, 485–86, 488, 519, 522–23

Alain, Marie-Claire, 505

Alard, Delphin, 61–62, 118, 142, 175, 182, 204, 209–10, 217–19, 258

Albert, Prince, of England, 205

Albin, Robert, 482

Alizard, Adolphe, 177

Alkan, Charles-Valentin, 48, 109, 149, 279, 542n. 23

Allard. *See* Alloud

Alloud, Auguste and Louis-Philippe, trombone, 67

Alsace and Lorraine, 104, 230, 242–43

Altès, Ernest, 38, 43, 65, 226, 260, 264, 268–69, 276–77, 296, 311

Altès, Henri, 43, 297

Ambroselli, Édouard, 51

Amédée-Lanneau, François, 144

American Federation of Musicians, 377

Amis de la Société des Concerts, Les, 58, 421

Andrade, Jean-Auguste, 48

André, Franz, 465

Angel records. *See* Pathé-Marconi

anniversaries of the society: 50th, 258–59; 150th, 15

Ansermet, Ernest, 485

Antwerp (Anvers): concerts in, 324, 332–33, 336, 350, 401, 424, 480; Flemish Opera, 476, 481

Appaire, Louis, 65

Aquila, concert in. *See* Italy

Arban, Jean-Baptiste, 103–4

Arbeau-Bonnefoy, Germaine, 453

archive of the society, 16–21, 301, 347, 435, 450

Archives Nationales, 21

Compositor:	G & S Typesetters, Inc.
Text:	10/13 Galliard
Display:	Galliard
Printer/Binder:	Sheridan